BOLSHEVIK CULTURE

STUDIES OF THE

KENNAN INSTITUTE
FOR
ADVANCED RUSSIAN STUDIES

THE WILSON CENTER

Experiment and Order
in the Russian Revolution

BOLSHEVIK
CULTURE

Edited by Abbott Gleason,
Peter Kenez, and Richard Stites

INDIANA UNIVERSITY PRESS
Bloomington

A Special Study of the Kennan Institute for Advanced Russian Studies
The Wilson Center
No. 5

Library of Congress Cataloging in Publication Data
Main entry under title:

Bolshevik culture.

(A Special study of the Kennan Institute for
Advanced Russian Studies, the Wilson Center; no. 5)
    Includes index.
    1. Soviet Union—Civilization—1917–   —Con-
gresses.   I. Gleason, Abbott.   II. Kenez, Peter.
III. Stites, Richard.   IV. Series.
DK266.4.B65   1985   947.084   84-48253
ISBN 0–253–31206–X

Contents

INTRODUCTION

Abbott Gleason

The chapters in this book were originally presented at a two-day conference at the Kennan Institute for Advanced Russian Studies of the Woodrow Wilson Center, Smithsonian Institution, on May 19 and 20, 1981. Participants in the conference aimed to examine the period around the Russian Revolution of 1917 in an effort to explain how in the course of a relatively few months and years what we call "Russian culture" began to change into something related, yet qualitatively different, usually referred to, equally generally, as "Soviet culture." This complex and subtle change entailed both the addition of new elements and the subtraction of old ones—and every kind of permutation of both. In the Russian Revolution the social groups that had dominated Imperial Russia, and the store of ideas, attitudes, and institutions that they had created over the centuries, were largely swept away. They were replaced by ideas, attitudes, and eventually institutions which were ultimately related to Russia's past but were also profoundly conditioned by the revolutionary beliefs and experiences of the new elite. Daniel Orlovsky's essay examines a preliminary phase of this process by focusing on the attempts of the Provisional Government—not surprisingly rather incoherent—to find a workable blend of old and new during its few months in power. Sheila Fitzpatrick contributes an essay to the current lively discussion as to precisely how the Civil War affected the mentality of Russia's leadership. That traumatic experience lent a concrete shape and coloring to the aspirations which Robert C. Tucker has analyzed by taking Bolshevism to be, among other things, a "culture in the making."

From our vantage point in the nineteen-eighties, we can see that some of the values and points of view which appeared to have been finished off in 1917 were more durable than had long been supposed, and less tied to the fate of the social groups that had initially put them forward. For example, the last decade has made clear that one does not need a patriarchal gentry in order to have a resurgence of Slavophile political romanticism. Nor, in a somewhat different vein, has the explicit internationalism of the Bolshevik point of view inhibited the steady growth of Great Russian nationalism, not least in the ranks of the successors of Lenin and Trotsky. The earliest development of what was to become the first ruler cult in the Soviet Union, as described by Nina Tumarkin, sheds further light on the difficulties facing the socialist minority, as they attempted to move the Russian masses, with their "traditional" culture.

To be sure, the full extent of these anomalies could not be discerned until long after the Revolution. Nevertheless, an intelligent observer of the revolutionary scene might have posited that the core of the new regime's values would result from the interaction of the political and cultural radicalism of the Russian intelligentsia (in particular its Marxist part), on the one hand, and the most deeply held values of the worker and peasant masses, on the other. The latter—particularly the vast majority still living in the village—remained the durable and central enigma of modern Russian history. But whether their deepest impulses were fundamentally collectivist or individualistic, brutally aggressive or self-sacrificing, religious or secular (or altogether devoid of such essentialist qualities), their attitudes would clearly exert a powerful shaping force on the nation, now suddenly devoid of its old elites.

If our hypothetical observer were of truly Tocquevillian discernment, it would not take much experience of the new Russia to suggest to him that there were some significant cleavages in the ranks of the intellectuals who had led the victorious revolution. The most influential, if not the numerical majority, took Marxism to be a straightforward guide to economic and political action, however great the difficulties which putting it into practice might entail. For them, as for the mature Marx, utopian extremism of any kind might be at best a byproduct of the decomposition of the old order (and a stimulus to it), but it could also easily turn out to be a harmful, politically dangerous roadblock for those anxious to get on with the business of building socialism. One might smile at the whimsical and evanescent communalism of university students; one might be intrigued, or merely annoyed, by the incomprehensible paintings and anti-bourgeois posturing of avant-garde artists. But it was most unlikely to suppose that the top Bolshevik leadership would accept the notion that the modernist "revolution" in the arts was the equivalent of the great social revolution which had just ended the Romanov dynasty's three-hundred-year reign and turned Russia's social order upside down. Attitudes among the political elite, profoundly practical, had been resoundingly vindicated by the events of 1917. The next thirty-five years of Russian-Soviet history would demonstrate the depth, as well as the limitations, of the realism which prevailed in this milieu.

But as one moved out and away from the centers of power, one encountered other people with quite different attitudes toward the Revolution. They were often enthusiastic and seldom totally hostile, but they frequently looked to just those dimensions of the Revolution which the Bolshevik leadership thought of as "utopian." Their interest was centered, in other words, on just how rapidly and programmatically the new regime would make good the hopes which the European Left had always placed on the revolution to bring about a radical transformation of human nature, ultimately the end of alienation. They anticipated "new men" and particularly (as Barbara Clements demonstrates) "new women," basing their hopes ultimately on apocalyptic interpretations of Enlightenment ideas about how human potential could be realized if and when people took their destiny into their own hands.

Some notion of culture, however inchoate, was clearly central to these hopes for transformation—whether it entailed the metaphysics of Suprematism, or that root-and-branch renovation of everyday life which the Constructivists demanded, an aspect of which is described by John Bowlt. Such people tended not to be "realistic," and the political leadership could certainly not count on them to order their priorities properly or to accept the postponement of their dreams with good grace. Richard Stites's essay in this collection deals most frontally with this mentality.

To these obvious sources of conflict in post-revolutionary Russia we must add a third and related one, which David Joravsky perspicaciously examines: the conflict between the intellectual underpinnings of Bolshevism, firmly rooted in the cultural world of nineteenth-century Europe, and the new science of the twentieth century, in terms of whose developing canons Bolshevism was crude and static. This cleavage was not initially so important as the utopian-realist one, but its significance would grow with time. The Bolsheviks claimed that they and their culture were "scientific," but those who were in the process of making the most important Russian contributions to science could not accept the materialist metaphysics of the nineteenth century, any more than the avant-garde artists who were drawn to the Revolution could easily come to terms with nineteenth-century realism as the basis for their art.

These, then, are some of the strands of the new and often contradictory culture so amply discussed in this book: varieties of Marxism; Enlightenment humanitarianism; utopian fantasy and millenarian faith; a pervasive belief in the transforming power of culture and equally pervasive disagreements and uncertainties about what culture actually was. In addition, there were the workers. Would they be the authors of the cultural transformation, as Marx had declared, or its object, as Lenin had suggested? James C. McClelland's essay suggests that even those who, like Anatole Lunacharsky, envisioned the active participation of the masses in socialist construction believed that a major effort to instill proletarian class-consciousness was necessary before this could occur.

These debates and discussions were carried on almost entirely in a few important urban centers. Stretching out boundlessly from these centers of debate and confusion lay the age-old world of the Russian countryside, which dominated the new Russia demographically, as it had the old. Before 1917, Slavophiles and Populists had glorified rural Russia and produced their divergent fantasies. Within two or three years of the Revolution, however, the influence even of militant Populist ideas was drastically contracting, as the Socialist-Revolutionaries succumbed to political failure and Bolshevik coercion. And yet, as Katerina Clark has shown, currents of anti-urban utopianism survived, fed by the experience of revolution and civil war.

But if some members of the intelligentsia dreamed of a world without cities, they were far outnumbered by those whose hopes and fantasies were urban, industrial, and futurist—social rationalists who exalted the city and the machine. Those who actually held power after the Revolution were far more inclined to the urban point of view. With the passage of time they too were possessed by fantasies of transformation, but unlike their unworldly intelligentsia confreres they did not lack the power to act them out. At all events, the new elite tended to regard the Russian countryside as irrational, filthy, economically backward, brutal, stunted—in almost every conceivable way antithetical to their vision of Russia's future. Marxism further suggested to them that rural Russia was a danger, for economic weight was always liable to become political power, and so it was desirable to rationalize and transform rural life as soon as possible. Beatrice Farnsworth's essay on village women explores some of the difficulties of this process and suggests its magnitude. At the close of the Civil War, few spoke for any version of the traditional ideologies of the countryside, which stretched defenseless, yet threatening, outside the walls of the Bolshevik citadels.

Despite the centrality of the concept of *culture* at the conference which produced these essays, there was a pronounced lack of certainty and precision among both the organizers and participants as to precisely what was meant by it. This anomaly was more than once remarked upon by the participants themselves, but it did not really affect the success of the conference or the value of the papers drawn from it. It was reassuring for the editors to be reminded that anthropologists themselves are far from agreeing about what culture is.[1] More important, in my view, is the fact that the historians who contributed to this volume, like many of their colleagues these days, have felt a tug from anthropology.

Several aims of the participants deserve special mention. Our contributors generally accepted that culture referred not merely to monuments or artifacts, but also to the transactions which produced them and the views of the producers. We intended to follow the current tendency to deemphasize high culture and investigate what ordinary people were reading and how they lived. We wanted to perceive orphanages and workers' apartments as "palaces of culture" along with museums (if not quite in the same way). We wanted to see the dynamics of village life in the early days of Communism as freshly as we could. And we tried to assimilate the aspirations of the intelligentsia and the political culture of the ruling elite to our more general notion. The "anthropological idea of culture" we aimed at involved a broadening, flattening, and democratizing of the term, together with an expansion of the field to be investigated. This somewhat tentative notion of culture allowed us to investigate much of what gave shape and texture to revolutionary and post-revolutionary Russia.

We did not deal with the non-Russian cultures of the multi-national Russian imperium, largely for two reasons. To have done so would have deprived this volume of its unifying focus on the Russian cultural core, which has always been the central fact of Soviet culture. Also, it would have been enormously difficult to deal in any serious way with the non-Russian parts of the Soviet world so soon after the Revolution, since their cultural interaction with the Great Russian heartland became substantial only at a later date.

The contributions to this book examine many of the central problems of Soviet culture. Peter Kenez has traced the origins of the Soviet attempt to create a new kind of newspaper with no news in it. Peter Juviler has recounted a chapter on the Promethean effort to substitute philanthropy for charity. Jeffrey Brooks has described the no less remarkable effort to change the reading of millions of people, while Richard Taylor deals with the early days of the art form that Lenin is alleged to have said was "most important" for post-revolutionary Russia: cinema. Even when we focused most directly on thought and thinking, we tried to bear in mind that these are social acts. Above all, perhaps, we tried never to lose sight of what Clifford Geertz called "the half-formed, taken-for-granted, indifferently systematized notions that guide the activities of normal men in everyday life."[2]

At the border of our temporal field of investigation, which begins "on the eve" and ends a few years after the Revolution, lies a much better mapped period: "the twenties." Although there is clearly some kind of overlap, these essays are not really about the twenties or even the early twenties. These terms denote, it seems to me, a better lit and more clearly demarcated field, dominated by the guideposts of political and economic history. In studying the twenties, one cannot escape dealing with War Communism, the Kronstadt Revolt, the political succession to Lenin, and other matters of comparable temporal specificity.

Beyond the twenties lies the period in which Stalin came to hold sway over the Soviet Union and the great upheavals which began in 1928 with forced collectivization and the First Five Year Plan. This period was certainly another watershed in the creation of Soviet culture; Sheila Fitzpatrick plausibly regards it as "cultural revolution"[3] and suggests that more of that revolutionary energy came from below than we have been accustomed to believe. Even if that is so, the forces unleashed in this later period meant the doom of what remained of modernist, avant-garde culture in the Soviet Union and the consensual achievement of a state-controlled mobilizational victorianism in the arts. Social mobility, as she has demonstrated, continued apace, but other forms of egalitarianism attenuated, as did creative freedom.

How to relate this second cultural revolution (if we may so refer to Stalinist cultural policies in the broadest sense) to the revolutionary culture whose formative phase we have examined is an aspect of one of the most bitterly contested issues in modern Russian historiography: the relationship between Lenin's Russia and Stalin's. None of the essays in this volume is directly concerned with this issue; the actors in our period believed themselves to be dealing with quite a different set of problems. Nevertheless, the shadow of the future hangs over the comparatively innocent period about which we have written and most of the participants, regardless of their perspective on the upheavals of the thirties, have discerned traces of the grim realism and ruthless *dirigisme* of Stalin's time. Maurice Meisner's fine conclusion enlarges the arena for discussion still further, by comparing the Russian experience of "cultural revolution" with the Chinese.

In conclusion, the editors would like to thank several colleagues who participated in the conference upon which this book is based and helped make it a success: Linda Gerstein, George Kline, Lars Kleberg, Anatole Kopp, Christina Lodder, Sidney Monas, William G. Rosenberg, S. Frederick Starr, and Robert C. Williams. Harvard University Press was kind enough to allow us to publish material which appeared in a somewhat different form in Nina Tumarkin's *Lenin Lives!* We are most grateful to the Woodrow Wilson International Center for Scholars, Georgetown University and the Research and Development Committee of the American Association for the Advancement of Slavic Studies for defraying the expenses of the original conference and some of the preparation of the manuscript. Rosemary Stuart, formerly of the Kennan Institute, made a substantial contribution to both conference and book. The Faculty Research Development Fund of Brown University helped with some of the costs of preparing the manuscript for publication.

NOTES

1. See, for example, the numerous definitions referred to in Clifford Geertz, "Thick Description: Toward an Interpretive Theory of Culture," *The Interpretation of Cultures* (New York, 1973).

2. Ibid., p. 362.

3. Sheila Fitzpatrick, *Cultural Revolution in Russia, 1928–1931* (Bloomington, 1978).

BOLSHEVIK CULTURE

[1] Iconoclastic Currents in the Russian Revolution: Destroying and Preserving the Past

Richard Stites

Blow up
Smash to pieces
The Old World!
In the heat of battle of the Universal Struggle
By the glow of flames
Show
No mercy—
Strangle the bony body of destiny!
                              V. D. Alexandrovsky, 1918

THEODOT: Will you destroy the past?
CAESAR: Aye! And build the future on its ruins.
        George Bernard Shaw, *Caesar and Cleopatra*

THE WORD ICONOCLASM is usually defined as either the destruction of hated images, idols, or icons; or a deep critique of a given cultural order.[1] The term "iconoclastic currents" in my title is a metaphor for the impulse, fed or reinforced by a revolution, to sweep away the memory of a hated past. In this essay I will talk about four of these currents of revolutionary thought and behavior: (1) the so-called mindless vandalism or wanton destruction usually associated with peasants in a rural milieu; (2) iconoclasm proper—the self-conscious removal or demolition of obvious artifacts of the old regime (statues, imperial regalia, etc.); (3) nihilism, or the repudiation of the old culture and art; and (4) anti-intellectualism, critical not only of past culture, but of intellectual elites. In my discussion of these categories—which often overlap—I shall try to show their relationship to each other, to their antecedents in Russian history, to similar phenomena elsewhere, and to the anti-iconoclastic feelings and policies of those in power. And I shall attempt to expose the complexity of motivations involved in smashing the emblems of the past. I will begin with a brief discussion of the nature of iconoclasm and conclude with an explanation of how these currents were opposed, controlled, and reversed by the Bolshevik authorities.

Iconoclasm has a very useful political, educational, and psychological role in times of violence. Smashing hated images and artifacts of the past can serve as a surrogate for, as well as a stimulus to, angry violence against human representatives of the old order. It can help erase reminders of previous holders of power and majesty. It makes way for the fashioning of new symbols and emblems of the revolutionary order. Unlike the medieval iconoclasts who smashed religious images because they thought such images evil, revolutionary iconoclasts cleared away the signs of the past in order to raise up new ones. Like the destruction of pagan images in Kiev after the conversion of Russia to Orthodox Christianity in the tenth century, revolutionary iconoclasm was a catharsis, a cleansing of the system, and a way to focus intense rage. Revolutionaries, like other kinds of leaders and political figures, know that surfaces and facades are very important, that it is essential to point the way to reality before one can begin the journey. They know that signs and symbols—and the very act of revising them—are able to mobilize certain sentiments of devotion and loyalty, and to evoke political and social dreams.[2] They also know the importance of the tactile and the visual in lands that are still very much illiterate.

Revolutions are a time for destruction, for smashing, for demeaning acts of mockery. In 1643, parliamentary agents broke into the Regalia Chamber of Westminster Abbey and made merry with crowns and coronation robes of England's hallowed monarchs, exposing the "sacred ornaments" to contempt and laughter. When the House of Commons later voted to melt down and sell the silver and gold in the royal regalia, the Puritans spoke of "detestable emblems of kings, their crowns, scepters and heathenish ornaments." A typical blend of contempt, hatred, and practical concerns, with a suggestion perhaps of a ritual of exorcism achieved by profaning the sacred. The successors of Charles I also came into power with dour faces turned against the art, the artifacts, and the frivolous ideas of the old order.[3]

In the French Revolution, the literal and the metaphorical sides of iconoclasm unfolded together. After the assassination of Marat, iconoclasm swelled into a tempest of burning and defiling of art, books, religious icons, and regalia; and an anti-art movement proclaimed that art corrupted morals and worked against republican simplicity and virtue. A law of 1792 announced that "the sacred principles of liberty and equality will not permit the existence of monuments raised to ostentation, prejudice, and tyranny to continue to offend the eyes of the French people . . . the bronze in these monuments can be converted into cannon for the defense of *la patrie*." It was during this great upheaval that the word "vandalism" was first coined. Henri Grégoire, an anti-iconoclast at the Ministry of Education, used it to indicate willful and ignorant destruction as opposed to legitimate political removal of repugnant visual reminders of the old regime.[4]

Social struggle in Russia was always strongly marked by iconoclasm. Both iconoclasm and vandalism accompanied the great peasant revolts of the seventeenth and eighteenth centuries, the Revolution of 1905–1907, and the Great Revolution of 1917–1921. Old Believers in the seventeenth century and the intellectual Bakunin in the nineteenth dreamed of "burning down all Russia"; and the "nihilist" Dmitri Pisarev invited his followers to strike out at random, destroying the worthless, in the process of which the worthwhile would survive the blows. Mystical anarchists around the time of the 1905 revolution hoped for a "universal beautiful fire that will consume the old world." One of them put it this way: "All history must be burned." The Revolutions of 1917 opened up new vistas for the destructive impulse—and not only the purely military one, such as the order given by General Khabalov during the February days to bomb Petrograd from the air.[5]

A word or two about a related matter—reversal and symbolic retribution. Rituals of reversal in medieval and early modern times were carried out at designated festivals when men would be ordered about by women, fools would be crowned kings, the lowly would be made the objects of mock reverence. Symbolic retribution occurs when punishment is accompanied by some reminder of the sociological irony of the punishment: jailers jailed, Muslims sewn into pigskins, peasant rebels roasted on a red-hot throne. Many instances and combinations of these occurred during the Russian Revolution—and they were used by both sides: putting mine operators down a mine shaft; wheeling bosses off the premises of a factory yard on a barrow; sending priests to the front with weapon in hand; stuffing the slit bellies of food requisitioners with grain; former servants lecturing to masters about the rules of the revolution; Makhno putting a policeman in his own former cell; ragged proletarians standing guard over a work detail of Land Captains, policemen, merchants, and gentry. There were even legends abroad in the early days of the Revolution that it was caused by Jews who wanted to ride Cossack horses and make their former owners walk, or that sailors wanted to ride inside the trams, a practice forbidden by the old order. These myths and episodes, so characteristic of all revolutions, were not reversal rituals, temporary rejection of normal life permitted in time of carnival; they were *tableaux vivants,* gestures bathed in revolutionary meaning and pointing toward a permanent new order of things. Those performed by revolutionaries were concrete embodiments of an abstract order—the laws and policies of the Bolshevik regime or of other ephemeral revolutionary governments.[6]

When Sergei Eisenstein edited the famous sequence in *October (Ten Days that Shook the World)* where workers in a conscious and mechanical act of urban iconoclasm are dismantling the statue of Alexander III—a monument rich in the imagery of the prerevolutionary order—he cut away to show the simultaneous rampages of peasants armed with scythes and heading for the nearest manor house.[7] He was clearly trying to show the underlying connection between urban revolution and rural rebellion. But historians, anthropologists, and revolutionaries themselves sometimes make a distinction between conscious iconoclasm and spontaneous vandalism. Is there such a distinction? Peasant vandalism, often called "the Red Cock" or rural rampage, was—like iconoclasm—physical destruction of things, some of which could be seen to have symbolic significance. But it is usually depicted as visceral, irrational, and unplanned. Did it in fact differ from iconoclasm in motivation, and style? Did urban iconoclasm sometimes resemble rural vandalism? Does the dichotomy have any meaning? Were those who put the torch to the prisons of Petrograd driven by different impulses than those who took the axe to the grand pianos of the manor houses?

In looking cursorily at behavior and motivation in rural destruction in the years 1905 to the end of the Civil War I have discerned no pattern of a single vandalist *mentalité* but rather a varying combination of envy, hatred, self-interest, and symbolism. Envy of the visibly larger portions of land and farm equipment, livestock, and useful implements; hatred for the supposed arrogance and indifference embodied in the embellishments of the rich; and self-interest in destroying premises and records of the landlord to prevent him from reestablishing himself. During the great pillages of 1905–1907, peasants burned or attempted to burn railroad stations, telegraphic lines, and the local school or teacher's home. Sometimes whole villages helped to destroy the orchards, houses, and barns of a landowner—suggesting collective responsibility and anonymity. The old, the women, and the more prosperous most often resisted; and young males most often instigated. Outside agitators on horse and bicycle were involved in some of the episodes, sometimes threatening to burn the peasants out if they did not take action against the landlord. In one case where a wineshop was burned, the motive was vengeance on the proprietor for having built it against local wishes; and here the women were energetic participants. In 1914, during the mobilization riots, similar things happened with no sign of a revolutionary situation at hand. Peasant recruits marching cross country got out of control, plundered estates, and urged local peasants to join them. Stations, shops, and homes were burned.[8]

The symbolic element was also present. In a study of 1917 in Saratov Province, Donald Raleigh finds that essential equipment was seized and divided, while fancy furniture, books, art works, and even parks and orchards were vandalized. John Keep's study of the rural revolution tells of how, in Tambov Province, peasants played the harmonica while igniting the mansions of the lord. In Ryazan Province, peasants merely emptied a manor house; but when a sailor arrived, he told them to chop it up and burn it down. Keep finds that the great majority of manors were left to rot or turned into schools that were hardly used during the Civil War. In an incident of 1922 in Nizhny Novgorod a soldier poked his bayonet in the parquet floors of an aristocrat's mansion and picked out the eyes of a Japanese carving. Keep and Raleigh use almost identical language in interpreting the events they describe. The former speaks of an archaic joy in destroying "symbols of their former subjection"; the latter of the destruction of "the symbolic vestiges of its subordinate economic position."[9]

The observations of contemporaries support this assessment. In surveying the devastation of art wrought by the Revolution, a commission for artistic preservation, headed by the noted art historian Igor Grabar and working closely with the Bolshevik government, reported a wave of destruction and burning in the summer of 1918 in which masses of art treasures perished or were stolen. The revolution and the Civil War, said the report, had resulted in "manor houses reduced to dust, slashed paintings, demolished statues, gutted palaces, and cathedrals destroyed by shells." Some of this of course was the offshoot of combat; but most of it was vandalism—the willful destruction or defacement of beautiful objects. The beauty of these objects, lamented the commission, was not appreciated by the peasants who saw in "pictures, sculptures, antique furniture, and musical instruments not works of spiritual value but only characteristic features of landlord life—a life alien to them."[10]

Let us take one more example—this time of essentially rural people set loose in a city. In December 1918, the Insurgent Army of the Ukrainian peasant anarchist Nestor Makhno entered the city of Ekaterinoslav. In addition to emptying the prisons, dousing them with kerosene, and keeping them in flames all through the night, they destroyed all archives, records, and libraries. But the most spectacular act of destruction took place in the streets adjacent to the railroad station. The shops and bazaars were put to the flame and Makhno himself mounted a three-inch cannon in the middle of the street and fired point blank into the tallest and most beautiful buildings.[11] Was this playfulness—the warrior ebullience and military macho which takes joy from ejaculating shells into a passive target, the kind so often noted in the Mexican Revolution? Was it an act of drunkenness, for which the *batko* was renowned? Was it deep hatred of the city on the part of enraged peasants? Was it a crude example of military tactics? Was it class war and political vengeance against the bourgeoisie? Or was it all of these things? However complex their motivations, by creating a spectacle, acts such as these were also symbolic.

There are, as I shall point out again presently, relatively few symbols, images, and icons to be found in the countryside.[12] The pattern of behavior in the revolutions of 1905 and 1917 seems to suggest that when peasants rampage, they like most of all to burn barns, pens, sheds, hayricks, stables, mills, and offices of the nearby lord or of the owner of a well-run farm. Much rarer is the burning of the manor house itself, an act found more frequently when town people are in the picture. If we juxtapose this fact with what was said about Makhno above, we have another startling example of the continuing "war between the city and the countryside."[13] When villagers do occupy manor houses, they take what they need and destroy the rest. Is this vandalism? Or is it rather "cunning of the peasant" who wants to keep the lord from coming back?[14] The fragmentary evidence hints that there might have been a difference between the "looting-consciousness" of local peasants and "burning-consciousness" of outsiders, almost invariably townsmen. The case of sacking railroad stations points two ways: it can be a very practical military decision in a land where punitive raids were deployed by rail and horse; or it can be a blow at the obvious link to the hated center from whence emanates all the trouble. This is clearly a topic which needs much more thorough and thoughtful investigation before we can speak glibly about the vandalistic mentality of the Russian peasant. One need only recall the burning of rental documents in France in 1789 to see that cool reason can ignite the hottest fires of devastation. If this is vandalism, then Bakunin, Trotsky, and Stalin must take their place in the annals of the vandals.[15]

In one of the few studies of the "crowd" in the Russian Revolution, Teddy Uldricks suggests that "Marxism served not so much to introduce sophisticated concepts of economic and social analysis to the worker and peasant as to create a new set of adversary symbols (e.g., the bourgeoisie, the capitalists, the imperialist powers) as the object of their semi-instinctive class hatred."[16] This seems clear enough, though the exact nature of the relationship between lower classes on the one hand and the objects and symbols of their hatred has never been adequately measured, or even examined. Let us look then at signs as objects of revolutionary destructiveness. For purposes of analysis, I have arranged them into three categories, partly inspired by the division made a century ago by the American philosopher Charles Peirce:[17] buildings and structures (indicating the presence of someone hostile); icons (images of hated figures); and symbols (indirect representations of abstract ideas, i.e., of power, inequality, repression).

If the Bastille of 1789 seemed to symbolize for some the entire ancient order in France, then certain kinds of buildings in Russia were also seen as centers and reminders of a detested world, as in the 1921 poster by N. N. Kogout showing a worker blowing up capital and simultaneously destroying the foundations of buildings and churches. When the SR terrorist Mariia Spiridonova was released by the Revolution from her Siberian prison, she had it blown up in the presence of the people. She repeated this performance all along the Trans-Siberian Railroad and when she arrived in Petrograd demanded that the authorities demolish the Peter Paul Fortress as well. Prisons would henceforth be unnecessary in revolutionary Russia—and the hated sight of them must be erased. Her emotional response recalls Hébert's demand during the French Revolution that all church steeples in Paris be leveled. During the February days in Petrograd people of the street—in an anonymous surge—invaded prisons, courthouses, and arsenals to blow them up or burn them out. Schlüsselburg was gutted, the Lithuanian Castle was demolished, but the Peter Paul Fortress was left unharmed. The process was repeated in local centers. There was no clearly discernible pattern and no element of ritual. Crowds apparently stood quietly and watched the blaze, as they would do in Catalonia in 1936 when dozens of churches were consumed in the flames. According to one eyewitness, the greater part of the burning in Petrograd during the February Revolution was functional, military, and political rather than symbolic: police stations and buildings sheltering snipers were the main targets, as well as courts, arsenals, and prisons.[18]

When we turn to icons, we find similar variation in behavior. A sampling of the press in the February Revolution reveals that, among other things, the citizens of Kansk-Eniseisk, far out amid the frozen wastes of Eastern Siberia, agreed to a proposal of local exiled revolutionaries to replace Alexander II with a monument to freedom fighters; that on March 18, a statue of Stolypin in Kiev was removed before a great throng of people; and that in the capital, rioters had demolished all the statues of monarchs inside the Arsenal before setting it on fire.[19]

But the process was by no means massive or complete. When it became clear to officials in Ekaterinoslav two weeks after the fall of the monarchy that it would not return, they quietly took down portraits of Nicholas II and hid them in attics in government institutions. The big ensembles of bronze and marble, with massive tsars seated on huge horses, did not fall to the fury of a symbolically vengeful mob. When the statue of Alexander III in Moscow was dismantled, a religious legend sprang up at once to the effect that the tsar's cross had disappeared during the "deromanovization." Could such features of royal regalia have played an inhibiting role for some people? The government decree on the dismantling of monuments raised to honor monarchs and their servitors was slow in coming—not published until Lenin's arrival in Moscow in April 1918—and tardy in execution as well. And it was emphatically qualified by exempting monuments which possessed historic or artistic value. Alexander III was the first to feel the force of the decree—he was particularly repugnant to revolutionaries (Lenin's brother had been hanged in his reign) and uncomfortably close to Bolshevik offices in the Kremlin. Lenin ordered him taken down and, with a trace of irony, replaced by Tolstoy who had been excommunicated by the Church. (The Tolstoy monument never materialized.) But the authorities were very modest in their campaign to "deromanovize" the cities. In Petrograd, Alexander III's equestrian statue on Resurrection Square near the station stayed around for years (it is now in the yard of the Russian Museum); and the world-famous representations of Peter (the Bronze Horseman on Decembrist Square), Catherine (near the Public Library on Nevsky), and Nicholas I (on St. Isaac's Square) are still there to dazzle foreign tourists and provincial Russians.[20]

Statues of tsars and princes and generals—Skobelev's figure was also removed—were virtual embodiments of reaction. But about religious icons, there was considerably more ambiguity. In the past, workers had sometimes struck out at the icons in their barracks at the onset of a strike, and orders were sent out during the Revolution and Civil War to remove them from public places such as hospitals. But crosses still adorned a conspicuous pinnacle of the Kremlin in 1920 and were still hanging in the Bolshevized Moscow Conservatory of Music in 1922—and probably much later. In the same year, women workers of a Moscow candy factory actually protested the removal of the icons by the plant manager. The problem with icons, crucifixes, and other Christian signs is that they represented someone far outside Russian politics: God, the savior, and the saints. Thus the graphic connection between them and either revolution or counterrevolution—in spite of conflict between Orthodoxy and Bolshevism—was more tenuous. Looting, defacing, and mockery occurred of course, but they were often closely tied to political or even economic acts (such as taking gold out of churches during the famine of the early 1920s).[21]

Tsarist emblems were more amenable to immediate removal and exchange in the symbolic war. During the February Revolution at the front, soldiers wore red ribbons on their sleeves, their weapons, and their vehicles and showed great anger at the display of tsarist emblems. Officers were arrested for breaches of symbolic etiquette and for calling the red banners "rags" and "babushka's underwear." The red banner, often fashioned out of makeshift materials, was the preeminent symbol of street disorders in the February days. At one of the first celebrations of the Revolution, on March 25, 1917, at the Mariinsky Theater, all Romanov eagles and coats-of-arms were removed; as an added touch, the ushers wore dirty jackets and the imperial box was filled with recent political prisoners. In Moscow, fire trucks with ladders and crews went round the town with iron hooks to pry off the eagles. In the capital a veritable hunt was mounted for imperial emblems; crowns and eagles were torn from gates and fences and even blown out with dynamite in some places. Signs were removed from store fronts and tossed onto the ice of the Neva. Eagles at the Alexander Theater were defaced. Piles of imperial arms and regalia from the Court Provenors' shops were made into giant bonfires. The Counterrevolution found its own symbol: at a performance of Tolstoy's *Living Corpse* at the Alexander Theater—where privileged audiences still prevailed—a gendarme appeared on stage with full-dress uniform and the crowd broke into an ovation. During the Civil War, the war of symbols continued: Komsomol pins were stuck through the tongues of Red nurses before they were hanged; Bolsheviks nailed epaulets into the shoulders of captured White officers.[22]

As in previous revolutions, places, things, institutions, and people were renamed to honor new heroes, commemorate dead ones, and eliminate odious associations. Towns were slow in receiving revolutionary appelations, but by May 1, 1924, the ancient map of all the Russias bristled with such places as Ulyanovsk, Leningrad, Sverdlovsk, Zinovevsk, Trotsk, Stalingrad, Dnepro-petrovsk, Luxemburg, Uritsky, and Pervomaisk (May Day). Streets like the Boulevard Ring in Moscow were renamed, in this case to divest the honest proletarian thoroughfare of association with decadent cafés and cheap novels. Ostap Bender in *The Twelve Chairs* almost lost himself in the welter of Soviet Streets and Lena Massacre Streets in a small provincial hole. The infection spread everywhere. The Tauride Palace became Uritsky Palace (for a time), factories were rechristened "Republic of Russia" and so on. Officers became commanders; sirs and madames became comrades. Words like governor, governess, lord, heir, prince, lycée, chambermaid, ambassador *(posol),* and minister *(ministr)* were abolished (though the last two were later reintroduced). Some young people in the Revolution thought that criminal argot ought to be the true language of the proletariat.[23]

Nowhere is the irony and pathos in all this instant innovation more apparent than in the renaming of people. Consider this partial list of names inspired by: (1) *heroes*—Vilen, Vilena, Ninel (Lenin spelled backwards), Budiona, Bukharina, Stalina, Vellington, Zhores, Mara, Marks, Engels, Robesper; (2) *ideas*—Revolution, February, May, October, Decree, Terror, Barricade, Commune, Shift, Smychka (alliance of peasant and worker), Will, Joy, Spark, Dawn, Vanguard, Alliance, Hero, Idea, Tractor, Electrification; (3) *compounds*—Vladlen, Remir (revolution and peace), Kim (Communist International of Youth); and (4) *popular misunderstanding*—Vinaigrette, Embryo, and Commentary! Like the French of a hundred years earlier, the Russian revolutionaries sought to reject names associated with religion and with the imperial family. Unlike the French, they invoked no classical style and ethos, an ethos that gave France not only the pseudoclassical canvases of David, and the fake Roman festivals that he composed, but also models of republican virtue—and a pool of names, Brutus, Gracchus, Pericles and all the rest. Though even here there was an analogy, since some Russians adopted, or contrived, antique Slavonic names, seen to be pure and prechristian, and therefore acceptable to the new revolutionary sensibility.[24]

It seems fairly clear—and hardly surprising—that in general there was much more symbolic behavior in the cities than in the countryside. Cities are replete with images: their horizontal space, transected by geometrically aligned streets, is itself a symbol of abstract order; their vertical space is filled with structures which graphically represent interdependence and inequality, power and alienation. Juxtaposition of contrasting things and persons is dense, speed and action apparent—symbols, signs, and names are everywhere. One hardly needs to take a step in order to perform a visible act of iconoclasm. Villages are often named for nature or nearby topographical marks, or they are neutral in meaning, and their single street of mud bears no magic name. Symbols, icons (except for religious ones), and centers of power are few—the manor, the station, a barracks, the church—and not so near at hand. They must be marched to and invested in a military maneuver. Peasant hosts seem most wanton and visceral in their urge to demolish when they take a city—we may recall Razin in seventeenth-century Astrakhan or Makhno in twentieth-century Ekaterinoslav. Though the examples I have given are few indeed—a handful of cities and rural places—it seems that in the mix of practical action, emotional drive, and symbolic behavior present on both kinds of spaces one finds much more of the last in an urban milieu.

In comparing rural vandalism with urban iconoclasm it seems clear that peasant destruction was permanently negative. Paintings were slashed and cellos were pulverized not in order to replace them with new objects reflecting peasant aspirations or revolutionary dreams. The "higher" consciousness of the iconoclasts—if one can call it that—consisted in removing artifacts of one culture in order to replace them with artifacts of another. Though the evidence is only suggestive, it is also probable that there was less of a carnivalic motif in urban destruction and defacing than there was in the countryside. Yet both vandalism and iconoclasm evinced mixtures of rational and emotional motivations, often inextricably fused. Both kinds of behavior were at various times used as media of publicity, vehicles for the kinesthetic exercise of power, and menacing signals of further and more ominous violence. Taken together with parallel movements of nihilism and anti-intellectualism, the war against images conducted by the iconoclasts and vandals seemed to portend an anti-cultural tempest of relentless power.

How is all of this related to "nihilism," which Berdyaev once defined as a secular version of religious asceticism that reviles art, thought, and religion as luxury? The word iconoclasm, as I have indicated, has both a concrete and an abstract meaning: the latter, like nihilism, has to do with a fundamental critique of a cultural order. The nihilism of the 1860s was destructive, generationally rebellious, materialist, ascetic, populist, elitist, utopian, and ambivalent. Pisarev's provocative invitation to smash the old has already been mentioned. Radicals debated in the 1870s about whether all culture would be rooted out after the revolution. Much has been written about Bazarov, the fathers and the children, and the generational revolt; it was still going on in the 1920s in remote villages where young militants harried old moderates. It hardly needs to be repeated that those identified as nihilist writers made a virtual cult of science and material progress. But their scientism was directed against soft culture and art—considered elitist; it was not the smug materialism of the West. The clerics' sons and the clerks—so despised by some historians—shunned luxury and wrapped themselves in a self-denying cult of sacrifice. Nihilists, even the earlier nonradical ones, hoped to spread the fruits of scientific progress to the masses, but were elitist in their ways of doing so. Their utopianism, dimly felt, caused painful ambivalence and feelings of guilt.[25]

The Futurist movement, the avant-garde in general, and the proletarian culture movement—Proletcult—were, to different degrees, heirs to this tradition. Soviet historians nowadays praise the cultural and organizational work of Proletcult during the Civil War but assert that some of their misguided leaders "took a nihilist" position toward the old culture. Pavel Lebedev-Polansky spoke of accepting the rich legacy of the past, but critically, and not in slavish obedience; and the critic Sanin was willing to accept selectively some older plays provided they were edited and purified for revolutionary purposes. But even these concessions were grudging and double-edged. A Proletcult speaker in December 1917 explained that old culture, "though sometimes valuable in form, was nevertheless for the most part vulgar and provocative in content and criminal in origin." Pavel Bessalko went further and announced that the proletariat did not need the past. In Tambov Province in 1919, local Proletcultists planned to burn all the books in the libraries in the belief that the shelves would be filled on the first of the new year with proletarian works! The generational struggle was clearly discernible in the movement as well, as when Bessalko said that the workers do not need "older brothers" such as Chekhov, Leskov, and Korolenko. Reverence for science was apparent in the machine-worship aspects of the movement and in the statement of the Tambov Proletcult speaker who warned his comrades against destroying works on such useful and venerable subjects as astronomy.[26]

Like those nineteenth-century nihilists who became radicals and "went to the people," the Proletcultists had a populist impulse: their mission was to smash what was repugnant in the old culture, build a new one, and take it out to the people. And they tried to do so in some very original and striking ways. But they often fell victim to elitism: when the Proletcult official who spoke of the virtues of astronomy heard of the book-burning plans of his comrades, he warned that "local people could not really understand the nature of the broad implications of the problem." Resolutions often affirmed the leadership role of a proletarian cultural vanguard analogous to the Party leadership—a chosen and "conscious" few who would have to lead and point the way. There was far more illusion—even utopianism—in the visions of organized iconoclasts, the Proletcult leaders, than in the acts of the physical iconoclasts who merely broke images and put up new ones: for they aspired to create among the workers and by the workers a whole new collective, machinery-oriented culture with little or no help from past traditions. And the fact that the Petrograd Proletcult set up shop in the opulent mansion that had recently sheltered the Hall of the Nobility while simultaneously proclaiming the criminality of past artistic affluence ought to remind us of Bazarov, the cultural vandal, breathing nihilistic fire as he roamed through the elegant parks of the Kirsanovs, partaking of fine cuisine, browsing in the library, and lingering in the salons of a country gentleman's estate.[27]

But these statements and gestures of a few of the more visible and vocal leaders ought not to mislead us about the inner aspirations of the mass membership of the Proletcult organizations. Recent and extensive research on the social history of Proletcult by Lynn Mally demonstrates clearly that the rank-and-file, and some of the leaders as well, were really hostile to destroying past culture. In the vast network of Proletcult studios, workshops, theaters, and cultural circles, classics of the past were cherished, read, and performed. Early organizers of classical concerts for the masses soon discovered that the works of Beethoven, Tchaikovsky, and Mussorgsky could, when properly introduced and glossed with social analysis, appeal mightily to hardened factory hands.[28]

The artistic Left—Futurists and other elements of the avant-garde—were perhaps the most self-conscious of all the cultural iconoclasts. Sergei Tretyakov captured the mood retrospectively in 1927:

All for combat!
Force is best.
A bullet in the brain
Of Basil the Blest.
Smash all the icons
And the signs They have made.
Explode the Iverskaya
With a hand grenade.[29]

The rhetoric of the Futurists was more outrageous than that of Proletcult. Mayakovsky loved to shout down "bourgeois" speakers; he wanted to level

"Comrade Mauser" at the orators of the past, to put Raphael and Rastrelli "against the wall" and to stop the useless museum work of "preserving junk." He and his colleagues rejoiced in mocking the culture of the past, not just anathematizing it. Meyerhold was "possessed by the spirit of iconoclasm"; Fyodor Kommissarzhevsky facetiously suggested that the Bolshoi be blown up by a bomb. The archetypal iconoclastic act of the Futurists during the Revolution was painting the trees near the Moscow Kremlin in glowing colors. Like their cousins and rivals, the Proletcultists, the Futurists expressed generational revolt, a worship of the machine, elitism combined with populism, and an elaborate dream of a new culture.[30]

But the differences in their iconoclastic impulse were distinct. They differed as to what could be preserved from the past. Doctrinally, Futurists tended to be vague and rhetorical, Proletcultists more specific and prosaic. The Futurists' outrageous style of iconoclasm contrasted starkly with the pious and didactic style of Proletcult. Proletarian culture wanted to communicate its messages among the working class and needed "realistic" content and form, whereas Futurists loved the arcane language of modernism and absurdism. This of course reflected the social bases of the two groups, as well as their relative closeness to European cultural movements. For although the notion of a "proletarian culture" was also a European import from German Social Democracy, it had become thoroughly Russianized. In terms of psychology, the Futurists were far more self-confident, "Western," and modish than the cramped, insecure, and ascetic members of the proletarian culture. It is not wise to speak sweepingly of the arrogance and fanaticism of revolutionary iconoclasm as some single and homogeneous phenomenon. Idols—and, metaphorically the culture of the past—can be smashed with hammer blows, burned, torn apart by hating hands, carefully sawed into pieces or melted down, ridiculed, or (as we shall see in the conclusion) carefully put away for other uses. The emotional insurgency of these small but influential movements in the Russian Revolution show dramatically to what extent the whole of the Russian cultural world had become an icon.[31]

I would like to discuss one more element of the current of iconoclasm in the Russian Revolution: anti-intellectualism and hostility toward the intelligentsia. One of the poignant aspects of the history of the Russian intelligentsia was its isolation, alienated from the masses and despised by the government, and often arrayed against itself. Lower-class anti-intellectualism is the hardest to talk about, although we know it was there. Peasants were bewildered by efforts of fine folk to "save" them and to labor, "like the sun," without pay on behalf of an ideal. Even the radical among the proletariat have told of their uneasiness in the presence of "real" intellectuals, their resentment of verbal facility and endless theorizing. The worker who aspired to replace the intelligent with a worker-intelligent could not but help feel the tension of upward mobility and loss of contact with former comrades. This is reflected both in memoirs and in popular tales about workers in the cheap press of the prerevolutionary period. The tsarist government's animosity to "intellectuals" as such—unless engaged in some acceptable service—expressed itself in many ways, the movement of police socialism of the last tsarist decades being one of the most famous.[32]

These currents were often churned up by storms of self-hatred among the intelligentsia itself. Sergei Nechaev, a would-be intellectual, wrote that "he who learns of the revolutionary cause in books will always be a revolutionary do-nothing." Richard Wortman has studied in *The Crisis of Russian Populism* the prominent strain of disillusionment among populists, their exaltation of the people, abasement of self, and desire to immerse that self in the common folk. Feeling and primitive impulse were often seen as superior to thought. When the Revolution broke out, Alexander Blok, who saw his own kind as parents and the proletariat as children, said: "If I were they I'd hang the whole lot of us." Gorky predicted that "the intelligentsia, the creator of spiritual sustenance," would be swallowed up by the peasantry who would absorb from the educated all that was useful to itself. The Revolution brought about in some ways a fusion of the separate currents of popular, governmental, and the intelligentsia's own anti-intellectualism.[33]

The *makhaevshchina*—the "anti-intellectual" teaching of Jan Waclaw Machajski—was an expression of this in the period of Marxist hegemony over the left, and it owes its origin to political traditions in neighboring Poland. Well before Mannheim and Michels, Machajski applied a sociology of knowledge to Social Democracy and pronounced it the self-interested ideology of the intelligentsia. His critique was therefore directed not at ideas or culture as such, but at the political uses of knowledge and against a coming elite of bureaucrats, scientists, privileged technocrats, and sacerdotal ideologues with a monopoly of knowledge, retained by means of inequality. Though Machajski's direct following was small, his distrust of the intelligentsia found sympathetic vibrations in the Russian labor movement and among certain anarchist groups (though he had opposed them too). There is also a note of violence in Machajski who warned that "the intelligentsia would perish not under the tsarist bullets but under the knife of the ragged tramp."[34] Some of his Russian followers extended his critique to culture and ideas in general. "All evil can be traced to ideology and to ideals," wrote one of them in 1906.[35] Another applied it to the entire history of the radical revolutionary intelligentsia, attributing the "deeds" of Zheliabov and Perovskaia to hypocrisy and egoism![36]

In the Russian Revolutions of 1917, these currents merged in a powerful stream of anti-intellectual statements and actions, some directed against people of ideas and skills, and some against ideas, words, and culture. Much of this flowed together with Proletcult, as in an article in *The Coming Culture,* "The Essence of the Intelligentsia," which defined that group as a "bourgeois concept that must vanish along with the bourgeois class." The anarchist Alexander Ge stated that specialists could be permitted to serve the state only with a weapon pointed at them; and Alexander Shlyapnikov—later a Left Communist—accused the party of pampering the specialists, people "from another world." Everywhere specialists not sufficiently protected by the Bolsheviks were harassed—some were murdered or driven to suicide up into the early 1920s. Nonspecialist intellectuals who possessed no particular patronage from the regime as did engineers, some artists, or officers were simply lumped together with the "burzhui," priests, landowners, and merchants and relocated from their homes, forced into work details, and in many ways demeaned and mistreated, if not imprisoned or shot. Rural teachers became a special target of abuse during the Civil War, and not only for their frequent sympathy with the enemies of Bolshevism. The whole surge of egalitarianism, fused with iconoclasm and hatred of authority figures of the past, worked to make life very difficult for the intellectual community who chose to remain in Russia after the Revolution.[37]

Anti-intellectualism was one of the things that divided the far left from the Left in the Russian Revolution. Anarchists and Left Bolsheviks and others seemed to share the view of the seventeenth-century radical English leveler Gerard Winstanley who noticed that "there are but few who act for freedom, and the actors are oppressed by the talkers and verbal professors of freedom."[38] Proletarian poets made mockery of the old intelligentsia in feuilletons, tales, and poems. The radical and experimental school movement often revealed a distrust of skill-mastery and pure learning: in one such school, Sheila Fitzpatrick tells us, everyone used a prompter in school plays because "it was considered shameful to know the part."[39]

Anarchists outdid all others in their hostility to "words" and "talk": "When will you leave off writing and passing resolutions?" asked Anna Vladimirova in September 1917. "When will this endless stream of words and documents cease at last?"[40] *Burevestnik* in January, 1918, went further: "Uneducated ones! Destroy that loathsome culture which divides men into 'ignorant' and 'learned'! They are keeping you in the dark."[41] The intimate link between iconoclasm and anti-intellectualism found lyrical and ominous expression in the same issue:

Destroy the churches, those nests of gentry lies;
Destroy the university, that nest of bourgeois lies.
Drive away the priests, drive away the scientists!
Destroy the false gentry and bourgeois heavens.
Smash these Peruns, gods, and idols.[42]

Vandalism, iconoclasm, nihilism, and anti-intellectualism—characteristic currents in the Russian Revolution and closely linked in their nature, their upward surge, and their decline. At various points in time and place, they possessed peasants and workers, soldiers and sailors, journalists and poets who longed to assault the Old. Sovdepia—as the Whites contemptuously called the Bolshevik ruled territory in the Civil War—was swathed in red, a new universe largely denuded of the old symbols and adorned with the new. After the war, the double-headed eagle vanished from Russian life except in the émigré centers stretching from Harbin to Paris. Whole classes were enveloped and vanished into the debris. The remaining purveyors of old values, the men and women who had lived only on ideas, were beset by the menace of an anti-intellectual storm. Why did the storm which built up a ferocious power in the early revolutionary years not blow away all traces of the old culture and its makers? Why does the modern tourist on a successful visit to Leningrad take in the Nevsky Prospect (once called Avenue of October 25th), the Peter Paul Fortress, the Winter Palace, St. Isaac's Cathedral, the Gold Room, the university, the Russian Museum, the Philharmonica, and the ballets of Tchaikovsky at the Kirov Theater? What happened to revolutionary iconoclasm?

Between November 6 and 8, 1918, in connection with the celebration of the first anniversary of the Bolshevik Revolution, Lenin participated in the festivities in a way that illustrated in capsule form his views of destruction and preservation. He left the Kremlin, a complex of architecture which he insisted on preserving but from whose premises he had banished the statue of Alexander III, and went into Red Square to attend the unveiling of the newly erected revolutionary monuments. His festive mood was marred by the sight of provocative and abstract decorations of the Futurist participants. In this revealing vignette, one finds displayed Lenin's fundamental intention to (1) pull down the more repugnant vestiges of the tsarist past; (2) retain those which had artistic and historic interest, as defined by the regime; (3) create a new world of symbols, glorifying the political counterculture of the past; (4) discourage excessive innovation.[43]

It is significant that the decree on *preserving* monuments of historical and artistic interest preceded that on the *removal* of those without such interest by more than four months. Though the latter was considered barbarous by some and though it certainly resulted in a rash of statue-breaking at the local level, its importance was greatly overshadowed by the other decree on protection and preservation. As in most revolutions, popular looting was curbed quickly and replaced by cultural "order." During the Provisional Government, scholars had urged turning palaces like the Catherine Palace of Tsarskoe Selo into museums for the people. In Petrograd after the coup, authorities refused even to locate wounded and sick refugees in buildings of historic value. Mansions of grand dukes and aristocrats were visited by teams from the newly formed Commissariat of the Property of the Republic who counted, catalogued, and remanded valuables to government bureaus. The buildings were then locked and guarded. Theaters were labeled "seats of culture of the Russian people." An analogous commission in the Moscow Kremlin gathered up works of art, designated certain buildings national property, and began restoration of edifices damaged during the November fighting. At Klin, local occupiers were chased out of Tchaikovsky's home by the Moscow Soviet because it was "a historically valuable property." The process was repeated in other centers. Bolsheviks even presented a monastery to a group of Tolstoyans to save it from vandalism by the local population. In the villages, Bolshevik authorities tried to prevent destruction of manor houses in order to use them as schools. By the end of 1918, there were 87 museums operating (compared to 30 before the Revolution); by the end of 1920, 550 old mansions and 1,000 private collections of art had been registered.[44]

One ought not to make too much of the famous story about how Lenin laughed at Lunacharsky's grief on hearing of the shelling of St. Basil's Cathedral. Lenin also wished to preserve the great historical and artistic monuments of the past, even those intimately and graphically tied to the name of Romanov. Lenin was a traditionalist in artistic taste and a political realist. He thought it was essential "to grasp all the culture which capitalism has left and build socialism from it." Proletarian culture, he taught, could not grow out of the brains of a few self-styled Proletcultists but had to evolve organically out of the past and the present. Lenin opposed indiscriminate smashing of those artifacts of the Russian past, just as he opposed intellectual-baiting. Had he lived, he probably would have opposed the epidemic of renaming which threatened to turn every other town into a "Lenin" and every theater into "October." The dilemma posed by the desire to "deromanovize" Russia graphically and to save the esthetic treasures of that dynasty was solved neatly and simply by the same mechanism used in the French Revolution of 1789: the museum. By placing crowns, thrones, and imperial regalia in a people's museum, the regime depoliticized them, neutralized their former symbolic power, and offered them as a gift to the masses who—by means of guides and rituals—were to view these artifacts as emblems both of a national genius and of an exploitative order which had used these works for private luxury or symbolic power. Bolshevik iconoclasm turned out to be the iconoclasm of disarming, demythologizing, and antiquarianism.[45]

Tombs of dead monarchs could be preserved and displayed; but imposing statuary—with few exceptions—could not. These were to be replaced, in

Lenin's plan for monumental propaganda, with statues to revolutionary and humanistic heroes of the past. The plan was simple: take down the old; put up the new; and invest the process of unveiling with elements of didactic ritual. Schoolchildren were to be taken to the monuments and told by guides of the exploits of the revered martyrs. And there was one more element in the plan: the appropriateness and accessibility of monuments should be checked first before unveiling them! The new monuments of 1918 celebrated three kinds of figures: European revolutionaries like Marx, Danton, Garibaldi, Blanqui, Fourier; Russian radicals like Radishchev, Herzen, Bakunin, Perovskaya, Chernyshevsky; and cultural figures thought to be "progressive" like Beethoven, Musorgsky, Tchaikovsky, Chopin (!). Except for a cubist statue of Bakunin, and a few others, these monuments were executed in the traditional style and were thus "accessible" to the masses. Ironically most of these early monuments were later taken away or simply deteriorated since they were made in haste and usually constructed out of nondurable materials like plaster. The new symbols that sprang up around the revolution were almost identical in motif to those of 1789: broken chains to evoke liberation; the harmony of exploited classes *(smychka);* fortresses stormed; the hydra of counterrevolution; daybreak, announcing a better world; the forge to fashion a new order; the New Man of toughness and honesty; the New Woman—grim, mannish, plain, and armed— and so on. Rituals, monuments, festive commemorations, funerals, and national emblems provided a new set of symbols to replace those of the past.[46]

Bolshevik political leaders showed a similarity to earlier revolutionaries by their preference for simplicity, strength, realism, heroism, piety, didacticism, and even sentimentality—and by hostility to the surrealist individualism of the Futurists. Proletarian iconography would be defined not by Proletcult or by the avant-garde of art but by Bolshevik leaders and cultural advisers of a cautious bent with an admiring eye to the past, concern about excessive negation of that past, and a sense of what kind of imagery could be rapidly assimilated by the untutored masses of the revolutionary state. The signs of an effete aristocracy could be banished to the museum; the excesses of ego-asserting Futurists could be toned down or curbed; and the "new" signs of Revolutionary order could be fashioned out of elements of the old. Iconoclasm seems so very Russian. But so does anti-iconoclasm. During the reign of Nicholas I, a man was put in a madhouse for hacking at the bust of the Emperor.[47]

Lenin's attitudes toward cultural nihilism and anti-intellectualism were, in a way, broader expressions of his view of symbols new and old. The subsequent story of the struggles between these currents and the government has been told many times; it is a story of sharp zig-zags in policy and emphasis ending in the Stalin solution.[48] Without raising the vexing and perennial question about the relationship between the Leninist beginnings and the Stalinist end, it can at least be said that Lenin and his major supporters saw from the very beginning the value of tradition in state-building. What needs to be done is to trace the origins of Soviet cultural policy back into the nineteenth century. Only this would put iconoclasm and cultural revolution in their proper perspective. "The breaking up, the smashing of something or other in general," wrote the philosopher Vasilii Rozanov in 1911, "is the first step toward culture."[49] In the Russian Revolution, it did not take long for that first step to be superseded by other steps—toward preservation, restoration, and the making of a revolutionary synthesis of the new and the old. In his craving for legitimacy and its signs, his desire to establish the new, his fear of an anarchic nonculture, Lenin may have given weight to the Freudian notion voiced by the anthropologist Geza Roheim that culture is composed of psychic defense systems against anxiety.[50] "The great danger against which mankind has evolved cultures," wrote Roheim, "is that of object loss, of being left alone in the dark."[51] Bolshevik leaders, like other Russian intellectuals, feared the blackness and void of barbarism. They needed a culture—as they needed technicians, specialists, and commanders—and they could not wait for the creation of a new one.

The anticultural and anti-intellectual menace in Russia in the years 1917–1918 may have been the greatest threat to culture in modern times. A veritable alliance—however unconscious—of urban iconoclasts and peasant vandals seemed to threaten the obliteration of the last remnants of an opulent national culture. Grabar, the learned and energetic promoter of art preservation, defined his task precisely as a dual struggle against the avant-garde artists in his commission who had contempt for "the old" and the rampaging peasants who were devastating public and private treasures of culture and history in their seemingly random and unarticulated fashion. Like the French iconoclasts in 1792, the former believed that "for every masterpiece that is lost, liberty [or Bolshevism] will produce a thousand." The preservers had a different view. A few days after the October seizure of power in Petrograd, *Izvestiia* addressed the mass readership of Soviet Russia:

> In addition to the fruits of nature, the laboring people have inherited enormous cultural riches—buildings of rare beauty, museums full of rare and marvellous objects, things that enlighten and inspire, and libraries containing vast intellectual treasures. All of this now really belongs to the people.

Like David and Lenoir in the French Revolution, the Bolshevik authorities and the cultural workers invoked the spiritual welfare of the people in their efforts to stem the roaring tide of cultural nihilism whipped up by the storms of the Russian Revolution.[52]

NOTES

1. V. K. Miuller, *Anglo-russkii slovar'*, 7 ed. (Moscow, 1960).

2. Ronald Firth, *Symbols—Public and Private* (Ithaca, 1973), 341.

3. Brian Barker, *The Symbols of Sovereignty* (Totowa, N.J., 1979), 53.

4. Stanley Idzerda, "Iconoclasm During the French Revolution," *American Historical Review*, LX/1 (October 1954), 16, 25, passim.

5. See James Billington, *The Icon and the Axe* (New York, 1966) for the "fire" and "axe" motifs in Russian history; Richard Pipes, *Russia Under the Old Regime* (New York, 1974), 236, 271; Bernice Rosenthal, "The Transmutation of the Symbolist Ethos: Mystical Anarchism and the Revolution of 1905," *Slavic Review* XXXVI/4 (December, 1977), 608–27; Allan Wildman, *The End of the Russian Imperial Army* (Princeton, 1980), 149.

6. Natalie Davis, *Society and Culture in Early Modern France* (Stanford, 1975); Harvey Cox, *The Feast of Fools* (Cambridge, Mass., 1969); Richard Stites, "Utopia and Experiment in the Russian Revolution," Occasional Paper, Kennan Institute for Advanced Russian Studies; Douglas Brown, *Doomsday, 1917: The Destruction of the Russian Ruling Class* (London, 1975), 95; A. V. Krasnikova, *My novyi mir postroim!* (Leningrad, 1967), 105–106; Jean Marabini, *La vie quotidienne en Russie sous la Révolution d'Octobre* (Paris, 1965), 52–64; Nestor Makhno, *Russkaia revoliutsiia na Ukraine*, 3 vols. (Paris, 1929–37), I, 127.

7. Richard Taylor, *Film Propaganda: Soviet Russia and Nazi Germany* (London, 1979), 94.

8. *Agrarnoe dvizhenie v Rossii v 1905–1906 gg.* [Trudy Imperatorskago Volnago Ekonomicheskago Obshchestva, Number 3, 1908] St. Petersburg, 1908, 49, 52, passim; S. M. Dubrovskii and B. Grave, *1905: agrarnoe dvizhenie v 1906–1907 g.g.*, I (Moscow, 1925), 44, 59, 74–75, 127–28, 134, 141–42, 144, 149, 151–54, 156, 166, 172 and passim; Wildman, *End*, 78.

9. Donald Raleigh, "The Revolutions of 1917 in Saratov" (Ph.D. Dissertation, Bloomington, 1979), 50, 107*n*, 103, 351 (quote); John Keep, *The Russian Revolution* (New York, 1976), 210, 212, 214 (quote), 399; Frederick Mackenzie, *Russia Before Dawn* (London, 1923), 274.

10. I. E. Grabar', A. A. Chaianov et al., *Kooperatsiia i iskusstvo* (Moscow, 1919), 1–27 (quotations, 27, 17).

11. Z. Iu. Arbatov, "Ekaterinoslav, 1917–1922 gg.," *Arkhiv russkoi revoliutsii*, XII (1923), 85–86, 97, 101; Makhno, *Russ. rev.*, I, 116–18, 135.

12. The most purely symbolic act of violence that I found to have occurred in the countryside took place on May 1, 1917 (a radical holiday), when Tambov peasants destroyed the family crypt of General Luzhenovsky (who had "pacified" them in 1905), then outraged and burned his corpse. *Delo naroda* (May 2, 1917), 4.

13. See the interesting essay by Jan Meijer, "Town and Country in the Civil War," in Richard Pipes, ed., *Revolutionary Russia* (New York, 1969), 331–54.

14. In one of the agrarian riots of 1905, the peasants burned "the raven's nest" (manor house), as they called it, so that the lord would have no place to live. Dubrovskii, *Krestianskoe dvizhenie v revoliutsii 1905–1907 gg.* (Moscow, 1956), 48.

15. See the comment by R. Pethybridge in *Social Prelude to Stalinism* (London, 1974), 280, on Bakunin and Trotsky.

16. Teddy Uldricks, "The 'Crowd' in the Russian Revolution," *Politics and Society*, 4/3 (1974), 397–413.

17. Firth, *Symbols*, 61. Peirce's terms are *index, icon,* and *symbol.*

18. V. L. Andrianova and S. G. Rutenberg, "Antireligioznii plakat pervykh let sovetskoi vlasti," *Ezhegodnik muzei istorii religii i ateizma*, V (1961), 203–204; Isaac

Steinberg, *Spiridonova* (New York, 1935), 158; Ernest Henderson, *Symbol and Satire in the French Revolution* (New York, 1912), 411; N. A. Morozov, "Kammennyi grob (Shlisselburgskaia krepost)," *Argus* (April 1917), 7–17; Raleigh, *Revolutions,* 126; A. Tarasov-Rodionov, *February 1917* (New York, 1931), passim. Tsuyoshi Hasegawa's recent study, *The February Revolution: Petrograd, 1917* (Seattle, 1981), shows how difficult it is to speak facilely about "rationality" in violent behavior: in "food pogroms," crowds not only took food and stole cash, but broke windows and shop equipment, thus combining need and anger. Pure hatred of Protopovov, the last tsarist Minister of Interior, surely outstripped the symbolic value of burning his apartment (with his wife still in it): pp. 81–82, 224, 303.

19. *Pravda* (March 23, 1917), 11; *Rabochaia gazeta* (March 21, 1917), 4; and *Rech* (March 7, 1917), 3.

20. Arbatov, "Ekaterinoslav," 84; Marabini, *Vie,* 202; V. Voinov, "Zhivopis'," in *Oktiabr'v iskusstve i literature, 1917–1927* (Leningrad, 1928), 59–73; V. D. Bonch-Bruevich, *Izbrannye ateisticheskie proizvedeniia* (Moscow, 1973), 65–68; Sheila Fitzpatrick, *Commissariat of Enlightenment* (Cambridge, 1970), 115; *Vestnik Russkogo Natsional'nogo Komiteta* (Paris), 8 (December 1923), 25, on the insulted but still standing statue of Alexander III. The SRs also blew up statues: After the SRs killed Volodarsky, the Bolsheviks erected a monument to him; SR terror squads dynamited it (Mackenzie, *Russia,* 49). For comparisons, see David Dowd, *Pageant-Master of the Republic: Jacques-Louis David and the French Revolution* (Lincoln, 1948).

21. V. F. Shishkin, "Propaganda russkikh sotsial-demokratami proletarskoi morali v kontse XIX–nachale XX v.," *Ezhegodnik muzei ist. relig. i ateizma,* VII (1964), 25–35; H. G. Wells, *Russia in the Shadows* (London, 1920), 149; Iu. V. Keldysh, *100 let moskovskoi konservatorii* (Moscow, 1966), 104; Diane Koenker, *Moscow Workers and the 1917 Revolution* (Princeton, 1981), 64; Library of Congress, Manuscript Division, Babine Papers, Section I (1917–1919), Box 1; for more on desecration and revolutionary blasphemy, see Stites, "Soviet Atheists in the 1920s," an unpublished paper.

22. Wildman, *End,* 223–25, 242; Hasegawa, *February,* 248, 283, 287–88; Brown, *Doomsday,* 88; *Dlia narodnogo uchitelia* (Moscow), 9 (1917), 16; Marabini, *Vie,* 74–75; Claude Anet [pseud. of J. Schopfer], *Through the Russian Revolution* (London, 1917), 56, 64; A. L. Fraiman, *Forpost sotsialisticheskoi revoliutsii: Petrograd v pervye mesiatsy sovetskoi vlasti* (Leningrad, 1969), 351.

23. A. M. Selishchev, *Iazyk revoliutsionnoi epokhi: iz nabliudenii nad russkim iazykom poslednykh let (1917–1926)* (Moscow, 1928), 15, 69, 74, 189, 193, and passim; Bernard Comrie and Gerald Stine, *The Russian Language Since the Revolution* (Oxford, 1978), 1, 21, 142, 156, and passim. See also Ilf and Petrov, *The Twelve Chairs* (New York, 1961), 35; Paul Dukes, *Red Dusk and the Morrow* (New York, 1922), 290; James Riordan, *Sport in Soviet Society* (Cambridge, 1977), 137; and Viktor Shklovskii, "Lenin, kak dekanonizator," *Lef,* 5 (1924), 53–56.

24. Selishchev, *Iazyk,* 190; Comrie, *Russ. Lang.,* 187–191.

25. Nicholas Berdyaev, *The Origins of Russian Communism* (Ann Arbor, 1960), 45; Daniel Brower, *Training the Nihilists* (Ithaca, 1975), 15, 31, 27; Abbott Gleason, *Young Russia* (New York, 1980), 72. For echoes in the 1920s, see the interesting chapter, "The Last of the Hamlets," in Maurice Hindus, *Broken Earth* (New York, 1926), 248–71.

26. *Sovetskaia intelligentsiia* (Moscow, 1977), 45. On Proletcult, see: G. S. Ignatev, *Moskva v pervyi god proletarskoi diktatury* (Moscow, 1975), 328–33; Sanin, "Teatr dlia rabochikh," *Vestnik truda,* 4–5 (April–May 1921), 81–84; discussion and documents in Lars Kleberg, *Teatern som Handling; Sovjetisk avantgarde-estetik 1917–27* (Stockholm, 1980), 5–51; P. Gorsen and E. Knodler-Bunte, *Proletkult,* 2 vols. (Stuttgart, 1974–75); Fraiman, *Forpost,* 344–53; Yu. I Ovtsin, *Bol'sheviki i kul'tura proshlogo* (Moscow, 1969), 81–94; Fitzpatrick, *Commissariat,* 70, 92, 239. The

Tambov episode in: II Tambov Conference of Proletcult and Cultural-Educational Organizations, December 1, 1919, from TsGALI, 1230–1–1519; this reference courtesy of Bengt Jangfeldt of the University of Stockholm.

27. Ignatev, *Moskva*, 334; M. Grishin, "Proletarskaia kul'tura," *Griadushchee*, 1 (1919), 11, 20; Sanin, "O rabochem teatre," 52–64; Fraiman, *Forpost*, 344.

28. My deep thanks to Lynn Mally of the W. Averell Harriman Institute for the Advanced Study of the Soviet Union at Columbia University for sharing her knowledge and insights on Proletcult with me. For classical music and the working class, see Stites, "Music and Revolution: the Utopian Moment," an unpublished paper.

29. *Novyi Lef*, 10 (October 1927), 3.

30. Edward J. Brown, *Mayakovsky* (Princeton, 1973), passim; Fitzpatrick, *Commissariat*, 124–28, 149; Ilya Ehrenburg, *First Years of the Revolution, 1918–21* (London, 1962); Boris Schwartz, *Music and Musical Life in Soviet Russia 1917–1970* (New York, 1972), 27; Anatole Kopp, *Changer la vie, changer la ville* (Paris, 1975), 142–44. Cf. *Lef*, 4 (August–December 1924), 16–21 on the alleged "utopianism" of the artistic left.

31. In addition to the above, see: B. V. Pavlovskii. *V. I. Lenin i izobrazhitel'noe iskusstvo* (Leningrad, 1974), 55–62; L. Kleinbort, "Rukopinsnye zhurnaly rabochikh," *Vestnik Evropy*, 7–8 (July–August 1917), 292; and the excellent discussion by Bengt Jangfeldt, "The Futurists and Proletcult," in his *Majakovskij and Futurism 1917–1921* (Stockholm, 1977), 72–91.

32. For some features of proletarian attitudes, see: Reginald Zelnik, "Russian Bebels" pt. II in *Russian Review*, 35/4 (October 1976), 424, 429–30, 433; Wildman, *The Making of a Workers' Revolution* (Chicago, 1967); Jeffrey Brooks, "The Kopek Novels of Early Twentieth Century Russia," *Journal of Popular Culture*, XIII/1 (Summer 1979), 85–97; and M. Gorky, *Revoliutsiia i kultura* (Berlin n.d.—after 1917), 77.

33. Gleason, *Young Russia*, 359; Philip Pomper, *Sergei Nechaev* (New Brunswick, 1979); Richard Wortman, *The Crisis of Russian Populism* (Cambridge, 1967), passim; Avril Pyman, *The Life of Aleksandr Blok*, II (Oxford, 1980), 257 n.4, 343; Gorky, *O russkom krestianstve* (Berlin, 1922), 42–44.

34. Machajski quoted in R. V. Ivanov-Razumnik, *Chto takoe 'makhaevshchina'?* (St. Petersburg, 1908), 87. This is a very influential, but by no means fair, treatment of Machajski's ideas. Machajski's Russian followers tended to be more anti-intellectual as such than he.

35. Quoted from *Buntar'* (December 1906) in I. I. Genkin, "Sredi preemnikov Bakunina," *Krasnaia Letopis'*, 1(22), 1927, 187–88. There is a big literature on this subject. See J. W. Machajski [A. Ch. Volskii], *Umstvennyi rabochii* (St. Petersburg, 1906). Two good commentaries, with references: Paul Avrich, "What Is 'Makhaevism'?" *Soviet Studies*, XVII (July 1965), 66–75; and A. D'Agostino, "Intelligentsia Socialism and the Workers' Revolution: The Views of J. W. Machajski," *International Review of Social History*, XIV/1 (1969), 54–89.

36. E. Iu. Lozinskii, *Chto zhe takaia, nakonets, intelligentsiia?* (St. Petersburg, 1907), 88–96. The sentiments in this little-known literature were far more hostile and vicious toward the intelligentsia than those expressed in the *Vekhi* campaign a few years later—and from a wholly different perspective.

37. *Griadushchaia kul'tura*, 1 (1918), 20; *KPSS v glave kulturnoi revoliutsii v SSSR* (Moscow, 1972), 46; S. A. Fediukin, *Velikii Oktiab'r i Intelligentsiia* (Moscow, 1972), 82; Kendall Bailes, *Technology and Society Under Lenin and Stalin* (Princeton, 1978), 59–60; D. Fedotoff White, *The Growth of the Red Army* (Princeton, 1944), 107–108; Fitzpatrick, "The 'Soft' Line on Culture and Its Enemies: Soviet Cultural Policy, 1922–1927," *Slavic Review* XXXIII/2 (June 1974), 274–8; *Bulletin of the Russian Liberation Committee* 40 (November 22, 1919), 2 (on teachers). For the appearance and the fears about anti-intellectualism in 1917–1918, see the very important article by Charles Rougle, "The Intelligentsia Debate in Russia 1917–1918," in Nils Åke Nilsson,

ed., *Art, Society, Revolution: Russia 1917–1921* (Stockholm: Almqvist and Wiksell, 1979), 54–105.

38. Quoted in V. Haynes and O. Semyonova, eds., *Workers Against the Gulag* (London, 1979), 4.

39. Fitzpatrick, *Commissariat*, 53.

40. Quoted in Avrich, *Anarchists in the Russian Revolution* (Ithaca, 1973), 95.

41. Ibid., 48.

42. Ibid. See also *Proletarskie poety pervykh let Sovetskoi epokhi* (Leningrad, 1959), 106, 208–209, 244–45.

43. See Ignatev, *Moskva*, 320 and the notes below.

44. *Muzykalnaia zhizn' Moskvy v pervye gody posle Oktiabria* (Moscow, 1972), 62; *Istoriko-revoliutsionnye pamiatniki SSSR* (Moscow, 1972), 4–6; *Iz istorii stroitel'stva Sovetskoi kul'tury: Moskva, 1917–1918 gg.* (Moscow, 1964), passim; V. Kurbatov, *Argus* (April 1917), 85–90; Fraiman, *Forpost*, 337–49, idem., *Revoliutsionnaia zashchita Petrograda v Fevrale-Marte, 1918 g.* (Moscow, 1964), 173–77; Marabini, *Vie*, 145, 177; *Petrogradskii Voenno-revoliutsionnyi Komitet: dokumenty i materialy*, 3 vols. (Moscow, 1966–67) I, 205; Ignatev, *Moskva*, 283, 319–28; K. Petrus, *Religious Communes in the U.S.S.R.* (in Russian) (New York, 1953), 62; Iu. S. Kulyshev and V. I. Nosach, *Partiinaia organizatsiia i rabochie Petrograda v gody grazhdanskoi voiny (1918–1920 gg.)*, Leningrad, 1971, 298; Ovtsin, *Bol'sheviki*, 64–71; *Vestnik Oblastnogo Kommissariata Vnutrennikh Del*, 1 (September 1918), 174—on the struggle for preservation in the rural areas; Pavlovskii, *V. I. Lenin*, 49; *KPSS vo glave*, 39. See Rougle, "Intelligentsia Debates," for the 1917 controversies on preservation.

45. Fitzpatrick, *Commissariat*, 13–14; N. S. Khrushchev tells his version of the St. Basil's episode in *Novyi mir*, 3 (March 1963), 19; Pavlovskii, *V. I. Lenin*, 1–33, 47—on Lenin's cultural tastes in the formative years; Ovstin, *Bol'sheviki;* Bailes, *Technology*, 52; Ignatev, *Moskva*, 317–18; Shklovskii, "Lenin," 53; Idzerda, "Iconoclasm"; Nina Tumarkin, *Lenin Lives!* (Cambridge, 1983), passim.

46. Pavlovskii, *V. I. Lenin*, 14–15, 51–53; *Iz. ist. stroitel'stva*, 15; Mikhail German [Guerman], *Art of the October Revolution* (New York, 1979), 15–16, 177–91; Kulyshev, *Partiinaia*, 298; *Muz. zhizn Moskvy*, 71; Kopp, *Changer*, 156 n.1; Voinov, "Zhivopis," 64; Henderson, *Symbol*, 46–47, 53, 66, 74, 77, 81, 84–85, 114, 115 (these illustrations may be instructively compared with those in any standard collection of Soviet posters, art, and symbols in the early years, such as the Guerman book cited above or B. S. Butnik-Siverskii, *Sovietskii plakat epokhi grazhdanskoi voiny, 1918–1921* [Moscow, 1960]. See also Dowd, *Pageant Master*).

Perhaps the most revealing episode of Lenin's handling of the monuments question was his treatment of the obelisk raised to honor the Romanovs on the Tercentary celebrations of 1913 in the Alexander Gardens adjoining the Kremlin. On hearing of plans to demolish the obelisk, Lenin ordered that it be retained, the offensive double-head eagle to be taken from the pinnacle, and the names of the tsars replaced by the names of More, Campanella, Winstanley, Fourier, Chernyshevsky and other thinkers and revolutionaries (*Istoriko-revol. pam.*, 15–16, with picture).

47. For some interesting remarks on the relationship between cultural taste and social-political values, see Dowd, *Pageant Master*, 2, 22, 130–35; and Conrad Donakowski, *A Muse for the Masses: Ritual and Music in an Age of Democratic Revolution, 1770–1870* (Chicago, 1977), 190. The bust incident is related in A. I. Herzen, *My Past and Thoughts* (New York, 1974), 81, n.4.

48. For the further development of these themes, see Bailes, *Technology;* Fitzpatrick, "The 'Soft Line'," and her *Education and Social Mobility in Soviet Russia 1921–1934* (Cambridge, 1980); Avrich, "What Is 'Makhaevism' "; and Fediukin, *Bor'ba s burzhuaznoi ideologiei v usloviiakh perekhoda k NEPu* (Moscow, 1977), 150–51, 199.

49. V. V. Rozanov, *People of the Moonlight* (1911), in *Four Faces of Rozanov: Christianity, Sex, Jews, and the Russian Revolution*, trans. S. Roberts (New York, 1977), 89.

50. Firth, *Symbols*, 152. See also 341 and 364–67.

51. Geza Roheim, *The Origin and Function of Culture* (New York, 1943), 77.

52. See Grabar, *Novaia zhizn'* (Moscow, 1937), 274; *Koop. i iskusstvo*, 8–21; and *Moskva*, 3 (March, 1962), 148 for the *Izvestiia* quotation. For anti-iconoclasm in the French Revolution, see: S. Lacroix, ed., *Actes de la Commune de Paris*, 7 vols. (Paris, 1899), VI, 300; John Moore, *A Journal During a Residence in France . . . 1792*, ed. R. Anderson (Edinburgh, 1820), 34–35 (quotation); Joseph Billiet, "The French Revolution and the Fine Arts," in T. A. Jackson, ed., *Essays in the French Revolution* (London, 1945), 200; G. Sprigath, "Sur le vandalisme revolutionnaire (1792–1794)," *Annales historiques de la Revolution francaise*, 242/No. 4 (1980). I am indebted to Professor R. Emmet Kennedy of George Washington University for the last reference.

[2] Lenin's Bolshevism as a Culture in the Making

Robert C. Tucker

THERE ARE GOOD grounds for regarding Bolshevism as a millenarian movement. If we do so, the insights of recent anthropological scholarship into the nature of millenarian movements as new communities or new-cultures-in-the-making become highly pertinent to the study of early Bolshevism. As one anthropologist has expressed it, "The hypothesis that millenary activities predicate a new culture or social order coming into being . . . is a fair one. Certainly it is more scientific to regard these activities as new-cultures-in-the-making, or as attempts to make a new kind of society or moral community, rather than as oddities, diseases in the body social, or troublesome nuisances to efficient administration—though of course they may be all these as well. Finally, of course, a millenarian movement is a new religion in the making. New assumptions are being ordered into what may become a new orthodoxy."[1]

Millenarian movements, sometimes also called *cults* and by the anthropologist Anthony F. C. Wallace *revitalization movements,* typically draw their followers from among the disadvantaged or distressed groups in a society. In his interpretation of early Christianity as a millenarian movement, John G. Gager emphasizes the central role of a "messianic, prophetic, or charismatic leader" in such a movement, and points out that the movement's adherents envisage the coming of a heaven on earth via the displacement or radical reversal of the existing social order.[2] Thus we are dealing with what is in essence a revolutionary, albeit also it may be a religious, phenomenon. From the anthropological point of view, the crucial fact is that there arises in the movement itself, within the pre-millenial here-and-now, a new community with a certain set of beliefs, values, and practices that may be destined to become foundation stones of a new established culture *if* the movement achieves wordly success.

A full-scale analysis of early Bolshevism as a millenarian movement with Lenin as its prophet or charismatic leader is beyond the scope of the present paper. It is addressed to the more limited task of examining the mental structure of Lenin's Bolshevism, particularly as expressed in *What Is to Be Done?*, as an implicit design for the new sociopolitical world, the party-state political culture, which came into being in the aftermath of the October Revolution of 1917.

I.

We have Lenin's word for it, in *"Left-Wing" Communism: An Infantile Disorder* (1920), that Bolshevism arose in 1903 "as a current of political thought and as a political party."[3] The apparent reference was to the conflict over paragraph one of the Party Rules at the Russian Social Democratic Workers Party's constitutive Second Congress, in the aftermath of which the term "Bolshevism" began to be used for the faction that Lenin led and the party concept that it represented. But Lenin's account of Bolshevism's origin leaves out the part he himself played in originating the current of thought and founding the party. If 1903 was the year of Bolshevism's birth as a current and a movement, the act of conception took place in 1902 in Lenin's mind as expressed in *What Is to Be Done?*, which formulated the "hard" concept of party membership that caused the contention at the Second Congress and the resulting division of the Russian Social Democrats between Lenin-supporting "Bolsheviks" and Martov-supporting "Mensheviks."

In appearance a treatise on how to make a revolution, especially under the then-prevailing police state conditions of Russia, the pamphlet advanced the thesis that the right kind of revolutionary party organization was a necessity in order that a mass revolutionary movement might develop and a revolution occur. Such a party should be small in numbers and composed chiefly of full-time professional revolutionaries thoroughly versed in Marxist theory, totally dedicated to the party's goal of realizing the Marxist revolutionary project, and so skilled in the art of conspiracy, of underground political activity, that they could evade the Okhrana's equally skilled effort to detect and apprehend them. They would work in small groups under centralized direction of the party's leadership, developing the revolutionary mass movement under party guidance which would eventually sweep away the Tsarist autocracy.

All this underlay Lenin's Archimedean metaphor, "Give us an organization of revolutionaries, and we will overturn Russia!"[4] Revolutions do not simply come, he was contending, they have to be made, and the making requires a properly constituted and functioning organization of revolutionaries. Marx proclaimed the inevitable and imminent coming of the world proletarian socialist revolution. Lenin saw that the coming was neither inevitable nor necessarily imminent. For him—and this was a basic idea underlying the charter document of his Bolshevism, although nowhere did he formulate it in just these words—there was no revolution outside the party. *Nulla salus extra ecclesiam.*

So strong was his emphasis upon the organizational theme, so much was his treatise concerned with the organizational requisites for the revolutionary taking of political power, that it has been seen by some as in essence a prospectus for Bolshevism as a power-oriented "organizational weapon." Such was the thesis of a book of that title, which argued that "Bolshevism calls for the *continuous* conquest of power through full use of the potentialities of organization," and that "it is Lenin, not Marx, who is communism's special hero, for it was Lenin's form of organization, with its implications for strategy, that gave birth to communism as a distinct trend within Marxism."[5] Again, Merle Fainsod saw in *What Is to Be Done?* the main vehicle of "the organizational concepts of Lenin" and "the seminal source of the organizational philosophy of Bolshevism."[6] True enough, but how adequate? I wish to argue that to reduce Lenin's Bolshevism to the striving for total party power through organization, and *What Is to Be Done?* to organizational philosophy, is to miss its essential meaning as the document that prefigured the appearance in Russia after 1917 of the Soviet culture, in other words, as a new sociopolitical world in the making.

Marx had seen in the modern proletariat a revolutionary class, a "dehumanization which is conscious of itself as a dehumanization and hence abolishes itself."[7] From the start a revolutionary class "in itself," its destiny was to become a revolutionary class also "for itself," in consciousness. This must come about owing to the developmental dynamics of the capitalist production process. To the proof of this proposition Marx devoted *Capital*. He was mistaken in the belief that the proletariat was inherently a revolutionary class and must necessarily become more and more revolutionized by capitalism's inner laws. Upon Marx's mistake—whether or not he realized it was that— Lenin based Bolshevism. It rested upon the sound but radically un-Marxist (in the Marx-Engels sense) proposition, for which he could and did cite Karl Kautsky as authority: "The history of all countries shows that the working class, exclusively by its own effort, is able to develop only trade union consciousness, i.e., the conviction that it is necessary to combine in unions, fight the employers, and strive to compel the government to pass necessary labour legislation, etc."[8]

Revolutionary consciousness, on the other hand, comprised understanding of Marxist theory, belief in the need for and desirability of a socialist revolution, commitment to the Marxist revolutionary project. Initially the prerogative of an educated minority, it could be brought to workers only "from without," by the efforts of the revolutionary Social Democrats as an organized body of the elect, the "conscious" ones. The mission of the revolutionary party was to propagate political (i.e., revolutionary) consciousness among the working class, spontaneously awakening to the need for a struggle but which on its own, spontaneously, would not acquire political consciousness of the Social Democratic kind. Thus, Lenin was laying the foundation of a party of missionaries engaged in propagating the Marxist faith.

To grasp his Bolshevism as a mental structure, it is of utmost importance to see that he was concerned to spread revolutionary political consciousness not simply among the workers as a class but among—in his own words, repeated over and over in *What Is to Be Done?*—"all classes." The argument by which he sought to establish the necessity of an all-class approach was a tortured one:

> Class political consciousness can be brought to the workers *only from without,* that is, only from outside the economic struggle, from outside the sphere of relations between workers and employers. The sphere from which alone it is possible to obtain this knowledge is the sphere of relationships of *all* classes and strata to the state and the government, the sphere of the interrelations between *all* classes. For that reason, the reply to the question as to what must be done to bring political knowledge to the workers cannot be merely the answer with which, in the majority of cases, the practical workers, especially those inclined toward Economism, mostly content themselves, namely: "To go among the workers." To bring political consciousness to the *workers,* the Social Democrats must *go among all classes of the population;* they must dispatch units of their army in *all directions.*[9]

On this shaky basis (shaky from the standpoint of Marx's Marxism), Lenin kept stressing the theme of "all classes" and "all strata." "We must 'go among all classes of the population' as theoreticians, as propagandists, as agitators, and as organizers. . . . The principal thing, of course, is *propaganda and agitation* among all strata of the people."[10]

Never before, it seems, had such an explicitly "all-class" approach been promoted by a Marxist revolutionary; never had Marxism's proletarian class emphasis been accompanied by and overlaid with such a concern to draw elements of all strata into the movement. Very likely this gave expression to the *narodnik* revolutionary outlook that Lenin had imbibed, as he showed at various points in *What Is to Be Done?,* from those Russian revolutionaries of the sixties and seventies whom he so greatly admired. For all his doctrinaire Marxism and insistence that class struggle is a motor force of history, he was bound to oppose the idea of a separate proletarian class culture. His "all-class" Bolshevism would make this Marxist *narodnik* the principled foe of the Proletcult that he became. His anti-Proletcult resolution of 1920[11] was prefigured in *What Is to Be Done?*

However weak the Marxist *logic* of going among "all classes," the real basis for doing so was strong. Lenin was sensitively aware of the discontents and grievances that many individuals in all strata of Russian society harbored against the Tsarist order. Although the working class was, as he said, the "ideal audience" for the Social Democratic political pedagogues, being most of all in need of the "political knowledge" that they had to impart, there were millions of working peasants and artisans who "would always listen eagerly" to the party agitators' political exposures of Russian conditions. There were aroused university students, unhappy *zemstvo* employees, outraged members of religious sects, and mistreated teachers, all of whom must be made conscious of the meaning of such facts of Russian life as "the brutal treatment of the people by the police, the persecution of religious sects, the flogging of peasants, the outrageous censorship, the torture of soldiers, the persecution of the most innocent cultural undertakings, etc." Especially could their indignation be aroused if news about these matters were brought to them vividly and regularly by an all-Russian party paper, smuggled in from abroad, which would function as a "collective propagandist and collective agitator."[12]

The organizational concepts of *What Is to Be Done?* belong in the frame of this reasoning about the teaching of anti-regime political consciousness as the prime function of the revolutionary party, its way of preparing for the eventual overthrow of the Tsarist state by mass revolutionary action under the party's guidance. The revolutionaries would form a sort of brotherhood (an "order of sword-bearers," the impressionable Stalin would later call it) functioning conspiratorially and under centralized leadership as Marxist-trained political tutors of large numbers of non-party people receptive to their message. Their medium of operation would be worker study-circles, trade unions, and other local groups, in which they would form nuclei of revolutionary consciousness—party cells. Here Lenin drew upon his own experience of underground propaganda work as one of the organizers in 1895 of the short-lived St. Petersburg Union of Struggle for the Liberation of the Working Class, and upon the larger experience of "the magnificent organization that the revolutionaries had in the seventies, . . . which should serve us all as a model. . . ."[13] The all-Russian party paper, drawing its material from revolutionaries working in these clandestine circles and being distributed by them, would constitute an organizational training ground in revolutionary work.

Such was Lenin's plan for an organization that "will combine, in one general assault, all the manifestations of political opposition, protest, and indignation, an organization that will consist of professional revolutionaries and be led by the real political leaders of the entire people."[14] He admitted that the plan was at best, so far, a "dream," but invoked the authority of Pisarev for the idea that "the rift between dream and reality causes no harm if only the person dreaming believes seriously in his dream, if he attentively observes life, compares his observations with his castles in the air, and if, generally speaking, he works conscientiously for the achievement of his fantasies."[15]

To understand Lenin's political conception in its totality, it is important to visualize that he saw in his mind's eye not merely the militant organization of professional revolutionaries of which he spoke, but the party-led popular *movement* "of the entire people." The "dream" was by no means simply a party dream although it centered in the party as the vanguard of conscious revolutionaries acting as teachers and organizers of a much larger mass following in the movement. The dream was a vision of an anti-state popular Russia raised up by propaganda and agitation as a vast army of fighters against the official Russia headed by the Tsar; and of this other, popular Russia as an all-class *counter-community of the estranged,* a mass of people trained to revolutionary consciousness by its party tutors and dedicated to the goal of a revolution that would rid Russia of its "shame and curse," as Lenin called the autocracy.

Of course, the dream was not realized, despite Lenin's determined, persistent efforts in the ensuing fifteen years to make it come true. His fantasy-picture of a collective of like-minded revolutionaries functioning harmoniously in a centralized organization remained just that. For the actual Bolshevik party as it evolved under Lenin was and remained a faction-ridden grouping of ever disputatious Russian revolutionaries. Nor did he realize his dream of forming under the party's leadership a great popular following that could and would destroy the Tsarist order in a victorious mass revolution and thereby become "the vanguard of the international revolutionary proletariat,"[16] making Russia the spearhead of world revolution. Prior to 1917, the party acquired nothing like a mass popular following.

Yet it was this party that managed to take over and hold onto political power in the new Time of Troubles unleashed by the World War. That momentous turn of historical circumstance gave Lenin the opportunity to attempt, from positions of power, from above, to translate his old dream into sociopolitical reality. Then it turned out that what in fact he had done, albeit unwittingly, in *What Is to Be Done?* was to sketch out the prospectus for a new culture: the tutelary party-state that he sought to construct and set on its course during his few remaining years.

II.

Is the rise of the Bolshevik party-state, the single-party system, to be explained as a consequence of the adversities experienced by the fledgling revolutionary regime in the time of the Civil War when it was beset by hostile forces? In *The Revolution Betrayed,* Trotsky argued that such was the case. During the Civil War, he wrote, the (socialist) opposition parties were forbidden one after another. "This measure, obviously in conflict with the spirit of Soviet democracy, the leaders of Bolshevism regarded not as a principle, but as an episodic act of self-defense."[17] Citing that statement as his authority, Isaac

Deutscher later reformulated the argument in more forceful terms: "The idea that a single party should rule the Soviets was not at all inherent in the Bolshevik programme. Still less so was the idea that only a single party should be allowed to exist."[18]

A Bolshevik only from 1917 and a unique political personality among Bolshevik leaders thereafter, Trotsky was a dubious source of authoritative testimony on this critically important point. Whether or not the idea that "a single party should rule" inhered in the Bolshevik party's programmatic declarations, it was present in the Bolshevism that prevailed in history, namely, Lenin's. When he wrote *The State and Revolution* while in hiding during the summer of 1917, seeking to show the Marxist propriety of seizing power by violent means and establishing a "dictatorship of the proletariat," Lenin revealed in a single lapidary sentence that his Bolshevism envisaged this dictatorship in the form of a party-state: "By educating the workers' party, Marxism educates the vanguard of the proletariat, capable of assuming power and *leading the whole people* to socialism, of directing and organizing the new system, of being the teacher, the guide, the leader of all the working and exploited people in organizing their social life without the bourgeoisie and against the bourgeoisie."[19] On this crucial point, the treatise, which was largely a tissue of quotations from Marx and Engels, made no reference to those authority figures. There was none to make. It was not classical Marxism but Lenin's Bolshevism that conceived the proletarian dictatorship as a state in which a political party would have the mission to "lead the whole people to socialism" as their teacher, leader, and guide.

We have Lenin's further, later testimony to the fact that the party-state as a system had been latent in his Bolshevism from the start. In 1920, when the system was in its third year, he described in *"Left-Wing" Communism* how it worked. After observing that "no important political or organizational question is decided by any state institution in our republic without the guidance of the Party's Central Committee," he explained by the example of the trade unions, as formally non-party bodies with a mass membership at that time of over four million, that Communists made up the directing bodies of the vast majority of the unions and carried out the directives of the party in their trade-union activity. There were other mass organizations under party leadership, such as the non-party worker and peasant conferences, he went on, as well as the soviets and their congresses. Then he continued:

Such is the general mechanism of the proletarian state power viewed "from above," from the standpoint of the practical implementation of the dictatorship. We hope that the reader will understand why *the Russian Bolshevik, who has known this mechanism for twenty-five years and seen it develop out of small, illegal and underground circles,* cannot help regarding all this talk about "from above" *or* "from below," about the dictatorship of leaders *or* the dictatorship of the masses, etc., as ridiculous and childish nonsense, something like discussing whether a man's left leg or right arm is of greater use to him.[20]

In Lenin's mind, the Soviet system of rule by the Communist Party was not a post-revolutionary innovation, and not (as Trotsky said) "in conflict with the spirit of Soviet democracy." It was, rather, the institutionalization *in power* of a set of party-mass relationships that originated in the party's prehistory, in the experience of the underground circles in which he had been active around 1895 in St. Petersburg. The party-state of 1920 was the party-led movement of the early years in open ascendancy as a sociopolitical formation in Russia.

As such it was, in one very important aspect, a system of power, as Lenin was frank to acknowledge when he wrote here: "Without close contacts with the trade unions, and without their energetic support and devoted efforts, not only in economic, but *also in military* affairs, it would of course have been impossible for us to govern the country and to maintain the dictatorship for two and a half months, let alone two and a half years."[21] In practice, he went on, these contacts call for propaganda, agitation, and frequent conferences with influential trade union workers, and also for "a determined struggle against the Mensheviks, who still have a certain though very small following to whom they teach all kinds of counter-revolutionary machinations, ranging from an ideological defense of *(bourgeois)* democracy and the preaching that the trade unions should be 'independent' (independent of proletarian state power!) to sabotage of proletarian discipline, etc., etc."[22]

Lenin's arrogation of all power to the Bolsheviks in the new Russia, his resolute orientation toward making the Soviet state a Bolshevik-ruled party-state, is not to be explained by an urge to power for power's sake, but by an urge to power for the sake of leadership of the society by the sole political force (as he saw it) in possession of the Marxist truth as guidance for politics. The one-party system appeared a legitimate political formation on account of the teaching role that Lenin considered the party to be uniquely qualified to play. The party-state in all its spheres was to be a tutelary state, with the party as political pedagogue in non-party organizations such as the trade unions. "The conquest of political power by the proletariat is a gigantic forward step for the proletariat as a class, and the party must more than ever and in a new way, not only in the old way, educate and guide the trade unions, at the same time not forgetting that they are and will long remain an indispensable 'school of communism' and a preparatory school in which to train the proletarians to exercise their dictatorship, an indispensable organization of the workers for the gradual transfer of the management of the whole economic life of the country to the working *class* (and not to the separate trades), and later to all the working people."[23]

Viewing matters so, Lenin was bound to take the position that he did in the trade union controversy of 1920–1921. He could not accept the view of the Workers' Opposition that the workers, through their unions, should take over management of the economy without a long preparatory period during which they would be "schools of communism" in which the party would be teacher. That was "a deviation towards syndicalism and anarchism," as he put it, for "Marxism teaches . . . that only the political party of the working class, i.e., the Communist Party, is capable of uniting, training and organizing a vanguard of the proletariat and of the whole mass of the working people that alone will be capable of withstanding the inevitable petty-bourgeois vacillations of this mass and the inevitable traditions and relapses of narrow craft unionism or craft prejudices among the proletariat, and of guiding all the united activities of the whole of the proletariat, i.e., of leading it politically, and through it, the whole mass of the working people."[24] One can imagine the scathing comment that a resurrected Marx would have made about the failure of his disciple from the Volga to understand some fundamentals of what "Marxism teaches."

In Lenin's Bolshevism, however, the workers after the revolution required party tutelage. Responding to Trotsky's platform for statification of the trade unions, he said that "this is not a state organization, not an organization for coercion, it is an educational organization, an organization for enlistment, for training, it is a school, a school of administration, a school of management, a school of communism."[25] The local soviets, too, were, in Lenin's eyes, fundamentally a school, a training ground: "Only in the soviets does the mass of exploited people really learn, not from books but from their own practical experience, how to construct socialism, how to create a new public discipline, a free union of free workers."[26] Indeed, all the non-party mass organizations of the Soviet system were conceived as party-taught, party-led, and party-organized schools in a tutelary state, Lenin's pedagogical polity.

III.

Thus Lenin's Bolshevism remained in power essentially what it had been from the start, an orientation on party tutelage of a popular movement toward a revolutionary goal. The goal having been attained in a negative way—the destruction of the Tsarist order—it now turned into the goal of constructing a socialist society in a new Russia defined officially as soviet in its political organization but not yet socialist as a society.

Socialism connoted a highly cultured society. In the heady atmosphere of 1917, when he was obsessed with the need to nerve the party leadership for a seizure of power in what he sensed was but an interregnum, Lenin had conjured up, perhaps in his own mind as well as in others, a vision of Russia as ripe for early, indeed virtually immediate socialist transformation.[27] By 1919–1920, he took a much longer view. The transformation of Soviet Russia into a socialist country would be the work of a generation, if not more. Consequently, Lenin's Bolshevik Marxism came to make provision for a "transition period" not envisaged in classical Marxism, a post-revolutionary period of transition *to* socialism.[28] What was to be done under these conditions was what had seemed to him in 1902 the thing needing to be done: the organization of revolutionaries, as a vanguard, as organized Marxist consciousness, must assume a tutelary role of leadership of the entire people, excluding interference by other parties misguided in their socialism, specifically the Mensheviks.

So the concept of a movement remained central in Lenin's Bolshevism. He saw the new society of the Soviet but not-yet-socialist republic as a *society in movement* save that now it was a constructive movement for the creation of socialism and ultimately communism. Such a thought had been in his mind, in an anticipatory way, before the taking of power. He had written in *The State and Revolution* that "*only* socialism will be the beginning of a rapid, genuine, truly mass forward movement, embracing first the *majority* and then the whole of the population, in all spheres of public and private life."[29]

A *locus classicus* of his subsequent thinking along these lines is his speech of October 2, 1920, to the Third All-Russia Congress of the Communist Youth League. To build communism (he could just as well have said socialism) involved a lengthy learning process, he argued; it meant first of all, "learning communism." This was not at all a matter simply of mastering Marxist theory, nor was it a matter of acquiring a "proletarian culture" in a class sense of the term. For "only a precise knowledge and transformation of the culture created by the entire development of mankind will enable us to create a proletarian culture." Learning communism meant, moreover, acquiring the skills needed for the economic revival of Russia along modern technical lines, on the basis of electrification, for which purpose mass literacy and technical knowledge were requisite. Hence the Communist Youth League must become fundamentally a teaching organization, from whose practical activity any worker "can see that they are really people who are showing him the right road." In conclusion, Lenin said that the generation of people now at the age of fifty (he was fifty then) could not expect to see a communist society. "But the generation of those who are now fifteen will see a communist society, and will itself build this society. This generation should know that the entire purpose of their lives is to build a communist society."[30]

A human society is not merely a large collection of people living in an organized way on a certain territory and interacting with one another on the basis of some institutionalized division of functions. Such a grouping of people does not form what may properly be called a "community" or "society" without a sense of common involvement in a meaningful enterprise, some consciousness of kind transcending, though probably including, a common language and symbols. This may be called the society's sustaining myth. In a certain sense the myth *is* the society; or to put it otherwise, the society has its real existence in its members' minds. Lenin, despite the opposition he had shown in the inter-Bolshevik controversies of earlier years to the ideas of Bogdanov, Lunacharsky, and others concerning a "usable myth" for socialism,[31] was himself engaged here in an historic act of mythologizing. He was putting into words the central, sustaining myth of Soviet society, laying the foundation of Soviet Communism as a culture. In the Leninist canon, to be a Soviet citizen was to be a member of a goal-oriented all-Russian collective of builders of socialism and communism.

There were different grades of membership. To belong to the Communist Party or the Communist Youth League was, by his definition, to be a *conscious* builder, one dedicated to the collective purpose as a personal life-purpose. It was to be a member of the leadership cohort in the constructive movement for the post-revolutionary transformation of the society into a socialist one. As Lenin put it to the Communist Youth League: "You must be foremost among the millions of builders of a communist society in whose ranks every young man and young woman should be. You will not build a communist society unless you enlist the mass of young workers and peasants in the work of building communism."[32] Enlisting was basically an educational enterprise: the transmitting of literacy, technical skills, and above all political consciousness, including dedication to the goal, to millions of not-yet-conscious builders of the new society.

As an heir of the nineteenth-century Russian Westerners, Lenin considered the learning of Western ways, the adoption of the organizational and technological achievements of what to him were the more cultured countries, to be a most important part of the learning process comprised in the building of communism. Thus his enthusiasm for the adoption of America's "Taylorism" in Soviet Russia. Thus his injunction, at the very time when Germany imposed a "Tilsit peace" on Russia at Brest-Litovsk, to learn from the Germans. "Yes, learn from the Germans! History is moving in zigzags and by roundabout ways. It so happens that it is the Germans who now personify, besides a brutal imperialism, the principle of discipline, organization, harmonious cooperation on the basis of modern machine industry, and strict accounting and control. And that is just what we are lacking. That is just what we must learn."[33]

Toward the end, he decided that learning to work cooperatively was the crux of socialism's construction in Russia. He elaborated this theme in "On Cooperation," one of the set of last articles that constituted his valedictory to the party and country. Going back to the "old cooperators" (he mentioned Robert

Owen in this connection but might just as well have chosen Fourier, whose projected *phalanstères* excited the imagination of Lenin's old idol Chernyshevsky), he proposed that "the system of civilized cooperators is the system of socialism." To enlist the whole population of Russia in cooperative societies was thus the main content of the building of socialism. State financial backing for cooperatives would be one way of doing so, but chiefly it was a problem of educational work, of "culturalizing" *(kul'turnichestvo)*. A whole historical epoch, comprising one or two decades at a minimum, would be required to carry out the "cultural revolution" needed in order to educate the Russian peasant to the advantages of the cooperative way: "But the organization of the entire peasantry in cooperative societies presupposes a standard of culture among the peasants (precisely among the peasants as the overwhelming mass) that cannot, in fact, be achieved without a cultural revolution. . . . This cultural revolution would now suffice to make our country a completely socialist country; but it presents immense difficulties of a purely cultural (for we are illiterate) and material character (for to be cultured we must achieve a certain development of the material means of production, must have a certain material base)."[34]

Such was Lenin's final word on what it would mean to build a socialist society. His heavy emphasis upon "educational work" as a long-range process of persuasion in the setting of a party-led movement of the entire people to socialism was in keeping with his Bolshevism's master theme, enunciated over twenty years before. It was still a matter of "consciousness" overcoming popular "spontaneity" by a pedagogical process. Now it had reached the point of conceptualizing Soviet Russia as the scene of a culture-building culture. Needless to add, the program for a cultural revolution presented in "On Cooperation" had nothing to do with the politico-cultural witch hunt that Stalin sponsored under the name of "cultural revolution" in 1928–1931. That episode in the later history of Soviet Russia had as little claim to being the cultural revolution conceived by Lenin as Stalin's terroristic collectivization of the peasants had to being the "cooperating of Russia" envisaged by Lenin.

When Soviet studies emerged as a branch of academic scholarship in the 1940s and after, it became customary to treat Soviet Communism as, in essence, a system of power, or total power. *How Russia Is Ruled,* by Merle Fainsod, stands as a monument to that understanding of the object of study, but it is only one of many. Although it had come or was coming true at the time when these works appeared, the image of the object as a system of power was wanting in historical accuracy. Soviet communism had been designed by its principal founder as in essence a new culture containing *within* itself a system of party-state power. From Lenin's movement "dream" of 1902 to his post-revolutionary dream of a society in party-led movement toward socialism and communism there was a straight line of continuity. Both before and after 1917, he and others tried to translate the dream into sociopolitical reality. The conquest of real political power in the Revolution made a huge difference by creating all sorts of possibilities for success in the culture-building effort that had not existed before 1917. Nevertheless, the venture was showing itself to be beset with enormous difficulties while Lenin still lived, and the appearance in the year of his death of Stalin's *Foundations of Leninism,* where the mass organizations that Lenin conceived as "schools of communism" were characterized mechanistically as "transmission belts" of party rule, was a symptom of a process then in full swing: the conversion of the tutelary state designed but at most only partially realized under Lenin into the system of total power that Soviet communism finally became.

There was a fundamental flaw in Lenin's design for a tutelary state in a culture-building culture, one that he might have foreseen but seemingly did not. The organization of professional revolutionaries imbued with Marxist consciousness was bound to turn into what it did become and would have become in time even if a Stalin had not sharply accelerated the process by murder and repression of old revolutionaries: an organization of professional party-state functionaries mouthing Marxist-Leninist ritual language and imbued with a spirit of self-seeking. Then the party-state would be confronted with the dilemma inherent in its self-proclaimed role as a political mentor of the masses: what grounds do the party-state monopolists of power have for asserting the continuing legitimacy of their tenure as political teachers when their pupils the people have reached maturity at graduation time?

NOTES

1. Kenelm Burridge, *New Heaven, New Earth: A Study of Millenarian Activities* (New York: Schocken Books, 1969), p. 9.

2. John G. Gager, *Kingdom and Community: The Social World of Early Christianity* (Englewood Cliffs, N.J.: Prentice Hall, 1975), p. 21. Professor Gager cites I. C. Jarvie, *The Revolution in Anthopology* (Chicago: Henry Regnery, 1957), on several of the attributes of a millenarian movement.

3. *The Lenin Anthology,* ed. Robert C. Tucker (New York: W. W. Norton, 1975), p. 553. See also his statement (ibid., p. 554) that "Bolshevism arose in 1903 on a very firm foundation of Marxist theory."

4. *What Is to Be Done?,* in *The Lenin Anthology,* p. 79.

5. Philip Selznick, *The Organizational Weapon: A Study of Bolshevik Strategy and Tactics* (New York: McGraw-Hill, 1952), pp. 17, 41.

6. Merle Fainsod, *How Russia Is Ruled,* revised ed. (Cambridge, Mass.: Harvard University Press, 1963), p. 39.

7. Marx and Engels, *The Holy Family: A Critique of Critical Criticism* (1845), *The Marx-Engels Reader,* ed. Robert C. Tucker, second ed. (New York: W. W. Norton, 1978), p. 132.

8. *What Is to Be Done?*, in *The Lenin Anthology*, p. 24. In 1902 Kautsky denied that socialist consciousness is the necessary result of the proletarian class struggle, and wrongly asserted that this denial was in accord with Marx's position. For Lenin's citation of Kautsky, see ibid., p. 28.

9. Ibid., p. 50.

10. Ibid., p. 52.

11. For the resolution's text, see ibid., pp. 675–676.

12. Ibid., pp. 43, 55, 102.

13. Ibid., p. 85. The reference, he explained, was to the *Zemlia i Volia*.

14. Ibid., p. 60.

15. Ibid., p. 106.

16. Ibid., p. 22.

17. Leon Trotsky, *The Revolution Betrayed* (New York: The Pathfinder Press, 1972), p. 96. The book originally appeared in 1937.

18. Isaac Deutscher, *Stalin: A Political Biography*, second ed. (New York: Oxford University Press, 1967), p. 224.

19. *The State and Revolution*, in *The Lenin Anthology*, p. 328.

20. *"Left-Wing" Communism*, in *The Lenin Anthology*, pp. 553, 572–573. First italics added.

21. Ibid., pp. 572–573.

22. Ibid., p. 573.

23. Ibid., pp. 574–575.

24. "Draft Resolution on the Syndicalist and Anarchist Deviation in our Party," in ibid., pp. 497–498.

25. "O professional'nykh soiuzakh, o tekushchem momente i ob oshibkakh t. Trotskogo," V. I. Lenin, *Polnoe sobranie sochineniia*, 5th ed. (Moscow, 1963), Vol. 42, p. 203.

26. "Tezisy po II kongressu Kommunisticheskogo Internatsionala," in ibid., Vol. 41, pp. 187–188.

27. See especially his essay "Can the Bolsheviks Retain State Power?" (September 1917), where he wrote: "The big banks are the 'state apparatus' which we *need* to bring about socialism, and which we *take ready-made* from capitalism; our task here is merely to *lop off* what capitalistically mutilates this excellent apparatus, to make it even *bigger*, even more democratic, even more comprehensive. Quantity will be transformed into quality. A single State Bank . . . will constitute as much as nine-tenths of the *socialist apparatus*." *The Lenin Anthology*, p. 401.

28. Marx foresaw an immediate post-revolutionary period of transition "between capitalist and communist society," but envisaged society in this transition period as already rudimentarily communist (or socialist, a word he used interchangeably with communist). On this, see his remarks in "Critique on the Gotha Program" (*The Marx-Engels Reader*, pp. 531, 538). Lenin's Bolshevism inserted a period of transition *to* socialism after the political revolution of October 1917 by which his party took power.

29. *The Lenin Anthology*, p. 382.

30. "The Tasks of the Youth Leagues," in *The Lenin Anthology*, pp. 664, 666, 673, 674.

31. For the use of this phrase and a discussion of "collectivism" as socialist myth, see Robert C. Williams, "Collective Immortality: The Syndicalist Origins of Proletarian Culture, 1905–1910," *The Slavic Review*, Vol. 39, No. 4 (September 1980), pp. 392–395.

32. *The Lenin Anthology*, p. 667.

33. "The Chief Task of Our Day" (1918), in ibid., pp. 436–437.

34. Ibid., pp. 710–713.

[3] The Provisional Government and Its Cultural Work

Daniel T. Orlovsky

"Sufficient unto the day is the evil thereof"—this is natural, this is right; however, the present day has "two evils": the struggle of the parties for power and the development of culture. I know that the political struggle is a necessary matter, but I accept this matter as an unavoidable evil. For I can't help seeing that (under the conditions of the present moment and in view of some of the peculiarities of the Russian psychology) the political struggle renders the building of culture almost impossible.

The task of culture—to develop and strengthen a social conscience and a social morality in man, to develop and organize all personal abilities and talents—can this task be fulfilled in times of widespread brutality?

. . . the revolution was made in the interests of culture and it was precisely the growth of cultural forces and cultural demands that called the revolution into being.

The Russian, seeing his old way of life shaken to its foundations by war and revolution, is yelling high and low for cultural aid.

Maxim Gorky, *Novaia Zhizn'*, May 18, 1917

TRANSFORMATION OF THE basic structures of any society—whether they be social, socio-psychological, or institutional—requires fundamental changes in the "learned repertory of thoughts and actions" and in their symbolic forms of transmission. Consequently, any theory of revolution that seeks to explain both the breakdown of Old Regimes and ultimate historical outcomes must take into account society's cultural dimension.

Unfortunately, the most widely heralded modern theories of revolution lack precisely this dimension. Theda Skocpol's notion of "social revolution," despite its evident strengths, may stand as a paradigm for teleological approaches that ignore culture and assume transformation.[1]

In *State and Social Revolutions* Skocpol defines social revolution as follows:

rapid basic transformations of a society's state and class structures accompanied and in part carried through by class-based revolts from below. Social revolutions are set apart from other sorts of conflicts and transformative processes above all by the combination of two coincidences: the coincidence of societal structural change with class upheaval; and the coincidence of political with social transformation. . . . What is unique to social revolution is that basic changes in social structure and in political structure occur together in mutually reinforcing fashion. And these changes occur through intense sociopolitical conflicts in which class struggles play a key role.[2]

According to Skocpol her theory is different from others because it identifies a "complex object of explanation of which there are relatively few historical instances"; and because her "definition makes successful sociopolitical trans-formation—*actual change* of state and class structures—part of the specification of what is to be called a social revolution." The problem with this approach is twofold. First of all it assumes transformation on the basis of external social and economic and political forms rather than their human content. Skocpol offers no explanation of survivals *(perezhitki)*, the curious mixing of old culture and new that any serious student of revolution faces again and again at almost every point in the historical process. While Skocpol's structural approach sheds light on the demise of Old Regime political structures and authority it offers no insight into the construction of new regimes and the new men and women who bring the new forms to life and who themselves are supposedly transformed in the process. Second, Skocpol's theory assumes that the realm of culture, of the linguistic and symbolic, the entire mental world of a society is somehow separate from the social and political structures that may be "transformed" in a revolution. In this vision, governments and institutions are what they proclaim themselves to be and social change is measured by the degree to which previously downtrodden social groups begin to share in political power and improve their economic well-being. There is no attempt to go beneath the surface of either the temporal order of events or the new forms of the revolutionary state or society.

We need not be content with this kind of theory of revolution. A good many serious thinkers, Marxists included, have maintained that superstructure, the realm of culture and subjectivity, of human mediation between the material world and the order of events, may have an autonomous existence. It is as if, to take 1917 as an example, class conflict had two mutually reinforcing realities—one clearly embedded in the economic and social realities of the era that had an enormous impact on the course of events and a second that was linguistic and symbolic, but no less real and no less (and possibly even more) capable of shaping events by altering the way people perceived reality. A theory of revolution should embrace such symbols and other cultural products as well as the patterns of perception, behavior, and organization that are themselves part of the culture undergoing transformation. An examination of how the structures that generate culture and its institutions interact with material conditions and other external influences may serve as a corrective to interpretations of revolution that embody the dominant western belief that history (diachrony) is dominant over structure (synchrony) in determining the course of events for all societies at all points in time. It may be, after all, that revolutions are profoundly conservative processes in terms of culture as distinct from measurable changes in social structure, mobility, organization of the economy, and the like. Explanations of revolution that embrace culture must consider both structure and event; they must go beneath formal institutions and laws to grasp their dynamics as cultural repositories and artifacts. If revolutionary theory and practice are to produce desired transformations, they must take account of the collective mentality and how to communicate with it, mobilize it, and change it.

One of the most important weaknesses of the Provisional Government as a revolutionary regime was its inability to generate an effective cultural policy. At the outset it approached the cultural question with an idealistic but vague sense of the need for cultural transformation, derived from the traditional values and ideologies of the intelligentsia who made up its ruling parties. Broadly speaking this meant the democratization and liberation of culture— liberation from the oppressive hand of Tsarist censors and the bureaucratized academy, for example. Thus, from the beginning there was a tension in the government's cultural work between a sense of cultural mission that fell short of mobilization and a desire to decentralize and dismantle the Tsarist controls and apparatus. Though many of its domestic programs in addition to those directly related to the arts or education had far-reaching cultural implications, these remained for the most part poorly advertised and not easily understood by workers, peasants, and soldiers. The Provisional Government's failure to win social support for its revolutionary program may be traced in part to the tension and incoherence in cultural policy mentioned above. The Provisional Government's attitudes and policies toward culture, therefore, can help explain the government's inability to build a revolutionary state capable of mobilizing the population to attain transformation.

When the cultural question is isolated and when the cultural dimensions of the traditional categories of social, political, and economic change are considered, the Provisional Government experience sheds light on the process of revolution in Russia. The Provisional Government experience brings to the fore problems and patterns that were faced by all regimes in the revolutionary situation. From this perspective we can see that early Bolshevik cultural policy and institutions and certain patterns of relationships between state, intelligentsia, cultural interest groups, and the masses all had their antecedents in the crucible of 1917 and in some cases even under the Old Regime. This is the same as viewing patterns of post-October party organization and state building as having antecedents in the experiences of party and soviets in the months prior to October.

In the Provisional Government's cultural policy as in its general domestic policy we find an ambivalent lack of focus that derived from the clash between principles and ideology on the one hand and the relentless pressures exerted upon the regime by the social and economic crises of 1917 on the other. And we find the same heavy hand of the past, in the form of political and institutional traditions and the mentality of elites and the masses alike, which so easily frustrated even the most inspired policies of transformation. To take just one example to be considered later in detail, the Provisional Government began by allowing the representatives of cultural institutions considerable latitude in administering former state and private theaters, concert halls, academies, and other educational institutions of the arts, and in labor relations with artistic workers of all sorts. Yet this desire to decentralize and move toward artistic "self-government" could not be fulfilled in the maelstrom of 1917. The various permutations of viewpoint and ideology in the successive Provisional Government coalition cabinets helped to produce a cultural policy that was both institutionally and ideologically fragmented. The escalation of demands from below in the artistic world and from within artistic institutions brought forth increasing controls from above—first from within the institutions themselves (where old hierarchies were reconstituted) then from state power, which ironically used as one of its power bases the autocracy's Ministry of the Imperial Court.

It was this institutional and ideological fragmentation and the growing reliance on old patterns of hierarchy and authority that minimized the impact of *Kulturträger* sentiments among Provisional Government officials. It was not that these figures lacked awareness of the "culture question." For example, N. N. L'vov, the Commissar of State Theaters, put it succinctly in the heady days of March: "The task of the state theaters is to serve the free *narod* and to educate it with artistic and moral ideals."[3] General A. Verkhovsky, the last War Minister of the Provisional Government and a man close to the troops, refers frequently in his memoirs to the psychology of the mass. Verkhovsky, who won the support of many leftists for his post-Kornilov reforms and futile attempts to end the war, wrote that reforms and peace were necessary to "create the necessary break in the psychology of the masses."[4] He understood that part of the effectiveness of the Bolshevik slogans was their "mythic" quality: "In the primitive psychology of the crowd everything is simple and clear. Everything is possible, and thus the masses follow these new words that promise them everything quickly and without any efforts."[5] Verkhovsky also understood the need to talk to the representatives of the masses in the Soviet in "revolutionary language that is understandable to them." Fëdor Stepun, an intellectual who for a time headed the "Cultural Enlightenment" Section of the War Ministry, also discussed the spiritual, symbolic, and religious dimensions of the revolution and the Provisional Government's failure to connect with the masses through effective propaganda and education.[6] The list of believers in cultural mission also included Prince G. L'vov, A. Shingarëv, I. Tsereteli, and others.

We shall examine the Provisional Government's cultural policy in the following areas: 1) political culture; 2) education and religion; 3) the administration of culture (art, theater, music, etc.); and 4) attempts to create new symbols and rituals, to use the arts, broadly conceived, to begin the process of culture change, and thereby to secure the gains of the revolution.[7] In each area, as we shall see, Provisional Government initiatives were later taken up more forcefully by the Bolsheviks, who had a much clearer sense of the cultural requirements of their constituency and far fewer inhibitions about the use of state power to effect culture change.

Perhaps the most ambitious Provisional Government legislation (and many would argue its most spectacular failure) occurred in the area of administrative reform or in "state building," where the government clearly attempted to modify not only key formal institutions of the Old Regime but the political culture that supported them. The Provisional Government's initial thrust was to break up the old Tsar-centered, highly personalized, clannish, bureaucratic politics and administration, substituting for them rule of law, separation of powers, self-government, and the primacy of institutions over personalities. In this as in so many Provisional Government policies, the legislation carried on the traditions of the reformers of the nineteenth and early twentieth centuries.[8] Democratization and extension of the zemstvo to the *volost'*, removal of police power from the bureaucracy, creation of the administrative courts to hold officials accountable before the law, the Constituent Assembly—all of these reforms were meant to break the cultural code of autocracy, to provide an institutional framework for the nurturing of a new politics and therefore of a new political behavior on the part of all classes.

As we know, the Provisional Government found it virtually impossible to graft new institutions such as the *volost'*, zemstvo, and administrative courts onto provincial society, which organized its own governing institutions in the countryside. The peasantry clearly did not perceive or believe that the new Provisional Government–sponsored institutions represented, in theory at least, significant departure from traditions. Or perhaps they understood only too well and instinctively worked to protect themselves and their way of life from all outsiders. The Provisional Government in any case could not sell the program of self-government, separation of powers, and breaking the culture codes of autocracy, and bit by bit during 1917, in an effort to establish effective authority, was drawn back into traditional Russian administrative patterns[9] as the power of the ministerial bureaucracy and police reappeared. Perhaps the most instructive event in terms of political culture was the emergence of Kerensky as a kind of Tsar figure, a farcical but logical repetition of the requirements of the culture for a "leader" and the reassertion of personal power over law.[10] Other devices, mixing old and new, were the lame attempts of Kerensky's government to build social support through pseudoparliamentary consultative organs such as the Moscow State Conference and Council of the Republic, or Pre-Parliament. As contemporary accounts attest, these bodies were ceremonially opened with the conscious political aim of building consensus for Provisional Government policy. The historical reference points were the State Duma and the various consultative bodies, such as the Zemskii Sobor, that had existed in myth, in life, and in numerous projects during the preceding centuries of Russian history. These non-institutions failed, however, to unify elites or provide legitimacy for the regime in part, as eyewitnesses observed, because the symbolic dimension of these bodies, rooted in Russia's past, could no longer strike a responsive chord among either the elites or the masses. In short, as with Kerensky's pathetic effort to become the "leader," he and his government failed to establish a charismatic "political center" necessary for mass mobilization in politics.

In education and religion where the state had long been dominant, the government moved to complete long stalled reforms from the agenda of the Old Regime that involved decentralization and debureaucratization.[11] There was legislation to restore autonomy to higher educational institutions, to democratize the schools, and to unify vocational and general or classical education at the secondary level into one system that would permit transfers at all levels between different types of schools without penalty. The government also decreed the absorption of the widespread network of church schools into the secular system, and, as in the case of police power, made gestures toward turning over a share of the administration of education to the new organs of self-government and education councils in the provinces that were to include representatives of society. There were plans to open new universities—for example, in Siberia. These efforts built upon initiative taken by state and society prior to 1917, such as the People's University, the women's courses, the private gymnasia, research into child psychology, the program of Minister of Education Ignat'ev in 1916 that emphasized the practical and vocational for peasants and workers.

The educational reforms of the Provisional Government also built upon already well established initiatives of the zemstvos and the state in the area of village primary education. The goal here was to further the spread of literacy, to "enlighten" the dark masses. In primary education, it would appear that the Provisional Government simply desired the pre-revolutionary educational establishment to continue its brand of cultural work, for there is no record of significant Provisional Government legislation in this area and no conscious policy of mobilization. Everyone of course favored literacy; but what kind?[12] For Provisional Government intellectuals, many of whom had been active in education administration under the Old Regime, enlightenment in the countryside always retained something of an abstract flavor—the imposition of an alien world view upon little-understood peasants. Although the teacher's union, the Central Executive Committee of the Soviet, and the State Education Committee all spoke of enlightenment and culture change in the countryside, it would take the advent of Soviet power and a regime less ambivalent toward the use of state power to launch new campaigns in the education of the peasantry.

Concern with literacy and education could be found among the intelligentsia of the revolutionary democracy centered in the soviets. At the first all-Russian Soviet Congress in June, for example, soviet representatives launched a sharp attack against the inactivity of A. A. Manuilov and the Ministry of Education.[13] Much hostility was vented at bureaucratic and centralized education, the powerlessness of the new State Education Commission and other matters that had long occupied the intelligentsia. There was the usual argument that education rightfully belonged to the organs of self-government, and appeals for more pay and higher status for teachers, open access, adult education, new textbooks consonant with the revolution, and purges in the Ministry of Education apparatus.

Indicative of intelligentsia cultural concern at the Congress was the speech of the delegate Porshnev on education outside the school *(vneshkol'noe obrazovanie)*. Porshnev framed his argument in the classic *Kulturträger* terms of the intelligentsia, claiming that education outside the school was crucial for "the cultural development of the country." He accused the Ministry of Education of inaction and gave the zemstvos credit for what little had been accomplished despite money shortages and ill-defined jurisdictions. Porshnev emphasized the problem of learning retention and recidivism in literacy. He believed that the government had to reach men and women at age twenty or older when they were becoming active participants in the economic and political life of the country. The alternative was the specter of *nevezhestvennost'*, rudeness or low cultural development. For Porshnev, Russia still lacked the obvious support mechanisms and institutions for cultural development—libraries, peoples' houses and universities, courses, lectures, readings, excursions, and books and publications of all sorts. Culture, he concluded, "is especially necessary now in revolutionary times. We know how difficult political liberty is to establish in a revolution when the revolutionary masses do not have a simple or clear notion of freedom of speech or assembly, or the aggregate of all civil liberties." Porshnev claimed that the cultural issue was crucial as a question of basic democracy that was a precondition for building socialism and he castigated his fellow delegates at the Soviet Congress for their preoccupation with the political struggles that in his view could only be resolved in cultural terms.

The Provisional Government did take some initiatives in adult and external education that were interrupted by the October Revolution, though taken up later by the Bolsheviks. There are scattered newspaper reports for October 1917 of the activities of the Assistant Minister of Education, Countess S. V. Panina, who at the time headed a Special Conference on adult and external education.[14] Panina pushed for increased facilities for adult education, and for people's libraries with special sections for beginning readers. She demanded 36,000,000 rubles in the 1918–1919 budget toward these ends, and she hoped to establish such special sections in some 30,000 libraries.[15] Again, it should be emphasized that the goal was general education and literacy, which was very much in the tradition of Russian liberalism. It is impossible to judge just what kind of educational synthesis might have in time emerged under Provisional Government guidance from the interaction of society, educational professionals, and the state; yet we should remember, as Sheila Fitzpatrick has shown, that the Bolsheviks, despite a much greater sensitivity to the issues, had no ready solution either to the quest for a unified education policy or the even greater problem of using such a policy to transform culture.[16]

In religious affairs, we may cite the Law on Freedom of Conscience of July 14, 1917, and the establishment of a Ministry of Religion to replace the Holy Synod.[17] Government and church leaders alike envisioned a revitalization of the Orthodox Church through completion of the administrative, educational, and social reforms begun during the nineteenth century.[18] The official goal of governmental and church reformers was to create—after more than a century of effort and education—an educated and "cultured" parish clergy that might take its place as a force for the spiritual well being, enlightenment, and indeed Christian social harmony of the peasantry. The first Minister of Religion was A. G. Kartashëv, a former professor at the St. Petersburg Theological Academy, who was sympathetic to the Orthodox Church and its own goal of revitalization. Kartashëv was also close to intelligentsia circles that had come back to Orthodoxy in the years prior to the revolution. Yet the Provisional Government as a whole, consisting as it did of many socialists as well as westernized liberals hostile to Orthodoxy (and indeed to state interference in religious life or to religion itself), did not produce a new secular religion on the model of what, for example, the God Builders among the Bolsheviks wanted to offer. Taken alone, the desire to remove the worst constraints of state tutelage in spiritual life was not enough to provide substantial spiritual revitalization for any segment of Russia's fragmented population, especially under the chaotic economic and political conditions prevailing in 1917.[19]

The Provisional Government's attempts to administer culture centered around such issues as censorship, the debate over the creation of a Ministry of Culture, and the Provisional Government's role as heir to the Old Regime's network of theaters, conservatories, museums, and the like. The revolutionary regime was forced to administer and devise labor and artistic policies for these institutions, even while the much larger issue of the relationship of the state to high culture remained undecided.

On April 27, 1917, the Provisional Government abolished preliminary dramatic censorship, the Main Directorate of Press Affairs (and its apparatus), and other related censorship institutions. Supervision of all public performances was entrusted to the relevant commissar of the Provisional Government or to the person or institution acting in his stead.[20] The government retained the right to intervene in public performances in cases in which public order was threatened. The result of these decrees was a change in the repertory of state and private theaters alike. Now it was possible to perform certain "realist" plays, among them the works of Gorky, that had been banned by Tsarist censorship. This development was viewed by artists and government intellectuals as an important step in the "democratization of culture," but these decrees left unresolved the question of who was really to administer theaters and similar artistic institutions. Ought there to be collegial forms of self-government within the institutions that were to determine artistic (and economic) policy? Should one retain the old administrative system of the institutions under Provisional Government tutelage in the form of commissars? Or should the Provisional Government itself step in as a new regulator and administrator of the arts?

As 1917 wore on the Provisional Government was drawn into all sorts of labor disputes in theaters formerly under the jurisdiction of the Ministry of the Imperial Court as well as into debates among the purveyors of high culture and the intelligentsia as to the proper relationship between the state and the arts and about the desirability of creating a new Ministry of Art to promote cultural policy as well as to preserve the artistic and historic monuments of the past. Prior to the February revolution, primary responsibility for the preservation of such cultural artifacts and the administration of royal theaters, museums, and certain institutions of artistic education had belonged to the Ministry of the Imperial Court. In free democratic Russia such a ministry could no longer exist, in name at least, and its responsibilities and apparatus were placed under the guidance of F. A. Golovin as Commissar of the former Ministry of the Imperial Court.

In the early months of the revolution, Golovin organized a series of special conferences with representatives from the artistic and literary world (the first of these was the so-called Gorky Commission) to plan the preservation of cultural monuments and to grope toward some new general principles of collaboration between the state and the representatives and institutions of "culture."[21] In early September this conference began to "meet in earnest" after the traditional summer lull in the world of high culture, but unfortunately we possess only a few tantalizing hints of its activities during the remaining weeks of the Provisional Government's existence. Those hints suggest that the policy of the conference had been reduced to measures to preserve or, more accurately, to protect from vandalism and theft the art treasures and monuments of the past.

This emphasis on preservation is symptomatic of the Provisional Government's failure to win popular support: the treasures and monuments of the past were seen by many workers and soldiers as remnants of the Old Regime they had come to loathe. In emphasizing preservation the Provisional Government showed itself to be inattentive to this mass constituency and its aspirations. Only up to a point was the Provisional Government willing to nationalize the property of the royal family, and it certainly had no intention, given its respect for private property, of nationalizing the private collections of the elite.

The issue of whether to create an arts ministry was even more divisive. Despite long debates in artistic and governmental circles during 1917, a Ministry of Art was never created. Indeed, similar debates about the efficacy of such a bureaucratic organ took place during the early years of the Soviet regime with much the same result. The very fact that a debate about such a ministry could take place at all in the "new democratic" Russia, that a ministry, in form so symbolic of the hated state guardianship of the arts and culture under the Old Regime, could be viewed as desirable or even necessary by artists themselves (not to mention government representatives) reveals an organizational imperative that could not be ignored by either the state or the cultural world. On the one hand, from stagehands in individual theaters through academies and conservatories to the level of national unions, artists and cultural workers had organized early in 1917 into unions and other organizations to promote their interests and visions of "cultural construction" and to shed the constraints of state power. On the other hand the state still existed, although in weakened form, and the ministerial organs of that state power remained as the most viable mediator between the interests of the state and those of the creators of culture—high and low.[22]

Artists both desired and feared creation of a Ministry of Art. It quickly became clear in the 1917 debates that despite many artists' fierce desire to keep the state out of cultural affairs completely, it was impossible to do so, not only because the art world required patronage but even more importantly because the artists viewed the organizing power and moral force of the state as essential to the revolution's cultural mission among the masses.[23]

Once the Provisional Government (and later, the Bolsheviks) decided to have any sort of cultural policy—either purely bureaucratic or in partnership with representatives of culture—the inherited institutional setting and the traditional patterns of politics pointed logically to a central ministry to create and implement it. The same considerations led to the creation in 1917 of Ministries of Labor, Social Welfare, and Religion and to an abortive plan to create a Ministry of Health and a Council of Nationalities. It was also evident in the push for a central organ of economic planning—the ill-fated Economic Council and Economic Committee that may be seen as forerunners of the post October Supreme Council of the National Economy *(Vesenkha)* and its provincial organs.

Different artists and intellectuals feared, however, that a ministry might be seized by one particular esthetic movement and used to batter the others into submission. Given inherited patterns of organization in the arts and political life, writers and artists recognized that a ministry might be desirable for representing the interests of the art world. Since the Provisional Government had chosen to continue ministerial politics and ministerial government, the art world required channels into the bureaucratic world, as well as an apparatus. As one commentator put it, "We need a ministry as a sign of the state importance of art, as representative of its interests. Now there is a new regime and things cannot possibly run the old way. The Ministry is necessary as a mediator between artists and society and as a real expression of the people's love and respect for native creativity." Already there were signs of the later Soviet scramble for control of the cultural apparatus and a feeling on the part of some that bureaucratic organization of the arts was desirable if it supported the correct revolutionary artistic movements and cultural policies.

In its attempts to use the arts or various types of cultural workers to reach the masses, either for propaganda purposes, or directly to shape the new revolutionary culture, the Provisional Government undertook sporadic initiatives that pointed the way toward Bolshevik cultural policy. Yet the Provisional Government created no "cultural center," no equivalent to *Narkompros* under Lunacharsky, and the leaders in the Provisional Government coalitions showed little concern for defining a cultural policy. Furthermore, the programs and activities that did get off the ground were directed toward an ill-defined audience, an amorphous mass. The Provisional Government developed few institutional mediators of culture, no organizations to rival the cultural and enlightenment sections of the soviets in 1917. Here we must note that both the soviets in 1917 and the Bolsheviks had the advantage of a class-oriented cultural policy and the grass roots organization necessary to begin to implement it.

An example of the Provisional Government's direct use of art for propaganda was the effort to organize a day of support for the government's Liberty Loan in the spring of 1917. The newspaper *Birzhevye vedomosti* reported on May 2, 1917, that the Ministry of Finance had made an appeal to the art world of Petrograd to engage in "constructive state work."[24] The ministry wanted the artists, writers, and musicians of the capital to bring to the organization of that day "all our creative enthusiasm. Let artists express the entire brilliance of their fantasies, design a great variety of posters . . . take to the streets with art of all forms, not to collect money but to popularize the all-national loan . . . take it to the villages and peasant huts . . . wear beautiful costumes, decorate the streets." Poets and writers were to prepare a single-issue newspaper with verse, interviews, and articles extolling the loan.

On May 25, in large letters, the headlines of the same newspaper proclaimed:

> 25 May art will be with you
> On the streets of Petrograd
> Artists of all theaters, painters
> poets and musicians
> will bring out their creations and raise your spirit
> Citizens! It will be "Liberty Loan" Day

Liberty Loan day itself involved demonstrations, processions, performances, and speeches, and was viewed in the bourgeois press as a huge success. *Birzhevye vedomosti* reported that the public manifestation of art in the streets had "a great influence in its uplifting of the mood of the masses among whom is seething the passion of the struggle for the new and precious freedom."[25]

At the same time the Provisional Government appeared insensitive to the mood of urban workers and soldiers. Its failure to build new shrines and symbols that would be meaningful to these groups may be seen in the aftermath of the solemn funeral on March 23 for the victims of the February revolution at Marsovo Pole. Newspaper reports later in April called attention to the lack of upkeep of the mass graves. What was to have been a revolutionary shrine had been allowed to degenerate into a "*market* square." What was to have been a "holy place" was strewn with cigarette butts and refuse, with few traces of the flowers or flags that had marked the funeral itself. Though the Petrograd Soviet also bore responsibility for the funeral and upkeep of the shrine, newspaper reports claimed that a feeling of disgust existed among older peasants and young soldiers who interpreted the situation as the result of the *government's* indifference to the sacrifice of the dead.[26]

Bringing culture, art, and information to the masses was a prominent idea among Provisional Government and Soviet activists in 1917. The Provisional Government (and the soviets) used plenipotentiaries, instructors, and commissars to prepare the population for the elections to the Constituent Assembly and for elections to self-government organs.[27] The Ministry of Education organized two-week lecture courses for these instructors and recognized and began to implement the idea that rural teachers and students on vacation ought to be mobilized for "cultural work" in the countryside, as had been suggested by the congress of the teachers' union in the summer of 1917.

In the War Ministry, the Culture and Enlightenment Section of the Political Directorate was particularly active. In late September the Section organized a book and library department to regulate the delivery of printed literature to the army.[28] The War Ministry noted that scholarly and popular works as well as textbooks and classics had disappeared into the black market because of severe shortages. Its Culture and Enlightenment Section therefore attempted large-scale acquisitions of printed literature for distribution at the front. In October the Section moved to engage drafted teachers and trained them for educational and cultural work at the front, and on October 15 a conference of delegates from military-cultural organizations from the front was held in Moscow.[29] Earlier in 1917, the War Ministry had organized "shock theater troupes" of drafted actors at the front to build morale. (It was apparently difficult to decide what to perform to attain the desired end. The troops rejected plays whose themes described *byt'*—everyday mores and life—and which carried heavy-handed moral messages, preferring instead "the heroic and the comic.")[30]

The Provisional Government, in conjunction with artists' organizations of the state theaters, orchestras, art schools, conservatories, and other institutions, worked to bring high culture to the new democratic audiences, and indeed to export cultural events, exhibitions, and the like to the countryside and working class districts of the cities. Special people's concerts were performed by the state symphony orchestra, and the regular programs of the ballet, symphony, and theaters often included speeches by government and soviet officials and ceremonies honoring revolutionary heroes of the past and present. At such gatherings the Marseillaise and other hymns were sung and indeed the state sponsored competitions for the writing of new "people's hymns" and offered support for the creation of new revolutionary works in the "democratic spirit."[31] By September there were district mobile troupes of young artists from both state and private theaters who took their productions to workers' districts. Again, the Provisional Government was in a sense in competition with the cultural work of artists' organizations themselves and of course with the programs of the cultural sections of the Moscow and Petrograd Soviets. On October 16, the Moscow Soviet announced a program to bring the masses to museums and exhibits (many newly created as a result of the revolution) and to organize theater troupes. The soviets processed many reports of grass-roots urban or provincial cultural organizations and noted their many complaints about the lack of direction and interest on the part of municipal self-government organs (the new local administration of the Provisional Government).

By 1917 movies were the most popular of all forms of urban mass entertainment, and the Provisional Government took its first hesitant steps toward using the movie industry for propaganda purposes. For example, on August 3, the Skobelev Committee asked V. L. Burtsev to edit a film on the reign of Nicholas II to show not only the causes of the collapse of the Old Regime, but also "the gradual destruction of the idea of Tsarism."[32] This was viewed as a first step in fulfilling the rich potential of putting history on film.[33]

In late May a report from the meetings of the Union of Artists *(Soiuz deiatelei iskusstv)* indicated the creation of a new organization entitled the Soviet for the Projection of Learning and Enlightenment, a film group whose program was to use the screen to propagandize for "knowledge, freedom, law, and autonomy."[34] The group wanted to organize a wide network of movie theaters in cities and villages, and to organize lectures on science, art history, and methods of political organization. Film screenings were to be accompanied by musical performances, artistic demonstrations, and exhibitions of paintings and sculptures in the foyers. Nonetheless, the Provisional Government did not fully grasp the potential of film as a cultural medium, did not follow through with contacts and support of the film industry, and developed no sustained program of film propaganda during 1917.

In addition to the various plans to create reading and tea rooms, as well as lecture halls, we should mention some Provisional Government programs in the area of artistic education. Besides palaces, orchestras, and theaters, the government had inherited the Academy of Art and its subordinate network of art schools. Responding after some months to the demands of the art establishment for autonomy, in August it issued a new charter for the Academy that was meant to break its suffocating stranglehold on art training. The charter recognized the preeminence of the Academy in Russian artistic life, especially in the academic study of art, but removed the provincial art schools from its control and democratized the administration of the central academy itself.[35] Thus, the Provisional Government tacitly recognized the need for new artistic centers and also for broadly based artistic (and musical) education in the provinces.

It should be noted, however, that the Provisional Government, as successor to the autocracy and its bureaucratic apparatus, found itself in the position of having to manage state artistic institutions. It could not easily mediate numerous labor disputes in theaters and conservatories. In fact, government officials spent much time in 1917 retrenching and attempting to restore Old Regime forms of theater management in the face of rising demands from the newly created and ostensibly autonomous organizations of artistic personnel. It proved far more difficult than either the artists or the Provisional Government anticipated to break authoritarian structures of management and state patronage in the arts.

After October the same tensions would emerge between the demands of artists for artistic freedom and their desire for support from the state. Bolshevik leaders themselves were reluctant to choose between preserving the high culture of the past and promoting the militant Proletcult as the truly revolutionary approach to culture change. As was the case for the Provisional Government, the institutions and culture (the structures) that the Bolsheviks sought to transform exerted their own powerful influence on the genesis of governmental cultural policy.

The Provisional Government cancelled many Tsarist holidays while retaining those with "general state significance," but offered nothing to replace them, not even a holiday that might come close to rivaling the workers' own holiday, May Day. The government could express concern for vandalism of cultural treasures and attempt to stop their export from Russia, but in the chaos of 1917, it could develop no sophisticated museum policy.[36] We might go further and say with Freud that revolutions require powerful creation myths to sustain them, something akin to the idea of a "big bang," and here too the Provisional Government was able to achieve little.

In retrospect, we can see that the Provisional Government was able to take the first steps toward a "cultural policy" under the broad rubrics of "democratization" of the arts and culture and "freedom" from state interference, but it had little idea of its possible mass constituency, little notion in the short run of how to create or channel culture change to achieve hegemony in the Gramscian sense. According to Gramsci, "the ruling class reaffirms its hegemony through the mediation of culture." The hegemonic class requires the mediation of culture to attain the "political, intellectual and moral leadership over allied groups." Hegemony is achieved at the moment when a class becomes aware of extra-economic links to other sectors of society, a moment when the corporate interests of a purely economic class are transcended. It is a purely political moment when superstructure (the political and cultural) clearly dominates and unity is achieved by the mediation of an ideology (myth, including symbols, etc.) that provides a moral unity that spreads throughout society.[37]

Gramsci spoke of culture in an anthropological sense. As he used the term and as Kroeber and others use it, culture refers to the "patterns, explicit and implicit, of and for behavior acquired and transmitted by symbols, constituting the distinctive achievement of human groups, including their embodiments in artifacts. The essential core of culture consists of traditional (i.e., historically derived and selected) ideas and especially their attached values; culture systems may, on the one hand be considered a product of action, on the other as conditioning elements of further action."[38] Even from a materialist perspective, culture is here viewed as the "learned repertory of thoughts and actions exhibited by members of social groups—repertories transmissible independently of genetic heredity from one generation to the next. The cultural repertories of particular societies contribute to the continuity of the population and its social life."[39] Without entering at this point the debate between structuralist and materialist conceptions of culture, we may say that both points of view embrace not only what we ordinarily consider high culture but also the values and behavior of the masses. Culture represents patterns of thought and behavior, a "semiotic field" to be interpreted as one interprets an "assemblage of texts."[40]

Cultural work as used here means any attempt either to use culture to establish hegemony in the Gramscian sense, or to change or transform the elements of culture to accomplish at the deepest levels the revolutionary goal of transformation—of the individual and his or her mentality, social groups, and institutions. Thus it is clear that cultural work must be at the very center of a revolutionary regime's activities, and this the Bolsheviks understood better (as they did the nature of power) than did the heterogeneous Provisional Government with its fragmented executive apparatus.

The Provisional Government, consisting as it did of disparate social groups and representatives of both the bourgeoisie and revolutionary democracy, could never really speak for one hegemonic social or political group. Furthermore, those shared ideals its members did possess, and more importantly the sense of cultural mission of most Russian intellectuals and professionals, were never adequately developed. Despite its many accomplishments, the Provisional Government failed in its cultural work to create hegemony and its higher cultural-moral synthesis. The problem of culture would remain as a legacy to the Soviet regime—and cultural transformation a necessary goal for the makers of a new society and new men and women, even as culture determined the parameters of the effort.

NOTES

1. See Theda Skocpol, *States and Social Revolutions: A Comparative Analysis of France, Russia and China* (Cambridge, England, 1979), especially 3–43.

2. Ibid., pp. 4–5.

3. *Birzhevyia vedomosti,* March 16, 1917.

4. A. Verkhovskii, *Rossiia na Golgofe* (Petrograd, 1918), 112–37.

5. Ibid., p. 116.

6. Fëdor Stepun, *Byvshee i nesbyvsheesia,* 2 vols. (New York, 1956), vol. 2, 47–58, 97–98.

7. Several works that touch upon Provisional Government cultural policy are the

essays by Nils Åke Nilsson, Charles Rougle, and Lars Kleberg in Nilsson, ed., *Art, Society, Revolution: Russia 1917–1921* (Stockholm, 1979); Sheila Fitzpatrick, *The Commissariat of Enlightenment: Soviet Organization of Education and the Arts under Lunacharsky* (Cambridge, England, 1970), 89–161; and G. I. Il'ina, *Kul'turnoe stroitel'stvo v Petrograde: Oktiabr' 1917–1920 gg* (Leningrad, 1982).

8. I draw this conclusion on the basis of my current work on a book to be titled *Bureaucracy and Revolution: The Russian Provisional Government of 1917 and the Creation of the Soviet State*.

9. Daniel T. Orlovsky, "The Ministerial Bureaucracy and the February Revolution," paper presented at the National Seminar for the Study of Russian Society in the Twentieth Century, University of Pennsylvania, January 1983.

10. Ibid.

11. See the documents in Robert P. Browder and Alexander F. Kerensky, *The Russian Provisional Government, 1917*, 3 vols. (Stanford, 1961), vol. 2, 771–839, and James C. McClelland, *Autocrats and Academics: Education, Culture and Society in Tsarist Russia* (Chicago, 1979), 29–55.

12. Ben Eklof, "Peasant Sloth Reconsidered: Strategies of Education and Learning in Rural Russia Before the Revolution," *Journal of Social History* (1980), 350–85, discusses the widely divergent types of literacy, some of which have little if any impact on culture change.

13. *Pervyi vserossiiskii s"ezd sovetov: Stenograficheskii otchët* (Moscow-Leningrad, 1930–31), vol. 2, 273–93.

14. *Vestnik Vremennago pravitel'stva*, October 5, 1917.

15. Ibid., October 10, 1917.

16. Fitzpatrick, *Commissariat*, 26–58, 89–161, and James C. McClelland, "Utopianism versus Revolutionary Heroism in Bolshevik Policy: The Proletarian Culture Debate," *Slavic Review*, vol. 39, no. 3 (September 1980), 403–25.

17. Browder and Kerensky, *The Russian Provisional Government*, vol. 2, 810–17.

18. See Gregory Freeze, *The Parish Clergy in Nineteenth-Century Russia: Crisis, Reform, and Counter-Reform* (Princeton, 1983). On church reform and the Sobor see Roman Rossler, *Kirche und Revolution in Russland: Patriarch Tikhon und der Sowjetstaat* (Cologne, 1969), 1–34; A. V. Kartashëv, "Revoliutsiia i sobor 1917–1918 gg.," *Bogoslovskaia mysl'* (1942), 75–101; and Igor Smolitsch, "Die russiche Kirche in der Revolutionszeit von März bis October 1917 und das Landeskonzil 1917 bis 1918," *Ostkirchlichen Studien*, 14, 1965, 3–34.

19. Ibid.

20. Browder and Kerensky, vol. 1, pp. 227–228

21. The details are drawn primarily from the "Art in Revolution" column of *Birzhevyia vedomosti*, March–September 1917, and E. A. Dinershtein, "Maiakovskii v fevrale–oktiabre 1917 g.," *Literaturnoe nasledstvo*, 65, 541–576. See Fitzpatrick, *Commissariat*, 89–161.

22. *Birzhevyia vedomosti*, March 26, April 7, April 12, May 7, July 16.

23. Ibid.

24. *Birzhevyia vedomosti*, May 2, 1917.

25. Ibid., May 25, 1917.

26. Ibid., May 26, 1917.

27. Ibid., April 15, 1917.

28. See reports in *Izvestiia, Vestnik vremennago pravitel'stva, Birzhevyia vedomosti, Novaia zhizn'*.

29. *Vestnik Vremennago pravitel'stva*, September 29, 1917.

30. Ibid., October 15, 1917.

31. *Birzhevyia vedomosti*, August 4, 1917.

32. Details from daily newspapers mentioned in notes above.

33. *Birzhevyia vedomosti,* August 3, 1917. Richard Taylor, *The Politics of the Soviet Cinema, 1917–1929* (Cambridge, England, 1979), 21–25.

34. Ibid.

35. *Birzhevyia vedomosti,* May 31, 1917.

36. Il'ina, *Kul'turnoe stroitel'stvo,* 167–85.

37. See the essays in Chantal Mouffe, ed., *Gramsci and Marxist Theory* (London, 1979), and Walter L. Adamson, *Hegemony and Revolution: Antonio Gramsci's Political and Social Theory* (Berkeley, 1980).

38. A. Kroeber and C. Kluckhohn as quoted in Marvin Harris, *Cultural Materialism: The Struggle for a Science of Culture* (New York, 1979), 280.

39. Harris, *Cultural Materialism,* 47.

40. Ibid., 281–82. See also Clifford Geertz, *The Interpretation of Cultures: Selected Essays* (New York, 1973), and the same author's *Negara: The Theatre State in Nineteenth Century Bali* (Princeton, 1980), 3–10, 121–36.

[4] The Civil War as a Formative Experience

Sheila Fitzpatrick

IN RECENT YEARS, a number of historians have suggested that the Civil War deserves a larger place in our picture of the evolution of the Bolshevik Party and the Soviet regime.[1] The presumption is that "the origin of the Communist autocracy" (to quote Leonard Schapiro's title) may lie in the Civil War experience rather than in Marxist-Leninist ideology, Lenin's natural authoritarianism, or the conspiratorial traditions of the pre-revolutionary party. Historiographically, such a suggestion falls within the framework of "revisionism," meaning a critical reappraisal of the totalitarian model and, in particular, its applicability to the pre-Stalin period of Soviet history.

The Civil War, Stephen Cohen writes,[2] "had a major impact on Bolshevik outlook, reviving the self-conscious theory of an embattled vanguard, which had been inoperative or inconsequential for at least a decade, and implanting in the once civilian-minded party what a leading Bolshevik called a 'military-soviet culture.'" In similar vein, Moshe Lewin had earlier noted that the Soviet regime in Lenin's last years "was emerging from the civil war and had been shaped by that war as much as by the doctrines of the Party, or by the doctrine on the Party, which many historians have seen as being Lenin's 'original sin.'"[3] Commenting on the relevance of the Civil War experience to Stalin and Stalinism, Robert Tucker concludes:[4]

> War Communism had militarized the revolutionary political culture of the Bolshevik movement. The heritage of that formative time in the Soviet culture's history was martial zeal, revolutionary voluntarism and *elan*, readiness to resort to coercion, rule by administrative fiat *(administrirovanie)*, centralized administration, summary justice, and no small dose of that Communist arrogance *(komchvanstvo)* that Lenin later inveighed against. It was not simply the "heroic period of the great Russian Revolution," as Lev Kritsman christened it in the title of the book about War Communism that he published in the mid-1920's, but above all the *fighting* period, the time when in Bolshevik minds the citadel of socialism was to be taken by storm.

Reading these characterizations of the Civil War experience, scholars who have worked on any aspect of the early Soviet period are likely to have an intuitive sense of recognition and agreement. The behavior, language,[5] and even appearance of Communists in the 1920s was redolent of the Civil War. The Civil War provided the imagery of the First Five-Year Plan Cultural Revolution, while War Communism was the point of reference if not the model for many of the policies associated with the industrialization drive and collectivization.[6] Moreover, many of the Old Bolsheviks, for whom the *pre-revolutionary* experience in the party remained vivid, had the sense that the Civil War had remoulded the party, not necessarily for the better. The new cadres of the Civil War cohort, they suspected, had brought back into civilian life the habits acquired in the Red Army, the Cheka, and the requisitions brigades.

Robert Tucker's contention that the Civil War experience deeply influenced Soviet political culture seems indisputable. But can we carry the argument further, and show that this was a crucial determinant of the Bolsheviks' subsequent policy orientation and form of rule? Can we demonstrate that the Civil War pushed the Bolsheviks in directions they would otherwise not have taken? There are, after all, different types of formative experience. Some are predictable rites of passage; others are not predicted but can be accommodated within a previously established framework; and a third category of experience conflicts so sharply with previous expectations that the previous framework has to be changed. Which of these categories do we have in mind when we speak of the formative experience of the Civil War?

The present paper examines these questions, first in relation to the Civil War as a whole, and then in relation to different aspects of the Civil War experience: 1) international revolution and nationalism, 2) dictatorship versus democracy, 3) centralization and bureaucracy, 4) terror and violence, 5) the Bolsheviks and the working class, and 6) the Bolsheviks and culture.

THE CIVIL WAR

In discussion of the Civil War experience, it is sometimes implied that the Civil War was an accidental or aberrant occurrence, deflecting the Bolsheviks from the course they had chosen in the first eight months after the October Revolution. This was the premise of many Soviet works published after Khrushchev's Secret Speech of 1956, and it is also detectable in Gimpelson's recent "*Voennyi kommunizm*" (1973). It is associated with an emphasis on "Leninist norms" and Stalin's divergence from them.

But the Civil War was not an act of God which the Bolsheviks could not predict and for which they had no responsibility. Civil war was a predictable outcome of the October coup, which was why many counselled against it. The Bolsheviks had another option in October 1917 in Petrograd, since the Second Congress of Soviets was expected to produce either a Bolshevik majority or a majority in favor of "all power to the soviets" (as it did); but Lenin insisted on preempting the Congress's decision by a largely symbolic armed insurrection organized by the Bolsheviks. Lenin, of course, had been writing for some years that the hope for revolution lay in the conversion of imperialist war into civil war. At the very least, one must conclude that Lenin was prepared to run the risk of civil war after the October Revolution.

However, it was not just a question of Lenin's attitudes. The Bolsheviks were a fighting party *before* the Civil War, associated with the Moscow workers' uprising in December 1905 and with crowd demonstrations and street violence in the capitals in the spring and summer of 1917. The "Peace" slogan from Lenin's April Theses (with reference to Russia's participation in the European war) gives a quite misleading impression of the party and what it stood for. This was clearly indicated in the first weeks of October, when a German attack on Petrograd seemed imminent and the city's workers were in a mood to resist: the Bolsheviks' popularity continued to rise (despite earlier accusations that Lenin was a German agent) because they were associated with belligerent readiness to fight class enemies and foreigners; and it was Kerensky and the Army High Command that were suspected of weakness and an inclination to capitulate to the Germans.

Looking at the situation in Baku in January 1918, shortly before the local Bolsheviks staged their own "October Revolution," Ronald Suny notes that they expected that this would mean civil war, and moreover "the approaching civil war appeared to the Bolsheviks not only inevitable but desirable." He quotes the Bolshevik leader Shaumian—a Bolshevik moderate in many respects—as writing that[7]

> Civil war is the same as class war, in its aggravation and bitterness reaching armed clashes on the streets. We are supporters of civil war, not because we thirst for blood, but because without struggle the pile of oppressors will not give up their privileges to the people. To reject class struggle means to reject the requirements of social reforms for the people.

Suny's conclusion, I think, is applicable not only to Baku but to the Bolshevik Party as a whole. The Bolsheviks expected civil war, and doubted that they could achieve their objectives without it. In terms of my classification of formative experiences above, the Civil War was a predictable rite of passage.

This point may be extended by considering the two analyses of the Civil War that were most commonly made by Bolsheviks in the 1920s, and shaped their thinking on many other questions. First, the Civil War was a class war—a war between the proletariat and the bourgeoisie[8] or, in a slightly more complex analysis, a war between the "revolutionary union of the proletariat and the peasantry" and the "counter-revolutionary union of capitalists and land-owners."[9] Second, international capital had rallied to the support of the Russian propertied classes, demonstrating that Russia's revolution was indeed a manifestation of international proletarian revolution,[10] and underlining the serious and continuing threat posed by the "capitalist encirclement" of the Soviet Union.

These were not new ideas derived from the experience of the Civil War. Class war was basic Marxism—and, as an analysis of the contending forces in the actual Civil War, the scheme of proletariat versus bourgeoisie had many deficiencies. The role of international capital was familiar to Russian Marxists not only from Lenin's *Imperialism* (1916) but also, in a more direct sense, from memories of the French loan of 1906 that enabled the old regime to survive the 1905 Revolution. Foreign intervention during the Civil War certainly could be seen as a demonstration of internationalist capitalist solidarity, though at the same time it demonstrated that the solidarity had limits. But it was an analysis based on *à priori* knowledge that sometimes led the Bolsheviks into misinterpretations, for example of the strength of Western European support for Poland in 1920.[11] All in all, the Civil War provided dramatic confirming evidence for Bolshevik views on class war and international capitalist solidarity.

INTERNATIONAL REVOLUTION AND NATIONALISM

The experience of the Civil War period that strikingly failed to confirm Bolshevik expectations was the collapse of revolution in Europe, and the fact that the Bolsheviks' Russian Revolution survived in spite of it. In Marxist terms, the anomaly of Russia's "premature" proletarian revolution could be handled by the argument that the "weakest link" of the capitalist chain had broken first, and the other links would follow. The Bolshevik leaders repeatedly said in 1918–19 that their revolution could not survive and achieve socialism without revolutions in the more developed countries of Europe. But the outcome contradicted at least the first part of these statements, and the Bolsheviks had no choice but to reassess their ideas in the light of a situation they had not expected.

It was certainly a dramatic disillusionment (though one suspects that *successful* proletarian revolutions in Germany and Poland might have had even more traumatic consequences for the Bolsheviks in the long term). At the same time, there were other experiences contributing to the erosion of Bolshevik internationalism. In principle, the Bolsheviks supported national self-determination.

In practice, with regard to the non-Russian territories of the old Russian Empire, they very often did not. This was partly a result of the complexities of the Civil War situation in border areas, with nationalist groups sometimes being supported by foreign powers and nationalist regimes sometimes tolerating the presence of White Armies (as in the Ukraine) and forbidding access to the Red Army. It was also partly the result of ethnic-social complexities inherited from the old Russian Empire, for example the existence of a largely Russian working class in Ukrainian industrial centers, and of a substantial contingent of Russian workers along with the Armenian and Azerbaidzhani population of Baku. In such cases, the Bolsheviks in Moscow could regard themselves as supporting the local working-class revolution, whereas the local non-Russian population would see them as supporting fellow Russians and the old Russian imperialist cause. But these are not total explanations of the Bolsheviks' policies on the non-Russian territories of the old Empire, especially the policies in the form they had assumed by the end of the Civil War. The Bolsheviks *were* acting like Russian imperialists, and of course they knew it. As Stalin, the Commissar for Nationalities, wrote in 1920:[12]

> Three years of revolution and civil war in Russia have shown that without the mutual support of central Russia and her borderlands the victory of the revolution is impossible, the liberation of Russia from the claws of imperialism is impossible. . . . The interests of the masses of the people say that the demand for the separation of the borderlands at the present stage of the revolution is profoundly counter-revolutionary.

It is possible that the Bolsheviks were always a more "Russian" party than we usually imagine. David Lane has pointed out their comparative success with *Russian* workers in 1905–1907, as opposed to the Mensheviks' success with non-Russians;[13] and Robert Tucker's discussion of Stalin's assumption of a Russian identity together with a Bolshevik one[14] suggests some interesting questions about other Bolsheviks. There is some indication that in the prewar years the Bolshevik *komitetchiki* (professional revolutionaries) in Russia hit very hard on the theme of the workers' exploitation by *foreign* capitalists. Be that as it may, the Bolsheviks entered the Civil War perceiving themselves as internationalists and unaware that they had any significant Russian identity. In the course of the Civil War, they saw the failure of international revolution, found themselves adopting quasi-imperialist policies, became defenders of the Russian heartland against foreign invaders and, in the Polish campaign in the summer of 1920, observed not only that Polish workers rallied to Pilsudski but that Russians of all classes rallied to the Bolsheviks when it was a question of fighting Poles. These experiences surely had great significance for the future evolution of the Bolshevik Party and the Soviet regime.

DICTATORSHIP VERSUS DEMOCRACY

As Cohen and others have pointed out, the Bolsheviks were not a highly centralized and disciplined elite party in 1917, and Lenin's prescriptions in *What Is to Be Done?* (1902) applied to the special circumstances of conspiratorial party organization in a police state. But by 1921, the Bolsheviks were stressing party discipline and ideological unity to the point of a ban on factions, had largely nullified the political power of the soviets and consolidated a centralized, authoritarian regime, and were about to force the dissolution of the remaining opposition political parties. Was all this a product of the Civil War rather than of pre-revolutionary party tradition and ideology? Had the Bolsheviks been pushed in the direction of authoritarian centralization when there was an alternative democratic path they might have taken?

There can be little doubt that the Civil War tended to promote administrative centralization and intolerance of dissent, and the process has been well described in a recent book by Robert Service.[15] The question is whether there was a Bolshevik democratic alternative. Let us forget, for a moment, about *What Is to Be Done?* and consider Lenin's theory of proletarian dictatorship as described in two works written in 1917, *Can the Bolsheviks Retain State Power?* and *State and Revolution*. One thing that Lenin makes extremely clear in these works is that by dictatorship he meant dictatorship. The proletarian dictatorship would take over state power, not (in the short term) abolish it. In Lenin's definition, state power was necessarily centralized and coercive by its very nature. Thus the regime that would lead Russia through the transitional period would be a coercive, centralized dictatorship.

As described in *State and Revolution*, the organization of public life under socialism would bear many resemblances to soviet democracy. But socialism was a thing of the future; and in the meantime, Lenin seemed to regard soviet democracy as a kind of training ground in which the citizens would practice their democratic skills while the dictatorship ran the state. There may have been another Bolshevik view on the soviets, but if so, it made little impact. All the leading Bolsheviks were fond of the soviets, but after October, none seem to have taken them very seriously.

It has been suggested that the Bolsheviks were not necessarily committed to the one-party state when they took power.[16] This is surely untenable as far as Lenin is concerned (did he not, after all, write *Can a Coalition of Socialist Parties Retain State Power?*), but other Bolshevik leaders were initially more sympathetic to the idea of coalition, though this seemed to be based on a judgment that the Bolsheviks could not survive alone. There were many inhibitions about outlawing opposition parties, and the Civil War did help to salve Bolshevik consciences on this score. But, before the Civil War began, the Bolsheviks had not only taken power alone but also dispersed the Constituent Assembly when it came in with an SR majority. Surely the Bolsheviks had chosen their direction, even if they had not decided how fast to travel.

The issue of internal party factions is perhaps more complicated. Before the revolution, the Bolsheviks had been distinguished from other socialist parties by their intolerance of factions and groupings, and by Lenin's special status as leader. But this relates primarily to the party-in-emigration, which after the February Revolution merged with the most prominent *komitetchiki* to form the leadership of a rapidly expanding Bolshevik Party. The party became more diverse as it expanded, and there were frequent disagreements, communications failures, and local initiatives in 1917. Factions, however, were a phenomenon of the post-October and Civil War period, the first emerging over the Brest Peace with Germany early in 1918. Since the Bolshevik Party was in process of becoming the sole *locus* of political life, it is reasonable to hypothesize that in some circumstances it might have chosen to institutionalize diversity and disagreement within its own ranks—in effect, loosening the one-party system by developing a multi-faction party.

This did not happen, but it is difficult to pin the responsibility squarely on the Civil War. For one thing, the factions were a Civil War phenomenon, and the ban on factions was imposed after the Civil War victory. For another, the factions came out of the Old Bolshevik intelligentsia: the lower-class rank-and-file of the party seem to have perceived them as *frondistes*, and only the Workers' Opposition made a real impact outside the party's top stratum. Finally, the desire for unity was very strong, and not simply a matter of expediency. The Bolsheviks really did despise "parliamentarism" (including parliamentarism within the party), associating it with decadent bickering and the loss of a sense of purpose. As Kritsman put it, proletarian rule "exud[es] a monistic wholeness unknown to capitalism, giving a foretaste of the future amidst the chaos of the present."[17] The factions detracted from the monistic whole, and this may well have been the basic reason that they failed to take root in the Bolshevik Party.

CENTRALIZATION AND BUREAUCRACY

The "bureaucratic degeneration" of the Bolshevik Party (to borrow a Marxist concept often used by the oppositions of the 1920s) can certainly be traced to the Civil War period. But this surely is just a pejorative way of stating the obvious fact that, once having taken power, the Bolsheviks had to start governing, and the Civil War was the event that first drove this fact home. Of course, the Bolsheviks did not necessarily realize the full implications of taking power in 1917. The idea of bureaucracy was abhorrent to them, they had vague hopes that the soviets would render bureaucracy unnecessary, and they often referred to the fact that under socialism the state would wither away. But, as Lenin pointed out, it was not going to wither during the transitional period of proletarian dictatorship. The Bolsheviks quickly reconciled themselves to the need for "apparats" (a euphemism for bureaucracies) and "cadres" (their term for Communist officials and managerial personnel), at least in the short term.

It is true that non-bureaucratic organizations—soviets, factory committees, Red Guard units—played an important role in 1917, but had disappeared or become much less important by the middle of 1920. However, the shift from non-bureaucratic to bureaucratic organizational forms cannot be attributed solely to the exigencies of the Civil War. In October 1917, the Bolsheviks' first act in power was to announce the creation of Sovnarkom, a cabinet of ministers (people's commissars) in charge of different branches of the central bureaucracy, headed by Lenin. This act was quite unexpected, since the slogan "All power to the soviets" implied an intention to abolish the Provisional Government, not to create a successor institution (Sovnarkom) with new Bolshevik personnel. In the following months, the elected provincial soviets started setting up departments with permanent, appointed staff, drawing on what remained of the old local-government and zemstvo organizations: these departments took instructions from both the local soviet executive committee and the appropriate central People's Commissariat (Health, Finance, Agriculture, etc.). Thus the process of formation of a state bureaucracy for the new regime was well under way before the outbreak of the Civil War.

But it is certainly possible to argue that the Civil War left a permanent mark on the nature of Soviet bureaucracy. The policies of War Communism— extensive nationalization of industry, state distribution and the prohibition on private trade, requisitioning, the aspiration toward state economic planning— required a large and complex bureaucratic structure to deal with the economy alone. These bureaucracies, moreover, dealt with many aspects of life that had not hitherto been subject to direct state regulation, even in Russia. They were generally ineffective. But in concept, if not in practice, there was a totalitarian, dehumanizing aspect to War Communism that Bukharin and Preobrazhensky projected in their contemporary *ABC of Communism* and Zamiatin satirized in his anti-utopian novel *We* (1920).

The Red Army—the largest and best-functioning Soviet bureaucracy of the Civil War years—also left its mark, both because it provided an organizational model for other bureaucracies and because, after the Civil War, demobilized Red Army veterans streamed into civilian administration.[18] The Red Army was a regular army (despite early controversy on the matter in the Bolshevik Party); and, as in other regular armies, discipline was imposed on officers and men, violations were harshly punished, the officer corps (*"komandnyi sostav"*) was distinguished from the rank-and-file soldiers, and orders were transmitted downward through a hierarchy of command. In principle, it was a single voice that commanded, in contrast to the collegial forms of leadership used elsewhere in the early Soviet bureaucracy. But in practice (see below), authority was often shared between a non-Communist military commander and a political commissar.

The Red Army's political commissars were appointed, not elected like representatives of the Army's party organizations in the early months of the war. This caused problems within the community of Red Army Communists, and in October 1918 all elective party committees above the level of the basic party cell in the Red Army were abolished.[19] Here too the Red Army set a precedent which, without being directly emulated outside the military sphere, may have contributed to the bureaucratization of the Bolshevik party through the appointment rather than election of party secretaries.

While elections were retained in all other types of party organizations, the trend toward *de facto* appointment of local party secretaries by the Central Committee apparat was clearly visible by the end of the Civil War. This reflected both the center's effort to increase control over local organs, and the fact that the party committees were strengthening their position *vis-à-vis* the soviets and thus becoming important institutions of local government. "Appointmentism"—and particularly the political use of the Central Committee Secretariat's power to appoint and dismiss—was one of the issues in the factional disputes of 1920–21, with the Democratic Centralists arguing that it was undemocratic and contrary to party traditions.

But there was no grass-roots movement of support for the Democratic Centralists, and one reason may have been that party tradition was actually quite ambiguous on this point. There was the tradition of 1917–18, when local party committees were exuberant, assertive, and often effectively independent of any central control. But there was also the pre-revolutionary tradition, which was not so much undemocratic as simply different. The *komitetchiki* had always moved around, more or less on the instructions of the Bolshevik Center abroad, organizing local party cells, reviving moribund organizations, and generally providing local leadership until they were arrested or moved on to another town. In the underground party, the sending of cadres from the center had normally been welcomed rather than resented; and this was still often the case in the early soviet years, when local organizations were often left leaderless as a result of Red Army and other mobilizations. The party—like the other revolutionary parties—really did not possess a strong tradition of election of local officers. It was not so much that an old custom was flouted during the Civil War as that a new custom failed to develop.

TERROR AND VIOLENCE

Next to the Red Army, the Cheka was the most effective and visible institution created during the Civil War years. It was also, like the Red Army, a new institution with no direct line of descent from its Tsarist predecessor. In fact, it operated quite differently from the old Okhrana, though the later Soviet security agencies tended to fall back into the old mould. The Cheka was an instrument of terror and class vengeance, not a routine bureaucracy. There was no advance plan to create such an instrument (the immediate justification for its creation was the looting and urban disorder that followed the October Revolution). But its existence was quite compatible with Lenin's statements in 1917 that the proletarian dictatorship must use the coercive power of the state against counter-revolutionaries and class enemies.

The Cheka worked within a framework of class justice, meaning differential treatment according to social position, and, in practice, punishment of "socially alien" individuals without regard to any specific criminal or counter-revolutionary acts. It was a weapon for "the crushing of the exploiters." It was not constrained by law, could dispense summary justice, and used punitive measures ranging from arrest, expropriation of property, and the taking of hostages to executions.

If one takes Bolshevik statements of the time at face value, they saw terror as a natural and predictable outcome of the Revolution, and found any other reaction extremely naive. They were not even prepared to make *pro forma* apologies for bloodshed, but instead tended to flaunt their toughness or speak with an Olympian smugness that was calculated to infuriate other intellectuals. Lenin set the pattern, but others were not far behind: Bukharin, for example, wrote sententiously that[20]

> Proletarian coercion in all of its forms, beginning with shooting and ending with labor conscription, is . . . a method of creating communist mankind out of the materials of the capitalist epoch.

But such statements should not be taken at face value. Whatever their intellectual expectations (and there is no reason to think that the Bolshevik leaders ever anticipated terror and violence on the scale that actually occurred during the Civil War), the old Bolshevik leaders had not led violent lives and could not fail to be emotionally affected. They were simply taking Isaac Babel's "no-comment" response to violence (in the *Konarmiia* stories) one step further by loudly asserting that they were neither surprised nor shocked at what they saw.

Thus one must assume that the Civil War terror was one of the major formative experiences for the Bolshevik leadership, as well as for the large number of Bolshevik cadres who served in the Cheka at this period before moving into other work in the 1920s. But in trying to define the nature of the experience, we are forced into the realm of speculation. In their own consciousness, as well as the consciousness of others, the Bolsheviks shared collective responsibility for bloodshed. Their statements admitting and justifying it were on record. If the sense of a higher purpose ever failed, they would have to see themselves as partners in crime. If they fell from grace with the party, or themselves became victims of terror (as happened to a large proportion of the surviving leaders of the Civil War period in 1936–38), there would be many Soviet citizens who felt that they had it coming to them.

But the experience could also be interpreted in another way. It could leave the impression that terror worked—after all, the Bolsheviks won the Civil War, and the regime survived against quite considerable odds. It could be seen as evidence that revolutions are fuelled by the baser passions of the lower classes, as well as their nobler aspirations, and that the terrorizing of an elite can have political payoff. W. H. Chamberlin, noting the Bolsheviks' success in tapping "the sullen dislike which a large part of the poor and uneducated majority of the Russian people had always felt for the well-to-do and educated minority," concluded that[21]

> The course of the Revolution . . . indicated that the poorer classes derived a good deal of satisfaction from the mere process of destroying and despoiling the rich, quite irrespective of whether this brought about any improvement in their own lot.

The same point was made in rather startling form by Lev Kritsman in his *Heroic Period of the Russian Revolution,* when he described how the former exploiters were "pushed out of Soviet society, shoved into a corner like rubbish that could barely be tolerated," sent to prison or concentration camp, or conscripted into forced labor:

> This ruthless class exclusivism, the social annihilation of the exploiting classes, was a source of great moral encouragement, *a source of passionate enthusiasm* [Kritsman's emphasis] for the proletariat and all those who had been exploited.[22]

THE BOLSHEVIKS AND THE WORKING CLASS

Both in 1917 and 1921, the Bolsheviks saw themselves as a party of the working class, although in 1921 the proportion of working-class members was 41 percent as against 60 percent in 1917,[23] while the party's leadership throughout the period came primarily from the intelligentsia. But the relationship of the party and the working class had changed considerably during the Civil War years. In mid-1917, the proletariat's strength seemed enormous: this was partly because the proletariat actually was enormous, if one followed the

Bolshevik practice of including not only the urban working class but also the millions of soldiers and sailors conscripted for the First World War. Furthermore, the workers, soldiers, and sailors were giving enthusiastic support to the Bolsheviks. Spontaneous proletarian organizations like the factory committees and soldiers' committees were endorsing the Bolsheviks, and the Bolsheviks endorsed them in return.

In 1921, by contrast, more than half the industrial working class had vanished from the hungry towns and idle factories—some to the Red Army, some into the new administrative organs, but most into the villages, where to all appearances they had been reabsorbed into the peasantry. Factory committees had given way to appointed managements. The Red Guards had been replaced by the Red Army, over five million strong. But by 1921, demobilization of the Red Army was in progress, and the Bolsheviks saw many of their former soldier-proletarians turning overnight into peasants or, still worse, into "bandits" spreading disorder in town and countryside. There were workers' strikes and rumors of increasing Menshevik influence in the factories. Finally, the Kronstadt sailors revolted against the rule of the "commissars" in the spring of 1921.

These were traumatic experiences for the Bolsheviks—Kronstadt as a symbol of repudiation by the revolutionary proletariat; the mass disappearance of workers into the villages as a token of the weakness and instability of the class in whose name the Bolsheviks had taken power. True, the Bolshevik leaders were to some extent protected against disillusionment with the working class by the fact that they had never been totally illusioned: the idea that the working class could fall from "proletarian consciousness" or fail to reach it had always been present in Lenin's writings, and it was in such circumstances that the party's role as the "vanguard of the proletariat" became particularly important. But were the experiences, as many Western historians have suggested, so traumatic that the Bolsheviks thereafter lost all hope of the working class and retained only a nominal proletarian identity?

This was not the case—or at least, not yet. As will be clear to any reader of Bolshevik debates throughout the 1920s, the Bolsheviks continued to see themselves as members of a proletarian party. At the beginning of the decade, no party faction caused such concern to the leadership as the Workers' Opposition (the only faction with real support from Communist workers). In the later succession struggles, the votes of the *factory* cells were considered crucial, and may in fact have been so. In 1924—with the working class strengthened and reconstituted as a result of the revival of industry—the leadership announced the "Lenin levy," a campaign to recruit workers into the party with the aim of reestablishing the numerical predominance of the proletarian group. The result was a massive recruitment of worker Communists that continued until the moratorium on party admissions at the beginning of 1933.

All this indicates a genuine and continuing interest in the working class, but one that was quite narrowly focused. It was not really an interest in workers as workers, or the class as a class. It was an interest in workers (particularly skilled workers with some education) as party members and potential cadres. This too was a product of Civil War experience—or, strictly speaking, the first Bolshevik experience of ruling, which coincided in time with the Civil War. The Bolsheviks found that in order to rule they needed cadres (administrators, managers, military commanders, political commissars, Chekists, government officials, and so on). They assumed without discussion or hesitation that the best source of cadres was the working class. Ideally, a worker would go through the basic training of party membership before taking on cadre responsibilities, that is, becoming a full-time administrator. But in the Civil War period (as later during the First Five-Year Plan), the need for cadres was so great that non-party workers were often directly "promoted" into cadre jobs. At first, vague ideas were expressed about the periodic return of cadres to the factory bench, to recharge the proletarian batteries and reestablish "contact with the class." It was probably impracticable; at any rate, it was not seriously tried. Cadres remained cadres, unless they were incompetent or positively desired to resume life as workers, which few did.

Thus, part of the Civil War experience for the Bolsheviks was learning what they meant by proletarian dictatorship. They meant a dictatorship in which a large proportion of the executants were former workers.[24] The party's link with the working class was a functional necessity rather than (or as well as) an idealistic commitment. This was the other side of the coin of class war; as the mighty were humbled, the lowly—or some of the lowly—had the chance to rise and take their places.

THE BOLSHEVIKS AND CULTURE

When Bolsheviks talked about culture in the 1920s, they often contrasted the tough policy line, characteristic of the party's young Civil War recruits and associated with a militant "Civil War" spirit, with the soft approach typical of Old Bolshevik "civilian" intellectuals like Lunacharsky.[25] Toughness meant impatience with or even hostility to the old non- or anti-Communist intelligentsia, especially those teachers, professors, and so on who had "shown their class face" by associating with the Whites. Softness meant a protective attitude toward the old intelligentsia, and left open the possibility that the Communist in question shared old intelligentsia values.

Some similar dichotomy on cultural policy—partly generational, partly linked with class background—would have emerged in the Bolshevik Party after the Revolution whether there was a Civil War or not. However, Civil War circumstances undoubtedly contributed to shaping it, just as they produced the visual signs (Army tunics and boots, conspicuously carried weapons) that distinguished tough young Bolsheviks from soft middle-aged ones. In some areas, Civil War influence can be clearly traced. In adult education, for example, the Red Army's Political Administration—which by the end of the Civil War overshadowed the equivalent state agency (though the latter was headed by Lenin's wife Krupskaia) as well as the party Central Committee's agitation and propaganda department—developed agitational techniques that seemed flashy and superficial to someone like Krupskaia, who looked back nostalgically to the workers' study circles and reading groups she had known in the early days of the Social Democratic movement in Russia. "When the Civil War came to an end," Krupskaia complained, "an enormous number of military workers poured into [civilian adult education], bringing all the methods of the front into its work," with the result that the whole thing became shallow and routine, and popular initiative was stifled.[26]

In the arts, as in politics, the Civil War was a period of factionalism. The Bolsheviks tried not to align themselves with any particular cultural trend, although "left" groups like the Futurists and Proletcultists declared themselves for the Revolution early on and achieved temporary leadership and high visibility.[27] The leftist groups often demanded monopoly rights and suggested that other, competing artistic groups should be suppressed, but Lunacharsky's Commissariat of Enlightenment opposed this.[28] All the same, it was a time of extensive state intervention in culture, analogous to the state intervention in the economy associated with War Communism. Publishing, theatres, and the film industry were nationalized; virtually all surviving cultural organizations received state subsidies; and individual members of the intelligentsia depended on the rations they were given by state agencies like Lunacharsky's Commissariat. There was some ideological motivation to state intervention, but much of it was simply a response to the economic plight of culture and the culture-bearers. Most of the subsidies and nationalization disappeared with the introduction of NEP, which spelled disaster for the Futurist and "proletarian" groups that had failed to find a popular audience. But at least one Civil War legacy remained: in the late 1920s, a new proletarian-cultural organization (RAPP) with roots in Proletcult, connections in the party leadership, and an ethos that glorified the Civil War[29] achieved a short-term "hegemony" in literature and terrorized the unreconstructed bourgeois poets and dramatists.

An important component in the Bolsheviks' attitude to culture was necessarily their relationship with the intelligentsia (here used broadly in the sense of educated and professional elite). Traditionally, the Russian intelligentsia had thought of itself as classless. But the events of 1917–18 challenged many of the intelligentsia's old assumptions, including its long-standing radicalism and anti-bourgeois (in the sense of anti-Philistine) sentiments. Most educated Russians opposed the Bolshevik Revolution. As their material conditions deteriorated, nostalgia for the past and even recognition that their past had been privileged grew apace. To the Bolsheviks, the intelligentsia was "bourgeois" and part of the old privileged classes.[30] This could lead to the stark conclusion that all members of the intelligentsia were counter-revolutionary class enemies, as indeed many Bolsheviks believed. However, the party leadership's attitude was always a little more ambiguous. In the first place, as Lenin argued forcefully, the Bolsheviks needed the services of educated professionals, especially in key sectors like transport, the armed forces, and banking where few if any Bolsheviks had expertise. In the second place, most of the Bolshevik leaders were themselves members of the intelligentsia in terms of social origin, education, and cultural habits.

The outbreak of the Civil War made the class allegiance and potential loyalty of one section of the intelligentsia—military officers—an immediate and urgent question. Trotsky argued that regardless of the danger of defection and betrayal, officers of the old Imperial Army must be used in the Red Army, because the Bolshevik Party and the working class had only a small number of people (mainly NCOs from the old Army) with the necessary experience and training. With Lenin's support, though against considerable opposition in the party, this policy was adopted. The Red Army not only took volunteers from the old officer corps but also conscripted persons in this category. About 50,000 of them were serving in the Red Army by the end of the Civil War. The Tsarist officers who served as commanders in the field were under the close supervision of political commissars, whose duties included countersigning the commanders' orders.

The relationship between political commissar and Tsarist officer during the Civil War provided a model for Red/expert relationships in the civilian administration and the economy as well as the military throughout the 1920s. In functional terms, the model worked quite well, but there was another side to the question. Some of the old officers drawn into the Red Army—how many is not clear[31]—betrayed their new masters by deserting, communicating with the Whites, or committing acts of sabotage. This is the kind of literal betrayal that civilian professionals in peacetime have few opportunities of committing; yet in the Cultural Revolution at the end of the 1920s, engineers and other members of the intelligentsia *were* accused of such crimes, and threatened with the corresponding penalties. Just as the Red Army of the Civil War years provided the model for working with bourgeois experts, so it also established the mode in which experts were later to be suspected and condemned.

It became clear during the Civil War that a strong vein of hostility to the intelligentsia—Makhaevism or, in common parlance, "specialist-baiting" (spetseedstvo)—ran through the Bolshevik Party and the working class, despite efforts by Lenin and other leaders to discourage it. The terror, in which members of the intelligentsia probably suffered disproportionately,[32] intensified passions on both sides. Large-scale emigration of professionals, many of whom left with the retreating Germans in 1918 or with the White Armies later, was yet another demonstration to suspicious Bolsheviks that the basic loyalties of the intelligentsia lay elsewhere.

Thus, treatment of the intelligentsia was a controversial issue within the Bolshevik Party in the Civil War years. Lenin and Trotsky consistently argued that cooperation with the intelligentsia and access to its culture and skills were imperative for the new regime. Others disagreed, starting with the Military Oppositionists who in 1918 objected to the cooption of Tsarist officers into the Red Army. Lower-class Bolsheviks who were suspicious of the bourgeois, non-party intelligentsia often also had a wary and critical attitude toward Bolshevik intellectuals, even though (or sometimes because) the party's leaders were of this group. In the party debates of 1920, oppositionists linked the issue of party democracy and the alleged authoritarianism of the Central Committee with the intelligentsia/proletarian division in the party, implying that Bolshevik leaders were behaving "like the old bosses" to the party's working-class rank and file,[33] and suggesting that the leaders' willingness to use bourgeois experts was related to the fact that they came from the same class.[34] At times, attacks on the intelligentsia leadership by members of the Workers' Opposition appeared to have anti-Semitic overtones.[35]

One of the few party leaders who shared the keen distrust of the old intelligentsia common in lower ranks of the party was Stalin. He had first-hand experience during the Civil War of the treachery and what he perceived as the incompetence of Tsarist officers drafted into the Red Army; and he was known to sympathize with the Military Opposition on this issue, even though leadership solidarity and loyalty to Lenin caused him to keep silent in public.[36] Almost certainly Stalin's hostility extended at least in some degree to the Bolshevik intelligentsia (excluding Lenin). A few years after the Civil War, he wrote with evident satisfaction that, as far as party leadership was concerned, the heyday of the Old Bolshevik intellectuals was past.[37]

All the same, the legacy of the Civil War in culture was ambiguous, even in Stalin's case. Episodes like the Cultural Revolution of the late 1920s can be linked with various aspects of the Civil War, including enthusiasm for proletarian culture and suspicion of the old intelligentsia and its potential for treachery. But the Bolsheviks also acquired other kinds of attitudes and policies during the Civil War: for example, general agreement on the need to "use" bourgeois specialists (which implied something like an alliance with the old intelligentsia), disillusionment with ultra-radicalism in the arts, a commitment to respect the cultural heritage, and a habit of tolerating cultural diversity. These became part of NEP cultural policy under Lenin. With the notable exception of cultural diversity, they were also part of Stalin's policy of "Great Retreat" in the 1930s.

CONCLUSION

The current interest in the Civil War as a formative experience is related to the effort to find a new explanation for the origins of Stalinism—to move the "original sin" (to borrow Moshe Lewin's phrase) from the theoretical premises of *What Is to Be Done?* to the actual circumstances of the Bolsheviks' first years in power. There is a *prima facie* case to be made for this interpretation. The Civil War circumstances encouraged or even required centralization and bureaucratization, provided a justification for coercion and terror against class enemies, and led to the formation of a "tough" Bolshevik position on culture and the partial discrediting of the popular-enlightenment ideals and relative cultural liberalism of the older generation of Bolshevik intellectuals. The party emerged from the Civil War as an "embattled vanguard," lacking social support, isolated, disappointed with the proletariat, and suspicious of and hostile to the old intelligentsia. The insistence on monolithic party unity exemplified by the ban on factions came after the Civil War, but could well be seen as a response to Civil War experience. Many Bolsheviks got their first administrative experience in the Red Army or the Cheka; and in the years following the Civil War, the party owed much of its coherence to the bonds forged among comrades in arms. Moreover, the majority of Communists and cadres of the 1920s had entered the party either in 1917 or the Civil War years; they knew the pre-revolutionary party only by hearsay (and misleading hearsay at that, given the process of rewriting party history that began after Lenin's death).

However, there are important qualifications to be made on the significance of the Civil War experience relative to earlier party experience, tradition, and doctrine. Granted that the Bolshevik Party after February 1917 scarcely embodied the principles of Lenin's *What Is to Be Done?* (1902), were the premises of Lenin's *Can the Bolsheviks Retain State Power?* (October 1917) equally irrelevant to the subsequent form of the Bolsheviks' "proletarian dictatorship"? The latter work suggested that the Bolsheviks would establish a centralized dictatorship, substitute Bolsheviks and "conscious workers" (the terms are used interchangeably) for the "130,000 landowners" who had previously staffed Russia's state bureaucracy, and use coercion against class enemies. This is quite an accurate prediction of what happened during the Civil War. One should perhaps give Lenin a little credit for leading his party the way he wanted it to go, just as one should give Stalin some credit for being a faithful Leninist.

The Civil War gave the new regime a baptism by fire. But it was a baptism the Bolsheviks and Lenin seemed to want. The Bolsheviks were a fighting party—even a street-fighting party—in 1917: that was one of the main reasons for their popularity with workers, soldiers, and sailors. Their manner of taking power in October was almost a provocation to civil war. This was tough-minded, if it was a conscious strategy, but tough-mindedness was an old Bolshevik quality. In any case, it made some sense in political terms. A civil war, if the Bolsheviks could win it, represented the best hope of consolidating the new regime, whose position at the beginning of 1918 was extremely precarious. The predictable costs of a civil war—social polarization, violence, wartime emphasis on unity and discipline, wartime centralization, and emergency rule—were costs that the Bolsheviks were ready or even anxious to pay. The benefit, of course, was that the Revolution should have its "heroic period" of struggle and emerge strengthened and legitimized by victory.

My conclusion is that the Civil War was indeed a major formative experience for the Bolsheviks. But I see it as an experience of much the same type as Alexander Herzen's famous disillusionment with Europe when he observed the cowardice of the French liberal bourgeoisie during the 1848 Revolution in Paris. Herzen (as Martin Malia argued in his intellectual biography) left Russia in 1847 fully prepared to be disillusioned with Europe and disgusted with European bourgeois liberals; and he was lucky enough to find the occasion justifying disillusionment. The Bolsheviks, similarly, had the formative experience they were looking for in the Civil War. It was the formative experience for which their past and thoughts had prepared them.

NOTES

1. The question was raised first in an interesting book of essays on the 1920s: Roger Pethybridge, *The Social Prelude to Stalinism* (London, 1974).
2. Stephen F. Cohen, "Bolshevism and Stalinism," in Robert C. Tucker, ed., *Stalinism* (New York, 1977), pp. 15–16.
3. M. Lewin, *Lenin's Last Struggle* (New York, 1970), p. 12.
4. Robert C. Tucker, "Stalinism as Revolution from Above," in Tucker, ed., *Stalinism*, pp. 11–12.

5. On "militarization" of language, see A. M. Selishchev, *Iazyk revoliutsionnoi epokhi. Iz nabliudenii nad russkim iazykom poslednikh let (1917–1926)* (2nd ed., Moscow, 1928), pp. 85–96.

6. See Sheila Fitzpatrick, "Cultural Revolution as Class War," in Fitzpatrick, ed., *Cultural Revolution in Russia, 1928–1931* (Bloomington, Ind., 1978), pp. 18–19, 25. See also Piatakov's comment on collectivization, quoted in Robert W. Davies, *The Socialist Offensive* (Cambridge, Mass., 1980), p. 148.

7. Ronald Grigor Suny, *The Baku Commune 1917–18* (Princeton, 1972), pp. 207–208.

8. S. Gusev, *Grazhdanskaia voina i Krasnaia Armiia* (Moscow-Leningrad, 1925), p. 52.

9. L. Kritsman, *Geroicheskii period velikoi russkoi revoliutsii* (2nd ed., Moscow-Leningrad, 1926), p. 66.

10. Kritsman, p. 47.

11. Norman Davies, *White Eagle, Red Star* (London, 1972), pp. 167–88.

12. Quoted in E. H. Carr, *The Bolshevik Revolution 1917–1923* (London, 1966), vol. 1, pp. 387–88.

13. David Lane, *The Roots of Russian Communism* (Assen, Netherlands, 1969), pp. 52–58.

14. Robert C. Tucker, *Stalin as Revolutionary* (New York, 1973).

15. Robert Service, *The Bolshevik Party in Revolution, 1917–1923: A Study in Organizational Change* (New York, 1979).

16. See, for example, Roy A. Medvedev, *Let History Judge. The Origins and Consequences of Stalinism* (New York, 1973), pp. 381–84.

17. Kritsman, p. 78.

18. See Pethybridge, *Social Prelude to Stalinism*, pp. 120, 287.

19. Service, p. 94.

20. Stephen F. Cohen, *Bukharin and the Bolshevik Revolution* (New York, 1973), p. 92 (from Bukharin's *Ekonomika perekhodnogo perioda* [1920]).

21. W. H. Chamberlin, *The Russian Revolution* (New York, 1965), vol. 2, p. 460.

22. Kritsman, pp. 81–82.

23. T. H. Rigby, *Communist Party Membership in the USSR 1917–1967* (Princeton, 1968), p. 85. These are official Soviet figures. "Workers" means persons who were workers by occupation on the eve of the Revolution.

24. See Sheila Fitzpatrick, *Education and Social Mobility in the Soviet Union 1921–1934* (Cambridge, 1979), pp. 14–17 and passim.

25. This argument is developed in my article "The 'Soft' Line on Culture and its Enemies: Soviet Cultural Policy 1922–27," *Slavic Review*, June 1974.

26. *Sovetskaia pedagogika*, 1961 no. 11, pp. 144–45.

27. On the Futurists' brief dominance of IZO, see Bengt Jangfeldt, "Russian Futurism 1917–1919," in Nils Åke Nilsson, ed., *Art, Society, Revolution, Russia 1917–1921* (Stockholm, 1979), pp. 109–21. On Proletcult in its heyday, see Sheila Fitzpatrick, *The Commissariat of Enlightenment* (London, 1970), pp. 89–109.

28. Fitzpatrick, *The Commissariat*, pp. 123–26.

29. Fitzpatrick, "The 'Soft' Line," loc. cit., p. 279.

30. Bolshevik protectors of the intelligentsia like Lunacharsky sometimes argued that it was in the nature of an intelligentsia to serve the ruling class without being a part of it, implying that the pre-revolutionary Russian intelligentsia was not exactly bourgeois, though close to it. But most Bolsheviks took the simpler view.

31. For discussion of this question, see S. A. Fediukin, *Sovetskaia vlast' i burzhuaznye spetsialisty* (Moscow, 1965), pp. 48–94.

32. This is the impression of many witnesses, although of course much of the testimony comes from members of the intelligentsia. S. P. Melgounov, a distinguished

émigré historian, writes in his *The Red Terror in Russia* (London, 1926), p. 140, that he made a count of deaths from the terror, broken down by social group, based on newspaper reports in 1918. Out of a total of 5,004 victims, 1,286 are intellectuals and 1,026 hostages (described by Melgounov as "from professional classes exclusively").

33. See, for example, Sapronov, in *IX konferentsiia RKP(b). Sentiabr' 1920 g. Protokoly* (Moscow, 1972), pp. 159–60.

34. See remarks by Zinoviev and Sapronov in ibid., pp. 144 and 193.

35. The point about the Workers' Opposition's hostility to the Communist intelligentsia was most strongly made at the Tenth Party Congress by two Jewish delegates, both of whom used pogrom imagery. On the forthcoming general party purge, Iaroslavskii said: "People suggested that we should not only purge the party of direct offspring of the bourgeoisie who had somehow stained their reputations, but rather launch a general attack on offspring of the bourgeoisie. From these suggestions, comrades in the provinces could draw the conclusion: 'Beat up the intellectuals [*Bei intelligentsiiu]*'" (*Desiatyi s"ezd RKP(b). Mart 1921 g. Stenograficheskii otchet* [Moscow, 1963], p. 263).

Rafail added: "The 'Workers' Opposition' goes in for intelligentsia-baiting [*intelligentoedstvo*] in the sense that it thinks that the whole problem lies in our directing organs and the fact that intellectuals occupy places everywhere. And comrade Iaroslavskii is quite right when he says that, just as the backward masses of workers and peasants used to think that everything stemmed from the fact that there were a lot of 'Yids' everywhere, so this anti-intellectualism is the basic thing that is wrong with the position held by the 'Workers' Opposition' . . ." (ibid., p. 274).

36. See Service, p. 102.

37. This comes from a 1925 letter to Arkadi Maslow cited in Ruth Fischer, *Stalin and German Communism* (Cambridge, Mass., 1946), p. 436. The letter was subsequently included in Stalin's *Works,* vol. 7 (Moscow, 1954).

$$\begin{bmatrix} 5 \end{bmatrix}$$ The Myth of Lenin during
the Civil War Years

Nina Tumarkin

THE LENIN CULT as a pervasive feature of Soviet political practice emerged in full force in the weeks following his death in 1924. Almost at once it reached its most intense phase, which lasted for the better part of two years. After that it assumed the status of a formal state religion, an organized system of rites and symbols whose collective function was to arouse in the cult's participants and spectators the reverential mood necessary to create an emotional bond between them and the Communist Party, personified by the symbolic Lenin. This formalized veneration of Lenin as the Party's sole divinity persisted until the end of the twenties, when the emerging cult of Stalin began slowly to eclipse it.

The foundation of the Lenin cult was laid during the Civil War years. Its elements and builders were diverse. Workers, peasants, Party agitators, and the highest Party dignitaries came to laud Lenin as a leader of genius. This development was not an organized progression. It was a response evoked in part by Lenin's strong leadership, but to a far greater extent by the political imperatives that called for dramatic images and symbols to legitimize the Bolshevik regime. Published agitation about Lenin began to spread his idealized image across Russia. That image was varied during the Civil War years, and provided the basis for the myth his later cult was to celebrate.

THE LENIN MYTH BEGINS

In the first ten months following the October Revolution Lenin was barely perceptible as a public figure beyond the speeches he delivered before live audiences. His widow, N. K. Krupskaia, later recalled that in the first weeks

This essay is adapted from Chapter 3 of Nina Tumarkin, *Lenin Lives! The Lenin Cult in Soviet Russia* (Cambridge, Mass.: Harvard University Press, copyright © 1983 by the President and Fellows of Harvard College), by permission of the publisher.

of Bolshevik rule "nobody knew Lenin's face. . . . In the evening we would often . . . stroll around the Smolny, and nobody would ever recognize him, because there were no portraits then."[1] His first official photographic portrait was made in January 1918, a realistic depiction of a very tired man.[2] It was reproduced on the first published poster of Lenin. Bland and spare, it bore the simple caption of his name and government title.[3] In the same year, 1918, the Petrograd Soviet published an advertisement for its official organ, *Izvestiia*, which manifested Lenin's elevated stature as founding father of the new regime: two portraits of identical size were symmetrically placed on the page—one of Lenin, the other of Marx.[4] In the press, Lenin was not singled out for praise or even special attention, except immediately after the seizure of power when the new leader was honored with a brief biographical sketch in *Izvestiia*[5] and a smattering of verse. The most extravagant example of Leniniana in this period was a poem by Demian Bednyi, soon to become the Bolshevik poet laureate. Entitled "To the Leader" *(Vozhdiu)*, it was a piece of occasional verse written for May Day 1918, and was filled with religious imagery. "You were in a distant land, / But in spirit you were with us always,—/ There grew, page by page, / The Holy Bible of Labor. . . ." Every day was fraught with danger, the poet continues, reminiscing about 1917, the danger of "open assault / And the crafty designs of a hidden Judas."[6]

No Judas did appear, but there was an open assault on Lenin on August 30, 1918. On that morning Moisei Uritsky, head of the Petrograd Cheka, was murdered. Later in the day Fania Kaplan, an anarchist of Socialist-Revolutionary persuasion, shot and wounded Lenin. That shooting spurred the first major concentration of Leniniana and marked the first occasion on which Lenin evoked extravagant praise simultaneously from diverse sources. This was the first event in the gradual emergence of the cult of Lenin.

The central press immediately launched a campaign of agitation, vowing to avenge the treacherous attacks. Uritsky was lauded with eulogies and poems in memory of the "fallen leader."[7] But overwhelmingly the agitational focus was Lenin. The first official response to the shooting came from Iakov Sverdlov, president of the Soviet's Central Executive Committee. Calling him the "genuine leader of the working class," Sverdlov said that "the role of Com. Lenin, his significance for the working movement of Russia, the working movement of the whole world," was "acknowledged among the broadest circles of workers of all countries." He vowed that in response to this attack on its leaders the working class would rally and unleash a merciless mass terror against the enemies of the revolution.[8] Kaplan was speedily executed, and, although she had not been connected to any organization, hundreds of people were arrested in reprisal for the shooting.

The country was already in the grip of civil war and the attack on Lenin was interpreted as an act of war. Lev Trotsky, leader of the Red Army, hurried to Moscow from the Kazan front. In an address to the All-Union Central Executive Committee on September 2, he spoke of Lenin's struggle against death as a "new front," for Kaplan's bullets had been a direct attack on the Bolshevik regime. Trotsky affirmed his faith in Lenin's victory, but at the same time observed that no other defeat would be as tragic for the working class as the death of Lenin. Lenin was the "leader of the new epoch," and the "greatest human being of our revolutionary epoch." Trotsky was well aware that "the fate of the working class does not depend on individual personalities." But, he continued, the individual can help the working class to fulfill its role and attain its goal more quickly. Lenin, he said, was brought forth by Russian history for the new epoch of "blood and iron" as the "embodiment of the courageous thought and the revolutionary will of the working class." Lenin's greatness as a revolutionary leader lay in his unshakable will, unusual perspicacity, and his acute "revolutionary gaze."[9] Trotsky's speech was a deliberate agitational weapon; it was published not only in the press, but in pamphlet form, together with a speech by Lev Kamenev, head of the Moscow Soviet, in an edition of one million.[10]

On September 6, in Petrograd, Grigory Zinoviev, the chairman of its Soviet, made a long address which was also published in book form (200,000 copies).[11] Its tone combines religious fervor and melodrama. He began by saying that for the entire previous week every honest Russian worker had but one concern: would the leader recover? Zinoviev then provided the happy news that Lenin had indeed recovered from his wounds. The speech was purportedly a factual biography of Lenin. But Zinoviev selected his facts carefully. He began, for example, by saying that Lenin's father came from peasant stock; he neglected to add that by the time Vladimir Ul'ianov was born, his father had achieved hereditary nobility.[12] Zinoviev depicted Lenin as a saint, an apostle, and a prophet. He described Lenin's long years in emigration as the trial of an ascetic: "He lived like a beggar, he was sick, he was malnourished—especially during his years in Paris."[13] Lenin came to be the "apostle of world communism." *What Is to Be Done?* Zinoviev called the "gospel" *(evangelie)* of the Iskraists. And then Lenin grew into a leader of cosmic stature, a mover of worlds:

> Someone powerful and strong has disturbed the petty-bourgeois swamp. The movement of the waters begins. On the horizon a new figure has appeared. . . .

> He is really the chosen one of millions. He is the leader by the grace of God. He is the authentic figure of a leader that is born once in 500 years in the life of mankind.

There is no reason to doubt the sincerity of Trotsky's and Zinoviev's praises of Lenin. The Bolshevik seizure and retention of power had been a remarkable achievement and Lenin's leadership had been a crucial component of its success at every stage. Moreover, their speeches were calculated to show that they perceived the assassination attempt as a declaration of war on the Bolshevik leadership, an attack that warranted mass reprisals. Lenin had only been wounded, not killed, and yet hundreds of Socialist-Revolutionaries were executed in the "Red Terror" on the grounds that their party had attacked the embodiment of the entire proletariat. These top Communist dignitaries had begun to create their myths of Lenin.

The process must have been at least partly conscious. Trotsky and Zinoviev were the most renowned orators in the Party. They doubtless understood the effect and significance of every phrase, every image with which they described the stricken leader. They were setting the tone of respect, reverence, and fervent solidarity that reflected the official Party position on Lenin. As they sought simultaneously to inspire anger toward the Socialist-Revolutionaries and praise of Lenin they were laying down the fundamental tenet on which the Lenin cult would be based: loyalty to Lenin and the Party he founded meant death to his opponents and detractors. Fervent love and undying hatred were to accompany each other and were invariably to be expressed together in the flood of articles unleashed by the attempt on Lenin's life.

One of the most striking was written by Lev Sosnovsky, a Bolshevik journalist who was editor of *Bednota*, a newspaper aimed at the broad mass of peasant readers. Two days after the shooting Sosnovsky wrote an article in *Petrogradskaia pravda* in which he described Lenin in Christlike terms—a formula he was to repeat after Lenin's death.[14] First he spoke of Lenin as a symbol to workers of the whole world, a symbol of the struggle for peace and socialism. Then he added a corollary inversion common to the Leniniana that followed the attempted murder. Capitalists, he wrote, hate Lenin for that very reason; they see him as their main enemy. He went on to speak of Lenin as a leader of such universal stature that Italian mothers, according to their tradition of naming their children after heroes, were now naming their babies after him. Sosnovsky devised a Christlike formula for Lenin: "Lenin cannot be killed . . . because Lenin is the rising up of the oppressed. Lenin is the fight to the end, to final victory. . . . So long as the proletariat lives—Lenin lives. Of course, we, his students and colleagues, were shaken by the terrible news of the attempt on the life of dear 'Il'ich,' as the Communists lovingly call him." Il'ich is the mortal man and Lenin is the immortal leader and universal symbol. "A thousand times [we] tried to convince him to take even the most basic security precautions. But 'Il'ich' always rejected these pleas. Daily, without any protection, he went to all sorts of gatherings, congresses, meetings." The mortal man exposed himself to danger, but Lenin cannot be harmed. Again the Christ parallel is striking. Lenin's wounding appears as a voluntary sacrifice of a man who consciously made himself vulnerable.[15]

Lenin's sacrifice and martyrdom was the theme of one of the many poems the shooting inspired:

> You came to us, to ease
> Our excruciating torment,
> You came to us as a leader, to destroy
> The enemies of the workers' movement.
> We will not forget your suffering,
> That you, our leader, endured for us.
> You stood a martyr. . . .[16]

Other poems called Lenin a martyr, suffering for the salvation of the poor.[17] He was an "enlightened genius," a "dear father," a "savior."[18] And finally he was a cross between Christ and St. George.

> Great leader of the iron Host,
> Friend and brother of all oppressed people,
> Welding together peasants, workers, and soldiers
> In the flame of crucifixions.
> Invincible messenger of peace,
> Crowned with the thorns of slander,
> Prophet who has plunged his sword into the vampire,
> Fulfiller of the fiery dream. . . .[19]

The popular avowals of Lenin's martyrdom were probably not responses to institutional directives. At this time no apparatus existed to indicate appropriate epithets and images, although the press of Moscow and Petrograd was making an attempt in this direction. Some historical process was turning Lenin into a "passion-sufferer" resembling the medieval saintly princes whose sanctity derived from the tragic ends they met as princes.[20] Like the officially sponsored cult of Alexander II after his assassination in 1881, the cult of Lenin had its beginnings in the public avowals of his voluntary self-sacrifice for his people. But Lenin's superhuman stature was complicated by the fact that he had martyred himself—and then survived. Some literature immediately following the incident attributed his physical survival to a miracle.

A dramatic example demonstrates the syncretism of ideology and mysticism that came to characterize the later cult of Lenin. An article in a Moscow regional newspaper said that it was only the will of the proletariat that had saved Lenin from certain death. "The history of firearm wounds during the last war is full of truly 'miraculous' occurrences . . . when a little notebook, medallion, or even button deflected a bullet and saved a person's life." But those involve shots at a great distance. Lenin's "murderess" fired point-blank. A few centimeters to the left or to the right and the bullet that pierced his neck would have killed him. The bullet in his shoulder could have penetrated his lung. Not a button and not a medallion, but the "will of the proletariat" intervened to save

Lenin, whose trust had made him open to attack.[21] This story is reminiscent of those which filled government and church publications in Russia after an unsuccessful attempt on the life of Alexander II in 1866. The gunshots missed the emperor due to the "Divine Hand of Providence" which caused the bullets to whiz past their target.

Whatever popular rumors there may have been to the same effect, the stories about Alexander were officially generated. What of the stories about Lenin in 1918? What does it mean to have Lenin portrayed as a martyr or a recipient of supernatural grace? Were the authors of poems and eulogies expressing their real feelings or were they deliberately attempting to create a myth with which to mobilize readers? These questions can have no definitive answers. It is certain, however, that the flamboyant poetry and prose about Lenin sparked by the shooting were *not* modeled on what appeared in the central press. Only Zinoviev's writings matched the extravagance of what was published in local newspapers, and his speech was published a full week after the assassination attempt. The mythologizing of Lenin began immediately after the event. Probably some journalists and poets expressed sincere sentiments of sorrow and anger in the vocabulary that came naturally to them. Others may have consciously attempted to paint Lenin in forms and colors they believed would move their readers. And many simply were expressing solidarity with the Bolsheviks in the strongest language available to them. Doubtless all of these elements were at work in this earliest mythologizing of Lenin, but the wish to demonstrate solidarity probably comes closest to an inclusive explanation of the flamboyant and quasi-religious rhetoric eulogizing Lenin in September of 1918. The Civil War was on and the Kremlin had not waited to unleash its "Red Terror" as an immediate response to what it perceived as an attempted Social-ist-Revolutionary coup d'état. It was a time to demonstrate loyalty clearly and sharply.

Feelings of religious veneration and political loyalty spring from a common source in the human psyche, and no gradual secularization had effected a separation between the two in the minds of the common people. Saints' lives, the favorite reading of the peasantry, had provided a political vocabulary even for many members of the revolutionary intelligentsia, particularly those from the provinces who were only a generation or two removed from humble origins. Moreover, the highly developed demonology of Russian popular religion included constant tensions between good and bad spirits, saints and devils. The language of this culture provided the earliest vocabulary of the emerging Lenin myth. It was evident in the popular mythologizing about Lenin that counter-posed him to a monstrous and demonic enemy. A memorable example is provided in an article published in a provincial weekly of the Military-Revolutionary Committee of the Moscow-Kiev-Voronezh railroad:

The counterrevolutionary hydra, as the devoted companion and consistent betrayer of all good, truth, and justice, is extending its poisonous tentacles from the depths of the nether regions, searching for a weak spot on the body of the world revolution. . . . This sea creature, a marvel of ugliness, a freak of nature, a fright to the world—called octopus at sea and the bourgeoisie on land—is a freak of nature, blind at birth and a result of the demon's own creation in the world. . . .

And so on August 27, the organized enemy of Soviet Russia—the bourgeoisie— and its devoted companions, the social-traitor "Chernovites" committed an un- heard of crime against the laboring class of the entire world—they shot point blank at Lenin, the leader of the world proletariat . . . the sole idol and divinity of the working class, the poorest of the peasantry, of every honest man and citizen of the entire world, and all of mankind. . . .[22]

The author of this powerful if confused prose was an unsophisticated repre- sentative of the common folk, most likely a railroad worker. His writing is ungrammatical and the primitive imagery could only reflect the popular imag- ination. The sentiments in this piece and others like it were doubtless genuine and indicate that Lenin's shooting had moved at least some portion of the Russian populace to envision Lenin in terms that transcended the natural world.

At the same time the central press sought to publicize this spontaneous adulation of Lenin and to set an example for its readers. It published numerous messages of goodwill to Lenin and letters to the editor praising the wounded leader. One letter noted that Christ died saying, "Forgive them Father, for they know not what they do." But Lenin's opponents knew very well what they were doing. "Do they not know that Lenin is the world beacon, the light of whose love illuminates all the dark corners of human suffering?"[23] Three weeks after the shooting *Petrogradskaia pravda* even *reprinted* a peasant's letter originally published in a provincial newspaper. "And when the little father [*tsar'- batiushka*] with God's help was overthrown, the SRs appeared, but we, the rural poor, waited for the party that would give us the land. After the land decree of November we peasants were overjoyed. 'Who, then, is this good person who did everything so cleverly?' We read the signature on the decree— 'Lenin.' " The letter ends, "Faith in the priest has fallen away and interest in and love for Lenin have grown."[24] The republication of this letter is an example of a very early step in the creation of Lenin's cult, for it seeks to arouse positive feelings for Lenin not through direct praise, but through a conscious underlin- ing of his purported strong relationship with the people.

While Bolshevik journalists were eager to strengthen the emotional bond between Lenin and the populace, they also followed the Party leadership in working to *standardize* Lenin's public persona, to establish an official bio- graphical depiction of Lenin that would make the leader an effective political symbol within the framework of Marxist ideology. An acceptable standardiza-

tion of Lenin's image was not effected until after his death in 1924, when the
organized cult of his memory was in full force. But the process began immediately after the assassination attempt, when the Central Executive Committee rushed into print two biographies of Lenin for mass consumption, one
aimed at workers and the other at peasants. These biographies were clear and
deliberate attempts to establish Lenin's impeccable credentials as a focus of
political loyalty for the Russian people, who, until the shooting, knew little
about him.

Emilian Iaroslavsky, who was to head the Institute of Party History in the
1930s, wrote his biography, *The Great Leader of the Workers' Revolution,* the
day after the shooting. In it Lenin is depicted as above all else beloved by
the working class. In 1917 when the order went out for his arrest, it was
the Petrograd workers who protected him "for the October revolution, of which
he was the soul, the brain. . . . The Bourgeoisie does not yet know . . . how dear
this person is to the working class." And we the old Party workers, wrote
Iaroslavsky, know that even when we disagree with him—he is better than all
of us.[25]

The Peasant Department of the Central Executive Committee also published
a biography of Lenin. The pamphlet's title reflected its theme: *The Leader of
the Rural Poor, V. I. Ul'ianov-Lenin.* One hundred thousand copies were
published, an enormous edition testifying to the fact that it was destined for a
mass readership. "The history of the Russian peasantry has its bright heroes,"
it begins. "There are not many of them—Stenka Razin, Pugachev, and a
few intelligentsia-populists who considered themselves friends of the peasantry. . . ." But recent history has brought forth a new hero "whose name is always
on the lips of the entire peasantry. In the past two years this hero appeared in the
dark Russian countryside with a brightly burning torch, and is scattering the
blinding sparks of his fiery brain far beyond the borders of Soviet Russia. The
wireless radio catches these sparks and sends them out across the surface of the
globe. This hero is Vladimir Il'ich Ul'ianov-Lenin." Even though Vladimir
Il'ich can rightly be called the leader of the socialist revolution in Russia and the
world, the Russian countryside considers him above all "*its* leader-hero." The
next sentence, which leads directly into the biography, exemplifies the conscious distortion of Lenin's career that was the *leitmotif* of this agitational
pamphlet: "Vl. Il'ich's entire life, all his teachings, his literary and political
activity, were inseparably linked with the countryside." He was always the
friend of the poor peasant, while the Socialist-Revolutionaries are the friends of
the landlords. When the SR party tried to kill him, it was "fate" that saved him
as well as his "iron heart in an iron organism," wrote the author. The biography
ends with a pure fabrication about the shooting. When the would-be assassin
fired, the workers began to panic, but "Vl. Il'ich shouted to them, 'Comrades,

order! This is not important—maintain order!'" This shows Lenin's spiritual nature, concludes the author. "To him it was not important that he was being killed on behalf of the toilers—it was only important that the toilers themselves not cease even for a moment their organized struggle. . . . Such is our glorious leader, our dear Vladimir Il'ich. . . ."[26]

Lenin made a quick recovery from his wounds, returning to work within two weeks of the incident, and the flurry of Leniniana subsided.[27] But the cult of Lenin had been set on its course, although no one at the time would have predicted its future development. The attempt on Lenin's life had brought forth a new rhetorical convention for expressing solidarity with Bolshevik policies: extravagant adulation of Lenin. This had taken many linguistic forms. Some of the imagery was religious, some was folkloric, some came from the language of war. All of it was emotional and intense. Its range reflected both the social and cultural heterogeneity of its users and the richness of revolutionary rhetoric in this early, formative, period of Soviet culture. More than a decade would pass before it was pruned and molded into a standardized rhetoric of uniform formulae, epithets, and clichés. The cult of Lenin played a primary role in this process by providing an official object of Communist enthusiasm whose exalted status ultimately gave the highest authorities in the Party the full power to determine the language fit to describe him.

In 1919, the year following the shooting, Lenin inspired isolated paeans and poems. But the next spring he once again evoked collective praises from the highest Party dignitaries. These were occasioned not by some threat to Lenin either from a political opponent as in 1918, or from illness as in 1923. The occasion was Lenin's fiftieth birthday, April 22, 1920.

LENIN'S FIFTIETH BIRTHDAY

In the spring of 1920 the eventual Red victory in the Civil War was already apparent, and popular discontent with War Communism was making itself felt. The failed socialist revolution in Germany in the fall of 1918 and the gradual restoration of capitalist economies in Europe after the end of World War I had destroyed the hope—shared by virtually all Bolshevik leaders in 1917—of an imminent westward spread of revolution. Soviet Russia was isolated and faced the difficult transition from war to peace, from revolutionary struggle to the extraordinary task of consolidating power and restoring the ravaged economy. The "nationalities question" loomed progressively larger as the central Party organization worked to control the non-Russian areas of the empire. Lenin's personal grip on the Party was tightening as its new organizational apparatus moved to replace the *soviet* rule of Russia.

The Eighth Party Congress in the spring of 1919 had confirmed the creation of the Politburo and the Organizational Bureau (Orgburo) as part of a general centralizing tendency within the Communist Party. Party discipline was defined as adherence to the following maxim: "All decisions of the higher jurisdiction are absolutely binding for the lower."[28] As a wartime measure this ruling was acceptable to the Party at large, but in March and April of 1920, with the end of hostilities in sight, the growing centralism of the Party provoked strident opposition at the Ninth Party Congress. Lenin, who had, as always, made the opening speech, was singled out for attack by delegates opposed to what they perceived to be an attempt at dictatorship of the Party by its center. Lev Kamenev responded: "Yes, we have administered with the aid of dictatorship. . . . We must develop a dictatorship based on complete trust that we have taken the correct line. . . ." In 1919 a Party faction known as the Democratic Centralists launched a vocal opposition to War Communism and the increasing centralization of the Party. At the Ninth Party Congress one of its leaders, Lev Sapronov, warned of the possible consequences of the continuing domination of the Party by its higher bodies:

> I then put this question to comrade Lenin: Who will appoint the Central Committee? You see, there can be individual authority here as well. Here also a single commander can be appointed. It does not appear that we will reach this state, but if we do, the revolution will have been gambled away. . . ."[29]

The acrimonious congress closed on April 5, 1920. Little more than a fortnight later came Lenin's fiftieth birthday. The highest Party officials seized on the occasion and turned it into a rally in support of Lenin and his continuing domination of the Party. At the same time, *Agitprop,* the newly formed Agitation and Propaganda section of the Party's Central Committee, used his birthday to launch an agitational campaign around Lenin. This marked the next stage in the emergence of the Lenin cult.

On April 23, 1920, the central press was filled with greetings, paeans, and poems honoring Lenin's fiftieth birthday. *Pravda* and *Izvestiia* devoted almost all their news coverage to the event and, in particular, published articles praising Lenin written by leading members of the Party.

Trotsky wrote a piece in which he strove to compensate for the internationalism of Marxism by depicting Lenin as above all a *Russian* leader. His article, "The National in Lenin," postulated that Lenin was the symbol of the new Russian nation, and that those who opposed him opposed Russia. In this piece Lenin was, in a curious way, an idealized peasant. "This most indisputable leader of the proletariat not only has the outward appearance of a *muzhik* [peasant], but also . . . the inner being of a *muzhik*." Lenin was a combination of Russia old and new; his was the shrewd wisdom of the Russian peasant developed to its highest degree and "armed with the latest word in scientific thought." Lenin embodied the vital forces of Russia and was thus a true national leader. In order to make his point, Trotsky even compared Karl Marx unfavorably with Lenin. Marx wore a frock coat; Lenin would never wear a formal frock coat. But then Marx's whole style was rich, elaborate, and German. Lenin's was simple, ascetic, utilitarian, and Russian.[30]

Both Zinoviev and Stalin addressed themselves to Lenin as creator and moving force of the Communist Party. "To speak of Lenin is to speak of our Party," said Zinoviev. "To write a biography of Lenin is to write the history of our Party." Lenin is to the Communist Party what Darwin was to the natural sciences and Marx to political economy. Lenin had steered his Party to power in Russia with his "iron hand, great heart, and intuitive genius."[31] This was a reminder to the Party—without Lenin none of them would have been where they had arrived. Stalin's praise of Lenin centered on a talent that later proved to be dangerously developed in Stalin himself: the ability to identify enemies early and the resolution to break with them. Stalin approvingly quoted the nineteenth-century German socialist Lassalle as saying: " 'The party becomes strong by purging itself.' "[32]

Nikolai Bukharin was editor of *Pravda* and the Party's best known theoretical spokesman. His speech, "Lenin as Revolutionary Theoretician," reflected his own proclivities. Lenin, he said, must finally be recognized not only for his genius as a revolutionary tactician and leader, but for the great theoretician that he is. Lenin founded a whole new theoretical school, and his April Theses have become the "gospel" of today's workers' movement.[33] Sosnovsky's peasant-oriented newspaper, *Bednota,* sent greetings to Lenin on behalf of all its readers and called his fiftieth birthday "a bright holiday on which all minds and hearts are directed to him who gave his entire life and all his strength to the cause of the emancipation of labor."[34]

The evident purpose of this press campaign was to strengthen the perceived legitimacy of the Party's centralized authority by concentrating it in the titanic talent and personal heroism of its idealized ruler. Lenin's supporters self-consciously equated him with the Party and its policies, and confirmed the convention of praising Lenin as a desirable expression of solidarity with the direction the regime was taking. They were turning him into a mythical figure within the Party and, by celebrating the anniversary of his birth as a holiday, they were making him a focus of Party ritual. The tone of the campaign differed markedly from the strident articles bearing a spontaneous stamp of shock and anger after the shooting incident of 1918. The birthday paeans were formal, ceremonial, and deliberate.

But that did not necessarily make them insincere. With the Civil War nearly over, Lenin had shown that he could indeed lead his party to power and retain that power in the face of extraordinary obstacles. Furthermore, Lenin had proven himself to be the most successful of all Social Democratic leaders, even though before 1917 not the Russian but the German Social Democratic Party had reigned supreme in international socialism. In 1920 Lenin was not only the head of the first state to call itself socialist, but also the acknowledged leader of the international Communist movement. In this Lenin's followers undoubtedly took pride. Their claims for his internationalism may have represented an effort to bolster national pride in a Russian leader, and, at the same time, an attempt to strengthen Lenin as a symbol of political legitimacy in the eyes of the non-Russian peoples of the former empire. This last was to be a major factor in the Lenin cult after 1924, when a flood of Leniniana was produced in every republic, accompanied by avowals that Lenin was beloved by this or that national minority. Even before 1920 some poetry honoring Lenin had come from the pens of non-Russian poets. In 1919 an Armenian poet had lauded Lenin as a "genius, fighter, leader," and in the same year the Kirghiz bard, Toktogul, wrote a poem entitled, "What Kind of Mother Gave Birth to Such a Son as Lenin!" The focus on Lenin's birth gives this poem a classically mythical quality: "Lenin was born for our happiness. / He became leader for our happiness."[35]

Lenin's fiftieth birthday inspired a wave of occasional verse. Demian Bednyi's poem described Lenin as captain of the ship of state, guiding his vessel past dangerous rocks and through turbulent storms.[36] Another poem portraying Lenin as captain was consciously modeled on Walt Whitman's elegy on the death of Lincoln, "O Captain! My Captain!" The poet, a Siberian, dedicated to the sacred memory of Whitman "this joyful hymn to My captain."

> Lenin! O Lenin! Your immutable fate
> Has shown the world a resplendent path! . . .
> O! Then live! Your abundant genius
> We need like the sun in our life and death struggle. . . .[37]

Vladimir Mayakovsky also dedicated a birthday poem to Lenin and began with a dramatic justification of it:

> I know—
> It is not the hero
> Who precipitates the flow of revolution.
> The story of heroes—
> is the nonsense of the intelligentsia!
> But who can restrain himself
> and not sing
> of the glory of Il'ich? . . .
> Kindling the lands with fire
> everywhere,
> where people are imprisoned,

like a bomb
the name
explodes:
Lenin!
Lenin!
Lenin! . . .
I glorify
in Lenin
world faith
and glorify
my faith.[38]

Mayakovsky's affirmation of faith in Lenin was echoed in the press campaign of April 23, 1920, which deliberately stressed the emotional bonding between Lenin and the *narod*. An article in *Bednota* maintained that "the toiling masses strongly believe in their leader." *Bednota* also published a reminiscence about the peasant response to the Decree on Land in October 1917. "What a wizard that Lenin is!" a peasant said, on learning of the decree. "The land belonged to the landlords, and now it is ours." "But won't he cheat us?" asked his neighbor. The author of the memoir next recalls explaining that Lenin had dedicated his whole life to the people. Then, he claims, all the twenty or so peasants gathered at the meeting during which the interchange took place "in one voice shouted: 'Such a man won't cheat [us]!' " The same newspaper carried an article by a peasant woman who had been to see Lenin in the Kremlin and had found him "more hospitable and concerned than words can say—just like your own father."[39] Not just the press but also agitational posters stressed the theme of Lenin's link with the *narod*. A special poster published for his birthday showed a portrait of Lenin and a peasant and worker gazing up at him. The caption read: "Long live our Il'ich!"

The change in the depiction of Lenin in posters at the end of the Civil War reflected his progressive development into a cult figure. Early posters of Lenin published in 1918 and 1919 had been little more than blown-up photographs of the leader's unsmiling face. But gradually he came to be portrayed with more dynamism. One poster, published in 1920 in Baku, shows Lenin standing atop a Grecian temple, his arm extended, finger pointed ahead, his face full of grim determination. The caption reads: "A specter is haunting Europe, the specter of Communism." In the same year the graphic artist Deni published a playful poster—a cartoon of Lenin perched on top of the globe with a broom, sweeping away capitalists and kings.[40] In 1922 the Moscow Party Committee published a poster in which Lenin stands on a globe with outstretched arm; behind him are the rays of the rising sun.[41] The image of Lenin in posters had shifted from a passive to an active one. He was becoming the subject not of mere portraiture, but of an iconography.

The demonology of Soviet agitation and propaganda developed more quickly and effectively than did its hagiography, and was to have a long and complex history. The double images of good and evil, monsters and heroes, were to reinforce each other and intensify after the Civil War, when the complement of designated enemies grew larger and larger, and drew closer and closer to the sacred Party nucleus. The war was fought against class enemies, Mensheviks, Socialist-Revolutionaries, foreign interventionists, White armies, but it would not be long before state enemies were to include Party factionalists, trade union spokesmen, and the sailors of Kronstadt who rose in rebellion against the regime in March of 1921. Finally, after Lenin's death, they were to be joined by members of the Politburo—first Trotsky and then, one by one, Lenin's oldest lieutenants, as the grisly purge of the 1930s was set in motion. As the line separating good from evil, friend from enemy, grew thinner, as the "enemies' " purported claims grew greater and greater, so they were depicted in terms and images that were increasingly monstrous.

Concomitant with this process was the deification of Lenin. Neither the demonology nor the hagiography of Party mythology was fully standardized until Stalin was in firm control of Soviet Russia, but the process of their creation had begun during the Civil War with the widespread agitation that sought to arouse mass hatred of the enemy and devotion to the idealized personification of the Party in the person of its founder and leader. When Lenin fell ill in 1922, a centralized and expanded apparatus of agitation and propaganda sought to perpetuate his authority, despite his incapacitation, by establishing the first institutions of the Lenin cult. When he died in 1924, this apparatus went into a frenzy of activity and spread across the land the trappings of a nationwide cult of his memory.

NOTES

1. N. K. Krupskaia, "Lenin v 1917 godu," *O Lenine: sbornik stat'ei i vystuplenii* (Moscow, 1965), p. 54. This article was first published in *Izvestiia*, January 20, 1960.

2. M. S. Nappel'baum was the photographer (L. F. Volkov-Lannit, *Lenin v fotoiskusstve* [Moscow, 1967], p. 82.)

3. Poster No. 37428–45, 1918, Poster collection, Lenin Library, Moscow.

4. B. S. Butnik-Siverskii, *Sovetskii plakat epokhi grazhdanskoi voiny 1918–1921* (Moscow, 1960), p. 688.

5. "Vladimir Ul'ianov (N. Lenin)," *Izvestiia*, November 5, 1917.

6. *Pravda*, May 4, 1918.

7. See, for example, *Petrogradskaia pravda*, August 31, 1918; *Krasnaia gazeta*, August 31, 1918.

8. *Krasnaia gazeta, Izvestiia*, August 31, 1918.

9. L. D. Trotskii, "O ranenom," *O Lenine, materialy dlia biografa* (Moscow, n.d.), pp. 151–156.

10. L. Kamenev and L. Trotskii, *Vozhd' proletariata* (Moscow, 1918).

11. L. V. Bulgakova, comp., *Materialy dlia bibliografii Lenina, 1917–1923* (Leningrad, 1924), p. 203. The speech was also published simultaneously in French, German, and English (G. Zinoviev, *Sochineniia*, Vol. XV [Leningrad, 1924], p. 297).

12. This misleading statement was edited out of the later edition of the speech published in 1924 in Zinoviev's collected works, Vol. XV, pp. 5–50. Lenin's paternal grandfather was a tailor. Lenin's father was an inspector of schools.

13. Lenin always lived in physical comfort during his emigré years. His Paris apartment in particular was large, light, and elegant (N. Valentinov, *Maloznakomyi Lenin* [Paris, 1972], pp. 59–64.

14. *Pravda*, January 27, 1924.

15. L. Sosnovskii, "K pokusheniiu na tov. Lenina," *Petrogradskaia pravda*, September 1, 1918.

16. Akim Stradaiushchii, "V. Leninu," *Bednota*, September 11, 1918.

17. G. Gulov, "Dorogomu tovarishchu Leninu," *Bednota*, September 17, 1918.

18. F. K-v, "Mirovomu vozhdiu proletariata V. I. Leninu," *Bednota*, September 12, 1918.

19. Iona Brikhnichev, "V. I. Leninu," *Proletarskii sbornik*, Bk. 1 (Moscow, 1918), p. 18, cited in M.E.O., "Vozhd' mirovoi revoliutsii," *Zheleznyi put'*, No. 8, March 1919, p. 4.

20. Michael Cherniavsky, *Tsar and People: Studies in Russian Myths* (London and New Haven, 1961), pp. 13–14.

21. N. Al-ov, "Takova volia proletariata," *Okar'* (Organ moskovskogo okskago oblastnogo komiteta), September 6, 1918.

22. I. Lipatnikov, "Udar v serdtse," *Vestnik glavago voenno-revoliutsionnago komiteta Moskovsko-Kievo-Voronezhskoi zheleznoi dorogi*, September 9, 1918.

23. *Izvestiia*, September 3, 1918.

24. "Derevenskaia bednota o tov. Lenine," *Petrogradskaia pravda*, September 21, 1918.

25. E. Iaroslavskii, *Velikii vozhd' rabochei revoliutsii* (Moscow, 1918), pp. 12, 14.

26. A. M.....v (Mitrofanov), *Vozhd' derevenskoi bednoty, V. I. Ul'ianov-Lenin* (Moscow, 1918).

27. According to V. D. Bonch-Bruevich, it was Lenin himself who ordered that the press cease publication of his praises (V. D. Bonch-Bruevich, *Vospominaniia o Lenine* [Moscow, 1965], pp. 337–340).

28. Robert V. Daniels, *The Conscience of the Revolution* (New York, 1960), citing Resolution of the Eighth Party Congress, "On the Organizational Question," *CPSU in Resolutions*, I, p. 444.

29. Daniels, *Conscience of the Revolution*, citing Ninth Party Congress pp. 77, 57–68.

30. *Pravda*, April 23, 1920. This speech was reprinted in Trotskii, *O Lenine*, pp. 145–150.

31. *Pravda*, April 23, 1920.

32. Ibid.

33. Ibid.

34. *Bednota*, April 23, 1920.

35. Akop Akopian, "V. I. Lenin"; Toktogul, "Chto za mat' rodila takogo syna, kak Lenin!" *Lenin v sovetskoi poezii* (Leningrad, 1970), pp. 73–76.

36. *Pravda*, April 23, 1920.

37. Adrian Vechernii, "Vozhdiu mirovoi revoliutsii," *Vlast' truda* (Irkutsk), April 23, 1920, cited in *Lenin v sovetskoi poezii*, pp. 79–80.

38. V. V. Maiakovskii, "Vladimir Il'ich," *Sochineniia*, Vol I (Moscow, 1965), pp. 172–174. Maiakovskii first read this poem at a meeting of publishers honoring Lenin on April 28, 1920. It was first published in *Krasnaia gazeta*, November 5, 1922.

39. *Bednota*, April 23, 1920.

40. Butnik-Siverskii, *Sovetskii plakat*, pp. 654, 625.

41. Poster No. 4416–55, Poster Collection, Lenin Library, Moscow.

[6] Cultural Revolution and the Fortress Mentality

David Joravsky

FROM THE START cultural revolution involved ambivalent torments, occasionally eased by utopian fantasies. Political and social revolution joined the Bolshevik Party with the masses in opposition to the favorite parties of the intelligentsia and the privileged classes, and the Bolshevik leaders were acutely aware that the political enemy had a monopoly of "culture." The masses were *nekul' turnye,* uncultured—uncivilized would be the nearest English term. They could seize farms and factories, but did not know how to run them efficiently, in the modern way. The culture they lacked was much more than technical knowledge or refined manners. In the vocabulary that the Bolshevik leaders shared with the intelligentsia at large culture meant all such elements fused in *samodeiatel'nost',* the intelligent self-activation of modern people. Culture meant striving for emancipation from the realm of darkness *(tëmnoe tsarstvo),* as Dobroliubov had named the vicious circle of *samodurstvo* and *obezlichenie,* self-assertive pigheadedness and self-effacing irresponsibility—the mutual stultification of the foot-stamping master and the grovelling slave. Educated *chinovniki* (government functionaries) and merchants could be in that dark realm along with illiterate peasants and alcoholic workers. Independent, critically thinking individuals were supposed to win emancipation from it, along with wrathful peasants and workers, whose liberating anger was supposed to light the way out of the darkness.[1]

Such were the terms, such was the mode of analysis that attended the emergence of the self-conscious intelligentsia in the mid-nineteenth century. Those terms, that mode of analysis, were still keenly alive in the minds of the Bolshevik leaders and their "cultured" adversaries, as the sudden disintegration of the tsarist state transformed opposed strategies of liberation into the life-and-death politics of civil war. The Bolsheviks lunged for power on behalf of "uncultured" masses, hoping for postrevolutionary help from the "cultured" adversary—the intelligentsia—who might be angrily uncooperative after political defeat. And in fact, two days after the Soviet regime was decreed, Lunacharsky, the first Commissar of Enlightenment, warned that "functionaries without ideas *(bezideinye chinovniki)* are rather likely to come to our side, while all the officials with ideas *(ideinye rabotniki)* stubbornly defend their opinion that our regime is a usurpation."[2] The Bolsheviks themselves seemed to be entering the realm of darkness, the vicious circle of *samodurstvo* and *obezlichenie*.

Lenin sometimes issued such warnings, but other times he swung about and claimed that revolting workers and peasants were turning themselves into cultured agents of modernization. At a terrible lowpoint in the Civil War he angrily denied any need for the hostile intelligentsia; they were "lackeys of capital who fancy themselves the nation's brain. In fact they are not the brain but the shit."[3] That outburst was a momentary extreme, but it vividly revealed the potentially violent ambivalence that attended the Bolshevik efforts to enlist the intelligentsia in the cultural revolution. At the point of a gun the intelligentsia were asked to teach the masses *samodeiatel'nost'*, the intelligent self-activation of culturally modern people. Under duress they were to draw the masses away from the heritage of duress, from *samotëk*, planless drift, and from *stikhiinost'*, the ancient "elementalism" that knows only inertial torpor or anarchic chaos. (The Greek root is still alive in Russian as *stikhiia*, the elements or chaos. We should stop translating *stikhiinost'* as spontaneity, which means freely willed activity. That is *samoproizvol'nost'*.)

Leninist fear of *stikhiinost'* and *samotëk*, elementalism and drift, was one of many signs that Bolshevik leaders shared the widespread misgivings among educated Russians concerning "the people" *(narod)*, in particular, concerning their capacity to rule before they had absorbed modern culture. Such fears were at the center of Bogdanov's insistence that cultural revolution, the achievement of cultural hegemony by the lower classes, must accompany their rise to political hegemony lest the lower-class democracy of the soviets become a hollow pretense.[4] Such fears were also widely expressed in warnings that even with the discipline of the Bolshevik Party the hegemony of the lower classes might lead to a barbarization of culture. The Bolshevik replies to those warnings were sometimes as much confession as rebuttal. President Kalinin, for example, wondered whether a barbarization of culture might not serve progress in the long run, as it had in the downfall of the Roman Empire.[5] Commissar of Enlightenment Lunacharsky was less apocalyptic and more typical of ordinary Bolshevik thinking when he assured the Academy of Sciences that the political triumph of the lower classes was not a threat to culture, because the masses had created a dictatorial regime that was a friend of modern culture. Genuine self-government, he promised, would not come until the masses were enlightened.[6] In the meantime he expected the old "bourgeois" intelligentsia to help raise a new, red, Soviet intelligentsia out of the lower classes, in other words, to transmit their knowledge, their culture, without the non-Marxist ideologies that saturated it.

That tangle of ambivalent hopes and anxieties dragged the Bolsheviks into offensives on two ever-widening sectors of the cultural front: against the "uncultured" tendencies of the masses, and against the subversive tendencies of the intelligentsia. Shouting hollow claims of victory, the Bolsheviks staked out fortified outposts in alien territories. They called themselves comrades of the natives on both fronts, while they knew that they were a tiny army of occupation, struggling to avoid assimilation by the "uncultured" masses on the one hand, by the subversive intelligentsia on the other. My military metaphors are drawn from the Bolshevik vocabulary of the time, but I am obviously twisting their words to expose an underlying hysteria, a self-deceiving response to intolerable realities, which expressed itself in boasts of a new culture created by campaigns against the old. The most striking evidence of that hysterical self-deception is to be found in the utopian fantasies that proliferated in the early years of the Revolution. The "T-N-B-ers," to take an extreme little example, preached the Theory of the New Biology: culture consists of mental phenomena, which are reducible to conditioned reflexes, and thus all the paraphernalia of past and present culture have been an upper-class mystification, to be replaced as expeditiously as possible by efficient proletarian gestures and grunts.[7]

But utopian fantasies rapidly withered away while the cultural revolution continued. The strongest evidence of continuing self-deception in it is the long-term pattern of thought control, which was largely restricted to political thoughts in 1917–21 but expanded thereafter into every field of learning and art. Of course I am taking advantage of hindsight; the study of history would be impossible without hindsight. The significance of a brief period of upheaval is revealed in its long-term consequences. They show something in the cultural revolution far deeper than the initial political differences between the intelligentsia and the Bolshevik regime, or the early dreams of an instant leap into some streamlined future. Political opposition withered away even more quickly than utopian fantasies, but wishful thinking about learning and art was thrust upon the intelligentsia by squads of ideologists who were themselves ultimately absorbed and chastised by a rapidly growing apparatus of bureaucratized ideology.

Let us set aside the conventional handwringing, the sanctimonious sermonizing, and confront with puzzled whys and wherefores the most persistent and the most baffling feature of the cultural revolution. (Also the most universal: this feature appears even more fiercely in the Chinese than in the Russian revolution, and it persists in gentler forms even in liberalized Yugoslavia.) Let us see if historical analysis can explain the Communists' conflict with modern high culture, which has erupted at one time or another in virtually every field of learning and art.

The conflict has followed a long historical curve. It rises from faint signs of incipient tension in the prerevolutionary era, through steeply climbing outbursts of controversy after the victory of political revolution, reaches a tormented plateau of protracted warfare in the era of high Stalinism (or Maoism, or Castroism, or . . .), and then declines slowly toward sullen toleration of autonomous thinkers and artists after the Great Leader has taken down to the tomb the magic of exorcising contrary spirits with the disciplined cheering of masses, the rhythmic waving of some little red book. The particular social and political circumstances of individual countries shape the variable slope of that long curve, but some ineluctable conflict of ideas must be its essential driving force. Inherent in modern high culture, in the works and thoughts of intellectuals and artists, there must be some qualities that provoke Communists to blind rage, and what is worse, to insistent shouting that blind rage constitutes a great new vision. The problem is to discover what those qualities may be, to see if historical analysis can explain the intense, persistent conflict between the beliefs of Communist revolutionaries and the inherent tendencies of high culture in the twentieth century.

This will not be another extravagant sermon on the monstrous historical consequences of "the Communist idea," in the style of Berdiaev or Solzhenitsyn. With humble arrogance the empirical historian accepts such extravagant prophesying, as evidence of the conflict of beliefs that is to be explained. The empirical historian is a bully of humility. He defers to all the contentious prophets of a bygone age of faith, and thus depreciates them all. He grubs for essential qualities in contingencies, in correlations between evolving mentalities and other social processes. First and foremost in the study of cultural revolution he notes the most obvious correlation: The Bolshevik and all other indigenous Communist revolutions (repeat indigenous; exclude revolutions imposed by foreign armies) have occurred in backward provinces of modern culture, not in metropolitan centers. That correlation is as striking in cultural as in socioeconomic development. It must have some deeper significance than the occasion it provides for superficial derision of Karl Marx's pioneering effort to correlate cultural patterns with socioeconomic formations.

Poring over many conflicts in various fields of learning and art, one discovers a common pattern, endlessly repeated with many variations. In backward or underdeveloped countries modern high culture is the concern of a special class, the intelligentsia, which is pulled in three different directions by its commitment to advanced culture in the context of backwardness. Faith in modern culture as a worldwide communion of thinkers and artists tends to pull the intelligentsia in a prophetic direction, toward a visionary realm above contemptible praxis, politics included. Faith in modern culture as an organizing ideology in the struggle against backwardness tends to pull the intelligentsia in a practical direction, toward engagement in such mundane or even sordid affairs as politics. Professionalization is a third vector and an extremely attractive one, for it combines the prophetic, the practical—and the comfortable. At least that seems to be the ideal future that beckons in advanced countries, where thinkers and artists have become modern professionals, that is, paid specialists in mental labor, with only a pleasant little aura of the exalted obligations that bind *Kulturträger* in backward lands to lives of sacrifice and danger. In revolutionary Russia that aura was not a pleasant little residue but a highly charged field of force, pulling the swelling ranks of professionals in opposed directions and generating repeated thunderbolts with the attendant friction. The most explosive friction, as it turned out, was *within* the Communist mentality, where all three trends contended with each other as inarticulate self-contradictions, which found expression, as they were brought toward conscious expression, in delusions, anger, even violence.

These generalizations concerning the troubled history of group mentalities have been abstracted from the exemplary troubles of individual minds. Exceptionally articulate individuals are especially valuable; by their stress on contrasts and matter-of-fact acceptance of similarities they illuminate the background majorities. Consider the *intelligent* who, in the midst of the Civil War, brought Marxism-Leninism and psychological science into a confrontation that no one else had ever attempted. He was Pavel Petrovich Blonsky (1881–1941), a psychologist and pedagogue, an avid seeker of truth in speculative philosophy, an ardent devotee of the people's liberation, and—luckily for the historian—a compulsive bearer of witness whose autobiography reveals more than he intended.[8] He was born to the impoverished gentry, sufficiently déclassé to hate the system that nurtured a sense of nobility and simultaneously mocked it, in soul as well as status. His father earned a meager living as a clerk and deliberately elevated his mind to a stoic dignity, flying out of temper only when his wife asked him to go buy something or talk business with someone. An older brother cultivated important people in hope of juridical positions that conferred status with little or no pay until one was past thirty. His mother approved such dignified careerism, while despising fawning in hope of immediate reward. She grimly pinched pennies to keep the family in respectable clothes and genteel occupations, and passed on to Pavel, as he genially confesses, a penny-wise-pound-foolish way with money. His obsession with small change was imposed by wretched circumstance; he rose above it with his lordly disdain for big money.

As a university student Blonsky joined the Socialist Revolutionary Party, and suffered repeated jailings during the first revolutionary upheavals in 1904–1906. But he also managed to become a professional in the emerging discipline of experimental psychology, with a special interest in educational applications. Thus he hoped, as the revolution seemed to ebb away, that he could serve the people as a scholar and pedagogue, and earn a meager living in the process. He taught at various secondary schools and pedagogical institutes, published many scholarly pieces, and found himself drawn into the faculty of Moscow University half against his will, full of ambivalence and moral doubt. Like a character from Chekhov—Dr. Astrov perhaps, in *Uncle Vanya*—Blonsky endowed his mundane career with the aura of a stoic *Kulturträger* by confessing the failed hope, the absurd struggle to achieve a purpose for struggle, which was especially acute in Russia:

> It has long since become a hackneyed phrase to say that our time is one of intensified criticism, or rather, of skepticism. Our favorite writers, our journalism, our literature, the mood of people all about us—all are full of negation, exhaustion, an avid lust for some temple that is still uncreated. We have been moving along a road littered with the ruins of shrines, and our gait is sometimes indecisive and uncertain, sometimes nervously hurried and unnaturally bold, like the gait of people who are tired of wandering and are rushing to rest somewhere, no matter where. And behind us our younger brothers are coming; their negation is even stronger, their exhaustion even more unbearable.[9]

Those were indeed hackneyed phrases when Blonsky published them, in 1908, age twenty-four. He was confessing a fashionable mood that Chekhov captured with exquisite art in, say, "The Duel," a tale of violent tension between a do-nothing humanist, who justifies lethargy by mouthing an ideology of decadence, and a fearfully active scientist, who nearly kills the flaccid humanist in his rage for the progress of the race. The near murder shocks both into disillusion with grand ideology. They are converted to humble faith in useful labor without exalted visions, since "No one knows what's really right." That well-known line of Chekhov's—"*nikto ne znaet nastoiashchei pravdy*"[10]—could have served as the motto of the many *intelligenty* who were turning into professionals. It was a motto implicitly at odds with the Communist claim to know real *pravda*, the fusion of factual and moral truth, of science and humanism. The humble realism of professionals was also at odds with another part of the Communist mentality, the defiant romanticism that finds human value in revolt against brutish reality.[11] Blonsky's talk of the "younger brothers" with their "unbearable exhaustion" and terrible "negation" revealed his sympathy with such wild romanticism, his self-critical revulsion against the professional's life of small deeds and limited expectations.

A harsh sociologist would note that philosophical skepticism and modest devotion to humdrum labor are an evasion of dangerous tension. They are a convenient ideology for modern professionals; they reassure specialists in mental labor who have surrendered grand vision to the powers that be, or to a dead past, or, in such violently "developing" countries as Russia, to revolutionaries. The great majority of the Russian intelligentsia were strongly attracted to the low-lying dignity of the professional surrender, and on that basis, in the course of the Civil War, an explicit compromise was arranged. The new regime would buy the services of silently hostile specialists. The disapproval of Bolshevism by the overwhelming majority of the intelligentsia would be tolerated on condition that the disapproval be unorganized, politically inactive, not expressed in print.[12]

That compromise was intolerably unprincipled to minorities on both sides of the barricades. On one side some of the anti-Communist *intelligenty* emigrated. On the other, some Bolsheviks demanded the suppression of "bourgeois" high culture. (The culminating symbol of that violent reaction was the highly publicized banishment of 161 scholars in 1922, chiefly social theorists and philosophers.)[13] And at the barricade itself a handful of thinkers, Blonsky among them, sought to transcend a purely political compromise between the Bolsheviks and the intelligentsia. They began to seek an accommodation of Bolshevism with high culture on a principled level, within such professional fields as philosophy and psychology. In the language of the time, they sought "recognition" *(priznanie)* of the revolution, in intellectual thought as well as political submission.

With respect to political ideology "recognition" was brief, brusque, crude. Blonsky did not reason his way out of Socialist Revolutionary ideology in any systematic manner. He simply turned away, as a convert takes the decisive step from darkness to light, saving reason for the other side, in the world lit up by his new faith.[14] "October clearly showed me the two sides of the barricade; I perceived keenly that there can be no middle ground, and since November of 1917 I have known the joy of being on the side of the people."[15] Indeed, that slam-bang manner of the convert, the abrupt dogmatic choice that protects the mind against the torments of unbridled reason, extended far beyond political ideology. It resounded time and again in Blonsky's new writings on philosophy and psychology, most strongly in denunciations of the metaphysical philosophy that had absorbed much of his energy before the revolution. He now accused it of being an upper-class mystification, without making any serious effort to prove the accusation by reasoned argument.[16] Analogous denunciations of psychological science seemed to point toward simple suppression of it too, along with the philosophies and the political ideologies of the class enemy. But consistently or not, Blonsky continued to be a professional philosopher and psychologist. He sought to go beyond denunciation, to transform both disciplines so they might serve the politically victorious lower class in its struggle for a new socialist culture. He tried especially to transform psychology into a science that would harmonize with Marxism in revolutionary theory, and would be practically useful in socialist education.

Just think: in backward Russia, during the darkest days of civil war and famine, an *intelligent,* converting to Bolshevism, strove against the tendency of his class to split the professional from the political mind, and thus made the first effort to create a Marxist psychology. Physically indistinguishable from the political pamphlets of the time (brittle pulp paper, either yellow-brown or gray, with print so coarsely smudged as to be illegible in places), Blonsky's two little treatises of 1920–21 were an unprecedented intellectual venture.[17] They were the first effort anyone had ever made anywhere to reconcile revolutionary Marxism and professional psychology, each of which claimed scientific understanding of human beings.

For the previous forty years the advanced centers of modern culture, especially the German-speaking centers, had poured out streams of publications on Marxism and on psychology, separate streams. No one had seriously confronted the obvious question whether they might be compatible with each other. Both Marxists and professional psychologists had been prudently purblind, sufficiently sophisticated or modern to ignore such troublesome questions. The new science of psychology could be regarded as a useful technical specialty linked to medicine or pedagogy; or it could be considered largely theoretical and ideological, though increasingly separate from philosophy. Prerevolutionary Marxists dropped rare occasional remarks that pointed inconsistently in both directions.[18] Psychologists never discussed the possible significance of Marxism for their science or their science for Marxism. Only when revolution and civil war pressed the intelligentsia of a backward country into political submission to Marxist-Leninist rule did a psychologist abandon professional prudence and try to show that Marxism and psychology were complementary approaches to an understanding of human beings.

If there was heroism in the project—and I think there was—it was the absurd heroism that typifies synthetic theorizing about human beings in our century. To specialists drowning in an irresistible tide of fragmentation Blonsky threw little cries to rise above the flood on revolutionary wings. His treatises were synthetic in the mocking sense—ersatz, artificial, inauthentic—that twentieth-century chemistry has poured into a once dignified term. He skimmed over the hard problems that had caused psychology to split away from philosophy, and were causing psychology to split further into incompatible schools. He dredged up theories of the mind proposed by a variety of thinkers—from Hume and Kant to Titchener and Freud; even Jacques Loeb's and Ivan Pavlov's reduction of mind to neural reflexes—and threw them together with Marxist declarations that modes of production are the expression and the determinant of the evolving mind. Striving for synthesis, he achieved eclectic clutter. And all his inconsistent hypotheses for a science of the mind were intermittently subverted by his denunciation of psychological science as an obfuscation, which diverts one from action to change the world into academic exercises at interpreting it.[19]

Blonsky's synthetic heroism is mildly amusing—or mildly depressing, if one yearns for coherent understanding of the mind—until one reflects on the ominous context and portent. His were not treatises for sequestered psychologists in an advanced country, where politicians and intellectuals minimize conflict by a sullen divorce of political leadership from professional thinking. Within the psychological profession Blonsky was offering a platform for active "recognition" of a newly victorious, urgently dictatorial political ideology that called itself science. If political leaders would ever assert their authority on that platform, psychologists would have little or no professional authority to serve as a counterweight. Unlike physicists or biologists, they lacked a clear set of commonly accepted principles and well proved knowledge. They were fragmented into schools and trends, each incompatible with the other, and all presenting claims of knowledge on the very subject—human beings, their behavior, their minds—where political leaders are practical experts and masters—*scientific* masters, the Communists claim.

An ominous portent is not a seal of doom. The effort to create a Marxist-Leninist psychology could have proceeded along such eclectic, pluralist lines as Blonsky projected, and it could have been ignored by political leaders, as it was when he projected it. Lenin had some of Blonsky's work in his personal library,[20] but there is no evidence that he or any other of the highest leaders paid any serious attention to the call for a Marxist psychology before 1923, when *Agitprop* deliberately raised the problem among psychologists—with eclectic and pluralist discussion as the result while NEP endured. Yet very early, in the midst of the Civil War, the highest leaders went out of their way to persuade Ivan Pavlov that there was an exceptionally honored place for him in revolutionary Russia, in spite of his strongly expressed disapproval of Bolshevism. And many years later, in the era of high Stalinism, that incongruous kowtow to Pavlov in 1920–21 would be hailed as the first move toward the suppression of eclecticism and pluralism in psychology, toward official "recognition" of Pavlov's "teaching" *(uchenie)* as the only correct embodiment of Marxism-Leninism in psychology.

To understand those paradoxical developments one must be constantly aware that they were paradoxical developments, that is, illogical and unforeseen results of a complex historical process. It is mythic invention to attribute to Lenin and his comrades foreknowledge of a Stalinist goal, or even a clear conception of elementary issues in their unexpected entanglement with psychology and neurophysiology. As they repeatedly confessed, they approached Pavlov's "teaching" with the simple credulity of laymen contemplating natural science, not as lordly ideologists laying down the principles of Marxist psychology. His dogs salivating to ringing bells were a symbol of the scientific way to understand the mind, by reducing it to associative functions of the nervous system. Marx and Engels had ridiculed the ideology of physiological reductionism back in the 1860s and '70s, but the Bolshevik leaders venerated natural science and were therefore quite vulnerable to the popular view of Pavlov as the experimenter who had turned the ideology into hard science. In vivid lectures and essays he had been showing how to reduce mind to neural matter in experimentally proven fact, not in abstract speculation. That at any rate was his central argument, and to some extent the Bolshevik leaders were persuaded, for his lectures were collected and published in fulfillment of a 1921 decree signed by Lenin himself.

Yet Lenin was quite chary of explicit commitment to Pavlov's "teaching," perhaps because he had used his wartime leisure in Swiss exile to study Hegel. His philosophical notebooks of 1914–16 contain decidedly mentalistic speculations about approaches to a scientific understanding of the mind.[21] There are no Pavlovian speculations in the notebooks, or in any of his writings; not a word to support the Stalinist myth that Lenin started the official "recognition" of Pavlov's "teaching" as the embodiment of Marxism in psychology. His only significant comment on the famous physiologist occurred in a narrowly practical letter to Zinoviev, of June 25, 1920.[22] It was exclusively concerned with the awkward problems raised by Pavlov's threat to emigrate, since the terrible deprivations of the time made it virtually impossible for him to continue his normal work at home.

Lenin wrote that it would

> hardly be rational to permit Pavlov to go abroad, for he has previously spoken out openly in this sense, that, being a truthful person, he will be unable, in case appropriate discussions are started, to refrain from speaking out against the Soviet regime and Communism in Russia.
>
> At the same time this scientist constitutes such a big cultural value [bol'shuiu kul'turnuiu tsennost'] that it is impossible to think of keeping him in Russia by force, in conditions of material deprivation.[23]

Therefore, Lenin argued, Pavlov should be treated as an exceptional case. His food ration should be made extraordinarily large and he should be given an especially comfortable place to live. In a government decree spelling out the details, which was published in February 1921 over Lenin's signature, exceptional provision was also ordered for Pavlov's scientific work, and the State Publishing House was directed to use the best available materials to publish a deluxe collection of Pavlov's essays and lectures during the past twenty years, the time he had been working on conditioned reflexes. The cryptic character-ization of Pavlov in Lenin's letter—"such a big cultural value"—was slightly expanded but hardly clarified in the decree: "Academician Pavlov's absolutely exceptional scientific achievements . . . have significance for the toilers of the entire world."[24] Evidently Lenin was unwilling or unable to venture even a sentence or a phrase that might help the toilers to understand the significance of Pavlov's scientific achievements as distinct from his scandalously anti-Communist ideology.

An outside observer with the advantage of hindsight can see why Pavlov's achievements seemed so exceptional. They glowed against a dark background of prevailing backwardness, the backwardness of Russia among scientific nations, the backwardness of psychology among the sciences. Pavlov was Russia's only Nobel laureate, and he had won that distinction in the natural sciences, as a physiologist not as a psychologist. For the most recent period in his long life—he was born in 1849—he had been claiming to extend the indisputable methods of the natural sciences to the study of the mind, and the public took his success for granted. He was the down-to-earth provincial Russian physiologist who was overcoming the mystical confusion of cosmo-politan psychology.

With respect to political ideology, on the other hand, Pavlov had the ordinary views of the learned estate, and not of Russia alone. Like the German *Gelehrten* whom he admired, he professed haughty disdain for "politics," a disdain that was actually a masked submission to those who wielded political authority, whether the Kaiser's, the Tsar's, or Lenin's.[25] The chief difference between the German and the Russian mandarins was the underlying satisfaction that the Germans felt for their old regime, in contrast with the dissatisfaction of the Russians, who eagerly welcomed the fall of their emperor. The February Revolution prompted many scholars and scientists to descend from Olympian silence on politics, or to rise from silent submission to political authority—in any case, to speak out. In April 1917 Pavlov took part in an academic celebration of the dawn of Russian democracy. His speech focused on the hope that the new freedom would enable Russian science to escape from shameful backwardness. Germany was the ultimate model to catch up with and surpass. Its supremacy in science and technology, he argued, explained Germany's success in fighting against countries that were superior in population and resources.[26]

On that grossly political level Pavlov's ideology was quite common, easily distinguishable from his exceptional position in science, and easily denied printed expression under the Bolshevik regime as it had been under the tsarist regime. (Later on, when the Bolsheviks turned openly to the job of making Russia stronger than Germany, he would have access to a political forum once again.) But within the writings that he offered as science, ideology was intricately entangled with psychology and even with neurophysiology. "The Reflex of Freedom," to take the most egregious example of the messy mixture, was a lecture he gave in May 1917, published in a medical journal in 1918, and included in the 1923 volume that was published on Lenin's say-so.[27] The essay began with purely factual observation, but quickly revealed the theoretical difficulties that saturate factual observation in psychology. About two dogs in a hundred could not be trained to stand quietly in harness on the laboratory table and thus to respond with appropriate variations of saliva flow to ringing bells, flashing lights, electric shocks—the "indifferent stimuli" that the dog's central nervous system was forced to associate with the periodic appearance and non-appearance of food. The two-percent minority salivated profusely and continuously all the time they were on the table, as nervous people in unsettling circumstances sweat and fidget. That anthropomorphic insight—or pathetic fallacy—was Pavlov's.[28] With it he unwittingly confessed that he was still trapped in the common habit of inferring mental states from external behavior—in short, reading the minds of other creatures—even though he endlessly insisted that he had escaped from such subjective mindreading.

Many such anomalies attended Pavlov's shift from purely physiological studies of the digestive system, which had won him a Nobel Prize, to studies of conditioned reflexes, which were winning him popular fame as a psychologist. His central claim to fame was the rigorously objective method that he brought to psychology, the replacement of "introspection" by a physiologist's correlation of physical stimuli and physical responses. Or so he believed, and the public innocently accepted his self-evaluation. They did not ask, for example, whether pure objectivity was not violated before the supposed beginning of the conditioning experiments. Before data were recorded Pavlov and his assistants made friends with the dogs, and thus prepared them to be calm in the laboratory situation, so that the stop and go of their salivation might fit the stop and go of the "indifferent stimuli." Absolute objectivity, the complete elimination of subjective interaction between humans and higher animals—or even more among humans—may be impossible to the extent that the creatures are conscious of themselves and each other. Edward Thorndike, the American pioneer of behaviorism, unwittingly illustrated this great difficulty in a different way. He did not train his cats to go calmly into his experimental puzzle boxes. He thrust them in snarling and clawing, which injected a different kind of unmeasured subjectivity into his subsequent measurements of their behavior.[29]

The tunnel vision of masterful specialists protected Pavlov and Thorndike from such crippling criticisms of their experimental route to important findings, and the public was correspondingly blinkered, calmly prepared to accept reinforcement of the mechanical spirit of the age. Even such a sophisticated critic of mechanism as Bertrand Russell was unaware of the great incongruities between aspiration and achievement in Pavlov's "teaching."[30] Psychologists and neurophysiologists of rival schools—indeed, some of Pavlov's own disciples who turned to questioning—hardly reached the public with their specialized criticisms of his methods and conclusions. He maintained his self-assurance and his reputation by ignoring most criticisms, in public at any rate. In private he brushed most of them aside with an increasingly short temper, as his capacity for self-criticism was worn away by fame and old age. He was especially incensed against fellow specialists in neurophysiology who noted that his neurological explanations of conditioning were purely imaginary and—worse yet—increasingly at odds with the accumulating data of rigorous brain studies.[31]

Yet great technical knowledge was *not* necessary to appreciate how extravagantly speculative and ideological Pavlov was in his supposed physiology of "higher nervous activity," as he preferred to call the mind. In essays like "The Reflex of Freedom" he flouted scientific rigor in the most obvious ways. He not only imagined a "reflex of freedom" to explain the continuous salivation of exceptionally nervous dogs. He derived it from the unchained lifestyle of hypothetical stray dogs, which he imagined to have been the progenitors of the nervous creatures that salivated profusely and continuously on the laboratory table. On the other hand, he speculated, chained yarddogs had probably been the progenitors of the calm dogs that salivated and stopped as the experimentor dictated. The compliant majority exhibited yet another physiological fantasy, "the reflex of slavery"—and so did many Russians. "How often," Pavlov exclaimed, "in what varied ways, has the reflex of slavery appeared on Russian soil, and how useful to become conscious of it! . . . [For then one can] suppress that reflex by systematic measures, by successful inhibition."[32]

Pavlov was a typical modern scientist in his willful ignorance of philosophy, his contemptuous indifference to the philosophical tradition from which he had escaped, he thought, into the verified truths of experimental science.[33] The paradoxical combination of determinism and voluntarism, the hope that personal freedom and dignity can be won by submission to impersonal necessity, can be found in Stoicism and Christianity as well as Marxism and behaviorism—and in Pavlov's supposedly physiological "teaching." Insiders, participants in a particular school, are usually unaware of the broad underlying affinity, and grow angry when they sense it. One school's sense of exalted submission to the necessities of god or nature is a repulsive caricature, an abomination, to a rival school. In a private letter to a disciple in Canada Pavlov praised "the sense of human dignity" that had prompted the exceptional man to emigrate. "All around me," he wrote, "I am astounded to observe the absence of that sense. People who have been thrown into prison two or three times quite without grounds, like dogs being tied to a stake, forget it so quickly, without recognition of spiritual defeat."[34] In public writing Pavlov carefully avoided such harsh comment, and his Bolshevik critics showed reciprocal restraint. They limited themselves to a brief exchange of courteous polemics in 1923–24, when Pavlov included "The Reflex of Freedom" in his collection of scientific essays, and lectured medical students on the superiority of his "teaching" to the pseudoscience called Marxism.

In the preface to the 1923 book Pavlov inserted another ideological challenge to Marxism, which seems quite daring, but only when we compare it with the complete suppression of such challenges since the twenties. By comparison with the ideological conflicts of the half-century preceding 1917, Pavlov's challenge to Marxism in 1923 is extremely muted and brief. With the progress of the natural sciences, he observed, the human mind was achieving astonishing technical triumphs, but

> the same human being, with the same mind, governed by some dark forces acting within itself, causes incalculable material losses and inexpressible suffering by wars and by revolutions with their horrors, which take man back to bestial relationships. Only the ultimate science, the exact science of man himself—and the most reliable approach to it from the field of all-powerful natural science—will lead man out of the present darkness and cleanse him of the present shame of interpersonal relations.[35]

As revolutionaries, the Bolsheviks could hardly ignore the assertion that revolution is, like war, a regression to bestiality. As Marxists, they could hardly ignore the assertion that only a physiological approach could reach a genuinely scientific understanding of human beings. The challenge was all the more provocative since Pavlov, in a 1923 lecture, repeated and enlarged on his criticism of Marxism as a pseudoscience of human behavior. He did that in the introductory lecture to his course on physiology at the Medical Academy, which seems to have achieved limited distribution in published form, for student use. The highest political ideologists—Zinoviev, Trotsky, Bukharin—replied at length in *Pravda, Izvestiia,* and in *Red Virgin Soil,* the major journal of high culture.[36] Their central problem was to draw a line, or erect a wall, which would separate Marxism, the science of social evolution, from Pavlov's "teaching," the supposed physiology of the mind. Yet they inconsistently regarded Marxism as a comprehensive philosophy, with important critical implications for the science of the mind, and they could not even think of the opposite possibility, that the science of the mind might have critical implications for Marxism. In short, they could not confront the clash of principles that required a wall to keep the peace.

Serious criticism of Pavlov would have drawn Bolshevik ideologists into the question: What is a reflex in physiological fact, as distinguished from metaphorical fictions like the reflexes of freedom and of slavery? Trotsky and

Bukharin simply brushed those fantasies aside with a little genial laughter. Certainly they did not get deeply involved in analysis of Pavlov's "reflex of purpose." It is closely akin to the so-called orientation reflex, the alert focusing of the animal's attention on some item of interest, if I may use the everyday language that describes behavior by unashamedly attributing mental qualities to pricking of ears, pointing of head, and stiffening of body. Holistic concepts like the orientation reflex were and still are very hard to place on one or another side of the lines that arbitrarily separate physiology from psychology and both from evolutionary studies, Marxism included. Yet Zinoviev, Trotsky, and Bukharin avoided such problems not only in their public criticism of Pavlov, but even in their private thinking. We can penetrate that sanctuary, though behaviorists would forbid the trespass, not only by noting the obvious sincerity of their uncritical praise for Pavlov's physiological "teaching." We also have a private letter that Trotsky wrote to Pavlov in 1923, in which he endorsed the widespread notion that Freud and Pavlov were working toward a unified science of the mind from opposite ends of a mountain shaft, Freud from the psychological top down to the physiological bottom, Pavlov from the bottom up.[37] Trotsky respectfully asked Pavlov's opinion, but Pavlov disdained to reply. (Or Soviet editors have concealed a reply that they cannot approve.)

In any case, the highest Bolshevik ideologists had no thought of venturing into Pavlov's domain, and thus could not perceive how extravagantly speculative he was there, in his supposed physiology. They simply took it for granted that his "teaching" was natural science, not to be criticized by laymen. They also were confident that it was materialist in its philosophical essence, though Pavlov denied that.[38] Bukharin was especially insistent on this point. He simply ignored the neo-Kantian argument, which Pavlov approved, to the effect that his analysis of phenomena left the problem of mental or material essences unresolved. Bukharin declared Pavlov's "teaching" to be "a weapon in the iron arsenal of materialist ideology."[39] Since Bukharin was becoming the Party's chief ideologist, as Lenin declined to the grave (or rather, to mummified eternity in a glass case), those words quickly became an official catch phrase. They would be repeated even by sophisticated critics of Pavlov's "teaching," in jarring dissonance with their arguments that it was inadequate to explain the mind, and even inadequate as physiology.[40] Willy-nilly the chief ideologist had struck the characteristic pose of *samodurstvo,* and deferential specialists would respond with the bowing and scraping of self-effacing *obezlichenie.*

All that lies beyond the temporal limits of this book, in the complex Soviet discussions of psychology and neurophysiology during the mid and late twenties. The point here is the self-contradictory mixture of tension and forbearance that set the framework for those discussions. Pavlov and the Bolshevik leaders touched swords in 1923–24, and quickly backed away from all-out combat.

They protected themselves from damaging conflict over irreconcilable differences by agreeing on the common view of the natural sciences—and supposed natural sciences—as an area of miraculous certainty in an otherwise uncertain world, as the sacrosanct realm of the purely technical. In this respect Trotsky and Bukharin uncritically shared the spirit of our century. They praised an allegedly physiological "teaching" which, they cheerfully admitted, they were incompetent to judge.[41] Such protestations of the layman's incompetence were—and are—part of the blinkered vision that enables twentieth-century leaders to go on preaching grand old ideologies which are deeply at odds with the basic assumptions of many scientific disciplines. Pavlov on his side quickly retreated to the characteristic diplomatic silence of scholars and scientists, who forbear making a big issue of ideological disagreements with their political masters—or with scholars and scientists in rival schools and disciplines.

Yet at the very same time Blonsky's effort to transcend the genteel disintegration of high culture was being endorsed by *Agitprop,* and turned into a continuing campaign.[42] In January 1923 K. N. Kornilov astonished the first postrevolutionary Congress of Psychoneurology with a call for Marxist transformation of the human sciences.[43] The "recognition" of Marxism preached by Blonsky was henceforth to be official policy. A devilish confusion resulted—with a certain excitement, to be sure, the tawdry, feverish excitement that colored so much of high culture in the 1920s. Virtually all the invisible colleges or schools of psychology and neurophysiology found Marxist spokesmen. There were Soviet Marxist versions of Freudianism, of *Gestalt,* of behaviorism, of comparative animal psychology (as ethology was then called), of cognitive psychology, and of course of physiological psychology—itself divided into the rival schools of Pavlov and Bekhterev, and others I will not here trouble you with. There would even be splendid beginnings of the philosophical brooding over psychology that would be called Marxist existentialism when it was reinvented much later in Western Europe.[44]

Nevertheless, in spite of all the diversity that these Soviet thinkers of the twenties would share with their colleagues in the West, they would exhibit one characteristic in common, a distinctively Soviet innovation in the high culture of the twentieth century. All would be part of a professed effort to achieve unity in the human sciences "under the banner of Marxism." To use the brutally plain language of George Chelpanov, all the discussants subjected themselves to the "dictatorship of Marxism."[45] Chelpanov was the dean of Russia's experimental psychologists, who was removed from the central Institute of Psychology, which he had founded and directed until 1923. He was removed because he was too free with such plain talk, too explicit in arguing that the drive to unify the human sciences entailed either an eclectic pretense of unity or the subjection of rival schools to a single one, such as "reflexology."

Chelpanov's greatest offense was to invoke Marxism against the drive for a

Marxist psychology. Properly interpreted, he argued, Marxism required a continued effort to divorce philosophy from experimental psychology, which should strive to be as factual, as philosophically neutral, as mathematics or physics.[46] The ideological authorities would not allow that viewpoint to be thoroughly examined, even though—or because—it was so strongly implicit in the distinction that they themselves persistently made between Pavlov's admirable science and his deplorable political ideology. The fragmented high culture of the twentieth century was to be hammered into unity "under the banner of Marxism."[47] Anyone who challenged the possibility of such unification—such philosophizing with a hammer, to borrow Nietzsche's ominous phrase—became an outcast. And of course excommunications *can* achieve unity of culture, within a state church belligerently fortified against the divisive opinions of heretics and heathens.

Let me repeat. Ominous portents are not a seal of doom. Many evidences of the fortress mentality appeared in the Soviet Marxist state church of the twenties, but the dominant tone was openminded creativity in the search for Marxist unity of high culture. Eclectic pretensions of unity sanctioned a reality of pluralism in the search. We all know how brief that golden age of fairly free discussions proved to be. By 1929 angry impatient hands would seize weapons from Bukharin's "iron arsenal of materialist ideology" to beat down eclectic pretensions and achieve monolithic unity by subjecting all rivals to a single school within each discipline. No doubt the chief cause of that cultural cataclysm in 1929–32 would be the resurgence of the civil war mentality among political leaders. But we must recognize the cultural tensions that helped to inflame their political minds. The Bolshevik Party was never intended to be a debating society, as its leaders have been insisting since 1901. Yet modern high culture has irresistibly generated debating societies even—or most of all—among those who are most intent on transcending its fragmentation. Those Bolsheviks who have believed that such transcendence is to be achieved through practical assault on Russia's backwardness would reveal the most intense yearning for a unified culture, and the most intense intolerance of debate.

NOTES

1. See N. A. Dobroliubov, *Sobranie sochinenii*, vol. 5 (Moscow, 1962) for the seminal essays, "Tëmnoe tsarstvo," and "Luch sveta v tëmnom tsarstve," originally published in 1859 and 1860. Note the Soviet editor's ambivalent commentary, pp. 560–561.

2. Quoted by Sheila Fitzpatrick, *The Commissariat of Enlightenment* (Cambridge, 1970), p. 12, from Novaia zhizn', 1917, No. 176, p. 3. I have altered her translation to reproduce in English Lunacharsky's contrast between *bez'ideinye chinovniki* and *ideinye rabotniki*.

3. Lenin, *Sochineniia,* 4th ed., vol. 44, p. 227. For more detailed analysis of Lenin's—and other leaders'—mixture of attitudes toward the professional class, see Joravsky, *Soviet Marxism and Natural Science, 1917–32* (New York, 1961), Chapter 4.

4. See especially Z. A. Sochor, "Was Bogdanov Russia's Answer to Gramsci?" *Studies in Soviet Thought,* Feb. 1981, pp. 59–81.

5. M. I. Kalinin, "Nauka i liudi truda," *Novaia Petrovka,* 1923, No. 3–4, p. 7.

6. *Pravda,* 1925, Sept. 8.

7. See Joravsky, as cited in note 3, pp. 93–95.

8. P. P. Blonskii, *Moi vospominaniia* (Moscow, 1971).

9. Blonskii, "Fridrikh Paul'sen kak filosof i pedagog," *Voprosy filosofii i psikhologii,* 1908, *kniga* IV (94), p. v.

10. Chekhov, *Polnoe sobranie sochinenii,* vol. 7 (Moscow, 1977). See especially pp. 688–707 for the rich editorial notes on the ideological disputes that were in Chekhov's mind when he wrote this story.

11. See, e.g., Trotsky's apostrophe to the twentieth century, as quoted in Isaac Deutscher, *The Prophet Armed* (New York, 1954), pp. 54–55.

12. See Joravsky, as cited in note 3. For a convenient list of Soviet historical studies, see L. V. Ivanova, *Formirovanie sovetskoi nauchnoi intelligentsii (1917–1927 gg.)* (Moscow, 1980), pp. 3–9.

13. *Pravda,* 1922, Aug. 31. For evidence of Bolshevik ambivalence and bad conscience, in 1922 and at present, see B. A. Chagin and V. I. Klushin, *Bor'ba za istoricheskii materializm v SSSR v 20-e gody* (Leningrad, 1975), pp. 73–74. The exiles were, and still are, pictured as the last agents of enemy ideology doomed to extinction by the revolution, yet they are also pictured as dangerous people since many Soviet people would respond favorably to the ideology of these enemy agents, if they had not been exiled.

14. I am drawing on Tolstoy's vivid analysis of conversion, in his *Confession.*

15. *Golos rabotnika prosveshcheniia,* 1922, No. 6, p. 43. Cf. Blonskii, *Moi vospominaniia* (Moscow, 1971), pp. 143ff, for his account of the letters he published in *Izvestiia* immediately after the Bolshevik seizure of power. He objected to the teachers' strike against the new regime, and was accordingly censured by the Teachers' Union.

16. See Blonskii, *Reforma nauki* (Moscow, 1920), and *Ocherk nauchnoi psikhologii* (Moscow, 1921), passim.

17. Ibid.

18. See, e.g., the references to psychology, as indexed in G. V. Plekhanov, *Izbrannye filosofskie proizvedeniia,* vol. 5 (Moscow, 1958), p. 884. Note that Plekhanov, who came to intellectual maturity in the 1870s, still shared some of the interest in physiological psychology that characterized radical intellectuals in the mid-nineteenth century. Lenin, who came to intellectual maturity in the 1890s, shared the indifference of his generation. In a forthcoming book I will deal with this archaizing tendency of the cultural revolution, that is, the tendency to revive troublesome issues and failed solutions.

19. See works cited in note 16. For a convenient though somewhat tendentious précis, see A. V. Petrovskii, *Istoriia sovetskoi psikhologii* (Moscow, 1967), pp. 33–36; and A. A. Smirnov, *Razvitie i sovremennoe sostoianie psikhologicheskoi nauki v SSSR* (Moscow, 1975), pp. 135–137; and M. G. Iaroshevskii, *Istoriia psikhologii* (Moscow, 1966), pp. 525–527.

20. See the editorial introduction to Blonskii, *Moi vospominaniia,* pp. 5–6. Note that

Lenin had several of Blonskii's works on various subjects, especially education, and that he took notes on one of them, "where Blonskii wrote about the significance of technology in the development of modern society."

21. See Lenin, *Sochineniia*, 4th ed., vol. 38 (Moscow, 1958), especially pp. 350 and 357–361.

22. Ibid., vol. 44, pp. 325–326.

23. Ibid.

24. Ibid., vol. 32, p. 48. See a photograph of the celebrated document in K. A. Lange, *Institut fiziologii imeni I. P. Pavlova* (Leningrad, 1975), p. 15. A complete translation is in B. P. Babkin, *Pavlov, A Biography* (Chicago, 1949), p. 165. The ideological explanation on p. 164 is as fanciful in its way as the Stalinist myth is in its. Babkin was an anti-Communist Pavlovian who emigrated to Canada.

25. Cf. Fritz Ringer, *The Decline of the German Mandarins: The German Academic Community, 1890–1933* (Cambridge, Mass., 1969); Paul Forman, "Scientific Internationalism and the Weimar Physicists: The Ideology and its Manipulation in Germany after World War I," *Isis*, June, 1973, pp. 151–180; Joseph Haberer, *Politics and the Community of Science* (New York, 1969). For the neatest statement of Pavlov's attitude, see his 1904 autobiographical essay, in Pavlov, *Polnoe sobranie sochinenii*, vol. 6 (Moscow, 1952), pp. 441–444. Note especially the simple declaration: "Foreign travel was valuable to me chiefly because it acquainted me with a type of scientist, such as Heidenhain and Ludwig, who invested their whole lives, all its joys and grief, in science and in nothing else."

26. *Rechi i privetstviia, proiznesennye na trekh publichnykh sobraniiakh* (Petrograd, 1917), organized and published by Svobodnaia assotsiatsiia dlia razvitiia i rasprostraneniia polozhitel'nykh nauk. Pavlov's speech was omitted from both editions of his supposedly complete works, but it has recently been republished—with some surreptitious alterations, to tone down the tribute to German science—in *Neopublikovannye i maloizvestnye materialy I. P. Pavlova* (Leningrad, 1975), pp. 74–76.

27. Pavlov, op. cit. in note 25, vol. 3, *kniga* 1, pp. 340–345. For an English translation, see Pavlov, *Lectures on Conditioned Reflexes* (New York, 1928), pp. 282–286.

28. Ibid., p. 283.

29. For an incisive sketch of Thorndike's work, see E. G. Boring, *A History of Experimental Psychology* (New York, 1950), pp. 561–564. The subjective element in the famous experiment was called to my attention by a lecture of Julian Jaynes, who had vivid slides to show the cats' frightful state of mind as they were thrust into the puzzle box.

30. See Bertrand Russell, *The Scientific Outlook* (New York, 1931), pp. 45–56 and passim. Thanks to T. W. Heyck, who called this book to my attention.

31. A full analysis of Pavlov's development will be given in my forthcoming book, *The Psychology of Stalinism*. The neatest evidence of his inability to take criticism seriously may be found in his response to Karl Lashley's experimental testing of Pavlov's views on the role of the cortex in conditioning. See Pavlov, "The Reply of a Physiologist to Psychologists," *The Psychological Review*, March 1932, pp. 91–127. Cf. the letter from one of Pavlov's disciples to another, sometime between 1933 and 1935: "But no one argues any more. This has become bad taste. In this his age is apparent. In our day he would have refused a piece of bread for the sake of an argument or a fight!" Savich to Babkin, in the papers of B. P. Babkin at McGill University.

32. Pavlov, op. cit. in note 27.

33. The neatest example of Pavlov's attitude to philosophy is to be found in *Psikhiatricheskaia gazeta*, 1917, No. 8, pp. 200–205. This exchange with the Petrograd Philosophical Society has been omitted from both editions of his supposedly complete works.

34. Pavlov to B. P. Babkin, Oct. 23, 1924, in the papers of Babkin at McGill University.

35. Pavlov, *Polnoe sobranie sochinenii* in note 25, vol. 3, *kniga* 1, p. 17.

36. See Zinoviev's speech to the First All-Russian Congress of Scientific Workers, published both in *Izvestiia* and in *Pravda, Nov.* 25 and 27, 1923, and separately. Trotsky's speech to the same meeting, also published originally in *Izvestiia* and *Pravda,* was conveniently reprinted in Trotsky, *Sochineniia,* vol. 21 (Moscow, 1927). The rebuttal of Pavlov is on pp. 264–266. Bukharin wrote the longest reply: "O mirovoi revoliutsii, nashei strane, kul'ture i prochem (otvet prof. I. Pavlovu)," *Krasnaia nov'* 1924, Nos. 1, 2, separately as a pamphlet, and in Bukharin, *Ataka* (Moscow, 1924).

37. Trotsky, *Sochineniia,* vol. 21 (Moscow, 1927), p. 260.

38. See, e.g., Pavlov's explicit declaration: "I cannot agree that my methods constitute pure materialism." Op. cit. in note 33, p. 202. Until the mid-thirties, when Pavlov died and the Stalinist myth emerged in full force, Bolshevik commentators showed constant awareness of the contrast between his agnostic position in philosophy and the materialism that they found implicit in his work.

39. Bukharin, *Ataka* (Moscow, 1924), pp. 171 ff.

40. See, most notably, L. S. Vygotskii, "Psikhologicheskaia nauka," in *Obshchestvennye nauki SSSR, 1917–1927* (Moscow, 1928), pp. 32 and passim. Cf. his comment on conditioned reflexes in *Psikhologiia i marksizm* (Moscow, 1925), pp. 175–176.

41. See works cited in note 36.

42. A. B. Zalkind, who was a leader in the campaign, dated it from 1919, but added that "it took serious shape beginning in 1922 in the depths of the psychophysiological section of the Institute of Communist Education, which was created on the initiative of the *Agitprop* Section of the Central Committee, and after that quickly spread to broad circles of scientific and public people." *Vrachebnaia gazeta,* 1930, No. 1, p. 52. The ambiguity of the reference to *Agitprop* is Zalkind's, not mine. If the archives contain better evidence of a more direct role played by *Agitprop,* Soviet scholars have not found such evidence, or have withheld it, though they like to attribute initiative and guidance to "central party organs."

43. K. N. Kornilov, "Sovremennaia psikhologiia i marksizm," *Pod znamenem marksizma,* 1923, No. 1. Cf. *Psikhologiia i marksizm* (Moscow, 1925), p. 233, for Kornilov claiming that his speech of January 14, 1923, was "the first time in the Russian literature that the question of 'psychology and Marxism' was placed on the agenda."

44. T. I. Rainov, "Otchuzhdenie deistviia," *Vestnik kommumisticheskoi akademii,* 1925–26, Nos. 13, 14, and 15. In some of his publications L. S. Vygotskii hinted at ideas which were fully expressed in an article that waited fifty-five years to be published. See "Istoricheskii smysl psikhologicheskogo krizisa," in his *Sobranie sochinenii,* vol. 1 (Moscow, 1982), pp. 291–436. Cf. the analysis by Alex Kozulin, "Vygotsky and Crisis," *Studies in Soviet Thought,* vol. 26 (1983), pp. 1–8.

45. See Bukharin, "Kul'turnyi front i intelligentskii pessimizm," *Pravda,* June 24, 1923, which dates Chelpanov's remark "a year ago." Cf. Iu. V. Frankfurt, "Ob odnom izvrashchenii marksizma v oblasti psikhologii," *Krasnaia nov',* 1925, No. 4, p. 186, for another polemic that dates the remark "in 1922." Unfortunately, I have been unable to find the original source of the remark. Cf. Bukharin, *Ataka* (Moscow, 1924), p. 133, for another polemic against Chelpanov's plain talk, in which Bukharin distinguishes between sincere ideological conversion, "even if under the pressure of the abovementioned dictatorship," and insincere conversion, which results in smuggling of enemy ideologies.

46. See G. I. Chelpanov, *Psikhologiia i marksizm* (Moscow, 1924), and *Psikhologiia ili refleksologiia* (Moscow, 1926).

47. That was the title of the chief philosophical journal of Bolshevism, *Pod znamenem marksizma,* which began to appear in 1922. Cf. Bukharin's declaration that

"the old world has no future, [and] therefore it has no great unifying idea that would rally people together, that would cement their relationships." *O mirovoi revoliutsii, nashei strane, kul'ture i prochem* (Leningrad, 1924), p. 36. The unconscious implication, that a "great unifying idea" is a consequence of a future history—in short, that it does not exist at present—almost emerged into conscious expression in Bukharin's speech to the Fifth Comintern Congress. See *Pravda,* June 29, 1924. Note the passage where Bukharin decries the tendency toward Hegelianism among Western Marxists and the tendency toward "agnostic positivism" among Russian Marxists, and demands a clause in the Comintern program that will insist on a genuinely revolutionary Marxist world view, "a rather elastic formula" but essential for unity.

[7] The Utopian and the Heroic: Divergent Paths to the Communist Educational Ideal

James C. McClelland

AN OVERVIEW OF Bolshevik efforts to introduce social and cultural change during the years immediately following the revolution would highlight two basic facts: the existence of wide disagreements and debates among the Bolsheviks themselves concerning what kind of measures were most urgent and desirable, and the unreality or inapplicability of virtually all of their conflicting plans in view of the harrowing political, social, economic, and cultural conditions of the time in Soviet Russia. Bolshevik policy in many areas can be viewed as the product of this combination of extravagant hopes, sharp debates, and dismal realities.

What was the nature of the debates on social and cultural issues among Bolshevik leaders at this time? It is possible (with hindsight) to detect a definite pattern of debate, a bipolar clustering of opinion on several related matters, which we must recognize in order fully to understand the issues involved. One set of opinions, which I shall call "utopianism," held that the most urgent task facing the new government was to implement measures that would immediately benefit the people in whose name the revolution was being fought, that would develop a proletarian class-consciousness within the population, and that would enlist the active participation of the masses themselves in the revolutionary process. Only then, it was thought, would Bolsheviks enjoy true mass support; only then would it be possible to establish the economic foundations for socialism. The second outlook, which can be termed "revolutionary heroism," maintained that a drastic advancement of the industrial economy was the most urgent need and that such a campaign must precede, not follow or accompany, efforts to produce a new political and cultural outlook on the part of the masses. Tied to the ethos of war communism, this view insisted that in order to attain the socialist goal, militaristic methods must be used in the social-economic sphere regardless of the hardships they might impose or the opposition they might arouse from the public at large. The leading stronghold of utopianism was Lunacharsky's Commissariat of Enlightenment *(Narkom-pros)*, while the main source of inspiration for revolutionary heroism was Trotsky's Red Army.

In terms of program, the two positions were diametrically opposed, and the year 1920 witnessed increasingly intense debates between the representatives of each. On one point, however, they were quite similar: each persuasion, in its undiluted form, was characterized by fervent radicalism, extremist hopes, and reckless impatience to revolutionize existing institutions. Efforts by some (including Lunacharsky) to stake out a moderate position while accepting the basic assumptions of one or the other position were generally unsuccessful. As a consequence, both approaches were discredited by the near-collapse of the economy at the end of 1920. Although the utopian-heroic debate would erupt again during the Cultural Revolution of 1928–1931, it was relegated to the background during the pragmatic years of the New Economic Policy.

Issues which exemplify this pattern of debate include labor and trade union policy, the role of women, the question of proletarian culture, and reform of education at all levels.[1] This paper will examine the utopian-heroic conflict in secondary education, where the vehement debate of 1920–1921 might well be summed up in the phrase, "polytechnism vs. monotechnism."

"At the present moment," declared Lunacharsky in a speech on August 26, 1918, "the government is confronted with one task: how to impart to the people as quickly as possible the huge amount of knowledge they will need in order to fulfill the gigantic role which the revolution has given them."[2] One might have thought that the primary task of the Soviet government in August 1918, was to defeat the White armies, but Lunacharsky made no reference to the spreading Civil War in his speech. In fact, during the first two years after the revolution, Lunacharsky and his *Narkompros* colleagues formulated their ambitious reforms generally without reference to either the military conflict or the economic disintegration that were devastating so much of the country and preoccupying the attention of other Bolshevik leaders. The result was a *Narkompros* reform program that was drawn up and promulgated without the participation of other Soviet agencies and that was to prove strikingly out of touch with prevailing political, social, and economic realities.

The major educational reform at this time was the statute on the "Unified Labor School" *(Edinaia trudovaia shkola*, hereafter abbreviated ULS), signed by Lenin and published September 30, 1918.[3] The goal of the decree was nothing less than to cast all existing schools in the country into a single mold. With one stroke of the legislative pen, the complex tsarist system of gymnasia, realschulen, pro-gymnasia, primary schools, upper primary schools, and parish schools was abolished. In its place, the decree called for the establishment everywhere of nine-year educational institutions, divided into primary (I *stupen'*) and secondary (II *stupen'*) schools. Education was to be free, coeducational, and compulsory for children between the ages of eight and seventeen. It was hoped that the establishment of a unified network of this nature would guarantee free access to education for children from all classes, in particular from the proletariat and peasantry.[4]

In addition to providing increased accessibility, the ULS reform was intended to make the new schools polytechnical in nature. Polytechnism, as understood by Krupskaia and Lunacharsky, was an eclectic concept that drew on the educational theories of Georg Kerschensteiner and John Dewey as well as on random comments by Karl Marx. In general, it postulated that pupils learn better by active doing than by passive reading or listening, and that most of the subjects to be studied in school should be related to the general theme of labor and the economy. The goal was to prepare the future workers to become "masters" *(khoziaeva),* with a good overall understanding of the economy as a whole, rather than the mere cogs in the economic system they had allegedly been under capitalism.[5]

How these principles could be translated into practice, however, was not at all clear, and vagueness and disagreements on this point seriously weakened the polytechnical position. There were two main positions on this issue within *Narkompros* during 1918–1919. The Petrograd group, led by Lunacharsky, thought that in addition to academic studies secondary school pupils should learn various skills, such as lathe work and soldering, and undertake part-time work in factories under direct pedagogical supervision. More radical—and more widely accepted among *Narkompros* officials in the early years—was the position of the Moscow group, which included V. M. Pozner, P. N. Lepeshinsky, and V. N. Shul'gin. They sought the complete transformation of the traditional school into a communal type of institution which would be economically self-sufficient through the work of its pupils.[6]

But if unable to agree on what exactly a polytechnical school *was,* most *Narkompros* figures did agree on what it was *not.* It was neither a strictly academic school on the one hand, nor a narrow trade school on the other. Furthermore, they all endorsed the basic utopian premise that a new educational system, however organized, would play an extremely important role in the construction of socialism. As Krupskaia (Lenin's wife and a leading *Narkompros* official) had put it before the revolution, a true labor school organized by a working-class government would be no less than a "tool for the transformation of modern society."[7]

In view of the conditions of the time in war-ravaged, poverty-stricken Russia, the statute on the Unified Labor School could only serve as a declaration of intent, and, as events were to prove, a highly unrealistic one at that. At that time school buildings located in civil war zones were frequently requisitioned for military use, the ranks of teachers were seriously depleted and those that remained were close to starvation. In short, it was difficult enough to staff and operate existing schools, let alone add to their number and carry out comprehensive reforms. Nonetheless, the basic principles of the ULS received the complete support of Lenin, and were in fact written into the new party program of March 1919. Point 12(1) of the program, which had primarily been written by Krupskaia herself, called for "The provision of free and obligatory general and polytechnical education (which will familiarize the pupil with the theory and practice of all main branches of production) for all children of both sexes until 17 years of age." Point 12(3) called for "The complete realization of the principles of the Unified Labor School, . . . a close connection between studies and socially productive labor, and the preparation of well-rounded members of communist society."[8]

What were the results of the efforts during the years 1918–1919 to convert existing schools into polytechnical institutions? By the end of 1919, it appears, the Moscow line in particular and the *Narkompros* policy in general had met with virtually complete failure. Local officials, including communist ones, reacted to the new educational principles with misunderstanding and even hostility. Some local authorities deliberately ignored the law requiring the separation of church and state, petitioning, in the name of the public, for the right to retain religious lessons in the schools. Krupskaia, in a six-week trip down the Volga in the summer of 1919, was shocked to discover that there were virtually no properly functioning labor schools in existence, and that local cadres were largely indifferent to education. *Narkompros* leaders had purposely declined to formulate and distribute detailed curricular instructions out of fear of inhibiting the spontaneity and initiative of local teachers. The result, however, was that while a variety of approaches was tried in the larger cities and in experimental schools, on the whole the majority of teachers had absolutely no idea what was expected of them and most teaching, when it occurred at all, followed traditional patterns. Where efforts were made to create "school-communes" the "labor" of the pupils usually boiled down to chopping wood and performing janitorial work with the result, according to one critic, that the pupils became dirty instead of becoming educated. Pozner stirred up a hornet's nest by simply closing the best technical schools in Moscow without being able to replace them with functioning polytechnical schools.[9]

It is not surprising, therefore, that *Narkompros* came under increasing criticism throughout the year 1919 for its polytechnical policies. Under the leadership of Lunacharsky, it began to modify its initial policies. By the end of the year the Moscow group had been discredited and removed, work was about to begin on the formulation of standardized curricula for all polytechnical schools, and Lunacharsky had made the first of many statements defending polytechnism in principle while admitting past mistakes and granting the need, given present conditions, for greater priority to vocational education.[10] These measures, however, were insufficient to satisfy his opponents. Criticism continued to mount until early 1920, when a new educational agency, based on the principles of revolutionary heroism, was created as a direct challenge to *Narkompros*.

By the end of 1919 it appeared that the Civil War had finally come to an end. The armies of Denikin, Kolchak, and Yudenich had been decisively defeated, and neither the forthcoming Polish invasion nor the last-ditch regrouping of White forces around Baron Wrangel was at that time foreseen. The time had come, it seemed, to transfer attention from the military front to the so-called second front—the restoration of the national economy.

It would be difficult to exaggerate the extent of the economic crisis confronting the government at this time. A large percentage of the industrial base had been either destroyed or badly damaged. Under normal conditions southern Russia supplied fuel, iron, steel, and other raw materials to the industries of central and northern Russia. But southern Russia had been occupied by the Whites during a large part of the Civil War, and when the Bolsheviks regained control, they discovered that the coal mines of the Donetz valley had been flooded, and the other industries destroyed. The destruction was so vast that even by the end of 1920 the coal mines produced less than one-tenth and the iron-steel works less than one-twentieth of their prewar output. Further complicating an economic recovery was the virtually complete standstill of the transport system. Railway track and bridges had been destroyed during the war, and rolling stock had not been renewed and rarely repaired since 1914.[11]

Recovery was made more difficult by a second aspect of the crisis—the melting away of the country's industrial labor force, both skilled and unskilled. Most workers had never severed their ties to the village, and many of them reacted to hard times by returning to the countryside where they would be closer to the food supply. Many others had been mobilized by the Red Army, but their return home after the fighting had stopped was greatly impeded by the transportation breakdown. As a result, cities experienced a serious decline in population between 1917 and 1920—Moscow lost 40 percent of her population, Leningrad more than 50 percent, Kiev 28 percent, Kazan 23 percent.[12] A recent and careful study calculates that the number of industrial workers declined from a high of 3.6 million in 1917 to a low of 1.4 million in late 1919. The dissolving of the proletariat into the peasantry is further illustrated by the fact that workers and their families comprised only 10.4 percent of the population of the entire country in 1924 compared with 14.6 percent in 1913, whereas the peasantry increased its relative weight from 66.7 percent to 76.7 percent.[13] The normal material incentives for attracting workers to the cities and factories were unavailable to the government in 1920 in view of the runaway inflation, which made currency virtually worthless as a medium of exchange, and the failure of the system of rationing and social maintenance to provide sufficient wage payments in kind. Under such circumstances the most elementary economic problem of apportioning sufficient manpower for the fulfillment of basic tasks assumed huge proportions.

It was Lev Trotsky who proposed the methods that were chosen to meet this challenge in January 1920. Then at the pinnacle of his career, the fiery Commissar of War had been brilliantly successful in whipping the Red Army into a victorious fighting unit. His principles were strict centralization, ruthless discipline, and passionate exhortations for sacrifice from the rank and file. Why not apply the same methods to the equally staggering problem of economic restoration?

The crux of Trotsky's program was the "militarization" of labor, which would subject all able-bodied citizens to "labor conscription" *(trudovaia povinnost')* whereby, under threat of military discipline, they would be obliged to perform labor for the state and could even be sent to distant parts of the country for this purpose.[14] In view of the country's desperate need for skilled labor, Trotsky's plan called for a rejuvenation of vocational education. When the *Narkompros* leadership got wind of the project, it "sharply protested," fearing that vocational education would be taken out of its hands, narrowly construed, and divorced from the principle of polytechnism.[15] These fears proved justified. The Central Committee approved a modified version of Trotsky's plan on January 22, 1920, and *Sovnarkom* decrees of January 29, signed by Lenin, established a new organ called the Main Committee of Vocational-Technical Education (*Glavprofobr*).[16] As a concession to *Narkompros, Glavprofobr* was administratively located within the Commissariat of Enlightenment, and Lunacharsky became its nominal chairman. In fact, however, it was granted considerable administrative autonomy, its own budget, and an advisory council in which representatives of *Vesenkha* (the supreme economic council), the trade unions, and the economic commissariats easily outweighed those of *Narkompros.*[17] Its real leader was O. Iu. Shmidt, a mathematician and subsequent polar explorer, an ardent vocationalist and opponent of polytechnism. Although Lunacharsky, as always, tried to make the best of the situation and mediate between the two camps, in fact the lines were drawn for a struggle between the utopian-minded polytechnists in *Narkompros* and the zealous vocationalists in *Glavprofobr*.

The difference between the two groups was fundamental. Whereas Lunacharsky thought that socialism could be achieved only by educated, class-conscious workers, and Krupskaia regarded the labor school as a "tool for the transformation of modern society," Shmidt, himself only a recent convert to Marxism, argued the opposite:

> Marxists, or anyone whom life has taught to think in Marxist terms, know that it is not words, it is not studies, it is not upbringing that creates new people, but a change in the economic structure . . . if socialism is not accomplished in the economic sphere, all attempts to accomplish it in the school will be in vain.[18]

Shmidt and other vocationalists did not regard education as unimportant, but merely insisted that it be strictly subordinated to the needs of the economic system. B. G. Kozelev, a leading trade unionist and member of the *Glavprofobr* collegium, called on the governmental economic organs, especially *Vesenkha,* to draw up a detailed plan providing precise estimates of the number of specialists that would be needed in each area of the economy in future years. *Glavprofobr* would then adjust its admissions quotas and allocate its resources among the different vocational schools under its jurisdiction accordingly.[19]

The *Glavprofobr* enthusiasts thus envisioned their committee as a production organ *par excellence*. Its job was to produce trained human specialists. It would receive orders for specified quantities and types of its goods from *Vesenkha.* The source of its raw materials would be unskilled trade unionists and youth currently enrolled in secondary and higher education. The distributing organ, which would send the finished products to their place of employment (under threat of compulsion, if necessary) would be *Glavprofobr*'s twin, the recently established Main Committee for Universal Labor Conscription *(Glavkomtrud).*[20]

It was fantasy to think that such a well-oiled coordination could be achieved under the chaotic conditions of 1920. *Vesenkha* had never been a strong organ and furthermore was led by A. I. Rykov and V. P. Miliutin, both moderates who had opposed Trotsky's plan for the militarization of labor from the beginning. Given the economic conditions of the time, *Glavprofobr*'s principles were every bit as impractical as *Narkompros*'s. Nonetheless, *Glavprofobr*'s plans for vocational education did receive important support in April from the Third All-Russian Congress of Trade Unions—support that was doubly significant because the previous year's congress had adopted strikingly different resolutions calling for the development of a proletarian culture and the inclusion of general subjects such as political economy and business management in all vocational education curricula.[21] Still more important was strong support for vocationalist principles from a completely new and unexpected source—the recently established Commissariat of Education of the Ukrainian Soviet Socialist Republic.

The policies of Ukrainian Commissar of Education G. P. Grinko and his deputy Ia. P. Riappo are prime examples of the heroic approach to education. Their uncompromising opposition to the institutional status quo was even more extreme than that of the Moscow group of the Russian *Narkompros*. "The worker-peasant revolution of the twentieth century," wrote Riappo in 1922, "will produce not reform of the former institutions, but revolution. . . . Attempts to rebuild the old institutions are completely hopeless. . . . We must approach the question as though we were confronted by a completely clean slate."[22] As early as August 1920, Grinko had attacked the Unified Labor School of the Russian *Narkompros* on the grounds that it represented an insufficient break with the "bourgeois" academic school of the past. Like some of the ultra-utopians in the RSFSR, he and Riappo tended to regard the school itself as only a transitional institution which should be replaced as soon as possible with children's colonies that would fulfill the functions of both family and school. Where they strongly differed from all their Russian counterparts, however, was in their insistence that education at the secondary and higher level should be directly coordinated with the needs of economic reconstruction. Whereas the Russian *Narkompros* had during its first two years closed some well-equipped vocational schools, the Ukrainian *Narkompros* adopted the opposite policy of closing several functioning schools of general education.[23] One of Grinko's theses approved by the Second All-Ukrainian Congress of Education (August 1920) read,

> Under the circumstances of extreme economic impoverishment, . . . when the need for a qualified working force . . . has become the decisive factor in economic reconstruction, vocational-technical education must become the foundation of the entire system of education.[24]

Knowledge acquired in a vocational school, according to Riappo, was not an end in itself, but only a means of preparing the student for a definite vocational specialty.[25]

Riappo wrote at one point that the Ukrainian educational system of "monotechnism" would only be valid for the transition stage between capitalism and socialism.[26] But, like Trotsky's unblushing defense of forced labor, Grinko and Riappo tended to make a virtue out of the necessity of vocational education. Grinko insisted that it should not be viewed as an external appendage to general education, but rather as its very source and basis. They both regarded Lunacharsky's ideal of a well-rounded, harmoniously developed personality as a bourgeois remnant, to which they counterposed their own ideal of "Homo technicus," who would achieve his fulfillment through participating in the building of a technological society.[27]

Among the policy issues that divided the Russian *Narkompros* from *Glavprofobr* and the Ukrainian *Narkompros* in 1920 were higher education, adult education, and the organizational structure of the commissariat itself. But it was the secondary school issue that was the most divisive and bitterly disputed. On the one hand was the original *Narkompros* position that all children should attend a nine-year, general educational, polytechnical labor school from age eight to seventeen. This position had the great advantage of being enshrined in the party program of 1919; it had the great disadvantage of having failed miserably during the first two years of its attempted implementation. The other position maintained that vocational (or "monotechnical") education must begin no later than age fifteen. Before that, there could be a seven-year school (although the Ukrainians much preferred a network of children's homes or colonies) in which children would learn one or more trades or skills. In addition to the seven-year school, however, the existing network of trade and vocational schools would be maintained and even expanded. Graduates of the seven-year school could go on to a four-year technicum and a few could go on to a specialized higher educational institute, in which the curriculum would be shortened from five years to three.

In one sense, all the participants in this debate were living in a world of unreality. For the majority of Russian children, especially in the countryside, the question was not whether they would attend a seven-year or nine-year institution, a polytechnical or a trade school, but whether they would attend any school at all. Only half the school-aged children of tsarist Russia were enrolled in schools in 1914, and official enrollments in Soviet Russia dipped below the prewar level during the years 1921 to 1925.[28] In 1925 fewer than fifty percent of those children who did enter school completed as much as three years of schooling. Only 16.2 percent of all urban and 1.9 percent of all rural primary schools offered the full five years of instruction.[29] The situation was better in the capitals, but by and large the participants on both sides of the Bolshevik educational debate were dealing with hopes and dreams, not with real possibilities.

Lunacharsky's leadership of the polytechnical camp was wobbly, to say the least. Throughout 1920 he proved willing to concede most of the essential points while still proclaiming the general principles that were in fact being sacrificed. He admitted past failures, which he attributed primarily to the Civil War and the government's inability or unwillingness to allocate sufficient resources to culture and education. He acknowledged, in view of the economic crisis, the need for *Glavprofobr*, granted that vocational education could begin even as early as age fourteen, and welcomed the continued existence of vocational schools, especially those in or near factories, for youth who were not attending the general schools.[30] But he warned, in his characteristically half-pompous, half-eloquent style, against letting this trend go too far:

We understand that the ruined Russian economy needs specialists, but must continually bear in mind that it was precisely to acquire, in the course of many years, genuine culture, to achieve true consciousness of its own human worth, to enjoy the salutary fruits of contemplation and sensibility that the working class has overthrown the rule of capital. . . . It is essential that the organizers of the Unified Labor School fully recognize the tremendous importance of the task which *Glavprofobr* must fulfill—the task of adapting the growing new school generation to the urgent economic demands which the country is experiencing at the moment. On the other hand, *Glavprofobr* officials must understand that we are living in a socialist society, where it is impossible to consider only the needs of production and where to overlook the human being in favor of production will no longer be permitted by the proletariat itself.[31]

Other *Narkompros* leaders (especially Krupskaia) and many teachers refused to accept their commissar's concessions. The issue was an emotional one—everyone remembered how the tsarist Ministry of Education had aroused both liberal and radical anger by creating a vocational school network that was clearly intended to keep middle and lower-class children from improving or even questioning their status. Trying to appear reasonable before a clearly hostile audience of educators in September 1920, Shmidt denied that either he or *Glavprofobr* was in favor of narrow specialization. But he labeled polytechnism under present conditions utopian and argued that the last two years of the nine-year school should have a definite vocational bias.[32] His views were sharply opposed at the conference by Pokrovsky and Krupskaia.[33] In late October Shmidt claimed that *Narkompros* was trying to establish the educational system of a full-fledged communist society without considering the necessity of a long transition period, and complained that *Glavprofobr*'s efforts had been stymied by a lack of cooperation from *Narkompros*.[34]

It seemed clear that the dispute would have to be resolved by higher authority, and at the end of October Lunacharsky seconded Grinko's proposal to Lenin that a special party conference on education be convened by the Central Committee.[35] The conference met in Moscow from December 31, 1920, to January 4, 1921. To the dismay of the participants, only two members of the Central Committee showed up (Zinoviev and Preobrazhensky) and they did not take an active part in the deliberations.[36] With Krupskaia absent because of illness and Lunacharsky all too willing to compromise, the vocationalists were clearly in the ascendant. The adopted resolutions called for a seven-year, not a nine-year school, so that the age of fifteen became the definite transition point between general and vocational education. A new set of factory schools for proletarian youth were to be established alongside the seven-year schools, and the very idea of a general educational school for youth which did not provide a definite vocational specialty was condemned as a vestige from the bourgeois past.[37] Although the resolutions did contain some concessions to *Narkompros* principles, Grinko and Shmidt were essentially correct when they claimed after the conference that their principles had triumphed.[38]

A relatively new figure at the conference was E. A. Litkens, who had in October been given the job of carrying out an administrative reorganization of *Narkompros*. His plan, based largely on the model of the Ukrainian Commissariat of Education, would have underlined the importance of age fifteen as a transition point by creating a Main Administration of Socialist Upbringing *(Glavsotsvos)* with jurisdiction for schools and educational activities up to age fifteen, beyond which schools would be regarded as higher educational institutions and would be under the jurisdiction of *Glavprofobr*. (Previously the Russian *Glavprofobr* had enjoyed jurisdiction over only higher technical institutes, not universities, and had only vaguely defined rights to assist in the drawing up of curricula for the upper grades of the nine-year school.) A civil war veteran and protégé of Trotsky, Litkens was clearly in the heroic tradition and unsparing in his criticism of *Narkompros* for its slowness to adopt new militaristic approaches to cultural and educational work among the masses.[39]

Lunacharsky, in a remarkable report to Lenin at the close of the conference, appeared satisfied with its results. It was true, he said, that several of the resolutions reflected the Ukrainian viewpoint, but the differences between the Ukrainian and Russian *Narkompros* had by now been reduced to matters of detail. Furthermore, the RSFSR contingent, including himself, Pokrovsky, Litkens, and Shmidt, found themselves much more united at the conference than they had been in the past.[40] Krupskaia, however, was not at all pleased when she learned the results of the conference, and fired off a letter of protest to Lenin.[41] And Lenin, as it turned out, needed little urging at this point to involve both himself and the Central Committee in the controversial issue of polytechnism.

Previously Lenin had said relatively little about the reform of educational institutions, although he had of course supported both the Unified Labor School concept and *Glavprofobr*'s militarization policies. As the Civil War was winding down in the fall of 1920, he focused his attention on the chief problem that would confront him for the few remaining years of his life—how to progress toward a communist society in a country having a devastated and underdeveloped economy and a rural and unenlightened population. He hit upon the idea that the best way to restore both industry and agriculture on a modern technological basis was by means of extensive electrification throughout the entire country. In November he coined his famous slogan, "Communism is Soviet power plus the electrification of the whole country," and in December the Eighth All-Russian Congress of Soviets endorsed his program of mass electrification *(Goelro)*. Lenin was convinced, however, that electrification in particular (as well as the construction of communism in general) would succeed only if understood by the population as a whole, rather than by just the handful of engineers and technicians (or Communist Party activists) that would be most directly involved.[42] This consideration helped to breathe new life at this time into his dormant belief in polytechnism.

A clue to Lenin's thinking on the subject can be found in his October 1920 speech to a *Komsomol* congress, in which he emphasized that the long-term task of creating a new society required a very broad educational background rather than narrow political indoctrination.[43] More specific were two brief notes (written November 29 and December 8, 1920) on the reorganization of *Narkompros,* in which he suggested that it might be possible to abolish (!) *Glavprofobr* and merge its schools with the polytechnical schools of *Narkompros.*[44] But it is in his marginal notes to a set of theses which Krupskaia had prepared for the Party education conference of December–January that the fullest expression of Lenin's educational ideas can be found.

In the theses themselves Krupskaia had reaffirmed the original *Narkompros* position that the full nine-year polytechnical school was extremely important, both for the pupils and for society.[45] Lenin's hurriedly scrawled comments contained both criticism and support for his wife. He objected to the general tone of the theses, which he believed was overly abstract and out of touch with reality. He wanted Krupskaia to defend the *principle* of polytechnism more cogently. But he then insisted that the "extremely severe economic condition of the country" required the "immediate and unconditional merger" of the upper grades of the ULS with existing vocational schools, though he stressed that in the process the curricula should be broadened and narrow specialization avoided. Furthermore, he emphasized that a number of steps should be taken *"immediately"* in the direction of polytechnical education, such as visits to the new electrical stations combined with experiments and demonstrations designed to show the limitless practical applications of electricity, similar excursions to state farms and factories, and the "mobilization" of engineers, agronomists, and other practicing specialists to give lectures and demonstrations. Secondary schools should turn out trained metal workers, joiners, and carpenters, but these graduates must also be equipped with general and polytechnical knowledge. He urged Krupskaia to draw up in detail a "minimum" of knowledge that all schools should impart in general or polytechnical subjects, such as the principles of communism, electrification, agronomy, and the like. In a final parting shot—not at Krupskaia but at her enemies—he wrote, "Grinko, it appears, has been making an ass of himself, *denying* polytechnical education (perhaps in part also O. Iu. Shmidt). *This must be corrected.*"[46]

The evidence does not support the conclusions of historians who have regarded Lenin's notes as representing a sharp change in his attitude toward polytechnism or as a blunt dismissal of Krupskaia's most treasured ideas.[47] To be sure, he did in effect support the lowering of the age at which vocational training would begin. But he had clearly hinted at this change earlier, and, more importantly, he continued to support the principle (at least as he understood it) of polytechnism itself. His primary grievances were with the vocationalists, and when he criticized Krupskaia, it was not so much for her continued support of polytechnism as for her inability to express its principles in clear, practical language.

When Lenin received the results of the Party education conference, therefore, he was more than ready to take action. In early February 1921 he sharply criticized the resolutions of the conference, reminding the participants that according to the party program the proper age for the transition from general to technical education was seventeen. The lowering of this age to fifteen, he insisted, must be regarded as only a temporary, practical necessity of the present and should not be defended, as some had done at the conference, as an act of principle. Furthermore, even in the present, polytechnical principles should be incorporated into vocational education wherever there was even the slightest possibility. The very use of the term "monotechnical education" was, fumed Lenin, "fundamentally incorrect, totally impermissible for a communist, indicating ignorance of the program and an idle fascination with abstract slogans." (That the very concept of polytechnism itself might be an "abstract slogan" was a possibility that Lenin apparently did not stop to consider.) The fundamental defect in the work of *Narkompros* and *Glavprofobr,* he said, was the lack of experienced educators and administrators on their staffs. Lunacharsky and Pokrovsky were the only ones who could be called "specialists." The task of all the others was not to engage in empty theorizing, but to find and utilize the skills of those (even if they be bourgeois in origin) who were experienced specialists in the field of education.[48]

Although spared the brunt of Lenin's attack, Lunacharsky's conciliatory behavior was nonetheless included in the criticism, as he himself realized. He wrote rather sheepishly to Lenin that he fully agreed with Lenin's points, but that at the conference and at other times in the past he had lacked the ability and the persistence to put them into effect. "Now we shall correct this," he concluded.[49] Shmidt was not so easily convinced. After continuing to defend his position in a prolonged and bitter debate with Krupskaia in the pages of *Pravda,* he was removed from his position as the head of *Glavprofobr* by the Central Committee.[50]

What, then, was the ultimate outcome of this dispute? In practical terms it was a compromise, with some of the vocationalist measures being adopted in practice while polytechnism was reaffirmed in principle. But at a higher level the implication of Lenin's policy (in this area as in the trade union dispute at the same time) was that *both* revolutionary heroism *and* utopianism were wrong insofar as both had demanded a radical transformation of existing institutions that had proved beyond the power of the young regime to achieve. His rejection of the heroic, militaristic approach of war communism was, at this point, decisive. His rejection of utopianism (which, after all, had been enshrined in his own work, *State and Revolution*), was more ambiguous, for he continued to believe that some of its principles (such as polytechnism) were important, indeed essential, while nonetheless realizing that the practical realities of the time imposed very serious limitations on their implementation.

What principles, then, *did* Lenin advocate at this time? Basically, a renewed emphasis on the importance of organizational control by the Communist Party (or the Soviet state), an approach that had been associated with Lenin ever since his *What Is to Be Done?* in 1902, but which had been relegated to the background during the revolutionary years of 1917–1920. Herein lies the explanation for the continuing interest Lenin demonstrated throughout early 1921 in the administrative reorganization of *Narkompros*. *Sovnarkom* had issued a decree dealing with this reorganization on February 11, 1921,[51] but well after that date Lenin continued to press Litkens to continue working on the job. "Do not," wrote Lenin to Litkens on March 27, "tear yourself away from your *organizational-administrative* work. From you and *only* you we will strictly and quickly (in about 2–3 months) demand results. . . . Focus *all* attention on that."[52] For if there were to be fewer efforts to change the *nature* of schools in particular or society in general, then there would need to be more efforts to achieve administrative *control* over the *existing*, imperfect, and unreformed institutions. This Leninist emphasis on organizational control rather than radical change in *either* the utopian or heroic direction amounted to a third major approach to the communist ideal, an approach that would predominate during the decidedly *non*-revolutionary years of the New Economic Policy.

NOTES

1. For a more elaborate presentation of these categories, see James C. McClelland, "Utopianism Versus Revolutionary Heroism in Bolshevik Policy: The Proletarian Culture Debate," *Slavic Review*, vol. 39, no. 3 (Sept. 1980):403–25. For application of

this approach to higher education, see McClelland, "Bolshevik Approaches to Higher Education, 1917–1921," *Slavic Review*, vol. 30, no. 4 (Dec. 1971):818–31. Another leading utopian figure was Aleksandra Kollontai. See Barbara Evans Clements, *Bolshevik Feminist: The Life of Aleksandra Kollontai* (Bloomington, Indiana, 1979), and Beatrice Farnsworth, *Aleksandra Kollontai: Socialism, Feminism, and the Bolshevik Revolution* (Stanford, 1980). During the years 1918–1921, Nikolai Bukharin embraced the principles of both utopianism and revolutionary heroism. In 1921 he abandoned the heroic outlook, after which he became more moderate in general while leaning toward the utopian view on the priority of cultural over economic needs and of persuasion over force as a means of achieving social change. See Stephen F. Cohen, *Bukharin and the Bolshevik Revolution: A Political Biography* (New York, 1973).

2. A. V. Lunacharskii, "Rech' na I Vserossiiskom s"ezde po prosveshcheniiu" (Aug. 26, 1918), in *A. V. Lunacharskii o narodnom obrazovanii* (Moscow, 1958), p. 33. This volume hereafter cited as *O nar. obr.*

3. *Dekrety sovetskoi vlasti*, 4 vols. (Moscow, 1957–68), 3:374–80.

4. Lunacharskii, "Osnovnye printsipy edinoi trudovoi shkoly" (Oct. 16, 1918), *O nar. obr.*, p. 523.

5. Ibid., passim; N. K. Krupskaia, "Narodnoe obrazovanie i demokratiia" (1915), in Krupskaia, *Pedagogicheskie sochineniia v desiati tomakh*, 11 vols. (Moscow, 1957–63), 1:249–350, passim (these volumes hereafter referred to as Krupskaia, *Ped. soch.*); Krupskaia, "Zadachi professional'nogo obrazovaniia," *Narodnoe Prosveshchenie: Ezhenedel'noe prilozhenie k Izvestiiam VTsIK*, no. 2, June 1, 1918 (this journal hereafter referred to as *NP*, weekly); Krupskaia, "Vneshkol'noe obrazovanie v novom stroe" (Aug. 1918), *Ped. soch.*, 7:15.

6. Valer'ian Polianskii, "Kak nachinal rabotat' Narodnyi Komissariat Prosveshcheniia (lichnye vospominaniia)," *Proletarskaia Revoliutsiia*, vol. 49, no. 2 (Feb. 1926):52–53; idem, "Trud vospitatel'nyi i trud proizvoditel'nyi v novoi shkole," *Proletarskaia Kul'tura*, no. 4 (Sept. 1918):18–22; V. N. Shul'gin, *Pamiatnye vstrechi* (Moscow, 1958), pp. 43–44; P. V. Rudnev, "K istorii razrabotki programmy partii po narodnomu obrazovaniiu," in N. K. Goncharov and F. F. Korolev, eds., *V. I. Lenin i problemy narodnogo obrazovaniia* (Moscow, 1961), pp. 206, 211–12; Sheila Fitzpatrick, *The Commissariat of Enlightenment: Soviet Organization of Education and the Arts under Lunacharsky* (Cambridge, 1970), pp. 26–34; Oskar Anweiler, *Geschichte der Schule und Paedagogik in Russland vom Ende des Zarenreiches bis zum Beginn der Stalin-Aera* (Heidelberg, 1964), pp. 102–17, 145–55.

7. Krupskaia, *Ped. soch.*, 1:350.

8. *KPSS v rezoliutsiiakh i resheniiakh s"ezdov, konferentsii i plenumov TsK*, 7th ed., 3 vols. (Moscow, 1954), 1:419–20. See also Rudnev, "K istorii razrabotki programmy."

9. A. G. Kalashnikov, ed., *Pedagogicheskaia entsiklopediia*, 3 vols. (Moscow, 1927–29), 1:1033–34; Fitzpatrick, pp. 54–57; Polianskii, "Kak nachinal," pp. 52–53; A. N. Veselov, *Professional'no-tekhnicheskoe obrazovanie v SSSR: Ocherki po istorii srednego i nizshego proftekhobrazovaniia* (Moscow, 1961), pp. 135–36.

10. Lunacharskii, "O zadachakh professional'no-tekhnicheskogo obrazovaniia v Rossii" (1919), *O nar. obr.*, pp. 539–46; idem, "Iz doklada na III sessii VTsIK VII sozyva" (Sept. 26, 1920), ibid., p. 129; idem, "O shkole rabochei molodezhi" (1921), ibid., pp. 174–75; Fitzpatrick, pp. 59–61; Veselov, pp. 134–37; F. F. Korolev, *Ocherki po istorii sovetskoi shkoly i pedagogiki, 1917–1920* (Moscow, 1958), p. 247.

11. Isaac Deutscher, *The Prophet Armed: Trotsky, 1879–1921* (New York, 1965), pp. 486–92. There was only minimal improvement during the following year. Total production of 1921 as a percentage of 1913 production was 30% for coal, 43% for oil, 2.8% for pig iron, 4.4% for bricks, and 29.8% for railway freight. *Narodnoe khoziaistvo*

SSR: Statisticheskii spravochnik 1932 (Moscow–Leningrad, 1932), pp. XXXIV–XXXV, XLII–XLIII.

12. Ibid., p. 405. Carr cites still higher figures. See E. H. Carr, *The Bolshevik Revolution, 1917–1923*, 3 vols. (Baltimore, 1966), 2:197–98.

13. E. G. Gimpel'son, *Sovetskii rabochii klass, 1918–1920 gg.* (Moscow, 1974), pp. 76–94, esp. p. 80; *Narodnoe khoziaistvo SSSR, 1922–1972: Iubileinyi statisticheskii ezhegodnik* (Moscow, 1972), p. 42.

14. *Pravda*, Dec. 17, 1919, reprinted in L. D. Trotskii, *Sochineniia*, 21 vols. (Moscow, 1924–27), 15:10–14. See also Carr, 2:211–16.

15. *TsGA RSFSR*, f. 2306, op. 1, ed. khran. 320, pp. 5–6.

16. Trotskii, *Sochineniia*, 15:107–14; *Sobranie uzakonenii i rasporiazhenii rabochego i krest'ianskogo pravitel'stva RSFSR*, 1920, no. 6, arts. 41–42 (hereafter cited as *SU*). *Glavprofobr* was based on an already existing vocational committee within *Narkompros*, but it became, as was intended, much more powerful and autonomous than its predecessor.

17. The membership of the council is listed in *TsGA RSFSR*, f. 2306, op. 1, ed. khran. 320, p. 66.

18. O. Iu. Shmidt, "O Glavprofobre," *Vestnik professional'no-tekhnicheskogo obrazovaniia*, no. 3–4 (Aug.–Sept. 1920):3. Hereafter cited as *Vestnik*.

19. O. G. Anikst, ed., *Professional'no-tekhnicheskoe obrazovanie v Rossii za 1917–1921 gg.: Iubileinyi sbornik* (Moscow, 1922), p. 14; B. G. Kozelev, "Prof-tekh. obrazovanie, kak ocherednaia zadacha khoziaistvennogo stroitel'stva," *Vestnik*, no. 1 (May 1920):9–10.

20. Ibid.; see also Shmidt's speech in *2-ia sessiia sovprofobra i s"ezda gubprofobrov 20–25 okt. 1920 g. (Protokoly zasedanii)* (Moscow, 1921), p. 29.

21. Iu. Milonov, ed., *Putevoditel' po rezoliutsiiam vserossiiskikh s"ezdov i konferentsii professional'nykh soiuzov* (Moscow, 1924). Cf. pp. 185–88 (1919 resolutions) and 253–60 (1920 resolutions).

22. Quoted in I. Krilov, *Sistema osviti v Ukraini (1917–1930)* (Munich, 1956), p. 39.

23. Lunacharskii, "Iz doklada," *O nar. obr.*, p. 129; idem, "Rech' na III s"ezde RKSM" (Oct. 2, 1920), ibid., p. 151.

24. Grinko's theses are reprinted in Krilov, p. 44.

25. Ia. P. Riappo, *Sistema narodnogo prosveshcheniia na Ukraine: Sbornik materialov, statei, i dokladov* (Kharkov, 1925), pp. 168–69.

26. Ibid., p. 175.

27. See speech by Grinko in *2-ia sessiia*, pp. 21–23; Anweiler, pp. 175–76.

28. *Narodnoe khoziaistvo 1932*, p. 507.

29. Kalashnikov, 2:174–75.

30. Lunacharskii, "Osnovnye voprosy novogo fronta" and "Deklaratsiia o professional'no-tekhnicheskom obrazovanii v RSFSR," *Vestnik*, no. 1 (May 1920):3–4, 12–16; "Iz doklada," *O nar. obr.*, pp. 119–43; "Edinaia trudovaia shkola i tekhnicheskoe obrazovanie" (Oct. 1920), ibid., pp. 156–63.

31. Lunacharskii, "Edinaia trudovaia shkola," pp. 159–60.

32. Shmidt, "O Glavprofobre," and "Shkola 2-i stupeni (Tipy i uklony)," *Vestnik*, no. 3–4 (Aug.–Sept. 1920):3–7, 12–14.

33. P. V. Rudnev, "Iz istorii bor'by za Leninskii printsip politekhnicheskogo obrazovaniia (Fevral' 1920 g.–Fevral' 1921 g.)," in Goncharov and Korolev, eds., *V. I. Lenin i problemy narodnogo obrazovaniia*, p. 253.

34. *2-ia sessiia*, pp. 27–28.

35. *Literaturnoe nasledstvo*, vol. 80, *V. I. Lenin i A. V. Lunacharskii: Perepiska, doklady, dokumenty* (Moscow, 1971), p. 224. Hereafter cited as *Lit. nas.*, vol. 80.

36. Ibid., p. 239.

37. The resolutions of the conference are reprinted in *Direktivy VKP(b) po voprosam prosveshcheniia,* 2nd ed. (Moscow, 1930), pp. 313–22.

38. *Prilozhenie k biulleteniu VIII s"ezda sovetov, posviashchennoe partiinomu soveshchaniiu po voprosam narodnogo obrazovaniia* (Moscow, Jan. 10, 1921), pp. 4–5, 7. See also Shmidt, "Pervyi god raboty Glavprofobra," *Vestnik,* no. 9 (Feb. 1921):13.

39. *Prilozhenie k biulleteniu,* pp. 2–3, 16.

40. *Lit. nas.,* vol. 80, p. 239.

41. Rudnev, "Iz istorii bor'by," p. 264.

42. V. I. Lenin, *Polnoe sobranie sochinenii,* 55 vols. (Moscow, 1958–65), 41:307, 42:30, 141, 160–61. Hereafter cited as *PSS.* See also Carr, 2:369–72.

43. Lenin, "Zadachi soiuzov molodezhi," *PSS,* 41:298–318.

44. Ibid., 52:21–22, 42:87.

45. Krupskaia, "Tezisy o politekhnicheskoi shkole," *Ped. soch.,* 4:35–37.

46. Lenin, "O politekhnicheskom obrazovanii: Zametki na tezisy Nadezhdy Konstantinovny" (late Dec. 1920), *PSS,* 42:228–30. Quotation on p. 230. Emphasis in original.

47. Respectively, Fitzpatrick, *Commissariat,* p. 197, and Robert H. McNeal, *Bride of the Revolution: Krupskaya and Lenin* (Ann Arbor, Michigan, 1972), p. 206.

48. Lenin, "Direktivy TsK kommunistam-rabotnikam Narkomprosa" and "O rabote Narkomprosa," *PSS,* 42:319–32. Quotation on p. 323.

49. *Lit. nas.,* vol. 80, p. 244. For cautiously optimistic accounts of the conference by Lunacharskii and other *Narkompros* spokesmen, see *NP,* weekly, no. 79, Feb. 20, 1921 (published early March).

50. *Lit. nas.,* vol. 80, pp. 246–48.

51. *SU,* 1921, no. 12, art. 78.

52. Lenin, *PSS,* 52:112. Emphasis in original.

[8] Lenin and the Freedom of the Press

Peter Kenez

THE BOLSHEVIKS WON the Civil War because they proved themselves superior to their opponents in two crucial areas of struggle: organization and propaganda. The embodiment of Bolshevik principles of organization was the Party. It brought a unity of purpose to the revolutionaries and it enabled them to build a rudimentary form of administrative structure, which, in turn, helped them to overcome the forces of anarchy. The Party was also a crucially important instrument in spreading the revolutionary idea. Both contemporaries and historians, friendly and hostile, have given credit to the Bolsheviks for their propaganda skills. Indeed, an appreciation of the significance of winning over the uncommitted marked all aspects of their activities: Lenin's government framed its decrees as propaganda tools; it organized institutions, such as the youth movement (Komsomol) which helped in mass mobilization; it sent thousands of agitators into the villages; it used conventional means, such as the press, and unconventional ones, such as sending agitational trains and boats into remote areas.

The Bolsheviks were fortunate that their past as revolutionaries helped them to develop precisely those weapons which proved crucial in the conditions of the Civil War. As Leninists they understood the significance of organization and discipline and as revolutionaries they saw as one of their major tasks the development of programs and the attractive presentation of those programs. The only serious opponents of the Bolsheviks were the army officers, and how different their background was! They had learned to despise politics and therefore they did not understand the essentially political nature of the Civil War, but perceived it as a series of military encounters in which their task was to command and the duty of the Russian people was to obey.

Let us examine here how the Bolsheviks used one major instrument of propaganda, the press. This is an interesting and important subject, for newspapers played considerable role in moulding public opinion. Also, since the history of the early Soviet press is tantamount to a history of Soviet censorship, the examination of this subject will give us revealing glimpses of the attitude of the leaders at the moment of their victory on such a large and elusive issue as their concept of political freedom.

- 1 -

Revolutionaries were also journalists; much of their activity consisted of writing articles, and editing and distributing small newspapers. V. I. Lenin stood out among his colleagues in his unusually clear understanding of what newspapers could accomplish and therefore in his more self-conscious use of the press. In his writings he gave an impressive analysis of the role of the newspaper in the revolutionary movement. As always, he was most insightful and clearsighted when dealing with the problems of organization. In a short but important article published in 1901, "Where to Begin?" he argued that the most important immediate task of the socialists was to establish a national newspaper. In the process of putting the paper together the party would develop. He also wrote that the work of carrying out propaganda was an instrument of propaganda itself. His insight that propaganda and organization are opposite sides of the same coin established a major principle of Bolshevik policy-making even after the Revolution.

Soviet publicists made Lenin's sentence famous by quoting it endlessly: "The newspaper is not only a collective propagandist and a collective agitator, it is also a collective organizer." Lenin went on to explain:

> The mere technical task of regularly supplying a newspaper with copy and of promoting regular distribution will necessitate a network of local agents of the united party, who will maintain constant contact with one another, know the general state of affairs, get accustomed to performing regularly their detailed functions in the all-Russian work and test their strength in the organization of various revolutionary actions.[1]

In his major and seminal work, published in 1902, *What Is to Be Done?*, Lenin returned to the same theme. It is characteristic of the down-to-earth quality of his thinking that in this study, in which he stated the theoretical premises of Bolshevik ideology, he devoted an extraordinary amount of space to the mundane questions of organizing a single newspaper. His arguments served an immediate purpose: he wanted to strengthen the position of the *Iskra* group, publishers of the first Marxist national newspaper, within the socialist movement. *Iskra,* among whose six editors Lenin was one, indeed played a crucial role in directing nascent Russian social democracy.

Throughout his life Lenin continued to pay great attention to journalism. He wrote articles for the obscure papers which his faction published in exile.

When, after 1905, tsarist censorship relaxed to such an extent that it was possible to print Bolshevik papers in Russia, Lenin followed their editorial policy from exile with great care. The most important of the Bolshevik papers was *Pravda,* which came out in St. Petersburg between 1912 and 1914. In the course of these two years Lenin published 265 articles in it.[2] When he settled in Cracow and the Austrian police questioned him about his profession, he could answer not untruthfully that he was a "correspondent of the Russian democratic paper, Pravda."[3]

In spite of Lenin's remarkable energy and talent, however, it would be a mistake to imagine that the pre-revolutionary Bolshevik press was fundamentally different from the press of the other revolutionaries. All revolutionaries operated in the same environment: they had to battle the censor, they constantly needed money, and they tirelessly and tediously polemicized against one another. Comparing the main Menshevik paper between 1912 and 1914, the daily *Luch,* with a circulation of 9,000–12,000, and *Pravda,* which had a somewhat larger circulation, one is struck by the similarities in style and content.[4]

The February Revolution was a turning point in the history of the Bolshevik press: since all censorship was temporarily abolished, for the first time the socialist newspapers had to compete with old, established, and well-financed papers for a mass audience. In perspective it is hard to evaluate how well the Bolsheviks did in this competition. On the one hand it is evident that support for the Party's position grew by leaps and bounds. In the course of a few months Party membership more than quadrupled, and, even more importantly, the Leninist position, which had only small support among the workers at the time of the collapse of the Romanov monarchy, by November acquired the support of the majority of the workers in the two capitals and a powerful following among the soldiers of the enormous Russian army. That the Bolsheviks were skilled propagandists and that their newspapers made a contribution to the spreading of their message is self-evident. On the other hand it is doubtful that the Bolsheviks can be credited or blamed for the collapse of the Provisional Government. It seems more plausible that the Bolsheviks simply benefited from the weakness of their opponents. On the basis of painful experiences of war and revolution, a crucial segment of the Russian people came to hold opinions which the Bolsheviks had already propounded. The Leninists did not disorganize the army nor did they make the peasants rebellious; but they were ready to take advantage of both these developments. A close examination of the history of the press in 1917 suggests that the Bolshevik newspapers were not superior to other socialist and non-socialist papers. Their victory came in spite of the fact that the bourgeois press continued to dominate the medium.

The Bolshevik press, and the socialist press as a whole, grew impressively.

The first issue of *Pravda* appeared on March 5, and it was soon followed by a large number of provincial papers, of which the one published in Moscow, *Sotsial-Democrat,* was the most important. Later the Party also published papers specifically for peasant and soldier audiences.

However, this achievement must be placed in context. In the course of 1917 the combined circulation of all Bolshevik papers probably never surpassed 600,000.[5] This was much smaller than the circulation of popular non-socialist papers such as *Kopeika* or *Malenkaia gazeta.* Lenin estimated that in the summer of 1917 the combined circulation of all socialist papers was less than a quarter of all newspapers printed, and of course the Bolshevik press was in a greatly disadvantaged position even as compared to the papers of the Socialist Revolutionaries and Mensheviks.[6] Non-socialist politicians had an immensely easier time communicating their positions. Their papers were financially strong and had a loyal readership acquired through the years.

The Bolsheviks could not compete for journalistic talent. The major Kadet paper, *Rech',* and other dailies such as *Novoe vremia* and *Birzhevye vedomosti,* were clearly better written and had broader coverage of events. Although the Bolsheviks did not disdain demagogy in their papers, neither did their opponents. For example, at one point, the Bolsheviks accused Kerensky of wanting to hand over Petrograd to the enemy in order to rid the country of the revolutionary center. The anti-Bolsheviks, in turn, charged Lenin with being a German agent.

But the attack on the Bolsheviks was not limited to a press campaign. Following the disturbances of the July days, a detachment of Cossacks destroyed the editorial offices of *Pravda.* The paper could reopen only some weeks later, under a different title. Further, it is clear that army authorities did everything within their power to prevent the circulation of antiwar propaganda, i.e., Bolshevik papers, within the army. The military postal service, for example, frequently confiscated papers sent through the mail.[7]

- 2 -

The Soviet press came into being in a historically unprecedented situation: it was created and protected by a one-party revolutionary state. This fact essentially determined its character. It is understandable that the Bolshevik papers, once relieved of the pressure of competition, developed characteristics which were unique at the time. The decisive development was the immediate suppression of the free press.

Ideologically Lenin was prepared for such a move. It is not that he had advocated censorship before. The Bolsheviks, as a revolutionary underground party, had to battle censorship, and it was natural that in their writings the revolutionaries should denounce tsarism for its restrictions on the freedom of the press. Nor did Lenin advocate the institution of censorship after the victory of the socialist revolution. Neither Lenin nor anyone else envisaged the circumstances in which the Bolsheviks would emerge victorious. The revolutionaries assumed that the revolution would be carried out by the great majority of the people and, consequently, the question of repression would not even arise. However, Lenin was never a liberal. He placed little value on "formal" freedoms, such as freedom of the press, and it was clear from his writings and actions that he would not hesitate to take steps, however brutal, when the success of his movement was at stake.

In retrospect, the first warning signal was contained in *What Is to Be Done?* After his famous denunciation of spontaneity Lenin wrote:

Since there can be no talk of an independent ideology formulated by the working masses themselves in the process of their movement, the *only* choice is—either bourgeois or socialist ideology. There is no middle course (for mankind has not created a "third" ideology, and, moreover, in a society torn by class antagonisms there can never be a non-class or an above-class ideology). Hence, to belittle socialist ideology *in any way, to turn aside from it in the slightest degree* means to strengthen bourgeois ideology. There is much talk of spontaneity. But the spontaneous development of the working class movement leads to its subordination to bourgeois ideology. . . .

A few paragraphs later Lenin went on:

But why, the reader will ask, does the spontaneous movement, the movement along the line of least resistance, lead to the dominance of bourgeois ideology? For the simple reason that bourgeois ideology, being far older in origin than socialist ideology, is more fully developed and has at its disposal *immeasurably* more means of dissemination.[8]

It is a peculiar notion that bourgeois ideology is more effective because it is older and it is somewhat surprising to find Lenin, the defender of Marxist orthodoxy, arguing that socialism was insufficiently developed, but he was unquestionably correct in maintaining that the bourgeoisie possessed far better means for spreading its ideas. Lenin would return to this point again and again, and it ultimately came to be a justification for censorship. However, the main significance of these passages is in showing that even in this early period Lenin did not accept the principle that one fights ideas with ideas and that he did not trust the workers to arrive at "correct" conclusions if two sides of an ideological issue were presented. It would be an exaggeration to say that these statements from *What Is to Be Done?* implied approval of censorship, but they are certainly consistent with Lenin's attacks on the freedom of the press two decades later.

It was during the 1905 revolution that Lenin first explicitly discussed the question of the freedom of the press. In his article "Party Organization and Party Literature" he argued that literature should be party literature, and that the literature of the proletariat should be under the control of the organization of the workers, i.e., the Russian Social Democratic Workers Party. Literature should be an instrument in the class struggle.[9] To those who objected that such a development would result in control of creativity he responded with two arguments: First, while individuals have the right to say anything they desire, organizations have the right to exclude those who do not agree with their fundamental principles; second, talk about absolute freedom of the press is hypocrisy since in bourgeois society the writer depends on those who finance him.

In 1905 Lenin did not foresee that his party soon would be in a position to suppress the opposition. He was preparing for a period when the workers would struggle against the bourgeoisie and only begin to organize for a socialist revolution. Under the circumstances suppressing non-socialist papers was not an issue, because it was not a realistic possibility. Once again, however, Lenin made it clear how little regard he had for the "bourgeois" notion of free expression. Most disconcertingly, in "Party Organization and Party Literature" he failed to draw a distinction between literature and journalism. Present advocates of artistic freedom in the Soviet Union cannot find much encouragement in it.

The February revolution made freedom of the press a practical issue. The Bolsheviks supported the efforts of the Petrograd Soviet to close down reactionary-monarchist papers. Lenin had only scorn for the March 10 decision of the Soviet which reversed itself and allowed papers to appear without previous permission.

The traumatic events in Petrograd in early July and the new opportunities presented by the failure of the Kornilov mutiny changed Lenin's tactics in the revolutionary struggle in general and his attitude to the press in particular. In his article "How Can We Assure the Success of the Constituent Assembly?" published on September 15, he wrote:

> The capitalists (and many SRs and Mensheviks following them either through misunderstanding or inertia) call freedom of the press that situation in which censorship is abolished and all parties freely publish any paper they please. In reality this is not freedom of the press, but freedom for the rich, for the bourgeoisie to mislead the oppressed and exploited masses.[10]

Lenin proposed to remedy this situation by suggesting that the Soviet would declare a monopoly on printing advertisements. This move would undermine the financial strength of the bourgeois press and help the socialists. Then he went further. He realized that in the short run what mattered most was the availability of paper and printing facilities. Therefore he proposed the expropriation of all paper and printing presses and their distribution according to the political strength of the parties in the two capitals. Simultaneously, in another article, Lenin advocated closing down the major bourgeois papers such as *Rech'* and *Russkoe slovo*.[11] He did not make it clear how the two sets of suggestions could be reconciled. After all, the Kadets did have substantial voting strength in Petrograd and Moscow.

Throughout the years, in his fundamental views, Lenin was remarkably consistent concerning the freedom of the press. It is true that in the fall of 1917 he did not renew his call for party-mindedness as developed in his 1905 article. But the reason was not a newly found liberalism. His article "How Can We Assure the Success of the Constituent Assembly?" was addressed to the socialists in the Petrograd Soviet. It is unlikely that he expected them to adopt his ideas, but he certainly hoped to score debating points. On the other hand, in September 1917 Lenin did not yet envisage a one-party regime in which only a single voice could be heard. Had his recommendation been followed the Russian people could have heard a multiplicity of views. This was, of course, not the policy which the Bolsheviks followed after they seized power.

On October 25 the Bolsheviks struck, seizing the Winter Palace, the ministries, the post and telegraph buildings, and the printing presses of *Russkaia volia*. The next day the Military Revolutionary Committee (MRC) issued a resolution temporarily forbidding the publication of bourgeois papers and counterrevolutionary publications.[12] It is not necessary to search for ideological reasons for preventing the publication of hostile declarations and manifestos. It is perfectly understandable that during the period of transition extraordinary measures had to be taken. Another and far more important question was what attitude the new authorities would take toward freedom of expression once their rule was established.

On October 27 the Council of Commissars (Sovnarkom) published its decree on the press.[13] This decree, after repeating Lenin's views on the bourgeois notion of the free press, gave Sovnarkom the right to close down newspapers which advocated resistance to the new authorities or attempted to "sow disorder by the publication of clearly slanderous misstatements of facts." The last paragraph asserted that the decree was temporary and after the return of normal order complete freedom of the press would be assured.

A few days later, on November 4, an important debate erupted in the Executive Committee of the Soviet (CEC) concerning the decree. The issue was even more profound than freedom of the press. It was what kind of regime would follow the revolution. At the time it was unclear whether the exclusively Bolshevik Council of Commissars could retain power, or whether the Bolsheviks would accept a compromise and bring the Socialist Revolutionaries and Mensheviks into the government. The majority of the supporters of the October revolution hoped for a socialist coalition. It was demanded in forceful terms by the Union of Railroad Workers, who possessed considerable power through their ability to call a strike. The idea of coalition was obviously attractive to an important segment of the Bolshevik leadership. The issue of coalition and the issue of freedom of the press became intertwined. Obviously it was not possible to attempt to suppress the publications of the moderate socialists while at the same time trying to induce them to participate in the government. It seems fitting that the first crucial and bitter debate which took place within the Soviet leadership concerned free expression.

The Central Executive Committee of the Congress of Soviets had 67 Bolshevik, 29 Left SR, and 20 other socialist members.[14] When the Sovnarkom issued its decree on the press, the CEC did not object. The revolutionaries understood that the exceptional circumstances necessitated exceptional measures. Ten days later, however, when the issue was thoroughly discussed, circumstances had changed. The dispute which took place was remarkable not because of the profundity of the views expressed but because the two points of view, both expressed with great passion, represented real and irreconcilable differences in the vision of the coming socialist order.

B. F. Malkin, a Left SR and the editor of *Izvestiia,* said:

> We firmly repudiate the notion that socialism can be introduced by armed force. In our view socialism is a struggle not merely for material advantages but for supreme human moral values. The revolution's appeal lies in the fact that we are striving not just to fill our hungry bellies, but for a higher truth, the liberation of the individual. We shall win not by closing down bourgeois newspapers but because our programme and tactics express the interests of the broad toiling masses, because we can build up a solid coalition of soldiers, workers and peasants.[15]

Later, in the heat of the debate, he responded to an opponent: "You are dishonouring the socialist movement by depriving it of its moral force."[16] V. A. Karelin, another Left SR, argued in terms of political expediency. In his opinion suppression of views would only make those more attractive. Prominent Bolsheviks such as Iu. Larin and D. B. Riazanov also spoke up in the defense of freedom of expression.

The Leninists, by contrast, were willing to subordinate all values to the immediate interests of the revolution. In their position one can sense a certain ambivalence. They defended suppression by pointing to immediate and presumably temporary needs, but at the same time they made it clear that in any case they had little regard for "formal" notions of freedom.

V. A. Avanesov said:

We defend the freedom of the press, but this concept must be divorced from old petty-bourgeois or bourgeois notions of liberty. If the new government has had the strength to abolish private landed property, thereby infringing the rights of the landlords, it would be ridiculous for Soviet power to stand up for antiquated notions about liberty of the press.

His resolution included these sentences:

The restoration of so-called "freedom of the press," i.e., the return of the printing press to the capitalists, poisoners of the people's consciousness, would be an impermissible capitulation to the will of capital, a surrender of one of the most important strong points of the workers' and peasants' revolution, and thus indubitably counterrevolutionary.[17]

Lenin based his argument both on expediency and on principles. He put it picturesquely: "If we want to progress toward social revolution, we cannot allow the addition of lies to the bombs of Kaledin."[18] He went so far as to say that allowing "bourgeois" papers to exist was the same as ceasing to be socialists. The Leninist position prevailed. Avanosov's resolution was adopted by a vote of 34 to 24 with one abstention.[19] It was at this point that people's commissars V. Nogin, A. Rykov, V. Miliutin, and I. Teodorovich resigned.[20]

The November 4 meeting of the CEC was a turning point in the history of the revolution. One can well imagine that had Lenin's opponents possessed more political acumen the outcome of the vote would have been different. The concept of the future, inherent in the thinking of the defenders of the freedom of expression, was obviously profoundly different from that of Lenin. On the other hand the likelihood is that if the revolutionaries had repudiated Leninist methods, the regime would not have lasted very long. The events which took place between February and October 1917 proved that Russia could not be administered in accordance with liberal principles. Those who refused to learn this lesson were condemned to defeat. Lenin, after all, was correct: the new regime could not tolerate freedom of criticism, nor could it repudiate terrorist methods.

The adoption of Avanesov's resolution did not immediately result in Bolshevik monopoly of the press. First of all, the Leninists did not yet desire such a monopoly. It was one thing to advocate suppression of forces hostile to the revolution and quite another to claim that there could be only one correct interpretation of all political events. Time had to pass before the Bolsheviks came to this view. But even if the Bolsheviks did secretly desire such a monopoly, it was good politics to proceed gradually. Prematurely frightening the uncommitted might have had dangerous consequences. But most importantly, the Bolsheviks lacked the means to suppress all enemies, real and potential. The control of the new regime over the workers of Moscow and Petrograd was weak, and control over the rest of the enormous country was minimal. As a consequence, the first eight months of the Bolshevik regime represented a twilight period for the Russian press. It was a period in which liberal and socialist journalists tried to defend themselves by rallying public support and by attempting to circumvent the regulations of the new authorities. Meanwhile, the Bolsheviks were making increasingly successful efforts to impose order on the country and to undermine the strength of their enemies; only when they considered themselves strong enough did they carry out frontal attacks.

The Bolsheviks' first obstacle was the Menshevik-dominated Printers' Union. The printers' opposition to the press decree surfaced even before the CEC debate. On November 1 the Union notified the MRC that if the press decree was not rescinded, "the Union would use all available means for pressure," i.e., it would strike.[21] On November 6 a meeting of Union representatives passed a resolution (171 to 69) which made the threat explicit.[22] The MRC was forced to engage in discussions with the printers in which the arguments used at the CEC meeting were repeated. The printers proved themselves to be just as eloquent defenders of freedom as the socialist politicians. However, the position of the printers was seriously weakened by the fact that the Bolsheviks controlled a large enough minority to shatter solidarity in case of a strike. At a time of extremely high unemployment the Bolsheviks were able to prevent a strike.

As in all other aspects of national life, great confusion prevailed in the regime's policy toward the press during the first weeks following the October takeover. The MRC or the Sovnarkom frequently closed down newspapers which then simply changed their names and continued to appear. *Rech'*, for example, appeared under five different names in the course of a few weeks, and the SR paper, *Volia naroda*, had six different names.[23] The Bolsheviks arrested editors and journalists, but almost all of them were freed within a few days. Furthermore, the situation varied a great deal from city to city. In Moscow, for example, repression was far less severe than in Petrograd. The Moscow MRC went on record in support of free expression at the same time that the CEC in Petrograd reaffirmed Lenin's position. The decree issued on November 6 forbade only the printing of proclamations calling for armed struggle against Soviet power, but allowed all papers to publish.[24] Indeed, moderate socialist publications continued to appear in Moscow relatively undisturbed until March 1918, when the government moved to that city. In the rest of the country the situation varied depending on the views and power of the leading local Bolsheviks. In the first few months hundreds of newspapers were closed down in provincial cities.

During the transition period the Bolsheviks often did not feel strong enough to carry out frontal attacks and therefore turned to indirect means. In the early days of the regime they confiscated the presses of such major papers as *Rech'*, *Novoe vremia, Birzhevye vedomosti, Zhivoe slovo,* and *Kopeika.*[25] These presses were taken over by Soviet publications. The confiscation of the printing facilities was, of course, a heavy blow to the "bourgeois" papers. They were forced to find smaller presses and contract their work. The newspapers which managed to survive did so with greatly reduced circulations. The most serious problem faced by all the newspapers was a shortage of paper. Publications tried to protect themselves by hiding their paper supplies. As early as October 26 the MRC ordered a complete inventory of paper[26] and a few days later forbade the removal of paper from Petrograd.[27] However, in the confusion it was relatively easy to disobey the MRC; indeed, it was necessary to do so in order to stay in business. But when the Bolsheviks did succeed in confiscating the scarce material, their action was often tantamount to closing down a hostile newspaper.

As compared to the confiscation of presses, paper, and newsprint, the regulation outlawing the printing of advertisements was only a petty harassment. Lenin first presented this idea in September 1917 and clung to it with a lack of realism that was uncharacteristic of the great revolutionary leader.[28] On his initiative the Sovnarkom passed a regulation on November 15 according to which only government publications would be allowed to print advertisements after November 22, 1917.[29] The newspapers resisted and the Socialist press which, by and large, had not carried advertisements, started to do so as a gesture of solidarity. A. I. Minkin, the commissar for press affairs, who foresaw the difficulties, asked for and was assigned a hundred sailors from the MRC to overcome resistance.[30] In many localities the local Soviets failed to take any steps to carry out this particular decree. After the end of the Civil War Lenin himself admitted that outlawing advertisements had been a mistake.[31] It created a great deal of resistance and focused hostility on the Soviet regime, while at the same time exhibiting the powerlessness of the new government. Worst of all, the damage inflicted by this regulation on the bourgeois press was trivial: with the economy of the nation in ruins, advertisements were no longer an important source of financial strength.

The relative impunity with which the new authorities could be defied was one small indication of the weakness of Bolshevik rule; the country was close to anarchy. The Leninists attempted to gain strength by broadening their base and included a few Left SRs in their government, the Sovnarkom. Perhaps not surprisingly, in this atmosphere of constant crisis the victorious revolutionaries regarded press attacks as dangerous. However, since they did not always have the strength to suppress offending newspapers, they followed an inconsistent policy, closing down some papers for small violations of the law while allowing others to publish truly subversive material.

In order to bring a system into this confused situation, the Left SR Commissar of Justice, I. Z. Shteinberg, on December 18 issued regulations for setting up revolutionary tribunals for press matters. For publishing falsehoods, the regulations called only for a printed retraction and the payment of a fine. Shteinberg allowed the closing down of a newspaper only in extreme cases and after repeated warnings. The Bolsheviks found such regulations far too lenient and circumvented Shteinberg by their use of the Cheka, which, of course, remained safely in their hands. The jurisdictional struggle which erupted between the Commissariat and the Cheka was resolved by Sovnarkom in favor of the Cheka. First, on January 24 the Sovnarkom decided that while revolutionary tribunals would deal with newspapers as collective entities, the Cheka could continue to arrest and punish editors as "counterrevolutionaries." Second, four days later Sovnarkom issued its own regulations for the operation of revolutionary tribunals. While the Commissariat of Justice previously intended to punish only those who printed falsehoods, the new regulations were aimed against those who printed "anti-Soviet material," obviously a much broader and vaguer category. Sovnarkom's punishments were also more severe: jail or exile.[32]

A study of the material of the revolutionary tribunals gives interesting glimpses of those confused days. One newspaper, *Novyi vechernyi chas* (New Evening Times), was closed down because it had frightened the people by drawing attention to the possibility of Japanese intervention. Clearly, in order to suppress, it was not necessary to show that the paper had written something untrue. One of the first papers to suffer was the major Menshevik daily *Den'*, which was charged with having changed its title several times in order to escape repression; having written that the Bolsheviks had intended to hand over Petrograd to the Germans; having described Bolshevik rule as unstable; and having reported on conflicts between the workers and the government.[33] We will never know for certain, but it seems likely that none of the leading Bolsheviks appreciated the irony of the situation. After all, *Pravda* itself not so long ago had frequently found it necessary to change its name; and the Bolsheviks' papers had also accused the government—with no justification whatever—of wanting to hand over the capital to the enemy. The Bolsheviks genuinely, if self-servingly, believed that morality did not exist aside from the standpoint of class. The same act had different meaning depending whether it was committed by the Mensheviks or by the Bolsheviks, because the Mensheviks were "objectively" the enemies of socialist revolution, and therefore of the genuine interests of the working classes.

The signing of the Brest-Litovsk treaty caused great dissension, the withdrawal of the Left SRs from the government—and a new series of repressive measures. But the final attack on the non-Bolshevik press occurred only in June–August 1918. After that time in Soviet Russia only one point of view could be expressed in the newspapers. Why did Bolshevik tolerance come to an end at this particular moment?

To some extent the Leninists simply responded to the moves of their opponents. The abortive Left SR rising in early July ended all possible hopes for cooperating with other socialists. During the late spring and early summer of 1918 the Civil War in the east and in the south assumed ever more serious proportions. Red terror and White terror obviously reinforced one another.

It would be naive, however, to regard the Bolsheviks as merely reactive and to see the repressive regime which emerged from the revolution as entirely the result of the bitterness of the Civil War. The existence of the Red regime was threatened more seriously during the first half of 1918 than during the second. In the first months of that year the regime was almost destroyed by sheer anarchy, by the inability of the Bolsheviks to feed the cities and make the state machinery function. In the second half of 1918 Bolshevik rule became more repressive at least partly because now the Bolsheviks had more strength with which to suppress. The final closing down of all liberal and socialist newspapers in the middle of 1918 was a natural step in the process of ever-increasing repression.

- 3 -

What kind of press did the Bolsheviks create in an environment in which their monopoly was assured? There was general agreement among the revolutionaries who concerned themselves with journalism that the press functioned poorly and could not carry out its assigned tasks: to mold opinion, to organize, and to win over the uncommitted. Observers criticized the content and format of the press and also recognized its technical poverty. Worst of all from the point of view of the Soviet leadership, the circulation remained low.

Immediately after the November revolution the Bolsheviks enjoyed the fruits of victory. They confiscated the paper supply, machinery, and buildings of the "bourgeois" papers as spoils of war. On October 27 *Pravda* took over the presses of *Novoe vremia*. On the same day MRC of Petrograd gave the presses of *Den'* to *Derevenskaia bednota* and those of *Rech'* to *Soldatskaia pravda*.[34] According to a Soviet historian the Bolsheviks had confiscated thirty presses by the end of 1917, seventy by July 1918, and ninety by the end of that year.[35] The Soviet press was based on these confiscated goods. As a result, in the course of

1918, the Bolsheviks managed to increase the circulation of their papers tenfold.

The most difficult problem continued to be a lack of paper and newsprint. In 1914 the Russian Empire produced 33 million puds of paper, but in 1920, the worst year, Soviet Russia produced only 2 million. The paper shortage in 1920 was so great that the Sovnarkom was willing to use its precious supply of foreign currency and buy 400,000 puds from Estonia.[36] The paper which was available was poor in quality, often hardly better than wrapping paper. The situation was almost as bad with regard to newsprint, the quality of which was so poor that on occasion entire columns were completely unreadable.

The shortage of paper inevitably resulted in a fall of circulation. Many papers closed down, the publication schedule of others became erratic, and such major papers as *Pravda* and *Izvestiia* appeared during the second half of the Civil War in editions of only two pages. *Izvestiia* had the largest circulation in 1919, appearing in 300,000 to 400,000 copies depending on the availability of paper. The average figure for *Pravda* was 130,000.[37] Such popular papers as *Krasnaia gazeta,* published in Petrograd as an evening daily, had so little newsprint that they did not accept individual subscriptions, preferring to send their copies to institutions with larger readership.[38]

The newspapers also suffered from a lack of trained personnel. The Menshevik-dominated Printers' Union continued to be hostile. There was a great need for typesetters and for people capable of operating the machinery. As a result the appearance of the newspapers was poor. Trotsky addressed a gathering of printers with these words:

> Comrade printers, our printing technique is terrible. Whole series are so blurred that you cannot make out a single line. The number of misprints, jumbled lines are innumerable. To the person who for ten years has become accustomed to reading papers and understands a phrase from two words, it is difficult, often times impossible, to decipher the idea of our newspaper articles. Under the circumstances, how much more difficult it is for the young Red Army soldiers, often semi-literate?[39]

Looking at issues of *Pravda, Izvestiia,* and *Petrogradskaia pravda,* to mention only the best papers of the time, one is struck by the dullness of format. The Bolsheviks had learned nothing of the techniques of the yellow press. The central papers did possess means to reproduce drawings and caricatures, but photographs never appeared.

Distribution was a major problem. The postal service did not function adequately, and, at least during the beginning stages of the conflict, it was in the hands of non-socialist workers. Since postal workers often refused to deliver Bolshevik newspapers, these had to be sent surreptitiously in parcels and virtually smuggled from one place to another by traveling soldiers and activists, just as before the October revolution. Local party organizations constantly complained that newspapers and other propaganda material did not arrive from the center. *Pravda,* for example, wrote on October 27, 1918, that the Vitebsk party committee had received only two or three copies of *Izvestiia* per month.[40] In 1957 Soviet historians published the correspondence between the Secretariat of the Party's Central Committee and local party organizations in 1917 and 1918. Complaints about the unavailability of newspapers in the villages are a constant refrain in the letters.[41]

Another difficulty in the development of the press was the lack of qualified journalists. The Soviet regime faced the problem of not having enough trained people in almost every area of reconstruction, but the shortage of journalists was an especially difficult problem. The regime could hardly entrust to potential enemies the sensitive matter of conveying its point of view. The task did not attract party activists. Newly converted but uneducated soldiers and workers were capable of carrying out oral agitation among workers and peasants, but of course could not write effectively. Among the top leaders, journalism did not have as much prestige as work on the front, in industry, or in administration. Lenin had to admonish his colleagues repeatedly to write more often for the newspapers. Naturally, in the provinces skilled and reliable journalists were even more scarce and as a result the state of local journalism was pathetic.

Since every army unit and local soviet wanted to have its own paper, even though they were incapable of publishing effective propaganda, there was a great proliferation of publications. At the end of the Civil War there were more periodicals printed in Russia than there had been in peacetime. Soviet historians today use these figures to show how quickly the press developed, but at the time the leaders well understood that a few strong papers would have been more beneficial than many weak ones, and they regarded proliferation both as a sign and a cause of weakness.

The Party wisely stressed the need to improve agitation among the peasantry. This policy was used to justify claims for paper on the part of local organizations. However, it was one thing to publish a newspaper and another to carry out successful agitation. The provincial papers failed to make contact with village life. By and large they reprinted articles from *Pravda* and *Izvestiia* and filled their pages with the texts of laws and regulations. Without village correspondents their information on village life came from hearsay. They appeared irregularly and their "original" articles were even duller than the ones they copied from the central press. At the same time a large share of the central papers was sent outside of the main centers. In 1920, for example, out of 350,000 copies of *Izvestiia*, 279,000 were sent out of Moscow; of the 250,000 copies of *Pravda* only 41,000 remained in the capital. *Bednota,* aimed at the poor peasants, was distributed almost entirely in the villages.[42]

The Red Army was politically a most powerful organization. During the second half of the Civil War when the number of civilian papers declined for lack of resources, the military press continued to expand. At the end of 1918 there were 90 newspapers published by various military units and in the course of 1919 their number grew to 170.[43] For the army distribution was, of course, no problem and the investment in indoctrination definitely paid off.

Agitation among the soldiers was a relatively easy task compared to creating a network of newspapers for the entire country. Journalists and party leaders alike were aware of the technical and ideological weaknesses of the press and discussed these problems repeatedly. L. S. Sosnovsky, editor of *Pravda*, reported to the 8th Party Congress (March 1919) on the situation of the press. He talked about the confusion in the provinces concerning the financing of newspapers. He complained about the ideological unreliability and lack of education of provincial editors and journalists.[44] Then he submitted a set of resolutions which the congress accepted. This was the first:

> The general weakening of party work at the time of the civil war badly damaged our party and soviet press. A general weakness of almost all party and soviet publications is a remoteness from local and often from general political life. The provincial party and soviet press almost completely ignores local life and chooses its material on general issues extremely unsuccessfully. They print long, uninteresting articles instead of responding with short, simply written articles to the main issues of national and local life. On occasion entire pages are filled with decrees, instead of explaining in a simple and understandable language the most important points of the decree. Newspapers print rules and regulations of different offices and departments instead of making from this material a lively chronicle of local life.[45]

The resolution blamed the failures of the press on the fact that most experienced party leaders paid too little attention to newspapers. In view of the importance of propaganda, the Congress directed local party organizations to assign their most experienced and talented people to press work. It assigned the task of supervising the local press and commenting on questions of party construction to the central press. The task of local papers was exclusively to appeal to a mass audience, to discuss their problems in a simple language. That the resolution had little effect can be seen from the fact that the 11th Congress in 1922 found it necessary to repeat all the main points.

Two congresses of journalists at the time of the Civil War, in November 1918 and in May 1919, also looked for ways to improve the work. The deliberations show that the Soviet press was still in a formative stage and that the journalists held a variety of opinions on how best to shape its character. The first congress was addressed by such major figures of Bolshevism as Kamenev, Radek, Lunacharsky, and Kollontai.[46] All speakers agreed that the press should pay more attention to life in the villages and factories. There was, however, an interesting disagreement over the question of audience. Sosnov-sky argued that all papers should be written for simple people, but the resolu-tion of the congress spoke of "leading" papers and "mass" papers. In fact, however, the intellectual level of such "leading" papers as *Pravda* and *Izvestiia* was not appreciably higher than that of the local papers, even if those in the capitals were more professionally produced.

The journalists devoted considerable attention to the organizational aspect of their work. A resolution called for the establishment of a Central Council of Journalists (Tsentrosoviet) which would not only protect the professional interests of journalists, but would also be responsible for such matters as distribution of paper and information. Nothing came of these plans. Tsentroso-viet was an organization of little influence which within a few months ceased to exist. The Party was not about to give control over crucial matters to an outside authority; the journalists were simply disregarded. The political-ideological orientation of newspapers and the appointment of cadres continued to be the responsibility of the Central Committee of the Party; distribution of paper, newsprint and machines was handled by the Central Economic Council (VSNKh), and the Sovnarkom set up the Russian Telegraph Agency (Rosta) for distribution of information.

The mood and character of the second congress of journalists in May 1919 were altogether different.[47] The organizers had learned that in the developing system there was to be no such profession as journalism, but simply a party function for publishing newspapers. The press would have no other task than to spread and advertise the policies and decisions of the Party. But the Party did not support even such a modest conception. The newly elected Central Com-mittee of journalists soon fell apart when the Party sent its members to different parts of the country. The party had no interest in supporting even the slightest degree of professional independence of journalists; it wanted no mediators between its policies and the publicizing of these policies.

The years of the Civil War were the formative period of the Soviet press. The Bolsheviks repudiated the principles governing the "bourgeois" press but they did not have clear ideas on the kind of newspapers which would be appropriate in the new age. There were no models to follow, and many questions. What subjects should the communist press emphasize? What should be the style? On what level should the journalists address their leaders? Lenin made a major contribution to the discussions in an article in *Pravda* in September 1918.

"About the Character of Our Newspapers" began with the practical statement that it was necessary to write simply and concisely for the masses. Lenin recommended that in order to be effective, journalists should deal with concrete situations. But he went much further. He argued that Soviet newspapers should devote less attention to politics.

Instead of 200–400 lines, why don't we talk in 20–10 [*sic*] about such matters as the treachery of the Mensheviks, who are the lackeys of the bourgeoisie, or such as the Anglo-Japanese attack for the sake of reestablishing the sacred rule of capital, or such as how the American billionaires gnash their teeth about Germany. These matters are simple, well-known and to a considerable extent already well understood by the masses.[48]

What should the press write about then? In Lenin's opinion more attention should be given to economics. He did not have in mind, however, the discussion of such issues as war communism, the effects of outlawing free trade in grain, or the consequences of workers' control of the factories. He wanted detailed reports of which factories did their work well and which ones did not; how successes were achieved; and, above all, he wanted to unmask the guilty—those who did not do their work. They were class enemies. The press should be an instrument of the dictatorship of the proletariat exposing those who through poor work in fact helped the enemy. The article concluded:

Less political noise. Less *intelligent*-like discussions. Closer to life. More attention to how the masses of workers and peasants *in fact* build something new in their everyday work. More *documentation* of just how *communist* this new is.

Lenin was implying that there was no point in discussing the political and economic issues of the day, for those had been decided. It is significant that this article was written exactly at the time when the last vestiges of a critical, non-Bolshevik press had disappeared. There remained no one to polemicize against. Politics as a conflict of opinion, as a presentation of alternatives, no longer existed. The public sphere of discussion was drastically narrowed and remained so for decades.

It would be naive to think that the Soviet press developed as it did because editors followed the advice of the founder of the system. But Lenin's article was prophetic. Today's *Pravda* would please him: the journalists admonish workers to do their job well, they single out specific factories for praise or blame and they most certainly waste no space on "*intelligent*-like" discussion of large political issues in terms of alternatives.

This brief report on the early history of the Soviet press shows that the evidence does not support claims for a decisively important role of the press in the battle for public opinion. The peasantry was still largely illiterate and the printed word was not the most suitable instrument for winning them over. Furthermore, the Bolsheviks faced insuperable technical difficulties: there was a chronic shortage of paper and the communication system barely functioned. Nor can it be said that the Bolsheviks were particularly innovative in this field. Journalism was a rather insignificant sideline for the most able leaders. Bolshevik superiority over their enemies in using the press for propaganda had a single cause: they were much more methodical in suppressing opposition. It is not, of course, that the generals were the followers of John Stuart Mill, deeply committed to free expression. However, they were nineteenth-century men and had a much more naive understanding of the role of ideas. They were content to suppress overt opposition, while allowing the expression of heterogeneous views. For example, under Denikin's rule trade unionists, Mensheviks, and Socialist Revolutionaries more or less freely published their newspapers. The Bolsheviks, by contrast, represented the wave of the future.

NOTES

1. V. I. Lenin, *Polnoe sobranie sochinenii.* 5th ed. Moscow, 1967–70, Vol. 5, pp. 11–12.

2. *Russkaia periodicheskaia pechat'*, (1895–Okt. 1917) Sbornik Moscow, 1957, p. 199.

3. S. A. Andronov, *Bol'shevistskaia pechat' v trekh revoliutsiiakh.* Moscow, 1978, p. 138.

4. *Russkaia periodicheskai pechat'.* p. 195.

5. Kh. M. Astrakhan and I. S. Sazonov, "Sozdanie massovoi bol'shevistskoi pechati v 1917 godu," *Voprosy istorii,* 1957, No. 1, p. 98.

6. Lenin, *PSS.* Vol. 34, pp. 209–210.

7. V. P. Budnikov, *Bol'shevistskaia partiinaia pechat' v 1917 godu.* Kharkov, 1959, p. 106.

8. Lenin, *PSS.* Vol. 5, pp. 39–41.

9. Ibid., Vol. 12, p. 101.

10. Ibid., Vol. 34, pp. 208–212.

11. Ibid., Vol. 34, pp. 236–237.

12. A. Z. Okorokov, *Oktiabr' i krakh russkoi burzhuaznoi pressy.* Moscow, 1970, p. 168.

13. *Pravda,* October 28, 1917.

14. L. Schapiro, *The Origin of Communist Autocracy.* 2nd ed. London, 1977, p. 69.

15. John Keep, ed., *The Debate on Soviet Power.* Minutes of the All-Russian Central Executive Committee of Soviets. Second Convocation, October 1917–January 1918. Oxford, 1979, p. 75.

16. Ibid., p. 76.

17. Ibid., p. 70.

18. Unfortunately this crucial sentence is mistranslated in Keep. In his version: "If we are moving toward social(ist) revolution, we cannot reply to Kaledin's bombs with bombs of falsehood." p. 75. See Lenin, *PSS.* Vol. 35, p. 54.

19. Keep, p. 76.

20. Ibid., p. 78. D. Riazanov, N. Derbyshev, Commissar of press affairs, I. Arbuzov, Commissar of state printing works, K. Iurenev, Commissar of Red Guards, G. Fedorov, head of the labor conflict department in the Commissariat of Labor, Iu. Larin also associated themselves with Nogin's statement and resigned. A. Shliapnikov expressed his agreement without resigning.

21. *Petrogradskii Voenno-Revoliutsionnii Komitet. Dokumenty i materialy*. Moscow, 1966–67, 3 volumes, Vol. 1, p. 530. See also discussion in Okorokov, p. 193.

22. Ibid., pp. 144–146.

23. A. A. Goncharov, "Bor'ba sovetskoi vlasti s kontrrevoliutsionnoi burzhuaznoi i melkoburzhuaznoi pechatiu (25 Okt.–Iul 1917 g.)" *Vestnik MGU Zhurnalistika*, 1969, No. 4, p. 16.

24. Okorokov, p. 271.

25. Goncharov, p. 14.

26. *PVRK Documents*, Vol. 1, p. 130.

27. Okorokov, p. 212.

28. Lenin, *PSS*. Vol. 34, pp. 208–213.

29. Okorokov, pp. 222–229.

30. *PVRK Documents*. Vol. 3, p. 232.

31. Lenin, *PSS*. Vol. 44, p. 200.

32. Okorokov, pp. 251–255.

33. Ibid., pp. 258–261.

34. *PVRK*. Vol. 1, pp. 162–163.

35. Okorokov, p. 325.

36. N. Meshcheriakov, "O rabote gosudarstvennogo izdatel'stva," *Pechat' i Revoliutsiia*, 1921, No. 1, p. 9.

37. D. Lebedev, *Shest' let moskovskoi pechati 1917–1923*. Moscow, 1924, p. 22 and p. 27.

38. C. S. Sampson, "The Formative Years of the Soviet Press: An Institutional History, 1917–1924," Ph.D. dissertation, Univ. of Mass., 1970, p. 126.

39. L. Trotskii, *Sochineniia*. Vol. 21, p. 243. Also in Sampson, p. 96.

40. *Pravda*, October 27, 1918.

41. *Perepiska sekreteriata Ts.K. RSDRP(b) s mestnymi organizatsiiami Noiabr' 1917g fevral' 1918g*. Moscow, 1957.

42. Lebedev, p. 79.

43. A. Berezhnoi, *K istorii partiino-sovetskoi pechati*. Leningrad, 1956, p. 6 note.

44. *Vosmoi s"ezd RKP(b) Mart 1919 goda Protokoly*. Moscow, 1959, pp. 295–296.

45. Ibid., pp. 436–437.

46. A detailed description of the conferences and its resolutions can be found in I. V. Vardin (Mgeladze), *Sovetskaia pechat'. Sbornik statei*. Moscow, 1924, pp. 126–130.

47. Ibid., pp. 130–132.

48. Lenin, *PSS*. Vol. 37, pp. 89–91.

[9] The Breakdown in Production and Distribution of Printed Material, 1917–1927

Jeffrey Brooks

THE SPREAD OF printed material in late imperial Russia depended on the functioning of a market economy.[1] Enterprising publishers, often of lower-class origins, made fortunes satisfying the tastes of readers from the same social stratum, who, in turn, gradually discovered the printed word as a source of information and entertainment. A brisk commercial trade in books, pamphlets, and newspapers developed in the late nineteenth and early twentieth centuries in the cities, and, more importantly for Russian development, in the countryside. The often crude commercial publications were supplemented by materials intended for the school system and also by a significant quantity of propagandistic state and Church publications, and by publicistic works from various other sources. Though some of these sponsored materials found a popular readership, many did not, and the experience of ordinary people with the printed word outside the school system depended largely upon the more numerous commercial publications, which educated Russians of various political persuasions viewed with distaste.

In times of war, revolution, natural and economic calamity, people's desire to follow the events of the day is keener than usual. During the last decade and a half of the old regime, when the Russo-Japanese War, the 1905 Revolution, the Stolypin reforms, World War I, and the February Revolution came in rapid succession, ordinary people increasingly looked to the printed word to orient themselves in their rapidly changing environment. On the eve of the October revolution there was a substantial reading public of unsophisticated and relatively new readers accustomed to seeking out newspapers, such as *Gazeta kopeika* (The Kopeck Newspaper) and *Russkoe slovo* (The Russian Word), and other printed materials for news, information, and entertainment. By purchasing printed material that they themselves considered valuable, ordinary people were acting primarily as consumers, but to the extent that in doing so they gained useful knowledge they were also investing in their future, and, in a sense, in the modernization of Russia from the bottom up.

In replacing the market with a command economy under conditions of wartime devastation, Bolshevik administrators swept away the consumer-oriented commercial publishing and distribution network. The result was a breakdown in the circulation of printed material in the popular milieux. For this reason, although the 1920s was an exciting period in the culture of the avant-garde, ordinary people's contact with the printed word during this period was sharply curtailed.

The breakdown in production and distribution of printed material had several dimensions and occurred for a number of reasons. Material and equipment shortages made production difficult in the first years of Soviet power. The book and newspaper industries suffered all of the familiar problems of retail trade after the revolution: the destruction of the old distribution system of shops and merchants, price and currency fluctuations, and the severing of the information flow between consumers and producers. The crisis in publishing had an additional ideological component: political priorities rather than consumer demand were the primary determinants of what was published. The effect of this multidimensional breakdown in the popular media was to exclude many people, particularly rural readers, from the flow of reliable information at a time when their need for it was heightened.

Crisis followed crisis in publishing during the period of War Communism and much of the New Economic Policy. Available figures suggest that production of books and pamphlets fell rapidly in 1918–1919 and continued to decline until 1922, before rising to prewar levels by 1924 or 1925, as indicated in Table 1 (Appendix). The fall in production was precipitous even when the decreased size of the empire is taken into account; only a quarter of the number of copies and titles produced in 1917 was issued in 1920 and 1921. Figures on newspaper production are less available and more difficult to interpret, since the definition of a newspaper varied. The figures shown in Tables 2 and 3 suggest that newspaper production and circulation dropped considerably after the revolution. The lowest point with respect to the number of dailies in the three years for which figures are available is 1925, when there were only 107, compared with 836 in 1914, the peak year in the prerevolutionary period. Even by 1928, the number of daily newspapers had not reached half that of 1914.

Data on the circulation of newspapers are incomplete and difficult to interpret. The pre–World War I figures used for comparison by contemporary Soviet specialists ranged from 2.7 to 3.7 million daily copies.[2] Figures given for the daily circulation of Soviet newspapers on Press Day in 1923 and 1924 were 1 million for 1922, 1.9 million for 1923, and 2.5 million for 1924, as shown in Table 3. Available figures show a sharp rise in the number of copies to 6.7 million in 1925, but this seems to reflect a great expansion in publications other than dailies, as well as a new way of counting.[3] The pre-1925 figures represent a substantial drop not only from 1909, but also, more importantly, from the greatly expanded wartime production, when the circulation of *Gazeta kopeika* and *Russkoe slovo* approached and sometimes passed a million copies a day.[4] The circulation of six of the largest Soviet newspapers for 1919 through 1924 did not rise above a peak of 1.3 million in 1924, as shown in Table 3. Circulation of all newspapers dropped sharply with the institution of the NEP, when newspapers had to be sold, rather than given away. The circulation of the Bolshevik paper for the peasants, *Bednota* (The Poor), the cheapest and most widely distributed of the dailies, fell from 500,000 copies on January 10, 1922, when the New Economic Policy was apparently applied, to 200,000 on January 17, 1922, after which the editors ceased to provide this information.

The decline in production and circulation of newspapers and books was felt in the cities, but it was in the countryside (where 71 percent of the nearly 60 million literate people lived, according to the 1926 census) that the shortage was most acute.[5] A journalist traveling through the south reported in *Pravda* on August 11, 1923, that newspapers were not always available even at the largest city railroad stations. An investigator sent into Voronezh Province by the Press Section of the Party to evaluate the success of rural papers found whole areas, including a large trading village with an agronomy school, that had not received a paper for a month or more.[6] There were few books in the villages either, complained the author of the lead editorial in the journal *Knigonosha* (Book Carrier) on April 29, 1923. An investigator sent to the province of Orel by the central state publishing house, Gosizdat, to see what peasants were reading reported in *Pravda* (July 26, 1923) that the few newspapers and magazines that reached the *volost'* level were read only by Komsomols and Party members; "the rest of the village lives by rumor."

Official awareness of these difficulties sharpened in the spring of 1924, and the subject was raised at the Thirteenth Party Congress, at which the slogan "face to the village" was proclaimed. Not only were there no newspapers in the countryside, complained Krupskaia, in a speech printed in *Pravda* (May 4, 1924), but in some cases it proved impossible for peasants to subscribe even when they wished to do so. Requests for papers went unanswered, and even those who succeeded in placing a subscription could not be assured of getting their paper. "The receipt of newspapers has been greatly reduced in comparison with prerevolutionary times," she concluded. The problem Krupskaia identified was not solved in 1924 or 1925, despite the new attention to the need for books and newspapers in the countryside.

Problems of production were in part the result of a shortage of machines and paper. Machines wore out, and there were difficulties producing and importing new ones. The number of rotary presses, flatbed presses, and lithograph and typesetting machines in operation fell to roughly two-thirds of prewar levels by

1924–26, as shown in Table 4. A substantial number of smaller, more primitive machines, for which no prerevolutionary figures are available, were functioning, but the number of these also fell between 1921 and 1926. Paper was always in short supply. The quantity of paper and cardboard produced fell to a low of less than 10 percent of 1913 levels during 1919–21, and the industry recovered gradually, reaching the 1913 level only in 1928/29, as shown in Table 5. The problem was greatest during the period of War Communism (1918–21).[7] Expenditures on imports of paper were substantial, particularly after 1924.[8]

Production difficulties affected quality. The printers of *Rabochaia Moskva* (Working Moscow), a paper with a circulation of 62,000 in 1923,[9] apologized to readers in the February 2, 1923, edition for the poor quality of the newspaper, and blamed the presses, typesetting machines, and inferior ink and paper. In the first anniversary issue, on February 7, 1923, workers complained that the paper was sometimes impossible to read because of smudged ink. Newspapers often appeared late; street sales and distribution of *Rabochaia Moskva* did not begin until 9:00 A.M., after Moscow workers were already at work. Distributors did not get to the printing plant until 7:00 A.M. As late as 1928, printing of some large morning papers was not finished until afternoon.[10]

As production difficulties reduced the flow of new material, existing prerevolutionary stocks of books and pamphlets were depleted either by direct destruction or by disorganized distribution, which often had the same effect. Stocks of books held by capitalist enterprises were confiscated in 1918 and 1919, and in 1920 whatever remained was nationalized, along with many personal libraries.[11] Confiscated books were given away, sent to various institutions, and, during the civil war, to the army, or pulped. A great quantity of prerevolutionary popular literature and religious works met the latter fate.[12] Remaining stocks of prerevolutionary books were sold off cheaply in 1924 in the major cities by state enterprises trying to improve their finances.[13]

The destruction of the prerevolutionary distribution system made it difficult to deliver to readers the newspapers and books that were produced. Prerevolutionary commercial publications had been sold through a network of city bookstores and kiosks, railroad stands, and rural general stores, and by hawkers and peddlers who visited fairs, markets, and villages. Non-commercial distribution through schools, adult education institutions, churches, zemstvos, volost' centers, and the military was well developed. Soviet authorities initially relied on the administrative and propaganda apparatus, and on *Tsentropechat'* (Central Press), which took over the remnants of A. S. Suvorin's prerevolutionary system of 1,660 kiosks, 40 percent of which were in railroad stations.[14] During the NEP, Tsentropechat' was replaced by *Kontragenstvo Pechati* (The Press Contracting Agency). This agency opened 400 railroad kiosks from March 1922 to July 1923, primarily in remote places along the route, and 200 kiosks were also opened in the city of Moscow, according to *Pravda* (July 6, 1923). An example of the disorganization in newspaper distribution at this time was the running battle between the managers of Kontragentstvo and *Izvestiia* in 1922 and 1923, when Kontragentstvo disrupted the distribution of *Izvestiia*, and made it an "underground" publication, according to an official spokesman.[15]

Distribution of books as well as newspapers developed slowly. The number of Soviet bookstores rose from several hundred in 1922 to nearly 1,200 in 1924, compared with 2,000 to 3,000 prerevolutionary shops.[16] The number of bookshops in Moscow and Leningrad did not approach prerevolutionary levels even in 1927. In that year there were 259 shops in Moscow and 161 in Leningrad compared with roughly 500 in Moscow and 341 in St. Petersburg in 1906.[17] Small private traders operated briefly in 1923, mostly in the used book trade, but by 1924 they were abandoning their shops and becoming street peddlers, as currency fluctuations and other unfavorable conditions made settled trade risky.[18] Early Soviet book distribution was almost exclusively urban. There were fewer than 400 regular retail book outlets outside provincial cities at the end of 1923, and about 700 in 1927, compared with 1,800 before the revolution.[19] Efforts to boost rural distribution were intensified after the Thirteenth Party Congress in 1924, through utilization of the postal system and consumer cooperatives. There were 6,500 postal distribution points and 4,000 consumer cooperatives with bookshelves by 1926, and 1,000 other cooperative distribution points, according to a commentator in the early 1930s.[20] The effectiveness of the postal and cooperative distribution system, however, must be questioned. Publishers had difficulty with the post before the 1924 Congress. The editors of *Bednota* complained in an editorial on December 19, 1922, that the mail was generally ineffective as a means of distributing newspapers, since it hardly functioned in the countryside. There were complaints from readers of *Bednota* in 1924 that they received newspapers in bundles of 10 issues at a time, or a month's subscription at once.[21] The situation probably improved after 1924, but complaints continued. Postmen and cooperative employees were often uninterested in book distribution.[22] In the late 1920s peasants who wanted books and periodicals were often unable to get them, according to M. I. Slukhovskii, who used letters to *Krest'ianskaia gazeta* (The Peasant Newspaper) and other sources to study the peasant reader. Peasants either did not know how to order under the new system or were discouraged by lack of cooperation on the part of sales personnel.[23] Attempts to develop a network of itinerant book peddlers similar to the prerevolutionary one failed, since the traders were classified as members of the bourgeoisie, heavily taxed, and deprived of voting rights.[24]

With the chaotic distribution system of the early 1920s, publishers found it easier to deliver to institutions and groups rather than individuals. Newspaper distribution was based on "collective demand," and compulsory group subscription to newspapers was the general practice in 1923 and 1924.[25] A directive was issued against such subscriptions, but the practice remained widespread in the mid-1920s. Only about 13 percent of the copies of workers' newspapers (including, one assumes, *Pravda* and *Izvestiia*) were distributed by direct subscription, according to a 1926 commentator, compared with about a third of the newspapers for peasants and members of national minorities.[26] Worker papers were distributed primarily through trade union and Party organizations, and peasant papers through paid agents, such as school teachers or rural newspaper correspondents. Distribution of periodicals by collective subscription had declined to 14.5 percent by fiscal year 1927/28, but 39 percent of all book sales were to collective subscribers. Most of these sales were probably of propaganda and school and library books.[27]

Book and periodical trade suffered from the confusion of price changes and income redistribution in the twenties, as did all retail trade. A pood of rye was worth ten small booklets of the sort sold by colporteurs before the war, but only one in the fall of 1923.[28] Despite efforts to reduce the price of printed materials, prices remained high for the agricultural population throughout most of the 1920s,[29] and peasants, in the words of a Soviet investigator, dreamed of the good old days when "people's books" sold for kopecks.[30]

During the NEP publishers were supposed to sell profitably what they produced, but with reduced demand and drastically curtailed distribution capability, profits proved elusive. Only slightly more than half of the 151 million rubles worth of books and pamphlets produced from 1921 through 1925 were sold.[31] The rest accumulated in warehouses until they were pulped at the end of the twenties.[32] Publishing losses declined in 1926 and 1927, but the industry did not begin to show a profit until 1928.[33] Difficulties in accounting and management continued throughout the decade, and currency fluctuations made financial accounting more complicated. The Worker-Peasant Inspectorate complained in 1924 that Gosizdat had no idea what was in stock, and often published works that were already oversupplied.[34] A number of firms went "bankrupt," including the anti-religious house, Bezbozhnik, and central publishers such as Gosizdat, Priboi, and Molodaia gvardiia experienced serious difficulties.[35]

Newspapers were not expected to show a profit, but their managers were under pressure to minimize losses. In 1926, publishers lost .57 kopecks for each copy of a workers' paper printed, 1.83 kopecks for every copy of a peasant newspaper, and 6.45 kopecks per copy for newspapers for national minorities, according to I. Vareikis.[36] In the same year, *Pravda* and *Izvestiia* sold for five kopecks a copy, *Krest'ianskaia gazeta* for three kopecks, and provincial papers

for four to seven kopecks.[37] Some central newspapers, such as *Pravda,
Izvestiia, Gudok, Krest' ianskaia gazeta,* and *Rabochaia Moskva,* were profit-
able in 1928, largely due to institutional advertisements and paid announcements.[38]

Concomitant with the many difficulties in supply and distribution of printed
materials throughout the decade was a significant drop in consumer demand. In
part this was due to economic factors, such as the relative decline in agricultural
incomes and the relative increase in the price of books. Much of the decline in
demand, however, was a response to the decision on the part of the Soviet
publishing monopoly not to print types of literature that had been popular
before the revolution. What was produced by private publishers under Soviet
authority (5 percent of all copies in 1925) was either insufficient or unsuitable
for the mass of ordinary people.[39] In the prerevolutionary period, belles lettres,
light fiction, song books, almanacs, and religious works constituted the bulk of
the commercially marketed materials for the common reader.[40] Reader reactions to early Soviet publications were noted in published studies of readers.
The tradition of studying the reader was well established in the prerevolutionary period, and was continued, in modified form, throughout the 1920s.[41] M.
A. Smushkova, who surveyed the reader studies published to 1926, commented that workers enjoyed belles lettres with social themes, but that peasants
were, on the whole, dissatisfied with the reading material available to them.[42]
The hostility and incomprehension of the peasants toward propagandistic
works and speeches of Bolshevik leaders were reported in a variety of other
studies.[43] M. I. Slukhovskii observed that these works appeared to be intended
for village activists, and not ordinary readers.[44]

Among the most successful propagandistic works for the peasants were
historical stories based on the lives of revolutionary heroes. The peasants
wanted to read something that engaged their emotions, as had the prerevolutionary tales and saints' lives. One reader wrote to *Krest' ianskaia gazeta* in the
mid-1920s that the biographies of revolutionaries "acted on me more strongly
than the suffering of the great martyr Saint George."[45]

The emphasis in Soviet book and pamphlet publishing was on political
issues, propaganda, social commentary, and school books. The seven authors
published in the largest number of copies by Gosizdat from 1919 to 1926 were
Lenin (7.5 million), Stalin (2 million), Bukharin (1.2 million), Trotsky (1
million), Plekhanov (.6 million), and Marx and Engels (.5 million.)[46] These
seven authors accounted for 6 percent of the copies published by Gosizdat, and
probably a larger proportion of the production of the specialized political
publishers. School books accounted for about two-fifths of Gosizdat's production, social science about a quarter, and publications for the peasants, including
both propaganda and agronomy, about one-fifth. The remainder was composed

of popular science, belles lettres, children's books, reference works, and books for the military.

Soviet publishing statistics have several peculiarities. In a command economy, changes in publishing policy could be abrupt, and the quantities of certain types of materials rose or fell sharply. Comparisons with prerevolutionary figures are necessarily somewhat arbitrary, and it is important to remember that significant quantities of publicistic and propagandistic material were published before the revolution, particularly during World War I. Tables 6, 7, 8, and 9 show the relative quantities of works on different subjects published after the revolution, with some comparison with the earlier period. Categorizations frequently overlapped; for example, social, economic, and political works, including Leninism, and Party literature comprised about a quarter of the titles from 1923 through 1925, but political titles also appeared among the popular science and children's books. According to another categorization, between two- and three-fifths of all titles published from 1921 through 1927 were "social science," broadly defined to include school books.

As a result of changes in economic policies and political developments, much of the agitational material and topical social commentary became obsolete soon after it was published. Local Party and GPU authorities received a directive in 1923, in which they were instructed to remove pre-NEP political and informational materials from small libraries.[47] Librarians were also responsible for purging their local holdings, and the greatest vigilance was urged in the case of small libraries serving workers and peasants.[48]

More than the presence of anti-religious books, the absence of religious books caused a serious break in the reading habits of many ordinary Russians. Anti-religious works comprised less than one percent of the number of copies of Soviet books published from 1921 to 1927. Slukhovskii reported that a number of investigators agreed that anti-religious works were poorly received in the villages.[49]

In the area of applied knowledge, which included industrial and technical information, agriculture, medicine, and other topics, reader interest coincided with the publishing monopoly's willingness to produce. Popular science and technology comprised a fifth of the titles published from 1921 to 1927, and a smaller proportion of the total number of copies. Reader studies indicated that peasants wanted books on agriculture.[50] In book requests to *Krest'ianskaia gazeta* in the mid-1920s, agriculture occupied first place.[51] In 1925, after the Thirteenth Party Congress, twice as many copies of agricultural works (3.7 million) were issued as in 1910, though there were fewer titles.[52] Among the large circulation editions were titles such as *Electricity and the Tractor in Agriculture,* works to encourage the planting of clover and abandonment of the three field system, and books on bee keeping and hog raising. Nevertheless, the peasants were not always satisfied with the agricultural literature provided, either because the instructions were not applicable to their region or because information was lacking on how to put suggestions into practice and where to get the necessary tools and materials.[53]

Despite ideological approval of works on applied technique, Soviet publishers left unsatisfied demand for many works conveying practical knowledge. Peasants wrote to *Krest'ianskaia gazeta* in the mid-1920s requesting books on handicrafts and trades.[54] This interest was interpreted as a response to the falling agricultural prices and an effort on the part of many individual peasants to find alternative means of livelihood.[55] Publishers had difficulty keeping up with the demand for works in popular science. The works of the prerevolutionary populizers were considered unsatisfactory by the end of the civil war, although those of N. A. Rubakin had been printed in large editions in 1919. Attempts to create a substitute for works like Rubakin's were not immediately successful.[56] The demand for printed information about laws, taxes, and the general economic and legal developments affecting rural Russia was also difficult for Soviet publishers to satisfy, since the rules were constantly changing. Peasants and peasant correspondents sent *Krest'ianskaia gazeta* many requests for information on land and forest use rules, credit, insurance, taxes, and other legal matters.[57] Such information had been provided in part by almanacs that were published in over 10 million copies in 1910.[58]

The most dramatic departure from the prerevolutionary publishing tradition came in the area of belles lettres and popular fiction. In 1910, 7.6 million copies of works of belles lettres were published in Russian. Additional fiction was included among the nearly 15 million copies of "people's books," and 2.6 million copies of detective stories also appeared.[59] In 1922, only 3.5 million copies of belles lettres appeared, and the category "people's books" no longer existed. These works were about ten percent of the total number of copies issued in 1922, as shown in Table 8. After 1922 a decision was made to increase substantially the publication of belles lettres, largely in response to growing inventories of unsold works. Soviet production neared the 1912 level of 33 million copies in 1925 and 1926. This figure was substantially exceeded in 1927 when 46 million copies of works of belles lettres were published.

The writings of the classical Russian writers dominated Soviet belles lettres particularly after the establishment of a state publishing monopoly over the works of 57 "classical writers" in 1918.[60] The works of these writers comprised a substantial proportion of all works published from 1918 through 1923. After that, although the numbers of these works published continued to increase, the relative share of the classics declined with respect to all belles lettres.[61] Many works of Russian classics had been issued in prerevolutionary "people's editions," and the early Soviet emphasis was not a departure from earlier practices.[62] The quantity of classical works available was probably no greater than before the revolution. In 1909, the works of nine classical authors were issued in 1.7 million copies in "peoples' books" alone, in addition to regular belles lettres.[63] According to a 1928 study, only in 1926 and 1927 did works of classical authors begin to arrive at Moscow trade union libraries in adequate quantity.[64] Readers wrote to *Krest'ianskaia gazeta* in the mid-1920s that they could not get copies of works by Nekrasov and Kol'tsov, or those of Soviet writers.[65]

Works by new Soviet writers and translations of certain foreign authors were also widely published in the 1920s. Among the new writers were proletarian and communist authors such as Gladkov, Neverov, Serafimovich, Furmanov, and also some fellow travelers, such as Seifulina and Romanov.[66] Works by Jack London, Upton Sinclair, and H. G. Wells were published in hundreds of thousands of copies in the 1920s. These Soviet and foreign works were reported to have been favorably received by workers, but less so in the village. According to many investigators, the peasants valued truth and realism, and had little tolerance for works that did not conform to their criteria.[67] Idealistic works about the revolution, the civil war, and socialist construction did not find a friendly audience in the countryside. Nor did writers such as Sinclair and Wells. Peasants were confused by the futuristic works that were popular among some Bolsheviks, and often had difficulty knowing whether they were true or fiction. One rural correspondent wrote to *Krest'ianskaia gazeta* for more information on Wells's *War of the Worlds*. He explained that it was his understanding that the book was about Martian polyps who landed in England or France, were smothered by the air, and then preserved in alcohol in a zoo. His question was, "Is it true or not that this affair took place in the nineteenth century?"[68] This reader expressed the confusion undoubtedly shared by many of his contemporaries in evaluating science fiction. The Soviet publishing monopoly produced revolutionary propaganda that told rural readers that many of the "facts" of their prerevolutionary political and religious knowledge were fiction, and, at the same time, distributed imaginative works that only sophisticated readers could identify as fiction.

More than what they chose to publish, what authorities decided not to publish affected the reading of common people. Soviet publishers eschewed the boulevard novels,[69] detective adventure stories, song books, and literature of the prerevolutionary colporteur *(lubochnaia literatura)*, as well as prerevolutionary light literature by respected authors such as Mamin-Sibiriak, because they believed that such reading inhibited the enlightenment of the common people. Popular light literature became scarce and *lubochnaia literatura* vanished. A peasant wrote to *Krest'ianskaia gazeta* in the mid-1920s that the old chivalry tales, story books, pilgrimage accounts, and saints' lives had "all been smoked up, so that the trunks and shelves that earlier were filled with these books" were empty.[70] Though of questionable literary merit, these materials had served as a means for the common people to develop and confirm new values, ideas, and symbols in the rapidly modernizing environment.[71] Even familiar fairy tales were often revised by prerevolutionary authors eager to take into account the new values and experiences of their readers. Popular religious materials had also been redesigned to conform to changes in readers' tastes. There was no replacement for this lost literature in the early years of Soviet power.

Soviet investigators who studied reader tastes and responses reported a serious shortage of books suitable for the peasant reader. "The peasant reader, the principal purchaser of books in the present period, remains virtually inaccessible," I. Vareikis commented in 1926.[72] "Until recently there was no literature for the peasant at all," wrote Smushkova, also in 1926.[73] Slukhovskii commented in 1928 that urban warehouses bulged with unsold books, while there was nothing to read in the villages.[74]

Children's books may have been another area in which Soviet publishers were slow to satisfy reader demand. Children's literature comprised 4 percent of all titles published in the empire in 1912 and 5 percent of all copies, but these works were only one percent of all titles published in 1922 and 3 percent of those published in 1923.[75] In 1924, the proportion rose to 5 percent and in 1925 to 7 percent. M. I. Slukhovskii nevertheless made reference in his 1928 study of peasant readers to "a real children's book famine," and some reports he gathered from the countryside indicated that children could find nothing to read once they left school.[76]

Newspapers, like books and pamphlets, changed in the postrevolutionary period, in accordance with the ideology, aesthetics, and political strategies of Bolshevik planners. Journalism, more than books and pamphlets, was the medium for communicating the Bolshevik message to the common people. The prerevolutionary big city dailies intended for diverse readership and more numerous smaller papers aimed at select audiences were replaced by central institutional organs, such as *Pravda* for the Party and *Izvestiia* for the government, and large papers for separate classes, such as *Rabochaia gazeta* (The Workers' Newspaper) and *Krest'ianskaia gazeta*. "*Rabochaia Moskva* is the real workers' newspaper, fully responsive to the interests of the Moscow workers," read an advertisement in that paper (December 27, 1923). The editors of *Bednota* promised that their readers would learn: 1) the laws about land, 2) how to increase the harvest, 3) where to get seeds and implements, 4) how to increase income from livestock, 5) how to cure livestock, 6) the decrees of the government, 7) all the laws about taxes, 8) all the most important news.[77] Peasant-oriented stories dominated the peasant papers, as shown in Table 10.

For example, *Krest'ianskaia gazeta* on February 9, 1926, carried the features "How to Promote Peasant Goods," "What the Peasants Say," and "Soviet Construction in the Village."

Workers were expected to have wide interests. Stories about workers and the economy occupied much of the space in the workers' papers. Characteristic stories in *Rabochaia Moskva* on February 3, 1923, were: "The Current Question of the Alliance (smychka) between City and Village," on page one, and "Workers' Insurance," and "The Workers Organize Their Cooperatives," inside the paper. According to a study of *Rabochaia gazeta* readers in the mid-1920s, workers read the "Worker Life" section of that paper, but were dissatisfied by the lack of critical coverage of subjects such as workers' rights, housing, and unemployment.[78]

Foreign affairs was emphasized in the Soviet press, as it had been before the revolution. It was prominent in the first page of the three newspapers sampled in 1922–23 and 1926, as shown in Table 10. Those who replied to the 1924 survey of *Rabochaia gazeta* indicated that they read the foreign affairs section first.[79] Ia. Shafir, who conducted the *Rabochaia gazeta* study, suggested that the predominant interest in foreign affairs could be explained by concern about war and hopes for revolution elsewhere.[80] A more likely explanation is that early Soviet readers were interested for the same reasons as prerevolutionary ones, probably a mixture of general curiosity and concern about a world of which they had recently become more aware.

Domestic politics and Party affairs were problem areas for Soviet journalists, and coverage diverged sharply from prerevolutionary practice. Despite threats of government retaliation, prerevolutionary editors had included much information about government policy and politics in their papers. There was less intelligible coverage of domestic political issues in Soviet papers. *Rabochaia Moskva* contained articles about the government and about the Party, but these were either summaries of official announcements, speeches, or laudatory descriptions of local Party activity. The "Party Life" section of *Rabochaia gazeta* was sharply criticized by respondents to the 1924 survey as boring, uncritical, and remiss in unmasking abuses, but the editors were unable to formulate a policy on how to present the Party to the satisfaction of readers.[81] Readers likewise criticized *Rabochaia Moskva* on the first anniversary of the paper, February 7, 1923, but in this case, too, the editors confessed themselves helpless to improve coverage.

Conspicuously absent from the Soviet papers were the human calamities, disasters, and crimes that were the focus of much reader attention in the prerevolutionary popular press. Trotsky, writing in *Pravda,* July 1, 1923, complained of the general unwillingness of journalists to write about difficulties and the sensational events that were exciting much of the population. In his view, people were interested in the seamy side of life, and because bourgeois papers used this material to stimulate "an unhealthy curiosity" and to play on "the worst instincts of man" was no reason for the Soviet press to ignore it. Such topics could be used to dispel superstition and show up bourgeois morality, Trotsky suggested, and if the Soviet press turned its back on the curiosity of the common people, they would get their information from less reliable sources on the street.

The occasional journalistic forays into the realm of crime and disaster were brief and didactic, such as *Rabochaia Moskva*'s coverage of a 1923 mass murder. Whereas the editors of the prerevolutionary boulevard newspapers such as *Gazeta kopeika* used such events to attract readers with extended and sensational coverage, their Soviet successors had different objectives. The 1923 murders were discussed on page four of a single issue on June 7, after the criminals had already been sentenced and shot. Although the crimes were described, the emphasis was on instruction as Trotsky had suggested, rather than an appeal to what he considered unhealthy curiosity. The man was identified as a wife and child beater, a churchgoer who liked to get drunk with priests, and the woman as a glutton. Economic crimes loomed large in the Soviet press during the NEP, and the headline "Our Court: Sentence for Exploitation," which appeared in *Bednota* on January 5, 1923, was not atypical.

Present only in greatly diminished form were the entertainment and light reading features that had brought many new readers to the prerevolutionary dailies. The snappy feuilletons and serialized potboilers that were standard fare in *Gazeta kopeika* and some other popular papers seldom appeared in the Soviet press.[82] When such material was printed, it was usually political. Demian Bednyi's poems about foreign affairs and a novel about the Civil War, *For Soviet Power,* were published in *Rabochaia Moskva* in February 1922. The peasant papers were almost devoid of such material, but what appeared sometimes represented an abrupt departure from the hardheaded emphasis of the rest of the newspaper. For example, in a short serial titled "Bread from the Air (in the Not Too Distant Future)," the editors of *Bednota* regaled readers with a tale of the production of flour and meat by microbes, without human labor.[83]

The decision to exclude light fiction and amusing reportage from the newspapers was a conscious one. Newspapers were intended to provide serious information, and not to entertain readers, even though editors realized that entertaining material was in demand.[84] The Soviet papers did include reports on cultural subjects, book reviews, and articles on theater and schools, as had the prerevolutionary papers.

An important difference between the pre- and postrevolutionary papers was the lack of advertising. There was some private advertising during the NEP, but most of the space allotted to advertisements in the Soviet newspapers was used for announcements of state institutions and firms.

Postrevolutionary print culture differed from its antecedents in language as well as content. The language of successful prerevolutionary publications developed gradually over decades. Soviet publishing officials jettisoned this language, partly because they were unfamiliar with it, and partly because they wanted new words for the novelties of revolutionary life. As a consequence, the Bolsheviks presented the common reader with a confusing array of unfamiliar words, phrases, and neologisms. Readers of *Rabochaia gazeta* complained in 1924 that they needed "ten dictionaries" to understand the paper, and that explanations for "scientific" and "foreign" words were needed.[85] When the paper was read at factories, listeners were confused by the most common Soviet abbreviations and acronyms. Readings of *Krest'ianskaia gazeta* to soldiers stationed in Moscow in November 1923 revealed similar linguistic incomprehension.[86] A speaker at a Leningrad conference of propagandists urged his listeners to translate the peasant newspapers into more familiar speech before reading them aloud to villagers.[87]

Several lists of words not understood by the common people were compiled at trial readings of popular publications, usually in Moscow, or from letters to newspapers.[88] The different lists hardly overlap, suggesting that the words included were chosen from a much larger pool of unfamiliar words. Words relating to politics, agriculture, science, and industry as well as literary expressions appeared frequently. Words essential to the Bolshevik world view such as 'democracy,' 'imperialism,' 'dialectic,' 'class enemy,' and 'socialism' were reported to be unfamiliar to readers or listeners. Political and economic terms such as 'trust,' 'syndicate,' 'blockade,' 'SSSR,' 'budget,' 'deficit,' and 'balance' were not understood. Abbreviations for organizations, such as 'Komsomol,' and scientific terms, such as 'nitrogen,' and 'microbe,' left readers puzzled. In many cases, the concepts communicated by these words were unfamiliar to common readers, and the words themselves were often Russifications of foreign terms, making them appear doubly strange. A peasant from Vladimir wrote to *Krest'ianskaia gazeta* in the mid-1920s to complain that books were written "not in peasant language, and, it is possible to say, not in Russian, but in political language."[89] In addition to its initial unfamiliarity, the language of the revolution changed rapidly as new words were used to describe policies and campaigns.

According to the 1926 census, there were nearly sixty million literate people in the Soviet Union.[90] One million copies of daily newspapers were published in 1922, and 2.5 million in 1924. Those among the common people who read the newspapers and other publications in the first decade of Soviet power were probably primarily urban inhabitants with both special interest and opportunity. Party members and others in responsible positions were told to subscribe to newspapers, and there were over a million party members and candidates in 1926.[91] There were almost two million Komsomols at the end of 1925.[92] There was also a large number of worker-peasant correspondents who were supposed to investigate local abuses, and were paid for their submissions to the press. Their numbers increased from 50,000 in 1923 to 250,000 in 1926, and roughly half of these were in the countryside.[93] The small number of newspapers relative to the numbers of correspondents and people affiliated with party organizations suggests that these readers probably accounted for many of the subscriptions to Soviet newspapers. Whether the news went beyond this circle of readers depended largely on the relations between non-party common people and the representatives of officialdom.

Because of the limited quantity of popular printed material, its difficult language, and, for most readers, its lack of appeal, it is most likely that common Russians read less in the decade after the revolution than they had in the decade before. The reduction in the role of the written word in people's lives was greatest in the countryside, where the potential modernizing role of printed material was greatest. In this respect during the first decade of Soviet power prerevolutionary trends were reversed. Cultural differences between country and city grew. A number of investigators reported an increase in superstition among rural people, outbreaks of wild rumors, and confusion about who ruled the country.[94] Literacy itself may have lost some value to people who could find nothing they wanted to read.

The establishment of a viable Soviet publishing industry took a decade and perhaps more. The change from the diversity of prerevolutionary literary culture to the Soviet alternative was accomplished only with a considerable disruption in production, distribution, and consumption of the printed word. When Soviet authorities jettisoned established publishing institutions, distribution networks, cadres of writers, types of publications, and familiar popular vocabularies and literary formulas, they naturally disrupted the circulation of the printed word. The authorities' rejection of consumer preference as a guide to what should be published also resulted in a sharp break in the reading practices of ordinary people, who were unable to circumvent official policies. The shortfall in the availability of information in printed form probably affected Soviet society in a variety of ways at a time when the electronic media of film and radio were not yet sufficiently established to serve as effective substitutes. In politics, a lack of information about the new government and its policies may have contributed to a pattern of authoritarian relations between rulers and ruled. In the economy, a lack of information probably raised production and distribution costs, as producers had more difficulty locating inputs, and consumers no longer had the advertisements that appeared in the prerevolutionary press. The scarcity of printed material resulted in increased reliance on oral communication and oral traditions. The interruption in the flow of information changed political, economic, and cultural life, and was part of the cultural and intellectual reality of everyday life in the early years of Soviet power.

APPENDIX

TABLE 1: Quantity of Books and Pamphlets Published in All Languages[a], 1912–1927 (in Thousands)

	All Titles	All Copies
1912	34.6	133,562
1917	13.1	140,000
1918	6.1[b]	77,700
1919	3.7[b]	54,600
1920	3.3[b]	33,800
1921	4.1[b]	28,300
1922	7.8[b]	34,000
1923	10.8[b]	67,000
1924	13.1[b]	110,000
1925	26.3	278,000
1926	28.4	206,000
1927	27.7	212,000

Sources: G. I. Porshnev, *Etiudy po knizhnomu delu* (Moscow-Leningrad, 1924), pp. 31–35; N. F. Ianitskii, ed., *Kniga v. 1924 g. v SSSR* (Moscow, 1925), pp. 16, 18, 57; *Statistika proizvedenii pechati vyshedshikh v Rossii v. 1912 r.* (St. Petersburg, 1913).
[a]Data for the year 1912 indicate that 1,116,000 copies of 27,400 titles were published in Russian alone. Data for Russian titles are not available for the other years.
[b]I used figures given in Porshnev for these years; Ianitskii (p. 57) gives higher figures, particularly for 1923 and 1924. He lists 18.6 and 29.1 thousand titles for these years. I have no explanation for the discrepancy. Porshnev's figures are closer to those available by subject. See Table 7.

TABLE 2: Newspapers and Periodicals Published in the Russian Empire and Soviet Union

	Twice Daily	Daily	2–4 Times Weekly	Weekly	Total
1910	6	506	202	633	1347
1914	12	824	240	691	1767
1915	10	584	176	512	1282
1924		150	150	348	648
1925		107	129	298	534
1928		201	254	247	702

Sources: Statistika proizvedenii pechati v Rossii v 1910 g., 1914, 1915 (St. Petersburg, 1911, 1915, 1916), pp. 111,113,99; *Kniga v. 1924 g. v SSSR* (Moscow, 1925?), pp. 75, 83; *Kniga v 1925 g.* (Moscow-Leningrad, 1927), pp. 93–95; *Piatiletnii plan khoziastva pechati SSSR* (Moscow, 1929), pp. 82, 102.

TABLE 3: Number of Daily[a] Copies of Soviet Newspapers
(in Thousands)

	1917	1918	1919	1920	1921(end)	1922	1923	1924
Pravda	30	80	138	250	265(250)		80	400
Izvestiia	35		452	350	350(275)		180	350
Bednota		50	240	570	350(275)		49	55
Rabochaia gazeta						—	150	200
Krestianskaia gazeta							50	124
Gudok			30	30	—	60	100	190
Total Copies			830	1200	945(800)	60	609	1319
Copies of All Soviet Papers			—	—	—	993[b]	1882	2520

Sources: Vertinskii, *Gazeta v Rossii i SSSR* (Moscow-Leningrad, 1931), pp. 135–39, 148–150; V. Molotov, *Politika Partii v derevne* (Moscow-Leningrad, 1926), p. 24; *Izvestiia*, May 4, 1924, *Rabochaia Moskva*, May 5, 1923.
[a]Except for *Krest'ianskaia gazeta,* which was published weekly.
[b]This figure from *Rabochaia Moskva*, May 5, 1923, for August 1922 may represent the low point in the conversion to NEP conditions. *Izvestiia* (May 4, 1924) gives 2.7 million copies for January 1922 and 1.4 million for December 1922. *Bednota* (May 4, 1924) gives its circulation for 1923 as 30,000 and 1924 as 60,000 and the 1924 circulation of *Krest'ianskaia gazeta* as 200,000.

TABLE 4: Number of Printing Machines, 1912–1927

	Typesetting Machines	Rotary Presses	Flatbed Presses	Litho-graphs	Ameri-kanki*	Other
1912	560	182	5340	640	—	—
1921	411	147	4270	570	1987	3689
1924	348	135	3378	531	1140	3658
1926	407	119	—	420	945	3607
1927	493	—	3522	—	1174	4405

Source: Piatiletnii plan khoziaistva pechati SSSR (Moscow, 1928), p. 174.
*"Amerikanki" were small typographical machines invented in the middle of the nineteenth century and widely used then.

TABLE 5: Paper and Cardboard Production, 1913 through Fiscal Year 1928/1929

	Tons	% of 1913
1913	392,000	100.0
1918	70,100	17.9
1919	29,700	7.6
1920	34,700	8.9
1921	30,900	7.9
1921/22	34,200	8.7
1922/23	71,400	18.2
1923/24	126,300	32.2
1924/25	233,000	59.4
1925/26	263,000	67.1
1926/27	300,400	76.6
1927/28	321,500	82.0
1928/29	405,000	103.3

Source: Piatiletnii plan khoziaistva pechati SSSR (Moscow, 1929), p. 197.

TABLE 6: Subjects of Soviet Books as a Percent of All Titles

	1923	1924	1925
Social, Economic, Political (including Leninism and party literature)	20.5	30.0	23.6
Scientific and Popular Scientific (except exact sciences)	14.9	22.0*	14.0
Exact Sciences	10.1	—	6.3
Children and Youth	3.5	5.5	6.9
School and Pedagogical	9.9	9.8	10.3
Bibliography and Reference	6.3	6.3	7.4
Belles Lettres	13.0	9.7	9.1
Departmental (Vedomstvennaia literatura)	15.0	10.3	11.7
Other	6.8	6.4	8.7
Totals	100.0	100.0	98.0**

Source: Kniga v 1925 (Moscow-Leningrad, 1927), p. 62, and material from Table 7.
*In 1924, this number includes the exact sciences, too.
**The total equals only 98 percent in the source.

TABLE 7: Subjects of Books and Pamphlets, Published in
All Languages 1912–1927

Subject Code[a]	Number of Titles							
	1912	1915	1921	1922	1923	1925	1926	1927
0	2,266	1,561	71	217	365	1,018	1,134	1,071
I	353	105	22	76	79	147	142	139
II	3,659	2,216	14	68	136	192	149	133
III	10,423	9,360	2,465	4,871	3,389	10,512	11,220	10,381
IV	1,154	937	41	148	206	453	493	563
V	1,548	1,333	184	589	913	1,462	1,499	1,519
VI	3,286	2,253	845	1,794	1,653	4,952	5,297	4,720
VII	1,689	1,422	78	213	222	494	653	782
VIII	7,317	4,895	308	1,038	1,567	2,607	2,985	3,602
IX	2,936	1,961	102	328	470	1,430	1,100	1,208
Totals	34,631	26,043	4,130	9,342	9,000	23,267	24,672	24,118

Sources: Statistika proizvedenii pechati, vyshedshikh v Rossii v 1912 godu (St. Petersburg, 1913), pp. 2–5, *Statistika proizvedenii pechati, vyshedshikh v Rossii v 1915 godu* (Petrograd, 1916), pp. 4–9, N.F. Ianitskii, *Knizhnaia statistika sovetskoi Rossii, 1918–1923* (Moscow, 192?), p. 35, *Piatiletnii plan khoziaistva pechati SSSR* (Moscow, 1928), p. 67.

[a]0 General: books, libraries, bibliographies, almanacs, encyclopedias, dictionaries.
I Philosophy: philosophy, psychology, logic, ethics.
II Religion: religion and atheism.
III Soc. Science: sociology, historical materialism, statistics, politics, economics, finance, government, law, army-navy, insurance, education, transport, metrology.
IV Philology: linguistics, foreign languages, Russian language.
V Exact Science: natural science, mathematics, astronomy, physics, chemistry, geology, biology, botany, zoology.
VI Applied Science: medicine, veterinary science, engineering, mining, transport technology, agriculture, printing, accounting, trades, crafts, building.
VII Art: art, architecture, music, theater, sculpture, games, sports.
VIII Belles Lettres: theory and history of literature, criticism, foreign and Russian literature.
IX History: history, geography, biography.
Note: Children's stories and popular songs were usually included in subject VIII in the Soviet period, and school books were allocated by subject. I have reclassified prerevolutionary headings as follows: school materials (II=15%, IV=45%, V=20%, VI=10%, IX=10%), children's books (II=20%, VIII=80%), and "people's publications" (II=35%, III=5%, V=5%, VI=5%, VIII=50%).

TABLE 8: Subjects of Books and Pamphlets, 1912–1927
(in Millions of Copies)

Subject*	1912 In All Langs.	(In Russian)	1915 In All Langs.	(In Russian)	1922	1925	1926	1927
General	22.3	(17.6)	11.7	(9.3)	1.6	16.4	11.6	14.7
Philosophy	.8	(.6)	.2	(.2)	.2	.9	.7	.8
Religion	22.4	(16.2)	14.6	(11.3)	.2	2.8	.9	.6
Social Sciences	14.1	(12.4)	31.2	(29.6)	12.1	94.6	68.8	75.7
Philology	9.2	(8.3)	8.8	(8.0)	3.0	19.5	12.9	12.5
Exact Sciences	6.6	(5.9)	5.5	(5.0)	3.4	12.7	10.9	8.9
Applied Sciences	13.3	(12.1)	6.1	(5.6)	7.7	40.1	31.7	21.3
Art	2.1	(1.9)	1.8	(1.7)	.4	3.2	4.0	4.6
Belles Lettres	33.4	(28.1)	22.2	(19.5)	3.5	30.3	30.1	46.4
History and Geography	9.5	(8.3)	5.9	(5.4)	1.9	21.5	7.6	9.0
Totals	133.7	(111.4)	108.0	(95.6)	34.0	242.0	179.2	194.5

Sources: Statistika proizvedenii pechati, vyshedshikh v Rossii v 1912 godu (St. Petersburg, 1913), pp. 2–5, Statistika proizvedenii pechati, vyshedshikh v Rossii v 1915 godu (St. Petersburg, 1916), pp. 4–9, Pechat' RSFSR v 1922 godu (Moscow, 192?), p. 27, Piatiletnii plan khoziaistva pechati SSSR (Moscow, 1929), p. 67.

*See Table 7 for an explanation of subject categories. Slight differences between these totals and those in other tables are due to rounding. Substantial differences between the totals for 1925–27 and those given in Table 1 are apparently due to the quality of the data.

TABLE 9: Subjects of Soviet Books
(in Percent of Printers Sheets)

	1925	1926	1927
General	7.9	8.1	9.2
Philosophy	0.0	.5	.3
Religion	1.0	1.0	.4
Social Science	38.4	36.5	33.7
Philology	13.9	13.9	13.6
Exact Sciences	7.6	8.9	8.3
Applied Sciences	10.7	13.6	11.2
Art	.9	1.1	1.4
Belles Lettres	8.7	11.4	16.7
History and Geography	10.3	5.3	5.3
Totals*	99.4	99.8	100.1

Source: Piatiletnii plan khoziaistva pechati SSSR (Moscow, 1929), p. 67.
*Totals do not equal 100.0 due to rounding.

TABLE 10: Newspaper Content (in Percent of Total Space)

	Gazeta kopeika		Rabochaia Moskva		Bednota		Kres'ian-skaia gazeta
	1913	1917	1922	1923	1922	1923	1926
Foreign affairs	12	10	10	20	15	18	12
Domestic politics	4	8	5	2	5	0	0
Urban life (Workers)	5	9	20	21	0	0	2
Rural life (Peasants)	1	0	7	1	30	19	35
Economy	0	1	3	7	6	19	16
"Party life"	0	0	9	7	1	3	5
Culture and education	5	5	10	7	1	2	4
Entertainment/fiction	11	13	5	2	10	2	4
Police and law	8	3	1	3	5	4	0
Happenings and news briefs	9	9	3	7	2	0	2
Agronomy and science	0	0	1	1	17	14	4
Religion	1	1	3	2	5	3	0
Army/WWI	0	17	5	2	2	3	5
Headlines	1	0	0	0	0	4	0
Ads	43	24	18	16	0	4	4
Other	0	0	0	0	0	4	4
Total*	100	100	100	98	99	99	99

Sources: Gazeta kopeika, January 4–10, 1913, and 1917, Rabochaia Moskva, Feb. 17, 19, 21–26, 1922, and Feb. 2–4, 6–10, 1923. Bednota, Jan. 3, 5–6, 10, 12, 13, 15, 1922, and Jan. 4–5, 10–14, 1923. Krest'ianskaia gazeta, Feb. 2, 9, 16, 23, March 2, 9, 16, 1926.
*Total may not equal 100 due to rounding.

NOTES

1. I am grateful to the International Research and Exchanges Board, Fulbright-Hays, and the National Endowment for the Humanities for support. I thank Jean Hellie, Richard Hellie, and Arcadius Kahan for their comments, and Louise McReynolds for her assistance.

2. *Izvestiia*, May 4, 1924; N. S. Vertinskii, *Gazeta v Rossii* (Moscow-Leningrad, 1931), p. 139.

3. *Kniga v 1925 godu* (Moscow-Leningrad, 1927), pp. 84, 96–97. Many of the newspapers were weeklies rather than dailies.

4. A. Z. Okorokov, *Oktiabr' i krakh russkoi burzhuaznoi pressy* (Moscow, 1970), p. 55.

5. *Vsesoiuznaia perepis' naseleniia 1926 goda,* volume 17 (Moscow, 1929), pp. 2–3, 48–49.

6. Ia. Shafir, *Gazeta i derevnia* (Moscow-Leningrad, 1924), pp. 94–98.

7. G. Mezhericher, "Bumazhnaia promyshlennost' " *Narodnoe khoziaistvo,* Nos. 6–7 (1921), pp. 96–105.

8. *Piatiletnii plan khoziaistva pechati SSSR* (Moscow, 1929), p. 198.

9. *Rabochaia Moskva,* February 7, 1923. There was also a rural supplement with a circulation of 20,000, according to the same article.

10. Ibid., p. 181.

11. *Izdatel'skoe delo v pervye gody Sovetskoi vlasti (1917–22)* (Moscow, 1972), pp. 72–73, 128–29.

12. V. Smushkov, "Raspredelenie proizvedenii pechati," *Pechat' i revolutsiia,* No. 1 (1921), pp. 38–39.

13. *Kniga v 1924 g. v SSSR,* N. F. Ianitskii, ed. (Moscow, 1925?), p. 218.

14. A. I. Nazarov, *Oktiabr' i kniga* (Moscow, 1968), p. 227.

15. *Izvestiia,* July 3–7, 1923.

16. *Kniga v 1924,* p. 210–11. V. R. Leikina-Svirskaia, *Russkaia intelligentsiia v 1900–1917 godakh* (Moscow, 1981), p. 121, puts the number of bookshops at 2,000 in 1910.

17. *Piatiletnii plan,* p. 223; *Knizhnaia letopis',* No. 1 (1907), p. 19, and No. 6 *(1907),* p. 27. The 1906 St. Petersburg figure includes *Knizhnye sklady, magaziny, lavry.* The Moscow figure given is 584 points at which books were sold, but this also includes kiosks. In 1890, N. A. Rubakin counted 205 bookshops in Moscow and 142 in St. Petersburg. (Rubakin Archive in the Manuscript Division of the Lenin Library, fond 358, k. 12 d. 16.)

18. Ibid., p. 212.

19. G. I. Porshnev. *Etiudy po knizhnomu delu* (Moscow-Leningrad, 1929), pp. 33–34. The 1927 figure excludes bookshelves at cooperatives and post offices. It is unclear what exactly is included in the prerevolutionary figure.

20. Cited in A. A. Govorov, *Istoriia knizhnoi torgovli v SSSR* (Moscow, 1976), p. 93.

21. *Bednota,* May 4, 1924.

22. *Piatiletnii plan,* pp. 219–20, and M. I. Slukhovskii, *Kniga i derevnia* (Moscow-Leningrad, 1928), pp. 148–51.

23. Slukhovskii, pp. 150–51; and A. Meromskii and P. Putnik, *Derevnia za knigoi* (Moscow, 1931), pp. 31–32.

24. Slukhovskii, p. 158.

25. I. Vareikis, *Zadachi Partii v oblasti pechati* (Moscow-Leningrad, 1926), p. 8.

26. Ibid., p. 8. M. Kalinin claimed in *Bednota,* May 4, 1924, that the number of individual peasant subscriptions to that paper rose from 7,000 in 1922 to 30,000 in 1923, and 60,000 in 1924. This was the full circulation of the newspaper.

27. *Piatiletnii plan*, p. 229.
28. *Bolezni nashego pechatnogo dela* (Moscow, 1924), p. 12.
29. Porshnev, p. 35.
30. Slukhovskii, p. 159.
31. Porshnev, pp. 44–45.
32. *Piatiletnii plan*, p. 222.
33. Ibid., p. 277.
34. *Bolezni nashego pechatnogo delo*, p. 5.
35. *Piatiletnii plan*, p. 276.
36. Vareikis, p. 10.
37. Ibid., p. 9.
38. *Piatiletnii plan*, pp. 283–84.
39. *Kniga v 1925*, p. 43.
40. *Vystavka proizvedenii pechati za 1909* (St. Petersburg, 1910), pp. 15–18.
41. Jeffrey Brooks, "Studies of the Reader in the 1920s," *Russian History*, Nos. 2–3 (1982), pp. 187–202.
42. M. A. Smushkova, *Pervye itogi izucheniia chitatelia* (Moscow-Leningrad, 1926), pp. 10–22, and Smushkova, *Bibliotechnaia rabota v derevne* (Moscow-Leningrad, 192?), p. 76.
43. B. Bank and A. Vilenkin, *Krest'ianskaia molodezh i kniga* (Moscow-Leningrad, 1929), p. 210; and Meromskii and Putnik, p. 159.
44. Slukhovskii, pp. 70–71.
45. Ibid., p. 81.
46. Porshnev, p. 63.
47. E. H. Carr, *Socialism in One Country*, vol. 1 (New York, 1958), pp. 65–66.
48. A. Pokrovskii, "O chistke bibliotek," *Krasnyi bibliotekar*, No. 1 (1923), pp. 13–20.
49. Slukhovskii, pp. 86–89.
50. *Massovyi chitatel' i kniga*, N. D. Rybnikov, ed. (Moscow, 1925), p. 39.
51. Slukhovskii, p. 27.
52. Compiled from *Knizhnaia letopis'*.
53. Meromskii and Putnik, p. 166; B. Bank and A. Vilenkin, *Derevenskaia bednota i biblioteka* (Moscow-Leningrad, 1927), p. 79; Bank and Vilenkin, 1929, pp. 178–79; Slukhovskii, pp. 64–66.
54. Slukhovskii, p. 27.
55. *Bolezni nashego pechatnego dela*, p. 11.
56. Ibid., pp. 13–14; Slukhovskii, p. 67.
57. G. Kh. Ryklin, *Kak sovetskaia pechat' pomogaet krest'ianinu* (Moscow-Leningrad, 1926), p. 31.
58. *Statistika proizvedenii pechati vyshedshikh v 1910 godu* (St. Petersburg, 1911), p. 2.
59. Ibid., p. 2.
60. Maurice Friedberg, *Russian Classics in Soviet Jackets* (New York, 1962), pp. 15–41.
61. Ibid., pp. 184, 190–91.
62. Jeffrey Brooks, "Russian Nationalism and Russian Literature: the Canonization of the Classics," in *Nation and Ideology: Essays in Honor of Wayne S. Vucinich*, eds. Ivo Banac, John G. Ackerman, and Roman Szporluk (Boulder, Colo., 1981), pp. 315–34.
63. *Vystavka proizvedenii pechati*, p. 16.
64. *Chto chitaiut vzroslye rabochie i sluzhashchie po belletristike* (Moscow, 1928), p. 20; G. Neradov, "Proizvodstvo klassikov," *Biuleten' Gosudarstvennogo izdatel'stva*, Nos. 31–32 (23 August 1928), p. 3.

65. Slukhovskii, p. 16; see also Meromskii and Putnik, p. 149.

66. *Chto chitaiut vzroslye rabochie*, pp. 14–19; and B. Bank and A. Vilenkin, 1927, p. 39; Bank and Vilenkin, 1929, p. 35.

67. Smushkova, *Itogi*, pp. 13–16; Slukhovskii, pp. 102–22.

68. Slukhovskii, pp. 110–20.

69. Cheap fiction was serialized in newspapers and sold separately at newsstands. *Lubochnaia literatura* was the term used for the Russian equivalent to English chapbooks and penny dreadfuls, but the term was also used more generally to apply to all cheap popular literature. See A. V. Blium, "Russkaia lubochnaia kniga vtoroi poloviny xix veka," in *Kniga issledovaniia i materialy, sbornik xlii* (Moscow, 1981), pp. 94–114.

70. Slukhovskii, p. 16.

71. I discuss some of the ways in which novels serialized in *Gazeta kopeika* served this purpose in "The Kopeck novels of Early Twentieth Century Russia," *Journal of Popular Culture*, Vol. xiii, No. 1 (Summer 1979), pp. 85–97, and more generally in *When Russia Learned to Read, 1861–1917*, forthcoming from Princeton University Press.

72. I. Vareikis, p. 26.

73. Smushkova, *Bibliotechnaia rabota*, pp. 75–76.

74. Slukhovskii, p. 42.

75. *Statistika proizvedenii pechati vyshedshikh v Rossii v 1912 godu* (St. Petersburg, 1913); N. F. Ianitskii, ed., *Kniga v 1924 v SSSR* (Moscow, 1925), pp. 28–29; *Kniga v 1925 godu* (Moscow-Leningrad, 1927), p. 62.

76. Slukhovskii, p. 115.

77. *Bednota*, June 16, 1922.

78. Ia. Shafir, *Rabochaia gazeta i ee chitatel'* (Moscow, 1926), pp. 143–54.

79. Ibid., p. 100.

80. Ibid., p. 108.

81. Ibid., pp. 171–79.

82. Brooks, "The Kopeck Novels of Early Twentieth Century Russia," pp. 85–97.

83. *Bednota*, February 6, 13, 17, 1923.

84. Shafir, *Rabochaia gazeta*, p. 196.

85. Ibid., p. 221.

86. Shafir, *Gazeta i derevnia*, pp. 75–89.

87. *Derevenskaia politprosvetrabota* (Leningrad, 1926), pp. 220–21.

88. Smushkova, *Itogi*, pp. 37–39; Ia. Shafir, *Gazeta i derevnia*, pp. 71–72, 75–82; Slukhovskii, pp. 119–21; and Meromskii and Putnik, pp. 170–71.

89. Meromskii and Putnik, p. 169.

90. *Vsesoiuznia perepis'*, pp. 48–49.

91. *Pravda*, May 22, 1924; and *Istoriia kommunisticheskoi partii sovetskogo soiuza*, vol. 4, part 1 (Moscow, 1970), p. 480.

92. Ralph T. Fisher, *Pattern for Soviet Youth* (New York, 1959), appendix B.

93. *Sovetskaia demokratiia*, ed. Iu. M. Steklov (Moscow, 1929), p. 203; A. Glebov, *Pamiatka sel'kora* (Moscow, 1925), p. 5.

94. Slukhovskii, pp. 93–95; Shafir, *Gazeta i derevnia*, pp. 113–28.

[10] The City versus the Countryside in Soviet Peasant Literature of the Twenties: A Duel of Utopias

Katerina Clark

THE TWENTIES MIGHT be called the most utopian of all the Soviet decades. The utopian impulse was felt in those years not only among the Bolsheviks and other enthusiasts for the Revolution but among many of the uncommitted intellectuals as well.

Two periods during this decade were especially utopian: the first corresponds approximately to the years of revolution and War Communism, 1917–21, and the second to the years of the First Five-Year Plan, 1928–31. Between the two came a less sharply defined period (the years of NEP), when the utopian impulse was still felt but was diluted by other currents.

The peasant question, and peasant literature as well, were among the special foci of utopian dreaming and striving in the twenties. There are obvious reasons why this should have been so. For instance, since the peasantry was that social class or category in old Russia which had been hardest to fit into the traditional Marxist models for revolution, it provided a good sandbox where the theorists could play about. Above all, however, the intellectuals of the twenties had behind them a tradition over half a century old of thinking up schemes to save the peasant from his grim lot, and of romanticizing the peasant and his commune.

Before the Revolution, there had been no consensus among intellectuals about what to do with the peasant. Thinking about the peasant and his lot had been inextricably bound up with the great either/ors over which the intelligentsia had been agonizing in trying to decide Russia's way forward. Should they modernize the country, or revive traditional Russian social and economic forms? More specifically, should they look to the great cities and cultural centers of Europe as models, or favor the more chaotic, higgledy-piggledy, Russian-style hamlets and small towns? The traditional Russian town might be more "backward" if measured by a European yardstick but, some argued, was more organically Russian, offered an atmosphere less stultifying and unhealthy, and was superior "spiritually" as well. In the twenties, these old dichotomies resurfaced in the debates and literature on the peasant, albeit in slightly altered form (for instance, the industrialized American city had eclipsed the European city as a model). In literature, one could talk of a "duel of utopias" between the anti-urbanists and the urbanists, with anti-urbanist ideology dominating during the first utopian phase of the twenties,[1] and the urbanist during the second.

The Bolshevik experiment, on the whole, stood for what might be called the "urbanist" side of the various dichotomies—after all, theirs was to be a "proletarian" revolution. The "vanguard" of the proletariat was to overthrow the stagnant, bourgeois order and institute a new age of efficiency, increased industrialization and technology, universal education, and so on. This was to be effected in a country that was overwhelmingly peasant, but the blueprint for the village was largely a subfunction of the urban model. Under the rubric "*smychka,*" or "alliance" between town and country, some of the peasantry were to be coopted into the urban labor force, and as for the rest, their lot was to be improved by bringing the "city" to the countryside with modernization, large-scale, mechanized agriculture, education—and all those "*lampochki Il'icha*" (Ilyich's lightbulbs).

During the Civil War, despite the chaos and hardship in rural areas, the regime's policy in the countryside reflected, in Moshe Lewin's words, "the general current of Utopianism which prevailed within the Party. Collectivist organizations in rural areas . . . received a vigorous stimulus."[2] The cause of peasant enlightenment was not neglected, either. At the First All-Russian Conference of Party Workers in November 1919, it was proposed to set up a network of special reading rooms or "*izby chital'nye*" in the villages as a "base" from which the cause of fostering education and greater consciousness among peasants might be prosecuted. Before long, the number of *izby chital'nye* burgeoned to 80,000.[3]

Such utopian gestures notwithstanding, it could not in fact be said that in the early twenties the Party paid much attention to the lot of the village *per se,* and especially not to providing literature for it. Admittedly, the peasantry were largely uneducated or poorly educated, but at the same time, according to the 1926 census, it was in the countryside that 71 percent of the literate people lived. As Jeffrey Brooks has shown, the early twenties saw a radical decline in the number of newspapers and book titles produced for the rural reader.[4] The means of distribution for such materials were inadequate, and in many areas virtually nonexistent. Also, such titles as were published for peasant readers were often unappealing to them and not read.[5]

During the first half of the twenties there was no major, Party-oriented peasant literature. In the prestigious "thick journals" such works about peasants by committed writers as did get published were primarily about their role in the Civil War (e.g., D. Furmanov's *Chapaev* of 1923 or A. Serafimovich's *The Iron Flood* of 1924), or about the woman question (such as L. Seifulina's *Virineia* of 1924). This is by no means to say that peasant writers or the old peasant questions were ignored in fiction. At this time varieties of peasant literature were extremely popular.

The leading peasant writers in the first utopian phase were all non-Party. They—Petr Oreshin, Pimen Karpov, Shiriaevets (the pseudonym of Aleksandr V. Abramov), Sergei Klychkov, Nikolai Kliuev, and to some extent Sergei Esenin—more or less formed a group and shared a common biographical pattern.[6] They were all born in villages between 1887 and 1895. After receiving some education (in many cases fairly rudimentary), they gravitated to Moscow or Petersburg where they joined literary circles and began publishing during the decade leading up to the Revolution. After the Revolution, which they all greeted with enthusiasm, they typically became founding members of the Peasant Section of Proletcult (founded 1918) and later joined the Union of Peasant Writers. Thus they might seem to represent the voice of the peasant in the post-revolutionary era.

In reality, however, they had been coopted, to varying degrees, into the ranks of the urban bourgeois intelligentsia. They were its exotics, its "folk." Before the Revolution they had learned the advantages of wearing a peasant shirt if one wanted to gain entry into the salons of the élite. The majority of the peasant writers were then heavily influenced by Symbolism, a West European importation which dominated Russian literature at the turn of this century. They sought approval and guidance (and in some instances received it) from such leading Symbolists as Blok and Bely. They were also patronized and organized into literary groups by the Acmeist poet S. Gorodetsky who, on the eve of the Revolution, tried unsuccessfully to unite the Acmeists and the peasant writers in a group called the Guild of Poets. Kliuev, the peasant writers' leading ideologist, tried to educate himself to compensate for his deprived background and read much of the abstruse Western philosophy and mysticism which engrossed certain sections of the intelligentsia at the time; his reward was to be accepted as an interlocutor by some leading thinkers of the day, and to become a darling of the highbrow intelligentsia.[7] Even Mandelshtam, himself something of a cultural snob, was an admirer of Kliuev. Esenin, on the other hand, attracted interest more by his outrageous behaviour and verse, which appealed to the current vogues for decadence and anarchism; he found his greatest readership among urban youth.

Ironically, this particular generation of peasant writers, though influenced by a literary movement which began as an echo of Western trends, espoused an anti-Western ideology, known as "muzhik socialism" or "Kliuevism." This ideology was basically a Slavophile variant of populism, but with anarchistic coloring. Its adherents were anti-Western, anti-urban, against all government, and, though most were religious, many were against the organized Orthodox Church, preferring more spontaneous folk expressions of a combination of Orthodox faith and pagan beliefs. They wanted power and land for the peasant, but only so that he might lead an idyllic Russian peasant existence, unhindered by bureaucrats.

As this program suggests, the peasant writers' attachment to the urban highbrow intelligentsia was fraught with ambivalence and tensions. After the Bolshevik Revolution, however, the two groups were close for a time. They stepped out into the post-revolutionary era in an alliance—a movement known as Scythianism—which was to become the most popular literary movement in Russia during the first utopian phase. The Scythian movement was led by urban bourgeois intellectuals like Blok, Bely, Ivanov-Razumnik, and Pilniak (who was admittedly a provincial, but from the town rather than the village and with professional training). The peasant writers were junior partners in it, but most of the above-named were either members of the Scythian group, or contributed to its almanac, *The Scythians,* of 1918.

Scythianism viewed the Revolution—the "proletarian" revolution—as the triumph of the Russian village over the urban way of life. It was able to do so because it found a role for the Revolution in a version of the old Slavophile lament about Russia's downfall under Peter the Great. During Peter's reign, the lament would have it, a new way of life, a way antithetical to Russian traditions, had been imported from Europe and imposed on the country. The Scythians rejoiced in the overthrow of the Old Order because it was, as Pilniak reminded his readers *ad nauseam,* the Old Order of Peter, Catherine, et al. which had taken a "straight edge" to higgledy-piggledy old Russia and replaced it with the loathsome "straight roads," "granite," and "cast iron." These writers saw the Revolution as expressing the rage of the Russian peasant who had been kept in check so long by the alien, oppressive system. In all the violent upheaval and chaos, the peasant had effectively dismantled the city and returned Russia, willy-nilly, to her natural, anarchic state.

The peasant writers among the Scythians were the more aggressively anti-urban. After a brief flurry of enthusiasm for the new age, they soon began to expose in their writings the evils of industrialization and urbanization, and to attack those contemporary writers of both the avant-garde and the "proletarian" camp who sang the praises of the smokestack, the blast furnace . . . the city.[8]

Their views on these particular issues were widely shared at the time, for the first utopian phase was marked by anti-urbanist writing. There were, for instance, the peasant utopias, such as Esenin's long poem "Inonia" (written January 1918) and Chaianov's *Journey of My Brother Aleksei to the Land of*

Peasant Utopia, Part I of which he published in 1920 under the pseudonym Iv. Kremnëv (Part II was never passed by the censor). These works were country cousins of the anti-utopias attacking the urbanist ideal which were written at the same time, such as Zamiatin's *We* (written 1920–21), and Lunts's *City of Truth* (published posthumously in 1924). The authors of these anti-urbanist tracts were almost all from the urban bourgeoisie (except for the déraciné Esenin). Thus we find the first utopian phase of the twenties marked by an urbanist anti-urbanism in literature.

Of the various anti-urbanist utopias dating from these years the one which gives by far the most comprehensive account of the utopia is Chaianov's *The Journey.* In this book, following the conventions of utopian literature, Chaianov takes his hero, Aleksei Kremnëv, away from the society to which he is accustomed (in this case Moscow of the early twenties) to a society separated radically in time and space: Aleksei falls into a swoon and wakes up sixty years later, in 1984 *(sic),* to find Moscow completely changed. A second, peasant revolution of 1934 has succeeded the Bolshevik one and has implemented the anti-urban dream.

One of the earliest reforms instituted by the new peasant government has been to reduce all cities to a population not exceeding 20,000. This they have done first by relocating the rail centers and factories to a radius some distance from each city. Next, all the "huge stone edifices" Pilniak so deplored in the modern Russian city were systematically demolished, leaving primarily wooden buildings of the seventeenth and eighteenth centuries, no higher than two stories. The resulting vacant spaces are used as parklands: the urban metropolis has become like the "hamlet from Northern Russia"; in other words an ideal has been realized very like the one Solzhenitsyn was to propose much later in his *Letter to the Soviet Leaders* (1974).[9]

An important principle behind this radical move was to break down the distinction between town and country: that great gulf is reduced to a mere difference between the more and the less densely populated areas. The cities are now of such low population density that they stretch for many miles. The aim is not just to have fewer people per square mile, however; the rural way of life is privileged over the urban. Most of the population lives on individual farms, one per family as in old Russia, and of about 3–4 desyatins in area. Although relatively small, these farms are spectacularly productive, yielding 500 poods per desyatin instead of the normal 40. The reasons for this are never satisfactorily explained but include the greater consciousness and commitment on the farmer's part and the fact that the weather is now controlled by magnetic fields.

This is not the only example of fuzziness in Chaianov's account of the peasant utopia. His failure to explain satisfactorily how his society achieved economic prosperity is in part because many of its policies involved turning back the clock. *The Journey* is not merely an anti-urbanist tract, but distinctly neo-Slavophile. The peasant society it extolls has made a conscious effort to revive old Russia and the pre-Petrine way of life; the strong, patriarchal family is a cornerstone of the new society; all dwellings are built in styles which predate Western influence, and their decor is traditional, usually with a profusion of icons; the old Russian games, such as knucklebones, have been revived as national sports; the guards wear the uniforms of the streltsy from the days of Aleksei Mikhailovich; and the protagonist who is the chief spokesman for the new society is named Minin, presumably after one of the men who saved Russia from foreign dominion during the Time of Troubles.

It is clear that what is intended is to revive not just the trappings of the old way of life, but also that elusive quality, Russian spirituality, the purported loss of which in the new materialist society has troubled many a thinker in the Soviet period, right down to Solzhenitsyn and others in the present day. Although Chaianov mentions schemes for ensuring that the farmers have economic incentives, for rationalizing farm methods, and so on, it is evident that in the peasant utopia the aim of gaining true spirituality has priority over all economic and organizational considerations. For instance, although Minin admits that the manual methods of farming he advocates are less productive, he chides Aleksei for being too "American" in wanting to see more mechanization; Minin justifies his farming methods by referring to some vague "law of diminishing fertility of the soil," but it is clear that in the best traditions of Tolstoy he believes in what field work can do for your soul.[10] Chaianov is cagey— presumably for reasons of censorship—about whether Russian Orthodoxy is the national religion of his peasant utopia, though he hints occasionally that the country has become a theocracy.[11] It seems likely that at the very least the lives of the citizens are permeated with a secular religiosity derived from Russian traditions.

Although Chaianov's *The Journey* contains many such points of difference with Bolshevik thinking, one can find considerable common ground between the two. In particular, both believe the ideal society can be reached by social engineering and by raising the consciousness of the masses. They both stress in their formulae for social engineering the regenerative power of sports and rhythmic gymnastics, and of course labor (in the case of *The Journey*, the faith in labor's formative influence on the individual is so great that all youths have to undergo two years of compulsory military/labor service even though, thanks to various inventions, conscription has been rendered redundant for military purposes). They also both believe culture must play a crucial role in forming the superior man and a superior society.[12]

Like the Bolsheviks, the founding fathers of the peasant utopia were particularly concerned to overcome the chronic cultural backwardness of the village.

Indeed, many of the measures they adopted to this end are not unlike programs adopted in the Soviet Union to bring culture to the people (such as traveling exhibitions of art and special boarding schools for the gifted). The principal panacea used in the peasant utopia, moreover, is quite uncharacteristic of anti-urbanist utopias: the new society uses various futuristic forms of rapid mass transit and commuter airplanes to ensure that no man lives more than an hour's travel from a cultural center, thus eradicating the village's traditional isolation and cultural deprivation.[13]

Chaianov's position, then, differs from Kliuevism in that he does not advocate turning one's back on the achievements of industrialization and modern social theory, and retreating to the idyllic hamlet in the Russian forest. Rather, he advocates a synthesis of the old and the new in the service of abolishing the evils of the modern metropolis. Thus his theories more directly rival those of the Bolsheviks than does "muzhik socialism."

Culture and art play a much more crucial role in Chaianov's utopia than they do in the Bolshevik world, however, and in this respect *The Journey* stands more in the tradition of the other peasant utopias of the early twenties. Whereas the Bolsheviks saw art as providing an adornment for the citizens' lives and spiritual enrichment, in the peasant utopias art and aesthetic sensibility are the key or mainspring of each utopian scheme: the utopias are not, at base, written to advocate a return to peasant society or rural life. That is a *means* rather than an end, the actual *telos* being to maximize the aesthetic in both the environment and the inner life of man. Several peasant utopians, such as Kliuev, stress the crucial role the various peasant arts and crafts play in giving peasants an aesthetic and moral sensibility without which life becomes sterile and meaningless.[14] Chaianov, for his part, calls ordinary citizens in his realized utopia "creators," and their leaders and planners "artists."[15] Moreover, there is a very telling incident in the closing chapters of *The Journey*. An attack from Germany is repelled decisively, thanks to the Russians' futuristic technology. The Germans ask for peace, and offer to pay reparations in any form, where-upon the Russians request paintings from German museums by Botticelli and other masters, plus—as if an afterthought to show this really is a peasant utopia—a thousand pedigreed cattle.

The peasant utopians of the early twenties can be seen, inasmuch as they privileged the aesthetic in their utopias, as close to another highly idealistic and extremist—utopian—movement of the same time, the avant-garde (i.e., groups such as the Futurists-cum-constructivists, and the writers and theater and film people connected with the Formalists. These groups saw the heightening of aesthetic consciousness in all citizens as a precondition for realizing a superior and socialistic society. Of course each of the various avant-garde and peasant utopian groups favored a different kind of art as the key to heightening aesthetic and moral sensibility: most peasant writers favored icons and peasant crafts; Chaianov mentioned them but mostly wanted the masses to be steeped in conventional, highbrow culture (he specifically rejected Futurist art[16]); the Futurists et al. favored modernist, experimental, and often non-representational art.

Thus, in a sense, in the early twenties the urbanist/anti-urbanist controversy was but one of many divisions within a general utopian movement. The various factions within the movement had in common a belief that in order to attain an ideal society the people had to "grow" in consciousness.[17] The anti-urban utopians and the avant-garde stressed the aesthetic as a crucial factor in raising consciousness, while the Bolsheviks stressed enlightenment, technology, and political and economic factors. The anti-urban utopians insisted that the city should be dismantled as a first step in providing an aesthetic and therefore beneficial environment for human development, while the avant-garde and the Bolsheviks hailed the city as the environment of the future. These differences notwithstanding, then, all three groups were clearly embroiled in the one utopian debate of the early post-revolutionary years.

As the twenties progressed, the divisions between the various participants in the debate widened, and the non-Party participants were progressively emasculated, especially in the late twenties. Thus the pattern of relatively *public* debate on these issues that was characteristic of the first utopian phase was to change radically by the end of the decade. As far as coverage of the peasant question in literature is concerned, a no less significant factor in the changes after 1922 was new directions in the Party itself.

As the country drew away from the Civil War (in which the peasantry had played such a crucial role) and the government put most of its efforts behind postwar reconstruction and modernizing the economy, the utopian phase in Party policy for the village came to an end. The *izby-chital'nye* were closed down, and many of the peasants who had joined communes during the period of War Communism soon left them.[18] Not that the Party had prosecuted its utopian policies in the village very aggressively between 1917 and 1921. With all its other crises and concerns during the Civil War, it had kept the cause of bringing socialism to the village somewhat on the back burner, which may in itself account for the fact that "peasant" literature of this period was dominated by non-Party intellectuals and anti-urbanists.

The popularity of anti-urbanist literature reached its peak in 1922, just after the Civil War, and fell away sharply thereafter. That is not to say that the peasant writers all stopped publishing. Esenin committed suicide in 1925; Kliuev found it increasingly hard to get published, especially after his "Lament for Esenin" came out in 1927. But several other peasant writers, notably Klychkov, published quite extensively in the mid twenties.

In the works of Klychkov and other peasant writers who continued to publish, however, one can detect a depoliticization of the manifest content. Whereas Klychkov was often heard in the immediately pre- and post-revolutionary period to propose that the peasant clear all non-peasant elements out of Russia—merchants, city dwellers, landowners, intellectuals, and clergy alike[19]—his poetry of the mid-twenties shows little of this bravado. Even his poem of 1926 with the forthright title, "We Have Strayed from the Paths of Nature," was much tamer than its title suggests.[20] Klychkov further adjusted to the times in that he followed the general drift of Soviet literature after 1924 by concentrating on long prose works rather than poetry as hitherto. He embarked on an ambitious nine-part epic about peasant life between the 1880s and the Revolution, *Life and Death*, only three disconnected volumes of which actually appeared. These novels represent something of a retreat in that they do not engage political themes very directly, and are highly reminiscent of pre-revolutionary Symbolist prose, except that in them Klychkov has made copious use of peasant speech. The works combine realistic description of peasant life at those times with fantastic events involving all manner of demons and the like from folk superstition.

Around 1926, as the anti-urbanist peasant writers were clearly waning in popularity and finding it harder to publish, a group of pro-urbanist peasant writers emerged for the first time as a group with any stature. In that year, the All-Russian Union of Peasant Writers (VKSP), to which had belonged most of the old-guard, anti-urbanist writers such as Kliuev, Oreshin, and Klychkov, was disbanded and a new All-Russian Society of Peasant Writers[21] (VOKP) formed. It was dominated by the new-guard, urbanist peasant writers. Most of the writers in this new guard had published before, but it was not until 1926 that their works had begun to attract much attention. No doubt the fact that the Party itself had begun to take much more interest in the peasant question around that time (in, e.g., the promuzhik versus pro-collectivization debates of 1925, and the discussions in the Communist Academy in 1926) was a factor in these writers' new prominence.

The biographies of the writers in this group (Aleksei Iakovlevich Doro-goichenko, Ivan Ivanovich Doronin, Petr Ivanovich Zamoisky, Ivan Ivanovich Makarov, Fedor Ivanovich Panferov, and Aleksei Artamanovich Tveriak) follow a fairly standard pattern. They were all born in rural Russia between 1894 and 1900, and the majority in 1900, i.e., five to thirteen years after the anti-urbanist peasant writers, a slight difference, but one which seems to have been crucial. Most of them were the children of poor peasants who joined the Party during the Civil War, or at least fought on the side of the Bolsheviks. After that, they either worked on a Soviet newspaper or joined a proletarian or peasant literary organization. Unlike the peasant writers who dominated Soviet literature during the first post-revolutionary utopian phase, the writers in this group had not published before the Revolution. It is hardly surprising that writers with this background—true sons of the Revolution, so to speak—became the spokesmen for the Party's urbanist vision for the village.

Prior to 1926, most of the literature produced by these Party-oriented peasant writers had been propagandistic and simplistic sketches and short poems. From 1926, however, they branched out into longer forms with, first, Doronin's seminal long poem "The Tractor Ploughman," hailed in those years as the first work to "speak for the new village, industrialized and electrified,"[22] and followed in the next year by the first novels on this subject. The most important of them was Dorogoichenko's *Bol'shaia Kamenka,* which was considered at the time to be peasant literature's answer to industrial fiction's *Cement* (by Gladkov) of 1925.[23]

Actually, the comparison with *Cement* could extend to most of these writers' fiction in the mid-twenties. Their novels were, for instance, all highly formulaic and didactic, though as in *Cement* the didacticism was relieved by a torrid love plot and by language that was more pithy than was to be allowed in later, socialist realist novels (not sufficiently relieved for the Formalist critic Eikhenbaum, however, who was most scathing of recent peasant fiction in a review).[24] Each work was obsessed with the way the new was superseding the old in the village, though in many cases an author would demonstrate this primarily in a love plot which showed how much more humane the new (Bolshevik) family morality was than the old, oppressive one upheld by the Orthodox Church. In consequence, his coverage of how the new economic and political order was introduced in the village often faded from view.[25] Presumably, this was done in the belief that his work would be read more readily that way.

These works were also like *Cement* in that the protagonists were frequently angry at the retreat from socialism in the NEP period, pushing, in this case, for more socialism in the village and expropriation of the wealthy peasants. As in *Cement,* the local bureaucracy was frequently represented as pusillanimous or lethargic, and the people took matters into their own hands out of frustration.[26]

The majority of these novels and long poems were structured as parables about how "the city" was brought to the village. A given work would open as an energetic young man from the city arrived in some rural village. Usually he was from these parts himself but had been away in the city for some time where he had acquired both technical or professional training, and Party membership (often as a sequel to serving in the Red Army during the Civil War). This young man, appalled at the backwardness of the village, would undertake to mobilize the local poor peasants, komsomols, and Party members, to organize some form of local collective with them at the core, and to introduce the new technology of the city. Significantly, however, the young agent of the "city" would not normally attempt to collectivize agriculture itself, but would rather set up a flour mill or saw mill, or organize an artel for manufacture or some other urban mode of production. This task would be accomplished with amazing dispatch, at which point, like the hero of a cowboy movie, he would move on, leaving behind folks who would miss him and a girl who would grieve, but knowing the good deed had been done—or as the hero Berezin put it in *Bol'shaia Kamen'ka*, "This place is not a village any more, but a veritable *'lampochka Il'icha.'* "[27]

As this quotation suggests, in these novels and long poems the symbolism of bringing the "city" to the countryside was no less important an element than the tale of how an agricultural collective was formed. In the majority of such works the authors, taking their cue from Lenin's maxim "Communism equals Soviet power plus the electrification of the entire country," had their heroes supervise construction of a local power station as the surest means of radical transformation from a backward village society of small individual households to an advanced, socialistic rural economy. It also became common to use some heavy-handed symbol for the triumph over the old by the new. Thus, for instance, in Doronin's "The Tractor Ploughman" a tractor runs over the old man of the village who had most vociferously opposed the new, and in Opalov's "The Water Meadow" the representative of the old, in this case an old lady, is electrocuted by the current of the new power station; in the latter work the author spells it out by remarking that the hero saw before him not only a dead woman, but something else that was dead and departing.[28]

Despite the viciousness of some of the symbols used in this kind of literature of the "new" village, these were days of innocence compared with what was to come in the later years of the collectivization campaign. It was then that the misguided old ladies were converted into positively sinister kulaks and serednyaks.[29] Most fateful for peasant literature in these years was not, however, the fact of collectivization itself. The initial collectivization drive more or less coincided with the second, urbanist utopian phase of the twenties during the years 1928–31 when the Party launched a "cultural revolution" and made a concerted effort to "proletarianize" all aspects of Soviet cultural life. These policies went hand in hand with the First Five-Year Plan program for rapid industrialization as the country's first priority. In short, this was the age of "the city," and, as a corollary, an age when all that "the village" stood for was held in low esteem; a standard item in the public rhetoric of those years was Stalin's dictum in "Foundations of Leninism" (1924) that "both in the material and the cultural sphere, the village follows, and must follow, the town."[30]

These policies were not exclusively negative in their consequences for the village. This was, after all, a utopian phase. Many of the policies for the village made during the cultural revolution were extremist, as utopian policies generally are, but they were also idealistic. For instance, a great deal of attention was paid to improving the cultural life and literacy in the countryside: campaigns were organized to collect books for village libraries;[31] writers were sent in brigades to rural areas where they were expected both to write enthusiastic accounts of the progress of collectivization, and to organize libraries in the villages and train kolkhozniks to be writers;[32] in these years many more resources were put into publishing works both by and for the peasant, and several new journals and newspapers for the peasant reader were founded such as *Zemlia sovetskaia* (1929–32) and *Perelom* (1931–32); literary circles were formed in the kolkhoz and there was a determined campaign to raise the percentage of kolkhoznik representation in the peasant writers' organization.[33] Of course, like all utopian schemes, many of these policies failed to pass the test of reality. Before long it became clear that, for instance, most of the literary circles in the kolkhozes existed on paper only.[34]

More dire in its consequences for peasant literature was the informing assumption behind many policies, an assumption linked with Stalin's dictum about the town leading the village, to the effect that the countryside, and all that went with it, was not merely more backward than the city but actively and insidiously retrograde. In both literature and the press of these years the old anti-urbanist claim of the early twenties that the village is somehow superior to the city was reversed to such an extent that many writers maintained there was something subhuman, even semi-bestial about the rustics,[35] and in criticism about peasant literature Marx's remark about the "idiocy of village life" became a catchcry.[36]

The peasant writer himself was fortunately not accused of semi-bestiality, but in these years he was regarded as manifestly inferior to the proletarian, and his works were never quite acceptable. The yardstick was militantly "proletarian," and most peasants failed to measure up to it. Much ink and breath were used in trying to decide where the peasant stood in class terms, and although the point was debated vigorously it was understood that he *should be*, and therefore *must become*, a proletarian.[37] The peasant writers were instructed to get closer to the proletarian writers' organization, RAPP, and accept its tutelage.[38] Groups of workers were asked to supervise the activities of the peasant writers' organization, VOKP.[39] And, finally, the name of VOKP, the All-Russian Organization of Peasant Writers, was changed in 1931 to VOPKP, the All-Russian Organization of Proletarian-Peasant Writers.[40]

Not surprisingly, spokesmen for the anti-urbanist position had little access to public forums during this period, and were generally persecuted. The old-style, anti-urbanist peasant writers, such as Kliuev, Klychkov, and Oreshin, became the targets of a concerted campaign led by self-styled "proletarian" critics.

Most were labeled "kulak"—ironically a label the now-ousted Trotsky had used for them in the early twenties.[41] Their response varied: Oreshin adapted his fiction to reflect more of the regnant obsession with class; Klychkov wrote spirited defenses of his position and was able to continue publishing until 1930, after which he had to eke out a living with such things as translations of folk epics by non-Russian Soviet peoples; Kliuev became even more intransigent, which meant he was no longer able to publish, but he survived as a poet by giving readings in private homes. Whether the anti-urbanist peasant writer made accommodations to the new political climate or not did not seem to affect his situation in the long run, however, for when the Writers Union was founded in 1932 the old-guard peasant writers were not admitted to it. Kliuev was arrested in 1933, and by the end of the thirties he, Klychkov, and Oreshin had all perished in exile or the camps.

The non-peasant anti-urbanists were not in a position of strength, either. Actually, some of them had died already (Blok in 1921, Lunts in 1924). Others, such as Ivanov-Razumnik and Chaianov, were repressed, while Pilniak and Zamyatin were both subjected to savage political campaigns against them (Zamyatin wrote to Stalin asking permission to leave the country and emigrated in 1931 and Pilniak was repressed in 1937).

The new-style, Party-oriented peasant writer who had emerged into prominence around 1926 was attacked like the anti-urbanist (though much less vehemently). He, however, showed no signs of pride and adjusted his writing as directed. The usual charge against him was that he had failed to show sufficiently cogently the link between the village and the towns. Even members of RAPP who were peasant writers, such as Panferov, the author of a classic on collectivization, *Brusski,* and Dorogoichenko (a writer who had been a Party member since 1919 and had helped establish Soviet power in Samara), came under attack.[42] Such writers always responded quickly. Panferov, for instance, altered Part II of *Brusski* (which appeared in late 1929) to give the "city" a greater role in collectivization. He showed no qualms about sacrificing consistency of plot or characterization as he hastily dispatched one of his peasant protagonists to a town where the young man's daily encounters with the mighty machine transformed him into a subject worthy of leading the collectivization drive back home.

One might be tempted to say that by 1931 the duel of utopias had been won by the urbanists, but this would be a premature and hasty conclusion. The urbanist utopian phase peaked in 1931, and before long thereafter a certain nostalgia for country life and nature began to creep into literature again, and has done so periodically ever since. Indeed, for most of the Brezhnev era so-called village prose, a movement with clear links to anti-urbanist peasant literature of the twenties, dominated *official* Soviet literature. For the past five years there has been a growing official reaction against this trend, but who can doubt that sooner or later the tide will turn again, for the city/countryside "duel" is a basic pattern of Russian intellectual life.

NOTES

1. Although the period of War Communism extended only through 1921 the literary expression of that era not only lasted through at least 1922, but actually peaked in that year.

2. Moshe Lewin, *Russian Peasants and Soviet Power,* tr. Irene Nove (Evanston: Northwestern University Press, 1968), p. 107.

3. Z. Bogomazova, "Metody i formy politprosveshcheniia v derevne (obzor novoi literatury)," *Pechat' i revoliutsiia,* 1925, no. 5–6, p. 312.

4. See chapter 9.

5. Ibid.

6. My source for all the biographies of writers, unless otherwise indicated, is the Soviet *Kratkaia literaturnaia entsiklopediia.*

7. Boris Fillippov, "Nikolai Kliuev, Materialy dlia biografii," in G. P. Struve and B. A. Fillippov, eds., Nikolai Kliuev, *Sochineniia,* v. I (Germany: A. Neimanis, 1969), p. 99.

8. E.g., "My rzhannye, tolokonnye. . . . Vy—chugunnye, betonnye" (a poem of 1918 addressed to Vladimir Kirillov), and "Tvoe prozvishche—russkii gorod" (probably written about the same time), in N. Kliuev, op. cit., pp. 483–85.

9. A. Solzhenitsyn, *Pis'mo vozhdiam Sovetskogo soiuza* (Paris: Y.M.C.A. Press, 1974), pp. 29–33. Cf. Iv. Kremnev, *Puteshestvie moego brata Alekseiia v stranu krest'ianskoi utopii,* Part I (Moscow: Gos. izd., 1920), p. 18.

10. Ibid., p. 21.

11. Ibid., p. 27.

12. Ibid., pp. 49, 50.

13. Ibid., pp. 16, 28, 48–49.

14. This idea is present in much of his poetry of the early Soviet years, but is especially expressed in his later poem "Pogorelshchina," which was never published in the Soviet Union, but is thought to have been written between 1926–28.

15. Chaianov, op. cit., pp. 29, 52.

16. Ibid., p. 10.

17. Cf. Chaianov, op. cit., p. 51.

18. Z. Bogomazova, op. cit., p. 312, Moshe Lewin, op. cit., p. 107.

19. Vladislav Khodasevich, *"Nekropol'." vospominaniia* (Brussels: Petropolis, 1939), p. 188.

20. "My otoshli s putei prirody," *Krasnaia nov',* 1926, no. 1, p. 121.

21. In 1929 the title was changed from Society *(obshchestvo)* to Organization *(organizatsiia).*

22. Mikh. Bekker, "Chelovek i mashina. O krest'ianskoi poezii," *Literaturnaia gazeta,* 1929, no. 20 (2 Sept.), p. 2.

23. *Istoriia russkogo sovetskogo romana,* Vol. I (Moscow-Leningrad: Nauka [Institut russkoi literatury, Pushkinskii dom], 1965), p. 208.

24. Boris Eikhenbaum, *Moi vremennik. Slovesnost', nauka, kritika smes'* (Leningrad: Izdatel'stvo pisatelei v Leningrade, 1929), pp. 123–24.

25. In one novel, Aleksei Tveriak's *Dve sud'by* of 1929, the story of how the central character, the Communist Egor, founded a cooperative brick factory in the village and led the peasants in communal farming is completely overshadowed by the story of his struggle with his brother Efim who attempts incest with their mother, rapes Egor's girlfriend and, when Egor later marries her (once he has overcome his old-fashioned scruples about marrying a fallen woman), Efim burns down their house, killing the wife; the young hero even kills his brother in vengeance.

26. Cf. esp. Aleksei Tveriak, *Na otshibe* (Moscow: Artel' pisatelej "Krug," 1926).

27. A. Dorogoichenko, *Bol'shaia Kamenka* (Moscow: Molodaia gvardiia, 1927), p. 207.

28. Cited in Mikh. Bekker, "Protiv uproshchenchestva. O krest'ianskoi literature," *Literaturnaia gazeta,* 1929, no. 8 (10 June), p. 3.

29. Cf. E. P. Shukhov, *Nenavist'* (1932), and Iv. Makarov, *Stal'nye rebra* (1929).

30. I. V. Stalin, *Sochineniia,* v. VIII, p. 78.

31. "Knigu v kolkhozy," *Literaturnaia gazeta,* 1930, no. 14, p. 1.

32. "Kolkhozy zhdut pisatelei," *Literaturnaia gazeta,* 1930, no. 24, p. 1.

33. E.g., L. Iavorskii, "Za vospitanie kadrov," *Literaturnaia gazeta,* 1930, no. 21 (May 26), p. 2; "Na puti k massovnosti," *Literaturnaia gazeta,* 1930, no. 52, p. 1; and O. Afanas'eva, "Za konsolidatsiiu krest'ianskikh pisatelei s massovym proletarskim literaturnym dvizheniem," *Literaturnaia gazeta,* 1930, no. 62 (Dec. 29), p. 1.

34. E.g., G. Tarpan, "Na vysshuiu stupen'," *Literaturnaia gazeta,* 1929, no. 53 (Oct. 2), p. 3.

35. "Privet s"ezdu krest'ianskikh pisatelei" (leader), *Literaturnaia gazeta,* 1929, no. 7 (June 3), p. 1.

36. "O krest'ianskom pisatele i krest'ianskoi literature," *Literaturnaia gazeta,* 1930, no. 14 (April 7), p. 1.

37. E.g., G. Fedoseev, "O tvorcheskom metode," *Literaturnaia gazeta,* 1930, no. 61 (Dec. 24), p. 3.

38. "Za reshitel'nuiu perestroiku ROKP," *Literaturnaia gazeta,* 1931, no. 69 (Dec. 23), p. 1.

39. E.g., G. Tarpan, op. cit.

40. "Peregruppirovka sil" (leader), *Literaturnaia gazeta,* 1931, no. 15 (March 19), p. 1.

41. Leon Trotsky, *Literature and Revolution* (Ann Arbor: University of Michigan Press, 1960), pp. 60–62, 91–92. This book was originally published in 1924, but comprises articles which Trotsky published earlier in the twenties.

42. E.g., for Dorogoichenko, G. Tarpan, op. cit.; for Panferov, "Puti krest'ianskoi literatury. Na plenume TsK VOKP," *Literaturnaia gazeta,* 1929, no. 32, p. 1.

[11] The Birth of the Soviet Cinema

Richard Taylor

MOST SOVIET HISTORIES of the Soviet cinema begin with a quotation attributed to Lenin, "Of all the arts, for us the cinema is the most important." Like that other famous statement on the arts that is attributed to Lenin, "Art belongs to the people,"[1] this remark comes down to us through hearsay, through an attribution recollected in the relative tranquility of later years, at a time when the remark itself had some political utility.[2] We should therefore treat it with some caution, at least as an expression of Lenin's view at the time. The real significance of such statements lies in the very political utility that they later acquired, when the longer term political function of the arts on Soviet society was being classified as a prelude to the "cultural revolution" that was to accompany the first Five Year Plan, and when, following the path indicated by Stalin,[3] political arguments were conducted by reference to citation from Lenin, rather as earlier generations, in western Europe at least, had resorted to arguments that revolved around differing interpretations of the Bible.

I have dealt at greater length elsewhere with the general problems that faced the Soviet cinema in the early post-Revolutionary years and, especially, in the Civil War period, 1917–21, and I shall therefore only summarize the situation in this paper.[4]

The first and most obvious question is why the Bolsheviks took the cinema so seriously. It is clear from the context, and from subsequent developments, that the Lenin quotation above refers not to the artistic qualities of film but to its potential as a weapon of agitation and propaganda. As such, the cinema had many points to recommend it. First, it was the only *mass* medium available in an era when radio and television were still waiting to be fully developed and exploited. In this connection, the cinema had certain advantages that were to survive the advent of the other mass media: even today the cinema is the only mass medium where each member of the audience is both alone and yet part of a crowd. Individual susceptibility to the volatility of crowd behavior is enhanced by the darkness of the cinema as the audience watches a larger-than-life, brightly illuminated image flickering on a screen before it. In the 1920s the cinema was, of course, still a silent medium and as such it communicated its message through predominantly or purely visual stimuli: its message had therefore to be simple and direct and, as a visual medium, its impact on the audience was, potentially at least, more profound. Untrammeled by limitations of language or literacy, a film could be shown (assuming the availability of the necessary technical facilities, and this was, of course, a big assumption) anywhere in the Soviet Union and its message immediately comprehended. In a country with such a varied linguistic and cultural heritage and such a backward educational level, the cinema was a godsend to the new authorities. One Soviet source commented: "The cinema is the only book that even the illiterate can read."[5]

In addition, the cinema was, by the standards of the time, a highly mechanized medium. The resources for the production and reproduction of film were expensive and highly centralized, and therefore relatively easy to control. A film could be sent out into the provinces and the central authorities could be reasonably certain that performances in Murmansk and Baku, Vladivostok and Minsk, would be virtually identical. The same could not be said, for instance, of a traveling theatre troupe. The cinema was therefore seen to be more *reliable*. Because of what came later to be called its "mechanical reproducibility,"[6] the cinema was also seen as a great unifying force precisely because audiences in different places could, at least in theory, see the same film at the same time.

The connection between the cinema and technology further enabled the authorities to link themselves in the popular mind with mechanization and with progress: "The cinema is a new outlook on life. The cinema is the triumph of the machine, electricity and industry,"[7] asserted one writer. Like machinery, the cinema was perceived to be a *dynamic* form, unlike, for example, the poster, which, even in the modified form of a ROSTA window, remained predominantly static: "The soul of the cinema is in the movement of life,"[8] claimed another. It is small wonder, then, that Łunacharsky argued that "The power of the cinema is unbounded."[9]

That, however, was the theory: the "great silent," as it was called, was to be *the* art form of the Revolution. Trotsky was to argue in 1923 that, whereas the Church in feudal society and the tsarist vodka monopoly in the period of capitalist transition had served as opiates to oppress the people, in socialist society the cinema could serve as the great liberating educational force.[10] But, in the years 1917–21, the Soviet authorities had to face more immediate tasks of political survival. Hence Lenin's astonishment when the Hungarian Soviet government under Béla Kun immediately nationalized all places of entertainment including cabarets.[11]

By 1917 the cinema had already established its credentials as the most popular form of entertainment for the urban population of the Russian Empire. But the industry was almost entirely in private hands and produced little other than the "psychological salon dramas" and the "love intrigues" that were later to be so violently denounced. The Provisional Government had initiated, albeit somewhat tentatively, an official newsreel designed to bolster public morale and strengthen the war effort. The Bolsheviks wanted to go further. Fear of their intentions drove most of the leading figures of the pre-Revolutionary cinema, from entrepreneurs like Khanzhonkov to stars like Vera Kholodnaia, first into hiding and then into exile. Those who left assembled in the Crimea which, partly because of its relative tranquility and partly because of its climate, became for a brief period something akin to the Hollywood of that period, a makeshift aspiring El Dorado.[12] The majority of those who fled south later emigrated, taking with them much-needed resources, talent, and expertise. Those who stayed behind in the cities of the north did so because they regarded the Bolsheviks as a passing, albeit irritating, phenomenon. Assuming, given the precarious position of the Bolsheviks, that the Revolution would be over and done with in six months, that the *ancien régime* would be restored, and that life would return to what they had come to regard as "normal," they took precautions to ensure that their equipment and materials did not fall into the hands of the Revolutionary authorities. They concealed their films and projection equipment from officialdom and frequently buried things in the ground, hoping to recover them when the going was good. It never was, of course, and this meant that the Bolsheviks were unable to realize the potential of the established cinema network for their own political purposes. As the supply of film stock (all of which had to be imported) dwindled due to the blockade, cinema theatres fell into disrepair, and electricity supplies were cut off,[13] the situation deteriorated even further.

Huntley Carter described the position in these terms:

I visited the "Mirror" kino in Tverskoi, another of Moscow's fashionable thoroughfares. As the name implies, the "Mirror" was once a hall of mirrors. When I saw it, it was the remains of mirrors, many of which got bent when the Reds and the antis were slaughtering each other. The decorated ceiling had been newly decorated by shot and shell, and had a special ventilating system introduced by the method of dropping eggs from aeroplanes. The windows were patched with odds and ends of timber, and the seats were in splints and looking unusually frowzy. Most of them were just plain wooden benches. Two dim lights made their appearance during the intervals which were pretty frequent. An ancient screen, suffering from jaundice, and a worn-out projector, buried in an emergency structure and half hidden by a dirty curtain as though ashamed of itself, completed the fitments.

The film was a genuine antique of pre-war Russian manufacture. It was in rags, and the reel was so broken that the "curtain fell" every few minutes.[14]

Bolshevik leaders hesitated to nationalize the cinema for fear that such a step would cause further retrenchment and disruption of the industry. Instead, local authorities were permitted and in some cases encouraged to take over a number of the cinemas in their area.[15] This action provoked a hostile reaction and a policy of noncooperation from the entrepreneurs' association,[16] which confirmed the Bolshevik authorities in their reluctance to nationalize. A Cinema Sub-Section was however established within the Extra-Mural Department of Narkompros;[17] hence initially the Soviet cinema was the responsibility of Lenin's wife, Nadezhda Krupskaia, who headed this department. Although resources were limited, the flight of so many of the personnel hitherto active in the cinema left an increasing proportion of cinema enterprises, *de facto* if not *de jure,* in the hands of organizations supporting the new régime. During the Civil War the Petrograd Soviet's film section, P.O.F.K.O., spread its influence throughout the northwestern provinces and assumed the acronym Sevzapkino. Similarly, by 1919 the Moscow Soviet's film section had expanded to the point where Lunacharsky deemed it appropriate to rename the section the All-Russian Photographic and Cinematographic Section (V.F.K.O.) and to take it directly under the wing of his own commissariat.[18] Headed by Dmitri Leshchenko, the former chairman of the Petrograd organization, the new section was to provide the basis for the nationalization that was finally decreed on 27 August 1919.[19] But nationalization on paper was not the same as nationalization in practice: there is evidence to suggest that the introduction of state control over even the central organs was not completed until late 1920[20] and, of course, the reemergence of the private sector under NEP was to delay the exercise of complete political control even further.[21]

Nationalization of the organization would in any case only provide a framework for political activity. As Lunacharsky himself put it:

> We need cadres of workers who are free from the habits and strivings of the old bourgeois entrepreneurial hacks and are able to elevate the cinema to the heights of the artistic and socio-political tasks facing the proletariat especially in the current period of intensified struggle.[22]

In 1919 the State Film School was established in Moscow under Vladimir Gardin, one of the few directors of the pre-Revolutionary cinema to have stayed behind.[23] As resources were limited, and film stock, in particular, was in short supply, the Film School concentrated on producing the short agitational films known as *agitki*. Of the 92 non-newsreel films produced by Soviet film organizations in the period 1918–20, 63 were *agitki* and most of them were less than 600 meters in length, or less than thirty minutes when projected.[24] The function of the *agitka* was to convey a simple message on a single subject with directness and economy. One such film, produced in Kiev in 1919 and entitled *The Asiatic Guest* (Aziatskaia gost'ia), dealt with the preventive measures to be taken against cholera.[25] Another, produced by the Moscow Film Committee to mark the first anniversary of the Red Army and called *The Fugitive* (Beglets), had this tale to tell:

> A backward Red Army soldier deserts from the front and returns to his village. The fugitive's brother, invalided in the Civil War, drives him out of the house. The front approaches the village. Realizing what the Red Army is fighting for, the deserter re-joins its ranks.[26]

Other contemporary problems provided the themes for other *agitki*. Lunacharsky himself wrote his first film script at this time. Called *Resettlement* (Uplotnenie), the film was produced in 1918 by the Petrograd Film Committee and directed by Aleksandr Panteleev. It told of the reactions of different members of a professional family when a worker and his family are resettled in the "surplus" living-space in their apartment.[27] *Resettlement* was however too long and too conventional in its melodramatic narrative format to be described in the strictest sense as an *agitka*. It belonged to another subgenre that was to play a significant role in the later Soviet cinema: the *agitfilm*. The *agitka* itself, the short direct film, was to exercise a decisive influence on the stylistic development of the Soviet film: the essence of economy and dynamism in the visual presentation of material was developed in the principles of editing, or "montage." The simple visual message had to attract and hold the attention of the audience and leave it with an impression of dynamism and strength. These principles were embodied in different ways in the theoretical writings of Lev Kuleshov, in the documentaries and manifestos of Dziga Vertov's Kinoglaz (Cine-Eye) group, in the films of Shub, Eisenstein, Pudovkin, and the FEKS group, notably Kozintsev. All these people cut their cinematic teeth in the fury of the Civil War.

The shortage of film stock meant that none could be wasted on experiments: what was shot *had* to be successful. For this reason Lev Kuleshov and his Workshop at the Film School spent much of their time in rehearsals, developing and refining his theory of the *naturshchik*, the actor with no conventional training, by miming the so-called *fil'my bez plënki* or "films without film."[28] In so doing, they laid the foundations for many of the techniques with which the Soviet cinema of the 1920s is so closely associated: they developed distinctive ideas on the style of acting appropriate for cinema and on the relationship between acting and montage. These ideas reached their zenith in Kuleshov's first full-length feature film, *The Unusual Adventures of Mr. West in the Land of the Bolsheviks*, made in Leningrad in 1924.[29] As Pudovkin, one of

Kuleshov's pupils, wrote later: "We make pictures—Kuleshov made the cinema."[30]

But, whatever the longer term advantages that were to be drawn from the experiences of this period, this was clearly no way to fight a Civil War—not, at least, to fight to win. Given that the conventional cinema network was largely *hors de combat*, the Bolsheviks were forced to turn elsewhere. To meet what was in effect a dire emergency they adopted emergency measures. Their needs were greatest in the front-line areas: to maintain the morale of their soldiers fighting at the front and to counteract the effects of White propaganda activities among the populations of newly recaptured areas. They needed a highly mobile and effective weapon and they chose to create a fleet of agit-trains.[31]

The first such train, named after Lenin, went into action among Red Army units in August 1918. It proved to be so successful that Trotsky ordered five more.[32] In January 1919 a special Commission was established to operate the planned fleet. Each train was distinctively and brightly decorated with paintings and slogans.[33] Artists of the caliber of Mayakovsky, El Lissitsky, and Malevich were employed, but their efforts were not always rewarded with success. Some of the initial designs were too abstract or fanciful to be readily understood by a mass audience, particularly one composed largely of illiterate and backward peasants. Dziga Vertov, who traveled on the "October Revolution" train with Kalinin as political commissar, described the effect of these paintings:

> It was not only the painted-up Cossacks depicted on the sides of the train whom the peasants called "actors"—they called the horses the same, simply because they were wrongly shod in the picture.

> The more remote the place, the less the peasants grasped the overtly agitational meaning of the pictures. They examined every picture carefully and every figure separately. Whenever I asked them if they liked the drawings, they would answer: "We don't know. We are ignorant folk—illiterate."

> But this does not stop the peasants, when talking among themselves, sniggering unequivocally at the horse "actors."[34]

Each train carried a small library, a printing press for the production of pamphlets, newspapers, and posters, an exhibition room, and a film section. The aim was both to distribute and to gather material. The cinema facilities played a significant part in attracting audiences to the trains, although the film makers confronted similar problems to those that the painters had encountered. Most peasants had never before seen a moving picture (or, indeed an image of an ordinary mortal!) and the effect was often very powerful. But Vertov argued that many peasants were confused by the "theatricality" of many *agitki:* they were after all unaware of the conventions by which the cinema of fiction conveyed its message. Nevertheless, in the first year of its existence, the "October Revolution" had provided 430 film showings for a total audience above 620,000 people.[35]

The agit-fleet also included the steamer "Red Star," which spent three months in 1919 sailing down the Volga. The political commissar was Molotov and the Narkompros representative Krupskaia.[36] The fact that people of the rank of Molotov, Krupskaia and Kalinin were spared from the center for these tasks underlines their political importance. According to Krupskaia, "Ilyich was raring to go himself but he could not leave his work even for a moment."[37] The cinema played an important role in the activities of the "Red Star" too. On its first voyage 199 film shows attracted 255,300 people, and on its second voyage in the summer of 1920, 202 shows attracted more than 294,000 people.[38]

Important though the agit-fleet was in forging new techniques of agitprop activity and in developing the new Soviet film style of dynamic montage, it would be foolish to imagine that, during the Civil War period, the emerging Soviet state was crisscrossed with traveling power-houses of propaganda. Even the places visited seem, at least in some cases, to have emerged unaffected.[39] For instance, when the "October Revolution" visited Irkutsk in 1919 its arrival and activities remained unreported in the local Soviet press, which was more concerned with reiterating that "Starvation, cold, misery and epidemics are the natural offspring of imperialism and its allies."[40] It is a significant comment on the state of the conventional cinema network at this time that the first thing that disappeared from the local newspapers when the Red Army arrived and *Svobodnyi Krai* (Free Region) became *Sovetskaia Sibir'* (Soviet Siberia) was the cinema advertisements. Since the cinemas had previously been indulging their audiences with *Innocence, Daughter of the Moon,* and *The Fall of Pompeii,* this is perhaps hardly surprising.[41]

By the end of the Civil War the cinema was still very much in a state of flux. With benefit of hindsight we can see that many important steps were taken toward the creation of a distinctively Soviet cinema during this transitional period. First of all, the nationalization decree of August 1919 laid the foundation of the institutional framework of the Soviet film industry. Although it was to be another ten years before the Party was to assume effective political control, a start had been made. The State Film School, the first such institution to be created anywhere in the world, began training, albeit on a very limited scale, the first cadres of Soviet film workers. By the end of the 1920s it would be pouring forth increasing numbers of technically qualified people. The desperate shortages of film stock and equipment, the need to cope with unheated studios and decrepit theatres, instilled into the new Soviet cinema a sense of economy in the use of resources that was to elevate cutting or montage—surely *the* distinctive feature of the "golden era of Soviet film"—to a central place in the later theoretical pronouncements of the varying schools of filmmaking that emerged around Kuleshov, Pudovkin, Eisenstein, Vertov, Shub, or the FEKS group. Most of these people had first entered the cinema in this period and several of them had played an active part in the film work of the agit-trains. In the period 1917–1921 therefore we can detect the birth of the Soviet cinema. But even as late as 1921, the longer term consequences of Civil War developments in the cinema could not be accurately foreseen, for the film was still very much the "art of the future."[42]

But if the achievements of the new Soviet cinema were still largely theoretical rather than practical, its theoretical achievements were nonetheless significant. One important pointer for the future, whose exact significance it would be difficult to exaggerate, was a collection of essays published by the State Publishing House in Moscow in 1919 under the auspices of Narkompros. Under the title *Kinematograf. Sbornik Statei* (The Cinematograph. A Collection of Essays) the collection dealt with several aspects of the role of the cinema in the creation of a new post-Revolutionary Soviet society. It was the first such collection of essays to be published anywhere in the world and this is in itself an indication of the practical importance attached to the cinema by the Soviet authorities.

The unsigned editorial that introduced the collection made the task of the Soviet cinema clear:

> Having won power and embarked upon a fundamental transformation of all spheres of social life, the laboring classes must tear this weapon from the hands of their exploiters and force it to serve them, their own interests, the great cause of socialism.
>
> For this, however, the cinema must take upon itself the task of the true enlightenment and cultural education of the masses—the deepening of the class-consciousness of the proletariat, the strengthening of comradely solidarity among the workers, the elevation of the revolutionary heroism with which is imbued the whole struggle of the working class for its emancipation and for the emancipation of all mankind.[43]

According to this editorial, "Truth and beauty must replace on the screen the seductive lies and embellished ugliness of the recent past. A mood of struggle and faith in victory must seize the hearts of the audience."[44]

The first and shortest essay in the collection elaborated on this theme: written by Lunacharsky, it was entitled "The Tasks of the State Cinema in the R.S.F.S.R.."[45] "It is," he wrote, "not simply a matter of nationalizing production and film distribution and the direct control of cinemas. It is a matter of fostering a completely new spirit in this branch of art and education."[46] He continued, "We must do what nobody else is either able or willing to do. We must remember that a socialist government must imbue even film shows with a socialist spirit."[47] Lunacharsky, whose position as People's Commissar for Enlightenment gave him ultimate overall responsibility for the cinema, was well aware of its financial difficulties. He therefore appreciated that "In the present impoverished state of the Russian economy we cannot count on . . . competing with foreign films or replacing Russian private films. In the end we might perhaps even borrow this kind of material."[48] On the other hand, the cinema had to be "imbued with a socialist spirit," and "There is absolutely no doubt that in this respect far more newsreel footage must be shot." The competing aims of commerce and ideology were to haunt the Soviet cinema into the 1930s. The eventual solution is foreshadowed in Lunacharsky's understandable if, from the artist's viewpoint somewhat ominous, conclusion:

> With our limited time and resources we must not mess around too much and, in choosing between two pictures of roughly the same importance and value, we must make the one that can speak to the heart and mind more vividly from the standpoint of revolutionary propaganda.[49]

The editors and Lunacharsky himself thus set the framework. Subsequent essays developed particular themes and it is clear from the editors' introductory remarks that the whole collection was intended merely as the first issue of what was supposed to be a regular journal. The back cover advertises the next issue, *Svetopis'*, (Light Play), which was never published. Not all the essays in *Kinematograf* are of equal importance.[50] But several presage the debates and polemics of the later 1920s.

The second essay in the collection, by F. Shipulinsky, was entitled "The Soul of the Cinema (The Psychology of the Cinematograph)."[51] The author was concerned to distinguish the unique features of the cinema which "sees everything, knows everything and shows everything to every one."[52] The message of a film was transmitted to the viewer through a linked series of images. The rapid movement of these images through a machine that projected them for the audience onto a screen produced for that audience the impression of movement. The human eye could only take in a limited amount of information at any one time and the cinema "therefore leaves us only with distorted, inexact and unclear images which are not impressed on our consciousness."[53] Indeed the projector's purpose was to keep the film going at a speed that would protect the audience from a clear perception of individual frames. Such a perception would disturb the image/message flow and break the cumulative effect of the film. As an integral part of the flow the individual frames act as "milestones on the broad path followed by our imagination,"[54] but in isolation the clear perception of an individual frame is like running into a brick wall.[55] In this argument we find the fundamentals of later principles of montage. More important at the time was that Shipulinsky, by distinguishing the unique features of the cinema, had established for it a place as a legitimate art form alongside, or perhaps even replacing, the theatre. Since the human eye perceived reality as it perceives the images in a film, as a continuous narrative of dimly remembered individual incidents given coherence only by reference to the whole, Shipulinsky concluded that the cinema was the ideal art form for the realistic depiction of life itself. He concluded, in Gogolesque fashion:

> The soul of the cinema is in the movement of life. The hum of the unfolding film is like the hiss of a troika passing over the potholes as it rushes along life's road with the poet of our imagination seated in it.[56]

The third essay, by S. Shervinsky and entitled "The Essence of the Cinematographic Art,"[57] was also concerned, as the title suggests, to delineate the distinguishing features of the new art form. He developed further the idea of editing: the cinema consisted in "alternation of facts" *(cheredovanie faktov)*. The film therefore relied upon a chain of succession. The collision upon which drama depended was as alien to the cinema as Shipulinsky's clear perception of the individual frame. Cinema was therefore not theatre. For Shervinsky silence was an essential characteristic of the cinema as art form, as it was to F. Kommissarzhevsky, the author of the fifth essay, "The Screen and the Actor," who was concerned to demonstrate the importance of movement in the expression of a character's internal emotional state. It was a lesson that was not lost on Kuleshov and his *naturshchiki* or, indeed, on Meyerhold and his theory of biomechanics.

In the seventh essay A. Toporkov examined the relationship between "The Cinematograph and Myth."[58] The cinema had justifiably been called "the art of the Hottentots."[59] It had demonstrated its potential by heroicizing the present; its heroes were types rather than individuals: "Individualism has not touched the cinema and this is only to the good."[60] The cinema was thus an inherently *mass* art form for the twentieth century in the same way that the drama had been a mass art form for the ancient Greeks. It displayed the same quality of mythic universality and the same claim to (and general acceptance as) the received truth: "From illusion it becomes reality, truth and even the norm."[61] The cinema as myth-maker presented the hero as a moral example for the mass, whereas other cultural forms, because of their socioeconomic associations, reflected the diversification of society into classes. Only the cinema was a uniting force: it alone united myth and reality, good and bad. "The cinema is illusion, recognized as truth."[62]

The tenth and last essay in the collection returned to the themes raised by Lunacharsky. In his "The Social Struggle and the Screen"[63] Kerzhentsev, the apostle of mass theatre, started from the premise that "The mass created the cinema's success."[64] As it was already a mass art form, the cinema's task was to involve the mass actively. A state cinema should involve mass participation: *Birth of a Nation* was cited as the model.[65] It should take its themes from the pages of the Communist Manifesto ("Open the first page of the Communist Manifesto and you will find dozens of themes"[66]) or the history of the workers' and peasants' struggle. The principal task however was to "achieve the transformation of the cinema from an instrument of amusement and entertainment into a means of education."[67] Here the role of the newsreel was to be pivotal. It could harness the natural curiosity and thirst for knowledge of the masses to the advantage of the authorities. The newsreel "is an indispensable tool which, in five to ten minutes, will provide audiences of all nationalities with an unforgettable illustration of the benefits of the October Revolution."[68] The Soviet newsreel (*pace* Vertov's later claims about showing "reality as it really was") was "in essence a cine-newspaper, which should not only respond to everything that happens, but should also illuminate it from a definite point of view."[69]

The conflicts that might arise from determining precisely whose point of view was to prevail—the filmmakers' or the Party's—were still in the future. As I have already argued, the shortages of basic essentials in the 1917–1921 period made all the arguments not only theoretical but hypothetical. The *Kinematograf* collection is important, however, not only as the first collection of its kind, not only as a clear statement of the Party's requirements, but as the seed of future theoretical debates and polemics. The germs of subsequent arguments about montage are to be found within its pages, as are the battles over the relative merits of documentary or fiction film. As Kerzhentsev concluded: "Practice will show what changes will have to be made to the present program."[70] The cinema was not yet the "most important of the arts"—it was still the "art of the future." But *Kinematograf* was very much a blueprint for that future art.

NOTES

1. Conversation recalled by Klara Zetkin and cited in: N. I. Krutikova (ed.), *Lenin o kul'ture i iskusstve* (Moscow, 1956), pp. 519–20.

2. From a conversation between Lenin and Lunacharsky in 1922, recalled by the latter in: G. M. Boltianskii (ed.), *Lenin i kino* (Moscow, 1925), pp. 16–17.

3. I. V. Stalin, *Problemy Leninizma* (Moscow, 1925).

4. R. Taylor, "A Medium for the Masses: Agitation in the Soviet Civil War," *Soviet Studies*, XXII, no. 4 (1971), pp. 562–74; idem, *The Politics of the Soviet Cinema, 1917–1929* (Cambridge University Press, 1979); idem, "From October to *October:* The Soviet Political System in the 1920s and Its Films," in M. J. Clark (ed.), *Politics and the*

Media (Pergamon Press, Oxford, 1979), pp. 31–42; idem, "Agitation, Propaganda and the Cinema: The Search for New Solutions, 1917–21," in N. Å. Nilsson (ed.), *Art, Society, Revolution: Russia 1917–1921* (Almqvist & Wiksell International, Stockholm, 1979), pp. 237–63.

5. Cited in: A. Goldobin, *Kino na territorii S.S.S.R. (Po materialam provintsial'noi pressy)* (Moscow, 1924), p. 64.

6. W. Benjamin, "L'Oeuvre d'art a l'époque de sa reproduction mécanisée," *Zeitschrift für Sozialforschung* (Paris), 1, (1936), pp. 40–63, translated as "The Work of Art in the Age of Mechanical Reproduction" in idem, *Illuminations* (Fontana, London, 1973), pp. 219–53.

7. I. Sokolov, "Skrizhal' veka," *Kino-Fot*, 25–31 August 1922, p. 3.

8. F. Shipulinskii, "Dusha kino," in: *Kinematograf. Sbornik statei* (Moscow, 1919), p. 20.

9. A. M. Gak & N. A. Glagoleva (eds.), *Lunacharskii o kino* (Moscow, 1965), p. 46.

10. L. D. Trotskii, *Voprosy byta. Epokha "kul'turnichestva" i eë zadachi* (Moscow, 1923), Ch. 3.

11. A. Iufit (ed.), *Lenin. Revoliutsiia. Teatr. Dokumenty i vospominaniia* (Leningrad, 1970), p. 199.

12. The atmosphere of the period is evoked in Nikita Mikhalkov's film *Raba liubvi (Slave of Love)* (Mosfilm, Moscow, 1978).

13. Taylor, *The Politics of the Soviet Cinema*, pp. 47, 65.

14. Cf. H. Carter, *The New Theatre and Cinema of Soviet Russia* (Chapman & Dodd, London, 1924), p. 240.

15. Taylor, *The Politics of the Soviet Cinema*, pp. 43–48.

16. For the relevant decree see: *Vestnik otdela mestnogo upravleniia komissariata vnutrennikh del*, 1918, No. 3, p. 1. For the reaction see: *Kinogazeta*, 1918, No. 3; *Mir ekrana*, 26 April 1918, p. 1; *Proektor*, 1918, no. 1/2, p. 1.

17. Taylor, *The Politics of the Soviet Cinema*, pp. 44–45.

18. Loc. cit.

19. *Izvestiia V.Ts.I.K.*, 2 September 1919.

20. A. M. Gak (ed.), *Samoe vazhnoe iz vsekh iskusstv. Lenin o kino*, 2nd ed. (Moscow, 1973), p. 52.

21. Until after the first Party conference on the cinema, held in Moscow in March 1928. The proceedings were published in: B. S. Ol'khovyi (ed.), *Puti kino. Pervoe vsesoiuznoe partiinoe soveshchanie po kinematografii* (Moscow, 1929).

22. Cited in: "Vysshaia kinoshkola strany. Beseda s A. N. Groshevym," *Iskusstvo kino*, October 1969, p. 41.

23. V. R. Gardin, *Vospominaniia* (2 vols., Moscow, 1949–52), Vol. 1, pp. 167–70, and also: V. Vishnevskii, "Fakty i daty iz istorii otechestvennoi kinematografii (Mart 1917–dekabr' 1920)," *Iz istorii kino*, 1 (1958), p. 71.

24. Based on information in *Sovetskie khudozhestvennye fil'my. Annotirovannyi katalog* (4 vols., Moscow, 1961–68), Vol. 1, pp. 5–26.

25. Ibid., p. 7.

26. Loc. cit.

27. Ibid., p. 6.

28. L. V. Kuleshov, *Stat'i. Materialy*, (Moscow, 1979), pp. 133–46; L. V. Kuleshov, A. Khokhlova, *50 let v kino* (Moscow, 1975), pp. 36–47; V. I. Pudovkin, "Masterskaia Kuleshova," *Iskusstvo kino*, January/February 1940, pp. 85–87.

29. *Sovetskie khudozhestvennye fil'my*, Vol. 1, pp. 65–66.

30. Pudovkin's introduction to: L. V. Kuleshov, *Iskusstvo kino* (Moscow, 1929), p. 4.

31. See above, note 4.

32. V. Karpinskii (ed.), *Agitparpoezda V.Ts.I.K. Ikh istoriia, apparat, metody i formy raboty* (Moscow, 1920), p. 6.

33. E. A. Speranskaia (ed.), *Agitatsionno-massovoe iskusstvo pervykh let Oktiabria* (Moscow, 1971), pl. 113–30.

34. S. Drobashenko (ed.), *D. Vertov. Stat'i. Dnevniki. Zamysli* (Moscow, 1966), pp. 89–90. A photograph of the horses can be found in: E. I. Vertova-Svilova & A. L. Vinogradova (eds.), *Dziga Vertov v vospominaniiakh sovremennikov* (Moscow, 1976), p. 12.

35. L. V. Maksakova, *Agitpoezd "Oktyabr'skaia Revoliutsiia" (1919–20 gg.)*, (Moscow, 1956), p. 11.

36. N. K. Krupskaia, "Po gradam i vesiam sovetskoi respubliki," *Novyi mir*, 1960, No. 11, pp. 113–30.

37. N. K. Krupskaia, *Vospominaniia o Lenine* (Moscow, 1957), p. 424.

38. Gak, p. 229, n. 188.

39. The Torsten Lundell collection of provincial Russian newspapers held at the Carolina Rediviva University Library at Uppsala, Sweden, is very revealing in this respect. I am indebted to the British Council (Younger Research Workers' Interchange Scheme) for funds to consult these materials.

40. *Sovetskaia Sibir'*, 17 December 1919.

41. Respectively advertised in: *Russkii vostok* (Chita), 29 March 1919; *Mysl'* (Irkutsk), 4 March 1919; *Svobodnyi krai* (Irkutsk), 25 February 1919.

42. Cf. G. M. Boltianskii, "Iskusstvo budushchego," *Kino*, 1922, No.1/2, pp. 6–7.

43. *Kinematograf. Sbornik statei* (Moscow, 1919), pp. 3–4.

44. Loc. cit.

45. "Zadachi gosudarstvennogo kinodela v R.S.F.S.R.," ibid., pp. 5–7.

46. Ibid., p. 5.

47. Loc. cit.

48. Loc. cit.

49. Ibid., p. 7.

50. For instance: A. Sidorov, "Kinematograf i izobrazitel'nye iskusstva," pp. 27–32; V. Sakhnovskii, "Fantasticheskoe v repertuare kinoteatrov," pp. 39–43; A. Chebotarevskii, "Kinematograf, kak metod," pp. 54–62; and N. Tikhonov, "Kinematograf v nauke i tekhnike," pp. 63–85.

51. F. Shipulinskii, "Dusha kino (Psikhologiia kinematografii)," pp. 8–20.

52. Ibid., p. 8.

53. Ibid., p. 11.

54. Ibid., p. 19.

55. Ibid., p. 16.

56. Ibid., p. 20.

57. S. Shervinskii, "Sushchnost' kinematograficheskogo iskusstva," pp. 21–26.

58. A. Toporkov, "Kinematograf i mif," pp. 44–53.

59. E.g., by Kornei Chukovsky in his *Nat Pinkerton i sovremennaia literatura* (Moscow, 1910), p. 26.

60. Toporkov, op. cit., p. 46.

61. Ibid., p. 47.

62. Ibid., p. 52.

63. V. (i.e., P. M.) Kerzhentsev, "Sotsial'naia bor'ba i ekran," pp. 86–94.

64. Ibid., p. 86.

65. Ibid., p. 87.

66. Ibid., p. 88.

67. Ibid., p. 89.

68. Ibid., p. 91.

69. Loc. cit.

70. Ibid., p. 94.

[12] Constructivism and Early Soviet Fashion Design

John E. Bowlt

A SPECIFIC EXAMINATION of fashion and textile design in a general discussion of early Soviet culture might seem, at first glance, to be peripheral to more traditional and apparently more central concerns such as architecture, the theater, and revolutionary poetry.[1] However, many of the artists whom we associate with the Russian avant-garde in painting and architecture just before and after 1917 gave particular attention to fashion and textile design. These artists for the most part gave the Bolshevik government their initial fervent support and, like the politicians, felt that the Revolution provided unprecedented opportunities for the creation of a genuinely new culture. Their argument was simple and persuasive: if the new, revolutionary man and woman were to be the initiators and bearers of a revolutionary culture, then the way they moved and dressed—the way they "looked"—should also reflect this enterprise. A principal task undertaken by experimental artists such as Alexandra Exter, Nadezhda Lamanova, Kazimir Malevich, Aleksandr Rodchenko, Vladimir Tatlin, and especially Liubov' Popova and Varvara Stepanova was to create just such a new look, a revolutionary dress that was to be simple, cheap, hygienic, easy to wear, and "industrial."

Most of these artists had practiced avant-garde art, particularly painting, before the Revolution and their rich experience, coupled with their inventive imagination and enthusiasm, produced some remarkable blueprints for clothes and fabrics just after the Revolution, although few projects were actually realized. In fact, for all their ostensible dedication to the revolutionary cause and their obeisance to the call to establish a revolutionary culture, the artists concerned were designing for a utopian world: for the most part, they were out of contact with the brutal reality of the new Russia and their visionary clothes designs were incompatible with its illiterate population, shoeless and in rags. Moreover, nearly all of these avant-garde artists had trained as studio painters. They had limited understanding of industrial design and perhaps, after all, consciously or unconsciously, they were simply investigating a more dynamic, more public medium to which they could apply the geometric, abstract compositions that they had been painting and sculpting before the Revolution. But in spite of these failings, they convinced themselves that they too were contributing to the foundation of a new proletarian culture and that their utilitarian, Constructivist esthetic was the true artistic counterpart to the social and political transformation of 1917.

The discipline of fashion design, especially fashion design of the 1920s, is still outside the main areas of academic inquiry, and except for a few scholarly analyses as, for example, Roland Barthes', it has not really been treated by scholars, largely because art history is still concerned primarily with the traditional fine arts, i.e., painting, sculpture, and architecture. Despite the considerable progress recently made in ethnic and folklore studies, in design and environment appreciation, there still exists an imbalance in scholarly interest between what are called conventionally the high arts and the low arts.

This orthodoxy, with its traditional objects for study, does have particular validity in certain periods of the development of art, but it is quite inadequate in the context of Russian, German, and Hungarian cultural developments just before and after the First World War. It is clear from the art of the Russian Revolution of October 1917 that its progressive styles in art—Futurism, Suprematism, Constructivism—were universal, intended to apply to art and to life without differentiation: it was essential "to reconstruct not only objects, but also the whole domestic way of life . . . both its static and kinetic forms."[2] If anything, the art of life, i.e., design, momentarily replaced the art of art. As a group of avant-garde artists declared in November 1921: "We consider self-sufficient studio art and our activity as mere painters to be useless. . . . We declare industrial art absolute and Constructivism its only form of expression."[3] One of the key areas to which the new artists gave their attention was textile and clothing design.

It is generally recognized that Constructivism received its primary stimulus as an art of design during the first years of the Soviet regime. Given its name in Moscow in 1921 by Kazimir Medunetsky and the Stenberg brothers, Constructivism evolved rapidly into a revolutionary, topical, and potential movement. However, it is wise to remember that the movement was not born in a vacuum and it should not be separated from its sociopolitical context (which we tend to do today through museum exhibitions, auctions, gallery sales, etc.). Constructivism did not regard itself as a school of permanent works of art. If, in the remote past, the work of art was created as a sacred act and as a metaphor for eternity, the Constructivism design and, indeed, much of the art related to it, such as the paintings of Mondrian and Malevich, was produced as a momentary gesture, an intended transience—the prelude to our own society of throwaway objects and built-in obsolescence. No doubt the leading Constructivists, such as

Laszlo Moholy-Nagy, Liubov' Popova, Alexander Rodchenko, Vladimir Tatlin, and Theo van Doesburg, would be appalled to learn that their various projects and sketches were being perpetuated in frames, in scholarly symposia, and museum catalogs. The question of impermanence and the Constructivist esthetic is a fascinating one and undoubtedly distinguishes this boldly twentieth-century movement from previous styles and artistic systems.

A second characteristic of Constructivism is the universality of its aspiration. During the 1920s, whether in Moscow, Berlin, Budapest, or Warsaw, one could have spoken of a Constructivist painting, a Constructivist plate, a Constructivist building, a Constructivist chair, a Constructivist dress, a Constructivist stage design, a Constructivist book cover, even a Constructivist garden. This had not normally been the case with art movements immediately preceding Constructivism. There was no Cubist architecture, there were no Symbolist chairs, there were no Realist dresses. But before that, in the era of the High Renaissance or Classical Antiquity, for example, an artistic term or esthetic was often applicable to cultural endeavors outside of painting, sculpture, and architecture. One can indeed refer to Renaissance furniture or Classical dress design, inasmuch as the societies so designated appear to have been cohesive, integrated, whole. The nineteenth century, with its social, political, and artistic fragmentation, destroyed this totality. Constructivism tried to synthesize the arts again, to put the pieces of that Victorian hero Humpty-Dumpty back together again.

These general remarks help to elucidate the derivation and development of Constructivist textile and dress design in post-revolutionary Russia. This particular medium, in fact, attracted many important artists, including Alexandra Exter, Kazimir Malevich, Popova, Rodchenko, Varvara Stepanova, and Tatlin, and it can be regarded as a microcosm of the entire Constructivist movement, for its artistic principles closely paralleled the principles supported by architects, book illustrators, and stage designers of the same period.

Although cultural life immediately after the October Revolution was confusing and in a state of flux, a number of important statements were made by politicians and their artistic sympathizers concerning the role and potential of art in the new society. Of course the central question was what kind of art could embody the aims of the Revolution. Answers were varied, although the notion of a proletarian art or proletarian style was discussed by all parties concerned. What exactly a proletarian art was, no one fully explained, although Trotsky tended to disregard it, arguing that any "proletarian" art would have to be a class art; and within a short time class divisions would disappear as a result of the international revolution. Consequently it was useless to consider the idea of a proletarian culture at all: a culture of some kind would emerge very soon, but it would not be "proletarian."[4] Other interpreters of proletarian culture, including Alexander Bogdanov, leader of the Proletcult movement, insisted that proletarian art was a mechanical, industrial art and that the concept of the inspired artist sequestered in his intimate studio was an anachronism: the revolutionary artist was the worker who freed himself from the weight of his cultural heritage and who worked in close proximity to the factory.[5]

A third interpretation of proletarian culture was that it must be international and "anonymous" since the Russian Revolution, it was argued, was only the first in a series of worldwide revolutions; proletarian art, therefore, must not rely on narrow, nationalist motifs but on forms that were neutral, untrammeled by parochial associations. This was allegedly one reason why abstract forms were offered by the new artists as the answer to this need; abstract form, they maintained, is international, independent of anecdotal, local content and readily accessible to the eye, whether in Russia, Europe, or the United States.

A fourth view of proletarian art maintained that it must be a dynamic, mobile, and variable art, because the Revolution was a perpetual and a universal one. A fifth point of departure had it that proletarian culture (or rather the proletarian style) must affect all of the new society, so that every aspect would reflect the socioeconomic revolution. This meant not only the more obvious manifestations of social structures, such as architecture and interior design, but also language, gestures, behavior, and dress.

To a greater or lesser extent these ideas can be discerned in Constructivist fashion design in Soviet Russia in the 1920s. Fashion, perhaps, is an inappropriate term here because of its immediate associations with Paris *haute couture*. The leading Constructivists, in fact, aspired to create a consistent, democratic style that would replace both the notion of a fashion for the elite and, no less important, the mass eclecticism of the post-revolutionary period. The sudden accessibility of luxury goods from abandoned aristocratic and bourgeois homes—Persian carpets, Sevres vases, and bamboo furniture—led to the most bizarre combinations in workers' and peasants' homes and clubs.[6] A similar clash of styles and ideas was evident in dress design just after the Revolution. Popova, Rodchenko, Stepanova, and Tatlin tried to counter this pluralism with a single, rational style when they turned to textile and dress design after 1923.

While the emergence of a distinctive Soviet style of textile and clothing in the early 1920s might seem surprising given the mediocrity of Soviet clothing design nowadays, it should be remembered that throughout the modernist period Russian artists gave particular attention to the design of fabrics and clothes, and that Popova, Stepanova, and their colleagues drew on an established tradition. In this connection, mention should be made of Lev Bakst, who represented the culmination of that process of stylization identifiable with pre-revolutionary design—with the *style moderne* exemplified by dressmakers such as Brisas, Florand, and Gindus (St. Petersburg) or Worth, Faquin, and Poiret (Paris). Bakst's immediate sources of inspiration in fashion were his own projects for ballet productions such as *Scheherazade* (1910) and *L'Oiseau du feu* (1910) in which he introduced radical conceptions of costume and decor, manifest less in the elaborate sensuality of the ensembles than in the underlying method of emphasizing and exaggerating the body's movement.

Bakst treated the body as the primary organizational element on stage (and in the salon) and hence as the determinant of the costume's "expression." This induced him not only to expose the body at certain strategic points but also to extend its physical movements outward and not to conceal them, as nineteenth-century European theatrical and social dress had done. Furthermore, Bakst used the feathers, pendants, veils, and loose trousers of his creations not as mere ornaments, but as functional devices to amplify and expand the actions of the body itself.

Of course, in the individual dress designs he produced after 1910, Bakst was often forced to contain this exuberance in order to conform to a client's taste, but even in his plainest pieces the absence of the corset and sometimes of the brassiere, the emphasis on the long, loose dress with flowing folds and a half-moon base maintained his conception of the female anatomy as a kinetic generator and not as a static "figure 8." In this lay the more "democratic" element of Bakst's design principles, i.e., the notion that every anatomy creates its own rhythms and that the looser the garment, the easier the projection of these rhythms becomes, whatever the proportions of the figure. Until the Revolution, Bakst was the arbiter of *haute couture* in Russia, as a glance at St. Petersburg fashion magazines for 1916–17 demonstrates immediately.[7]

Paradoxically, Bakst pointed to important concepts of dress construction which early Soviet designers, especially Popova, also supported and developed. Still, Bakst was both a creator of, and slave to, fashion. He created only for a small, wealthy class, and while his ideas of rhythm and freedom of the body were progressive, he himself did not regard them as the probable future trend. On the contrary, in 1913 Bakst envisaged a highly ornamental future design, rather than a simple, functional one.[8] But by 1922 we read in *Zrelishcha* that "people have fallen out of love with Bakst and have fallen in love with industrial clothing."[9] This rapid development from "artistic" to "utilitarian" levels of fabric and dress design—in broader terms, from "reproduction" to "construction"—was stimulated by the activities of many avant-garde artists involved directly or indirectly in applied art just before the Revolution.

For example, Natal'ia Goncharova made patterns in 1913 for embroideries and for over forty dresses, some of which were purchased by Natal'ia Lamanova, Moscow's most sophisticated couturiere. In 1915–16 Ol'ga Rozanova, one of the original exponents of Suprematism, applied dynamic combinations of color planes to textiles for dresses and accessories such as purses. In 1916 the painter Ksenia (Xana) Boguslavskaia, the wife of Ivan Puni, contributed three embroidery designs to the Petrograd "World of Art" exhibition; with Rozanova and Malevich, she participated in a special show of contemporary applied art in Moscow in 1917.[10]

The abstract designs of these painters were based on the same formal and textural contrasts evident in their studio paintings of the same period. Even though these designs were "painterly" and had no practical connection with the medium of embroidery or the material of cloth, they signaled a transition from the textile decoration applied in a sequential or "narrative" manner to the textile design used as a variable and versatile composition, in which the effect is not spoiled by a constant change of position. This concern with the visual universality of the fabric and the dress is central to Constructivist textile design of the early 1920s.

In view of the traditional reliance of the Russian clothing industry on the individual tailor and seamstress, and the sudden disappearance of that very class which had placed private commissions—together with the disruption of the textile industry in 1917—clothing design in the new Russia could scarcely be contemplated until the advent of more orderly conditions. Even the urgent need to create a Red Army uniform did not result in the production of a standardized pattern until after the Civil War in 1922. By then the inauguration of Lenin's New Economic Policy (NEP) in 1921 (a policy that allowed a partial return to a free enterprise system) had quickly brought forth a new bourgeois clientele and the return of the private tailor; the textile industry also began to recover from its stagnation, as materials and manpower increased. Moreover, the idea that studio art was a superfluous deception capable only of stylizing reality and not transforming it had rapidly gained ground by then. As the critic Osip Brik affirmed in his article "From Pictures to Textile Prints":

> The studio painting is not only unnecessary to our contemporary artistic culture, it is also one of the most powerful brakes on its development. . . . Only those artists who, once and for all, have broken with studio craft, who have recognized productional work in practice not only as an equal form of artistic labor, but also as the only one possible—only these artists can grapple successfully and productively with the solution to the problem of contemporary artistic culture.[11]

Some artists were already describing the abstract compositions not as self-sufficient entities, but as models or projects for the creation of new objects. Popova made this clear in her statement in the catalog of the exhibition "5 × 5 = 25" in 1921. "All the pieces presented here," she wrote, ". . . should be regarded merely as preparatory experiments for concrete constructions."[12]

And indeed, architectonic compositions of 1920–21 relied on principles such as asymmetry, stratification, and counterpoint, principles that she used in her textile designs of 1923–24.

At the end of 1922 Popova and Stepanova entered the design section of the First State Textile Print Factory, a huge complex in Moscow that, before the Revolution, had belonged to the German industrialist Emile Zindel. With the exception of Liudmila Maiakovskaia (sister of Vladimir Maiakovsky), who had been working as a designer at a local textile mill since 1910,[13] Popova and Stepanova were probably the first women artists to be employed as professional designers in the Russian textile industry.

It was a curious world that greeted them. Despite the resonant call from the avant-garde for a constructive and industrial art, the prevailing form of design at Soviet textile mills in the early 1920s was a pastiche of styles differing little from pre-revolutionary stereotypes. The ignorance and conservatism that Popova and Stepanova encountered on the factory floor contrasted sharply with the radical ideas on new Soviet dress that their intellectual colleagues were proclaiming. Indeed, the question "What should the new Soviet woman be wearing?" occasioned the most diverse answers. Certain extremists shouted "Away with Shame!" and advocated nudity as the only possible equivalent of technological, democratic form, an exhortation that culminated in a number of "Evenings of the Denuded Body" in Moscow in 1922.[14] Some championed throwaway clothing, referring to the paper clothing which, they alleged, America was already producing.[15] Others supported the idea of asexual, "universal" clothing, regarding the Isadora Duncan tunic as a plausible solution. Obviously, Popova and Stepanova found that they needed not only to design textiles, but also to formulate a total conception of what the new proletarian dress should be. Popova immediately came to terms with both problems.

Popova brought to the world of textile and dress design a rich and varied artistic experience. By the end of 1922 she had worked as a studio painter, a poster designer, and a stage director. She had moved rapidly from Cubism (she studied with Le Fauconnier and Metzinger in Paris in 1912–13) to her so-called painterly architectonics in 1916; she had taken part in major avant-garde exhibitions and had assumed artistic responsibility for important stage sets and costumes. Popova was one of the most serious and disciplined members of the Russian avant-garde, and however diverse her activities, she remained loyal to certain basic concepts of form and space.

As a matter of fact, the salient characteristic of Popova's architectonic paintings is the absence and not the presence of space. Often rejecting recognizable objects, collage, and lettering, Popova manipulated planes of color devoid of any allusion to three-dimensional space. To this end, she sometimes dis-

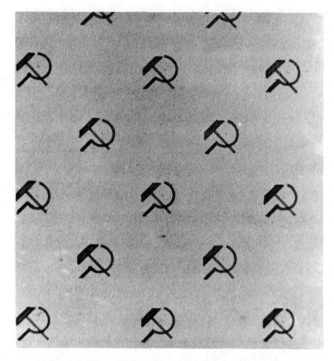

Liubov' Popova (1889–1924): Textile design, ca. 1923.
Gouache on paper. Private collection, Moscow.

missed the logical color progression of cool to warm (and vice versa) and used "non-sequences" in her paintings; she might place red above black but put pink underneath or she might place blue above yellow and then cause both to interpenetrate. However, Popova's apprenticeship to Le Fauconnier and Metzinger, her experience of Cubism, imbued her with a respect for the "object" and hence for the principle of construction. Popova also possessed the rare faculty of being able to think in terms both of two and of three dimensions, and ultimately she could not remain satisfied with the flatness of the pictorial plane. Her desire to reintroduce space as a creative element, encouraged by her friendship with the sculptress Vera Mukhina and with Tatlin, was even apparent in her occasional painted reliefs of 1916. But it was in her stage and textile designs that Popova finally gratified her wish to build with real materials in real space.

Even though Popova had no training in applied art, she immediately recognized the specific demands of the task before her and adjusted her conception of "artistic" space accordingly. Instead of dealing with a flat, two-dimensional surface (the canvas), she was now concerned with an undulating, three-dimensional solid (the body); instead of a static image that had to be viewed

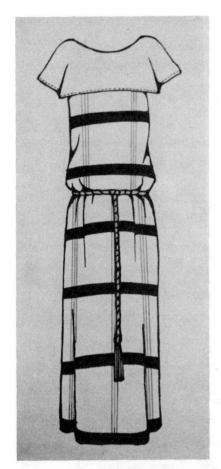

Liubov' Popova (1889–1924):
Dress design, ca. 1923.
Gouache on paper.
Private collection, Moscow.

frontally, she was now working with a mobile sculpture to be seen from many angles; instead of a decoration that followed a single, logical sequence, she now needed a design that would still give visual and psychological satisfaction when creased, rucked, or mixed with other forms. To this end, Popova used and emphasized simple forms for their maximum emotional effect.

In some of her compositions of 1920–21 Popova revived the sense of perspective by a method of linear stratification, i.e., the superimposition of a grid of regular or irregular lines on a complex of colored planes, the latter sometimes carrying letters or numbers to emphasize their flatness. Popova used a similar device in a number of her textile designs, superimposing a grid of diagonals on a series of verticals and horizontals or vice versa. Popova was also intrigued by the idea of syncopation and arhythmicality not only in sound (she was very interested in jazz) but also in visual imagery. She found, for example, that a counterpoint of regular and irregular forms produced a highly kinetic

Liubov' Popova (1889–1924): Dress design, 1924. Watercolor,
gouache, photomontage on paper. Private collection, Moscow.

effect (e.g., circles in a regular pattern containing irregular horizontals).
Popova's use of syncopation and occult symmetry brings to mind methods used
by Van Doesburg and Domela, and, in some cases, there are anticipations of
the Op-Art of Vasarely.

That movement formed the basis of Popova's art is clear not only from her
choice of specific geometric shapes (the triangle, the lozenge, the circle) which
produce a sensation of ascension and levitation, but also from her recourse to
the psychological game. For example, in one of her compositions of five
circles, the textile pattern acts as a juggler, interchanging sizes, sequences, and
combinations. Applied to a piece of clothing, i.e., placed into a condition of

movement, such designs lose none of their effectiveness, and, conversely, the designs continue to move even when the wearer is sitting. This visual result fit the conception of the emancipated Soviet woman who, reportedly, no longer needed to stay at home, but could lead an active, mobile life alongside her male colleagues. Despite the success and theoretical ingenuity of these designs, very few of them were implemented. Like her paintings, they call for direct psychological involvement on the part of the spectator, and unless the spectator is prepared to participate, the designs may seem facile and monotonous. No wonder, then, that simple working people, accustomed to vivid flower prints and the accessories of lace, paper flowers, and jewelry, requested that Popova "cover Constructivism with a haze of fantasy."[16]

Like Popova, Stepanova (married to Rodchenko) thought seriously about simplicity of design. Regarding emotion and illusion as alien to production or industrial art, Stepanova aspired to eradicate the "ingrown view of the ideal artistic drawing as the imitation and copying of nature; to grapple with organic design and orient it toward the geometrization of forms; to propagate the production tasks of Constructivism."[17] In keeping with their wish that the decorative and decorating aspects of clothing be abolished, Stepanova and Popova worked on various kinds of specialized clothing—the so-called *prozodezhda* (industrial clothing), *spetsodezhda* (special clothing), and *sportodezhda* (sports clothing). Stepanova argued that each profession—that of factory worker, doctor, actor, sportsman, etc.—demanded its own costume, which should be constructed according to the norms of convenience, hygiene, and expediency directed by that profession. As Stepanova wrote: "It is not enough to make a comfortable, clever costume design, one must *make* it and demonstrate it at work."[18]

Exciting examples of Stepanova's experimental costume design were her projects for sports clothes. Incorporating lightness of form (for mobility), economy of material (to keep down body temperature), and bright, emphatic colors (for identification on the athletic field), these designs rely upon function as the only possible "esthetic."[19] Rodchenko was also active as a textile and clothes designer at this time and produced his own *prozodezhda* in the form of a worker's coverall. But not only did the Stepanova and Rodchenko experiments contravene popular taste, a sympathetic, sophisticated manufacturer was also required to produce them—and no such person was forthcoming. Tatlin tried to solve the problem by designing clothes that could be assembled easily from cheap materials at home by the workman himself. Indeed, Tatlin made a coat and a suit in this way in 1924, although his proposal does not seem to have awakened mass enthusiasm. At this time Malevich, too, tried his hand at dress design, applying Suprematist compositions to standard forms, but these projects were never realized.

Varvara Stepanova (1894–1958): Designs for sports clothes,
1923. Reproduced from T. Strizhenova, *Iz istorii sovetskogo
kostiuma* (Moscow: 1972), p. 96.

In the drive for a simple and effective dress for the proletarian woman,
Nadezhda Lamanova played an influential role. As a celebrated couturiere
before the Revolution, Lamanova was one of the very few Soviet dress
designers to have had professional experience, and despite the abrupt shift from
aristocratic made-to-order to democratic ready-to-wear, she produced much
important theoretical and practical work. Although Lamanova did not possess
the artistry and inventiveness of Popova and Stepanova, she understood the
needs of the time, as she indicated at the First All-Russian Conference on
Industrial Art in 1919, where she proclaimed:

> [Art] must penetrate all spheres of everyday life; it must develop the artistic taste
> and feeling of the masses. Clothes are one of the most appropriate vehicles for this
> . . . in the clothing business artists must take the initiative and work to produce very
> simple but pleasing forms of clothing from simple materials, clothing which will be
> suitable to the new structure of our working life.[20]

Nadezhda Lamanova (1861–1941): Designs for sports clothes,
ca. 1924. Reproduced from T. Strizhenova, *Iz istorii sovetskogo
kostiuma* (Moscow: 1972), p. 55.

Like Tatlin, Lamanova was an early proponent of simple cut-out clothing
and home production. However, unlike her Constructivist colleagues, Lamanova regarded clothes design as her single, permanent profession. If Popova,
Rodchenko, Stepanova, and Tatlin turned to textiles and clothes as one more
potential channel for expressing their ideas on function and form, Lamanova
worked exclusively with clothes design, adjusting her skills to what she
understood to be the actual needs of the new woman. Consequently, although
Lamanova sympathized with the simple, geometric forms of the Constructivists, she was not deaf to the many requests for a more decorative, more
"feminine" kind of dress. To this end, Lamanova proceeded to design clothes
with elegant, i.e., classical motifs, with flowers, and with folkloristic images—while also producing items analogous to those of Popova and Stepanova. Unlike the primary representatives of Constructivism, Lamanova was
flexible in her esthetic criteria and more perceptive of the real tastes of the
average woman. Thanks to her common sense, Lamanova was able to cater to
various clienteles during her long professional life, practicing as an expensive
St. Petersburg designer, as a Constructivist—and also as a supplier of dress
designs for Stalin's more puritanical society of the 1930s.

The principle of maximum effect through minimum means, shared by
Lamanova, Popova, Stepanova, and Tatlin, differed considerably from the
methods of a rival group of textile and clothes designers in Moscow attached to

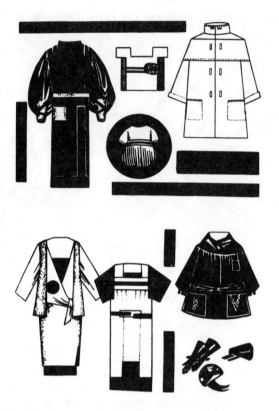

Alexandra Exter (1884–1949): Designs for ready-to-wear
clothes. Reproduced from T. Strizhenova, *Iz istorii sovetskogo
kostiuma* (Moscow: 1972), p. 75.

the so-called Atelier of Fashions.[21] This establishment catered to the new
Soviet bourgeoisie of the early 1920s, and although its most serious members,
Alexandra Exter and Mukhina, approached the issue of fashion design with
imagination, they did not achieve the purity and simplicity identifiable with the
Lamanova and Popova pieces. On the one hand, Exter declared that the dress
should consist of rudimentary geometric shapes and that certain materials were
appropriate to certain forms;[22] on the other hand, she added fur trimming to
sleeves, used Egyptian motifs, and included pearl necklaces and fans as
ornaments. Exter's tendency toward the extravagant—which must have
appealed to the bourgeois lady—attained striking results in the theatre and the
cinema as, for example, in the movie *Aelita* (1924). Just as Erté elaborated and
extenuated the elements of the Bakst costume, so Exter did the same with the
principles of Lamanova, Popova, and Stepanova. In other words, her creations

became, once again, esthetic objects and ceased to be "industrial constructions."

It is significant that, when looking at the Soviet dress designs of the early
1920s, especially from the Atelier of Fashions, we are reminded of contemporary Paris designs. Even Popova's dresses recall somewhat the European and
American fashions of the "roaring twenties," with their sacks and bucket hats.
This kinship with the mainstream of design did not particularly worry Exter or
Popova, but it did cause concern among the more committed socialist critics in
the Soviet Union. Their argument became a familiar one: if a revolution has
been made and if this has given rise to a new, radical society with new systems
and ways of life, then the artistic style of this new society should be distinctive,
immediately identifiable, unprecedented. It became especially clear at the
"Exposition Internationale des Arts Decoratifs et Industriels Modernes" in
Paris in 1925, where the Soviet Union was well represented, that new Soviet
design, while audacious, attractive, functional, had much in common with the
new wave of design in France, Germany, and the United States. The critic
Yakov Tugendkhol'd commented on this in his review of the Exposition:

> Many still think that Constructivism and non-objective art represent an extreme-
> ly leftist trend, identifiable precisely with our proletarian country. The Paris
> Exposition has revealed that Constructivism is identifiable equally with bourgeois
> countries too, where "leftist" bourgeois bedrooms . . . and leftist ladies' *manteaux*
> of ermine and sable are being made. . . . Does this mean that the revolutionary
> ideology is conquering the bourgeois consciousness, that it is entering the
> bourgeois world or, on the contrary, that these principles are really not so revolu-
> tionary? The latter, I would think.[23]

This argument served as a major weapon in the struggle against Constructivist
architects and designers from the late 1920s on and as a major stimulus to the
creation of a definite, distinctive, nationally identifiable style instead—Socialist Realism.

The Constructivist contribution to textile and clothes design in Soviet Russia
was brief but remarkable. Popova, above all, reached a new definition of
movement perceived visually and did, indeed, extend "art" into "life." Unfortunately, with her death in 1924 and Stepanova's shift of interest to printing and
photographic design, the Constructivist experience in textiles was soon forgotten. Ignoring the lessons of their elders, young designers at the key textile
centers either reverted to a Victorian floridity or they treated the textile as a
pictorial surface which could transmit an agitational or literary message. Of
course, the new figurative textiles were a direct response to public taste, but as
the critic Alexei Fedorov-Davydov wrote in 1931, they had little to do with
Soviet reality:

... all attempts to sovietize the textile design for garment fabrics ... have been confined to a very narrow choice of themes, in most cases lacking in any sociopolitical trenchancy. At best, the subject is a rather naive one—a Pioneer, a Red Army soldier on skis, a little head with a smile. . . . Pioneers on a piece of fustian . . . repeated endlessly in a single figure lose all representational value. . . . Or take the so called industrial motifs. . . . What's Soviet about them? Why does a mere tractor have to be a Soviet theme? There are actually more tractors in bourgeois America than in the USSR. . . .[24]

By the late 1920s it was clear that Soviet textile design had lost its clarity of purpose and, as in all spheres of design, the result was a curious eclecticism of styles. Abstract motifs vied with luxuriant cornucopias just as photomontage vied with the new Realist painting or the austere lines of reinforced concrete buildings contained soft couches, pouffes, bearskins, and classical vases. By the mid-1930s the contradiction was resolved, for art once again became "reproductional" and intensely decorative. Just as flowers are scattered above the tomb, so Soviet art reached its most florid phase at the sternest moment of Stalin's rule. The heroines of the revolution arose from the divans upholstered in material carrying industrial motifs in rococo settings and donned kerchiefs recounting complicated episodes from the Civil War; they drank tea from cups depicting Slavic fairy tales, entered Baroque subway stations, and went to work in Neo-Palladian office buildings. Such was the "haze of fantasy" which clouded the pure visions of Popova and her comrades, such was the monstrous mixture that liquidated Constructivist design.

NOTES

1. Part of this article appeared in an essay entitled "From Pictures to Textile Prints" in *The Print Collector's Newsletter*, New York, 1976 (March/April), 16–20.

2. N. Tarabukin, *Ot mol'berta k mashine* (Moscow, 1923), 23–24.

3. Quoted from V. Lobanov, *Khudozhestvennye gruppirovki za poslednie 25 let* (Moscow, 1930), 101.

4. L. Trotsky, *Literature and Revolution* (New York, 1924), Chapter 6.

5. For information on Bogdanov see Dietrich Grille, *Lenins Rivale. Bogdanov und seine Philosophie* (Cologne, 1966).

6. This was noted by David Arkin in his article "Iskusstvo veshchi" in *Ezhegodnik literatury i iskusstva na 1929 god* (Moscow, 1929), 437.

7. See, for example, *Damskii mir*, Petrograd, 1917, especially the January issue.

8. L. Bakst, "Kostium zhenshchiny budushchego (Beseda)" in *Birzhevye vedomosti* (St. Petersburg, 1913, 20 March).

9. V. Mass, "Pankrasy levogo fronta" in *Zrelishcha* (Moscow, 1922), No. 10.

10. See catalog of "Vtoraia vystavka sovremennogo dekorativnogo iskusstva," Moscow, 1917.

11. O. Brik, "Ot kartiny k sittsu" in *Lef,* Moscow, 1924, No. 2, 30–31.

12. L. Popova, untitled, unpaginated statement in the catalog of the exhibition "5 × 5 = 25," Moscow, 1921.

13. On Liudmila Maiakovskaia see V. A. Katanian, *Maiakovsky. Literaturnaia Khronika,* Moscow, 1961, pp. 10ff.

14. E. Kan, "Telo i odezhda" in *Zrelishcha,* 1922, No. 7, 16.

15. Yu. Annenkov, "Estestvennoe otpravlenie," in *Arena,* Petersburg, 1924, 114.

16. Quoted from T. Strizhenova, *Iz istorii sovetskogo kostiuma,* Moscow, 1972, 100.

17. Ibid., 97.

18. Varst (=V. Stepanova), "Kostium segodniashnego dnia—prozodezhda," in *Lef,* 1923, No. 2, 65.

19. It should be noted that Stepanova's sports designs found an important precedent in Bakst's costume designs for the ballet *Les Jeux* produced in 1913 with Nijinsky and Karsavina in the main roles.

20. N. Lamanova, "O masterskikh sovremennykh khudozhestvennykh kostiumov," in *Pervaia Vserossiiskaia konferentsiia po khudozhestvennoi promyshlennosti, avgust 1919* (Moscow, 1920), 37–38.

21. For information see the journal issued by the Atelier: *Atel'e mod,* Moscow, No. 1 (no more published).

22. Exter touched on this in her article which appeared in *Atel'e mod.* Extracts are quoted in Strizhenova, op. cit., 72.

23. Ia. Tugendkhol'd, *Khudozhestvennaia kul'tura Zapada* (Moscow-Leningrad, 1928), 130.

24. A. Fedorov-Davydov, "Iskusstvo tekstil'ia" in *Izofront. Klassovaia bor'ba na fronte prostranstvennykh iskusstv. Sbornik statei ob'edineniia "Oktiabr' "* (Moscow-Leningrad, 1931), 77–78.

[13] The Birth of the New Soviet Woman

Barbara Evans Clements

THE "NEW SOVIET WOMAN" is a familiar figure to most students of the Soviet Union. Born in the revolution and civil war, the Soviet heroine first appeared in periodicals as a nurse, as a political leader in the army, even as a combat soldier. She was modest, firm, dedicated, sympathetic, courageous, bold, hard-working, energetic, and often young. She gave no thought to her personal welfare. She could leave her children, although with regret, if she was needed at the front; she could put up with physical hardship, face combat and torture if captured, and even endure death, believing that her sacrifice had contributed to the building of a better world.[1]

The new Soviet woman has changed in significant ways since those early years when she made her debut as a heroine of civil war. Initially she was drawn from life. In 1920, 66,000 women were serving in the Red Army, comprising 2 percent of that force. Although the vast majority held support jobs in administration or medicine,[2] they often shared the dangers and difficulties of war with the soldiers, and their sacrifices were the more admirable because they were for the most part volunteers. Basing their portraits on these real women, Soviet publicists created the selfless revolutionary who was the first incarnation of the new Soviet woman. Later, in the twenties, the new Soviet woman continued to have the same character as the revolutionary heroine, but she was engaged in study or work in industry. In the late twenties she changed still further, as a more maternal woman began to win approval. The ideal Soviet woman of today grew out of the hybrid heroine of the thirties. The present ideal is dedicated, hard-working, and modest like her grandmother of the revolution, but she is also loving and maternal, the keeper of the family hearth.

Who created the revolutionary heroine, what purposes did she serve, and what does her later evolution reveal about the attempts of the early Bolshevik government to establish a revolutionary culture based on a new value system?

My thesis is a simple one: initially the Bolsheviks drew the new woman from life, but more importantly from their beliefs about what woman was and what she should be. They believed that the woman of the masses was both a conservative who could be an enemy of revolution and a long-suffering victim of oppression who must be liberated by revolution. The emancipated revolutionary woman already existed among the proletariat and in the party, the Bolsheviks believed, but in very small numbers. The vast majority of women were thus both victims and adversaries, whom the revolution must make over into free and equal beings. With these conceptions, a group of Bolsheviks began agitation and propaganda among women. During the civil war years, the vision of the emancipated woman they propagated was tempered because of the fear of female conservatism and because of inner-party opposition to feminism. During the N.E.P., the ideal was further altered as part of a syncretism between radical Marxist and traditional Russian values. The Stalinist ideal which emerged was a blend of the old and the new, as were most Stalinist values.

To understand this process we must begin with the interpretation of the nature and condition of women in Russia that the Bolsheviks held on coming to power. The official party view, set forth in the writings of the leaders of work among women—Nadezhda Krupskaia, Aleksandra Kollontai, Inessa Armand, and Konkordiia Samoilova—was that the masses of Russian women were suffering meekly under the heavy oppression of class and family.[3] The woman of the peasantry and the proletariat was, to quote Gorky, a "soft, sad, and submissive" creature who bore every hardship which a cruel world could inflict on her with simple resignation.[4] Deeply maternal, she devoted herself to caring for her husband and children, even though men often abused her. This romanticization of the poor Russian woman (the noblewoman was dismissed as a parasitic member of an exploiting class) had been formulated originally by the populists of the mid-nineteenth century, and had been most eloquently expressed by the poet Nikolai Nekrasov. Nekrasov in turn drew on ancient myths, most notably the Christian, which sanctified woman as suffering servant.

Thus the Bolshevik idealization of woman had its roots in Russian and Western European socialism, in romanticism, and in older traditions. It was part also of the socialist belief in the nobility of all the oppressed, and is different from the Bolshevik idealization of the man of the lower classes only in the extent to which the idealization of woman included praise for her docility. But the praise was always uneasy and the idealization tempered by mistrust. No revolutionary felt comfortable applauding the submissiveness of those he hoped to stir to revolt. And the praise for woman's natural virtue was also weakened by the belief that women were not merely more downtrodden than men, but also more conservative. There was some evidence to support this contention in the nineteenth century. Women did not join trade unions in large numbers. They attended church more regularly than men. They were illiterate and therefore more difficult to reach with printed propaganda. They considered politics a male preserve.[5] It took considerable faith for revolutionaries to see any virtue in this passivity. Most believed that centuries of oppression had made women long suffering and faithful, and also ignorant, religious, and apathetic. The Bolsheviks had similar fears about lower-class men, which they expressed for the most part in condemnations of the peasantry. With regard to women of both the peasantry and the proletariat, they admitted openly that they believed women to be a backward element which could threaten the success of the revolution.

There was less ambivalence toward women in the Bolsheviks' conception of what they would be after the revolution had swept away their ignorance. They would become "new women," a conception the Bolsheviks took directly, and at first without significant modification, from nineteenth-century feminism and socialism. The Europeans who played the leading role in developing this ideal were George Sand, Charles Fourier, Harriett Taylor and John Stuart Mill, August Bebel, and Henrik Ibsen. Although differing on the proper role of women in the family, these writers agreed that the defining characteristic of the new woman was independence from prescribed roles and male domination. She was an individualist, determined to pursue self-development, to seek, in Mill's words, "a life of rational freedom"[6] in defiance of custom and even of the legitimate claims of those she loved. Mill assumed, as did Bebel and most writers on the new woman, that she would choose to express her freedom in socially responsible activity, for neither Mill nor Bebel was inclined to embrace a pure, anarchic, self-indulgent individualism. Indeed, "rational freedom," the goal of liberals and socialists alike, demanded a high degree of commitment to the welfare of others on the part of men as well as women. Although the defining characteristic of the new woman was independence, it was an independence in which she chose voluntarily to serve society while serving herself.

The new, autonomous, socially responsible woman made her appearance in Russia with the opening of the debates on the woman question in the 1850s and found her most influential advocate in Nikolai Chernyshevsky. Vera Pavlovna, the heroine of Chernyshevsky's novel *What Is to Be Done?* (1863), became an inspiration for generations of radical women, including those Bolsheviks— Armand, Krupskaia, Kollontai, Samoilova—who were to play a direct role in creating the Soviet heroine. Through rejecting the control of her philistine parents, Vera Pavlovna obtains everything a free woman could want: a loving, supportive husband, beautiful children, good friends, and a worthwhile career. Elena in Turgenev's novel *On the Eve* (1860) was another of the new women of nineteenth-century Russian literature, more passionate than the rationalistic Vera Pavlovna, more decisive, and more clearly committed to political liberation. Elena, with her ardent social conscience, and Vera Pavlovna, with her stress on individual freedom, together exemplified primary aspects of the new woman for several generations of Russian radicals.

This vision of emancipated womanhood, expressed in fiction, found real-life embodiment in the revolutionary women of the 1870s. Inspired in part by fictional models, Sofiia Perovskaia and her comrades created the tradition of female participation in revolutionary parties. The Bolshevik leadership took its conception of the new woman from this blend of Western European and Russian ideals. She would be created from the masses of downtrodden women about whose attitudes and loyalties the Bolsheviks had grave doubts. It was with the goal of transforming illiterate workers and peasants into emancipated women that Bolshevik propaganda began during the civil war years to shape the image of the new Soviet woman.

The most active propagandists of this conception were the Bolsheviks who led the first efforts to organize working-class women, that is, Inessa Armand, Aleksandra Kollontai, Nadezhda Krupskaia, Konkordiia Samoilova, Klavdiia Nikolaeva, Liudmilla Stal, and Rakhil Kovnator, among others. The tasks of organizing women and of articulating new conceptions in order to organize them were left almost exclusively in the hands of these women of the party Woman's Bureau (the *Zhenotdel*), because most Bolsheviks simply did not think the work was very important. The party had long judged women's emancipation to be a lesser issue subsumed under the great task of bringing about revolution. During the civil war, Bolsheviks set the highest priority on military matters, and downgraded the worth of work among women as well as work in education or in other social services. For the same reasons the party spent little time discussing the woman question. Agitation and propaganda for general party or public audiences rarely mentioned women.[7] The consequences of all this were that propaganda among women and the conception of the new Soviet woman were initially developed by the *Zhenotdel* working without close party supervision.

The agitation addressed to working-class women in 1918 and 1919 took the form of pamphlets written by Kollontai, Armand, Samoilova, and others and newspaper columns written by the *Zhenotdel* organizers of work among women, not by the regular newspaper staffs.[8] This agitation sought to persuade women to aid the war effort by convincing them that the revolution was worth defending. The conceptions of woman propagated by these writings included woman as suffering victim occasionally, but far more commonly used was the negative view of woman as anti-revolutionary. Woman was passively watching the revolution, the pamphlets and columns declared, while her men fought and died for her. "We, whom nature has endowed with a special sensitivity of soul, a special ability to understand another's grief," wrote Gofanovich-Milovidova, a communist in the army in 1919, "we stand on the sidelines in this great cause—the emancipation of the oppressed and outraged."[9] The lower-class woman had been given freedom and equality by the Soviet government, but she was too ignorant to understand this, so she was allowing herself to be abused by her bosses and deceived by the priests.[10] The writers admitted that working women were sometimes openly critical of the Bolsheviks,[11] and they explained both the apathy of the majority and the hostility of the minority as a result of woman's backwardness. The word "backwardness" occurs repeatedly in these sources, as do references to "dark women." By contrast the columns praised women who had awakened from their ignorance to an understanding of the revolution as a great triumph for their gender and their class, and who had dedicated themselves to defending it against the capitalists and the landlords.

A disturbing insensitivity seems to pervade this agitation. Only rarely did writers show any sympathy for the terrible hardships that beset women in the civil war years—the hunger, cold, and disease with which they had had to cope. If ever there was a time when Russian women truly were suffering servants it was during the civil war, and yet the columns and pamphlets for the most part ignored women's struggle to survive and accused them of passivity if they could not find the energy to do volunteer work. Were the Bolsheviks callously refusing to understand the plight of working-class women in explaining their refusal to flock to public activities as a sign of their personal deficiencies, their backwardness? Some Bolsheviks no doubt felt that way, but not the leaders of the *Zhenotdel*. They chose to condemn women's passivity because they believed that women's welfare and the revolution would be advanced if women became involved in nursing the sick or organizing day care centers. Thus the *Zhenotdel* writers could not admit that very real problems were keeping most women occupied. Rather, they had to proclaim that women's attitudes were the obstacle preventing them from joining the revolution, and they had to ignore the privations that the government could do little to alleviate.

What of the subject that chiefly concerns us here, the creation of the conception of the new Soviet woman? Did the emancipated woman figure in the agitation addressed to working-class women? The answer is no, not in her fully developed form. The *Pravda* columns and the pamphlets presented female emancipation to proletarian women as a package of reforms which would make their lives easier, not as a program for the total restructuring of their lives, and therefore this agitation kept the new woman in the background. "Woman worker," a typical headline in *Pravda* proclaimed, "take your fate in your own hands, wake up, lift up your head. You are an equal creature."[12] Equality was explained as political rights, the right to divorce a cruel husband, equal pay for equal work, labor protection, and, in the future, help with childcare and housework. There was no glorification of women's domestic duties, no hymns to the happy homemaker like those which appeared in the thirties, but neither was there the wholesale assault on family roles which Bolshevik ideology promised. Women were assured that the state was not going to take their children away from them, only care for the youngest while the mothers were at work. "Free love" was defined as marriage based on friendship rather than male domination. Although Christianity was derided as prejudice and superstition, agitators did not deny that women had a right to practice religion. Anatole Lunacharsky, the Commissar of Enlightenment (Education) in an article in *Pravda* in 1919, gently explained that women could pray if they chose, but that they could not, as one woman told him she would, join the Communist Party and continue to go to church.[13]

The agitators urged women to support the revolution, therefore, not because the revolution was going to make them into new women, but because the revolution had already broken the power of the landlords and the bosses, and had given them political rights. Eventually it would make their lives easier. In return, women owed aid to the Soviet government. They had a duty to work hard in their jobs, to volunteer for public-works projects in their off hours, to organize facilities to help themselves, to visit wounded soldiers in the hospitals, to support their men at the front, and even to fight at the front themselves. They had been given much, they should take part in defending the revolution.

This elementary appeal was chosen because Armand, Kollontai, Krupskaia, and Samoilova believed that working-class women at best would be indifferent to theorizing about the new woman, and at worst would be hostile to the criticism of religion, family, and women's traditional roles implicit in advocacy of complete emancipation.[14] There is evidence provided by *Zhenotdel* workers that working-class women did openly condemn the Bolsheviks, although the extent of their opposition is unclear. The Bolsheviks may have overestimated the resistance of working-class women to their appeals, because they began with the assumption that working-class women would resist them. In any event it is clear that *Zhenotdel* workers found little in the behavior of proletarian women in 1919 and 1920 to contradict their belief in widespread female conservatism.

The *Zhenotdel* leaders also may have avoided an ardent appeal for the new woman in mass agitation because they feared that the party would charge them with encouraging feminism if they stressed women's emancipation too strongly. The party leaders insisted that agitation among women must do nothing to rouse "feminist" attitudes, which meant that such agitation must emphasize women's responsibility to the "general revolutionary cause," as the phrase went. Women were to be persuaded to work for the good of all, and to pursue their own special interests only to advance the revolution. In ideology and in policy the Bolsheviks had always subordinated women's emancipation to the greater goal of revolution for an entire society. Like most socialists, they did so out of a combination of legitimate ideological and tactical considerations, and unacknowledged prejudice.[15] Kollontai, Armand, Samoilova, and Krupskaia had dealt with this resistance for years, learning in the process to hedge their declarations of female emancipation round with assurances that women were seeking their own liberation as part of the general liberation.

Finally, there is some fragmentary evidence that the *Zhenotdel* leaders, the most feminist of Bolsheviks, themselves may have feared feminism among more politically aware working-class women, that is, may have feared that women, inspired by declarations of female emancipation, would begin to demand improvements in their lives which the government could not make. There were times when women at meetings organized by the Woman's Bureau criticized the party for not keeping its promises to them. For example, at a meeting in 1919 a factory worker asked why women were not getting equal pay for equal work. She was told by the conference organizers that women would be paid equally when they participated equally in the struggle.[16] *Zhenotdel* writings also contain brief references to women in the provinces organizing women's unions to press for better wages and working conditions. The *Zhenotdel* leaders in Moscow condemned these groups as feminist and ordered them disbanded.[17] Armand, Kollontai, and Samoilova wanted to bring women under Bolshevik leadership, not encourage them to question its shortcomings. In writing their agitation for lower-class women, therefore, the *Zhenotdel* workers developed a carefully crafted message designed to calm the opposition of traditionalist women, antifeminist Bolsheviks, and activist women alike.[18]

The *Zhenotdel* had not abandoned the new woman; its leaders simply did not feel that she should be presented to the masses of working-class women, so they saved her for propaganda designed for a more educated and therefore more trustworthy audience. Once a woman had mastered the basics of literacy and Marxism, then she was ready to be introduced to the new woman. Thus in the brochures and handbooks recommended to *Zhenotdel* workers and especially in *Kommunistka*, the journal of the *Zhenotdel*, the new woman figured more prominently than in the mass agitation of *Pravda* and the pamphlets.[19] In these publications, designed to teach communist women or fellow-travelers about organizational techniques and about the condition of women in Russia, Armand and Kollontai felt free to call for the creation of that fully autonomous creature who had completely rejected the past, economically, socially, psychologically. Theoretical articles such as Kollontai's on morality and the family, Armand's and Krupskaia's on the marriage law, or Krupskaia's on abortion, discussed the changes in relations between the sexes that were necessary to free women from slavery to men.[20] By and large, however, the editors of *Kommunistka*, led by Krupskaia, expressed their advocacy of the new woman not in theoretical essays but in biographical sketches of real and fictional women, thereby creating the Soviet heroine with whom we began. *Kommunistka* was not the only champion of the new woman; there were short stories, poems, and plays published elsewhere during the war years in which she appeared, but *Kommunistka* featured her so consistently and so prominently that its editors can justly be credited with playing a major role in the creation of the Soviet heroine.[21]

She was, above all else, a fighter who was willing to dedicate her entire life to the cause of advancing communism. Often of lower-class origins, she had fought her way out of the slavery which was a woman's lot, usually because the revolution in 1917 had shown her the truth. She had then gone on to work for the cause, as a political officer, nurse, or soldier, and had distinguished herself by her bravery, her selflessness, and her modesty (*skromnost'*, meaning in this context that she lacked the vanity commonly attributed to women). Zinaida Chalaia described such women as "bold, impetuous, practical, prudent, greedily drinking in all knowledge." Liudmilla Stal praised "the fire of their faith" and their "joy in labor."[22] If they had to die, they died with their faith undiminished, as did Ksenia Ge, a real communist who faced a White firing squad with the defiant shout, "I am dying for that blessed idea which you will someday understand."[23] So long as they lived, they worked tirelessly at whatever job the party gave them, putting duty ahead of all else. Inessa Armand became the shining example of such self-sacrifice, for she drove herself to the point of exhaustion in 1920, and then, forced by friends to rest in the Caucasus, she contracted cholera and died.[24] Women such as Inessa were praised for never losing hope, never faltering; they were a source of inspiration and comfort to their comrades. In a poem in *Pravda* in 1920 entitled "Woman Communist" a female soldier newly arrived at the front tells the men who greet her with hisses:

I have come from your sisters and brothers,
I can help you in your suffering,
I will brighten the horrors of death's embraces
Overcome hunger, cold, despair.[25]

Are these heroines the new women of the nineteenth century converted to communism and armed, or are they simply Bolshevik Molly Pitchers, the suffering servant in uniform doing all to help their men? The answer is that these are emancipated women, for they have rejected traditional female roles to serve, not men, but the cause, and they have done so, the articles often say explicitly, to escape bondage as women. In the mass agitation women were often called on to support the revolution as a way of helping their husbands or defending their children. In *Kommunistka* few such appeals to traditional loyalties were made. The writers even speak approvingly of the new women's decisions to leave their children. They are praised for their autonomy, and in this they are the direct descendents of Vera Pavlovna and Elena. In fact, they are more autonomous than Vera Pavlovna, in the extent to which they have abandoned family life. And they do so not simply to dedicate themselves to communism, thus exchanging one form of service for another, but to free themselves as individuals. It is only after emancipating themselves that they can dedicate themselves to society. Like Vera Pavlovna and Elena, they are individualists who serve the collective welfare. A poem from 1922 entitled "Daughters of October" sums up their virtues:

They came
Not in diamonds or flowers.
They were born in October
On the barricades, in the streets.

They wear finery: jackets, caps,
Blood red kerchiefs;
They shake hands until it hurts,
And their expression is bold, profound.

With the sound of new, red songs,
With cries of horror from the Philistines
They blow up the family's lamp molds*
Madly rejoicing in the light.

Love with censers, love with altars
They cast away, smiling—
Love is free, as themselves,
The boundaries are broken for them.

Not knowing the slave's boredom, they
Rush between life and labor
Pressing toward the springs of science,
Quenching their thirst for knowledge.

Their violent beginning
Opened the doors to a new age,
And shouted loudly to the world,
"I am a person."[26]

Most of the articles on the revolutionary heroine were more muted in their proclamations of women's sexual independence. In *Kommunistka,* as in agitation for less literate audiences, the Marxist belief in free love was acknowledged, but usually defined as a commitment to monogamous relationships

*Used to make ikon lamps.

based on mutual affection rather than economic dependence. Rakhil Kovnator wrote openly about a woman's right to "a free, independent attitude in her personal life" in *Kommunistka* in 1920, and Kollontai analyzed sexuality.[27] Other writers in *Kommunistka* avoided the issue, and this is evidence in these years before sexuality became a subject of general discussion that it was controversial. The writers also soften the individualism of the new woman somewhat by stressing her service to the cause as her chief virtue. Her individual emancipation is usually pictured as a means to the end of her apotheosis as communist. Thus, predictably, even in the most feminist of Bolshevik writings, woman's liberation is subordinated to the liberation of the whole, feminist goals to communist ones. Nevertheless, the new woman's emancipation *qua* woman was made more explicit and praised more loudly in *Kommunistka* than in the agitation designed for uneducated women.[28]

What functions did the new woman, now transformed into revolutionary heroine, fulfill in the *Kommunistka* articles and in other propaganda for communist women? She honored the dead and exhorted the living. Examples such as the peasant who became a communist after a lifetime of servility or the young machinegunner who held a bridge until reinforcements arrived reassured the Bolsheviks that the new woman was emerging from the sea of peasants whose hostility they feared.[29] The new woman also served as the regime's approved model of female virtue, the antithesis of the lethargic, obstructionist peasant. In approving her, the Bolsheviks declared the traditional conceptions of female virtue, and therefore traditional roles, obsolete.

Even in the earliest days of Soviet rule, however, *Zhenotdel* leaders felt that they had to make concessions to public and party opinion where women were concerned. The agitation addressed to mass audiences was cautious in its advocacy of female emancipation because of fears of rousing resistance among the masses and within the party. In the twenties the new woman began to be reshaped by party and public. Two initially unrelated debates began within the party that changed the revolutionary heroine—one the discussion of sexuality, which culminated in a rejection of the Marxist doctrine of free love, the other the marriage law reform, which in effect gave official blessings to the nuclear family. A detailed examination of these two developments is beyond the scope of this paper.[30] Suffice it to say that by the late twenties authoritative writers in the party press, reacting to what they perceived as promiscuity among the young, had declared monogamy and premarital chastity to be the ideals for Soviet youth. Paralleling this was a reform in the 1918 marriage law, issued in 1926, that guaranteed child support and alimony to spouses in common law marriages. In drafting this humane legislation, the leaders of the Commissariat of Justice rejected more radical proposals that childcare expenses be paid out of public funds, and affirmed the responsibility of parents to support their children, thereby taking the first major step toward endorsing the nuclear family as a fundamental institution of Soviet society.

Both these changes were part of a syncretism in progress between Bolshevik ideology and traditional Russian values, a syncretism apparent as early as the *Pravda* columns of 1919, that led by the thirties to the emergence of a modified revolutionary heroine. She was still an equal citizen and loyal worker, but she was also a devoted wife and mother, and she had lost most of her autonomy, the defining characteristic of the new woman. Rather than rejecting family roles, she fulfilled them perfectly; she was enmeshed in a web of responsibilities to husband, children, and society and beautified by her capacity to serve. In her ability to be all things—worker, wife, and mother—the Soviet heroine of the thirties resembled Nekrasov's valiant peasants, except that unlike Nekrasov, her Soviet mentors praised her service without qualification. The mass agitation of the civil war years had been careful not to attack widely held ideas about woman's nature and role in the family too directly. The pronouncements of the thirties—mass agitation, inner-party propaganda, and belletristic works—embraced the idea of woman as servant wholeheartedly.[31] It is tempting to conclude that having vanquished the benighted *baba* by educating her and bringing her to work in the factories or offices, the party felt free to merge the two images of women which Bolsheviks had always admired—the free communist and the long-suffering servant. No longer did woman's capacity for dumb endurance threaten to preserve an unjust society; now her mythical powers of service could be useful in strengthening a Bolshevik-dominated social system.

Yet it is insufficient to explain the changes in the new woman exclusively as a consequence of the Bolsheviks' self-serving manipulation of stereotypic images. Always a product of Bolshevik efforts to build public support by molding public attitudes, the new Soviet woman was from the first also an expression of their attitudes toward female emancipation. The party's program for female emancipation was weaker than the party endorsements of it suggested, because of the influence of traditional values within the party and because the Marxist analysis of the family was inadequate. Lower ranking members of the party, often poorly educated, probably understood little of Marx's and Engels's doctrines on the abolition of the family and free love.[32] Educated Bolsheviks familiar with proposals to socialize housework and childcare did not look beyond these to a consideration of new family structures until the twenties. Marx had declared that no one could predict the form relations between the sexes would take after the revolution, and in any event it was a matter of minor social significance. The bourgeois family would be abolished, women freed, and social control over sexual relations removed. Perfect freedom between women and men would then ensue. This utopian prospect and the

Marxist dismissal of the family as an institution derivative of economic forces prevented Bolsheviks from understanding the depth of human loyalties, including their own, to the division of power and roles within the family.

In the twenties, the ending of the war allowed the party to turn its attention to peacetime problems, among them the pattern of daily life that was emerging in the new Russia. This consideration naturally included an examination of male-female relations. Reacting to the dislocations caused by the years of war, some communists began to fear that widespread divorce and promiscuity were threatening the consolidation of social stability. These fears were probably exaggerated,[33] but the Bolsheviks perceived the sexual experimentation and marital instability of the twenties as a threat because they feared, rather than hoped for, the dissolution of the family. Faced with the task of governing an immense, war-ravaged country, they postponed the abolition of the family to a comfortably remote future. For the time being, they asserted, the family was essential to social order. Crucial to the survival of the family was the preservation of woman's nurturing roles and man's providing roles within it. Many also believed that they must preserve male authority, but this was so completely antithetical to party ideology that it could not be openly admitted.

A few quotations should serve to illustrate the reaction. In a 1926 article in the journal *Molodaia gvardiia,* Emelian Iaroslavsky, a middle-aged Bolshevik intellectual, discussed the dangers of "the sexual licentiousness which exists . . . among communists and in particular among the youth." "Now," he wrote, "you often meet worn-out youths, young old men who need a rest home, a sanitarium, because they already have led a life that many of us old men haven't led." Puberty generated sexual energy, Iaroslavsky declared, which either could be put to constructive use building socialism or squandered in self-indulgence.[34]

There was something of the universal parental lament over the waywardness of youth in Iaroslavsky's avuncular tone, and perhaps a touch of the envy of the middle-aged, too. Other Bolsheviks saw the alleged sexual excesses of the twenties as a problem of male appetites unleashed by permissive laws. A woman communist named Shurupova expressed this attitude with a nice peasant metaphor during the marriage law debate. "He took two wives," she said by way of example, "each gave him a baby, so he must pay both of them. It's nobody else's fault: If you like tobogganing, you must like pulling your sledge uphill." The issue was not perceived as trivial, for social order was at stake. Volkhova, a female communist from the provinces, summed up the fear of the consequences of liberated sexuality in her statement during the marriage-law debate:

> The majority of our rural population wish to preserve a system described as *domostroy* [patriarchal family relations], according to many of the speakers here. I

declare, comrades, that this is not true. But it is true that the villages do not wish to attract to the rural areas the marriage instability that exists in the towns. Who is responsible for the neglected children? The villages? The towns, begging your pardon. What will happen if 85 percent of the population of our country, formed of the peasantry, did as the towns do? We should flounder in disintegration.[35]

The solution in the view of many Bolsheviks was to restore stability to marriage by confining sex within it and by reaffirming woman's and man's responsibilities to each other and their children. It took but a small additional step to reach the syrupy descriptions of woman's domestic roles characteristic of the thirties. In the words of Stekha, the heroine of a 1937 novel, "a wife should also be a happy mother and create a serene home atmosphere, without however abandoning work for the common welfare. She should know how to combine all these things while also matching her husband's performance on the job."[36]

The *Zhenotdel*'s role in the definition of Soviet womanhood ended with the growth of party interest in matters once stigmatized as of secondary importance. The *Zhenotdel* relinquished that role openly in 1923, when Sof'ia Smidovich, then head of the department, announced in *Kommunistka* that hereafter the journal would be devoted exclusively to instructing *Zhenotdel* workers in organizational techniques. Smidovich advised female communists interested in "theoretical questions" to turn to "the party press," which meant, presumably, publications of a less exclusively female readership.[37] The debates over sexuality and the marriage law occurred instead in *Molodaia gvardiia,* published by the Komsomol (the overwhelmingly male party organization for young people), in *Pravda,* and in collections of articles issued in book form.[38] The *Zhenotdel*'s abdication of a role in the debates, save for occasional articles by Smidovich and a discredited Kollontai, resulted from the fact that the original leaders of the department were gone—Armand and Samoilova dead, Kollontai in exile, Krupskaia withdrawn first to Gorki to nurse Lenin and later to work in education, Stal and Kovnator moved off into editorial work elsewhere. It is doubtful, however, that even they could have defended the new woman against the party's reassessment, for the assimilation of traditional values into Bolshevik ideology was a virtually inevitable part of the formation of a broadly based, post-revolutionary culture. Some accommodation between Marxist feminism and ancient attitudes toward woman and family always comes as revolutionaries settle down into governors, and peasants move into the party.[39] In picturing the new Soviet woman as the ideal Soviet wife and mother as well as an equal citizen and worker, in stripping her of her autonomy and reasserting the importance of her maternal duties, the Bolsheviks were creating a heroine acceptable not just to themselves as rulers, but to the nation as well. The iconoclastic, individualistic new woman was a stranger in the family-centered, conformist world of the village.

Finally we must return to the point with which we began: the new Soviet woman was always a servant of the regime. A central question for the Bolshevik government of the twenties was order, how to restore order to a ruptured society, and the means chosen in all areas of Soviet life became increasingly authoritarian as the twenties gave way to the thirties. The resurgence within the party of traditional values regarding woman's responsibilities to the family was part of the growth of this authoritarianism. Seeking to establish control over Russia, the Bolsheviks shored up the two institutions—the state and the family—once condemned by them to extinction. As long as the party's attention had been occupied elsewhere, the Bolshevik feminists had been relatively free, although never completely free, to praise the new woman. The *Zhenotdel* knew, however, that the new woman had not been accepted by the people or the party, hence their caution in displaying her. Her liberated sexuality, her disregard for family were too great a threat to social order and to deeply cherished beliefs about human nature and sexual identity. Her individual emancipation always had to be limited by a clear definition of her responsibilities, she always had to serve ends greater than her own welfare. As they came to be defined, in the twenties and thirties, the ends were traditional—the preservation of established authority—and modern—industrialization. The responsibilities were traditional—preservation of the family—and modern—participation in work outside the domestic sphere. Thus the new Soviet woman finally became a syncretic creature, a blend of the feminist ideal, which in its individualism was essentially middle-class and liberal, with the socialist ideal, which found liberation in collective endeavor, and the older Russian ideal, which hallowed woman for her ability to serve the family. It was an awkward creation, as impossible of attainment by real women as the virginal virtue of the Christian saints had been, but it was more acceptable in its blend of the old and the new than the daughters of October. This is why the daughters of October, born in the freedom of the civil war years, did not survive the twenties.

NOTES

1. See for example N. K. [Krupskaia], "Inessa Armand," *Kommunistka*, no. 5 (1920), pp. 17–20; P. F. Kudelli, *Rabotnitsa v 1905 g. v Peterburge* (Moscow, 1926); *Zhenshchiny v revoliutsii* (Moscow: Politizdat, 1959); *Zhenshchiny russkoi revoliutsii* (Moscow: Politizdat, 1968); *Bez nikh my ne pobedili by* (Moscow: Politizdat, 1975).

2. P. M. Chirkov, *Reshenie zhenskogo voprosa v S.S.S.R. (1917–1937gg.)* (Moscow: *Mysl*, 1978), p. 156.

3. N. Krupskaia [pseud. Sablina], *Zhenshchina-rabotnitsa* (n.p.: Iskra, 1901); R.S.D.R.P., *Zhenskaia dolia* (Geneva: Iskra, 1905); *Listovki Peterburgskikh bol'shevikov 1902–1917,* 2v. (Moscow: Politizdat, 1939), 1:37–38, 183–84, 361–63, 379–81; 2:93–94; Kollontai, *Sotsial'nye osnovy zhenskogo voprosa* (St. Petersburg: Znanie, 1909); Inessa Armand, "Zhenskoe rabochee dvizhenie i voina," *Sotsial-demokrat,* no. 34 (1915), reprinted in Vsesoiuznaia kommunisticheskaia partiia (bol'shevikov), *Kommunisticheskaia partiia i organizatsiia rabotnits* (Moscow-Petrograd: *Kommunist*, 1919), pp. 47–50; K. Samoilova [pseud. N. Sibiriakova], "Avgust Bebel i zhenskii vopros," *Rabotnitsa,* no. 1 (1914), reprinted in *Vsegda s vami; Sbornik, nosviashchennyi 50-letiiu zhurnala 'Rabotnitsa'* (Moscow: *Pravda*, 1964), pp. 51–53.

4. M. Gor'kii, *Mat'* in *Sobranie sochinenii* (Moscow: Gos. izd. khudozhestvennoi literatury, 1960), 4:158.

5. There is manifold evidence for these observations, from nineteenth-century parliamentary debates to twentieth-century historical studies. For a recent example of the latter see Mary Lynn McDougall, "Working-Class Women During the Industrial Revolution," *Becoming Visible: Women in European History,* Renata Bridenthal and Claudia Koonz, eds. (Boston: Houghton Mifflin, 1977), pp. 255–79, esp. pp. 272–74. For a discussion of women's participation in the 1917 elections in Moscow see Diane Koenker, *Moscow Workers and the 1917 Revolution* (Princeton: Princeton University Press, 1981), pp. 203–204, 207–208. For an anthropologist's interpretation of female political participation see Jane Fishburne Collier, "Women in Politics," *Woman, Culture and Society,* Michelle Zimbalist Rosaldo and Louise Lamphere, eds. (Stanford: Stanford University Press, 1974), pp. 89–96.

6. Mary Wollstonecraft, *The Rights of Woman,* and John Stuart Mill, *The Subjection of Women* (London: Dent, 1955), p. 311.

7. For examples of general agitation in which women are rarely mentioned see the *Pravda* columns "Working Life" and "Red Army Soldier" for the civil war years. See also the Agitprop journals *Agit-Rosta* for 1920 and *Vestnik agitatsii i propagandy* for 1921–1922. There were occasional proclamations and leaflets issued by party committees or by commissariats addressed to women. For example see G. D. Kostomarov, ed., *Golos velikoi revoliutsii* (Moscow: Politizdat, 1967), pp. 186–88, and "Fevral'skaia revoliutsiia v dokumentakh," *Proletarskaia revoliutsiia,* no. 1 (13) (1922), pp. 282–84.

8. The columns or "stranichki" appeared first in the newspapers *Kommunar, Petrogradskaia pravda,* and *Krasnaia gazeta* in November and December 1918. *Pravda* began to publish a weekly column in the spring of 1919. The columns were the responsibility of the organizers of work among women in a given area. At their peak in 1921 there were some 80 stranichki being published in provincial newspapers, carrying a combination of articles sent from Moscow and local news. ("Otchet o rabote ot Ts.K. R.K.P. po rabote sredi zhenshchin s m. 1920 po fev. 1921," *Izvestiia Ts. K.R.K.P.(b),* March 5, 1921, pp. 29–30.) Many of the columns were discontinued in 1921 and 1922 when a paper shortage and N.E.P.-induced budget restrictions necessitated cutting down on features.

9. *Pravda,* December 14, 1919, p. 4.

10. See, for example, Ibid., June 12, 1919, p. 4.

11. Ibid., June 19, 1919, p. 4; July 3, 1919, p. 4; July 10, 1919, p. 3; July 17, 1919, p. 4; September 11, 1919, p. 3; October 16, 1919, p. 4; June 3, 1919, p. 2; October 24, 1919, p. 4. Evidence of this criticism also occurs frequently in the pamphlets cited below, note 18.

12. Ibid., September 4, 1919, p. 3.

13. Ibid., October 2, 1919, p. 3.

14. These fears are directly expressed in Ibid, July 31, 1919, p. 4; K. Samoilova, "O

rabote sredi krest'ianok," *Kommunistka*, no. 9 (1920), p. 33; Kommunisticheskaia partiia Sovetskogo Soiuza, *Vos'moi s"ezd, mart 1919 goda* (Moscow: Politizdat, 1959), p. 300.

15. For studies of socialism's espousal of women's rights see Marilyn J. Boxer and Jean H. Quataert, eds., *Socialist Women* (New York: Elsevier, 1978); Jean H. Quataert, *Reluctant Feminists in German Social Democracy, 1885–1917* (Princeton: Princeton University Press, 1979); Sheila Rowbotham, *Women, Resistance and Revolution* (New York: Vintage, 1974).

16. *Pravda*, June 3, 1919, p. 2. For additional references to criticism by women see note 11 above.

17. Ibid., June 3, 1919, p. 2; October 24, 1919, p. 4.

18. This summary is based on the following pamphlets: Ekaterina Arbore-Ralli, *Mat' i det'ia v Sovet. Rossii* (Moscow: Gosizdat, 1920); Kollontai, *Kak boriutsia rabotnitsa* (Moscow: Izd. VTsIK, 1919); Kollontai, *Rabotnitsy, krest'ianki i krasnyi front* (Moscow: Gosizdat, 1920); Kollontai, *Sem'ia i kommunisticheskoe gosudarstvo* (Moscow: Kommunist, 1918); Z. I. Lilina, *Nuzhna li rabotnitsam i krest'iankam Sovetskaia vlast'?* (Petrograd: Gosizdat, 1921); K. Samoilova, *Krest'ianka i sovetskaia vlast'* (Moscow: Gosizdat, 1921); Samoilova, *Rabotnitsy v rossiiskoi revoliutsii* (Petersburg: Gosizdat, 1920). It is also based on two Zhenotdel broadsides reprinted in Kostomarov, *Golos velikoi revoliutsii*, pp. 203–207, 210–214; and on the column "Stranichka zhenshchiny-rabotnitsy," *Pravda*, 1919–21. There were individual differences in the agitators—Inessa and Kollontai were more feminist than Krupskaia or Unskova (one of the main contributors to the *Pravda* column)—but these differences did not alter the central thrust of the agitation. The published materials used here cannot be augmented with speeches made to delegate meetings, a major form of mass agitation, because usually only the titles, not the content, of those speeches were reported in the press.

19. For the instructional materials for Zhenotdel workers see Vsesoiuznaia kommunisticheskaia partiia (bol'shevikov), Tsentral'nyi komitet, Otdel po rabote sredi zhenshchin, *Sbornik instruktsii otdela Ts.K. R.K.P. po rabote sredi zhenshchin* (Moscow: Gosizdat, 1920), especially pp. 44–50; V.K.P., *Kommunisticheskaia partiia i organizatsiia rabotnits*, especially pp. 12–16, 31–41. See also Kollontai's articles on the new woman, *Novaia moral' i rabochii klass* (Moscow: Izd. VTsIK, 1918).

20. Kollontai, "Sem'ia i kommunizm," *Kommunistka*, no. 6 (1920), pp. 16–19; Kollontai, "Tezisy o kommunisticheskoi morali," *Kommunistka*, no. 3–4 (1921), pp. 28–34; Inessa Armand [pseud. Elena Blonina], "Usloviia polnogo osvobozhdeniia rabotnits i krest'ianok," *Kommunistka*, no. 3–4 (1920), pp. 21–24; Krupskaia, "Voina i leto rozhdenie," *Kommunistka*, no. 1–2 (1920), pp. 16–19.

21. Xenia Gasiorowska (*Women in Soviet Fiction* [Madison, Wisc.: University of Wisconsin Press, 1968]) writes that "the very first 'New Woman' in Soviet literature" appeared in 1921 in A. Neverov's story "Marya the Bolshevik." (p. 35) There is evidence in the "stranichki" in *Pravda*, however, and also in an article by Rakhil Kovnator ("Novaia zhenshchina v revoliutsionnoi literature," *Kommunistka*, no. 5 [1920], pp. 32–35) that the new woman had been present in the very earliest Soviet literature, as she was in the propaganda.

22. Zinaida Chalaia, "Bortsy i stroiteli," *Kommunistka*, no. 10–11 (1922), p. 28; Stal, "Novye zhenshchiny," *Kommunistka*, no. 6 (1920), p. 19.

23. "Pamiati krasnykh sester," *Kommunistka*, no. 8–9 (1921), p. 40.

24. N. K., "Inessa Armand," *Kommunistka*, no. 5 (1920), pp. 17–20; L. Stal, "Pamiati Inessy Armand," *Kommunistka*, no. 12–13 (1921), pp. 9–12.

25. *Pravda*, January 18, 1920, p. 3.

26. Ksenia Bykova, "Docheri Oktiabria," *Kommunistka*, no. 10–11 (1922), p. 28.

27. Kovnator, "Novaia zhenshchina v revoliutsionnoi literature," *Kommunistka*, p. 33.

28. This summary is based on the materials on revolutionary women published in *Kommunistka* from 1920 to 1923. They total 47 columns and articles, far too many to list individually here. For a representative sample see the pieces cited above. See also "Biografiia rabotnitsy A. N. Razumovoi," *Kommunistka*, no. 4 (1920), p. 28; "Barmashikha," *Kommunistka*, no. 10–11 (1922), pp. 30–31; "Zhenskie tipy v povstanchestve," *Kommunistka*, no. 10–11 (1922), pp. 36–37. For examples of sketches of revolutionary women from other periodicals see Nogin, "Genkina, Ol'ga Mikhailovna," *Proletarskaia revoliutsiia*, no. 7 (1922):178–80; and G. Lelevich, "Chetyre mogily," Ibid., no. 6 (1922):14–23. These articles lack any reference to women's emancipation, in marked contrast to the sketches in *Kommunistka*.

29. "Odna i mnogikh (Dorogoi pamiati t. Barmashevoi)," *Kommunistka*, no. 3–5 (1922), p. 12; "Kommunistka-geroinia," *Kommunistka*, no. 5 (1920), p. 22.

30. For thoughtful discussions of these two issues see H. Kent Geiger, *The Family in Soviet Russia* (Cambridge: Harvard University Press, 1968), pp. 43–106; Richard Stites, *The Women's Liberation Movement in Russia* (Princeton: Princeton University Press, 1978), pp. 346–91.

31. For a discussion of Stalinist fictional heroines see Gasiorowska, *Women in Soviet Fiction*, pp. 51–60, 102–16. For examples from mass agitation see the magazine *Rabotnitsa*, especially issues from the late thirties. A typical pamphlet from this period is K. Nikolaeva and L. Karaseva, *Zhenshchina v boiakh za kommunizm* (Moscow: Politizdat, 1940).

32. This conjecture is based on the fact that in 1924, according to one survey, 91 percent of male party members only had a primary-school education or were "self-taught." Six percent had completed high school. Among female Bolsheviks (then approximately 9 percent of party members), 74 percent had primary schooling, 20 percent high school education, and 2 percent some higher education. (E. Smitten, "Zhenshchiny v RKP," *Kommunistka*, no. 4 [1924], p. 9.) Such low levels of literacy would suggest a fairly low mastery of Marxism, especially among those people who had joined the party since 1917. The literacy level also makes likely a common phenomenon among revolutionary parties: as ideology proceeds downward from an educated elite to an uneducated mass of followers, it disintegrates from a systematic whole created by intellectuals into a collection of slogans which speak to the needs of the followers. (Philip E. Converse, "The Nature of Belief Systems in Mass Publics," *Ideology and Discontent*, David E. Apter, ed. [New York: Free Press, 1964], pp. 206–61.) Among these slogans, the abolition of the family and free love never ranked very high, in part because they were middle-class ideas alien to workers and peasants, in part because the leaders thought the rank-and-file would reject them. Thus the rank-and-file were not equipped to master Engels' discussion of the family on their own and were not pushed to accept it by the leadership. For example, in 1919 Lenin refused to present the abolition of the bourgeois family as a plank in the new party platform to the Eighth Party Congress because he thought the delegates would be outraged by the proposal. (A. M. Kollontai, "Avtobiograficheskii ocherk," *Proletarskaia revoliutsiia*, no. 1 [1921], pp. 300–301).

33. For an article that argues that the young were not radical in their sexual attitudes and behavior, see Sheila Fitzpatrick, "Sex and Revolution: An Examination of Literary and Statistical Data on the Mores of Soviet Students in the 1920s," *The Journal of Modern History*, 50 (June 1978): 252–78. Much of the information used during the marriage law debate to demonstrate the urban family was disintegrating was so highly impressionistic and sensationalized that it casts doubt on the premise. See Rudolph Schlesinger, ed., *The Family in the U.S.S.R.* (London: Routledge and Kegan Paul, 1949), pp. 81–168.

34. Emelian Iaroslavskii, "Moral' i byt proletariata v perekhodnyi period," *Molodaia gvardiia*, no. 3 (May 1926), pp. 145–46, 149. The most famous and one of the earliest Bolshevik condemnations of youthful sexual license came from Lenin in his

1920 interview with Clara Zetkin. (Lenin, *The Emancipation of Women* [New York: International, 1975], pp. 104–108.)

35. Schlesinger, *The Family in the U.S.S.R.*, pp. 100, 147.

36. F. Panforov, *The Village Bruski* (Moscow, 1937), 4:132; quoted in Gasiorowska, *Women in Soviet Fiction*, p. 53.

37. Smidovich, "Znachenie 'Kommunistki' dlia raboty sredi zhenshchin," *Kommunistka*, no. 7 (1923), pp. 7–9. See also the article by Putilovskaia that asserts that in the past *Kommunistka* had engaged in insufficiently "concrete" and "factual" examination of the *byt*. ("Nash put'," *Kommunistka*, no. 7 [1923], pp. 15–17.)

38. In 1922, the Komsomol was 85 percent male, in 1927, 79 percent male. (Chirkov, *Reshenie zhenskogo voprosa v SSSR*, p. 173.) For collections of articles on male-female relations see *Brak i byt: Sbornik statei i materialov* (Moscow: Molodaia gvardiia, 1926); E. Iaroslavskii, *Voprosy zhizni i bor'by* (Moscow: Molodaia gvardiia, 1924); S. M. Kalmanson, *Polovoi vopros'* (Moscow: Molodaia gvardiia, 1924); L. S. Sosnovskii, *Bol'nye voprosy (zhenshchina, sem'ia i deti)*, (Leningrad: Priboi, 1926).

39. See, for example, Elisabeth Croll, *Feminism and Socialism in China* (London: Routledge and Kegan Paul, 1978); Barbara Wolfe Jancar, *Women Under Communism* (Baltimore: Johns Hopkins University Press, 1978); Susan Kaufman Purcell, "Modernizing Women for a Modern Society: The Cuban Case," *Female and Male in Latin America; Essays*, Ann Pescatello, ed., (Pittsburgh: University of Pittsburgh Press, 1973), pp. 257–71.

[14] Village Women Experience the Revolution

Beatrice Farnsworth

COMMUNISTS REGARDED peasant women as the "darkest," most backward layer of the Russian population, a dead weight and a potential source of counter-revolution. If women, who constituted the majority in the countryside, were to be drawn into the Soviet sphere, it would require a fundamental change in their outlook and values. From a "correct" Marxist standpoint, such an alteration in attitude could result only from deep economic changes in rural Russia. That such changes were occurring in the early years of the Revolution seemed questionable. The former landlord's land went to the peasants, but they continued to farm in traditional, inefficient, small-scale ways. Women carried on with their accustomed drudgery. Nevertheless, even before the end of the Civil War in 1921, Communists were attempting to a limited extent to induce a transformation in peasant outlook by introducing Soviet mores to women in the countryside. This essay looks at the interaction that resulted: how did the Bolsheviks attempt to reach women in the villages of Central Russia? How did peasant women respond to the new cultural values set before them?

Who was the Russian peasant? The answer has defied consensus. One commentator recently remarked of the peasantry that "no class or group in society has ever received such strikingly mixed notices from anthropologists, sociologists, and historians."[1] The self-governing communes in peasant villages have been idealized as exemplifying the principles of primitive communism, where, in contrast to the wickedness of the towns, the fruits of the social product went to all. The "peasant mind" has been depicted as "childlike" and "uncontaminated." At the other extreme were those who found such images deeply unrealistic. Lenin and Plekhanov attacked the nineteenth-century narodniki for believing in sentimental myths about the *mir*. Maxim Gorky tried to find the good-natured, thoughtful Russian peasant, the indefatigable searcher after truth and justice so movingly depicted in nineteenth-century Russian literature, but could only discover a person "half-savage, stupid, heavy. . . ."[2]

Oscar Lewis, Edward Banfield, and other social scientists have challenged many of the assumptions of Robert Redfield and his followers who found peasant societies to be smoothly functioning and well-integrated, made up of contented and well-adjusted people.[3] The critics came away from peasant communities with impressions of peasants as often fatalistic and supine, ignorant, dishonest, sunk in apathy and meanness.

The tenor of village life in Russia with its fist-fighting organized as entertainment, its fortune-telling, and its superstition suggests this latter view. The beauty of peasant folk art, its stories and songs tended to be obscured by the squalor of daily existence. By the turn of the century, moreover, urban tastes had penetrated those villages close to markets with well-developed patterns of peasants (mainly men) departing seasonally to earn money. One could find there cheap colored prints on the walls, card playing, city dancing and singing, and consulting of horoscopes. For a village to have few or no books was not unusual. Most of the peasants in Tver province were illiterate, although in some families old people did read aloud from prayer books. In villages in Voronezh province prior to the Revolution there were no libraries, the sole books there being gospels and prayer books.[4]

One should not, however, exaggerate village illiteracy. Viriatino, a village 200 miles southeast of Moscow in Tambov province, had a library in the local school with 153 books. According to teachers, young peasants who used the school library especially liked stories about peasant life and fairy tales. Literate adults more frequently read *The Lives of the Saints* or the Bible.[5]

The Bolsheviks, assuming with Marx and Engels a "rural idiocy," aimed at breaking down the old *byt'*—the complex of customs, beliefs, and manners that determined the peasants' daily life. From the outset, Bolshevik culture was didactic, moralistic, and atheistic, trying to rid the peasant not only of religiosity but of the ancient practices of lying, thieving, bribery, and swearing. Whenever a peasant was brought to court for stealing, making homebrew, or beating his wife or child, some official would launch into a lecture on why a Soviet citizen should abstain from such "bourgeois practices."[6]

At the simplest level Soviet culture meant hygiene and health care, and knives and forks rather than a wooden spoon dipping into a common bowl, a remarkable message to a peasant who may customarily have left human excrement to pile up around the hut.[7] Peasants began to accustom themselves to posters proclaiming: "Syphilitics, do not use alcohol," and "The louse is a carrier of Typhus."[8]

Knives, forks, and public health injunctions could be regarded as a minor affront to traditional ways. Atheism and the new iconography—Karl Marx flanked by Lenin and Trotsky on the walls of the village Soviet in place of St. Nicholas—were a graver threat.[9] Women, traditionally close to Christianity, saw their old faith attacked and slipping away and they feared that their husbands who ate meat on fast days and ceased going to church were damned. Ikons hanging in the corner of the hut, frequently side by side with lurid atheist posters, testified to the clash of cultures.[10]

The very organization of government within the village was alien. The *sel'sovet,* its basic element, was both imported and imposed. The number of peasants taking part in elections after the Civil War remained small (22.3 percent in 1922), and in many villages no more than 10 to 15 percent of the peasants would turn out to vote. Peasant lack of interest is understandable, since the *sel'sovet* was controlled by the authorities and its membership was decided upon by the Party in the district, in consultation with the local Party cell, if there was one. The peasants regarded the ancient *mir,* which had revived during and after the Revolution, as the actual village government.[11]

The Party staffed the *sel'sovet* with the village poor, the *batraki* and the *bedniaki,* or even workers sent out from the towns to strengthen the proletarian element.[12] Thus, this alien import, the *sel'sovet,* elevated those whom the more solid peasants regarded as riffraff.

An aspect of the new culture, then, was the sudden prominence within the village of its poorer inhabitants. Previously, the peasants regarded the village as a unity—the *mir.* Now they were told that it really consisted of three parts—the rich peasants, the middle, and the landless poor. Soviet culture from the outset forced on the peasant a model of class conflict.[13] The famous "Committees of Poor Peasants," backed up by detachments of the proletariat, who came from the towns in 1918 to requisition grain, reinforced the image.

With the infusion of Soviet politics into the village, language itself began to change. Peasants heard about People's Courts, "enemies of the working class," *kombedy, smychka, kommuna, delegatki, komsomol,* and *Commissar.*[14] The Party told the peasant woman that she was no longer a *baba.* An equal citizen now, she should forego the old term and call herself *krest'ianka.*[15]

The Communists gave a woman the right to seek a divorce.[16] Activists arriving in the village urged her to learn to read. But above all, Soviet culture was collectivist. The Bolsheviks would attempt to inculcate the religion of "we" and to break down the belief in "I." For women, this may have been the most alien message of all.

To understand how Soviet culture was perceived initially by the *baba* one must first know the values of peasant women, how they related to the values of the peasant community, and how they related to the values of men. A sexual division had to some extent always existed in the village. One need only recall the frequent references in literature to "the women," with the assumption that they were a group apart, to understand that women had their separate sphere in both the community and the household.

What were their values? The peasant woman was a housewife and she wanted to remain one. In a society in which marriage was the norm, most women lived with their husband's family after the age of 20.[17] The Revolution awarded woman full equality within the joint household. She was confirmed in her right to be designated as head of the family which might be large and complex (grandparents and married sons), or small and complex (parents, children, and perhaps a married brother), or more rarely, the small nuclear family common in Russia today.[18] Theoretically no longer subordinate to a patriarchal male, women might legally attend the village assembly *(skhod)* and participate in running the community,[19] but reports suggest that such female participation was uncommon. When one woman attended a village assembly in Smolensk province in 1922 she was greeted with abuse. In areas of Penza province in the mid-twenties, women lived as they had twenty years earlier, unaware of their legal rights.[20] Most married women continued to live in a household headed by a man and to focus narrowly on family, farm, and economic survival.

The household functioned according to a traditional division of labor. Men sowed, plowed, cut hay, prepared fuel, and tended the horses. In many families—especially in Northern areas where men were away for long periods earning wages—women also plowed and harrowed and cut hay, but generally they tended the cattle, worked in the house, and did a certain amount of field work.[21] In poorer families, girls and women might hire out as servants or agricultural day laborers.[22]

In a sense, peasant women also lived as hired laborers within their own extended households, with a mother-in-law distributing the tasks.[23] One authority on peasant life, commenting on the awesome mother-in-law and the quarrelsome sisters-in-law, concluded that it was good to marry an only son and best of all one whose father was a widower.[24] But *snokhachestvo* (sexual advances of the father-in-law) was another feature of the peasant milieu.

Given the harshness of women's lives, the female solidarity of which we have abundant evidence is scarcely surprising: rural women organizing as a group in times of stress; women plundering a local store in protest against high wartime prices; women day laborers refusing to work for a particular landlord who reduced the daily wage from 50 to 45 kopeks; soldiers' wives rioting and resisting separate consolidation of communal lands undertaken in accord with the Stolypin land reform.[25] But that such female cohesion persisted in the routines of daily life seems doubtful. Despite women's tendency to organize against perceived threats to their economic interests and despite their mutual dependence in matters of childbirth, relations among women forced by tradition and economics to live together were predominantly unpleasant. Within the household, tensions built not only over whether mother-in-law or daughter-in-law would predominate at the stove but between younger women who might resent the obligation to care for a sister-in-law's children.[26] In the larger community, malice and competition smoldered over the possession of a man and the birth—or lack thereof—of children.

Although Leo Tolstoy has described a young peasant woman who frankly expressed a sense of release at the death of a child,[27] such an example is probably far less common than that of another nineteenth-century Russian writer: "Peasants . . . view the birth of children as a sign of God's blessing on the parents, whereas not having children is considered a misfortune."[28] Beyond the question of the mother's relationship to the child was the fact that childlessness for the peasant woman was a painful situation which often constituted a source of moral humiliation. In the novel *Brusski,* the young peasant wife longs for a child and release from the mockery of the women at the spring who called her barren.[29] To be barren meant to be deprived of children through whom alone a woman could implant herself firmly in the family of her husband and be guaranteed comfort in her old age.[30]

Before turning to the peasant woman's relationship to property, it is important to understand how peasant property was held within the joint households of Central Russia. Traditionally, the male peasant, owning nothing privately beyond his personal possessions (clothing, harmonica), shared as coowner in the property of the household: hut, livestock, and tools. His earnings, even when he went away to work, generally went into the general holdings. The peasant's role as a joint owner, living in a commune that periodically redistributed the land, gave rise to considerable disagreement among scholars. Because the peasant's land was not truly his own, because his livestock, tools, and hut were held in common, because his outside earnings went into a common fund and he farmed in accord with decisions arrived at democratically by a village assembly within each commune, it has been suggested that the peasant was a natural socialist. Opponents of this view countered that far from being natural socialists, the peasants required the repartitional mechanism to reconcile their extreme competitiveness and self-interestedness. They pointed out that commune members were not equal either in income or resources, that the poorer peasant envied the better-off, on whom he might be dependent for loans, and that the more prosperous were able to manipulate the decision-making process in the assembly.

What needs to be emphasized here is that this controversy is relevant primarily to the male segment of peasant society. Women certainly did not live as socialists. They were not members of the decision-making village assembly and their earnings were considered private property. This last point needs explanation. Although the Land Code of 1922 accorded women equality as joint owners in the household,[31] their earnings—cash from specifically "female activities" such as selling eggs, mushrooms, and handcrafts, and from weaving and dyeing—were generally separate from common household funds, as had been the case before the Revolution.[32] A woman's dowry, frequently including some livestock, technically remained under her own control, to be passed on to her daughters. Consequently a woman's sense of private property was more developed than that of her husband. Unlike men who worked communally, many women lived, at least part of each day, by the capitalist ethic. The business of linen bleaching is an example: in certain areas women attending fairs solicited orders from other villages, thus developing a home industry.[33] The nineteenth-century historian Kovalevsky, speaking of the joint household, observed that if a movement in favor of private property could be detected it was only in the private earnings of women and girls.[34]

The need to earn and control money of her own is understandable, since it was the custom of the household that no family money was to be spent on the daughter-in-law. The family budget entitled her only to food, an overcoat, and shoes, and she was dealt a ration from the family supply of wool and hemp. What money the woman earned went for petty expenses such as soap, salt, matches, and kerosene. Any necessities for herself and her children had to be bought with her own money.[35]

The daughter-in-law protected what was hers. In the large, joint families of Tver province, small sheds were often built around the vegetable garden, one for each daughter-in-law. Here she could keep her personal property. If her husband brought her a gift upon his return from seasonal work, the wife might not use it as long as she lived together with her husband's relatives. Instead she would hide the item or give it to people whom she could trust until she and her husband separated from the joint family.[36]

Thus it was no surprise that the Bolsheviks met resistance when they called on the peasant woman accustomed to protecting her individual interests to act collectively for the general good. It was hard for the Russian peasants, who traditionally worked hardest on their own strips of land and who were some-times said to altogether lack a social conscience,[37] to understand the concept of mutuality between city and village. Now the peasant must give grain to the towns because the factory worker could not produce implements for the farms if he had no food. Peasants were exhorted to enter the Soviets, where they would work to help the widows and families of Red Army men. They were to construct shelters and nurseries for orphans and children of the village poor and they were somehow to absorb the uncongenial idea of work without pay.[38] This last injunction proved to be particularly awkward. When the question of wages for the delegates (women elected to receive elementary political training) came up in Kaluga province, the majority of them, not receiving any pay, simply refused to work.[39]

The absence of any general will to collectivity on the part of women is illustrated by their opposition to the early Soviet communes. Women reacted negatively, although they were promised more than their husbands. In 1919 *Pravda* reported that female antipathy was the chief obstacle to the formation of communes.[40] If they did go into the communes they usually held back from active participation.[41] Although the commune freed women from certain chores it required of them much more readjustment than it did of their husbands, who for the most part went about their accustomed agricultural work. Quarrels arose in the community kitchen and dining halls. Women did not like cooking for those outside their family, doing impersonal, menial jobs, or caring for the children of others. According to one source, the women engaged in all manner of recriminations and dodged the work. One reporter, sympathetic to the commune, found that women disliked the communal nursery as much as the kitchen and had to be rotated very often. Bickering and gossip were the rule.[42] But when they needed to, women did act collectively. Widows, especially, sometimes formed communes in order to support each other. The "Fortress of Communism" was started in the lower Volga region by seven women, some of them widows. Husbands joined upon release from service.[43]

The primary mediator between peasant women and the new political milieu was the Communist Women's Section, the *Zhenotdel*, founded at the end of 1919. Although the zeal of its leaders was impressive, it would be a mistake to assume that rural Russia was saturated with female agitators working to create "new women." Even by the end of the 1920s three-fourths of the villages had no organized Party activity,[44] and in the RSFSR alone there were 150,000 villages. Although Communists in principle favored bringing politically backward peasant women into public life, work among women in the war-ravaged countryside received low priority in the Party at large. The *Zhenotdel*'s female leadership constantly protested insufficient funding and shortages of qualified personnel,[45] and usually only part of a province experienced the Women's Section at all.[46] Activity might mean merely a poorly paid district organizer, knapsack on her back, going by foot 20 to 30 versts, from district to district.[47]

In general, it was the peasant woman who lived in semi-industrial areas like Iaroslavl and Gomel provinces who received the greater cultural impact, since *Zhenotdel* workers from the industrial areas of the province could be sent into the villages to spread the Party message. The purely peasant provinces had a less developed Party apparatus.[48]

Communist women appealed to self-pity, quoting Nekrasov's famous lines: "Oh Russian fate / Oh miserable women's fate / Is it really possible to find anything worse!"[49] Peasant women did work hard and for a longer day than men, as Figure 1 suggests.

According to a local doctor in Voronezh province at the turn of the century, women became ill and sought medical treatment at the Zemstvo facility more frequently than did men. That this report came from an area of extreme misery and low female literacy should serve to correct the popular image of backward *babas* relying solely on "wise men" and old women.[50] The death rate of women from the ages of 15 to 60 in these same Voronezh villages exceeded that of men.[51] Indeed, throughout European Russia, according to statistics for the period 1867–1881, women's death rate was higher than that of men. Statistics for 1896–1897 show women's death rate higher between the ages 10–39, 55–59, and 65–74. In 1908–1910, the death rate for women was higher up to age 40 and from age 60 to beyond 80. The higher male death rate from 40 to 60 reflected in statistics for 1908–1910 is presumably explained by the increasing hazards of factory work and migrant labor.[52]

Communists, responding to these gloomy statistics, offered rural women an image of a brighter, collectivist future: communal nurseries, kitchens, and laundries, to say nothing of equal access with men to positions in public life. These utopian and uniquely Communist promises and expectations were the ones the regime would most conspicuously fail to fulfill. Be that as it may, rural women reacted with suspicion to the phenomenon of zealous, urban females

Figure 1: Labor Distribution by Sex and Age in Volokolamsk Uezd

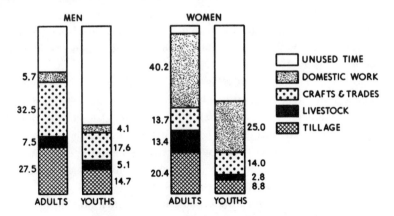

Source: A. V. Chayanov, *The Theory of Peasant Economy*, ed. Daniel Thorner, Basile Kerblay, and R. E. F. Smith (Homewood, Illinois, 1966, originally published Moscow, 1925), p. 180. Data was presumably collected between 1907 and 1913.

trying to change their lives. In villages where the Women's Section established summer nurseries they were perceived as a threat. Rumors circulated that once in them children were enrolled as Communists and taken from their mothers.[53] Upon occasion, women spoke with particular force against nurseries as indicated by the following resolution taken at a meeting of peasant women in Penza province: "The women's meeting . . . under the chairmanship of Evgeniia Romanovka, unanimously refuses to open and organize a kindergarten and nursery since in our community we don't have mothers who would refuse to bring up their children."[54]

Paradoxically, women complained that Communist investigators were interfering with traditional childraising, threatening to lock them up if they whipped their children. In order for peasants to understand urban concepts in child care, agitators resorted to dramatic devices which were occasionally effective: one was a symbolic "belt burying." Peasant women in Tver province would report that children were not being beaten because the family had "buried the belt."[55]

Communist rural activity included labor conscription, which was decreed in 1920. It was seen as a harsh intrusion by women who worked hard but at their own tempo and who resented regimentation. Although labor mobilization did not require change of location for peasant women with children under twelve, it did mean coerced and arduous work such as clearing snow from railway tracks.[56] Peasant attitudes toward work discipline were unequivocal and reflected work habits alien to modern, industrial efficiency. An American visitor approaching a group of women day laborers working in a *Sovkhoz* was told very frankly that no, life was not better for them than in the old Tsarist days. "We worked then from dawn to dark—but we didn't have to keep it up all the time. We could even stop to sing, and lie down in the sun and sleep when we wanted to and the foreman didn't mind—he did the same himself. But now they make us stick to our work."[57]

Another cultural change was the introduction of literacy classes for adults.[58] While education might be perceived by a minority of peasant women as an opportunity, literacy centers were irrelevant for many. Occasionally peasant women projected their own cultural values in opposition to those being imposed. One school teacher in Tver province tried to teach some peasant women to read and write. After the third lesson, they asked her for a printed cotton shirt apiece, as compensation for their loss of time.[59]

A certain number of women did become literate, often braving male disapproval. Since the literacy campaign was closely connected with the campaign against religion, orthodox priests took the lead in conducting agitation against literacy centers.[60] Men forbade their womenfolk to participate. Enthusiastic "liquidators of illiteracy" conducted covert propaganda in the villages against male tyranny and persuaded women to visit the centers by stealth.[61]

The Bolshevik idea that girls should attend school was also alien. In a village in Penza province peasants complained that in the old days girls did not go to school. Now a teacher agitates for their attendance and 18 girls immediately enter.[62] Yet, the number of girls in school there between 1922 and 1924 declined significantly. In some schools there were no girls at all. Traditionally, if a family were to make a sacrifice, it would be for the son. He would be going into the Army and it was inconvenient for a man to be illiterate. But for the girl to remain illiterate seemed no great misfortune. Frequently mothers prevented their daughters from going to school, arguing that the family could not afford it.[63] Those girls who did go to school often left before completing the course of study. On the other hand, girls in Penza province were attracted to the literacy center although they felt shy about attending. Reportedly they wanted a separate women's group.[64]

The same peasant woman who objected to her daughter going to school was encouraged, if she lived in a village where the Party was active, to achieve a different self-image—that of an effective and literate citizen, a member, it is worth noting, of a participatory democracy. She was told that if she learned to read, speculators would not be able to cheat her; if she were to take part in elections to district and village Soviets, they would not be dominated by kulaks and former shop and tavern keepers; if she used her right to vote, the Soviet would be made up of honest people who would defend the village poor; if she participated in the Soviets and in the district executive committees, the Soviets would care more about improving the life of women and children.[65]

Occasionally women were persuaded to enter the Soviet. More frequently they responded negatively:

> "I have small children at home and a farm. Therefore I have no time to work in the Soviet."
> "I am illiterate—what would I do in the Soviet and how will I be of use to the village?"
> "My husband is opposed."[66]

For the married peasant woman of average means living with her husband's family in a village that had experienced little or no organized Party activity, Soviet culture probably meant little besides the resented "tax in kind" that in 1921 replaced the forced requisition of grain. Or, if she traveled into the large towns, there was the "Agitation Point" (perhaps only a kiosk in a station), disseminating Bolshevik propaganda.

The new culture was experienced more intensely by the poor, especially single women householders, Red Army wives and widows. More vulnerable and generally older, they were the women most receptive to rural activists[67] and the most likely to attend their meetings. Of 134 delegates (63 of whom were peasants and 71 urban women) at a non-Party Conference in Orel province in 1923, the majority (70) were in the 25 to 45 age group. 49 were between 17 and 25 and 18 were older than 45.[68] The Party worker reporting on the Conference was gratified that there were also some young women present who left farm and children to attend. At a similar women's conference in the province of Nizhni-Novgorod that same year a large number of delegates, surprisingly, were under 30.

In general, young peasant women burdened with children were less responsive to the Party, while the young, unmarried woman was the least likely of all to participate.[69] Reports deplored the scarcity of girls in the rural komsomols.[70] In some there were no women at all, or at most, simply one in a cell of thirty—a result, in part, of parental disapproval of a Communist youth group perceived as immoral.[71]

The single woman householder—often a widow—had the most reason to react positively to the Communists. Her life was extraordinarily difficult. She was expected alone to raise children, to maintain the cattle, and to farm. A small percentage of these women moved into the category of the landless peasant—the *bobylok*. The majority of them farmed with varying degrees of success.

Party workers sought out the more outspoken among them. Occasionally a peasant woman would be persuaded to make public demands; A. Volkova from Smolensk province was probably one such recruit. In a letter to the journal *Kommunistka*, she called on the urban working women, the seemingly favored element in the Revolution, to "remember the peasant women." She read in the women's pages in *Rabochi Put'* about meetings for city women. She requested similar meetings for peasant women where questions could be answered about problems like the tax-in-kind.[72]

Volkova was typical of the minority of rural women who tended to become the "troublemakers," organizing other village women, attending Women's Section courses, and participating in meetings that today we would recognize as consciousness-raising and that in China would be called "speaking bitterness." At non-Party conferences, peasant delegates would be encouraged to talk about their own lives, not only about the hardship of their past, but also about their current exploitation both by kulaks and by male members of the Soviet power structure in the villages.

Women complained about the conditions of daily life which in some instances were made worse by the Revolution. Drunkenness, well known in the Russian village, continued to plague the countryside, even becoming a feature of local Soviet organs, which in the view of some peasants resembled taverns more than government institutions.[73] Drinking at home seemed to the women to have increased. In the old days there was a formal liquor monopoly. Now each muzhik distilled his own and life had become impossible for the woman.[74]

A twenty-two-year-old peasant woman in the province of Nizhni-Novgorod told of her experiences the previous year as a member of the Soviet. The kulaks proposed that she chair a work committee with the idea—as she now realized—of manipulating her. When she called them to task for their tax irregularities, they threatened to kill her. I don't go to the Soviet anymore, she told the conference. I am twenty-two and I still want to live.[75]

An older woman in the same area protested that the working woman in the city got four months maternity leave, while she had borne sixteen children (five of them buried) working continuously. Why weren't the peasant women given the same benefits as the city woman?[76] Distrust of the urban working woman was common among the peasant women, who complained about their exhausting work over a long summer day while the factory woman worked, in their view, not 24 hours but simply 8.[77]

At a meeting in Nizhni-Novgorod, women protested against the painful tax-in-kind and the cruelty of sadistic Soviet agents, who, instead of sympathizing with the difficulties of a Red Army man's wife and perhaps letting her off more easily, taunted the woman with outlandish requests, such as that she produce 60 identical black cats so that he could make a fur coat.[78] The Party worker noted that this was only one episode of humiliating injustice occurring locally at the hands of brutal collectors of the tax-in-kind. Indeed the hated tax appears occasionally as the hallmark of Soviet culture in the villages.

But not everyone felt this way. A peasant woman in Orel province recalled that in the past she had no land and the village called her a tramp. "Why? I was not a thief." Now she had 12 desiatins (1 desiatina = 2.7 acres) of land and the kulak who formerly had 40 had 8. She sold her son's miner's clothing and even managed to buy a horse. She lived well. It was warm inside in the winter. Still, she did not want to identify too closely with the Revolution. "They call me a Communist. But I am not a Communist."[79] Another woman explained that she had never before been at a conference. Nor had she known where the city was. But now it seemed to her that Orel was sitting right in her vegetable patch. She summed up the cultural impact of the Revolution on her life by noting that it had taken her out of the village.[80]

Bringing women together to express personal grievances and triumphs was a dramatic way of drawing them into the Soviet orbit. There were other ways: organizations among single women to purchase glass, firewood, and various supplies; and groups to develop summer nurseries which would work together to obtain local funds from committees of mutual aid, district executive committees, and local cooperatives.[81]

The peasants did not always accept the cooperation urged upon them by the authorities, although cooperatives were well known in pre-revolutionary Russia. They made excuses: the *baba* could not live without her daily trip to the city to sell milk and eggs from her own farm; or, peasants were not the kind of people to work together harmoniously.[82] Yet frequently cooperation succeeded.

Work artels brought change to the lives of those relatively few women involved.[83] A member of the *Zhenotdel* reported in 1920 a conversation with a woman who recalled that at first no one in the village wanted to hear about organizing an artel (a peasant association for the common cultivation of land). They told her to get rid of her Bolshevik ideas. But she persuaded other peasant women, especially Red Army wives who farmed alone, to join with her. Together they obtained seed in the city. Their two horses became the common property of the artel. Going beyond joint agricultural work, they organized a children's dining room with the help of the Soviet network. The *Zhenotdel* worker marveled that the artel was begun by the peasant women themselves, despite the mockery of the men. Yet we may assume an ongoing degree of *Zhenotdel* help in the form of encouragement, literature for the reading hut, and evidently the very sheets of paper (unavailable in the village) that the women needed to record the protocol of their meetings.[84]

Peasant women—again in the relatively few villages with energetic Party organizers—might experience the Bolshevik message at any level of daily life. Even allowing for the likelihood that Party workers exaggerated the degree of their actual accomplishments, the scope of agitation was broad.[85] On Sundays women were recruited, ostensibly to gather mushrooms and medicinal herbs, but in fact for political indoctrination. Dramatic and choral circles were created in the villages.[86] Dramatizations and concerts became an integral part of non-Party conferences. Indeed, in some instances, women would attend meetings only if a "spectacle" was on the program.[87] In reading huts, teachers read from scarce copies of the new Party journal, *Krest'ianka*.[88] In Leningrad there were excursions of peasant women to museums, and in Moscow to children's institutions, the museum of the People's Commissariat of Health, to lectures, and to movies.[89] Cultural innovation came to the village in the form of "magic lantern" (slide) exhibits and model vegetable gardens.[90] In the summer of 1920 on the steamship *Red Star* peasant women of the Volga region reportedly marveled at an exhibition of the uses of electricity in the countryside—how in several minutes it was possible from milk to make butter.[91]

The use of street theater was particularly effective in attracting large numbers of peasants, especially the dramatization of people's courts. In Saratov, the *Zhenotdel* presented a staged court on work deserters, gangsterism, sabotage, and "new women." In Ekaterinburg a performance of "the people's court" investigated the morality of "outrages" against women.[92]

In the semi-industrial areas, female Party workers were conscious of the need to develop ties between city and country women. Thus in Kiev, Kostroma, and Penza provinces, delegates' meetings were organized together with city working women.[93] With the same idea in mind, the Kiev all-city delegate meeting decided to take under its wing a district delegate meeting in Budaevka. For local women, the result was an increased urban presence in the village.[94] The Kiev *Zhenotdel* sought further to develop linkages by bringing groups of peasant women into the city to meet in conferences with urban working women. Despite the optimistic conclusions from Party workers that a tie was being forged between rural and urban women, the opposite may have occurred. Peasant women, as we know, resented the urban working woman as the dominant and favored class.[95]

A sampling of rural participation in the *Zhenotdel* network provides a sense of the scope of Communist activity among peasant women. Each woman drawn, however briefly, into the female political orbit was herself something of a cultural phenomenon when she returned to her village.

One report published in 1920 relates that non-Party district conferences of peasant women were conducted in approximately 60 provinces during the previous half year. In all 853 conferences took place,[96] each conference attended by around 200 people.[97]

Delegates' meetings among peasant women were usually conducted in areas having Communist Party cells (the Ukraine, Samara, and Riazan provinces were given as examples). Besides district delegate meetings, there were also village delegate meetings in those villages having large enough populations.[98]

The most important issues discussed at district delegate meetings concerned land and taxes. The tax-in-kind and the Land Code were laws about which the women were most troubled. Other topics of interest were the significance of the committees of mutual aid, the struggle against home-brew, the new rights of the peasant woman in Soviet Russia, hygiene, and the protection of mothers and infants.[99] Questions of antireligious propaganda were rarely put forth at delegate meetings in view, we are told, of the lack of skilful agitators available to propagate antireligious views.[100] Reports indicated that some delegate meetings were poorly conducted, touching not on issues of daily concern to women but on such matters as the international organization of women and Soviet industrialization. Delegates in these instances lost interest.[101]

In Kaluga province a Party worker reported that organizational activity was well developed in 89 districts (out of 176). Delegates worked in all sections of the District Executive Committees. The Kaluga province *Zhenotdel* in 1920–21 conducted 85 meetings at which a total of 4,500 women participated. Delegates' meetings of peasant women were created in 87 districts, drawing in around 5,000 peasant women.[102] In Siberia, there were 272 district organizers working among peasant women in 1921. In Ufa, Samara, Perm, Astrakhan, and Ekaterinburg provinces and in the Don area, the *Zhenotdel* assigned district organizers, conducted delegate meetings, and apportioned delegates to district executive committees.[103] In Saratov province in 1921 there were up to 1,000 peasant women serving as *praktikants,* receiving political indoctrination from the *Zhenotdel* and working in Soviet institutions, usually for three months.[104]

The concrete results of this spotty but frenzied activity, as measured by actual political participation, were small. In one area in Penza province a peasant woman was chosen as chair of the Soviet. At an *uezd* Congress of Soviets in Penza province out of 110 delegates there were eleven peasant women.[105] Occasionally one met a peasant woman who was a member of a District Executive Committee, a director of one or another section of the District Soviet, or a member of the board of the District cooperative. In 1923 it was estimated that peasant women made up 1.5 percent of the village Soviets. In about 36 provinces there were 1,022 women serving in the village Soviets.[106] A Communist reporter noted frankly that it was difficult even to draw peasant delegates into the Party.[107] According to statistics for 1920 there were 428 peasant women Communists in the 15 provinces surveyed.[108]

In comparative terms the number of peasant women touched by the political culture of the Revolution in its first years was no more than a few thousand, when the countryside of the USSR consisted of 18.5 million scattered small farms.[109] If only a portion of women became activists, we would like to know how many among the thousands attending meetings became sympathetic to Communism. The evidence, admittedly impressionistic, suggests relationships of a personal rather than an ideological nature. We are told that peasant women in Tver province were drawn to meetings because of a particularly charismatic female leader, but that when she left the area, participation fell.[110] We know that peasant women occasionally turned to the *Zhenotdel* as their advocate. In a village in Smolensk province a widow of a Red Army man, having been refused land by the sowing committee, asked for help from the delegate, who demanded that the woman receive the land to which she was entitled.[111] During War Communism Smolensk delegates intervened on behalf of pregnant women, citing their right not to perform forced labor. They had learned of this right in a report at a delegates' meeting. The chairman of the village Soviet was obliged to release the women from the assigned work.[112]

At a meeting in Orel province a district organizer told of a typical day spent gathering women for a meeting. Toward evening, she reported, you are tired of talking, you have not eaten, and your head hurts. But always there is some woman who invites you home for soup and bread, saying that since you teach us for nothing, you must come to us and eat.[113]

Communist women, heartened by such signs, believed they were influencing the peasants. Some Party workers reported that when women received special attention from the Communists, they began to favor the regime more than their husbands. In certain instances, we are told, Bolshevik rural activists failed to influence the men but succeeded in organizing the women, appealing to their underprivileged position.[114]

A peasant woman who became politically active was seized upon eagerly. The middle-aged F. O. Shupurova from Siberia, in the mid-1920s a member of the All-Russian Central Executive Committee, was depicted in Soviet newspapers more than a dozen times. A poor peasant, drawn into the *Zhenotdel* orbit and intrigued by literacy and ultimately by politics, she learned to read, each night mastering two or three letters.[115] Shupurova was exceptional. Most peasant women, especially married ones, rejected socialist dreams in favor of familiar security, however miserable it appeared to the urban outsider.

Despite the aura of political ferment surrounding the Communists, much of what the Bolsheviks accomplished in rural Russia in the early years of Soviet power falls into the category, not of radical cultural innovation, but rather of increased modernization along familiar lines. More peasant women learned to read. If as late as 1930 two thirds of the female peasant population were still illiterate, it was an advance over the pre–1914 era when in rural areas approximately nine tenths of the women were illiterate.[116] Nurseries gained acceptance. Organizing a day nursery became by the mid–1920s a Communist ploy for "catching" the *baba*.[117] But neither literacy nor summer nurseries can be separated from a modernization process that predated the Revolution.[118]

Not even those stalwarts whom the Bolsheviks called "new women," who dotted the rural Soviet network, were types unique to Bolshevism. Independent women, coping alone for much of the year because the men of the household were away at seasonal work, had already evolved in the nineteenth century.[119] The casualties of war, even without the Revolution, would have increased their ranks.

On the other hand, women's legal equality reflected in their right to seek a divorce was uniquely Soviet. The right to a divorce appeared as a revolution of its own in villages where before 1917 a husband might obtain the priest's help in retrieving a wife who had fled to her family. One peasant recalled how at age 17 she was married to a 40-year-old man who beat her. She wanted to leave him, but her mother warned that it would be a sin.[120] Instances of village divorce during the 1920s were not widespread, compared to the number of divorces in the cities, but their social impact exceeded their actual numbers. At village meetings peasants, associating marital instability with Soviet urban life, complained that divorce was becoming frequent.[121] By the mid–1920s most of the village lawyers' cases reportedly involved alimony.[122]

The new freedom of women to divorce, together with their status as equals in the joint household, also found expression in a reported wave of household partitioning initiated by women, in many cases as part of divorce settlements.[123] Delegates working within the *Zhenotdel* network became advocates of the property rights of peasant women.[124]

Bolshevik culture presented itself to rural women as an amalgam of socialist collectivism and feminist equality—concepts that proved difficult to reconcile in a milieu of small-scale private farming. The *Zhenotdel* exhorted peasant women to build communal facilities such as nurseries and to contribute their labor without pay for the common good. Simultaneously, it supported peasant women in defense of their property rights when they separated from joint households to form smaller, less efficient economic units. Thus, the voice of female Bolshevism found itself functioning both as a reaction and a vanguard, an untenable position that no doubt contributed to that institution's political demise in 1929.

Female privatism persisted, nourished by the peasant woman's new legal equality and undaunted by Communist collectivist slogans. Its tenacity is suggested by events at the end of the decade when the regime moved to replace individual farming with the collective farm. In 1930, Kaganovich would charge that peasant women were providing much of the resistance to collectivization.[125] His belief was supported in reports of the "25,000'ers" whom the Communists sent into the countryside as Kolkhoz organizers.[126] Female opposition to collectivization requires its own account, but we may briefly observe that peasant women fought in 1929 to preserve their poultry, livestock, and carefully wrought private economic arrangements.[127]

A final note. The popular term for these mass female outbursts against the kolkhozy was *babi bunt* (women's riot). In 1918 a Communist leader enthusiastically enjoined women to bury the demeaning label of *baba*.[128] But in villages women continued to refer to each other by the old term, even while participating in the new ritual of electing women to the village Soviet.[129]

Peasant women responded selectively, out of self-interest, to Bolshevik culture. They embraced equalizing features that gave them the right to initiate a household partition, to seek a divorce, or to participate in an election. Simultaneously, indifferent to incongruities, they clung to cultural symbols of the past.

NOTES

1. Jonathan Lieberson, "The Silent Majority," *New York Review of Books,* October 22, 1981, p. 36.

2. Ibid., p. 36. For peasant as "childlike," see Daniel Field, *Rebels in the Name of the Tsar* (Boston, 1976), pp. 213–15. For peasant as Communist, see Maxime Kovalevsky, *Modern Customs and Ancient Laws of Russia* (New York, 1970), pp. 61–62 (originally 1891).

3. For criticism of Redfield's assumptions, see Oscar Lewis, *Life in a Mexican Village, Tepoztlán Restudied* (Urbana, 1951), pp. 428–29.

4. See A. I. Shingarev, *Vymiraiushchaia derevnia* (St. Petersburg, 1907), reproduced in K. M. Shuvaev, *Staraia i novaia derevnia* (Moscow, 1937), p. 173.

5. On village culture, see Sula Benet, ed. and trans., *The Village of Viriatino* (New York, 1970), pp. 67, 134, 153–54; L. A. Anokhina, M. N. Shmeleva, *Kultura i byt kolkhoznikov Kalinskoi oblasti* (Moscow, 1964), pp. 183, 246–47; *Sotsial'no-ekonomicheskie preobrazovaniia v Voronezhskoi derevne (1917–1967)* (Voronezh, 1967), p. 282.

6. Maurice Hindus, *Broken Earth* (New York, 1926), p. 283.

7. Shingarev in Shuvaev, p. 200.

8. Joshua Kunitz, ed., *Russian Literature Since the Revolution* (New York, 1948), p. 74; for details on extent of syphilis in two Russian villages in Voronezh province, 1900, see Shingarev in Shuvaev, pp. 257–75.

9. "Andron Neputevyi," in A. S. Neverov, *Izbrannye proizvedeniia* (Moscow, 1958), pp. 315–16. For reference to Lenin and Trotsky, consult original edition. See translation in Elisaveta Fen, *Modern Russian Stories* (London, 1943), pp. 121–64.

10. Hindus, *Broken Earth*, p. 188, 194.

11. For statistics on Soviet village government, Moshe Lewin, *Russian Peasants and Soviet Power* (Evanston, Illinois, 1975), p. 81, 26.

12. Ibid., p. 81. A bedniak was a poor peasant. A batrak was an agricultural wage laborer employed by private peasants or by their communities.

13. For such a message directed to the peasants, see K. N. Samoilova, *Krest'ianka i sovetskaia vlast'*, p. 19.

14. On Communist language, see A. M. Selishchev, *Iazyk revoliutsionnoi epokhi: iz nabliudenii nad russkim iazykom poslednikh let. 1917–1926* (Moscow, 1928).

15. Beatrice Farnsworth, *Aleksandra Kollontai* (Stanford, 1980), p. 149.

16. See Decree on the Introduction of Divorce, December 19, 1917, in R. Schlesinger, *The Family in the U.S.S.R.* (London, 1949), pp. 30–32.

17. In 1926 the marriage age for women was raised from 16 to 18. See excerpt from "Code of Laws on Marriage and Divorce," Schlesinger, p. 155. But according to the census for 1897 only in the Transcaucasus and the Southern provinces of Central Asia was the average age of marriage below 18. For rural European Russia in 1897 the average age of marriage was 18 or over. In 1908 it remained roughly the same. See A. J. Coale et al., *Human Fertility in Russia Since the Nineteenth Century* (Princeton, 1979), pp. 152, 156.

18. See Land Code of 1922 for women's right to head a family. Schlesinger, p. 42. In 1890 the Senate ruled that women could be heads of household if this was in accord with local custom. See William T. Shinn, Jr., "The Law of the Russian Peasant Household," *Slavic Review* v. XX, Dec., 1961, p. 605. Custom usually stipulated that the father be head.

19. On the legality of women participating in the skhod, see V. P. Danilov, "Zemel'nye otnosheniia v sovetskoi dokolkhoznoi derevne," *Istoriia SSSR* vol. 1, no. 3 (May 1958), p. 98.

20. N. Rosnitskii, *Litso derevni* (Moscow-Leningrad, 1926), p. 112. Local customs varied. Prior to the Revolution, in Viriatino in Tambov province women, generally, were not allowed to take part in the council even when they became widows and heads of household. Benet, *Viriatino*, p. 45. On the other hand, Wallace describes female heads of household present at the village assemblies in northern provinces in the 1870s participating in matters relating to their own households. D. M. Wallace, *Russia* (New York, 1905), pp. 117–18.

21. V. G. Kartsova, ed., *Opyt istoriko-sotsiologicheskogo izucheniia sela "Moldino"* (Moscow, 1968), pp. 107–108. Hereafter, "Moldino."

.22. See Shingarev in Shuvaev, pp. 223–24, and Anokhina and Shmeleva, p. 25.

23. Anokhina and Shmeleva, pp. 175, 181.

24. M. Ia. Fenomenov, *Sovremennaia derevnia* (Moscow-Leningrad, 1925), part II, p. 20.

25. See A. N. Anfimov, ed., *Krest'ianskoe dvizhenie v Rossii v gody pervoi mirovoi voiny* (Moscow-Leningrad, 1965), pp. 149–50, 309–10, 333–34, 385–87, 401. Women resisted consolidation during the war because they feared that with their men away, they would be taken advantage of in any reallocation of property. Examples are drawn from the provinces of Saratov, Simbirsk, Kharkov, Kazan, Perm, Orel, Tomsk.

26. M. M. Gromyko and N. A. Minenko, eds., *Iz istorii sem'i i byta sibirskogo krest'ianstva v XVII-nachale XXv* (Novosibirsk, 1975), p. 24.

27. Leo Tolstoy, *Anna Karenina* (New York, 1961), p. 605. Observations on child care written by local doctors can be used to support assumptions both of maternal neglect and devotion. On attitudes toward infants, see David L. Ransel, "Abandonment and Fosterage of Unwanted Children: The Women of the Foundling System," pp. 189–217, and Nancy M. Frieden, "Childcare: Medical Reform in a Traditionalist Culture," pp. 236–262, in D. L. Ransel, ed., *The Family in Imperial Russia* (Urbana, 1978).

28. A. A. Titov, *Iuridicheskie obychai sela Nikola-Perevoz Sulostskoi volosti, Rostovskogo uezda* (Iaroslavl, 1888), pp. 51–52, as quoted by Antonina Martynova, "Life of the Pre-Revolutionary Village as Reflected in Popular Lullabies," p. 172 in Ransel, ed., *The Family in Imperial Russia.*

29. F. I. Panferov, *Brusski*, trans. Z. Mitrov and J. Tabrisky (Westport, Conn., 1977, reprint of 1930 ed.) p. 20.

30. Antonina Martynova, "Life of the Pre-Revolutionary Village as Reflected in Popular Lullabies," in Ransel, ed., p. 172.

31. The Land Code abolished the Stolypin land reform that had given the head of household sole ownership of land and house. Prior to the Stolypin laws, the property of the household was owned jointly by the family. The extent to which the women were considered partners in this joint ownership is not entirely clear. In the nineteenth century women, as a rule, did not take part in the partitioning of household property. See Shinn, p. 604, Wallace, p. 85. Kubanin claims that prior to the Revolution, sisters did not receive any of the property. See M. Kubanin, *Klassovaia sushchnost' protsessa drobleniia krest'ianskikh khoziaistv* (Moscow, 1929), p. 72. Stepniak, on the other hand, explains that sisters generally did not inherit from brothers because in marrying they went to another family and took with them a dowry. But a spinster sister or a widow who returned to live with her brothers would always receive her share from the tribunal. Stepniak (Kravchinskii, S.), *The Russian Peasantry* (New York, 1888), p. 80. According to Lewin, a woman would get something but not a full share.

32. On separate female property, see Shinn, p. 604, V. F. Mukhin', *Obychnyi poriadok' nasledovaniia v krest'ian'* (St. Petersburg, 1888), pp. 89–92, A. F. Meiendorf, *Krest'ianskii dvor* (St. Petersburg, 1909), M. Kovalevsky, *Modern Customs and Ancient Laws of Russia* (London, 1891), p. 59.

33. Benet, *Viriatino*, p. 41.

34. Kovalevsky, p. 59.

35. Benet, *Viriatino,* p. 102, Anokhina and Shmeleva, p. 175.

36. Anokhina and Shmeleva, p. 175.

37. On lack of social conscience, see Lewin, p. 22. A number of peasants did enter communes. But only a fraction of 1% ever joined. See Robert Wesson, *Soviet Communes* (New Brunswick, N.J., 1963), p. 6.

38. K. N. Samoilova, *Krest'ianka i sovetskaia vlast',* pp. 24, 29.

39. *Kommunistka,* no. 10–11 (1921), p. 46.

40. See *Pravda,* June 1, 1919, as cited in Wesson, *Soviet Communes,* p. 216.

41. Wesson, *Soviet Communes,* p. 216.

42. See Wesson, p. 216, and Sergei Tretiakov, *Vyzov* (Moscow, 1932), pp. 54, 58, 86–87, 103–104. Other sources on women in communes: P. Lezhnev-Finkovskii, *Sovkhozy i kolkhozy* (Moscow, 1928), p. 187; A. F. Chmyga, *Ocherki po istorii kolkhoznogo dvizheniia na Ukraine (1921–25)* (Moscow, 1959), p. 193; A. A. Bitsenko, *Sel'sko-khoziaistvennye kommuny* (Moscow, 1924), p. 29. Bitsenko notes the subordinate position of women communards.

43. Wesson, *Soviet Communes,* p. 112. See A. L. Strong, *The Soviets Conquer Wheat* (New York, 1931), pp. 121–22, on "Fortress of Communism." See A. F. Chmyga, p. 92, for widows organizing kolkhozy in early years of the Revolution.

44. Gail W. Lapidus, "Sexual Equality in Soviet Policy," in D. Atkinson et al., eds., *Women in Russia* (Stanford, 1977), p. 121.

45. See Farnsworth, *Aleksandra Kollontai,* pp. 284–308.

46. Thus in Gomel province out of 36 selected volosts systematic work was carried out only in 16. In Kursk province out of 36 volosts work was conducted in 32. *Kommunistka,* no. 10 (1923), p. 29. And the presence of the *Zhenotdel* did not necessarily mean substantial progress. For example, a report from Penza province in 1921 indicated that after a year of work the broad mass of women in the province were affected only slightly. Still, in 5 volosts 20 peasant women were elected to the Soviet. *Kommunistka,* no. 8–9 (1921), pp. 54–55.

47. *Kommunistka,* no. 10 (1923), p. 28. A report from Orel province pointed out that there were 45 volost organizers, nearly all serving without pay. Their work was of a low level. The women were young and fervent but ill-prepared. *Kommunistka,* no. 6 (1923), p. 38.

48. *Kommunistka,* no. 10–11 (1921), p. 43.

49. Quoted in Samoilova, *Krest'ianka i sovetskaia vlast',* p. 6.

50. See Shingarev in Shuvaev, pp. 171–72, for illiteracy, pp. 251, 275 for illness. In Kostroma province in the late nineteenth century, a doctor reported higher rates of illness among women. D. N. Zhbankov, *Bab'ia storona* (Kostroma, 1891), p. 4.

51. Shingarev in Shuvaev, pp. 298–99.

52. For statistics on death rates, see A. G. Rashin, *Naselenie Rossii za 100 let* (Moscow, 1956), pp. 203–5. Statistics for each period show a greater death rate for infant boys. See Zhbankov, pp. 4–5, 72, for adverse effect of migrant and factory labor on the life expectancy of peasant men.

53. Samoilova, *Krest'ianka i sovetskaia vlast',* p. 10.

54. *Kommunistka,* no. 12–13 (1921), p. 67.

55. Anokhina and Shmeleva, p. 266.

56. See *Krest'ianstvo i trudovaia povinnost'* (Moscow, 1920). For exemptions for women, see Farnsworth, *Aleksandra Kollontai,* p. 192.

57. Jessica Smith, *Woman in Soviet Russia* (New York, 1928), p. 33.

58. V. Ulasevich, *Zhenshchina v kolkhoze* (Moscow, 1930), p. 58.

59. John Maynard, *The Russian Peasant* (London, 1943), p. 174.

60. Sheila Fitzpatrick, *Education and Social Mobility in the Soviet Union, 1921–34* (New York, 1979), p. 162. An example of atheism in the village: in 1924 in Voronezh "Societies of the Godless" conducted antireligious lectures and conversations utilizing

village evening parties and reading huts. *Sotsial'no-ekonomicheskie preobrazovaniia v Voronezhskoi derevne (1917–67)* (Voronezh, 1967), p. 309.

61. Fitzpatrick, *Education and Social Mobility*, p. 162.

62. Rosnitskii, *Litso derevni*, pp. 92–93.

63. Ibid., pp. 92–93.

64. Rosnitskii, *Litso derevni*, p. 107. Although adults were generally adverse to the idea of literacy training, in those villages where cultural work was extensive, even older women went willingly to literacy centers. Ibid., p. 106.

65. Samoilova, *Krest'ianka i sovetskaia vlast'*, pp. 28–29.

66. D. P. Rozit, *Proverka raboty nizovogo apparata v derevne*, p. 79 (examples drawn from area of Urals).

67. See *Kommunistka*, no. 3 (1924), p. 26, and ibid., no. 12–13 (1921), pp. 66–67. The majority of peasant women in the Soviet were Red Army wives.

68. Ibid., no. 6 (1923), p. 39.

69. Ibid., p. 46. In the 1920s women without families, presumably widows, were those who participated publicly. See L. V. Ostapenko, "Vliianie novoi proizvodstvennoi roli zhenshchiny na ee polozhenie v sem'e," *Sovetskaia etnografiia*, 1971, no. 5, p. 101.

70. *Kommunistka*, no. 3 (1924), p. 26.

71. Ibid., no. 8 (1923), p. 20. For attitudes toward the Komsomol, see A. M. Bol'shakov, *Derevnia, 1917–27* (Moscow, 1927), pp. 321–36.

72. *Kommunistka*, no. 8–9 (1922), p. 35.

73. Rosnitskii, *Litso derevni*, pp. 38–39.

74. *Kommunistka*, no. 6 (1923), p. 39.

75. Ibid., no. 3–4 (1923), p. 46.

76. Ibid., no. 3–4 (1923), p. 47.

77. Ibid., p. 47.

78. Ibid., no. 8 (1923), p. 29.

79. Ibid., no. 6 (1923), p. 39.

80. Ibid., p. 39.

81. For collective purchasing organizations, see *Kommunistka*, no. 3–4 (1923), p. 52; no. 3 (1924), pp. 33–36; no. 7 (1924), p. 33.

82. Rosnitskii, *Litso derevni*, p. 54. For peasant distrust of cooperatives, ibid., pp. 52–55.

83. The number was small. By the mid-twenties, a friendly source indicated, over 500,000 women were members of consumer's cooperatives, 180,000 were members of *kustarnye* (handwork) cooperatives, and "a large number" belonged to the agricultural cooperatives. Smith, *Woman in Soviet Russia*, p. 43. (Geographical area not indicated.)

84. *Kommunistka*, no. 3–4 (1920), p. 30. The presence of two horses suggests a relatively prosperous artel. See V. A. Sidorov, *Klassovaia bor'ba v dokolkhoznoi derevne* (Moscow, 1978), p. 64.

85. See Rosnitskii, *Litso derevni*, p. 81, for indication that intentions of Communist activists were not always carried out.

86. Sometimes with unhappy results. Rosnitskii reports a husband in Penza province beating his wife for joining a choral circle. She remained in the group. *Litso derevni*, p. 113.

87. Smith, *Woman in Soviet Russia*, p. 37.

88. *Kommunistka*, no. 10–11 (1921), p. 47, for description of reading material in Saratov. See p. 48 for publications aimed at peasant women.

89. *Otchet otdela TsKRKP (b) po rabote sredi zhenshchin za god raboty* (Moscow, 1921), p. 28; *Kommunistka*, no. 6–7 (1922), pp. 6–7.

90. *Kommunistka*, no. 12–13 (1921), p. 55.

91. Ibid., no. 7 (1920), p. 34.

Village Women Experience the Revolutions   259

92. *Otchet otdela TsKRKP (b) po rabote sredi zhenshchin za god raboty* (Moscow, 1921), p. 27.
93. *Kommunistka*, no. 10 (1923), p. 29.
94. Ibid., no. 8 (1923), p. 29.
95. Ibid., no. 8–9 (1922), p. 35, on peasant resentment. "Patronage" *(shefstvo)* of city communists over village groups sometimes worked out badly and antagonized the peasants. For descriptions of Communist irresponsibility and insensitivity, see Rosnitskii, *Litso derevni*, pp. 107–108.
96. *Kommunistka*, no. 7 (1920), p. 33.
97. Ibid., no. 5 (1920), p. 15.
98. The age of the delegate was usually between 20 and 40. *Kommunistka*, no. 10 (1923), p. 29. A report from Penza province is indicative, however, of the underlying mood of the peasant women toward such public work. One woman, registering herself as a delegate in the hope that she would receive some benefit, crossed her name out when she learned that the delegate did not receive any special advantages. Rosnitskii, *Litso derevni*, p. 113.
99. *Kommunistka*, no. 10 (1923), p. 30.
100. Ibid., p. 30.
101. D. P. Rozit, *Proverka raboty nizovogo apparata v derevne*, p. 79.
102. *Kommunistka*, no. 10–11 (1921), p. 46; *Otchet otdela TsKRKP (b) po rabote sredi zhenshchin za god raboty* (Moscow, 1921), p. 25 (hereafter *Otchet*).
103. *Otchet*, p. 25.
104. *Otchet*, p. 21. *Praktikanty* received political indoctrination from the *Zhenotdel* and they served in Soviet institutions.
105. *Kommunistka*, no. 5 (1920), p. 15. But see Rosnitskii, *Litso derevni*, p. 112, on backward attitudes toward women in public life in other areas of Penza province.
106. *Kommunistka*, no. 8 (1923), p. 6. There were 50,000 village soviets in the RSFSR and 70,000 in the country as a whole. Lewin, p. 105. Few women participated politically in the first years of the revolution. In province, uezd, and volost congresses, there were never more than 4 women for every 100 men. Sometimes the proportion was as low as 0.5 women for every 100 men. Only in the city soviets was female participation higher. See tables in *Kommunistka*, no. 8–9 (1922), p. 5. As late as 1927 in Tver province only 32.5% of the women took part in elections to village soviets. *Sotsialisticheskoe stroitel'stvo v Tverskoi gubernii* (Moscow, 1927), p. 29, as cited in L. V. Ostapenko, "The Effect of Woman's New Production Role on Her Position in the Family," *Soviet Sociology*, v. 12, no. 4, 1974, p. 94.
107. *Kommunistka*, no. 1–2 (1920), p. 38.
108. The provinces were: Iaroslavl, Simbirsk, Vladimir, Severnaia-Dvina, Kostroma, Pskov, Kursk, Tver, Kaluga, Gomel', Briansk, Moscow, Nizhegorod, Ivanovo-Voznesensk, Samara. *Kommunistka*, no. 10–11 (1921), pp. 40, 42. Female membership in the Party for the same provinces was 6,499. Ibid., pp. 40, 42. The actual numbers were probably somewhat higher since there were no returns listed for Briansk or Moscow. Only 8 provinces listed any peasant women as members of the Party: Iaroslavl, Vladimir, Kostroma, Kursk, Gomel', Severnaia-Dvina, Nizhegorod, and Ivanovo-Voznesensk.
109. A. V. Chayanov, *The Theory of Peasant Economy*, ed. Daniel Thorner, Basile Kerblay, and R. E. F. Smith (Homewood, Ill., 1966, originally published Moscow, 1925), p. 265.
110. Bol'shakov, *Derevnia 1917–27* (Moscow, 1927), pp. 352–53.
111. *Kommunistka*, no. 8–9 (1922), p. 35.
112. Ibid.
113. Ibid., no. 6 (1923), p. 38.
114. Teodor Shanin, *The Awkward Class* (Oxford, 1972), p. 176.

115. Smith, pp. 41–42.

116. On literacy, 1930, see V. Ulasevich, *Zhenshchina v kolkhoze* (Moscow, 1930), p. 58. For pre–1914, A. G. Rashin, *Naselenie Rossii za 100 let* (Moscow, 1956), p. 294.

117. D. P. Rozit, *Proverka raboty nizovogo apparata v derevne* (Moscow, 1926), p. 80. Organization was slow. By 1924–25, Kaluga province had only 14 nurseries. Ibid.

118. Summer nurseries inaugurated by Zemstvos on a limited scale were an innovation of late nineteenth-century Russia. In 1898 the Voronezh provincial Zemstvo pioneered in the nursery movement. See Frieden, "Childcare: Medical Reform in a Traditionalist Culture," pp. 251–53. Also see Shingarev in Shuvaev, p. 271.

119. A locale in which women predominated because as many as 60% of the men were away at wage labor *(otkhodniki)* would be called a "babii" uezd. A. G. Rashin, *Formirovanie rabochego klassa Rossii* (Moscow, 1958), p. 364. Around 1900, for example, in Viazemskii uezd in Smolensk province, 61% of the grown men and 15% of the grown women were away working. For analysis of two female-dominated areas in Kostroma province, see D. N. Zhbankov, *Bab' ia storona* (Kostroma, 1891). See Smith, pp. 39, 41–42, for twentieth-century peasant new women. For fictional portrayals, see Iakov Korobov, *Katia Dolga* (Vladimir, 1958); *Mar' ia-bol' shevichka* in Aleksandr Neverov, *Izbrannye proizvedeniia* (Moscow, 1958), pp. 195–200; and *Virineia* in L. Seifullina, *Sobranie sochinenii*, vol. III (Moscow-Leningrad, 1929).

120. Smith, p. 42. Separation by mutual consent did, however, occur. Moreover, a woman who complained to the township court of serious maltreatment by her husband might, if she were lucky, and the judges well-disposed, receive permission to live apart from him. See, for example, a case in Iaroslavl province in 1869 in *Trudy Komissii po preobrazovaniiu volostnykh sudov*, vol. III (St. Petersburg, 1874), p. 158.

121. Schlesinger, pp. 147, 150. Registrar's Office statistics on divorces for one three-month period—October, November, December 1924—show that for every 10,000 inhabitants of district towns there were 7 divorces. In smaller towns for the same number of inhabitants there were 3 divorces, and for every 10,000 village inhabitants, 2 divorces. Thus in a year there would be approximately 28 divorces in district towns, 12 in smaller towns, and only 8 in villages for every 10,000 inhabitants. Schlesinger, p. 118.

122. Schlesinger, p. 151; Smith, p. 44.

123. M. Kubanin, *Klassovaia sushchnost' protsessa drobleniia krest'ianskikh khoziaistv* (Moscow, 1929), pp. 71–75. For laws regulating partition of the dvor, see E. Dombrovskii, *Krest' ianskii dvor i semeino-imushchestvennye razdely* (Moscow, 1926), and N. M. Tomashevskii, *Zakony o nasledstvennosti v krest'ianskom khoziaistve* (Leningrad, 1925).

124. *Kommunistka*, no. 10 (1923), p. 30.

125. Farnsworth, *Aleksandra Kollontai*, p. 320n.; Kaganovich's speech: *XVI S"ezd Vsesoiuznoi Kommunisticheskoi Partii (b). Stenograficheskii Otchet* (Moscow-Leningrad, 1931), p. 70. Also see M. Hindus, *Red Bread* (New York, 1931), pp. 49–50, and S. Tret'iakov, *Vyzov* (Moscow, 1932), pp. 223, 307. On the other hand, widows—especially *bedniaki*—or women with husbands away for years at wage work, were more inclined to join the kolkhoz. Anokhina and Shmeleva, pp. 32, 273.

126. See reports in *Materialy po istorii SSSR*, vol. 1 (Moscow, 1955), pp. 327, 347–48, 350, 354–55, 357–58, 364, 368.

127. See M. Fainsod, *Smolensk Under Soviet Rule* (Cambridge, Mass., 1958), pp. 253–54.

128. Farnsworth, *Aleksandra Kollontai*, p. 149.

129. Smith, pp. 35–36.

[15] Contradictions of Revolution: Juvenile Crime and Rehabilitation

Peter H. Juviler

Some day a historian of child welfare will record this striking contrast between unbelievable efforts to carry out lofty slogans about the happiness of children and the future society, and the harsh reality which sullied them and trampled them into the mud.

(M. N. Gernet, 1874–1953)

THESE WORDS BY an eminent Russian criminologist looking back over the early Soviet years speak directly to the theme of this chapter. It is an account of "lofty slogans" and "harsh reality," all right. And the point is that much of the harsh reality that sullied and trampled the ideals behind those slogans grew out of the originally unintended results of the very Bolshevik revolution which nurtured those ideals.

The original Soviet ideals for rehabilitating juvenile criminals and the nature and circumstances of their implementation demonstrate graphically that revolution serves better to restructure political authority than to reconstitute social authority. Moreover, the ideals and conflicts over these ideals, even the extent of their implementation, fall short of conveying the full impact of revolution on culture. The ultimate success or failure of revolutionary ideals, their remolding of culture, depends on their relation to existing attitudes but also on the outcome of the entire revolutionary process and cannot be understood apart from that broader context.

Between 1917 and 1924 the Soviet regime laid down the theoretical, legal, and institutional foundation in theories, laws, and institutions for the struggle to establish order-supporting authority over millions of homeless or untended children and adolescents, and to form the "new man" of the future socialist society. This account focuses on Soviet responses to juvenile crime in the context of the tsarist legacy; early Soviet non-punitive approaches; civil war breakdown and Bolshevik responses to juvenile vagabondage and crime; and the juvenile work communes. It will take up, finally, the retreat to more punitive alternatives.

AN INAUSPICIOUS LEGACY

Revolution follows political deauthorization, but more than political authority may collapse in the process. Russia's helter-skelter exodus from village to towns, accompanied by disastrous wars, rent the fabric of custom and authority. Peasant in-migration swelled the urban population threefold during the last forty years of the nineteenth century[1] and continued into the twentieth to crowd impoverished families into fetid tenements, with as many as eight persons in a room,[2] and to swamp welfare and order-keeping agencies.[3] Out of work but surrounded by stealable goods in the communal apartments, stores, and markets, many peasant lads drifted beyond any semblance of a family and community life. The research of Professor M. N. Gernet's Moscow University seminar on juvenile delinquency (1909–1911) found in the dossiers of nearly 3,000 cases ample proof of the role of poverty, unemployment, and the destruction of peasant culture and authority in fostering crime, and of the corrupting slum environment—the heavy drinking (a country pastime too), idling in taverns and billiard parlors, prostitution, robbable markets, pickable pockets in city crowds, and the dens for sleeping, carousing, consorting, and plotting.[4]

Many city youngsters lived desperately, like the boy known to us as "Ch." His mother, the Moscow court dossier read, worked in a factory; his father lived somewhere around the Khitrov market. Homeless and without steady work, Ch. fell in with some debauched newspaper boys, drank, "defrauded the public by selling old newspapers, shouting sensational headlines: 'Stolypin killed!' (Stolypin, the prime minister was assassinated later, in 1911), 'bomb explodes!' etc." Finally, as a beggar, he broke the window of a storekeeper who had refused him a handout and was sent to court.[5]

Indeed Russia's upheavals and blows from war on the home front hit juveniles hardest. Their convictions rose at more than twice the rate for adults, registering a 15 percent increase for the period 1890–1895 as compared with the period 1884–1889.[6] Convictions of juveniles after the Russo-Japanese War and 1905 Revolution registered an increase "without equal in the courts of Western Europe."[7] Felony convictions of juveniles again soared in World War I, by 75 percent between 1914 and 1916. War, the penologist P. I. Liublinsky wrote, "created millions of orphans . . . drove masses of refugees with small children from their homes, disrupted children's schooling, undermined their health by prolonged deprivation, forced tens of thousands of children into overtaxing work and subjected the children's delicate psyches to the pathological impact of inflamed wartime passions and the hubbub of black market speculation."[8]

Swarms of these children ended up homeless, like Ch., the newspaper boy. Predecessors of these *besprizorniki*—untended ones—had roamed Russia's streets and highways at least as far back as Petrine times,[9] but never in greater numbers than during the wartime twilight of the empire.[10] Because of government inertia and lack of funds, programs dealing with child vagrancy and crime voted at the All-Russian Conference on Wartime Child Care (March 1916) remained mere words. As war dragged Russia to defeat and collapse in 1916–1917, crime mounted ever higher; the revolutionary outcome of February–October 1917 caught up with and inundated the previously accelerating reform movement in juvenile justice led by jurists like Liublinsky and Gernet.[11] Clearly an inauspicious legacy awaited the reformers and their new Bolshevik governors. But the deep disorder of tsarist times seems idyllic compared with the consequences of the revolutionary conflict to follow.

"NO COURTS OR PRISONS..."

Bolshevik officials responsible for law and order were divided about how to deal with child criminals: reform juvenile justice by treating minors outside corrupting jails as malleable victims of the old order, or punish them as criminal enemies of society? With Lenin's backing, the reform got through the Council of People's Commissars as the decree of January 14, 1918.[12] Henceforth, the decree proclaimed, "there shall be no courts or prisons for children." The decrees raised the lowest age for criminal liability from the tsarist 10 years[13] to 17. Child suspects through age 16 were to be referred to newly created Commissions on Juvenile Affairs. These commissions were to be educational and welfare agencies as well as punitive boards, unlike the part-educational, part-punitive tsarist children's courts begun in 1910.[14] Children then in prison were to be released and, if need be, housed in reformatories. "When the legislators drafted the law," recounted V. I. Kufaev, criminologist and associate of Gernet, "they were more concerned about the harm lawbreaking might do to the child than they were about the harm it might do to the state, for that harm resulted from disorder in the life of the state."[15]

The new legislation represented at least a paper victory for Soviet reformers, communist and non-communist alike. They hoped to rehabilitate wayward children by making their environment more humane and secure, away from the repressive, punitive and criminogenic surroundings of tsarist correctional institutions, wherein most juveniles ended up housed with the adult criminals who became their law-opposing authority figures.[16]

BREAKDOWN

Meanwhile, Lenin's slogan of 1914—"Change world war into civil war!"— came home to roost in Soviet Russia, not as a means to a communist takeover, but as a consequence of it. Although devastation and hunger drastically depopulated the large cities, per capita rates of juvenile convictions rose so high that their absolute number increased as well.[17] *Vorushki,* the little thieves, were everywhere, it seemed. They stole food from stalls, luggage from travelers, money and property from friends and relatives as well as strangers. They could be dangerously violent, especially in the provinces, where crimes other than theft included timber poaching, moonshining, smuggling, horse stealing, and arson.[18] Criminologists found it particularly disturbing that even "under the rule of the proletariat" most juvenile criminals came from classes closest to the revolution: workers, peasants, artisans, and other persons of humble occupation. That things got worse in Soviet Russia after World War I while crime dropped in capitalist countries like England and Germany only hurt the more.[19] But at least in those days Soviet criminologists could make such comparisons.

Out of civil war came the dreadful famine of 1920–1921. Three out of ten children in the Volga region succumbed to starvation and disease before Russian and U.S. relief efforts could take effect. *Besprizorniki* formed marauding bands, joined in acts of cannibalism. Many tried to flee disaster on foot or stowed away on trains, along a doleful route marked by hundreds of thousands of little corpses.[20] Children's crime, up to then primarily urban, increased in the countryside, "especially in famine regions and regions of intensified civil war."[21]

The accumulation of war, civil war, and famine produced around seven million *besprizorniki*. But children's shelters could hold only 540,000 at their peak of capacity, and under conditions so dreadful that many inmates preferred to take their chances on the street.[22] Thronging the cities into the 1920s, groups and gangs of begging and pilfering *besprizorniki* took nocturnal shelter in empty railroad carriages, station closets, foul flophouses, giant tar cauldrons still warm from the day's work. Many were ravaged by syphilis or exposure or were addicted to cocaine. *Besprizorniki* accounted for 80 to 90 percent of all lawbreaking by juveniles.[23] Poor city children, too, joined the waifs. "It is not difficult," Kufaev noted, "to trace how a child coming from a poverty-stricken proletarian family unable to give him an education and job training, finds himself willy-nilly on the job market and, left to his own devices, becomes a *besprizornik*."[24] In-migration resumed and again schools and families lost control; authority broke down in the drunken social anarchy of factory barracks and slums which disgorged their neglected or abused child victims onto the streets as in the old days.[25]

Child vagabondage of the *besprizorniki* remained a "major social disaster" long after the period 1917–1924.[26] So did juvenile crime. While some jurists in 1917–1924 envisaged broad state programs of "social and legal protection for children," other jurists and the regime initiated steps to liberate women while reinforcing family obligations and assisting mothers, in order to bolster the child-rearing functions of that temporarily necessary relic, the family, and to enforce paternity and support obligations.[27]

But Russia's poverty dogged child care and rehabilitation at every step. Agencies competed for pittances. Conflicts arose "over whether desperately short funds should go to housing children sleeping in ruins, water conduits, and tar-heating cauldrons, or to training guardians competent to supervise children pulled off the streets."[28] State care of children had been the Marxists' goal for an age of affluence, but it was already being attempted in 1919 under conditions of last-ditch conflict and growing hunger. Children's needs for food, clothing, and shelter, even before the famine years, rapidly exceeded the capacity of children's homes.[29]

There was no affordable remedy for this situation. And competing priorities for what resources there were included lavish allotments sent abroad for the purposes of the Bolshevik-controlled Communist International and its member parties.[30] Moreover, economies decreed in 1922 as part of the "economic accountability" of the New Economic Policy increased unemployment and forced the closing of over half the children's shelters. Their capacity fell from an already inadequate 540,000 in 1921 to 280,000 by 1924 and lower thereafter.[31]

There was little or no coordination in child care and rehabilitation, at least through 1924. They remained under the competing jurisdictions of a number of agencies exercising Soviet state authority over children. These included the People's Commissariats of Enlightenment *(Narkompros)*, Health *(Narkomzdrav)*, and Social Security *(Narkomsobes);* the secret police;* the NKVD; and the People's Commissariat of Justice *(Narkomiust)*.[32] Given the importance of labor communes as exercises in rehabilitation, however, a few words are in order about their rival sponsors, *Narkompros* and the OGPU.

Feliks Dzerzhinsky's command of power and resources gave him an advantage over Commissar Anatole Lunarcharsky of *Narkompros*. Dzerhinsky had headed the Cheka since its founding in December 1917. He took over the NKVD in 1920, the People's Commissariat of Transport in 1921, and VSNKh, the Supreme Council of the National Economy, in 1924. Dzerzhinsky amply earned his reputation as "scourge of the bourgeoisie and faithful knight of the proletariat." But already in his revolutionary youth he had professed great love for children and special empathy for the homeless and hungry ones.[33] On January 21 of the dreadful year 1921 he achieved the formation of an interagency Commission to Improve Children's Life, which he headed with V. S. Kornev, Chief of Staff of the Cheka troops, as his deputy. The other five members of this seven-person agency to coordinate child welfare measures

---

*It was known by its acronym Cheka or VCheka until 1922, when it became the GPU in the People's Commissariat of Internal Affairs (NKVD) and in 1924 the OGPU, a separate agency again, attached to the Council of People's Commissars.

came from such concerned agencies as the Commissariats of Health, Food, and Enlightenment, and the Workers' and Peasants' Inspectorate (an agency of administrative inspection and control). Dzerzhinsky installed Chekists as heads of local branches of the commission.[34]

The Cheka's entry into the lists as savior of children created tensions with *Narkompros*, whose pedagogues saw themselves frozen out of influence with child welfare efforts. They also associated the Cheka with harsh discipline and with the possible intimidation of teachers. A *Narkompros* report of 1920 stated the official approach to wayward children: "We do not recognize juvenile crime. We know only sick children, spoilt by an ugly environment and education." Punishment, however, was not Cheka policy either in the early 1920s. Dzerzhinsky himself instructed the Commission to Improve Children's Life that "for children in Soviet Russia there are no trials and no imprisonment."[35] *Narkompros* girded itself to deal with sick, defective children. The Chekists involved were counseled, rather, to see the children as basically unspoiled victims of a sick society.

Out in the field, the Cheka used its centralized and pervasive machinery to dominate conflict-ridden attempts at rescuing children from the famine in 1921. It suppressed the private Committee for Aid to the Starving, imprisoning its leaders on charges of intriguing against the Soviet regime.[36] *Narkompros*, meanwhile, had begun to open a series of children's labor communes as part of its program for rehabilitating criminal and derelict juveniles, for rescuing them from the culture of the streets and turning them into carriers of the new culture of the coming socialist society.

COMMUNES

Architects of the brighter future, drawing up their plans amidst the ruins of the old society the revolution had helped shatter, pedagogues of *Narkompros* made NEP a period for experimentation and innovation in reeducation of a variety and boldness later unequaled in the USSR.[37] Stanislav Shatsky (1878–1934) personified the close connection *Narkompros* maintained between education and the rehabilitation of youth. Shatsky set up forerunners of the labor communes before the revolution. His "Cheerful Life" summer labor colony, organized in 1911 for working class children, anticipated the later *Narkompros* combination of socially useful work and general education as the foundation of character building.[38]

Educators shaping policy within *Narkompros* agreed that communes and schools should combine book learning with work training, that these institutions not only should reflect social change but should actively influence it by helping form the new socialist culture.[39] In the Russian revolutionary tradition the pedagogues extolled the collective side of the educational experience.

The educators disagreed among themselves, however, about whether the school would "wither away" entirely and about the relationship between the individual and the collective. What was the proper balance between the individual's development and the collective's ideals? Lunacharsky, who as head of *Narkompros* was the leading ministerial figure for education and culture in the USSR, depicted the struggle against "individualism" and for the new culture as the pursuit of an ideal "communal life based not on compulsion and the need of mankind to herd together for mere self-preservation, as it had in the past, but on a free and natural merging of personalities into superpersonal entities."[40] Quite in line with this vision of spontaneous collectivism was the child-centered, psychologized approach to ex-*besprizorniki* undergoing rehabilitation as sick and sometimes dangerous defectives to be isolated from society and cured after proper diagnosis, with the help of psychological techniques from the West.

Among the holdouts against this method was the most famous commune leader of all, the Ukrainian communist ex-schoolteacher Anton Makarenko (1888–1939). Makarenko is so well known relative to other commune leaders and so untypical of *Narkompros*'s pedagogues that I shall touch only lightly on him here, devoting this account mainly to lesser known figures and methods. It is worth pointing out, though, that Makarenko's method of rehabilitation featured tight, group-imposed discipline (ranging from persuasion to shaming, noncorporal punishment, and the ultimate penalty, expulsion from his Gorky Commune). A nucleus of dedicated communàrds loyal to Makarenko led the group, backed up by Makarenko's firm and fatherly presence, and by a quasi-military ritualism (drums, bugles, marching, guard watches, and ceremony). Makarenko's methods reflected his contempt for foreign pedagogy and for the standard *Narkompros* methods, which included delving into the past or the psyche of a new recruit to the commune. Eventually this difference of method resulted in bitter conflict with *Narkompros* and led to Makarenko's departure from *Narkompros* in 1927–1928 to open and head the OGPU's Dzerzhinsky Commune. After ten successful years, it was liquidated under Stalin, along with all other communes.[41]

Away from the rarified atmosphere of pedagogical debate, founders of communes out in the field had to improvise, to make a go of it in half-ruined estates, dilapidated former tsarist juvenile colonies, and converted jails. Because they normally functioned as closed institutions, the *Narkompros* communes were not always easy to distinguish from the juvenile colonies of imperial Russia. This situation changed in 1924–1925 as a result of gains made in *Narkompros* by environmentalists. One of them cited to the Second Psychoneurological Congress in 1924 the rehabilitation of 4,500 "defective" lawbreaking children in Petrograd simply by giving them decent housing, clothing, food, and schooling. These alleged criminals were not defective at all, she said, but "children warped by the abnormal life they had to lead and their abnormal upbringing."[42]

Indeed, by 1924, a turning point in *Narkompros* policy had been reached, bringing about the opening up of closed communes and orders for the introduction of vocational training everywhere. All institutions for "difficult" children were to resemble communes as closely as possible. This meant that they were to feature maximum possible voluntary recruitment, self-government, and socially useful work as part of the training for life. Behind these ideals, but still apparent to *Narkompros,* one must not forget, lay the hard facts of poverty, which often made it impossible "to satisfy the most basic needs of youngsters," let alone provide "the proper means of labor training." Moreover, the conditions, practices, and effectiveness of communes varied widely.[43]

One of the first, and apparently most successful, communes appeared in 1919, the year before Makarenko's. Its director, identified only as Mirandov, set up the Ulyanovsk Labor School-Commune on a ruined estate along the Volga. He and his counselors faced nightmarish difficulties in dealing with their first charges, ten criminals whose long prison records belied their youth. The staff had also to contend with local hostility and the famine of 1920–21 from which their farm never quite recovered. By 1925 they had four workshops and 50 communards—all full or half orphans. Material difficulties prevented them from taking in their full quota of 65. Mirandov, like Makarenko, insisted on complete trust between counselors and inmates. He had open doors from the beginning, and "neither guards nor watchmen, wardens, nor solitary confinement." He directed the waifs' street-developed initiative into a form of goal-directed participatory democracy, while the staff tried to make the work materially rewarding, useful, and promising of a brighter future. Self-organization, meaningful work, and trust became, as described in Mirandov's report, a model for other communes. From Mirandov they heard how,

> cut off from the city, situated in the remote countryside, we live as a close-knit family. Here we discuss all school matters and often private ones at general meetings. In the communal milieu nobody hesitates to seek support and sympathy when beset by personal troubles or grief. But the most potent source of revolutionary influence on the children we find to be organized collective work.[44]

The communes of *Narkompros* accepted children 12 to 16 years of age, either directly from the streets and orphanages or sent them by the Commissions on Juvenile Affairs, and kept them to the maximum age of 18. Labor communes of the OGPU took in largely an older contingent, mostly in the 16 to 23 range—boys and girls sent them by the Commissions on Juvenile Affairs or from prisons and labor camps, as well as stowaways found on trains. With ampler funds and older inmates, the OGPU communes were able to establish flourishing regular factories, not just rudimentary workshops and farms like those of *Narkompros*.

Dzerzhinsky began the OGPU commune program in 1924. To initiate it he called on Matvei Pogrebinsky, an intense young man who invariably wore a black karakul fur hat, and whose reputation for working well with youth went back to his Civil War service as a military commissar on the Siberian front against Kolchak. While working out plans for a commune, Pogrebinsky visited *besprizorniki* in their nighttime haunts to gauge their outlook and organization. He opened the first OGPU commune on August 18, 1924, in the beautiful estate of Bolshevo, which had once belonged to a chocolate manufacturer. Before its liquidation in 1937 (along with Pogrebinsky's), the Bolshevo commune had grown to over 1,500 communards, a self-contained youth town with factories for the manufacture of shoes, knitted goods, and skates.[45]

All differences of resources and methods aside, both the OGPU and *Narkompros* in their own ways contributed to the movement in the early Soviet years away from "coercive placement in institutions and coercive retention of an adolescent in them by such physical means as locks, bars, etc., which contradict principles of Soviet pedagogy and do not achieve their purpose."[46]

But the bars, locks, and fences of adult prisons and camps run by the NKVD and Cheka-GPU-OGPU awaited most juvenile criminals sentenced by the courts. The ideals and innovations of the communes affected only a small proportion of all *besprizorniki* and juvenile criminals.[47] Moreover, law enforcement authorities had by 1924 taken over from the educators the disposition of more and more cases involving minors. Even as the commune system expanded, criminal law retreated from the principle of "no courts or prisons for children." No account of rehabilitation would be complete without at least a brief glimpse of that retreat in criminal policy.

RETREAT

Its first legislative step was the Guiding Principles of Criminal Law, issued in 1919. True, on the reform side, the Guiding Principles stressed social causes of crime over individual choice, and affirmed the need to minimize suffering for the convicted. Also, the measure decreed that educational measures rather than criminal punishment be applied to juveniles, even over 16, but under 18 if acting "without reason," the old tsarist mitigating factor. But, on the other hand, the Guiding Principles lowered the minimum age of criminal liability from 16 to 14 for offenders acting "with reason," that is, with conscious intent to perform a criminal act.[48] A decree in 1920 changed the criterion for lowering the age of criminal liability to 14 from acting "with reason" to "incorrigibility by educational or medical means." The first detailed Soviet criminal code, that of 1922, incorporated past changes in juvenile liability since 1918 and marked a further retreat from the 1918 principles of "no courts or prisons" for minors by lowering the minimum age for unconditional criminal liability from 18 to 16. Also it lowered by two years, from 16 to 14, the minimum age at which minors could be sent by Commissions for Juvenile Affairs to court for trial.[49]

The case of a boy with the street-gang sobriquet of "Bulldog" will illustrate both contemporary procedure and a typical background of a juvenile criminal. Bulldog migrated from his village to Moscow with his parents before the Revolution, but his father died in a workers' demonstration in 1917. The death of his mother from tuberculosis orphaned Bulldog in 1923. He then ran away from a children's shelter where his brother had placed him, taking up the life of a *besprizornik* and professional thief. Several times he was picked up by the police at the railroad station where he had been preying on passengers, registered, and taken to a "reception and distribution center" of *Narkompros,* where he appeared before one of the Commissions on Juvenile Affairs.[50] These were three-person boards made up of a pedagogue from the education department of the borough soviet, a doctor from its health department, and a local People's Court judge.

Eventually the Commission sent Bulldog to court under the already mentioned provision of the 1922 Code that covered juveniles as young as 14 and 15, when (1) they were stubborn repeaters, habitual runaways from children's homes; or (2) had committed homicide, aggravated assault, rape, robbery, arson, counterfeiting, bribery, large-scale theft of socialist or cooperative property, and speculation.[51] Bulldog, who was a year or two under 16, was convicted of theft and was sent to a closed reformatory, *Mostruddom* (the Moscow Labor Home for Juveniles), run by the NKVD.

The purpose of *Mostruddom* was "to train minors in a work skill, make them morally aware, develop their higher cultural interests, broaden their mental horizons through schooling and vocational training [shoemaking, bookbinding, tailoring, etc.], and make them self-reliant citizens of the Soviet republic, aware of their rights and obligations." But from the moment a Black Maria or guarded foot convoy delivered Bulldog, Little Gypsy, Camel, Nikitka, and other ragged and vermin-ridden youngsters, they resisted these ideals and clung to street mores. Many of these youngsters sent to court by Commissions on Juvenile Affairs as incorrigible were "completely homeless, semi-literate, lacking work skills, with serious congenital deficiencies and the social maladjustments of abandoned, vagrant half-children/half-adults, deformed by the life experiences and sharing a thieves' code of honor." A favorite drink among them was vodka mixed with cocaine and gulped down. Many bore tattoos of their fantasy women on their arms or, in one case, on the penis, a psychiatrist of

Mostruddom noted. "Sometimes tattoos appear on buttocks (for example a cat on one side and a mouse on the other which move when their wearer walks) or on the back (a naked man on one shoulder blade and a naked woman on the other; when the shoulder blades are squeezed together, the man and woman move close together)." The *Mostruddom* staff could not stop the rape of weaker boys by stronger ones.[52]

What a contrast between *Mostruddom's* emphasis on correcting defects and the emphasis on the collectivist environment by Mirandov, Makarenko, and Pogrebinsky in their much more lightly staffed and open communes! And what a contrast between the approach of *Mostruddom* and that of reform-oriented criminologists like Vasily Kufaev. Kufaev, a major critic of *Mostruddom*, worked in the Department for the Social and Legal Protection of Minors of *Narkompros*, taught at the Second Moscow State University, and worked in the NKVD's Institute for the Study of Crime and the Criminal. Kufaev fought in the rearguard action of pedagogues in *Narkompros* and of reform-oriented lawyers like himself, Liublinsky and Gernet, against the growing reliance, already described, on physical coercion and criminal punishment for minors.[53]

At odds with Kufaev was Boris Utevsky, a partisan of *Mostruddom*. Utevsky also worked at the Institute for the Study of Crime, specializing in the criminal personality (a subject to which he returned after Stalin and until his recent death) and correctional policy. Utevsky sided with the NKVD against the approaches of educators and their jurist allies, approaches he considered sentimental and unrealistic. Kufaev insisted that a child who was treated like a criminal would soon become one, and believed that *Mostruddom*, with its bars and guards, had precisely this effect. Since the trend in pre-revolutionary Russian penology had been away from punishment toward treatment (as was still true in the capitalist countries of the West), it was all the harder for Kufaev to accept the Soviet retreat to more "sentences to deprivation of freedom," which he regarded as "a solution tried and already justly condemned in prerevolutionary times." Seconding Kufaev, Gernet added a vote for prevention: "Instead of sending a child to a little prison, one should send a pedagogue to seek out these waifs before they become lawbreakers . . . in orphaned families, tenements, in SRO 'corners,' in workers' families, on the squares, among the street hawkers."[54]

Utevsky countered with the assertion that only by using guards and locks to foil escapes could *Mostruddom* hold inmates long enough to reform them. Kufaev was wrong to assume that the inmates got there by chance. Questionnaires cited by Kufaev gave false statistics, for inmates understated their ages and concealed past criminal records whenever possible to avoid more severe punishment, and were much more hardened and habitual lawbreakers than

Kufaev's data showed.[55] Later, under Stalin, when labor homes like *Mostrud-dom* were being replaced by special trade schools (or simply, adult labor camps), Utevsky depicted *Mostruddom* as a failure.[56] Indeed, it appeared to have been that, despite the heavy staffing—nearly one staff member for every two of the 200 inmates.

Whatever their results, labor homes for juvenile lawbreakers like *Mostrud-dom* made little difference in the fate of most juvenile offenders because of their limited capacity. Nor did it make much difference that NKVD distribution commissions might send 16- and 17-year-olds to labor homes, considered "educational-punitive" agencies, instead of to regular correctional facilities, after their trials. The overwhelming majority of all teenagers, whether they were as young as 14 or as old as 17, had to go to regular adult places of confinement—prisons and labor camps. There the youths were housed with or near adults and, as before the revolution, were schooled to crime by the real authority figures in such places, the professional thieves. It was not only lack of space—administrators at places of confinement considered 16- and 17-year-olds to be adults.[57]

Hence, alongside the horrors of conflict which vitiated the "lofty slogans" in child rehabilitation, shortages and retreats in implementing them also moved rehabilitation back toward the policies of tsarist times, resulting in no rehabilitation at all for most juvenile criminals.

THE CONTRADICTIONS OF REVOLUTION

The early years of Soviet power brought diverse experimentation in the rehabilitation and upbringing of the decimated and devastated younger generation. Specialists in education, crime, health, and psychology, many of them already pioneers in rehabilitation before the revolution, received wide scope for their work. Among their achievements were the labor communes for juvenile lawbreakers and vagrants. Yet building a new socialist culture, a new set of values, meant not simply overcoming moral "survivals of the past." It meant also overcoming contradictions inherent in the very process of building a new political and social order: contradictions in perception and contradictions in the very process of revolution, between the ideals and the disorganizing chaos.

Contradictory trends in policy reflected conflicting assumptions. Proponents of decriminalizing juvenile offenses soon lost ground to officials who managed to lower the minimum age of criminal liability from 17 to 14. Specialists favoring non-prison approaches divided into those who favored some punishment and those who were for isolation, in reformatories; the environmentalists, who blamed crime on social conditions and shunned all coercion; and the defectologists, who sought to treat offenders as mentally ill or congenitally deviant. These contradictory trends in policy and assumptions also reflected interagency and intraagency competition.

If revolution was not immune to these familiar schisms in the correctional establishment, it brought its own contradictions, between ideals and the aftermath of upheaval. First of all, the numbers of *besprizorniki* overwhelmed child care facilities. Millions suffered or perished during the civil war period and in the aftermath. Again, despite the bright hopes for the new order, the overwhelming majority of juvenile criminals went not to the labor communes of *Narkompros* or the reformatories of the NKVD but to adult prisons and camps, as they had before the Revolution.

Toward the end of NEP a Soviet criminologist stated that the breakdown of law and order in his country was "not the result of 'the Bolshevik autocracy' as our enemies believe or wish to believe, but of the survivals of the old way of life . . . of the capitalist past and capitalist encirclement. . . ."[58] Indeed, the Bolsheviks faced an inauspicious legacy of unmanaged organization and mismanaged wars. Social authority had been breaking down and crime increasing since long before the Bolshevik Revolution. But the question remains, what did the Bolshevik Revolution itself contribute to the problem or its solution besides the greater possibility of implementing progressive ideals of upbringing and rehabilitation?

Did the Bolsheviks bring on the chaos described here because they liquidated private welfare agencies, eliminated the church's hold over the family and introduced freedom of marriage and divorce and other anti-patriarchal legislation?[59] Charges to that effect are hardly convincing. Before 1917 private agencies had failed to cope with the smaller number of *besprizorniki* and lawbreakers. There is no reason to believe that they could have coped with them after the revolution. The breakdown of the family had been spreading along with urbanization in the nineteenth and twentieth centuries. The impact of legal and policy changes after the Bolshevik Revolution paled alongside the real subversive forces at work among the masses of Soviet people—unleashed by the catastrophe of civil war and famine.

A basic contradiction of the Bolshevik Revolution, other than the paradox of an authoritarian liberation, was the contradiction between revolutionary ideals and the aftereffects of conflict. That conflict smashed existing culture and authority faster than revolutionary social engineering could replace them.

"Systematic efforts to prevent crime," a leading tsarist and Soviet criminal statistician wrote in 1918, "require expenditures of considerable resources and domestic tranquility in a society not distracted by political crises and intensified class struggle."[60] At the time he wrote these words, conditions could hardly have been more distracting. A physician active on Commissions on Juvenile Affairs attributed the torrent of *besprizorniki* and their crimes to the demoralizing hardships and rapid change "that come with every revolution."[61] But the hardships and the change occurred after the Bolshevik Revolution to an unprecedented degree, reflecting the particular inclusiveness of the struggle and far-reaching repressiveness of the Bolshevik regime.[62]

Feliks Dzerzhinsky more than once stated frankly what the conflict had meant. Victory won in the "bitter and bloody struggle" had been a "costly" one, damaging to children's well-being, he told the readers of *Izvestiia*.[63] Earlier he observed to Lunacharsky that "we are faced with a terrible calamity" among children, many of whom "have been crippled by the struggle and poverty."[64] This crippling aftereffect had a far greater impact in the 1920s than did the ideals of the new Soviet man. True, some youth workers extolled the romanticism of the *besprizorniki,* their street code of honor and collectivism, their rejection of the "philistine" dreams of the private, well-lined little nest.[65] Dzerzhinsky remained less sanguine. He feared that child vagrancy, "which after all takes such very monstrous and frightening forms as child crime and prostitution, threatens the younger generation with the gravest consequences."[66] I would agree with Lilge's conclusions that probably, among the *besprizorniki,* the greater number died of famine and epidemics, that others grew up into adult criminals, and "only a small minority were rehabilitated."[67] Military experiences of children in uniform instilled in some of them "a passion for bloodletting."[68]

The promoted achievers (the *vydvizhentsy*) of Stalin's control and purge apparatus would come out of the generation of those caught as youths in the devastation of 1917–1921. The political police recruited from among social outcasts and "saints," to be sure, but also from among sadists and perverts.[69] They became operatives who put away and liquidated many makers of the revolution, the "old Bolsheviks." They became criminals who, when caught and sent to labor camps, preyed on those same "politicals." Meanwhile Stalin, his way paved by the revolutionary single-party regime, liquidated any remaining measures of rehabilitation based on the old socialist and liberal ideals. Such were the contradictions of revolution, not simply concocted out of academic musings in a rarified atmosphere far from the scene, but generated and recorded in the heat of the struggle for power—and for a new culture.

NOTES

The opening quotation is from Gernet's introduction to the first edition V. I. Kufaev's *Iunye pravonarushiteli,* reprinted in ibid., (2nd ed.; Moscow, 1925).

1. Peter I. Lyashchenko, *History of the National Economy of Russia to the 1917 Revolution,* trans. L. M. Herman (New York: Macmillan, 1949), pp. 503, 544–55.

2. N. Mankovskii, "Sotsial'no-ekonomicheskie faktory detskoi prestupnosti v Moskve," in M. N. Gernet, ed., *Deti-prestupniki* (Moscow, 1912), pp. 238–47.

3. A. M. Rubasheva, "Ocherk sistemy bor'by s detskoi zabroshennost'iu i prestupnost'iu v Amerike i v Zapadnoi Evrope," in Gernet, *Deti-prestupniki*, pp. 483–524; E. Tarnovskii, "Voina i dvizhenie prestupnosti," in *Sbornik statei po proletarskomu revoliutsiiu i pravu*, Nos. 1–4 (1918), p. 114, quoted in S. S. Ostroumov, *Prestupnost' i ee prichiny v dorevoliutsionnoi Rossii*, p. 199.

4. Mankovskii, "Sotsial'no-ekonomicheskie faktory," pp. 238–47, 252–57; Aaron Zak, "Kharakteristiki detskoi prestupnosti," in Gernet, *Deti-prestupniki*, pp. 103, 107–10; 116–17; Aleksei Emelianov, "Prestupnost' nesovershennoletnikh po mirovym uchastkam Moskvy," ibid., pp. 136–37, 169–70, 224; I. M. Diomidov, "Alkogolizm kak faktor prestupnosti nesovershennoletnikh," ibid., pp. 364–66; A. N. Trainin, "Obshchie vyvody," ibid., p. 550; L. M. Vasilevskii, *Detskaia prestupnost' i detskii sud* (Tver': 1923), pp. 28, 38.

5. Mankovskii, "Sotsial'no-ekonomicheskie faktory," pp. 239, 244–45.

6. Zak, "Kharakteristiki detskoi prestupnosti," pp. 88–89, 94.

7. E. Tarnovskii, "Dvizhenie chisla nesovershennoletnikh, osuzhdennykh v Rossii za 1901–1910 gg." *Zhurnal ministerstva iustitsii*, No. 10 (1913), pp. 45, 48–49, cited in Ostroumov, *Prestupnost' i ee prichiny*, p. 194.

8. P. I. Liublinskii, "Okhrana detstva i bor'ba s besprizornost'iu za 10 let," *Pravo i zhizn'*, No. 8 (1927), p. 28; Ostroumov, p. 199.

9. N. I. Ozeretskii, "Nishchenstvo i besprizornost' nesovershennoletnikh," in E. K. Krasnushkin, et al., eds., *Nishchenstvo i besprizornost' nesovershennoletnikh* (Moscow, 1929), pp. 116–24.

10. Ostroumov, *Prestupnost' i ee prichiny*, p. 195; Emelianov, "Prestupnost' nesovershennoletnikh," pp. 256–63; Mankovskii, "Sotsial'no-ekonomicheskie faktory," pp. 240–41.

11. Vasilevskii, *Detskaia prestupnost'*, pp. 27–28; A. A. Gertsenzon, *Bor'ba s prestupnost'iu v RSFSR: po materialam obsledovaniia NK RKI SSSR* (Moscow: 1928), pp. 13–16; Liublinskii, "Okhrana detstva," p. 28; Iu. Bocharov, "Pervye detskie sudy po delam o maloletnikh v Rossii," in Gernet, *Deti-prestupniki*, pp. 525–32, 536–40. As a young radical criminologist, Gernet envisaged that gallows, prisons, corporal punishment would "wither away along with the old unjust social relations," to be replaced by "compulsory rehabilitation with the utmost humanity and respect for the inmates." *Obshchestvennye prichiny prestupnosti i sotsialisticheskoe napravlenie v nauke ugolovnogo prava* (Moscow, 1906), pp. 204–208.

12. *Sobranie uzakonenii rabochego i krest'ianskogo pravitel'stva*, hereinafter *SU RSFSR*, No. 16 (1917–1918), item 227.

13. S. Gurevich, "Otvetstvennost' iunikh prestupnikov po russkomu zakonodatel'stvu," Gernet, *Deti-prestupniki*, pp. 13–20.

14. Bocharov, "Pervye detskie sudy," pp. 525–42.

15. Kufaev, *Iunye pravonarushiteli*, p. 45.

16. Ibid., p. 42; M. K. Zamengor, "Mery presecheniia i nakazaniia, premeniaemyia k iunym prestupnikam," in Gernet, *Deti-prestupniki*, pp. 397, 409–10; P. Vsesviatskii, "Nesovershennotletnie v tiur'me," ibid., pp. 416, 421, 425–26; N. A. Okunev (the first justice of the peace to be assigned to children's court), *Osoby sud po delam o maloletnikh: Otchet na 1910 g.*, quoted in Emel'ianov, "Prestupnost' nesovershennoletnikh," ibid., p. 221, and see also pp. 227–32.

17. In 1917–1920, the urban population fell from 18 to 15 percent. Not until 1926 did industrial production and percent of urbanization regain 1913–1914 levels. Robert A. Lewis and Richard A. Rowland, "Urbanization in Russia and the USSR: 1897–1966" (mimeographed monograph, Columbia University); B. Ts. Urlanis, *Rost naseleniia v SSSR* (Moscow, 1966), p. 28; I. Iu. Pisarev, *Naselenie i trud v SSSR* (Moscow, 1966), p.

76. Petrograd's population fell from 1,217,000 to 722,000 in 1918–1921, but per capita crime rates of juveniles rose from 2.0 to 7.6 per 1000 inhabitants. Arrests of adults rose nearly 2.5 times in the Russian Republic between the first quarter of 1920 and the first quarter of 1922. Arrests of juveniles (under 18) rose nearly *four* times. P. I. Liublinskii in intro. to Vasilevskii, *Detskaia prestupnost'*, pp. iv–v.

18. Kufaev, *Iunye pravonarushiteli*, pp. 135–49, 61, 115–17, 122, 186–87, 218–25.

19. Ibid., pp. 195–98.

20. Vserossiiskaia tsentral'naia komissiia pomoshchi golodaiushchim V.Ts.I.K., *Itogi bor' by s golodom v 1921–1922 gg.* (Moscow, 1922), especially pp. 17, 31–32; V. Zenzinov, *Besprizornye* (Paris, 1929), pp. 72–94; Vasilevskii, *Detskaia prestupnost'*, pp. 38, 41–43.

21. Ibid., p. 38.

22. Estimates indicate that seven million is not excessive. M. Epshtein mentioned nearly seven million, "Besprizornost'" v SSSR," *Bol' shaia sovetskaia entsiklopediia* (1st ed.; Moscow), 5 (1927), p. 786; A. S. Griboedov in January 1924 cited N. K. Krupskaia's figure of seven million in G. Daian, "Vtoroi psikhonevrologicheskii s"ezd (okonchanie)," *Krasnaia nov'*, No. 3 (1924), p. 227; Liublinskii said six million children in the RSFSR needed shelter, with 540,000 places for them and two million in the Ukraine, "Okhrana detstva," p. 30; Zenzinov, *Besprizornye*, cited eight million from some sources, pp. 111–120. The textbook *Kriminologiia* (3rd ed.; Moscow, 1976), p. 291, mentions "over 4.5 mln. besprizorniki" at the beginning of the 1920s.

23. Kufaev, *Iunye pravonarushiteli*, p. 122; Zenzinov, *Besprizornye*, pp. 156–57; *Kriminologiia* (2nd ed.; Moscow, 1968), pp. 344–45.

24. Kufaev, *Iunye pravonarushiteli*, pp. 185, 188.

25. G. M. Min'kovskii, "Osnovye etapi razvitiia sovetskoi sistemy mer bor'by s prestupnost'iu nesovershennoletnikh," *Voprosy bor' by s prestupnost' iu*, 6(1967), p. 39; Liublinskii, "Okhrana detstva," p. 35; Zenzinov, *Besprizornye*, pp. 56–57.

26. S. Tizanov, "Ob uchrezhdeniiakh dlia trudnykh detei i podrostok v sviazi s planom bor'by s detskoi besprizornost'iu," in V. L. Shveitser and S. M. Shabalova, eds., *Besprizornye v trudovykh kommunakh: praktika raboty s trudnymi det'mi; sbornik statei i materialov* (Moscow, 1926), p. 13. Tizanov was head of the Department of Social and Legal Protection of Children in the Main Administration of Social Upbringing, RSFSR Narkompros. See also Epshtein, "Besprizornost' v SSSR," p. 786. Epshtein was head of that chief administration. Nearly a half century after his encounter with the *besprizorniki*, "begging or stealing and living as wild animals unconnected with normal community life," a visitor recalled that "At the time the tragic problem of these children seemed unsolvable." W. Averell Harriman, *America and Russia in a Changing World: A Half Century of Personal Observation* (Garden City, N.Y.: Doubleday, 1971), pp. 5–6.

27. Liublinskii in Vasilevskii, "Detskaia prestupnost'," pp. vii–viii; Ozeretskii, "Nishchenstvo i besprizornost' nesovershennoletnikh," pp. 126–28; E. V. Boldyrev, *Mery preduprezhdeniia pravonaruzhenii nesovershennoletnikh v SSSR* (Moscow, 1964), pp. 15–18; Liublinskii, "Okhrana detstva," pp. 30–31; V. Bil'shai, *Reshenie zhenskogo voprosa v SSSR* (Moscow, 1956); Rudolph Schlesinger, *Changing Attitudes in Soviet Russia: The Family in the U.S.S.R.* (London: Routledge and Kegan Paul, 1949), pp. 25–234; Fannina W. Halle, *Woman in Soviet Russia* (New York: Viking Press, 1933), pp. 93–217; Min'kovskii, "Osnovnyi etapi," pp. 40–41. Gail Warshofsky Lapidus, *Women in Soviet Society: Equality, Development, and Social Change* (Berkeley: University of California Press, 1978), pp. 57–63.

28. Gernet, foreword to Kufaev, *Iunye pravonarushiteli*, p. 10.

29. Intensified hunger began in 1919, before the main famine struck. See accounts by inmates of the Moscow Labor Home in B. S. Utevskii, *V bor' be s detskoi prestupnos-*

t'iu: ocherk zhizni i byta Moskovskogo trudovogo doma dlia nesovershennoletnikh pravonarushitelei (Moscow, 1927), pp. 104–105.

30. Gunther Nollau, *International Communism and World Revolution: History and Methods* (New York, Praeger, 1961), pp. 167–71.

31. Min'kovskii, "Osnovnye etapi," p. 43.

32. Ozeretskii, "Nishchenstvo i besprizornost'," pp. 126–35, 138–43, 145–50; Boldyrev, *Mery preduprezhdeniia,* pp. 15–18; Jennie Stevens, Georgetown University, has prepared a prepublication draft of "Children of the Revolution: Soviet Russia's Besprizorniki (Homeless Children) in the 1920s," forthcoming in *Russian History,* in which the organization and roles of agencies are treated in some detail.

33. Quotation is from party eulogy of Dzerzhinsky, A. A. Gertsenzon, *Ugolovnoe pravo i sotsiologiia* (Moscow, 1970), p. 264; Lennard D. Gerson, *The Secret Police in Lenin's Russia* (Philadelphia: Temple University Press, 1976), p. 122.

34. Gerson, pp. 124–25.

35. Quotations are from *Narkompros* report of 1920 and Dzerzhinsky's instructions to the commission, in Sheila Fitzpatrick, *The Commissariat of Enlightenment: Soviet Organization of Education and the Arts under Lunacharsky, October 1917–1921* (Cambridge: Cambridge University Press, 1970), pp. 229, 232–33.

36. Zenzinov, *Besprizornye,* pp. 74–92.

37. Maurice J. Shore, *Soviet Education: Its Philosophy and Psychology* (New York: Philosophical Library, 1947), pp. 16–18, 39–59, 129, 143. Political, educational, and cultural efforts to mold new people are summarized in Samuel Northrup Harper, *Civic Training in Soviet Russia* (Chicago: University of Chicago Press, 1929), pp. 1–38.

38. A. I. Kairov, et al., eds., *Pedagogicheskii slovar'* (2 vols., Moscow, 1960), II, pp. 680–81. On communes as part of Soviet experimentation and on Shatsky and P. N. Lepeshinsky (1863–1944) another commune pioneer, see Fitzpatrick, *The Commissariat of Enlightenment,* p. 50.

39. James Bowen, *Soviet Education: Anton Makarenko and the Years of Experiment* (Madison: University of Wisconsin Press, 1965), pp. 137–38; Shore, *Soviet Education.*

40. Shore, pp. 32, 138.

41. Frederic Lilge, *Anton Semyonovich Makarenko: An Analysis of His Educational Ideas in the Context of Soviet Society* (Berkeley: University of California Press, 1958); Bowen, *Soviet Education;* A. S. Makarenko, *Sochineniia v semi tomakh* (2nd ed.; Moscow, 1957–1958) includes autobiographical novels like *Pedagogicheskaia poema* on the Gorky commune; see n. 45 below on liquidations.

42. G. Daian, "Vtoroi psikhonevrologicheskii s"ezd (nekotorye itogi), *Krasnaia nov',* No. 2 (1924), pp. 155–66; No. 3 (1924), pp. 223–38. Quotation is from No. 3, p. 231. Sheila Fitzpatrick brought this to my attention.

43. "Ot redaktsii," in Shveitser and Shabalova, *Besprizornye v trudovikh kommunakh,* p. 6; "Instruktivnoe pis'mo glavsotsvosa ot 19/X-25g. No. 98206, O reorganizatsii uchrezhdenii dlia trudnikh detei i o postanovke v nikh rabote," ibid., pp. 174–77.

44. Mirandov, "Rabota Ul'ianovskoi trudovoi shkoly-kommuny pri s. Maksimovke," ibid., pp. 41–47. Quotation is from p. 48.

45. Ages are only approximate for many reasons, and are mentioned in the later Statute on Labor Communes for Adolescents, January 7, 1926 in ibid., pp. 171–74. On Pogrebinsky see M. Pogrebinskii, *Fabrika liudei* (Moscow, 1929); E. Vatova, "Bolshevskaia kommuna i ee organizator," *Iunost'* No. 3 (1966), pp. 91–93 (a source suggested by Sheila Fitzpatrick), which says on p. 93: "In 1937 Pogrebinskii perished at the age of 42 at the peak of his powers and talent. Bolshevo Commune also soon ceased to exist."

46. S. Tizanov, "Ob uchrezhdeniiakh dlia trudnykh detei i podrostok v sviazi s planom bor'by s detskoi besprizornost'iu," Shveitser and Shabalova, *Besprizornye v trudovikh kommunakh,* p. 14.

47. Ibid., pp. 13–14.

48. Decree of December 12, 1919, *SU RSFSR*, No. 6 (1919), item 590, Art 13.

49. Responsibility for ages 14 through 17 from "acting with reason," *SU RSFSR*, No. 13 (1920), item 83; changes in policy summarized in Kufaev, *Iunye pravonarushiteli*, pp. 27–76, and Boldyrev, *Mery*, pp. 12–21.

50. Bulldog is a typical street pseudonym supplied by me, for an anonymous *besprizornik* and criminal quoted in Utevsky, *V bor'be*, p. 106.

51. "Instructions to Children's Commissions," published by *Narkompros*, *Narkomzdrav*, and *Narkomiust*, Decree of July 29, 1920, *SU RSFSR* 1920, No. 68, item 308.

52. Utevskii, *V bor'be*, p. 7 (Statute of labor home, on goals, quoted by E. Shirvindt, in intro.), and pp. 36–44, 75–95.

53. Kufaev, *Iunye pravonarushiteli*, pp. 45–53; Gernet in ibid., pp. 12–13; Liublinskii's introduction to Vasilevskii, *Detskaia prestupnost' i detskii sud*, p. vi.

54. Gernet in Kufaev, *Iunye pravonarushiteli*, p. 26; Kufaev, ibid., pp. 52, also 16–22, 115–17; Vasilevskii, *Detskaia prestupnost'*, p. 55.

55. Utevsky, *V bor'be*, pp. 12, 13, 28, 31, etc.

56. B. S. Utevskii, *Sovetskaia ispravitel'no-trudovaia politika: Posobie dlia slushatelei pravovykh shkol* (Moscow, 1935), pp. 109–10.

57. B. Utevskii, "Itogi bor'by s prestupnost'iu nesovershennoletnikh," *Administrativnyi vestnik*, Nos. 10–11 (1927), pp. 56–61; there was room for only 1,883 inmates in RSFSR Labor Homes in 1926. There were about one million convictions in the RSFSR (Juviler, *Revolutionary Law and Order*, p. 31) and juvenile convictions were 4.7% of the USSR total (A. A. Gertsenzon, *Sovetskaia ugolovnaia statistika* (Moscow, 1937), p. 174. See also Kufaev, *Iunye pravonarushiteli*, pp. 50, 62–64; V. Iukubson, "Nesovershennoletnie pravonarushiteli v mestakh zakliucheniia," *Ezhenedel'nik sovetskoi iustitsii*, No. 18 (1923), p. 414, quotation from ibid., pp. 70–71.

58. Gertsenzon, "Osnovnye tendentsii dinamiki prestupnosti," p. 72.

59. Zenzinov, *Besprizornye*, pp. 14–25.

60. Tarnovskii, "Voina i dvizhenie prestupnosti," p. 199.

61. Vasilevskii, *Detskaia prestupnost' i detskii sud*, p. 63.

62. Zenzinov, *Besprizornye*, pp. 10–14; Bertrand Russell, *The Practice and Theory of Communism* (2nd ed.; London: George Allen and Unwin, 1949), p. 114.

63. Quotation from *Izvestiia*, March 23, 1923, by Gerson, *The Secret Police in Lenin's Russia*, p. 126.

64. Quotation from ibid., p. 123.

65. A. Zal'kind, "Besprizornost'," *Bol'shaia sovetskaia entsiklopediia* 5 (1927), pp. 784–85; Zenzinov, *Besprizornye*, pp. 33–34, 108; A. S. Makarenko, "O moem opyte," *O kommunisticheskom vospitanii* (2nd ed.; Moscow, 1956), p. 401.

66. Quotation from Min'kovskii, "Osnovnye etapi," p. 39. See also Zenzinov, *Besprizornye*, pp. 221.

67. Lilge, *Makarenko*, p. 14.

68. Gernet in Kufaev, *Iunye pravonarushiteli*, p. 8. See also Zenzinov, *Besprizornye*, pp. 189–90; Vasilevskii, p. 70.

69. Dzerzhinsky: "Only saints or scoundrels can serve in the GPU but now the saints are running away from me and I am left with the scoundrels." Quotation from Robert Conquest, *The Great Terror: Stalin's Purge of the Thirties* (New York: Macmillan, 1968), p. 544. Luminarsky, a character in a story by Alexander Rosen, had been raised in a children's home under a brutal director whom he learned to manipulate by denouncing others. Ibid., pp. 547–48. Simon Wolin and Robert M. Slusser, *The Soviet Secret Police* (New York: Praeger, 1957), p. 6, discuss the Cheka recruits.

Maurice Meisner

LENIN AND MAO TSE-TUNG, the leaders of the two greatest political and social revolutions of the twentieth century, were also advocates of "cultural revolution." Having achieved power in countries burdened not only by economic backwardness but also by the persistence of old feudal traditions and habits, both Lenin and Mao insisted that the modern cultural transformation of the masses was no less pressing a post-revolutionary task than that of modern economic development. For Lenin in the early 1920s, as for Mao three decades later, a "cultural revolution" was essential both for the industrialization of the largely agrarian lands they had come to rule and for the realization of the promised socialist goals of the revolutions they had led.

Yet "cultural revolution" had a far different (and far more radical) meaning for Mao Tse-tung than it did for Lenin. And the differences between the Maoist and Leninist conceptions of cultural revolution—a term which lacks any generally accepted Marxist definition—were closely linked to the different ways the two men approached several of the more crucial questions posed in the early post-revolutionary histories of Russia and China. If a socialist society presupposed a modern culture as well as a modern economy, then what was the proper Marxist understanding of the relationship between cultural and socioeconomic change? If socialist political power was perforce to be employed to complete the unfinished economic tasks of abortive capitalist regimes, then how were the means of modern industrial development to be reconciled with the ends of socialism? And if the envisioned new society demanded a new culture, as both Lenin and Mao believed, then how was the construction of a new revolutionary culture related to the cultural legacies of the past?

The dissimilar Leninist and Maoist responses to these dilemmas, which played no small part in molding the histories of the Soviet Union and the People's Republic of China, were not unrelated to differing conceptions of "cultural revolution." It is the purpose of this essay to explore certain of these differences, first, by clarifying the origins and nature of the Maoist idea of cultural revolution, and, secondly, by drawing some tentative comparisons between divergent Chinese and Russian usages of that most ambiguous but crucial notion in modern revolutionary history.

I. NATIONALISM AND CULTURAL ICONOCLASM IN CHINA

Mao Tse-tung was not the first Chinese author of the term "cultural revolution." The Chinese history of the concept of cultural revolution began with the beginnings of the modern Chinese intelligentsia at the turn of the century—and it is intimately related to the birth of modern Chinese nationalism and the strong strain of cultural iconoclasm which was perhaps uniquely intertwined with nationalist feelings among modern Chinese intellectuals.

The association of cultural iconoclasm with nationalism is a rather historically curious phenomenon. Nationalism, after all, presupposes a valued national past, and it is the general proclivity of nationalists to celebrate and glorify their particular cultural and historical heritage and use that heritage for modern nationalist ends. Yet this was not generally the case in China. It was not the case because Chinese nationalism originated not simply as a political response to the foreign imperialist onslaught against the old Chinese empire but also out of a long and agonizing process of intellectual alienation from traditional Chinese values and culture. And that process of intellectual alienation manifested itself around the turn of the century in the emergence of a modern Chinese intelligentsia whose eminently nationalist founders—most notably, Yen Fu and Liang Ch'i-ch'ao[1]—arrived at the conclusion that the basis of the power of the Western countries in the modern world was not simply their technological and material accomplishments but, more importantly, the Western ideas and values which (they believed) had produced those accomplishments. Strongly influenced by Social Darwinism, they concluded that the secret of the wealth and power of the West was to be found in Western ideas of progress and Western values of struggle, in the Promethean Western spirit which released human energies for the conquest of nature, modern economic growth, and the achievement of political and military power. The weakness and plight of China in the modern world, it followed, was to be explained by the absence of such dynamic ideas and values in the Confucian tradition.

The message was clear, however reluctantly arrived at, and the message was potentially iconoclastic: the survival of China in a world of rapacious modern nation-states was dependent on learning the wisdom of the West, and this implied discarding traditional Chinese values and cultural norms which were unsuited to the pursuit of modern nationalist goals.

The iconoclastic potential of Chinese nationalism soon revealed itself. From the nationalist questioning of the utility of the Chinese tradition it was but a short—yet fateful—step to questioning its moral validity as well. The most radical step was taken by the ardent Francophile Ch'en Tu-hsiu, the acknowledged leader of the westernized intelligentsia in the second decade of the century.[2] In founding the periodical *Hsin ch'ing-nien* (New Youth) in 1915, Ch'en inaugurated what came to be known as the New Culture Movement (1915–1919), the opening phase of the May Fourth era, and the young intellectuals who gathered around that most influential of journals undertook a wholesale critique of the entire cultural and historical heritage. Not only was traditional Chinese culture useless for China's survival in the modern world, they charged, but it was morally corrupt as well—and indeed had probably always been so. For Lu Hsun, China was burdened by "four thousand years of man-eating history," and the only hope was to "save the children" who might not yet be infected by the diseased culture and the cannibalistic society it supported.[3]

If the old culture was so utterly evil and so completely without redeeming features, as Ch'en and his colleagues believed, then the problems and plight of China could be resolved only by the most radical measures. Before a new culture based on the modern Western principles of democracy and science could be introduced, all vestiges of the old tradition had to be uprooted and destroyed, and the whole value system of the people had to be completely transformed. In the meantime, it was futile to participate in the politics of a society so diseased lest it result in one's own infection. Before effective political and social action could be undertaken, it was necessary to fundamentally change the culture of the nation and the psychology of its people. Thus the radical New Youth intellectuals called for a "cultural revolution" (wen-hua ko-ming) to annihilate the old and introduce the new. "Destruction before construction" was Ch'en Tu-hsiu's motto before it became Mao's injunction.

The term "cultural revolution," as it was employed by the radical intelligentsia in the second decade of the century, thus conveyed two notions that were to prove of enduring significance in the intellectual and political history of twentieth-century China: first, a virulently iconoclastic and totalistic rejection of the traditional Chinese cultural heritage, which was viewed not only as useless for the modern regeneration of China but also as morally evil and inherently corrupt; and second, an extraordinary emphasis on the primacy of ideas and consciousness in history, or what Lin Yü-sheng has termed "the cultural-intellectualistic approach,"[4] the belief that cultural and intellectual change is the essential prerequisite for effective political action and socioeconomic change.

Both of these notions were to become crucial elements in the dominant

Chinese variant of Marxism that eventually was to be canonized as "Marxism–Leninism–Mao Tse-tung Thought." And it was by no means fortuitous that the young Mao was an avid reader of the *New Youth* magazine and that the formative years of his intellectual development were molded by the writings of the iconoclastic intellectuals of the New Culture era.[5]

II. MAOISM AND THE CONCEPT OF CULTURAL REVOLUTION

If the Chinese concept of "cultural revolution" gives primacy to the role of ideas in history, then Mao Tse-tung surely must be regarded as the most ardent promoter and practitioner of the notion. For the Maoist version of Marxism-Leninism is above all characterized by an extreme voluntarist faith that people armed with the proper consciousness and will can surmount all material obstacles and mold social reality in accordance with their ideas and ideals. While Mao paid ideological deference to the presumably objective laws of historical development set forth in Marxist canonical texts, and perhaps derived from them some degree of assurance of a socialist future, he never acquired any real Marxist confidence in the workings of such objective historical laws. For Mao, history was determined by conscious human activity, and the most important factors in the making of history were how men thought and their willingness to engage in revolutionary action. From that belief flowed the enormous Maoist concern with developing and maintaining a "correct consciousness," the stress on "ideological remolding," and the emphasis on the techniques of "thought reform." Just as the maxim that "men are more important than machines" was the guiding Maoist principle for the making of revolution and the fighting of war, so the Maoist strategy of post-revolutionary socioeconomic development was based on a faith in the subjective factors in history, in what Mao so often celebrated as "the boundless creative powers" of the masses and their "inexhaustible enthusiasm for socialism." Mao shared with Martin Buber the "utopian" belief that socialism depends not so much on "the technological state of things" but rather "on people and their spirit."[6]

Closely associated with Mao's belief that consciousness is the ultimately decisive factor in history was a strongly iconoclastic condemnation of traditional Chinese culture, for "correct consciousness," in the Maoist view, demanded the total elimination of the pernicious influences of traditional values and ideas. Cultural iconoclasm and the stress on consciousness were combined in the enormous emphasis on "cultural revolution" in Mao's seminal treatise "On New Democracy," written in 1940. "For many years we Communists have struggled for a cultural revolution as well as for a political and economic revolution," Mao declared, stressing that the envisioned new society presupposed "a new Chinese national culture" and not simply a new political order. To be sure, Mao duly repeated the orthodox Marxist formula that a society's culture reflected its economic base and the social relations thereby produced, but his emphasis clearly was on the "tremendous influence and effect" of the cultural realm on the economic and political realms.[7]

China, Mao argued in "On New Democracy," was a country where capitalism had proved abortive and where, therefore, the bourgeois-democratic revolution had failed. It was thus a land which labored under the twin burdens of the "slave ideology" of an "imperialist culture" imposed from without and the persistence of the decadent Confucian values of its indigenous feudal culture. Unless both were "swept away," Mao maintained, "no new culture of any kind can be built up. There is no construction without destruction. . . ."[8] The destruction of the old was the prerequisite for the triumph of the new cultural movement born in the May Fourth era, a movement Mao described as the most "thoroughgoing cultural revolution since the dawn of Chinese history," not a bourgeois cultural revolution but rather one which he characterized as "part of the socialist cultural revolution of the world proletariat."[9] And the triumph of the new culture, in turn, was the prerequisite for political victory. "Revolutionary culture," Mao proclaimed, "prepares the ground ideologically before the revolution comes and is an important, indeed essential, fighting front in the general revolutionary front. . . ."[10]

The Maoist version of Marxism thus retained two essential beliefs that the young Mao Tse-tung had learned from the New Youth intelligentsia during the formative years of his intellectual development. First, the conviction that a cultural revolution was the prerequisite for political revolution, that correct ideas and values were the essential preconditions for effective political action—and thus the ultimately determining factor in history. Secondly, he retained an iconoclastic stance toward what was perceived to be the pernicious Chinese cultural-historical heritage, implicitly rejecting the accepted Marxist view that the new society would inherit the cultural as well as the material accomplishments of the past. Destruction, not inheritance, was the Maoist injunction.

Mao's enormous emphasis on the crucial importance of the cultural realm did not diminish during the post-revolutionary era. Even at the height of Chinese enthusiasm for the Soviet model of development in the early 1950s, Mao continued to stress the role of cultural factors in transforming the economic base. And in pondering the problem of inequality in post-revolutionary society and what he termed "the forces tending toward the creation of a new class," Mao, in a 1964 conversation with Andre Malraux, emphasized that "the thought, culture, and customs which brought China to where we found her [in 1949] must disappear, and the thought, customs, and culture of proletarian China, which do not yet exist, must appear."[11] Mao made only one concession to the cultural traditions of old China, drawing a distinction between the decadence of China's feudal culture and what he extolled over the years as "the fine old culture of the people which has a more or less democratic and revolutionary character."[12]

Perhaps this celebration of China's popular peasant culture, albeit a somewhat tepid celebration, offered psychological compensation for the emotional void left by the iconoclastic rejection of the Chinese past. Nonetheless, Mao left ambiguous (and the ambiguity was to remain) the role that folk culture was to play in what he hailed as China's newly emerging "proletarian culture."

Yet if Mao was searching for cultural compensation, he was to find it not so much in popular peasant culture but rather in the absence of culture in general. For Mao soon discovered socialist virtues in China's economic and cultural backwardness. "In history," he once remarked, "it is always people with a low level of culture who triumph over people with a high level of culture."[13] And the remark reflected a long-standing Maoist faith in the advantages of backwardness, a faith that received its most extreme cultural expression in the "poor and blank" thesis, the special revolutionary virtues that Mao attributed to the Chinese people in 1958: "Apart from their other characteristics, China's 600 million people have two remarkable peculiarities; they are, first of all, poor, and secondly blank. That may seem like a bad thing, but it is really a good thing. Poor people want change, want to do things, want revolution. A clean sheet of paper has no blotches, and so the newest and most beautiful words can be written on it, the newest and most beautiful pictures can be painted on it."[14]

What is suggested in this remarkable statement (certainly all the more remarkable for a Marxist) is a notion similar to that strain in nineteenth-century Russian Populist thought which celebrated the moral purity of backwardness and argued that a country relatively unencumbered by overly mature historical-cultural traditions was potentially more revolutionary and closer to socialism than the advanced capitalist countries of the West, staggering under the weight of morally decadent traditions. Mao Tse-tung, by declaring the Chinese people "blank," was driven by a similar utopian impulse to escape history and by an iconoclastic impulse to wipe the historical-cultural slate clean. The emotional void created by the iconoclastic rejection of the Chinese past was filled by an even more iconoclastic proclamation of the nonexistence of the past in the present. And thus a new culture, Mao seemed to believe, could be fashioned *ex nihilo* on a fresh canvas. Just as Herzen once declared that "we possess nothing," to affirm his faith in Russia's socialist future,[15] so Mao proclaimed China "a clean sheet of paper" and found in that alleged condition the promise of China's forthcoming cultural creativity and its future socialist greatness.[16]

Yet the "clean sheet of paper" Mao optimistically proclaimed China to be when he launched that massive utopian experiment known as the "Great Leap

Forward" campaign in 1958, was a canvas marred by all manner of political and ideological blotches, he pessimistically concluded in the early 1960s. That most extraordinary of upheavals Mao conjured up in 1966, and which he baptized "The Great Proletarian Cultural Revolution," was intended to remove the blotches.

It may seem odd to suggest that there was anything "cultural" about the Cultural Revolution which wracked (and nearly wrecked) China in the late 1960s. It was, after all, an era of massive political violence, power struggles at the highest (and lowest) levels of society, bizarre political rituals performed around the cult of Mao, and violent social conflict. Yet in one sense the Cultural Revolution was a profoundly "cultural" undertaking, and not primarily because it involved a twin assault on Western bourgeois culture and the vestiges of traditional Chinese culture, with Red Guards smashing recordings of Beethoven and old Buddhist relics with equal abandon. For the movement was launched by Mao and Maoists on the assumption that the existing state and party apparatus was dominated by "bourgeois ideology" (or, more precisely, by people who were deemed to be carriers of that ideology) and that, therefore, the political apparatus was producing capitalist-type relationships in society at large. It was an ideologically deterministic assumption resting on the proposition that the crucial factor in sociohistorical development is the consciousness of those who exercise political power. If Marx believed that "being determines consciousness," Mao believed that it was consciousness as such (mediated through political action and the state apparatus) that determines social being.

It is in this sense that the Cultural Revolution can broadly be characterized as "cultural," in the sense that it was assumed that the ultimately determining force in historical development is the ideas and values of people, that such ideas and values determine the uses to which political power is put, and that the latter in turn determines the course of history in general.

From this assumption it followed that the way to achieve socialism (or perhaps more precisely, to forestall what at the time was called the danger of a "bourgeois restoration," for the Cultural Revolution was motivated more by a fear of the past than a positive utopian vision of the future) was to revitalize the socialist spirit and ideals of the revolution, revolutionize the consciousness of the masses through political action, and thereby refashion a new state structure guided by "proletarian ideology."

Both the May Fourth Movement and the cataclysm of the late 1960s appear on the Chinese historical record as "cultural revolutions." The two were separated by half a century and took place under vastly different historical and political circumstances. Nonetheless, there are certain striking similarities between the cultural revolution the pre-Marxist Ch'en Tu-hsiu began from his underground sanctuary in Shanghai in 1915 and the one Mao Tse-tung launched fifty years later standing high atop the Gate of Heavenly Peace in Peking. Both began with the assumption that the problems afflicting Chinese society were fundamentally "cultural" in that they were rooted in basic defects in the realm of thought and values, and therefore it was assumed in both cases that a profound transformation of human consciousness was the essential precondition for correct political action and social change. Both cultural revolutions involved totalistic attacks against the hated traditions of the Chinese past—and, for Mao, the traditions of the Western bourgeois present as well. Ch'en condemned old Chinese cultural traditions (in traditionally demonic terms) as "savage beasts" and for Mao they appeared as "ghosts and monsters"—and the total destruction of all old "beasts" and "ghosts" was the first cultural revolutionary order of the day. In both cases the emergence of a new society presupposed the emergence of "new men," and the new men were to be young men, for only the youth were seen to be sufficiently uncorrupted by the traditions and moral evils of the past to be the creators of a new culture and the bearers of a new society. Ch'en began his iconoclastic crusade with a manifesto entitled "A Call to Youth" and named his famous periodical *The New Youth*. The cult of youth born in China's first cultural revolution was cultivated in Maoist ideology over the revolutionary decades, found renewed political expression in the aging Mao's desperate search for "revolutionary successors," and reached its ultimate and grotesque culmination in the Red Guard rampages of China's second cultural revolution. Both cultural revolutions soon turned political, the first perhaps because of fortuitous historical circumstances, the second certainly by grand design. And in the politicization of both cultural revolutions, young student activists served as catalytic agents in transforming "cultural revolutions" into massive political movements.

III. RUSSIAN AND CHINESE CONCEPTS OF "CULTURAL REVOLUTION"

If the notion of "cultural revolution" seems reasonably amenable to general definition in the intellectual history of twentieth-century China, as suggested in the preceding pages, this does not appear to be the case for Russia, where the term has been used in highly diverse ways and has been applied (both by Russian historical actors and by the historians who study them) to a bewildering variety of historical phenomena. In early twentieth century Russian history, the term "cultural revolution" variously refers to long-term processes of cultural change that accompany (or are produced by) long-term processes of socioeconomic change; to the intelligentsia's self-proclaimed duty to educate the "uncultured masses"; to spontaneous popular iconoclastic assaults against the cultural symbols of the past; to the Leninist emphasis on the need to learn the modern material and technological "culture" of the capitalist West in order to overcome the feudal habits and inertia of the Russian cultural-historical heritage; and, somewhat incongruously, to the imposition from above of Stalinist cultural, intellectual, and scientific orthodoxies during "the great turn" of 1928–31.

In view of this diversity of usage, it seems fruitless to undertake a general comparison of Russian and Chinese notions of "cultural revolution." Rather, the comparisons offered in the following pages largely focus on Maoist and Leninist conceptions.

Alexander Bogdanov was perhaps the most radical Bolshevik proponent of the idea of cultural revolution and the notion of proletarian culture.[17] Bogdanov's concept of cultural revolution, as David Joravsky points out, centered on the insistence that the achievement of cultural hegemony by the masses must accompany their rise to political hegemony.[18] Both Lenin and Mao shared the view that the cultural development of the people was essential for the construction of a socialist society, but they differed sharply on the means by which the masses would acquire modern culture and, more fundamentally, on the question of the relationship between cultural and socioeconomic change in the post-revolutionary era. Lenin, with an ardent faith in modern technology, assumed that the cultural uplifting of the masses—and thereby their capacity to govern themselves—would more or less naturally follow from processes of modern economic development presided over by a socialist regime. All energies, therefore, were to be turned to the task of the industrial transformation of backward Russia in the most rapid and efficient fashion. Mao Tse-tung, by contrast, believed that the cultural hegemony of the masses was not so much the product of, but rather the prerequisite for, modern economic development, at least insofar as the latter might contribute to a socialist historical outcome. In socialist economic construction, Mao emphasized time and again, "the important question is the remolding of the people."[19]

Mao also departed from Lenin (and from Leninism) on the question of who were to be the bearers of modern culture. For Lenin, the role of the intelligentsia remained decisive. Just as Lenin's conception of revolution demanded that the "revolutionary consciousness" of the intelligentsia be imposed on the spontaneous and amorphous movement of the masses, so his conception of post-revolutionary development assumed that properly politicized and technologically educated intellectuals would spearhead the modern industrial transformation of backward Russia and bring modern knowledge and culture to the masses in the process. By contrast, Mao Tse-tung, distrustful of intellectuals, retained a Populist-type faith in the spontaneous creativity of the masses and believed that a cultured people would emerge from the self-activity of the masses themselves and thereby realize his vision of a nation of "socialist-conscious, cultured laborers." The principle of "self-reliance" had an internal as well as an external dimension for Mao; just as the Chinese nation was to become economically self-reliant and not dependent on other nations (and especially not on the Soviet Union), so the Chinese people were to become self-reliant and not dependent on an intellectual-technological elite. "The masses must make themselves masters of culture and science" was the Maoist demand.

Mao further departed from Leninism in his conception of the relationship between town and countryside in the modern transformation of post-revolutionary society. Lenin retained the basic Marxist belief that the forces of modern historical progress resided in the cities, and from there were to be spread to the rural areas. The cultural enlightenment of the peasant masses (as well as their modern political, economic, and social transformation) was the task not only of urban intellectuals but also that of the urban working class. "It is our duty to establish contacts between the urban workers and the rural working people, to establish between them a form of comradeship," Lenin wrote in the early 1920s. "This is one of the fundamental tasks of the working class which holds power. To achieve this we must form a number of associations (Party, trade union, and private) of factory workers, which would devote themselves regularly to assisting the villages in their cultural development."[20] Mao Tse-tung, on the other hand, retained the powerful anti-urban biases bred during the revolutionary years. Just as Mao's revolutionary strategy took the form of mobilizing peasant radicalism in the countryside to "surround and overwhelm" the conservative cities, so his conception of post-revolutionary development centered on a perception that the rural areas were the true repositories of social and intellectual creativity. The cities remained under suspicion as the breeding places of ideological, moral, and cultural corruption. Whereas Lenin advocated sending members of the proletariat to the countryside to raise the cultural level of peasants, Mao advocated sending urban dwellers to the countryside to learn "proletarian virtues" from the peasants.

Robert Williams has pointed out that there were differences and ambiguities among the Bolsheviks on the question of "whether a proletarian culture was to evolve over a long period of time as a consequence of a transformation in social and economic relations, or to emerge rapidly out of a revolution and serve as a means for that transformation."[21] Here, Lenin (as opposed to Bogdanov) held to the orthodox Marxist view that culture would change rather slowly in accordance with, and following from, long-term processes of socioeconomic development. To be sure, Lenin emphasized the need to educate the masses (and especially the peasantry) to raise their cultural level and that this required a "cultural revolution." But he emphasized even more strongly—and here exhibited his characteristic technocratic bias—that "to be cultured we must achieve a certain development of the material means of production, [we] must have a certain material base."[22] Mao Tse-tung stood at the opposite end of the Marxist spectrum, maintaining quite explicitly and consistently that culture—in the form of "proletarian" consciousness, ideas, and values—was the essential condition for rapid economic development and for the socialist transformation of political and social relationships.

Reinforcing Lenin's belief that cultural development presupposed economic development was his reluctance to abandon the orthodox Marxist proposition that socialism presupposed capitalism, or, at least, a genuine socialist revolution presupposed the completion of the bourgeois-democratic phase of the revolutionary process. So long as the revolution remained isolated in backward Russia, it would be largely confined to "bourgeois" limits, Lenin believed, and thus when he spoke of the need for "cultural revolution" he generally referred to bringing "bourgeois culture" to the masses of workers and peasants who remained mired in "precapitalist" habits, customs, and methods of work. The building of a genuinely proletarian culture was a task to be carried out at an unspecified time in the future, and it was dependent on establishing its appropriate material and social prerequisites.

Mao Tse-tung, uninhibited by orthodox Marxist considerations on the relationship between economic and sociocultural change, saw China moving rapidly to socialism and communism through a process of "permanent revolution." For Mao, neither a socialist nor communist society was dependent on the prior development of material productive forces; rather, the essential condition was the "proletarianization" of the consciousness of the people, and this was to be accomplished by carrying out a series of proletarian "cultural revolutions."[23]

Perhaps the most radical difference between Lenin and Mao was on the whole question of the relationship of the new society to the cultural legacy of the past. Karl Marx, of course, assumed that socialism presupposed capitalism, and further assumed that a socialist society would inherit all the cultural as well as material accomplishments of its predecessors. Here, Lenin stood firmly in the classical Marxist tradition, however much he may have departed from original Marxist theory in other respects. As Richard Stites has noted, Lenin believed it essential "to grasp all the culture which capitalism has left and build socialism from it."[24] Lenin took it for granted that the new society would inherit both traditional Russian culture and Western bourgeois culture, save that the former would be purged of its baneful "Asiatic" elements. And he was generally hostile to the notion of "proletarian culture" and certainly to the radical iconoclasts of the Proletcult movement.

Mao Tse-tung, in striking contrast, believed that a new culture as well as a new history could be written on "blank" sheets of paper, and he rejected in highly iconoclastic fashion both traditional Chinese culture and the bourgeois culture of the modern West. Whereas Mao celebrated the potential socialist virtues of China's cultural "blankness," Lenin always deplored Russia's cultural backwardness—and, indeed, at the end of his life partly attributed the spiritual and political degeneration of the Revolution to the lack of *kulturnost*.

There are also enormous differences between Lenin and Mao on what David Joravsky has termed "the Communists' conflict with modern high culture."[25] This clash has manifested itself (to greater or lesser degrees) in the imposition of official orthodoxies over wide areas of intellectual, scientific, and artistic life; in the suppression of those who dissent from such orthodoxies; and in a Communist antipathy to "bourgeois specialists," sometimes accompanied by anti-intellectualism and a general distrust of specialization and professionalism.

It is of course impossible to cast Lenin as an opponent of "modern high culture." Both as a matter of personal taste and as a principle of public policy, Lenin had a keen appreciation of the literary and artistic, as well as the scientific, accomplishments of Western civilization. Moreover, he ardently advocated the need to learn the habits and mentalities necessary for modern technological efficiency; he praised the virtues of specialization; and he demonstrated a remarkable political tolerance for "bourgeois specialists," even those who were decidedly anti-Soviet in their political proclivities. As Sheila Fitzpatrick has noted: "Lenin had rejected the idea that cultural power, like political, could be seized by revolutionary action. Culture, in his view, had to be patiently acquired and assimilated; Communists must learn from 'bourgeois specialists' despite their identification with an alien social class; and refusal to learn was a sign of 'Communist conceit.' "[26]

While Lenin in no sense foreshadowed the later Communist conflict with "high culture," Maoism documented that conflict in abundant measure. The Maoist assault on "high culture" was twofold. It involved, on the one hand, the condemnation of traditional Chinese culture, which symbolized (in Maoist eyes) the pernicious influences of a hated past and which tended to be viewed as a gentry class culture rather than a national heritage. At the same time, the Maoist assault was directed against the bourgeois culture of the West. The latter, of course, was a far more alien phenomenon in the Chinese historical environment than it was in Russia, but for Mao bourgeois culture was rejected as alien more on political than on purely cultural grounds. For modern Western culture had come to China under the aegis of the foreign imperialist impingement, and its carriers were westernized intellectuals whom Mao and Maoists politically distrusted. The antipathy to bourgeois culture was reinforced by the powerful Populist strains in the Maoist mentality which manifested themselves (among many other manifestations) in a profound and abiding hostility to professionalism, to occupational specialization, to large-scale organization, to formal higher education—and indeed to all things which threatened to divide "the people."

If Mao's attitudes toward "high culture" differed sharply from those of Lenin, it would be rash to assume that Maoism should be equated with Stalinism in the cultural realm. To be sure, there are obvious similarities between Maoism and Stalinism, particularly in the imposition of official cultural orthodoxies, although the content of those orthodoxies was by no means identical. Yet Stalinism, after an initial onslaught against "high culture," proved amenable to conducting a celebration of the cultural-historical heritage to serve immediate nationalistic and political ends—and what was not of immediate political use was placed safely on display in the silence of the museum. Moreover, Stalinism soon accommodated itself to the technological intelligentsia by separating (however tenuously and uneasily) the realm of the purely technical from the political. And Stalinist policies fostered (and were designed to foster) the development of an elite of technological experts, occupational specialization, and professionalism in both economic and cultural life.

This was not the case with Maoism. The strongly iconoclastic character of the doctrine precluded any sustained celebration of the culture of the past, whether the high culture of traditional China or Western bourgeois culture. During the Maoist era, even the flexible device of Marxist historical relativism proved insufficient for iconoclasts in power to provide an honorable historical resting place for high culture. In the "Great Proletarian Cultural Revolution," even the museums were ransacked. And the powerful Populist strains in Maoism generated a continuous conflict with intellectual and professional elites, both inside and outside the state apparatus. It was not until the post-Maoist era that the Chinese Communist regime arrived at a Stalinist-type accommodation, allowing a relatively autonomous arena for the technological and cultural intelligentsias, and reviving the celebration of high culture both within and outside museums.

Lenin's notion of cultural revolution, like Mao's, was intended to prevent the degeneration of the socialist spirit and goals of the revolution during the lengthy era that would be required to carry out the modern economic transformation of a backward land. But Lenin's emphasis on the material prerequisites for cultural change, and his insistence on the need to overcome "precapitalist" cultural values and habits unconducive to modern economic development, lent themselves to Stalin's fateful decision to subordinate all social and ideological considerations to a crash drive for industrialization. To be sure, the term "cultural revolution," along with some of the utopian imagery associated with the notion in the early 1920s, was used and manipulated to mobilize popular energies during the frenetic years of the First Five Year Plan. But having served their initial economic and political purposes, both the term and the concept largely vanished in the Stalinist political terror of the 1930s and the subsequent institutionalization of the new Soviet order.

The Maoist version of the concept received cataclysmic political expression in the "Great Proletarian Cultural Revolution" of the late 1960s. But the results of the upheaval served to discredit the Maoist ideas which produced it—at least in the eyes of Mao Tse-tung's successors. It remains to be seen whether the concept of cultural revolution, which has so long been part of the consciousness of the modern Chinese intelligentsia, will survive the passing of the May Fourth generation of Chinese political leaders—or indeed whether it has survived the traumatic experiences of what now is condemned as "the Cultural Revolution decade" of 1966–76. The economically deterministic version of Marxism that has come to dominate post-Maoist Chinese Marxist theory, an ideology which rests on a faith in the workings of objective social laws and which (like its Soviet counterpart) places an enormous emphasis on "building the economic foundations for socialism,"[27] suggests that the fate of the notion of cultural revolution will not be very different in a modernizing China than it was in Stalinist Russia.

NOTES

1. The best intellectual biographies of Yen and Liang—and the most illuminating analyses of the origins and nature of Chinese nationalism—remain Benjamin Schwartz, *In Search of Wealth and Power: Yen Fu and the West* (Cambridge, Mass.: Harvard University Press, 1964), and Joseph R. Levenson, *Liang Ch'i-ch'ao and the Mind of Modern China* (Cambridge, Mass.: Harvard University Press, 1959). See also Joseph R. Levenson, *Confucian China and Its Modern Fate: A Trilogy* (Berkeley: University of California Press, 1968).

2. At the end of the decade, Ch'en was to become a convert to Marxism, a co-founder of the Chinese Communist Party in 1921, and the Party's first leader during the great revolutionary upsurge that ended in the bloody disaster of 1927.

3. Lu Hsun's famous story "The Diary of a Madman" appeared in the April 1918 issue of the *New Youth*. For an English translation, see *Selected Works of Lu Hsun* (Peking: Foreign Languages Press, 1956, Vol. I, pp. 8–21).

4. Lin Yü-sheng, *The Crisis of Chinese Consciousness: Radical Antitraditionalism in the May Fourth Era* (Madison: University of Wisconsin Press, 1979), esp. chapter 3. Professor Lin argues that the totalistic iconoclasm of the modern intelligentsia was itself partly molded by a traditional Chinese predisposition toward "a monistic and intellectualistic mode of thinking."

5. Mao's first published essay, a treatise on the virtues of physical culture (which also was rather iconoclastic in its time), appeared in the *New Youth* magazine in 1917.

6. Martin Buber, *Paths in Utopia* (Boston: Beacon Press, 1958), pp. 46–47.

7. "On New Democracy," *Selected Works of Mao Tse-tung* (Peking, 1965), Vol. II, p. 340.

8. "On New Democracy," p. 369.

9. Ibid., pp. 372 & 374.

10. Ibid., p. 382.

11. Andre Malraux, *Anti-Memoirs* (New York: Holt, Rinehart and Winston, 1968), pp. 373–74.

12. "On New Democracy," p. 381.

13. Mao Tse-tung, "Reading Notes on the Soviet Union's 'Political Economy,' " (1960) *Mao Tse-tung ssu-hsiang wan-sui* (Taipei, 1967), p. 240.

14. *Hung-ch'i* (Red Flag), June 1, 1958, pp. 3–4.

15. Alexander Herzen, "The Russian People and Socialism" (1851) in Herzen, *From the Other Shore* (London: Weidenfeld and Nicolson, 1956), p. 199.

16. Mao converted backwardness into a social as well as a cultural virtue. In his 1960 critique of the Stalinist strategy of development, for example, he arrived at the astonishing conclusion that "the more backward the economy, the easier, not the more difficult, is the transition to socialism." "Reading Notes on the Soviet Union's 'Political Economy,' " *Mao Tse-tung ssu-hsiang wan-sui* (Taipei, 1967), pp. 181–82.

17. For an analysis of Bogdanov's views on the role of culture in social and economic development, see James C. McClelland, "Utopianism versus Revolutionary Heroism in Bolshevik Policy: The Proletarian Culture Debate," *Slavic Review*, Vol. 39, No. 3 (Sept., 1980), pp. 403–25. While there are striking similarities between Bogdanov and Mao Tse-tung on this question, Bogdanov's emphasis on the primacy of the cultural realm seems to have lacked the radical political implications of the Maoist emphasis. One of the issues dividing Bogdanov and Lenin, as McClelland notes, was Lenin's fear that Bogdanov's interpretation of the relationship between "being and consciousness" would lead to the abandonment of revolutionary activism. (Ibid., p. 409).

18. See ch. 6.

19. Mao Tse-tung, "Reading Notes on the Soviet Union's 'Political Economy,' " *Mao Tse-tung ssu-hsiang wan-sui*, p. 182.

20. V. I. Lenin, *Collected Works* (Moscow: Foreign Languages Publishing House, 1970), Vol. 33, p. 466.

21. Robert C. Williams, "Myth and Authority in Early Soviet Culture," Kennan Institute Occasional Paper, p. 3.

22. V. I. Lenin, "On Cooperation," as quoted in ch. 2.

23. In the late 1960s Mao proclaimed that "The Great Proletarian Cultural Revolution presently going on is only the first of its kind. In the future other such revolutions will necessarily take place. . . . All Party members, and the population at large, must refrain from thinking that all will be smooth after one, two, three, or four Cultural Revolutions." Cited in Jean Daubier, *A History of the Chinese Cultural Revolution* (New York: Vintage Books, 1974), p. 265.

24. See ch. 1.

25. See ch. 6.

26. Sheila Fitzpatrick, "Cultural Revolution as Class War" in Sheila Fitzpatrick (ed.), *Cultural Revolution in Russia, 1928–1931* (Bloomington: Indiana University Press, 1978), p. 8.

27. On the character of post-Maoist Chinese Marxism, see Maurice Meisner, *Marxism, Maoism and Utopianism* (Madison: University of Wisconsin Press, 1982), ch. 8.

Contributors

John E. Bowlt, Professor of Slavic Studies at the University of Texas at Austin, has published widely on the subject of modern Russian art. Among his books are *Scenic Innovation: Russian Stage Design, 1900–1930*, and, coauthored with Nicoletta Misler, *Pavel Filonov: A Hero and His Fate*.

Jeffrey Brooks is Associate Professor of History at the University of Chicago. He has published widely on issues of cultural change in Russia. A forthcoming book is entitled *When Russia Learned to Read, 1861–1917*.

Katerina Clark is Associate Professor in the Department of Slavic Languages and Literatures, Indiana University, Bloomington. She is author of *The Soviet Novel: History as Ritual* and coauthor with Michael Holquist of *Mikhail Bakhtin*.

Barbara Evans Clements is Associate Professor of History at the University of Akron. She is the author of *Bolshevik Feminist: The Life of Aleksandra Kollontai* and of articles in *Russian History, Signs*, and *Slavic Review*.

Beatrice Farnsworth is Professor of History at Wells College. She is the author of *William C. Bullitt and the Soviet Union* and *Aleksandra Kollontai: Socialism, Feminism, and the Bolshevik Revolution* and is working on a study of Russian peasant women.

Sheila Fitzpatrick is Professor of History at the University of Texas at Austin. She edited *Cultural Revolution in Russia, 1928–1931*, and her most recent book is *The Russian Revolution*.

Abbott Gleason, Professor of History at Brown University, is author of *Young Russia: The Genesis of Russian Radicalism in the 1860s* and former Secretary of the Kennan Institute for Advanced Russian Studies, Wilson Center.

David Joravsky is Professor of History at Northwestern University and author of *Soviet Marxism and Natural Science, 1917–1932, The Lysenko Affair*, and the forthcoming *The Psychology of Stalinism*.

Peter H. Juviler is Professor of Political Science, Barnard College, Columbia University. He is the author of *Revolutionary Law and Order: Politics and Social Change in the USSR* and of many studies on Soviet family and criminal policy.

Peter Kenez is Professor of History at the University of California, Santa Cruz, and author of *Civil War in South Russia, 1918: The First Years of the*

Volunteer Army; Civil War in South Russia, 1919–1920: The Defeat of the Whites; and *The Birth of the Propaganda State: Soviet Methods of Mass Mobilization, 1917–1929* (forthcoming).

James C. McClelland is Associate Professor of History, University of Nebraska-Lincoln. He is the author of *Autocrats and Academics: Education, Culture and Society in Tsarist Russia,* and is presently at work on a study of higher education in the aftermath of the Russian Revolution.

Maurice Meisner is Professor of History at the University of Wisconsin-Madison. His books include *Li Ta-chao and the Origins of Chinese Marxism; The Mozartian Historian* (coeditor); *Mao's China: A History of the People's Republic;* and *Marxism, Maoism and Utopianism.*

Daniel T. Orlovsky is Associate Professor of History at Southern Methodist University. He is the author of *The Limits of Reform: The Ministry of Internal Affairs in Imperial Russia, 1802–1881.*

Richard Stites, Associate Professor of History at Georgetown University, is coeditor of *Red Star: The First Bolshevik Utopia* by Alexander Bogdanov and author of *The Women's Liberation Movement in Russia: Feminism, Nihilism, and Bolshevism, 1860–1930.*

Richard Taylor is Lecturer in Politics and Russian Studies at University College of Swansea, U.K. His publications include *The Politics of the Soviet Cinema 1917–1929; Film Propaganda: Soviet Russia and Nazi Germany;* and *The Film Factory: Soviet Cinema in Documents.*

Robert C. Tucker is Professor of Politics at Princeton University and author of *Stalin as Revolutionary, 1879–1929: A Study in History and Personality* and *The Soviet Political Mind.*

Nina Tumarkin is Associate Professor of History at Wellesley College and an Associate of the Russian Research Center, Harvard University. Her book, *Lenin Lives! The Lenin Cult in Soviet Russia,* won the Harvard Press Thomas J. Wilson Prize for the best first-book manuscript.

Index

Leninism, 287–91; and freedom of the press, 138–39, 141, 143
Letter to the Soviet Leaders (Solzhenitsyn), 179
Lewin, Moshe, 57, 176
Liang Ch'i-ch'ao, 280
Liberty, 45–46; and freedom of the press, 139
Libraries, 5, 11, 45–46, 158; on agit-trains, 195; in villages, 186, 239
Life and Death (Klychkov), 183
Lin Yü-sheng, 281, 292 n.4
Literacy, 44–46, 164–65, 226, 239, 253; of Bolshevik party members, 236 n.32; cinema not limited by, 191; classes for peasants, 246–47, 258 n.64; in countryside, 176, 186
Lower class, 13–14, 67; women of, 224, 226–27
Lubochnaia literatura, 160, 174 n.69
Luch, 133
Lu Hsun, 281, 292 n.3
Lunacharsky, 69, 70, 75 n.30, 94–95, 225, 267; and the cinema, 191, 193–94, 197–98; educational policy, 115–16, 117–18, 119–20, 121, 122–24, 126
Lunts, 187; *City of Truth*, 179

Machajski, Jan Waclaw, 14
Main Administration of Socialist Upbringing (Glavsotsvos), 124
Main Committee of Vocational-Technical Education (Glavprofobr), 119–20, 122–26
Makarenko, Anton, 267, 271
Makhno, Nestor, 3, 5, 10
Malevich, Kazimir, 203, 204, 205, 208, 213
Malkin, B. F., 138
Manor houses, 4, 5, 6, 17, 20 n.14
Maoism, 96, 282–86, 290–91
Mao Tse-tung: and cultural revolution, 279–80, 282–92, 293 n.17
Marriage: in peasant society, 241, 255 n.17
Marriage law, 226, 229, 231–32
Marx, 26–27, 87, 186, 239
Marxism, 6, 34, 38 n.28, 40–41, 60, 63; and cultural change, 279, 288–89, 292; and dictatorship of the proletariat, 31, 32–33; and education, 120; on the family, 230, 236 n.32; and historical progress, 288, 291; and Lenin's Bolshevism, 26–29; Maoist version of, 282–83, 285; party members' knowledge of, 236 n.32; and peasantry, 175, 238; and psychology, 102, 106–109; on state care of children, 265; on women, 221, 228, 230–32
Marxism-Leninism, 57, 97, 100, 101
Marxism–Leninism–Mao Tse-tung Thought, 282
Masses, 42–43, 114, 287–88; cinema for,

197, 199–200; and culture, 48, 50–51, 93–97, 287–88
Mayakovsky, Vladimir, 12–13, 88–89
May Fourth Movement, 281, 283, 285–86
Mensheviks, 26, 32, 34, 61, 68, 138, 142; and newspapers, 133, 134, 136, 140
Meyerhold, 13, 199
Military Revolutionary Committee (MRD): and the press, 137, 140–41
Millenarian movements, 25
Ministry of Art: proposed, 47–48
Ministry of Education, 45, 50–51, 123
Minkin, A. I., 141
Mir, 240
Mirandov, 268, 271
Modernism: and Futurism, 13
Monotechnical education. *See* Vocational education
Monuments, 7–8, 16–18, 23 n.46, 47
Moscow, 8–9, 118, 140, 155, 193
Moscow Soviet, 51, 193
Mostruddom (Moscow Labor Home for Juveniles), 270–72
Movies. *See* Cinema; Film industry
Mukhina, Vera, 210, 216
Museums, 16–18, 47, 250, 291
Muzhik socialism (Kliuevism), 177–78, 181
Myth, 3, 35, 42; and the cinema, 199; Lenin cult as, 77–90

Names, 9
Narkompros (Commissariat of Enlightenment), 70, 265–69, 270; and the cinema, 193, 197; educational policies, 115–18, 119, 121–22, 123–24, 125–27
"National in Lenin, The" (Trotsky), 86–87
Nationalism, 60–61, 280–81
Nationalities question, 61, 85
Nationalization, 48, 70, 154, 191–93, 196
Nekrasov, Nikolai, 221, 230, 244–45
New Culture Movement, 281
New Economic Policy (NEP), 70, 73, 115, 175, 208, 265; effects on publishing, 152–53, 154–55, 156, 163
New Man, 18, 261, 274, 286
New Soviet Woman. *See* New Woman
Newspapers, 29, 131–49, 161–65, 186; cinema advertisements, 196; production and distribution, 151–57, 164–65; and propaganda for women, 223–24, 226, 234 n.8, 235 n.18, 235 n.21; role in Lenin cult, 78, 80, 83, 86, 87
Newsreels, 192, 198, 200
New Woman (New Soviet Woman), 18, 220–33, 235 n.21, 253; clothing designs for, 209, 213, 215
New Youth (Hsin ch'ing-nien), 281–82, 286
New Youth intellectuals, 281, 283
Nihilism, 1, 10–11, 12, 18–19
Ninth Party Congress, 86

W9-BCX-688

Prison Journal, 1940–1945

EDOUARD DALADIER

Prison Journal

1940 – 1945

*with a foreword
by Stanley Hoffmann*

*compiled and annotated
by Jean Daladier with Jean Daridan*

translated by Arthur D. Greenspan

Westview Press
BOULDER • SAN FRANCISCO • OXFORD

The translation of this book was funded in part by the French Ministry of Culture.

English edition copyright © 1995 by Westview Press, Inc.

English edition published in 1995 in the United States of America by Westview Press, Inc., 5500 Central Avenue, Boulder, Colorado 80301-2877, and in the United Kingdom by Westview Press, 12 Hid's Copse Road, Cumnor Hill, Oxford OX2 9JJ

First published in 1991 in France as *Journal de captivité 1940–1945* by Calmann-Lévy

Library of Congress Cataloging-in-Publication Data
Daladier, Edouard, 1884–1970.
  [Journal de captivité, 1940–1945. English]
  Prison journal, 1940–1945 / Edouard Daladier ; with a foreword by
Stanley Hoffmann ; compiled and annotated by Jean Daladier with Jean
Daridan ; translated by Arthur Greenspan.
    p. cm.
  ISBN 0-8133-1905-6
  1. Daladier, Edouard, 1884–1970—Diaries. 2. Statesmen—France—
Diaries. 3. World War, 1939–1945—Prisoners and prisons—Diaries.
4. France—Politics and government—20th century. I. Daladier,
Jean. II. Daridan, Jean. III. Title.
DC397.D25A3 1995
940.5'7244'092—dc20
[B]   94-35523
                                                                          CIP

Printed and bound in the United States of America

⊗ The paper used in this publication meets the requirements
   of the American National Standard for Permanence of Paper
   for Printed Library Materials Z39.48-1984.

10   9   8   7   6   5   4   3   2

Contents

Foreword

Stanley Hoffmann

Edouard Daladier was one of France's most important statesmen between the two world wars. He had been the Prime Minister who signed the Munich Agreement in September 1938, at Czechoslovakia's expense, and he was also the Prime Minister who, one year later, declared war on Hitler's Germany after the Nazi invasion of Poland. When his government fell in March 1940, during the "phony war," he remained Minister of Defense in the final cabinet of the Third Republic, the cabinet headed by Paul Reynaud. This government presided over the collapse of France in seven catastrophic weeks in May–June 1940, split over whether to seek an Armistice, resigned, and was followed by the Pétain government, which promptly signed the Armistice, summoned the French Parliament, obtained full powers from it, and set up the Vichy regime.

Daladier was a member of a small but distinguished group of parliamentarians who were led to believe, or tricked into believing, that the Pétain government would keep waging war from North Africa, and who left France on a boat—the *Massilia*—that went to Morocco. There, they were promptly arrested and returned to France. Daladier was among the political and military leaders Vichy threw in jail and decided to try for the responsibility in France's defeat—it was never too clear whether they were being blamed for France's military incompetence or for having wanted to resist Hitler. A special court was set up in Riom (Auvergne) to try Daladier, Léon Blum, and the Generalissimo of 1940, Gamelin, along with a couple of minor figures. Even before the trial, Pétain condemned the accused to be detained in a fortress. The trial, in early 1942, was a disaster for Vichy and had to be suspended. Imprisoned now in another fortress (Bourassol), Daladier and Blum were delivered by Vichy to the Germans, who locked Daladier (along with Reynaud and Gamelin) in a "castle" in the Tirol. Daladier's diary covers these events, until his liberation by the Americans at the end of the war.

Few French politicians have had a more fluctuating reputation. Daladier was often seen as "exhibit A" of the kind of social ascent the Third Republic fostered. The son of a baker in Carpentras (Vaucluse), he was the typical *boursier*—the boy whose brilliance in school results, first in scholarships, and later in obtaining an *agrégation* in history and geography, a degree won through competitive examination, that allowed him to teach in high schools. He soon entered politics, as a Radical, and became mayor of Carpentras at twenty-eight, in 1911. He fought in World War I as a Sergeant and became a Deputy in 1919. The Radical Party was the very loose political force that dominated French politics from the beginning of the twentieth century to 1940. It was ideologically on the Left—the ardent champion of representative and (above all) secular government, of the public school system, and of the "principles of 1789"—and socially quite conservative, in line with the wishes of an electorate of peasants and petits bourgeois. Being a party of the Center, it could form coalitions either with those to its left (including the Socialists) or with more right-wing parties. Daladier, in the 1920s, was the leader of the left-leaning elements in the party and became its President in 1927. The rivalry between the younger Daladier and his former teacher, the mayor of Lyons, Edouard Herriot, who had been the luckless Prime Minister of the leftist Cartel des Gauches in 1924, but later agreed to take part in more conservative cabinets, marked the history of the party for many years.

Daladier, several times a Minister in the 1920s, specialized in foreign and defense matters. His reputation was that of a "Jacobin"—a tough and austere defender of the Republic, with a taste for action and (unlike Herriot) a distaste for rhetoric and sentimentality. There are two kinds of southerners in France: the sunny and loquacious ones (whose seriousness General de Gaulle, a man from the North, always questioned) and the taciturn, more melancholy ones. Daladier was clearly one of the latter. His reputation suffered when his first two experiences as Prime Minister turned out to fall far short of expectations. His nine-month-long Cabinet of 1933, following the 1932 elections that had favored the Left, proved, like its predecessors and successors, incapable of defining a clear financial policy to cope with the Great Depression. It fell when Daladier, under pressure from the Right of his party, took deflationary measures that those conservative Radicals deemed insufficient and that the Socialists, whose votes he needed, rejected. After the scandalous Stavisky affair, in which several Radical politicians were compromised and widely denounced as corrupt, Daladier became Prime Minister again—a week before the violent antiparliamentary riots of February 6, 1934, provoked by far-right "Leagues." Daladier, at first, seemed to want to react firmly in order to restore and maintain law and order; but some of his closest supporters abandoned him, and he resigned on February 7—a decision one historian has called the collective suicide of the Republic.[1] It led to a shift from left to right, which lasted two years; during that period, Marshal Pétain joined the Doumergue government and Pierre Laval became the Prime Minister of deflation.

It was at that time that the Popular Front emerged, at first as a popular reaction to the riots of February 6, 1934, later as a laborious alliance between three parties: the Communists, who adopted a stance of moderation and cooperation with the Socialist rivals and Radical bourgeois they had spent years denouncing, Léon Blum's Socialists (who had never been in power), and the Radicals. The latter were as usual divided, with Herriot at first quite reluctant. It was Daladier who led the Radicals into the Popular Front and went to rallies with Blum, Thorez (the Communist leader), and Jouhaux, the head of France's largest union, the CGT. Daladier became Minister of Defense in Blum's government after the Popular Front's electoral victory in 1936. Quickly, the Radical Party began to back away from Blum; overthrown by the Senate, he was replaced by a Radical (Chautemps). After the fiasco of a very brief second Blum Cabinet, the President of the Republic, Albert Lebrun, turned once more to Daladier in April 1938. This last Daladier Cabinet remained in power almost two years—an exceptionally long time in the Third Republic.

It was an important government. Gradually, within a few months, Daladier moved away from the Popular Front: By the fall of 1938, his Cabinet was an alliance of the Radicals and the moderate Right, strengthened when one of the more impressive (and unorthodox) conservative leaders,

1. Serge Berstein, *Histoire du Parti Radical*, vol. 2 (Paris: Presses de la Fondation Nationale des Sciences Politiques, 1982), p. 287.

Paul Reynaud, became Minister of Finance. Daladier and Reynaud reformed the 1936 legislation that limited work to forty hours a week (thus slowing down rearmament), and when the CGT imprudently called for a general strike, the government faced it down and prevailed. Daladier, for a while, became as widely popular as Poincaré had been in the mid- and late 1920s. He was seen, once more, as a man of firmness and authority; he was treated as a hero when he returned from Munich, having saved peace (but he, unlike Chamberlain, had no illusions about its duration and is reported, upon meeting mobs of enthusiastic well-wishers at the airport, to have exclaimed, in somewhat more pungent language: Fools!), and also when he reasserted France's rights and rule in Algeria and in the colonies, against Mussolini's claims. He was the first to launch an ambitious and coherent "family policy" in order to cope with France's demographic decline; and he heeded the public mood in trying to stem the flow of refugees and put many of them in camps.

After Hitler, violating his promises, occupied Bohemia, Daladier insisted on guaranteeing Poland's integrity. When the Hitler-Stalin pact made war inevitable, Daladier's steadily growing hostility to communism became more intense—after all, he had been in the process of negotiating an alliance with Stalin when the latter turned to Germany. After the declaration of war, Communist deputies were expelled from Parliament. Daladier, and much of the political class, championed a strategy of attrition against Germany. Daladier wanted to avoid at all cost a repeat of the bloodletting of World War I, in which 1.5 million Frenchmen—largely peasants and those other *petits* whom the Radicals represented—had been killed. Like Pétain in 1916–1918, he wanted to minimize French losses; hence the passivity of the French Army, locked in the Maginot Line, while Hitler destroyed Poland. The dominant strategic notion was that of a "peripheral strategy" that would go after supplies indispensable to Hitler: iron ore in Scandinavia, oil in the Caucasus. The French Right seemed more eager to fight Stalin (and help Finland, attacked by him) than to fight Hitler and help Poland. Daladier was accused—especially by the pacifist Laval—of not waging the war energetically enough. Sensing that his majority was waning, Daladier resigned, once again, as Prime Minister.

The diary shows what his main concern was after Vichy denounced and jailed him. He wanted to show that ever since 1936 he had launched an extensive rearmament program, and that France had in many areas (although not in aircraft) as much matériel as Germany. This is what he argued in Riom, where he and Blum turned the tables on Vichy: he, with his figures and facts, Blum with his eloquent defense of the Republic. Again and again, he pointed out that the defeat of France resulted not from a lack of preparation but from the incompetence of the High Command. Battling against Vichy's accusations, he had no time for self-criticism: Alas, the military leaders who proved so timid, unadapted to motorized warfare and *Blitzkrieg*, wedded to a defensive strategy that met the public's battle fatigue, yet contradicted France's alliance policies, were men Daladier had appointed or promoted or protected (like the mediocre Gamelin, whom he shielded from Reynaud's wrath).

For many people in France and abroad, he remains the man of Munich. This is, in a way, unfair. He signed that infamous agreement in part because Chamberlain insisted on appeasement and France alone wasn't strong enough to wage war on Hitler, in part because he was sensitive to the Sudeten Germans' demand for self-determination and critical of the way in which President Benes had handled them. But unlike many other *Munichois* who were either pacifists pure and simple or convinced that settling accounts with the Left, or with the Republic, in France was far more important than resisting Hitler, Daladier wanted to use the "reprieve" Munich represented in order to strengthen France's armies and to restore national unity and resolve. One problem, here, was the presence at the Quai d'Orsay of another Radical, Georges Bonnet, a genuine appeaser whose goals were quite different, and whom he didn't remove from the Foreign Ministry until after the war began. Daladier, whose instincts were often excellent, was frequently a willing victim of the Byzantine coalition politics of the Third Republic (and of his own party), and there was a constant battle between firmness and caution in his actions.

The diary shows a man who both relives a heavy past and defends his role in it, who blames those who took France out of the war in order to indulge in dreams of a reactionary "national revolution"—and also worries about the future of his country and of the world. He has nothing but contempt for *both* Pétain and Laval and gives a devastating account of the third great man of Vichy, Admiral Darlan. He realizes that the war cannot be won without American participation; but he is often morosely pessimistic about the course of the war—unlike Blum—and increasingly anxious about an outcome he foresees with great lucidity: Soviet domination of much of Europe (although he exaggerates the risk of a Bolshevized Germany, on the Polish model). He compares unfavorably the Allies' "abandonment" of Poland with what had happened in Munich. His references to de Gaulle in London and Algiers, to Gaullist propaganda, to the trials and political debates that took place in Algiers in 1943–1944, are often critical; he is clearly afraid that trials occurring while the war goes on will be anything but fair, and he wishes that the French people be consulted before any great political and social changes are carried out; in this respect, he remained a man of the Third Republic.

His combination of humanity and lucidity is evident in his remarks on Germany. He is far more distrustful of Germany than is Blum; but he acknowledges the force of German nationalism and condemns any policy of dismemberment (which de Gaulle pursued for a while). His reaction to learning about the atrocities in concentration camps is moving and strong, but he is not a seeker of revenge.

The reader of this diary will be entertained by Daladier's references to his relations with his many guards and jailers and with his companions of captivity: His sympathy for Blum and for the tennis champion, ex–Vichy Minister–turned–resister Borotra; his fairness toward the baffling and waffling Colonel de La Roque, the head of the largest right-wing League (and later party) in the 1930s—a man whose wolfish rhetoric scared the Left, but who turned out to be a sheep, and who supported Pétain after the defeat yet worked for the British intelligence service; and his old hostility toward Reynaud are all in evidence.

Two other points are worth noting. Daladier's captivity did not isolate him from what was happening. While jailed in France, he received lawyers and other visitors who kept him informed of the latest rumors and gossip, of the latest stories about that quaint Vichy regime that I once described as a pluralistic dictatorship, a conglomeration of feuding factions. In the Tirol, he had access to an extraordinary array of newspapers and radio programs.

Moreover, among his visitors in France there was the infamous René Bousquet, the head of Vichy's police and close collaborator of Laval, who played a large and sinister role in the deportation of Jews. Bousquet had been a "Popular Front Prefect," close to the Radicals. His conversation with Daladier on September 16, 1942, is triply fascinating. First, it reveals the calculations of many Vichyites, for whom German victory was likely: France in order to survive had to fit into the "new European order" and in the meantime could do no more than bow to German demands and plead for some of them to be softened. It is Bousquet who comes and tells Daladier that Vichy had to yield to the German demand that he be deported to Germany. Second, it shows that Bousquet did not want to burn his bridges with the leaders of the "old regime" (as Vichy called the Third Republic): He cultivated Daladier just as he established contacts with the Resistance (he befriended, among others, the young Mitterrand, then en route from his Pétainism of 1941–1942 to his resistance of 1943–1944). All these contacts helped him survive and prosper after the war—until his assassination by a madman in 1993. Third, it is clear from the tone of Daladier's entries that he kept some respect for Bousquet, unlike the strong dislike he had for Bousquet's bosses.

The publication of the diary in English should accomplish at least two things. It should revive interest in a man whom history has not treated very well—an imperfect politician, to be sure, part of a system of government whose vices overwhelmed its democratic merits (see for instance Daladier's account of press corruption), but a man of intelligence, integrity, patriotism, common sense, and culture (cf. his interest in Church history). And it should inform the reader about the extraordinary complexity of a period in which rival contenders fought murderously about France's direction and soul, in which uncertainty about the future obliged men and women to make an existential gamble about the outcome, based in part on what they expected but also on what they desired. Daladier never had any doubts about what he wanted for France, even when he wondered how long it would take for victory to come, and he lamented the fate of much of Europe when it finally occurred.

Preface to the English Edition

Jean Daladier

Even after fifty years, and in spite of the reams of documents now available, it remains difficult—especially in France—to form an objective view of what things were like in the period between the wars and in 1940.

The greater, the swifter, the more unexpected the disaster, the less people are willing to deal with it squarely. Once a certain threshold of suffering, shame, and humiliation is reached, actual facts become unimportant, analyses become bothersome. History falls prey to myth and rumor. People refuse to hear any more, but they still need someone to blame. In France, the strangest of bedfellows have come to speak about it in one voice, and the good people have remained mute.

Absolutely no one, with the notable exception of Hitler, had anticipated the collapse of the French Army and the Armistice, and even less so France's decision to collaborate with the victorious enemy without so much as a thought to continuing the fight from North Africa. Once that happened, it took acts of heroism to stand up to the Germans and Vichy's police and militia.

The Anglo-Saxons and the Soviets labored under the mistaken belief that, as in 1914, the French Army would be the main force in forging victory. France's Generals were under the same illusion. How could they not have seen that with a population of 40 million people, with 1.5 million men dead and even greater numbers wounded and disabled in World War I, the France that emerged so weakened in 1918 could not singly hold off a more populous and more highly industrialized German nation?

*   *   *

In Edouard Daladier's prison diary, one of the principal statesmen of the time provides answers to a good many of our questions. The portrait of the author that emerges is nonetheless one of a man unknown and misunderstood. He compiled this journal while in captivity, writing from one day to the next with no thought to publication; in fact, he didn't believe he would survive his imprisonment. The elegance of his style is hardly a drawback, nor is his humor.

Daladier was born in 1884. His family was poor. With the help of various scholarships, he was able to make his mark as a student and went on to become a history teacher. He developed a passion for politics, republican values, and democracy while still very young and devoted himself to their pursuit with a fervor that one would find surprising today. In 1914, he enlisted in the Foreign Legion. He spent four years in the trenches, and was wounded and cited for bravery on several occasions. During that time, he acquired a knowledge of war that was very likely the equal of those who have studied it from their armchairs.

Throughout his life, he worked to rearm France and reforge the coalition that had defeated Germany, as only its combined strength could have. He was disappointed with the Treaty of Versailles, which emerged from the war, knowing as he did that revenge lay foremost in Germany's mind. And indeed, German experts went quickly to work in the Soviet Union, developing new weapons and sharing their discoveries with the Soviets.

Daladier was first elected to Parliament in 1919. He went on to occupy several ministerial posts and finally reached a position where he could achieve his goals when he was appointed Prime Minister in 1933. It was he who initiated France's rearmament campaign. In response to Hitler's initiatives, he created the first motorized division, the forerunner of today's armored division, with tanks, artillery, and motorized infantry units.

At the same time, he worked to reconstitute the four-nation coalition of World War I. Although the British and Italians supported his efforts, he failed to convince Franklin D. Roosevelt or his special ambassador Norman Davis that in the face of the rising German peril it was in America's interest to renew these ties.

Several months after he became Prime Minister, his government was brought down by an alliance of Socialist and right-wing parties. His rearmament program was not implemented. In fact, the nation's military appropriations were considerably reduced, and by Marshal Pétain himself, who was Minister of War in 1934, which made it doubly surprising.

When he returned to power in 1936, in Léon Blum's government, he found that little had been accomplished by the War Ministers who had succeeded him. The French Army possessed a grand total of thirty-four tanks. The situation in England and the United States was not much different. That the danger that was Hitler could have been so completely disregarded boggles the mind. Not only had Germany's other political parties aligned themselves with the Nazis, but even the Vatican, in opposition to the Communists, had called for Catholics to vote for the Nazis.

*　　*　　*

In France, in the wake of the bloodletting of World War I, the economic crunch, and the general disillusionment, crises and confusion ran rampant. The Right was fighting the Left; there were the Communists, the Royalists, the Fascists. A much degraded republican parliamentarianism was foundering in demagoguery; Ministers had little more than token power; governments were brought down in a matter of weeks.

There were even secret organizations at work. One of them, the Cagoule, had the backing of a Marshal of France: Franchet d'Esperey. Loustanau-Lacau, Pétain's military Chief of Staff, was one of its members. (As the archives in Moscow have confirmed, the Soviets were directing and financing the French Communist Party.) The specter of communism turned many a Frenchman toward the Far Right. Much of the population favored Italy over Ethiopia, and Franco over the Spanish Republic.

Today, the methods and the conspiracies of those times are referred to with an affected wryness. But Léon Blum was wounded in the street, and Daladier's apartment was broken into in the middle of the night. Numerous others were physically set upon, and the attacks in the press were vicious to the point, to offer only one example, of driving journalist Roger Salengro to suicide.

Prime Minister again in February 1934, Daladier was confronted with the riots of February 6. Isolated, reluctant to call in the Army, he stepped down. Today we know that most of his principal subordinates were antirepublican. They gave ample proof of that in Vichy! Some of them even went on to play up to the Pretender to the French throne!

Was France actually on the verge of civil war? Whatever the case, after the defeat of 1940, these were the very same men who turned up in Vichy. The quantity of legislation that had been drafted before the French surrender is astonishing. As early as 1935, Laval had begun establishing ties with Pétain, the real head of the Army, and the candidate of both the Right and the Far Right.

Daladier joined with Blum and the Communists in launching the Popular Front. With their victory in the elections of 1936, they were able to institute the social reforms so desperately needed. Thus did Daladier exact his revenge on the rioters of February 6. But their very victory, along with the measures enacted by the Popular Front, was to constitute one more reason for the Right and the middle class to embrace the Vichy regime.

It was the Popular Front government, with Daladier as Minister of Defense, that initiated a rearmament program far greater even than that which France's military leaders had requested. In a nation as divided as France was then, whose industry was often outdated and unsuited to mass production, the difficulties of implementing a program of this kind were enormous. Conflicts flared with both unions and bosses. Daladier tried to negotiate. He aided certain enterprises and nationalized others. He broke the general strike. With the declaration of war, he outlawed the Communist Party and tracked down those who supported the Nazis. He believed that the possibility of war actually breaking out was very real. For him, that alone mattered.

He appointed Jean Monnet to head a purchasing commission sent to the United States and, with the help of Roosevelt, put through orders for large numbers of airplanes. This was to prompt some of his Ministers to issue complaints. Stettinius, Roosevelt's Secretary of State, later acknowledged that it was as a result of the French, and subsequently the combined French and British orders, that America was able to launch its arms manufacturing prior to 1939 and become the arsenal of the free world by 1941–1942. Daladier was fully aware of the time it took for a new industry to be able to function at capacity. He knew that it would take the French, too, at least four years, as it would the British.

But the crisis erupted in September 1938, when Hitler called for the Germans in the Sudetenland to be reincorporated into the Reich. There has surely been no paucity of statements about the Munich Agreement—acclaimed when they were signed, maligned ever after—but rarely are such pronouncements accompanied by fact.

At the end of World War I, it was Clemenceau who insisted that the Sudetenland be made a part of Czechoslovakia. The Czech President, Tomas Masaryk, was opposed but eventually yielded. Out of a total population of 13.5 million in Czechoslovakia, there were only 6 million Czechs (44 percent) and 3.5 million Germans. There were also Slovaks, Hungarians, and Poles, who more often than not were hostile to the Czechs. (Just recently, barely three years after it was liberated from the Soviet bloc, this same nation split in two.)

France had been so unwise as to guarantee Czechoslovakia's sovereignty on its own. The illusions that were born of the victory of 1918 lasted a very long time.

When Germany remilitarized the Rhineland in 1936, Daladier favored armed intervention. Merely a Member of Parliament at the time, he urged General Maurin, the War Minister, to intervene. Once that moment had passed, he felt that the balance of power had shifted: Germany's rearmament was an established fact.

In September 1938, the British were opposed to any form of armed intervention; in truth, they did not possess the force with which to intervene. Chamberlain, moreover, felt that an agreement could be reached with Hitler. The United States was still an unarmed nation at that point and wedded to its isolationist policies. The Soviets, in spite of what has since been claimed, kept equivocating and proposed to bring the matter before the League of Nations. France knew that it could not by itself oppose Germany, that it would take a multinational alliance to save Czechoslovakia and some two to three years to reestablish the balance of power.

Daladier signed the agreements—an act that would haunt him for the rest of his life. When he returned to France from Munich, he did not proclaim, as Chamberlain did, that he had brought "peace for our time."

Looking down on the crowd that had gathered to welcome him, he simp
muttered, "Goddamn fools!" and went back to Parliament to ask for a
even greater rearmament program. These are the facts; they speak fc
themselves.

In 1939, Daladier was to go even further. To avoid war, and in agree
ment with the Poles, he was prepared to negotiate the return to Germar
of Danzig and the Polish corridor. This time, it was Hitler who refusec
He attacked Poland, with the help of the Soviets. The same recognition c
France's vulnerability was to move Daladier to do everything he could t
avoid major battles in the months that followed. (Note that it was not unt
1942–1943 that victory finally swung over to the side of the Allies, and th;
it had effectively required an international coalition to turn the tide.)

By 1940, the rearmament objectives had been fulfilled. Shortages pei
sisted in certain areas, but overall, France was armed with a considerabl
stock of modern weaponry. The French, for example, had the same nun
ber of tanks as the Germans, approximately 2,800. Note, moreover, th;
when they were led into battle, the French troops fought bravely. Som
100,000 men died in action, in just a few weeks' time.

The Germans attacked at Sedan. Pétain had refused to defend th;
portion of the Ardennes region. General Billotte, in contrast, had long ar
gued that this was the sector through which the Germans would send thei
armored divisions. He believed that France was capable of sending a
equal number of tanks to blunt their attack and that it was time to reorga
nize France's defenses. The French High Command would have none c
it. On the eve of the German offensive, the command did not even believ
the pilot who reported the nighttime movement of huge numbers of en
emy tanks, driving on Sedan, headlights ablaze. The confidence tha
reigned was so great that certain military leaders even removed the ob
structions that had been set up along one of the main access roads.

Most of these Generals had performed admirably in World War]
They were still basking in past glory, maneuvering to outdo each other i
pride and ambition, as they looked across the border to their young Ger
man counterparts. Like the Prussian Generals at Iena before then
France's military leaders proved incapable of adapting to the unexpectec
Their mood swung from excessive confidence to utter panic, and fror

there to the absolute certainty that the German Army was invincible and would crush the British in a few weeks' time.

Even as late as 1942–1943, Pétain and the principal leaders in France were convinced that the Anglo-Saxons and the Russians would never be able to defeat the Germans. Pétain saw himself as one of several negotiators in a compromise peace settlement, as is clearly brought out in Daladier's journal. But the truth is that when the likes of Buisson, de Gaulle, and Perré were provided with the necessary firepower, France's young military leaders were able to score clear victories over the Germans. The story was much the same for the Air Force, which was supposedly outnumbered. The facts show that in the few weeks when pilots organized their own missions in the absence of orders from the retreating High Command, they shot down 900 enemy planes while losing only 400 of their own. One wonders what would have happened in the 1940 Battle of Britain had Göring's superior numbers been further reinforced by those 900 aircraft. Whenever able leadership was there—in Africa, Italy, and in France—French soldiers fought valiantly.

But instead of conferring the responsibility for regrouping France's forces to these younger leaders, Prime Minister Paul Reynaud called on Pétain and Weygand, both of whom were convinced that England would be overrun. They had no sense of America's strength and rejected out of hand the possibility of carrying on the war from North Africa. This is an issue that went unquestioned for years and years. We now know that putting up resistance in North Africa, with the men and matériel already in place, bolstered by whatever could have been transported from the mainland, was fully within the realm of possibility. France's fleet ruled the Mediterranean, seconded there by the British fleet. By then there was even an assembly plant for American planes in Casablanca. This was the most unforgivable error of all, the one that has been so carefully hidden over the years and that prefigured the total surrender of the Unoccupied Zone in November 1942, Pétain's and Weygand's refusal to leave for Algiers, and the absurd decision to scuttle the fleet rather than sending it off to join forces with the Allies.

In fact, Daladier, along with several Members of Parliament, left France in June 1940 to carry on the fight from Morocco. He was forcibly brought back, imprisoned, and indicted, first for having declared war on Germany, then for having failed to rearm the nation. His diary offers a scathing depiction of the scandalous Riom trial, suspended by Pétain once it became clear that it was proving detrimental to Vichy. Subsequently, Pétain allowed Daladier to be deported to a prison in Germany. The Riom trial proved that France had indeed been rearmed, a fact that the parties directly involved were to continue to deny for the next fifty years.

While in prison, Daladier wrote about the happenings and people in Vichy with an exactness and a lucidity that are bound to surprise. Even when he was isolated in Germany, he made observations on events past and present that are no less striking. And he gave voice as well to his profound disappointment as he witnessed the inadequacy of Anglo-Saxon policies and the skill with which Stalin went about colonizing all of Eastern Europe, including the very Czechoslovakia that Churchill had claimed he wanted to save in 1938. Following the war, countless people criticized the Munich Agreement, whereas those who expressed opposition to Soviet occupation were far less numerous. The leaders of the French Communist Party tried to obscure the statements they had made in Berlin in 1933, when they called for the liberation of the Sudeten Germans in Czechoslovakia. The Right added its voice as well. Between the end of the war and the early 1970s, former Pétainists and Communists were appointed to ministerial posts. The country began congratulating itself more and more openly for the approach adopted by Pétain, which, it was said, had spared France considerable suffering and paved the way for the Resistance. Others simply pretended that all of France had been in the Resistance. The state of confusion that reigned was the direct result of the country's general unwillingness to examine the past objectively.

Daladier was finally liberated, almost by miracle. As German soldiers were about to execute the remaining prisoners, an American detachment came to the rescue, aided by a German officer and his men. Daladier looked on in horror as this German officer, who had come to defend the lives of enemy prisoners, was killed before his eyes, when the war was in effect already over.

Back in France, Daladier became the scapegoat of both the Right and the Left, and above all the Far Left. He was nonetheless reelected to Parliament. "Munich! Munich!" they shouted, when he voiced his opposition to the war that was beginning in Indochina. They condemned him for having left France unarmed, even though the facts and figures were available to everyone. They condemned him for just about everything, and then some.

Remarkably, he never responded to the attacks and the slander. The consumer society—the world of mass media, advertising, and money—elicited from him only reactions of irony and indifference. He watched as veritable "collective memories" were forged, each by the design and within the limits of the prevailing interest groups or political parties. In Western democracies, there is simply no place for a lone individual and perhaps not even for grand principles. One has only to consider the way electoral campaigns are now financed and how mores have evolved.

In the trenches and in Parliament, in Ministries and prisons, this was a man who fought for republican ideals. For him, being a democrat involved a lifelong political and personal commitment tantamount to stoicism. He needed little to get by and left behind neither money nor possessions. He was emotionless when he testified at Pétain's trial, although Pétain had sentenced him to life in prison, slandered him, and handed him over to the Gestapo. He used to say, "Vengeance is just so much silliness." Those who betrayed him during his years of captivity shamelessly continued reaping benefits from it. He never said anything about it. Perhaps he had arrived at a true experience of freedom and found some form of hope for the future.

One morning in 1970, I listened as he scoffed at the hopes expressed by his physician and offered his farewell with a smile. He died the following day without the slightest fear, and without a word.

I came upon the old notebooks that made up his prison diary long after his death, in the bottom of a dresser drawer. When the book was published in France, I was surprised to receive so many letters from simple folk who had not forgotten him, and who perhaps shared with him the same almost indescribable form of hope.

June 1940: The Departure for Morocco

Jean Daladier

The British had offered Daladier refuge in London, but he preferred to leave for Morocco and continue the struggle from there, as France's leaders in Bordeaux[1] had agreed to do. He wrote the following:

"The government had stated that it would set up its base in North Africa and move all government offices there. Some members were to leave via various Mediterranean ports. Others, including myself, were to go to Le Verdon, where we would board the *Massilia* en route to Casablanca.

"I was anxious to meet with General Noguès.[2] I had appointed him Governor-General of Morocco and wanted to encourage him to carry on the fight.

"In Le Verdon, half of the Deputies who had been present in Bordeaux boarded the *Massilia*, along with General Michel, government personnel, and even Herriot's suitcases.

"We set sail on June 21, in spite of the German mines and the problems we had with the crew; they wanted to return to their families.

"We learned of the Armistice while at sea. The ship's commander categorically refused to alter his course and make for England.

"When we arrived in Casablanca, we were forced to remain on board. It was during that time that the official turnaround in France took place. In the radio and press campaigns mounted against us, we were being accused of desertion.

---

1. In the face of the German advance, the French government had moved from Paris to Tours and from there to Bordeaux in June 1940.

2. General Charles-Auguste Noguès. After having requested and been denied permission from Pétain's government to organize an insurgent military, General Noguès aligned himself with the Marshal. In 1942, Noguès's forces put up armed resistance to the Allied landing. He later sided with Admiral Darlan when the latter came to Algiers. He sought exile in Portugal.

"I finally met Noguès on June 27, in Rabat. 'The Army didn't lose the war,' he said. 'They never went to war.' We both thought that it would be possible to carry on the fight from North Africa, as did all the other leaders, even those in Black Africa and the Middle East.

"We had 270,000 men at our command and the capacity to mobilize them rapidly. We had arms, and even 1,800 top-flight warplanes. Airplanes I had ordered from the United States were to be delivered to Morocco, where assembly plants had already been set up. The Franco-British fleet ruled the Mediterranean. Five admirals had come to Casablanca, among them Laborde and Marquis. Darlan[3] had asked Noguès to set up a command post for him in Rabat.

"Spain was certain to remain neutral, given the exhausting civil war it had just been through and its need for American aid. On Tunisia's border with Libya, there were the Mareth fortifications I had had built.

"Noguès had already cabled Bordeaux several times. He was seeking government authorization to break with official policy and fight on, even if the government had to disavow its involvement in the process.[4] He agreed to send one final cable; it too went for naught.

On June 30, Members of Parliament were prevented from boarding ship and returning to France. They would not be allowed to do so until July 10, in order to deny them the possibility of voting in Vichy, where Pétain was granted plenary powers."[5]

---

3. Admiral François Darlan, who had become Commander in Chief of the Navy in August 1939.

4. While in Morocco, my father and I tried to meet up with the British and leave for London. A submarine was sent to pick us up off the coast of Casablanca. We were betrayed, however, and never found the skiff that would have taken us out from the beach. Other escape attempts failed as well. The Governor-General's office in Rabat managed to foil them all. We were eventually forced—with Noguès's consent, obviously—to leave Morocco under police escort and return to France, where my father was arrested.

General Noguès would later order his troops to fire on the Americans as they landed. He went on to align himself with Darlan and, subsequently, Giraud. After the war, he went into exile. Strange fellow, this General Noguès, who felt he had to ask the government for permission to rebel.

5. General de Gaulle pushed strongly for Noguès to refuse the Armistice and come to London to serve under him.

1940

September 6, 1940

We were having lunch at La Vernue, deep in the countryside near Vichy. André Borie and his family had been my warm and generous hosts for several days. I said to my friends, "It won't be long before I am taken into custody," but they were a little skeptical. "Why would they bother arresting you? The trial is being held right here in Riom.[1] The authorities will know exactly where to find you, since you notified the Minister of the Interior yourself."[2]

I had been warned two or three days before that I could expect to be arrested. The leaders at Vichy had already made up their minds, and there was no time to lose if I hoped to get away. Nonetheless, in view of General Noguès's decision not to make a stand in North Africa and the failed British attempts to spirit me to London, I was determined to face the ordeal in France. On September 3, a young inspector from the *Sûreté* even came to warn me that they would be coming to get me very soon. He offered to take me to Switzerland within a few hours. I thanked him but refused to go.

On September 4, the press published a statement issued by the government in which it claimed "the right to place in administrative detention those individuals deemed dangerous to national security or public safety."

---

1. Site of the court established by the Vichy government, where Daladier and other leaders of the Third Republic were to be tried.

2. Daladier notified him because the Ministry of the Interior is primarily concerned with matters of security and law and order. It oversees general administrative matters within France, such as elections, and virtually all administrative matters for France's territories overseas, but its principal function remains that of governing the nation's various police forces.

3

Nothing happened for the following two days. In fact, my friends at La Vernue were somewhat amused at my having gotten my papers together and carefully arranged them in two leather briefcases.

I harbored no illusions as to the impartiality of this supreme tribunal[3] —my sentence would undoubtedly come down directly from Pétain—but I felt I owed the people of this country an explanation. Had France been betrayed and if so by whom? And how? I was also afraid that by staying with Borie, I would be endangering him, but he absolutely refused to let me leave.

We went on with our meal. Suddenly, the little blonde serving girl came running up, all excited. "Madame, several cars have pulled in and are stopping in front of the house."

Brochet, the Director of the State Police, strode in. Looking important and solemn, he read aloud an order signed by Porte, the Subprefect of Monluçon, who had run for office in the Nièvre as a Popular Front candidate. In accordance with the law of September 4, 1940, and by virtue of the authority vested in Adrien Marquet,[4] Minister of the Interior, I was to be placed under house arrest in the château in Chazeron.

I dictated and signed a statement of protest, denouncing them for arbitrarily resurrecting a law intended to punish plots against the nation and acts of sabotage against the defense industry.

With the help of my son Jean and Dr. Mazé,[5] and in the presence of a kindly but talkative policeman, I quickly packed two suitcases. I took leave of Mme Borie and her daughters, who had received me in their home and been so gracious and considerate. When I started blaming myself for not having left sooner, they stopped me and hugged me. I told my son Jean to

---

3. La Cour Suprême de Justice: a Vichy institution created to try Third Republic Ministers et al. for entering and losing the war against Germany, in other words, to find scapegoats for the humiliating defeat of France.

4. Adrien Marquet had a hand in organizing Pétain's government in Bordeaux, where he was Deputy and Mayor.

5. Pierre Mazé, Secretary-General of the Radical-Socialist Party. As one of Daladier's close personal friends, he organized several attempts to rescue him. He played an important role in the Resistance and was eventually arrested by the Germans. He was liberated in 1945.

notify his brother, Pierre, and my sister so that they wouldn't be brutally shaken by reading the news in the morning papers.

We went outside. In spite of the gasoline crisis, there were five cars parked at the door, each of them packed with policemen. So much for the propaganda promoting a return to the land.[6]

One of the policemen, a pale, round-eyed, fat and fleshy fellow, tried to take a picture. Jean and Dr. Mazé lashed out at him, and he put down his camera.

I would never have guessed I rated a five-car procession. Marquet was doing things up right. We drove through Gannat, Aigueperse, and Châtel-guyon, with people stopping in the streets, staring at us as we went by. One of the cops began telling the story of his years on the force. I lit up my pipe and sat back.

When we came into Chazeron, I could make out in the distance the château tower, the crenellated ramparts, and the old black walls surrounded by pine trees, all of it taken over now by ravens and owls for a nesting ground. The gate is rather handsomely crafted, but the courtyard, with its well and a few dilapidated buildings, is overgrown with weeds. The grounds were teeming with state troopers and inspectors from the *Sûreté*, strolling about and puffing on cigarettes. Dozens of workers were repairing and patching things up, nailing in doors, boarding up windows, and installing lovely, brand new, sharply pointed bars. Their prisoner had arrived before they'd finished readying his prison.

I was told that the illustrious M. Marquet, the Minister of the Interior, had graced this run-down château that the government had requisitioned by visiting it personally.

That was to be his last official function. A few days later, he was removed from office by Pétain and replaced by Peyrouton,[7] a fitting reward

---

6. To counter what Pétain claimed to be the decadence that had brought about France's downfall, he promoted a return to the simpler, purer values of life in the countryside.

7. Marcel Peyrouton, Governor-General of France's overseas territories prior to the war, Pétain's Minister of the Interior in 1940, and Governor-General of Algeria after the Allied landing in North Africa. He was incarcerated at the end of the war.

for having betrayed the government in Bordeaux and having helped Pétain come to power. Word has it that he immediately set out for the Occupied Zone to spew out his rancor and offer his services to the Germans.

I sat down in the courtyard, with a policeman still right behind me. The gate opened and a limousine rolled in. Policemen and troopers ran up to greet it, but it turned out to be just Chavin. Several years ago I had named him Prefect of the Vaucluse and then Prefect in Constantine, after having decorated him with the *Légion d'honneur* in between. He is now Director of the *Sûreté*. With a crowd milling around him, our M. Chavin pretended not to see me, even though our eyes met several times. He walked by, passing just a few feet away, on his way to a tour of the château and what passes here for gardens. Then, once he had finished visiting the grounds, he headed back toward the gate at an angle, and doffed his hat in my direction from as far away as he could. I replied by tipping mine.

I was officially welcomed by M. Bartelet, the warden of this Bastille. We chatted for a while. He is a veteran from Lorraine, twice wounded and twice decorated in 1914. Briefly and discreetly, he shared his feelings with me about France's collapse, our surrendering in Bordeaux, and the path the Vichy government had taken since. Then he headed off to oversee the construction work.

Once the iron bars were finally secured, I moved into my cell, that is, my room. I was given two candles, since they hadn't finished wiring electricity for lights. A policeman and a state trooper settled in outside my door. I was free again, alone at last with my thoughts.

This is where I shall have to muster my strength. Ever since the capitulation in Bordeaux, life has left little more than an ashen taste in my mouth. In Morocco, when I realized that all was lost, I occasionally had thoughts of putting an end to it.

I'll have to fight the press, Laval's[8] slimy arrogance, and the Cour Suprême de Justice, even if I have to fight them on my own. I am alone with

---

8. As Vice Premier, Pierre Laval effectively shared power with Pétain in what was at best an uneasy association and at times an openly hostile one. He was the principal architect

the lions; it's up to me to charge forward and do battle without worrying about the outcome, so that the truth can be known.

It would have been criminal for France not to respect her commitment to Poland at a time when England was finally allied with us in a common cause, as opposed to the way things had transpired over Czechoslovakia. With Hitler reigning over Europe and Italy anxious to get in on the kill, he would have attacked us anyway, in which case the British would have stayed out of it. They would simply have looked after their colonial interests, confident that the United States would back them.

No one has yet said in so many words that France was responsible for this war, but that too will come. In the meantime, they are emphasizing what they call our state of military unpreparedness, for which I am supposed to be responsible. When the time comes, I'll show them figures that prove that the French Army was far better prepared in 1939 than it was in 1914. I'll point out the disastrous errors committed by our military commanders, whose superiors are now blaming my government. They are the ones who betrayed the trust we placed in them, that could have been placed only in them.

Night has fallen, a calm, starry night. I can hear the troopers and police inspectors changing shifts. Outside, the rain is coming down. If only it would go on raining for months, so that England might be spared the bombings and a German invasion. England is my only hope.

September 8, 1940

No visits and no mail since my imprisonment. Peyrouton, the Interior Minister, has gone too far. Even condemned men have those rights. Of course, since he is indebted to me for a good part of his career, the poor fellow won't dare lift so much as a finger to grant authorization.

---

of both the dissolution of the Third Republic and the implementation of the policy of collaboration. Because of his closer ties with the Nazis and his more overtly anti-Semitic acts, he has remained a far less controversial figure than Pétain. He was tried and executed at the end of the war.

Paul Reynaud,[9] who is also under arrest here at Chazeron, asked one of the guards if there had been bars on the windows before he got here. He hadn't noticed they were brand new. Typical Parisian.

When Lebrun[10] first made the decision to call upon Reynaud, I told him that he was turning to a man who would lead us to disaster. Not long after that, in London, Reynaud wondered aloud before a flabbergasted Jean Monnet,[11] "What would have happened to France had there not been those two votes that got me elected?"

He scornfully discarded my policy of temporizing until war supplies could arrive from the United States and until our own industry could swing into gear. He absolutely had to go to war, had to do what Clemenceau had done and make his mark on history. He ran off to London and within fifteen minutes had agreed to send an expeditionary force to Norway and to mine German canals and the Rhine with newly invented British explosives.[12] I was against the idea of an expeditionary force; I preferred blockading Norwegian ports. I opposed the use of floating mines at that juncture and said I would resign if they went through with it. I was convinced there would be retaliatory strikes against our aviation industry. Chamberlain sent me a kindly worded letter to persuade me, and Churchill came all the way to Paris to work on me, but I held out.

In the Senate, Reynaud hailed the naval victory the British won at Narvik and proclaimed: "Hitler's colossal strategic miscalculation."

Even before the truth about the Norwegian expedition was known, Reynaud set about assigning responsibility for the fiasco to Gamelin.[13]

---

9. Paul Reynaud, lawyer and statesman. He was Finance Minister in Daladier's government in 1938 and Prime Minister from March through June 1940. Imprisoned in France in 1940 and subsequently in Germany, he was liberated in 1945.

10. Albert Lebrun, President of France, 1932–1940.

11. Jean Monnet, later called "the father of Europe," presided over the Franco-British Economic Coordination Committee.

12. These floating mines proved to be ineffective.

13. General Maurice Gamelin. First in his class at the Saint-Cyr Military Academy in 1893, he rose to the rank of General at age forty-four. His leadership helped forge the victory at the Marne in 1914. He performed brilliantly as a commander, first with a brigade,

Reynaud brought a list of charges against him in meetings of the Cabinet and the War Council and discredited him in the eyes of public opinion. Twice Gamelin tendered his resignation, but Lebrun refused it each time.

In May, after a series of military setbacks, Reynaud finally managed to relieve Gamelin of his command, but he kept Georges[14] in charge of military operations in the Northeast. After declaring that he would defend Paris in house-to-house fighting if he had to, he cleared out of the city without warning by eight o'clock that night. I can't figure out why he resigned in Bordeaux while he still had the backing of the majority.

To top it off, he has just sent me a message that I should put the blame on Gamelin during the pretrial proceedings.

September 9, 1940

Just finished reading Voltaire on judicial errors in the eighteenth century. I learned this morning that General Gamelin is here. He had been at his friend Gaboriau's when they picked him up. Gaboriau walked out with him to the car and told the arresting officers: "The man you have taken into custody and who is leaving with you is alive. I assume he will be alive when he gets to Chazeron."

The Vichy mafia has probably hatched this plot to "save the honor of the Army," as they used to say back in the days of the Dreyfus affair.

According to the terms of Pétain's decree, only the "immediate subordinates" of Ministers can be held accountable. Gamelin, head of the Joint Chiefs for National Defense, was directly under me in the War Ministry. If he were to disappear, no other General could be charged. Only civilians would be tried, and they would be overwhelmed by Generals who would triumph in the courtroom—after failing on the battlefield.

---

then a division. He was named Chief of Staff in 1931, Inspector General in 1935, Supreme Commander in 1938. He held the position of Chief of Staff for National Defense until May 1940. He was imprisoned by the Vichy government, tried in Riom, and subsequently imprisoned in Germany. He was liberated in 1945.

14. General Joseph Georges, Commander in Chief of Operations in Northeastern France and Army Inspector General.

General Huntziger,[15] who was the first to suffer defeat in the war, the man who lost in Sedan, is today War Minister in the Vichy government.

My "head waiter" here, the policeman who brings in my meals, is an aviator from Lorraine with 1,500 hours of flying time. He has four children in Occupied France, two of whom are prisoners. "Weather like this," he said, watching the rain come down, "is a real problem for bombardiers. If only it could keep up and protect England."

Some of the policemen were in the last war, just as I was. One of them said to me: "Why shouldn't they hold out? Didn't we hold out at Verdun under the heavy artillery shelling?"

Tuesday, September 10, 1940

No newspapers and no visits. Peyrouton has really gone too far. There's a biting, cold wind; it's already autumn. If we stay here through the winter, this room will be ice cold. Even now I have to work with my hat on and blow on my fingers.

I spotted General Gamelin from my window. He seems to have aged considerably. The guards saluted him as he passed by. I first met him in 1933 in the War Ministry, when he was Chief of Staff and Weygand[16] was head of the General Staff.[17] I found him to be cultured and amiable and gifted with a sharp, clear mind. When I went before the Supreme War Council, he joined me in supporting a plan to extend fortifications up to Dunkerque.

---

15. General Charles Huntziger was named to the Supreme War Council in 1938. In 1939, he was put in charge of the Second Army, then of the Fourth Combined Armies Sector (the Ardennes region, where the Germans broke through). He headed the French delegation at the signing of the Armistice. Pétain appointed him War Minister in 1940.

16. General Maxime Weygand, who was Marshall Foch's Chief of Staff during World War I, became Commander in Chief of the French Army in 1930. Having retired in 1935, he was recalled to active duty in 1939 to head military operations in the Mediterranean. In May 1940, he replaced Gamelin as Supreme Commander. He was Minister of National Defense under Pétain from June to September 1940 and Pétain's representative in North Africa in 1940 and 1941. The Germans had him relieved of his duties, after which, in 1942, he was imprisoned in Germany.

17. The Chief of the General Staff was responsible for preparations for war. Command in time of war was the province of the Vice President of the Supreme War Council.

He had been an officer on Joffre's command staff, both in Charleroi and at the Marne, after which he brilliantly commanded a division and an army corps. He was the Poincaré brand of republican, neither Fascist nor Royalist like some of our Generals. After he was named to head the General Staff, by either Piétri[18] or Maurin,[19] our paths crossed again in 1936. I readjusted his budget requests upward and worked out a 14 billion franc rearmament program. I got Blum to back the plan, telling him that I would not go back to the War Ministry if he refused to release the funds.

In 1937, Chautemps[20] and Bonnet[21] turned down the increased budget requests that I judged necessary for our Air Force and our antiaircraft defenses. When I became Prime Minister in 1938, I insisted that we adopt a 20 billion franc program.

Now Marshal Pétain, General Maurin, and Fabry,[22] who was War Minister then, are holding me responsible. What did *they* do between 1934 and 1936?

I tried to lower the retirement age for Generals, but President Lebrun opposed it. Out of kindness or a sense of diplomacy, General Gamelin must have intervened with Lebrun and certain Members of Parliament. The fear of "jumping into the unknown" is a veritable disease in France. It's the Commander in Chief, and he alone, who names the members of the Supreme War Council who lead our armed forces, and he alone is responsible for them.

---

18. François Piétri, left-wing republican Member of Parliament, several times a Minister. He aligned himself with Pétain, who appointed him Ambassador to Spain from 1940 to 1944.

19. General Joseph Maurin, War Minister in 1936.

20. Camille Chautemps, Radical-Socialist, elected Deputy in 1919. He subsequently served as Prime Minister several times prior to 1938. He was a member of both Paul Reynaud's and Marshal Pétain's Cabinets in 1940. Having been sent by Pétain on a mission to the United States, he remained there for the duration of the war.

21. Georges Bonnet, Radical-Socialist Deputy who became Minister of Foreign Affairs in 1938 and Minister of Justice in 1939. He sided with Marshal Pétain.

22. Jean Fabry, Minister of War and National Defense under Daladier in 1934.

The tenure of men over sixty-two should not have been renewed automatically. I had drawn up reform measures, but with the coming of the war, I had to put them aside.

Gamelin favored intervening on the side of Czechoslovakia in 1938. Contrary to what has been reported in the press, it was in the face of England's reluctance and the frightening inferiority of our Air Force that he gave up the idea. If Reynaud wanted to relieve Gamelin of his command on May 19, 1940, why replace him with Weygand, who had never even commanded troops between 1914 and 1918? He would have done better to choose someone with combat experience.

I see Gamelin heading back to his cell, followed by police inspectors. He never speaks to them.

I've heard he has begun writing. He should keep in mind that the best defense is an aggressive offense.

Wednesday, September 11, 1940

Worked all day, reading through articles published by either Georges Bonnet or his cronies—Berl[23] perhaps, since he was appointed by him. They're signed XXX. "We lost the war, England is being showered with bombs; the time for discretion is over." Bonnet alone saw things clearly; Bonnet alone was a "true" pacifist.

After the Germans had abruptly broken off negotiations at 8 P.M. on August 31 and invaded Poland that very night, I always assumed that they were responsible for starting the war. Now it seems that the responsible parties were England and Lord Halifax, whom Bonnet used to call his friend.

None of these articles mentions the countless memos and statements by Bonnet in which he declared that France would intervene if Poland were attacked. Even I never went that far. I stated in March that I would

---

23. Emanuel Berl, writer and Editor in Chief of the left-wing weekly, *Marianne*, from 1933 to 1937. In 1940, he collaborated with Pétain, penning several of the Marshal's speeches.

not go to war over Danzig, that I would do so only if Poland were threatened with destruction. Beck, the head of government, relented and said that he would not undertake any military action if Danzig proclaimed itself a part of the Reich.

Bonnet is acting in the interests of the Vichy government and its deep-rooted hatred of the English. Last winter, when I offered Bonnet a position in my government, Pétain told me that the British didn't particularly care for him. The Vichy leaders are living under the illusion that a properly orchestrated hostility toward England will earn them better treatment from the Germans. As for Bonnet, he had schemed to get himself named Vichy's Ambassador to the United States, but Bullitt[24] saw this coming and made it known that the American government would not support the nomination.

Bonnet is now singing the praises of Mussolini and Ciano,[25] probably maneuvering for the vacated ambassadorship to Rome. These articles I'm reading could not have been published without the authorization and perhaps even the assistance of the government. Nowadays, *L'Action française* is France's *Journal officiel*. They ran an article setting forth Pétain's views on education. They would do better to set forth his views on the military: his opposition to armored divisions, his belief in fixed fortifications, and so on.

All the shopkeepers in France are being asked to place a portrait of the Marshal in their windows, and *France Soir* apparently wants to organize a contest!

As for Déat,[26] he claims our imprisonment was long overdue. He was

---

24. William C. Bullitt, American Ambassador to France from 1936 to 1940. He was a close personal friend of both Roosevelt and Daladier. In 1944, he enlisted in the First French Army.

25. Galeazzo Ciano, close associate and son-in-law of Mussolini; Minister of Foreign Affairs.

26. Marcel Déat was elected to Parliament as a Socialist in 1932 but broke with the SFIO to launch a reformist party in 1933. He favored appeasement with Germany and authored the well-known article "Die for Danzig?" in the daily *L'Œuvre*, a vehicle for German propaganda that he took over in 1940. He headed the pro-German movement in France and as such was opposed to even Vichy's policies.

Air Force Minister under Sarraut.[27] What did Déat do on March 6, 1936, when Germany marched back in to occupy the Rhineland? How many planes did he leave us with? In 1939, he added his signature to a defeatist tract and then claimed that he had merely acceded to a request made by Lecoin[28] and signed a blank page. Frossard[29] came and pleaded with me to let the matter go, and Monzie[30] intervened on his behalf, too.

One of the workers here told me that he had seen soldiers who cried from shame when they were captured, others who laughed and sang *Madelon*, and others still who climbed on the backs of German motorcycles. Then he said: "Who knows? The people who have put you in jail just might someday end up taking your place here."

It's not for me to undermine the wonderful optimism that allows him to go about his work with a light heart.

Mandel[31] got here Tuesday night. He is ill and confined to bed.

The weather has, unfortunately, been absolutely beautiful for the last three days and London is a patchwork of smoke and flames. To be sure, the death toll is not especially high, but what about the factories, the war industry, and the landing fields? Will the mass destruction be followed by an invasion?

---

27. Albert Sarraut, Radical-Socialist, several times a Minister beginning in 1914, including Interior Minister during Daladier's third government (1938–1940) and Education Minister under Reynaud (1940). He was first named Prime Minister in 1933, then again in 1936, and was in power when Hitler moved to occupy the Rhineland. He was imprisoned in Germany in 1944 and 1945.

28. A conscientious objector.

29. Ludovic-Oscar Frossard, journalist and Socialist politician. He was Public Works Minister in Daladier's third government and Information Minister under Reynaud in 1940. He sided with Marshal Pétain in 1940.

30. Anatole de Monzie, Deputy and Senator from the Lot, several times a Minister, including Public Works Minister in Daladier's third government (1938–1940). He had a hand in bringing the Vichy regime to power.

31. Louis Georges Mandel had been Georges Clemenceau's Chief of Staff before being named Minister of the Colonies in Daladier's third government (1938–1940) and Interior Minister under Reynaud in 1940. Pétain had him imprisoned in 1940. He was subsequently deported to Germany, then in 1944 brought back to France, where he was assassinated by the Vichy Militia in Fontainebleau Forest.

I admire the British. After France fell, they could honorably have signed a peace treaty. If they can hold out three months and the United States comes to their aid, maybe the idea of a French resistance force in North Africa will crystallize again. But haven't we already given away all our planes and disarmed our Navy?

Churchill will defend England village by village, house by house. His speech was an admirable display of courage, restraint, and dignity. He has reached a height of true grandeur. Roosevelt's speech was a poor one, at least from what I can gather from the summary in the newspapers. Obviously, he has to deal with the isolationists. England is my only hope. I am filled with admiration for their pilots, who every night have to fly through heavy antiaircraft barrages on their missions over Berlin, Hamburg, and Munich, whereas the German fighter pilots have the benefit of an elaborate warning system.

Is the British Air Force being supplied by the United States? In dealing with Curtiss and later with Glenn Martin in 1938, I was struck by their low production capacity. In the contract we signed, I even agreed to pay a share of the costs for expanding their factories, their retooling, and their hangar construction. I wanted to order 10,000 planes from them. I was opposed by Paul Reynaud and those working under him. They wanted to hold on to the greater part of the Bank of France's gold so as to bolster the franc. Now that France has surrendered, I hope the Americans have given Britain the airplanes I ordered from them. It buoys me to think that the French orders placed in 1938 and during the war significantly increased America's industrial potential, and that England might be reaping the benefits at least of this French initiative. But is their industrial base up to it? That is the main issue. It takes a good year to move from putting out a prototype to factory-line mass production.

When I look over these figures, when I consider the current situation of their industry and the time it will take to increase its capacity, and then the peril that now threatens England, I am overcome with a feeling of anguish.

September 12, 1940

Everyone's bustling about. The policemen in the next room are being moved out of their quarters.

They had a real sawmill going next door. There'll be a lot less snoring coming out of there now, but there must be some reason for the change. I wonder who the next prisoner brought in will be. Léon Blum?[32] All those vicious hatchet men writing for *Le Jour* and *Le Petit Journal* have been clamoring for his arrest. It might be someone else, but not a simple General, and certainly not one of those colonels I passed on the road up from Bordeaux, who were speeding south in their sedans to save their skins.

It's raining here at the château. If only a storm could rage and never die down! Nature could level the playing field that way. If she doesn't, the battle will become more and more lopsided.

I came across an excerpt from a speech Weygand made on July 2, 1939: "I believe that the caliber of the French Army is higher today than at any other time in its history. We have the highest-quality matériel, first-rate fortifications, excellent morale, and an outstanding High Command.

"No one among us wants war. But I state firmly that if we are forced to win new battles, win them we shall."

A pity he wasn't forced to win them.

There has been a complete turnover of the policemen working here. After a full week together, we had gotten used to them. Some of them shared our views and didn't especially try to hide it. One was a former student of mine from my days of teaching history in Marseilles, a fine young man who kept telling me, "Don't let your spirits drop, keep them up." I certainly hope I'll be able to keep them up, but learning to live in the absence of freedom is a painful experience.

---

32. Léon Blum was a Jewish intellectual and Socialist politician who is primarily remembered as the first leader of the Popular Front government in 1936. He was deeply involved in journalism, first as one of Jaurès's collaborators on *L'Humanité* and subsequently as founder of *Le Populaire*. Following the trial in Riom, he was handed over to the Germans and deported to Buchenwald. After liberation, he returned as the head of *Le Populaire* and became Prime Minister again in 1946, concerning himself then with establishing the institutions of France's newly formed Fourth Republic.

September 13, 1940

London subjected to massive bombings. German field communiqués. German war analyses. Excerpts from German newspapers. *L'Œuvre, Le Jour, Le Petit Parisien, Le Journal*, etc., how abject our newspapers are. I'm not sure which one of them takes the prize. Only Alexandre Varenne's *La Montagne* has maintained its dignity, and I can't figure out how he's managed to keep from being arrested.

I went for my usual walk in the courtyard. When I got back, I learned that my son Jean and Dr. Mazé had been granted permission to visit me. The order stipulates that M. Jean Daladier can see his father without a police inspector present, whereas one will have to be there when I speak with Dr. Mazé. The order is signed by the illustrious Chavin, Director of the *Sûreté*. But how is that going to work, since they'll come together? Am I supposed to ask the inspector to kindly step outside when I address my son and then ask him to come back in when I turn to Mazé? And why hasn't Dulot[33] been authorized to come and see me as well?

At around 6 P.M. three automobiles pulled into the courtyard. The idea flashed through my mind that it was Léon Blum. Looking out through the barred window, I watched a wide brimmed hat, a broad mustache, and a pince-nez emerge from the lead car. Blum calmly surveyed the château. His face looked weary. It's a long drive up from Narbonne. He climbed up the steps slowly, said a few words in the room next to mine, and that was all. They've hunted down the Jew and the Socialist, the man who was responsible for the agreements signed at Matignon.[34] The fact is, there is absolutely no reason for him to be charged with anything. The plutocrats are simply paying him back for having struck fear into them in 1936.

---

33. Charles Dulot was an economist writing for the daily *Le Temps*. He was a close personal friend of Daladier.

34. In June 1936, shortly after the Popular Front came to power, Blum presided over the signing of these agreements between labor (represented by the Confédération Générale du Travail [CGT], the Communist trade union organization) and management. Management agreed to recognize labor unions and union delegates and accepted the principle of collective bargaining. Loosely used, the "Matignon agreements" refer as well to the forty-hour workweek and paid vacations, which became law at the same time.

We created the Popular Front to fight off La Roque[35] and his Croix de Feu. We took them seriously. In 1934 they were well on their way on the road to power. The Popular Front did its most effective work before 1936; after that, they were undone by the Communists. Blum's mistake was in not forcing them to listen to reason, and yet he could easily have run the government without them. But he is a Marxist who believes in the existence of social classes and in the necessity or at least the inevitability of the struggle between them. He used to love it when he was called "comrade" by those clowns from the Metal Workers' Union who refused to put in additional hours for national defense until I put an end to their factory sit-ins and their strikes. Organizing sit-ins in factories that were turning out arms for the war effort was unconscionable. The forty-hour workweek was applied much too automatically and inflexibly for a time when the Germans were working far longer days and more productively.

I think that's the key. Blum could not conceive of a Socialist leader who didn't have the backing of every workers' group, especially just after the working class had finally been able to make some claim to unity. Yet he knew full well that the Communists were insidiously maneuvering to undermine what he was doing. He could have demanded that they toe the line and they would not have put up a fight.

He was often critical of me; in fact, he twice forced me out of power, first in October 1933, then in March 1940, and both times with Flandin's[36]

35. François de La Roque, an antiparliamentarian who became president of the Croix de Feu, a right-wing veterans' association that became increasingly politicized under his leadership. He participated in the riots of February 6, 1934. When the Croix de Feu was dissolved in 1936, along with the other Fascist leagues, he founded the French Social Party (PSF). He sided with Pétain in 1940 but was subsequently imprisoned in Germany and then again in France at the end of the war. (Cf. diary entries for January 1944.)

36. Pierre-Etienne Flandin, President of the right-wing Democratic Alliance in the Chamber of Deputies. He was several times a Minister beginning in 1924 and Prime Minister in 1934–1935. He was a Minister in Marshal Pétain's government (see the diary entry for December 15, 1940). Having been forced out of the government by the Germans in 1941, he left for North Africa in 1942 and was arrested in 1943. In 1945, he was sentenced to five years of national disgrace but won a reprieve for his role in the Resistance.

approval. But he is an upright, courageous man. If any of the people now slandering him had been in his shoes the day following the Armistice, they would have taken off for the United States or South America. I learned a thing or two about such matters from Bullitt.

I haven't seen Blum since June 17 or 18, when we were together in Pomaret's[37] office. We were both very shaken by the misfortunes our country was suffering, and we hugged each other in a mutually spontaneous gesture.

I can hear him walking about next door; I can hear him very clearly. We could communicate through Morse code if we wanted, but both of us have better things to do.

September 14, 1940

The sky is clear and illuminated by the insolent brilliance of the moon. Two days from now we'll learn about more bombings and perhaps the invasion of England.

Letters mailed September 8 have just reached me today, many of them bringing words of encouragement from good, simple folk.

I got a lovely letter from my son Jean. The ordeal he's going through is making a man of him, as I had fervently hoped it would. Many of the doors that used to open for him at the slightest touch are now bolted shut. He'll learn how low men can stoop and that, in the end, nothing ever comes easily.

If Doumergue,[38] Flandin, and Laval, who knew of and in fact denounced Germany's massive rearmament, had made a serious effort to rearm the nation, it wouldn't have fallen to me, beginning in 1936, to organize the war industry and produce all the equipment with which our armies went into battle. Everything had to be built from the ground up. I

---

37. Charles Pomaret, Socialist Labor Minister under both Daladier and Reynaud, then Interior Minister under Marshal Pétain. He sought refuge in Switzerland.

38. Gaston Doumergue, Radical-Socialist President of France from 1924 to 1931. He took over from Daladier as Prime Minister in February 1934 and later appointed Marshal Pétain to his first Cabinet position, Minister of War.

had to fight certain management groups and certain union leaders. We explained to them how serious the situation was and that the Fascist and Nazi movements they were fulminating against in their meetings weren't going to wait for us to draw up statistical charts and debate over them.

I can still see them snickering while Belin,[39] the Vice President of the CGT, looked on approvingly, as they awaited the publication of *Syndicats*, financed with money from secret funds.

September 15, 1940

Sometime near midnight, I was awakened with a start by howling winds. To the north of us, they were twisting trees and pulling pines and cedars right out of the ground. The sky was pale, the way it is just before daybreak. Policemen stood watching the storm through windows facing south. I hope the Nazi planes ran into this weather over the Channel.

At 8 A.M. a peasant cleaning woman said to me, "What horrible weather!"

"It was a beautiful night for England," I said.

"Oh it was," she replied. "In that case, I'm all for it. They're our only hope."

In spite of her errors and her shortcomings, England has never been as popular in France as she is today. Baudouin,[40] the financier turned Minister, our man of Fascist business matters, has been making speeches that so reek of the most mindless obsequiousness toward our conquerors that they have probably reinforced our admiration for the British. Somebody must have told him, and now he has stopped. Too bad.

September 16, 1940

This was a happy day. At 10:15 this morning, my son Jean and Dr. Mazé came into my room, preceded by the stuffy, solemn warden of this Bastille.

---

39. René Belin, left-wing union leader who in 1940 sided with Marshal Pétain. Pétain appointed him Labor Minister.

40. Paul Baudouin, Director of the Indochina Bank. Although Paul Reynaud had appointed him Secretary of the War Council, Baudouin went on to betray Reynaud by helping to bring the Vichy regime to power. Pétain named him Minister of Foreign Affairs.

We embraced each other. So many things have happened since I was arrested at La Vernue. I asked about Dulot. Mazé said that he was infuriated with the people at the Interior Ministry who refused to grant him permission to come and see me, which tells me that he is fine.

The three of us headed down to the vegetable garden for a stroll. In a gesture of tact and sensitivity that their chief would have severely reprimanded them for, the inspectors from the *Sûreté* sat apart on a bench, smoking and chatting together idly. With his keen doctor's eye, Mazé pointed out that, as was the custom many centuries ago, the château walls had been reinforced with animal bones embedded in the sand between the stones. "Too bad they weren't human bones," my son said. "That would fit in better with present-day local color." I gave him an affectionate slap on the back and we continued on our walk around the courtyard.

Near morning's end, the warden came in to say that Jean and Mazé could stay and have lunch with me, but in the presence of an inspector from the *Sûreté*. That was not about to keep me from saying all the lovely things I had to say about the honorable Minister of the Interior and the head of the *Sûreté*, our friend Chavin, whom I had once named Prefect of the Vaucluse.

Finally they had to leave. I said good-bye to them from behind the bars, as they were crossing the courtyard. They turned several times to wave back and disappeared behind the trees near the gate. I spotted them one final time after that.

That evening, the old police inspector who had accompanied us at lunch came into my cell, smiling. "I just got back from the village. There's a wine merchant there who picks up British broadcasts. They said that the English had shot down 185 German planes. You'll see, we're going to win this thing."

Tuesday, September 17, 1940

They do what they can to jam the radio, but there's always one frequency they don't manage to block out.

This morning, a carpenter working in one of the rooms repeated to me what they were saying about our arrests on British radio. He also recited several brief passages from one of de Gaulle's speeches. "Hell of a speech!" Then he added: "Before the last war, Laval was a revolutionary and a Socialist. Now he's rich and he owns a château and a few newspapers. Contractors direct us to buy our supplies from his company."

Looking out my window, I saw Mandel go by with his topcoat open and his hands, in the gray gloves he always wears, hanging freely at his side. I could hear his clipped speech resonating in the courtyard.

He has been accused of plotting against national security. They claim he tried to foment a rebellion in Africa, financed by Jewish Moroccans, and get himself named Proconsul or something of the sort. That was just a web of lies that he tore apart in Meknès, where he was initially interrogated. I heard that the Examining Magistrate from the military, who was in charge of the case, wanted to have it thrown out.

September 19, 1940

Every newspaper is running front-page headlines announcing that General Gamelin and I have been indicted. It's a press release from the Ministry of Justice. The tactic doesn't surprise me at all. They've got to keep the Krauts and their pals happy.

September 20, 1940

Received a letter from Roger Génébrier,[41] my friend in need, as I used to call him.

Over a three-year period, from 1937 through September 1, 1939, I earmarked more than 65 billion francs for national defense, 39 billion of that to the Air Force. If the various Prime Ministers and other Ministers directly involved, General Maurin, Fabry, and those who succeeded them between 1934 and 1936, had committed just half that much to rearming the nation, the situation would have been entirely different, but it was left to me to build from the ground up and produce all the modern weaponry we had at the time of the mobilization. Needless to say, the Generals who

---

41. Roger Génébrier, career public official. As Daladier's associate and faithful friend, Génébrier helped him throughout his captivity and took part in Daladier's various attempts to escape.

were defeated, prodded on now by Weygand, are all doing what they can to relieve themselves of their own responsibility and place it at my feet. But not one of them ever voiced a complaint, neither on August 23 nor after that, and especially not during my visits to the front. I defy them to show me one single letter in which they expressed reservations.

One of my regrets at being locked up here is that I can't put together a dossier made up of the firsthand accounts of those who actually fought in the war. How can I be expected to prepare my defense under these conditions?

September 21, 1940

I went to Riom at 2:30 P.M. and for three hours answered questions put to me by M. Lagarde, a member of the High Court of Appeals and the Examining Magistrate[42] for the case. His mind is already made up; he shares the government's opinion. Of course they had no trouble turning up all the accommodating souls they needed: Bonnet, naturally, the Army Generals, Weygand and Alibert,[43] Baudouin, and so forth. Barthe[44] did his part by rummaging through the trash and fishing out scraps of paper.

The prosecution's argument holds that the French government in power at the time was responsible for the war. I listened to M. Lagarde tell me how I should have insisted that England begin conscripting soldiers in 1936, and that in the face of their refusal, I should have signed a treaty with Germany and Italy! What a pity M. Lagarde wasn't Foreign Minister back then. Of course, our defeat is all the explanation they need. The same M. Lagarde was surprised when I read him a series of Bonnet's declarations in which he stated that any German threat to Poland would immediately

---

42. For criminal matters in the French legal system, an Examining Magistrate (*juge d'instruction*) is appointed to carry out an investigation and ultimately make the determination whether to indict. In U.S. terms, he is part police detective, part Grand Jury, and part pretrial prosecutor.

43. Raphaël Alibert, member of the Conseil d'Etat, France's highest juridical body. Prior to the war, he had close ties with right-wing extremists. He had a hand in the conspiracy in Bordeaux, helping and counseling Marshal Pétain, who subsequently appointed him Minister of Justice.

44. Edouard Barthe, Socialist Deputy who aligned himself with Marshal Pétain.

trigger France's intervention. He hasn't read the blue book, or any diplomatic dispatches or documents for that matter, only the Fascist newspapers that are subsidized by the Germans: *Gringoire, Candide, L'Œuvre,* and *L'Action française.*[45]

I have no illusions. I know they've already worked out the sentence to be rendered by this special tribunal, but I have to make a stand and let the truth come out.

September 22, 1940

The bombing of London has not let up; I read a statement issued by the Lord Mayor of the city. The important question is whether England is being supplied with significant numbers of aircraft from the United States and Canada. Without that support, they'll soon run out of fighter planes. The United States seems increasingly preoccupied with Japanese imperialism. Will Japan play the part that Berlin expects it to? If England should fall before winter comes, the fleet would head for Canada, Churchill said. We might see a huge Anglo-Saxon coalition that would include the United States and the nations of the Commonwealth.

Some of the members of the *Sûreté* have been dismissed, in particular two inspectors who had said hello to me and shaken my hand. Another inspector was dismissed for having committed the grievous crime of remaining in my room with me for a few minutes while I was having dinner.

September 23, 1940

I had been looking forward to a visit from Mazé and my son Jean but spent the day waiting for them in vain.

September 24, 1940

I was doing my best to get some work done when Jean and Mazé showed up, loaded down with packages like a pair of Santa Clauses. They had been

---

45. All four newspapers were politically far right, antirepublican, and pro-German. Before 1939, *Gringoire* had launched a series of attacks against Daladier that featured doctored photographs.

in the South: Orange, Carpentras, Marseilles. My sister is undaunted as always, preparing for the coming winter and doing whatever is necessary to see to my son's education. They saw our friends in Orange, who have remained faithful to me.

September 25, 1940

It rained all night. Water is seeping through the roof, spreading over the parquet floors.

The Japanese have landed in Indochina and taken over the airfields. Their planes will take off from there on bombing runs over China. A communiqué from pitiful M. Baudouin explains that our realistic approach to foreign policy *is* really the best one. General Catroux[46] has been relieved of his position as Governor-General of Indochina for simply trying to defend France's interests in Asia.

De Gaulle has been beaten back in Dakar.[47] The attack was poorly organized. He must have been misled by people in his entourage.

Alibert, the Minister of Justice, whose home had been searched by the police back when the Cagoule[48] was active, hasn't lost any time. He has put through one of those good old laws that was popular during the Second Empire, a statute approved by the Marshal, instituting a court-martial at which they can try de Gaulle's accomplices. It is, needless to add, a despi-

---

46. General Georges Catroux, Governor-General of Indochina in 1939. In 1940, when he tried to join forces with de Gaulle, Vichy dismissed him. He commanded the Free French forces in Syria and Lebanon. In 1945, he was named Governor-General of Algeria.

47. De Gaulle's Free French forces were repelled by Vichy's military as they attempted to seize the port city of Dakar.

48. The Cagoule was the name given by the press to the Secret Committee for Revolutionary Action (CSAR), an organization operating clandestinely, under the leadership of Eugène Deloncle and the patronage of Marshal Franchet d'Esperey. They possessed large arms supplies and boasted some 10,000 military and civilian members. The organization had close ties with Commander Loustanau-Lacau (see "1944," n. 9), who, while serving as Pétain's aide, helped organize an insurrection within the Army.

cable and outrageous piece of legislation. The spirits of Trestaillons[49] must be dancing with glee.

I've heard that a piece of property in the Indre belonging to the La Rochefoucauld family has been converted into a detention center for about sixty Socialists and Radicals. They were chosen from among those who voted against dictatorship at the National Assembly session held in Vichy. Pétain is on the job and giving a good imitation of Monck.

Friday, September 27, 1940

Ribet,[50] my lawyer, came to see me this afternoon, accompanied by his wife, who is also a member of the bar. He told me that the charges against me are grotesque, that they don't stand up in the light of day. He took a great many notes, as did Mme Ribet, who is lovely, alert, and resolute, and very patriotic as well. Whereas pimps and murderers have the right to have their lawyer present while they're questioned by the Examining Magistrate, we won't enjoy such privileges. Vichy has decided that the proceedings will be closed; Ribet won't be able to attend.

Grumbach,[51] Moch,[52] and either Auriol[53] or Dormoy[54] are being formally held in that little hotel in the Indre that Courrier had gone to fix up.

---

49. Following the defeat at Waterloo, the Royalists returned to power and began exacting revenge by instituting a court-martial for Napoleon's principal military leaders. In southeastern France, this *terreur blanche* assumed the form of mob violence and was at times reminiscent of the sixteenth-century religious wars, as in Nîmes, where Protestants were slaughtered by Catholic Royalists led by a street porter calling himself Trestaillons.

50. Maurice Ribet, World War I veteran and former President of the Bar Association. He was Daladier's lawyer during the trial in Riom. He was a republican and a man of great courage. He participated in Daladier's various plans to escape and became a close personal friend.

51. Salomon Grumbach, Socialist Deputy who left for North Africa on the *Massilia* in June 1940.

52. Jules Moch, Socialist politician and member of the Resistance. Between 1945 and 1958, he held several positions as Minister: Public Works, Defense, Interior.

53. Vincent Auriol, a Socialist who became Finance Minister under Léon Blum in 1936. In Vichy, he voted against giving plenary powers to Marshal Pétain and eventually made his way to London in 1943. He headed the Foreign Affairs Committee in Algiers and later served as President of France, from 1947 to 1954.

As M. de Carbuccia[55] would say (the same M. de Carbuccia who had received a medal for a wound in his heel that he got twenty days into the last war, after which he carefully spent the next four years waiting the war out), the weeding out continues.

September 28, 1940

The Examining Magistrate from Riom's Cour Suprême has come to Chazeron with a court recorder.

He questioned me about the causes of the war, our military preparations, and the delays in arms manufacturing resulting from the nationalization of certain industries and from the laws guaranteeing a forty-hour workweek, paid time off, and so on and so forth. The defeated Generals, and above all those who were most responsible for our defeat, have written up statements said to be terribly damning. Why didn't they write them up before the war, instead of assuring me that they were prepared and confident of victory? The person who seems to have gone furthest is the one and only General Georges, who was Commander in Chief of the front lines in the Northeast, where the Germans broke through. If there were weak spots in the front lines between Sedan and Mézières, if they weren't shored up in time with reinforcements, if there wasn't adequate matériel there, who is to be held responsible for that, if not the General in command of the area and the entire northeast region?

I asked to see a copy of those statements so that I could look them over and respond to them. The Examining Magistrate explained to me that it wouldn't be possible, for reasons of national security. I told him that it was a disgrace that he and the court would have to live with forever. He

---

54. Marx Dormoy, a Socialist who became Junior Minister under Léon Blum in 1936, and subsequently Interior Minister in 1937–1938. He voted against giving plenary powers to Pétain. On orders from the Vichy government, he was assassinated while under house arrest, apparently by terrorist elements of the Cagoule, an organization he had actively pursued while Minister of the Interior (see diary entries for July 24 and 31, 1941).

55. Horace de Carbuccia, Editor in Chief of the far-right weekly, *Gringoire*. He supported Marshal Pétain and the politics of collaboration.

started equivocating and said that those were the government's orders. I told him that in that case I wouldn't answer any more of his questions.

This is even better than the Dreyfus affair.

September 29, 1940

I waited for Ribet, but he didn't appear, probably because automobiles are not allowed on the roads on Sundays. Reread *Les Mémoires d'outre-tombe* again, the volume with the lovely narration of Chateaubriand's meeting with Charles X in Prague.

I heard that Reynaud expects to be released on his own recognizance.

September 30, 1940

A lovely day. Jean and Mazé stepped out of the mist that has settled over this crow's nest. We spent a good three hours together and, inexplicably, without any policemen lurking around. We just left the door to the room open. It's a small miracle.

Ribet arrived. He had met with the presiding judges in the Riom court. Some of them are feeling a kind of shame at having to sit in judgment at this trial, but they'll of course do as they're ordered. We sketched out a plan for my defense. I agreed with him that the verdict really doesn't matter. The government will dictate the verdict and might even have drafted it already. What counts is that we state the truth, that we let it be known and make it a part of the record. That is how we can best serve our country.

October 1, 1940

It rained all night. There were a few snowflakes in the morning. It rained throughout the day.

October 8, 1940

I haven't kept up with this diary for a week. Afternoons have been almost entirely taken up by meetings with Ribet or whatever reading I have been able to get done in the presence of the court recorder taking down the depositions of the military leaders here. What a pathetic lot they are. How could I ever have trusted such men? Yet they all conducted themselves honorably in 1914, although they were at considerably lower ranks then. On my brief official visits to the front, each of them had expressed the utmost confidence. Now they claim that they didn't have any weapons to fight with and that the battle was lost before the first shot was fired. They alternate between whining and bellowing.

The measure that Weygand pushed through to roll back the retirement age from sixty-two to sixty-five for members of the Supreme War Council was of disastrous consequence. I tried to get it repealed in November 1936 but ran into the opposition of the President of the Republic and General Gamelin, who had been named wartime Commander in Chief and who had absolute confidence in his fellow commanders. I should have held out. Of course, at the time, our military leaders were worried, or at least pretended to be worried, about certain incidents instigated by the Communists that I in fact decisively put down. I was told that if I named a new Supreme War Council at that point I would be sowing confusion in an already unstable structure. It was a major error not to have wiped that slate clean. What an amazing accumulation of incompetent individuals! What a bunch of weepers, whiners, and tremblers! They're armchair reactionaries made for political intrigue, each of them more a warmonger than a war maker, and all of them primarily interested in growing old and collecting their sizable pensions, not to mention the handsome income they receive from the various boards of directors they sit on. Weygand once launched a brilliant offensive against the Board of Directors of the Suez Canal and came away with some 400,000 francs a year to add to what was already a comfortable pension.

Others like them have lent their skills to the war industry or more or less directly to national defense. Some have gone into optics, some into oil. Once Weygand and others had taken that route, why wouldn't those who succeeded them? How could I not have gotten rid of pathetic old officers like Dufieux,[56] Prételat, Requin, and so many others of their kind? Poor old Gamelin pleaded their case with me from 1936 to 1939. Now that he is

---

56. General Julien Dufieux, Inspector General of Infantry and Tanks.

in Chazeron, they have shown their thanks by attacking him more con-
temptibly than anyone else testifying against him, whereas, when he was
Supreme Commander, they used to drip all over him with their flattery
and servility.

Dufieux was always moaning because he had not been given a medal.
Georges kept bowing and scraping, even though he was furious inside.
Prételat came and pleaded with me to name him Military Governor of
Paris (after Gouraud, a real hero, had vacated the position), swearing to me
with his hand on his heart that he was a republican and a friend of Paul-
Boncour[57] and Camille Chautemps. If I had pushed a little, I probably
could have gotten him to swear that he was a Freemason. These men were
born defeated, by virtue of their limited abilities, and they're the ones now
parading through the courthouse in Riom. Each of them shows up with his
list of charges, his little scraps of paper, and his big pile of crap. What a difference there is between them and the men who went into battle, like the
admirable General Frère and General Touchon; what a difference between them and real fighting men like Colonel Perré, the Commander of
the Second Armored Division, whose testimony, even if not entirely above
reproach, is still the word of a true soldier.

To lighten things up, we turn to *L'Action française*, where I see that our
favorite comedian, Charles Maurras,[58] has outdone himself—vilifying de
Gaulle, the British, and Churchill. The only people he hasn't worked over
are the Krauts. Then this hateful old man has the nerve to ask for contributions. He's also the only person encouraging people to turn informer.
Here too, he has had his comeuppance on occasion, but what does it matter to him if he has to retract what he writes from one issue to the next—
his slanderous comments have made their mark.

---

57. Joseph Paul-Boncour, leftist politician and former Prime Minister, who voted
against the establishment of Pétain's government in 1940.

58. Writer, political theorist, member of the Académie Française, who was a strong
supporter of Pétain. Maurras, a monarchist, was one of the founders of the nationalistic review *L'Action française*.

November 7, 1940[59]

On September 16, Mme Guyon, who is a close personal friend of Laval's, suggested to my secretary of many years, Mlle Mollet, that she go to see me in Chazeron; Pierre Laval would be pleased to supply her with the necessary authorizations. Mlle Mollet accepted the offer immediately; but instead of calling her back the next day, as had been agreed, Mme Guyon didn't get in touch with her again until October 2. Mme Guyon told her that she was dining with Laval that very evening and that she would call back the following day to let her know when she could make the trip. In fact, Mme Guyon didn't phone again until October 4, and then only to tell her that Laval could no longer procure the necessary authorizations. Mme Guyon carries a card with her, written in German, instructing German officials to consider her a German officer and treat her that way.

On September 20, M. Achenbach, who is with the German Embassy in Paris and whom Mlle Mollet had met, with my consent, several times before the war, called to say that he absolutely had to discuss with her certain matters of great urgency and importance.

They left together for Trouville on Saturday, September 21, at 9 A.M., accompanied by M. Jardin,[60] from the SNCF (French National Railroad). Their conversation lasted from 10 A.M. Saturday through Sunday evening. It dealt with the causes of the war, peace terms, the political climate in France, and the possibility of reuniting the country under the banner of the Radical Party! They asked about me and told her she could meet with me, after first meeting with M. Abetz, Germany's Ambassador to Paris. This is the very same Abetz that I had expelled from France as a spy before the war; now he is trying to enlist my support!

---

59. This is the story of the attempt by Abetz, Ribbentrop, Laval, Huntziger, Jardin, and Pétain to get Daladier to sign a document they had prepared showing Roosevelt to be a warmonger who had violated the laws of neutrality.

60. Jean Jardin, Laval's Chief of Staff in Vichy from 1941 to 1943. He was an associate of Raoul Dautry (see "1941," n. 25).

The following day, Mlle Mollet met with General Bineau[61] to apprise him of these conversations. He told her to keep him posted and, on arriving in Vichy, to inform General Huntziger, the only person with direct access to Marshal Pétain.

For several days, Achenbach, whom Mlle Mollet had advised of Mme Guyon's proposition, called to find out if she had in fact obtained the necessary papers. He had himself provided her with a Vichy pass valid for the week of October 13–20. When she spoke with him at noon on October 21 to ask him to extend it, he requested that she meet him at the Embassy immediately. There she would lunch with him and Ambassador Abetz.

Abetz had met with Laval and Alibert a day earlier. For the authorizations, he told Mlle Mollet to arrange for an appointment with Alibert as soon as she got to Vichy. Abetz and Achenbach were openly optimistic about the coming negotiations between the French and the Germans. They went back over the points they had raised in Trouville. They repeatedly asked her if there were any documents in Daladier's file proving that France had not wished to go to war, that it had done so only to fulfill a commitment, that Daladier would not have declared war had it not been for pressure from the British, who pledged complete cooperation, and had he not received the promise of American war matériel.

They said they had to have those documents by 10 A.M. the following day, October 22. Abetz knew that at 10 A.M., on the Ambassador's invitation, Laval would be leaving for a destination unknown to him and would end up face to face with Hitler in the latter's private train, somewhere in the countryside around Tours. Mlle Mollet told them that she would not be able to supply the documents in the allotted time. They pressed her to leave for Vichy and Chazeron at once. Achenbach gave her his word that Ribet's living quarters would not be searched before her return, although he knew that Ribet kept Daladier's file at his home, after having earlier entrusted it to the American Embassy in Paris.

---

61. General Henri Bineau was a Major General in September 1939. He was transferred to the War Minister's staff in January 1940 and subsequently became Pétain's Chief of Staff.

Mlle Mollet arrived in Vichy on October 23 but did not get to see General Huntziger until the 25th. She informed him of her conversations with the Germans. She also met with Alibert to request authorization to see me in Chazeron, but he put off giving her an answer. Then she heard that Laval wanted to see her. She went directly to his Ministry, where she was made to wait for a while before being informed that Laval had left and that she would be contacted by phone. It was not until Monday, October 28, that she learned from M. Anglade, Laval's Chief of Staff, and then from the Ministers of the Interior and of Justice, that she could meet with me in Chazeron without police inspectors present.

She got to Vichy at 5:30 that afternoon. M. Anglade told her that Brinon[62] had phoned from Paris several times in the course of the day to ask her to return there immediately, regardless of whether she had seen Prime Minister Daladier.

Nonetheless, she came to Chazeron on Tuesday morning at 8:45. I had been notified of her visit by M. Perrin, the warden of this bucolic Bastille, at 9 o'clock the previous evening. After relating all the conversations she had had, she told me pointedly that Abetz and Achenbach were in agreement with Laval and Pétain. All of them wanted a signed statement from me to be carried in the press and broadcast on the radio. I was to say that I hadn't wanted to go to war, that I had yielded under pressure from England and from the American Ambassador to Paris, who had promised to provide us with great quantities of matériel, but that now I was forced to acknowledge that England's aid had been seriously wanting just when we needed it most, and that the advice I had received from Mr. Bullitt was disastrous. Mlle Mollet showed me a typed draft of a statement drawn up along these lines, several paragraphs long. She added that Abetz and Achenbach thought the trial in Riom was absurd and that Laval and Brinon agreed. They were of a mind to let it drag on for a long time, perhaps until it was forgotten entirely. In the meantime, they could make my

---

62. Fernand de Brinon, newspaperman in charge of the Foreign Affairs desk at *L'Information.* He founded the Comité France-Allemagne in 1935. During the Occupation years, he was Vichy's representative to the German authorities in Paris. He was executed by firing squad in 1947.

stay at Chazeron far more enjoyable, starting right now, and allow someone close to me to keep me company, and so on. After thanking Mlle
Mollet for her trouble, I explained to her that if I ever signed a statement
of that sort, I might perhaps regain my freedom, but I would surely lose
my honor.

What do they expect to get out of this statement? First, it would
breathe new life into the violently anti-British campaign being waged in
French and German-Italian newspapers. Second, it would seriously implicate Bullitt, who is Roosevelt's personal friend, and present them both as
having insidiously played a role in our declaration of war and as presently
trying to bring the United States into it.

Wilkie is running on a strict isolationist platform. He is also apparently from a family of German immigrants, which has probably given
Ribbentrop the wrong idea.

Would such a statement from me mean better peace terms for France?
The German diplomatic corps might actually be working at cross-pur-
poses with the Reich's High Command, as was the case after Sadowa in
1866 and after Paris surrendered in 1871. It's perfectly conceivable that
they would prefer a policy of "collaboration," to use the term in vogue in
the French press, which has not yet figured out that this would guarantee
Germany control over our principal industries—metallurgy, mechanical
engineering, chemical engineering—and reduce France to the state of a
colony or a protectorate. As an approach, it is far less spectacular for the
victor and far less painful for the defeated nation than territorial annexation, but it is far more effective. It undermines virtually all the material
and moral reasons for revenge. In any event, even if I am wrong about the
"better peace terms" that Abetz and Achenbach are dangling in front of us,
a statement signed by me and issued from my prison cell in Chazeron
would have no sway with public or foreign opinion, in fact, no real impact
whatsoever. Besides which, isn't the policy of collaboration already a fait
accompli, given the meetings between Laval and Hitler and Pétain and
Hitler? Isn't our entire press urging us to collaborate? Hasn't Marshal
Pétain, with his last two public statements, already incriminated the government that was in office in September 1939 and condemned the pressure
that was supposedly brought to bear on us by England and international

Jewry? On the other hand, it is true that he has yet to implicate Bullitt and Roosevelt.

I told Mlle Mollet that I could certainly be mistaken and that if a statement from me could have a positive effect on the terms of the peace treaty, then in the sole interest of France, I was prepared to sign it unconditionally, but the French government would have to make that request of me. I was under the impression that Pétain was aware of these dealings, and Mlle Mollet confirmed that he was.

She left on Tuesday October 29 at around 10:30 in the morning and headed back to Paris in the Vice Premier's car, the same one that had brought her down to Chazeron. She was driven directly to the German Embassy and arrived there at 8 P.M. Achenbach apologized for having hastened her return to Paris, a decision with which he claimed Laval had concurred. Had she brought back any documents? Had she obtained a statement from me about the pressure exerted by England and the war supplies promised by the United States? They were needed to justify the lenient peace terms that were being negotiated. Mlle Mollet replied that she had not had the time to address issues of such moment. Achenbach caustically shot back that the other matter was no longer of interest to him, adding that counselor Ribet had come to see him on October 28 to request an extension for his pass to Vichy, and that in the course of their conversation, he asked Ribet whether there were any documents in the file relative to Britain's pressure and America's promise. Ribet had assured him there weren't. When Achenbach insisted that he return immediately to Chazeron to obtain the statement he wanted from me, Ribet had categorically refused.

At midnight on October 29, four German police officers showed up at Ribet's door with a search warrant. Having expected it, he had asked the head of the bar association to be present during the search. After poring over the file until 4 in the morning, the German officers left, taking with them a considerable number of documents. They came back for the remainder of the file the following morning around 10:30.

Mlle Mollet was to meet with either Laval or Brinon that same day, October 30. She saw Brinon and asked him to accompany her to the German Embassy. Achenbach told her that the search had been ordered only after she had failed to bring back a signed statement. The search had turned up a significant number of diplomatic memoranda and provided evidence proving that Bullitt had frequently met with Prime Minister Daladier in the days preceding the war. Abetz was present for part of the discussion. He claimed that Laval shared their views on all of this. Then he asked Mlle Mollet to head back down to Chazeron and emphasize to me how important this statement would be for France.

Mlle Mollet thus returned to Vichy on October 31. Laval had twice called his Chief of Staff Anglade from Paris to verify that the formalities for her meeting with me had been arranged. He had also called Peyrouton and requested that Mlle Mollet be allowed to see me without delay. Peyrouton admitted her and provided her with the necessary papers.

I met with Mlle Mollet at 10:30 on the morning of November 1, without having been told she was coming. She left me as dusk was falling, to keep an appointment with Laval in Vichy. She recounted the events of her last few days, adding that Laval had asked her to insist that I prepare a statement dealing with the causes of the war and assigning responsibility for it. She said that he would have it published immediately and that it would be in the best interests of the nation. It would be the first act of Franco-German collaboration and in the eyes of the Germans would justify more generous peace terms.

I thanked her and dictated a few comments, which she took down in shorthand, to be typed up when she got back. I noted first that at the same time as negotiations were being carried out with me, unannounced searches were being carried out at my lawyer's residence; second, that while Laval was imploring me to write that statement, his personal friends were submitting affidavits against me in Riom, in utter bad faith and with a hatred that spoke volumes. To be sure, this would in no way prevent me from performing any act whatsoever that might bring France more favorable peace terms, but I did not believe that the statement I had been asked to prepare would produce such a result.

I felt they should once and for all back up what they were saying with specifics. Until I was shown otherwise, I wouldn't believe that there was any more to it than what had been said in Marshal Pétain's speech and Laval's communiqué. Besides, I intended to present my account of what brought on the war in the courthouse in Riom. I added, moreover, that I could not submit a statement of that kind without first having it reviewed by my lawyer, and that it seemed reasonable to conclude that if Mlle Mollet had been asked to make a second trip to Chazeron, documents implicating Bullitt, the United States, and England had not been found among my papers. I said to her, "If you should see Laval this evening, who you said is expecting you, tell him to call counselor Ribet so that he can head back down here."

I was surprised to see Mlle Mollet again at 6 P.M. on November 2. She had not met with Laval but had managed to see General Huntziger. It was the latter's opinion that although the statement might conceivably be used against me at the Riom trial, it could improve chances for better peace terms for France. Mlle Mollet departed at 7:30. I have since learned that she and Mme Guyon were driven in an official limousine to Moulins, where a German officer and a car had been waiting for them since that morning. Because they arrived so late, they spent the night in a hotel before leaving on the following morning, Sunday, November 3.

On November 5, a Paris correspondent for the *Moniteur*, Laval's newspaper, submitted an interview Brinon had given to a "representative from the American press" with insinuations about the role played by "an unidentified high-ranking American official" and emphasizing France's position, etc., etc. It was a pathetic, ineffectual article. Anyway, it came too late; Roosevelt was reelected on November 5.[63]

I have not had to wait long to find out what all this means for me. The head warden has begun the paperwork for my incarceration.[64]

---

63. In this way, acting in secret, Daladier was able to buy a little time by misleading both the Germans and Vichy. Roosevelt would be grateful to him for this throughout the war.

64. In the middle of November, Daladier, together with Blum, Gamelin, and La Chambre (see "1941," n. 16), were transferred to a country estate at Bourassol, a few miles south of Riom. The dilapidated old house served as their new prison.

December 15, 1940

Yesterday morning, the head prison guard, looking furtive, came to me and said: "I heard that there was a sensational arrest in Vichy. And Mussolini has been assassinated and the Prince of Piedmont is marching on Rome." The Italians are intelligent and well informed, but I found it hard to believe that piece of "news."

As for the "sensational arrest," I had absolutely no doubt that the story was true and bet him that it was Laval, an opinion shared by Master Sergeant Passemard, an old, intelligent, kindly veteran of the Moroccan campaign, who is always trying to be helpful. He had been telling me these last few days that Laval's popularity had plummeted, even in the Puy-de-Dôme, where he is from, and that virtually everyone, from the upper middle class to the workers, was accusing him of corrupting officials, taking payoffs, and misappropriating public funds. British radio announcers keep labeling him a traitor, and British broadcasts are given considerable credit in Unoccupied France, just as they are in the Occupied Zone. I had also heard that Flandin had come down and set up residence in Vichy a few days ago. In the desert, when you see a jackal leave his lair, you know he's smelled the sweet scent of a carcass ... or a Minister's portfolio.

One of the young guards, Guichard, brought in the newspapers and left without saying a word. There were blaring headlines: "Pierre Laval No Longer a Member of the Government." "Laval Replaced as Foreign Affairs Minister by Pierre-Etienne Flandin." Marshal Pétain had given an eight-sentence speech on the radio that was reprinted in the newspapers: "I have just made a decision that I believe to be in the best interests of the nation. M. Pierre Laval is no longer a member of my Cabinet. M. Pierre-Etienne Flandin is now in charge of Foreign Affairs. Constitutional Act Number 4, naming my successor, is hereby rescinded. I have resolved to make this decision for compelling political reasons. It in no way alters our relationship with Germany. I remain at the helm. The National Revolution will continue to move forward." And as every drama has its light moment, a philosophy professor named Chevalier, with a particular gift for looking ridiculous, who has wooed and worn down every Cabinet for the last twenty years with his tedious flattery and platitudes, has been named Minister of Education.

So once again we find ourselves in the midst of a ministerial crisis. Ever since the creation of the New Order, whose continuity and administrative stability were to be its cornerstones, not a month has gone by without some palace revolution to purge a few Ministers and replace them with others. But today's is the most significant crisis of all. It is not just Vice Premier Laval who has been unseated, it's the heir apparent, the man Pétain had designated to succeed him when he leaves us for that paradise that awaits cautious warriors such as he. Laval had surrounded himself with men of action, all of them, like himself, thoroughly devoid of scruples, and they proved to be of tremendous help to him in Bordeaux, in anesthetizing Albert Lebrun and putting a stranglehold on Paul Reynaud and then, after they joined forces with the general staffs of Pétain and Weygand, in handing France over to the Germans. He spent more time in Paris than in Vichy, the better to play up to the victors, but in doing so—a fatal slip—he left the field open for his enemies, Alibert and Peyrouton. Laval was the man behind Déat's articles and similar pieces in other papers attacking his adversaries and the Royalist- and church-dominated government in Vichy. All of this he did as the German Ambassador, whom he had managed to win over, looked on indulgently. His frequent stays in Paris led to his downfall. How could he not have understood that? And when that little rat Montigny,[65] with his menacing mouth and his twisted nose, abandoned the Laval ship a few days earlier, how could the sly lord of Châteldon have failed to see the ominous meaning of that?

Peyrouton and Alibert would never have been able to accomplish this without the help of the coterie of officers in civilian clothes who surround and manipulate Pétain. Laval had threatened both of these Ministers, without ever translating talk into action, which is the ultimate act of imprudence. None of these people liked him. They found him insolent, vulgar, and underhanded. They were bruised by his appointment as heir apparent, and black and blue from the blows delivered by Déat and the pro-Laval press in Paris. But who would have guessed that the Marshal

---

65. Jean Montigny, unaffiliated member of the Left and close associate of President Caillaux. In Vichy, he voted to give Pétain plenary powers and was later named to the Conseil National, Vichy's pseudo-parliament.

himself, who ever since Doumergue's death had been young Laval's trump card, his associate and accomplice through all the twists and turns of French politics, who would ever have guessed that he would desert the cunning Auvergnard and throw him to the wolves, when he owed him so much? No one would have believed it possible. Apparently Pétain and his entourage finally made up their minds to do something about the domestic political situation.

Laval was toppled because he worked exclusively to promote his own interests. He saw himself as a führer, like Hitler or Mussolini, at the head of a one-party system, a French National Socialist Party, with Déat as a sort of party ideologist. National socialism or socialist nationalism, the name reads the same backwards and forwards—like Laval's.

"Compelling political reasons," Marshal Pétain is supposed to have said. I can't imagine any other kind. He specifically denied any departure from the policy of collaboration with Germany. Bringing in Flandin adds respectability. He was already pro-Hitler before the war, whereas Laval first adopted that line in Bordeaux. Besides, Hitler was consulted by Pétain about Flandin and approved the appointment. Our great patriot Pétain actually solicited the approval of the conquering enemy before naming his Foreign Minister. No French government in history ever stooped so low. Last of all, the Constitution that the National Revolution has been assembling piece by piece since July of this year is now the subject of an operation aimed at "arresting the spread." They've disposed not only of the heir apparent but of the very idea of having one. Should M. Pétain return to tending his olive trees or be called by the Lord, his successor will be chosen directly from among the members of the Cabinet. That's one fine conclave we can look forward to. In the meantime, they'll continue to be at each other's throats.

I never really got to know Pierre Laval until 1926, when we were both members of Briand's Cabinet.[66] In 1914, although he was barely thirty-one years old, he stayed riveted to his seat in the Chamber of Deputies. He re-

---

66. Aristide Briand, Socialist statesman, twenty-three times a Minister, Prime Minister eleven times.

mained there throughout the war, without ever once displaying a desire to breathe in the air of the trenches. At least he never gave a patriotic speech.

In truth, he quickly became a proponent of peace at any cost and, without involving himself directly, supported the Socialist Deputies and other Socialist Party members who went to Kienthal at the height of the war to confer with elected representatives from Germany. A little later, faced with the prospect of a long, drawn-out war, in a speech on the floor of Parliament that is painful to read today, he lent his support to a peace conference in Stockholm with Germany, sponsored by Socialists from a number of countries. This poor revolutionary Socialist, who could barely pay for the clothes on his back, suddenly became fabulously wealthy at the end of the war, at a time when many war profiteers were seeing their fortunes reduced to the subsistence level or going bankrupt. Their estates had been placed, as it were, in Laval's personal receivership.

He had had dealings with Stavisky,[67] who once presented him with a magnificent painting that hung in Villa Saïd, Laval's beautiful house on the Avenue du Bois, in appreciation for either his arbitrating some matter or his offering legal counsel. By intervening with Assistant Prosecutor Albert Prince, he had obtained a long series of postponements that amounted to a virtual dismissal of the case against Stavisky, which was of considerable benefit to the Foncière, headed by his friend Hudelot, a former Prefect. It later surfaced that these postponements had benefited Stavisky as much as they had Hudelot, and that disclosure led directly to Prince's suicide, which the Royalist clique naturally represented as a murder perpetrated by either the Freemasons or the police.

Laval was able to involve himself in these various machinations, once he had shed his Socialist garb, as Minister of Justice in the Briand-Painlevé government. Before the war, he was the capitalists' choice to defend their interests from within the government.

When he became Prime Minister, he held on to power for a time by buying off some of the more mediocre and compliant Deputies in Parliament. His associate Stora was specifically assigned to transact this dirty

---

67. Serge Alexandre, alias Sacha Stavisky, the man responsible for the financial scandal that served as a pretext for the riots of February 6, 1934.

business, and he did so masterfully. Laval used his position to enrich the people who backed him and, of course, himself, as in 1935 when he instituted the so-called deflationary policy, which consisted of lowering the wages and retirement benefits for people of modest means, thus carrying us out of an economic crisis on the backs of the neediest. With his hatred both for French democracy, which had never forgiven him for the values he had renounced, and for England and the United States, which had always viewed him with suspicion, he was also a voice within the government for international fascism. He acted as if he were Mussolini's friend; during the war in Ethiopia, he kept up a personal correspondence with him, which I had occasion to read while at the Quai d'Orsay, all of which placed him in a highly compromising situation. Officially, he upheld the League of Nations vote to impose economic sanctions on Italy, but in practice he did all he could to render the sanctions meaningless. After 1936, he became a constant table companion of, first, the Italian Ambassador, then, the Spanish Ambassador, and defended the interests of both of these countries against those of his own. In 1939, he voted in favor of war allocations but sided with Montigny, Brinon, Tixier-Vignancour, and the other defeatists on the Comité France-Allemagne, although he did so far more adroitly than any of the others.

France's defeat in July finally brought Laval his revenge and his triumph. In Bordeaux, he was able to achieve in the political arena what Pétain and Weygand had managed with the military: getting France to capitulate. He stormed into the Cabinet room with a group of defeatist Senators and Deputies behind him and put on a show of intimidation that he had been working up since May 19. Then, once a shattered Paul Reynaud had stepped aside, Laval set his sights on the seat of power, and as a result of the cowardice of the leaders of the Republic, instead of being thrown into jail with his accomplices, he became the virtual head of the government overseeing the capitulation. In a cynical book entitled, as one might imagine, *Toute La Vérité* (The whole truth), Montigny extols the victory of Laval and his gang. These days, he must be having it pulled off the shelves.

Was Laval actually arrested, as rumor has had it for the last two days? It wouldn't surprise me. Our conquering enemies have no reason at all to show him special consideration. They might be intimidated by his capacity for intrigue, although with Parliament having fallen into disgrace, he has become an infinitely less dangerous man. When there is no bargaining to be done, when there are no men to be bought and sold, there is little room for Laval to display his great talents, which are essentially those of a horse trader. He doesn't need a speaker's platform to be effective; in fact, he is generally ill at ease there, especially when launching extemporaneously into a heated debate. He prefers the back corridors of power and those parliamentary sessions that go on for hours, where he can flatter and corrupt and promise whomever he meets a few thousand francs, or civil service jobs, or a few positions as court reporter, or a Minister's portfolio or two. If Pétain has decided to bring down the man to whom he owes so much, clearly that man is no longer to be feared.

It might be a mistake for Flandin to start celebrating his newfound success. His career might turn out to be shorter than he expects, even if he did send congratulatory telegrams to Hitler and Mussolini two years ago.

December 17, 1940

Otto Abetz, Germany's Ambassador to France, arrived in Vichy on Monday evening, December 16. He was received the following morning at 10 o'clock by Marshal Pétain, in the Sévigné Pavilion. An infantry guard gave him military honors.

"The Chief of State invited him to an official luncheon in his honor, attended by Admiral Darlan, Minister of the Navy; General Huntziger, War Minister; and M. Baudouin, Special Counsel to the Executive." The Germans have remained loyal to their servants and their accomplices, the kind of loyalty common among thieves. Abetz stepped off the train in Vichy and was immediately surrounded by more than a dozen machine gun–toting German soldiers and policemen, who escorted him everywhere. I doubt very much that Abetz beat around the bush with Pétain. He must have demanded from him what Laval had already conceded: unobstructed passage across French territory for 300,000 German soldiers headed for Italy.

I have learned from one of the people who came to see me that Abetz met with Pierre Laval during the afternoon following yesterday's luncheon.

December 18, 1940

Today's newspapers are carrying the following item: "Marshal Pétain has met with Pierre Laval to discuss the general state of the nation." What a farce! They have put together a board of directors chaired by Darlan, with Huntziger and Flandin as vice chairs.

Darlan met with Hitler in his private train, near Beauvais. The skillfully worded terms of the Armistice worked out in June 1940 are long forgotten. The Germans keep piling on the demands, and Darlan and Pétain are their willing servants.

1941

January 2, 1941

As I reflect on the American elections and Roosevelt's new term, I am reminded of what Bullitt once told me, that Roosevelt would really be in a position to intervene in the war only if he were returned to office a third time.

There is no denying that the Americans harbored ill feelings about France's refusal to settle her debts from 1914–1918, or that they campaigned against us strenuously. In a phone conversation with Roosevelt in 1939, I went as far as to tell him that I wanted to pay them back what we owed. He laughed and said: "What for? I'd just put your check in the safe and never cash it."

January 7, 1941

Yesterday, having been elected President of the great American republic for a third time, Roosevelt went up to Capitol Hill and spoke to the Congress.

At a time when heroic England has refused Hitler's offers of peace and is alone in waging a debilitating war in the air and at sea, at a time when so many statesmen elsewhere have resigned themselves to the situation or become accomplices in it, Roosevelt hurled defiance at the world's dictators. He has been untiring in his skillful efforts to bring American public opinion to support his views. He has come an incredible way since his first term.

This marks the definitive break of the United States with the arrogant, isolationist policy that brought about the downfall of the League of Nations and was one of the essential causes of the second world war.

January 10, 1941

Why haven't Herriot[1] and Jeanneney[2] convened parliamentary sessions? What are they afraid of? It was their duty to do so.

January 21, 1941

The German-Soviet Pact has been reinforced. The "alliance cemented in blood" during the war against Poland is being further strengthened by significantly increased shipments of oil and wheat. The USSR has become vital to the Third Reich's interests and its principal supplier. These shipments have effectively neutralized the Allied blockade.

February 1, 1941

9:30 A.M. Ribet and Mazé. Once again we discussed the causes of the war and compared Bonnet's phone calls, which have been doctored, with the telegrams included in the blue book.

The Germans deliberately sought war; they made it inevitable. They were convinced, moreover, that they would be able to break the ties between France and England. I now believe that that was the point of the Italian proposal calling for a conference similar to the one held in Munich.

What really transpired between Ribbentrop and Bonnet in Paris in 1938? Which one of them is lying? From December to August, Bonnet acted as if Ribbentrop were the liar. It seems to me the opposite is true. I should review the facts to see if Bonnet didn't actually encourage Ribbentrop's Eastern European ventures.

For years now, I have thought that only America's industrial capacity could match Germany's. America's isolationism represented the greatest danger facing Western democracies. I was the first to order planes, convinced as I was that American industry, once its productive machinery had been set into motion, could match Germany's aviation production within two or three years.

---

1. Edouard Herriot, President of the Chamber of Deputies
2. Jules Jeanneney, President of the Senate.

Thanks to my friendship with Ambassador Bullitt, who is as much a Frenchman as the most patriotic Frenchman among us, I was able to get Roosevelt to intervene personally on several occasions. In particular, in May and October 1938, he helped us overcome a great many obstacles that confronted us when we tried to place orders with American factories. I can still hear that kindly voice of his, when I called him from Ambassador Bullitt's office, expressing his affection for France and offering me encouragement in my efforts on behalf of an Army fighting for freedom.

At the beginning of the summer of 1939, I was sufficiently worried about the worsening international situation to wonder whether the time had not come for America to step in on the side of Great Britain and France. In carefully worded terms, Bullitt put the question to Roosevelt and brought back his answer. Roosevelt felt that the majority of Americans still believed that the United States could, and should, stay out of European affairs.

Needless to say, the President said he would work through diplomatic channels to defend peace and the freedom of nations. If the situation were to worsen in Europe, he said, he would be able to intervene only after being reelected, and that could come to pass only if his health allowed him to run for a third term. That time is now at hand. On July 1, 1939, there were only 174,000 men in military service in America, all of them volunteers, spread out over 130 bases. There were few officers, and their equipment dated almost entirely from the last war. Beginning in May 1940, after Roosevelt's messages to Congress on May 16 and 31, the Army received appropriations of $2 billion, and that amount was subsequently increased in congressional committees. On September 16, the draft was put into effect, with the result that the number of men in service jumped almost instantly to more than 1.5 million. The training of officers was organized on a broad scale, and America's industry, with its enormous war potential, took on the task of equipping its Army, under the leadership of General Marshall, the Commander in Chief.

America's aviation industry had excellent prototypes to work with. They had been mass produced in 1938, thanks largely to orders placed first by France, then Britain, and finally France and Britain jointly.

By June 1940, French orders for American-built planes had risen to more than $500 million worth. So why did the French Air Force receive no more than 500 planes—all of them in fact excellent—during the war? In compliance with American laws, we had to wait three months before the embargo prohibiting the export of war supplies could be lifted, but the resulting delay could easily have been made up for by shipping parts, under the protection of our Navy. They could have shipped them to Caen and Bordeaux, where we had set up heavily protected assembly plants. Unfortunately, the French Air Force's High Command—without consulting me, but probably with the approval of the War Ministry—had them routed instead to Casablanca, where no such assembly plants existed, where everything had to be improvised. That is the principal reason—which I didn't know until it was too late—why France received only 500 planes. We could have been supplied with 1,000 warplanes to fight alongside our 2,000 modern French aircraft in May and June 1940. That is, if the Air Force High Command had wanted us to.

On June 16, 1940, Colonel Jacquin, the head of the French Air Force's mission in the United States, learned that the new government in Bordeaux was going to ask for an armistice. Pétain had the power to revoke Jacquin's authority or invalidate previously made agreements at any time. He could even have issued an order for the planes to remain in the United States. Colonel Jacquin courageously moved to transfer all the French contracts to the British purchasing commission that Purvis headed, thus allowing the war matériel intended for France to go to England, at a time that was critical for her salvation, in fact for all of Europe's salvation.

Prior to July 1, 1940, France and Britain, having been threatened and then attacked by Hitler, ordered a total of 10,000 aircraft. In the two and a half years from January 1, 1938, to June 30, 1940, the U.S. Army and Navy ordered a mere 5,400. In July 1940, the monthly output moved up to 550, and it continued increasing thereafter.[3]

In his admirable inaugural address, Roosevelt announced America's departure from her isolationist policies, her desire to become the arsenal of

---

3. In a speech given after the war, Edward R. Stettinius, Roosevelt's Secretary of State, noted that it was as a result of French orders first placed in 1938 that American industry had been able to supply the Allied forces beginning in 1942.

democratic nations, increase her military strength, and guarantee freedom of the high seas. This will surely draw America into war with Germany.

February 7, 1941

Meanwhile, Mazé went to Clermont Ferrand to meet with the brilliant young commander Jacquot,[4] who told him: "Everything I have learned has confirmed my belief that enormous blunders were committed by our military commanders. In fact, by the third day of the attack, there were no military commanders. There were neither orders nor chains of command. Large amounts of equipment were stupidly left sitting in hangars. The will to lead was totally absent.

"There was a complete collapse in French military thinking. The men who were responsible for the defeat are the men now reorganizing the French Army of the Armistice. General Huntziger, who bears greater responsibility than anyone, is absolutely loathed by everyone in the military."

They have been hounding Jacquot, but he is determined either to go on thinking his own thoughts or leave the Army.

Ribet and Mazé returned the same day, accompanied by Croquez, a young lawyer and veteran of the fighting in Belgium. He came to tell me that at 12:30 P.M. British radio had announced the capture of Benghazi.

What joy, what brightness filled this prison.

I spread the news, which everyone welcomed enthusiastically. The prisoners and the guards share similar feelings. In fact, the guards would much prefer to have other inmates, and they would be happy to handpick them from among the members of the Cabinet, or even better, from among those traitors in Paris who have been playing the role of Germany's valets for several years now. We have been following the British advance

---

4. Pierre-Elie Jacquot, a captain in the Third Bureau (Operations), who was in constant contact with Edouard Daladier's staff. He commanded a battalion from April to June 1940, then joined the Army's Resistance Forces (L'Organisation de la Résistance de l'Armée) in 1942. After having served as a colonel in the *maquis* and then in the Alsace-Lorraine brigade, he joined the First French Army. By the end of his career, he was an Army General and Commander of NATO forces at Fontainebleau.

together on maps. Their progress is continuing, through Eritrea, Somalia, and Abyssinia.

After my guests had left, I asked to see the prison guard, that is, the kindly prison guard, Passemard, who had been away that afternoon. I gave him the news. He gushed with emotion and shook my hand. We raised a glass to the capture of Benghazi.

February 25, 1941

Darlan has been handed the reins of power.

Mazé, who knew Darlan well, met with him for an hour in Vichy, at 11:30 in the morning. "I have seen Hitler; he agrees that I should be Prime Minister," Darlan said. "We have to defeat our enemy, England."

He was undoubtedly a less than scrupulous broker in the negotiations. The Germans have been pressuring Pétain, but then so have the Americans, for opposite reasons. Pétain had told Chauvel,[5] with whom he's very close, that he was afraid of the Germans.

Flandin has resigned. In an exchange of letters, the Marshal told him that "he had nobly sacrificed himself for France." That was followed by an item from the Havas News Agency exalting Flandin's sacrifice. It's a kind of hedge against the future, not unlike the waiting game almost everyone was playing before the war. By 1936, Flandin had been prepared to surrender anything he had.

Since then, we have been deluged with constitutional decrees. Darlan has been appointed Minister of Foreign Affairs, Minister of the Radio and the Press, and Minister of the Navy; he has even been named France's heir apparent, just as they use to do in the days of Hugh Capet.

In the meantime, all sorts of laudatory statements have been issued about his career and his person: "The grandson and great-grandson of sailors." Who were the parents?

---

5. Henry Chauvel, Edouard Daladier's second lawyer.

March 18, 1941

Saw Blum when he came back from his walk. He showed me the text of Roosevelt's speech, the speech of a nation at war: "The Vital Bridge Across the Ocean."

I find Blum's optimism frightening.

The British government will move to Canada if it has to, and the naval battle will continue.

The Krauts have opposed the release of Reynaud and Mandel. As for the Vichy government, they are annoyed with themselves for having demanded that we be put on trial, but they won't take any new initiatives. In Paris, they have freed Langeron.[6] He had been forced into retirement while he was being held prisoner!

March 20, 1941

Was absolutely delighted to see Roger Génébrier, a fine and faithful friend, the finest of them all. He recounted Peyrouton's ignominious attempts to have him demoted just because he is a friend of mine. Peyrouton had tried the same thing with his brother-in-law, Monnier, who is also a Prefect and one of my friends.

March 21, 1941

Ribet came by again at 10:30 A.M. He had met with Lagarde, who confirmed that the government was in the process of rewriting Constitutional Act Number 7, granting itself the authority to postpone ongoing trials whenever the interests of the nation so dictate. A fine example of new French law!

The truth is that neither Pétain, Darlan, nor Barthélemy[7] wants anything to do with this trial, even though they are the ones who initiated it. They are afraid there will be unavoidable incidents and a public indictment of military Generals. This is what Ribet thinks, and he so informed Le Trocquer, Blum's attorney.

---

6. Roger Langeron, former Prefect of Police.

7. Joseph Barthélemy, Minister of Justice.

Génébrier related the admissions and platitudes that constituted his talk with Chavin, better known as "tricky Chavin." Like so many others, Chavin and Peyrouton, who were once at my feet, have been unrelenting in their efforts to destroy the people close to me, who were once their friends.

March 23, 1941

Had lunch with Génébrier. He was in Paris the day after the government headed south. He found the city mournful, completely deserted. He had a difficult time finding an open restaurant. At the War Ministry, where it had been decided that an officer would remain in charge, he saw only one NCO, two antiriot policemen at the door, and, in place of the guard inside, Maury, the chauffeur!

He also told me about a conversation Ribet had had with Bonnet at the Hotel Pailleret. Bonnet was scared and spent two hours trying to defend his position. He protested that he had remained absolutely faithful to me, and so on and so forth. He added that the government was doing everything it could to save Gamelin. Some of my friends have joined up with the Vichy government.

Daridan[8] came to see me this evening. We went for a stroll in the courtyard. He is a good man. He spoke to me about the new Europe and the plans the English supposedly have for the future.

March 24, 1941

It has been rainy and bitter cold, but this afternoon, while he was out for his walk, Blum managed to find some sunlight. Sitting there with his beret,

---

8. Jean Daridan, career diplomat who prior to the war held positions on the staffs of Herriot and Paul-Boncour. After having worked with the French Committee of National Liberation in Algiers, he served in numerous government capacities, among them Ambassador to Japan and India. He was a close associate of Daladier's and provided the footnotes for the French edition of this diary. The English-language annotations are substantially based on his.

his long skinny body and walrus mustache, which is almost entirely white, he looked very much the prophet of Israel.

3 P.M. Théry and I discussed our reasons for being hopeful. He brought me copies of the depositions given by Happish and General Corap. The latter was not questioned once about the defeat at the Meuse. I continued reading Gamelin's memoirs and found his loyalty wanting on more than one occasion.

Then my former associate, Léonard,[9] arrived. He too had met with Commander Jacquot, who felt that Germany versus an England backed by the United States would be an even match. Jacquot stated that everyone in the Army was hostile to the High Command. It is his hope that if Germany should falter, the new French Army could play some role. There is enough equipment to arm 300,000 men. Young men have been sneaking illegally into the Unoccupied Zone to enlist.

Léonard said that in the winter of 1939, Pétain had told him that he didn't think Gamelin was fit to command the French Army. Léonard said that he then asked : "Have you informed Prime Minister Daladier of this?" Pétain answered, "No, let him handle it."

March 27, 1941

Mazé has been held up by the Germans, who have refused to give him a pass. The orders they have placed with French factories are for immediate delivery only, for the war will have been won by year's end, or so they claim.

Received a strange letter from a woman in Brittany telling me that the Germans had laid waste to the woods near her home and hidden camouflaged cannons and trucks there. Is this just one part of a more extensive operation in preparation for an impending invasion of England?

Chauvel confirmed that a new law has been enacted, modifying Constitutional Act Number 7 and allowing for the postponement of trials.

---

9. Roger Léonard, member of Edouard Daladier's staff from 1938 to 1940.

"That should be a good thing both for France and for you," he added. That is not my opinion.

Read a thoroughly disgraceful interview with de Brinon.

March 28, 1941

When the guard left his post momentarily, Spanien, one of Blum's lawyers, took advantage of the situation and stopped off to see me, after leaving his client. Blum wanted him to inform me of the coup d'état in Belgrade. Peter II is setting up a new government that will include every political party. Is this merely a matter of internal politics, or will it undermine their pact with Hitler and Mussolini? Whatever the case, it is a magnificent example of a popular uprising.

Blum, however, went even further, with his prophetic imagination conjuring images of a "German Army threatened on its right flank by the Greeks and on the left by the Turks." He gives me the shivers.

The British took Keran and Harrar at the very time Italian communiqués were claiming that all attacks there had been repelled.

March 28, 1941, afternoon

At 3 P.M. Théry came to see me at the prosecutor's request. He was flushed and visibly ill at ease. A few smoked sardines and a glass of the cognac Génébrier had brought me helped him find the nerve to show me an important document, one that they refuse to give me a copy of, on grounds of national security! "But," he said, "you can make your own copy."

It was the deposition of Colonel Rivet, a good man whom I knew well. He stated that the number of German tanks actually engaged in the Battle of France on May 10 was at most 3,600.[10] Well, on that same date, we had 3,000 tanks, with superior armor plating and superior weaponry. This is a vital document. The first part of it includes a rather hypocritical letter from Picquendar. Had our commanders done their duty, there is no reason why we should have been defeated.

---

10. In Vichy and even in London, the figure generally cited was 8,000. There were actually fewer than 3,000.

April 1, 1941

The Italian Navy has suffered another defeat in the Mediterranean. The Italian squadron was spotted by the RAF off the southwest coast of Crete. The *Littorio* was hit by a bomb and fled. The English squadron gave chase and sank three cruisers and two torpedo boats.

What overblown ideas we had about Italian naval power before the war. The Franco-British plan to secure the Mediterranean called for the entire French fleet and 200,000 tons of British shipping. This proves once again that we should have continued fighting in North Africa. We could have knocked out the Italians in a matter of weeks.

In 1939, I drew up a plan for the occupation of Salonika ... but the British were against it. They held certain illusions about Italy and wanted at all costs to appease her with concessions, French concessions, naturally.

3 P.M. Théry returned. He lives in Douai and has four kids. He was a prisoner in Germany in 1914. His father was mistreated by the Germans and eventually died from the abuse. He brought me greetings from the President and Vice President of the Army's National Federation of Volunteers.

April 6, 1941

Jean came. He has been a little discouraged by life in his high school in Marseilles. He kept coming back to this idea he has about going to England to enlist.

2 P.M. One of the guards, Lelauze, told me that Germany had attacked Yugoslavia. Belgrade is being bombed. Greece is at war; Thrace is occupied. Those are two great peoples.

Blum told me through his window that Hitler was going to run into the same kind of quagmire there that defeated Napoleon in Russia. I pointed out to him that this was a Russia with a network of roads and railroads and with aircraft flying overhead.

April 7, 1941

French newspapers have confirmed the German invasion of Greece and Yugoslavia.

Hitler claims, naturally, that Germany is merely defending herself against the Greek ogre and the Serbian bear that have attacked her. Anyone who doesn't revere slavery is an enemy of peace.

Russia had signed a nonaggression pact with Yugoslavia on the very day the Germans invaded.

The English have taken Addis Ababa. The Duke of Aosta and his Army have fled the city and taken refuge in the mountains. There are strikes and factory sit-ins in America, just as there were in France in 1936, and they are just as unconscionable.

In reading the newspapers, I learned that my apartment in Paris had been ransacked.

April 14, 1941

In spite of Blum's prophecies, the Yugoslav Army has been routed; they were taken by surprise in the middle of their mobilization efforts. There was a severe shortage of modern equipment. Just as in France and Poland, those Yugoslavs who either believed in Hitler or were on his payroll had a major hand in it. Bulgaria and Hungary are rushing in to get a share of the spoils.

Stalin and Matsuoka[11] have signed a treaty of friendship and nonaggression, leaving Japan free to take on the Americans.

I saw Blum with his daughter from my window. He remains optimistic. He thinks that the Sino-Russian pact has no real meaning. He also said that Yugoslavia and Greece could hold out for a month. He believes what he wants to believe.

April 15, 1941

The saddest day of all. According to a dispatch reprinted in *La Montagne*, the British are evacuating their troops from Greece.

I sent the following note to Blum: "Now Crete has fallen.

"Did you notice that the English neglected to destroy their airfields in the Northwest of the island prior to the German invasion?

---

11. Matsuoka Yosuke, Japanese Minister.

"I have a bad feeling about this.

"I fear that if American warships don't start protecting British convoys, the British government will have to retreat to Canada this summer.

"How could the 40,000 British soldiers stationed on Crete not successfully defend it?

"As for Admiral Darlan's speech, I think it is the work of a jackal. What about you?"

Blum sent back the following reply: "I saw in *La Montagne* that the criticism leveled against the English commanders, although by no means groundless, came from the Air and Sea Editor of the *Sunday Times.* Generals are the same everywhere.

"My feelings about the situation are not negative. Iraq was won back without a shot fired, which is a vital point; Hitler has got a lot riding on the Iraqi card. It took the Germans twelve full days of uninterrupted fighting to take Crete, with the English struggling under the worst conditions imaginable.

"With regard to the protection of convoys, Roosevelt made his position absolutely clear in the copy of the speech I gave you. It will be a good many weeks, in fact probably months, before they'll be able to attack England again.

"As for Admiral Darlan's speech, that is another matter entirely. I found it even more reprehensible than the previous one, but I interpret it differently from the way you do. First of all, it seems to me that his main idea is to put the Marshal in an untenable position. The Admiral believes that his time has come and he is growing impatient. Moreover, Germany's repeated attempts to provoke a split between England and France and between the United States and France are not signs of strength, quite the opposite. ... They show just how much the Germans need us.

"We now find Germany more and more deeply involved in a peripheral action in the Mediterranean, one that she would have given anything to avoid; it is costing her in troops, in troop carriers, in oil, and most of all, in time. She has had to postpone indefinitely launching a single, decisive strike, which has become increasingly risky. Months have gone by already. Read Roosevelt's speech again and take heart, the way he has."

In the April 13 issue of the *Journal de Genève*, René Payot offers a defense of Pétain in the following terms: "We must rally round our leader. ... The Armistice was the least harmful solution for the nation. ... The French psyche had been so perverted that it would have been impossible for us to follow the Queen of Holland's example and refuse to capitulate. ... The Marshal has opted for a reasonable approach, instead of a jingoistic one."

He went on to say that the actions de Gaulle was engaged in were dangerous for France and that peace alone could allow us to rebuild ourselves morally and materially, etc., etc.[12]

April 22, 1941

Jacomet,[13] the former Inspector General, has arrived. He too is to be interned here with us. He is accused of having failed to fulfill his professional obligations. I had heard that he was coming and so informed the guards, with the idea of offering him some small consolation.

I spotted him near the entrance. His back was hunched, his face pale, and his eyes looked hollow with fatigue. He seemed to be in a profound state of depression. The shock has apparently had serious consequences, or so I fear.

I asked my lawyers, Ribet and Chauvel, to go and give him my regards. Jacomet insisted on seeing me. I had them tell him that I would try to talk with him from my window tomorrow, when he went out for his walk. He assured me profusely of his undying loyalty. It all makes me very sad.

Word has it that the Germans have been exerting pressure to bring Laval back to head the government, which would carry with it the return of some 500,000 French prisoners, easier passage at the line separating Occupied France from the Unoccupied Zone, and probably the opportu-

---

12. In 1944 and 1945, the same Payot would be writing in the same newspaper as a fervent advocate of de Gaulle (see diary entry for January 6, 1945).

13. Robert Jacomet, Army Inspector General and Secretary-General at the National Defense Ministry until June 1940. He is one of the principal figures responsible for France's rearmament.

nity for the opening of preliminary peace talks. There might even be a secret clause in the deal calling for France's active participation in the fight against England, our former ally.

In fact, it appears that the German divisions in Cyrenaica moved across Bizerte and Tunisia.

This time, Laval will make himself out to be the adversary of the military establishment and a democrat seeking to bring Parliament together to govern with him in a cooperative effort.

He requested that Daridan come and see him, and Chauvel, too, in other words, my friends. He would like to have the support of the Radical Party. Laval is probably behind the party's convention in Nîmes, which he has organized to pull the wool over their eyes.

April 27, 1941

Swastikas are flying over the Acropolis!

Génébrier told me about the Radical Party convention in Nîmes. Few of my friends have remained faithful to me. Even Fabre, who owes me everything, wanted to attend. Maurice Sarraut[14] boldly wrote an article condemning the event. It had been organized behind the scenes by Vichy, to hoodwink the Radicals.

Mazé came; he had been in Brest. The English bombed the port and then the docks, inflicting serious damage to the *Scharnhorst* and the *Gneisenau* and various German installations in the city.

May 6, 1941

Blum called to me in the course of his walk in the courtyard. I opened my window and we chatted through the bars.

"Did you know that Iraq has been at war with England for the last two days?"

I said to him, "In my opinion, that is a serious blow." Then I added, "Mosul and the oil pipeline there are of major importance to the British fleet and their forces in Egypt. There is no doubt in my mind that these

---

14. Maurice Sarraut, owner and Editor in Chief of *La Dépêche de Toulouse*.

operations have been carried out by German and Italian troops. They have succeeded in bypassing Turkey. British reinforcements will have to be drawn from their troops in Egypt, who are already dangerously thin, and precisely at a time when Rommel's Army is being built up."

I told him that to my mind, American industry was not moving fast enough; they were turning out a mere 500 bombers a month and only 300 for England. As I saw it, that made for a very bad situation indeed. Blum would have none of it. He found support for his views in the fact that Hitler was no longer predicting victory by the end of the year.

"But Hitler never said that," I said to him. "That was Goebbels!" No matter. Nothing could shake the great prophet. He believed that the Iraqi business would be resolved in two days' time.

We spoke about the way Chavin, the Director of the *Sûreté*, had been denying us the right to have visitors. Chavin is avenging himself for all the kind things I did for him while he was under me.

Then we got around to talking about Vuillemin[15] and Guy La Chambre.[16] Blum has nothing but contempt for my former Minister, because of the perfidious comments about me that run through his deposition. He too was saddened to see Jacomet laid so low. I told Blum that he was doing much better and that he seemed to have gotten over the initial shock of being interned.

I watched Blum as he walked away in his handsome dark blue jacket and his gray hat. He looked incredibly youthful. If you want to grow old and do it right, you either have to remain optimistic like him, or egotistical like Pétain, or maybe both.

May 8, 1941

I managed to have a word with Blum and said to him: "The news from Vichy is not good. They have relaxed restrictions governing the movement

---

15. General Joseph Vuillemin, Air Force Chief of Staff and Commander in Chief of the Air Force 1938–1940.

16. Guy La Chambre, Radical-Socialist Member of Parliament. He was Air Force Minister in Daladier's third government (1938–1940). He voted in favor of granting Marshal Pétain plenary powers. He was imprisoned by Pétain in 1941.

of merchandise and currency across the line separating the two zones. From now on they'll allow regular postcards to go through. And the war debt will be reduced by 100 million francs per day. Hallelujah! In exchange, France will simply have to turn over Bizerte, Dakar, and Syria to the Germans."

Our sense of honor should prohibit us from doing anything whatsoever against our allies. We have become a nation of cutthroats. England is surrounded in the eastern Mediterranean and the Middle East. Gibraltar is threatened, and the route to the Cape has been cut off.

May 9, 1941

An item from the Havas News Agency sings the praises of Darlan and hails the greatest victory won since June 1940. After Montoire, our efforts at collaboration had produced nothing really positive. Fortunately, Darlan appeared on the scene. *Fiat lux*—how incredibly despicable!

In America, someone finally demonstrated a clear perception of the situation: Stimson, in a speech. As for Roosevelt, he has made progress. Let's just hope it is not too late and that they will finally start supplying England in significant quantities.

Jacomet has fallen prey to an idée fixe. I explained to him the real reasons for his incarceration. Every member of the Joint Chiefs is out to get him. He hasn't even had a chance to see Picquendar's new depositions attacking him.

May 10, 1941

I took great pleasure in reading Amédée Thierry's wonderful essays about the beginnings of monasticism in 1866 issues of *La Revue des deux mondes*. Read about Saint Jerome and the heresies in Early Christianity.

Was taken with Saint Jerome's admirable talent. He was a magnificent writer, capable of a dense, clear, and vigorous dialectic. Read his polemic with Augustine over the "Jewish bent" of Saint Peter's and Saint Paul's views and his exchanges with Rufin about Origen. Read about the life and impassioned movements of Early Christianity, about the breakup and the subversion of the Roman Empire, which dropped into the hands of the barbarians like rotten fruit falling from a tree, all of it recounted with the capture and pillaging of Rome merely as backdrop.

For the monks and the clerics, the City of God was far more important.

It made me think about my studies. After getting the *agrégation* in history, I began working on a thesis on Carolingian abbeys. Where has all that work gone? Why did I ever give it up? It could have brought me considerable pleasure. I could have been a historian instead of the eternal Sisyphus that every statesman is. I should have listened to Martonne.

Read some wonderful essays on the wars between the German states. The parallels between Bismarck and Hitler are obvious: their common desire to gain control over all of Europe progressively, and France's and England's blindness to it.

May 11, 1941

Paul Reynaud's birthday. It is also Joan of Arc day. The last celebration took place on May 11, 1939, with a military parade. *L'Action française*,[17] La Roque, Doriot[18] and some warmed over Catholics cheered their hearts out. I wonder why democratic parties have always eschewed this great celebration?

May 12, 1941

Passemard, the kindly guard, told me about the Joan of Arc festivities in Riom. A lot of people turned out. The school children all went to mass and to the stadium. There were a great many priests, too. Passemard saw people singing the *Marseillaise* who not that long before had been singing the Communist *Internationale* with their fists raised in the air. This is exactly what the Veterans' Legion does; it is the single-party-system party Déat

---

17. A Royalist newspaper, violently racist, supportive of Vichy and collaboration.

18. Jacques Doriot, who, before founding the French People's Party (the Parti Populaire Français, the PPF) in 1936, had been a union organizer and a Communist. During the war, he launched the Legion of French Volunteers (the Légion des Volontaires Francais, the LVF) to fight Russia alongside Germany. He wore the German uniform and took refuge in Germany in 1945, where he died under circumstances that remain unclear.

would like to have, but run by Doriotists and Royalists. And it's a lot shrewder than setting up an overtly Nazi party.

Fascism has surreptitiously settled in under the colors of the war veterans by virtue of their monopoly over certain privileges (ration cards, pensions, etc.). That is why the Royalists and other groups are fighting to get control over Déat.

May 15, 1941

Clapier[19] came to see me for the first time since I was arrested. Finding the moral courage for a mere visit apparently required months of prolonged reflection. From just after the last war, he followed me throughout my career as Director of my Cabinet. I made him what he is. He didn't even answer my telegram from Morocco in June 1940, sent via Hutin and the Navy, asking him to keep me informed about what was going on in France. He hid out at his place in La Bastide, then went back to Paris, knowing full well that my situation was critical and that we had to go on fighting in North Africa. He is a gullible man of bovine dullness, but a diligent worker with solid common sense and a man very easy to get along with, in spite of his conceit. My wife was right in her judgment of him.

He was very close to Darlan, who courted and flattered him to get into my good graces. In fact, it was Darlan who got him the pass that allowed him to come and see me.

May 16, 1941

Clapier came back at 11:30. He had seen Lagarde, who at first refused to allow him to see me again. He finally relented, although not without taking some measure of revenge—he had Lesueur and Baraveau question him. He will have to come back at 3 P.M. and give a deposition, after which he won't be able to return anymore. Prior to this trial, I knew very little about the legal world. I certainly know how it works now.

---

19. Marcel Clapier, who was associated with Edouard Daladier from 1920 on, was Daladier's Chief of Staff in 1940.

Chauvel came by at 5 P.M., but he had not seen Jean. He and Herriot were in the same train compartment, but they couldn't talk because they weren't alone. Herriot was wearing an old cap and looked fatter and older.

He had also met Wilhem, who before the war had obtained franchise rights for Krupp's all-terrain vehicle. They were magnificent machines. From 1935 to 1937, Colonel Lefèvre, who was at Vincennes, while claiming he was delighted with the vehicles, kept insisting on so many changes that after having complied with a few of his demands, Krupp and Wilhem finally gave up the idea of producing them in France.

Around midnight, I heard loud noises coming from bus and truck engines and saw armed, helmeted gendarmes in battle gear.

May 18, 1941

I have been in bed. Read Henri Bidou's *Paris*. It is a huge catalogue, with neither unity nor life to it, a massive, failed effort. It relates the history of the growth of Paris and the opening of new thoroughfares, but without any sense of the grandeur of the subject matter.

Worth remembering are the strikes that took place under Napoleon. There were some seventy to ninety thousand apolitical workers in Paris then. In the middle of a crisis, Napoleon is supposed to have said to Chaptal: "A man who can't find work is prey to any subversive who comes along. He can be led to revolt. I am more afraid of insurrections that come about because people don't have enough to eat than I am of a battle against two hundred thousand men."

Construction workers struck in 1806. In 1809, they struck at the Arc de Triomphe to get two additional paid hours of work, which they subsequently lost.

There was a strike during the coronation and, later, on the construction site at Notre-Dame. They ended up getting raises.

May 19, 1941

Things are happening in Bourassol. There were more gendarmes on motorcycles and in trucks, and fighter planes flying overhead, all apparently because the Cagoulards have been bragging that they are going to kidnap us and administer their own brand of justice. I have my doubts. I rather suspect that the government wants to get out from under the accusation that they are being too kind toward us. The government is afraid of *Gringoire, L'Œuvre,* and *Le Matin.*

May 20, 1941

German planes have landed in Syria, provoking a sharp reaction from England and the United States, where Roosevelt issued a statement that was a lot tougher than the one that appeared in the French press.

I think that Darlan and Pétain have made their decision and have effectively excluded Laval for the moment. They are pursuing his policies with perhaps even greater servility toward Hitler than Laval showed.

Blum explained to me the reason for all the gendarmes bustling about. It seems that stores of weapons hidden by the Cagoulards at the home of a certain Dr. Martin[20] have been discovered. Martin and Filhol, the killer of the Rosselli brothers, had bragged about pulling something off in Bourassol. Filhol is being actively sought everywhere, whereas Martin is in Vichy, as everyone knows. He is being kept there as bait.

In Syria, General Dentz[21] says that France will retain its control. … Ribet and Croquez came around 3 P.M. *Le Pilori* and *Le Matin* are trying to mold public opinion by publishing articles against the Jews and the Freemasons, who, according to them, are more and more entrenched in Vichy's Ministries. The politicians who were responsible for France's defeat will not even be brought to justice, etc., etc. These are the same blackmailers who have been on Hitler's payroll for a long time.

May 24, 1941

A speech of Darlan's was broadcast on the radio.

Back when Blum was the head of the government, Darlan tried every approach he could think of with Blum, Gasnier-Duparc, and me to get himself appointed head of the General Staff of the Navy. He would have

---

20. Dr. Henri Martin, one of the leaders of the Cagoule.
21. General Henri Dentz, Vichy's Commander of French forces in Syria.

liked to be named to the position before the departure of Admiral Durand-Viel, who was the target of his unrelenting sarcasm.

He also schemed to get himself named Admiral of the Fleet and even Head of the Joint Chiefs, which was absurd.

During my trip to Tunisia, he was constantly licking my boots. On August 26, 1939, he uttered not one word against our policy of support for Poland. In June of 1940, he cabled Noguès to have a personal command post set up in North Africa. The man's ambition knows no bounds. He outwitted Laval by fawning before Hitler even more than Laval himself.

I heard that Lagarde, one of the judges at the court of Riom, found Darlan's speech admirable.

May 26, 1941

The *Hood* has been sunk by the *Bismarck*. The British Navy suffered heavy losses. The Germans have widened their beachhead in Crete.

May 27, 1941

Wonderful article by Montégut in *La Revue des deux mondes* about Laurence Sterne, "the most ordinary man of genius ever." His *Sentimental Journey* is a true masterpiece. It gives you everything about the France of Louis XV: the good life in Paris and London, Diderot, Crébillon …

At 9 P.M. Passemard came to tell me that the British had sunk the *Bismarck*. From my room I could hear Blum shouting, "Hip, hip hurrah!"

May 28, 1941

Roosevelt made a speech on May 27. Blum showed me an unabridged version of it. His resolve is firmer than ever. He laid out what a world dominated by the Nazis would look like and skillfully showed how the standard of living of Americans would decline, how there would be a loss of independence and an end to the American way of life.

May 31, 1941

Pierre and Marie won't get here before 11 P.M. I'll have to ask Lagarde for permission for Pierre to speak with his own father. The last time they came, he informed them that a four-day visit was too long. He pretended to be consulting my file, which he had laid out on his desk, probably for the effect it would have on my young son.

The police here have been relieved. They assembled at noon but didn't leave until 3 p.m.; the Army hasn't changed. I went for my walk in the cesspool the courtyard has become. I was closely watched by a policeman and a guard. Hard to tell which of the two of them is the less polite. The guard is impolite in a more direct and insolent way. All week long, there have been more planes flying over Bourassol than there were over Sedan during the battle of the Meuse. They are rehearsing for Pétain's upcoming review of the military at Aulnat.

Read a fascinating article by Renan in *La Revue des deux mondes* (1866) about Joachim de Flore and the "Eternal Gospel": the rule of the Holy Spirit versus the simony and the lifestyles of the clergy.

He talks about the reasons for the Reformation that existed three centuries before Luther, about the eleventh- and thirteenth-century Renaissance movements and how colossal an error it is to reduce the Middle Ages to a monolithic period. He points out that the passion of the time was a burning one, but one limited in scope, and speaks of the Greek influences on Joachim de Flore and his disciples. "The Lord will raise his sword against the German empire, for it has been hard and cruel toward us." The monks Gérard and Léonard were sentenced to life in an underground prison, where Gérard died. His body was buried in the corner of the garden they used as a garbage dump.

June 1, 1941

Gamelin has taken communion for a second time, the first having been this past Easter.

A handicapped priest arrived by car at 8 a.m. with a portable altar, like the ones we had at the front. It would all be rather moving if Gamelin were actually sincere. Before the war, he was not a practicing Catholic and often mentioned his friendship with Sarraut. He added that if he had been a civilian he would have been a Radical. He converted in Chazeron. Legueu related the following exchange with the priest: "Father, can you teach me a short prayer that I could recite in the evenings while meditating." Somewhat embarrassed, the priest answered: "There is the 'Our Father. ... ' Let's recite it together," but Gamelin had forgotten it.

When he got to "Forgive us our trespasses as we forgive those who have trespassed against us," Gamelin said, "I'll never forgive Daladier." "You will have to," the priest told him. "Otherwise the prayer makes no sense." So Gamelin recited the sentence he had balked at.

I wondered what I had done to Gamelin, whom I had always supported, often at a cost to myself, and even when he was in the wrong. In reading his memoirs and the testimony he has given, I came to understand that what he holds against me are the official minutes of the meeting that took place on August 23, 1939, which indicate that all the people present voted in favor of our going to war.

His religious conversion has been followed by a political one. Gamelin now has the nerve to write that he merely went along with the government's decision to go to war and that he personally had been opposed to it. In truth, he advocated declaring war in September 1938; he even advised me not to divulge the actual state of our Air Force to the British. If I wanted to, I could have his letter included in the Examining Magistrate's dossier. With regard to Poland, he told me that it would be a great dishonor for France to refuse to come to its aid. Such is the measure of the man. I can't say that the rest of them are any better, but can they possibly be as hypocritical? I had always been struck by Gamelin's flabby handshake.

June 9, 1941

Sensational news: British and Gaullist forces have crossed the border into Syria.

June 10, 1941

Not a peep out of Pétain or Darlan. It is hard to understand.

June 11, 1941

Today is Saint Barnaby's day. Barnaby was the nickname we gave Pitous, my orderly during the War of 1914–1918. At 10 A.M. Jean brought me news that Blum later confirmed in a note: It would appear that the British and the Gaullist forces have encountered no resistance in Syria.

Darlan's latest speech made no mention of the Gaullist attack in Syria. He simply offered a sniveling justification of France's collaboration, with the Marshal portrayed as its leading proponent, naturally. He came up with this sordid turn of phrase: "Presiding over our defeat."

Jean said good-bye to me at 7 p.m. He'll get back to Marseilles at about 4 in the morning.

June 13, 1941

There has been fighting in Syria. And they said there weren't any Germans there.

June 15, 1941

Mazé came here from Brest, where he said that young men are being executed frequently. Mayor Gorjeu and a priest are forced to witness the executions, as are the mothers, fathers, brothers, and sisters of the condemned men. The priest tries to get them to keep their spirits up by telling them they are dying as good Christians and Frenchmen. They are dying as heroes.

June 20, 1941

Chauvel thinks that there will be war between the Russians and the Germans. This was the information he picked up from Ostrorog and a number of officers.

June 21, 1941

I passed on to Blum the news that Chauvel had brought me. He answered with a note and by giving me a copy of today's *Journal de Genève*. Is war between Russia and Germany imminent?

Blum's note, as handed to me by the guard, follows: "Thank you. I am sending you a copy of today's issue of the *Journal de Genève*. Take a look at the last page, with Vichy's correspondence relative to the conflict between Germany and Russia.

"British radio broadcast an ultimatum issued by Germany this morning. I have the feeling that Hitler wants to bring the situation to a head, whereas Stalin wants to drag it out.

"As for the events in Syria, I still have the impression that the operation will soon be brought to a close. There is a lot of bluffing going on.

"With regard to the trial, have you read, included in what Gamelin's come up with most recently, the copy of the letter Admiral Darlan sent him on September 17, 1938? It makes absolutely devastating reading now. If Admiral Herr gets to see it, it will not make him change his opinion of Darlan.

"The heat is killing me. My 'apartment' is absolutely unbearable.

"Best wishes, fraternal wishes. L.B."

June 22, 1941

I was coming back half naked from lying out in the sun, which I do during the time I am allotted for a walk, when a white dove came and landed on my head!

4 P.M. Mazé came here by bike. He had gone and waited for Lagarde after mass to ask him for a pass to see me, which Lagarde graciously gave him. With Germany having declared war on Russia, life at Bourassol will improve during the next few days.

Mazé traveled in trains bursting with "legionnaires," "fellows," and "youth group members." They were going to rally in Limoges, Aubusson, and all the other cities Pétain plans to visit. These are the military extras who do the cheering.

In Orange and Carpentras, Mazé saw our friends again, not all of whom have remained faithful.

He left for Paris at 2 A.M. to work on the plan from within the Occupied Zone.[22]

Alone in my cell this evening, I reflected at leisure on the events of the day.

---

22. The reference is to a plan to escape to England.

At 10 o'clock this morning, Renée Blum[23] informed us of the declaration of war Hitler had sent to Stalin. The guards and the gendarmes in Bourassol were as enthusiastic about it as the prisoners.

If Stalin had been allied with us in September 1939, as I repeatedly proposed to him, we wouldn't be caught in the Nazi nightmare today.

I spotted Gamelin from my window—unnoteworthy.

Once again the French Communists are going to be forced to "follow the Party line." They are going to be forced to become patriots again. Hitler has said that "Russia will be beaten, Russia will be crushed." Of course, Napoleon made it to Moscow and what did it get him? Most important is that England will benefit from a respite. In a release to the Havas News Agency, Vichy expressed its approval of the actions taken by Hitler, the man defending order against the evils of Bolshevism.

June 26, 1941

According to British radio, the fighting in Russia is fierce. It will be a number of days before we can get a clear idea of any kind.

June 29, 1941

I had one last lunch with Roger Génébrier. He left me at 4:30 to meet with Léonard at the *Café des Voyageurs* but came back at 6:30. I was surprised to see him again. He brought me two important pieces of information: Colonel Rivet, who has debunked the myth of the 7,000 tanks used in the German offensive, is prepared to testify and produce precise figures. Secondly, Jacquot has finished his interviews with two hundred heads of military units in which he inquired about the orders they had received from their superiors. The results are devastating. We didn't lose the war because of a lack of matériel; we lost it because of the mind-boggling incompetence of military leaders mired in the past.

---

23. Léon Blum's daughter-in-law.

July 1, 1941

2 P.M. I was visited by Guichard, a Deputy from the Vaucluse. He brought me cherries, a pipe, a pouch of tobacco, a pack of Boyard cigarettes, a box of matches, and a flask of brandy. He let me know how valuable it all was by telling me how much trouble he had had getting them. He thought my setup wasn't bad at all. Did he just come out of sympathy, or more likely curiosity, or was it out of a desire to be able to tell everyone about it back in the Vaucluse?

July 2, 1941

Pierre arrived unexpectedly at 11 A.M. while I was waiting for Ribet. He has grown thin and pale. He is a good-natured boy, so much like his mother. We talked about his studies and what he has been reading and working on, and for a few minutes I became a professor again. He seemed to like me in that role. We talked about Russia, England, and America. He remains a rabid Gaullist.

Ribet came around four that afternoon. We discussed the trial. People in Paris are beginning to see through it. The fellow in the cloakroom at the courthouse asked him, "How's Edouard doing?" and added, "I used to be a Communist, but now I'm all for him."

July 3, 1941

People have nothing but scorn for the French newspapers run by the Germans, especially for Déat. The French Hitlerites—Camelots du Roi, Doriotists, Cagoulards, revolutionaries in uniform, and mindless fanatics supporting totalitarian regimes—are all at one another's throats.

Ribet brought with him several different newspapers of this ilk, written by the visionary cranks working with Châteaubriand at *La Gerbe*, the scum at *Pilori*, who had already sold out before the war, Luchaire[24] and his

---

24. Jean Luchaire, Radical journalist. He launched the weekly *Notre Temps*, for which Otto Abetz wrote and which the German government subsidized from 1936 to 1939, then founded *Les Nouveaux Temps*. After 1940, he became the behind-the-scenes liaison between Laval and Abetz. He took refuge in Germany in 1944 and was executed in 1946.

cronies at the *Nouveaux Temps*, who have been taking payoffs forever, and of course the lily-livered Déat, who wanted peace right away, along with a few other little turds. That Déat is furious with the Veterans' Legion, which has become the only recognized political party, is comical, as every instance of a cuckold's fury is comical.

At around 3 P.M. the Ribets came to see me. We drew up a request for my provisional release and a letter to Pétain. I have no illusions about the outcome, but I'll wait and see. I had drafted a forceful, aggressive letter, but Ribet thought I should tone it down, which is the way the final version came out. I am not too happy about it.

Ribet met with Lagarde, who is considerably put out now at having to sit in judgment of this case. "We are in a terrible predicament," he told Ribet. "We have to act both as examining magistrate and judge. The situation is filled with pitfalls." Then he proceeded to rattle off all the practical difficulties without ever once elevating the discussion to matters of principle. He suggested that Barthélemy include in the Constitution he is drafting a High Court composed of magistrates elected by the High Court of Appeals, the Conseil d'Etat, and the Veterans' Legion. The court in Riom would function as an investigative commission. Not a word of these exchanges was reported to Allard this morning.

They absolutely loathe Darlan in Paris. He would like to use Hitler's methods to do what Hitler did, that is, bring all of France to march in step. But Hitler won majority support in Germany in free elections, by appealing to nationalist feelings and denouncing the Treaty of Versailles, and by decrying unemployment and calling for economic expansion. Darlan, in contrast, comes across like a servile partisan of surrender, a traitor, the man who is organizing France so that the Krauts can squeeze the most out of her. It is the very difference that sets the Restoration of 1814–1815 apart from the one that took place under Louis-Napoléon in 1852.

From here on in, the German thrust into Russia will advance very quickly to Petrograd, Moscow, and Kiev, with the Stuka dive-bombers undoubtedly playing a major role. Vuillemin wouldn't believe me when I told him of the panic the Stukas could create. What's worse, this is an aircraft that was invented by a Frenchman.

July 4, 1941

5 P.M. I saw Jacomet in the courtyard with his wife. As soon as he noticed me at the window, he came over and started talking about the trial, which is the only subject of conversation he is capable of. He has undertaken a huge project that could turn out to have considerable impact. What was the reason for the delays between the time the decision to order equipment was made and the signing of those contracts? Jacomet places responsibility squarely at the feet of Castelnau, who was in charge of that department. Castelnau was the engineer General who had Deloncle (a Cagoulard) freed at the time of the mobilization and got him a position in an armory under Dautry's jurisdiction.[25] Dautry felt uncomfortable enough to have him transferred to a Naval armory.

July 5, 1941

Darlan has dismissed Gasnier-Duparc, the Mayor of Saint-Malo, and made a number of harsh comments about his opposition to the great work of the National Revolution. They were old friends and neighbors, too. Gasnier had even pushed through Darlan's appointment as head of the General Staff of the Navy six months early.

Stalin is reported to have said that if necessary, he'll set up the command position of the Russian front in the Urals.

July 6, 1941

Vichy. Various War Tribunals have been sentencing people to three-year prison terms for possession of Communist tracts. Similar sentences were handed down for people who had maligned the Head of State.

Read excerpts from Stalin's speech in the July 5 *Journal de Genève*, which we received today. What a sorry explanation he offers for the German-Soviet Pact of August 23, 1939. Absolutely shameful! It is all so inept, with the exception of those moments when he falls back on Kutuzov.

---

25. Raoul Dautry, Arms Minister under Daladier. He was a former executive officer of the SNCF, the French National Railroad.

Jacomet thinks the Russians will draw the Germans all the way back to the Urals, but he is mainly thinking about the trial and all the bribing Brandt did. From what he says, Reibel,[26] a Senator, was Brandt's attorney, as was Bénazet,[27] who received some 50,000 francs from the Lorraine Corporation by bragging to them that he was the one who had got their tractors chosen. There was also the story General Sthelé told about a letter Bénazet had stolen.

Vichy's War Minister has reduced Jacomet's status to that of an "imprisoned officer," with a salary of 2,500 francs a month. And he has got his wife, his daughter, and his two grandchildren in Riom!

Monday, July 7, 1941

Ribet came back from Vals. He is defending Bretty's[28] and Mandel's interests. The latter's apartment has been taken over by an Anti-Jewry Board. Mandel has his own lawyer, who doesn't have the nerve to defend his client. He is not the only one.

Saw a photograph of Chautemps with his two- or three-year-old son in his arms. He got the pose just right. What a self-satisfied look. The country can fall apart …

Tuesday, July 8, 1941

Spent a wonderful afternoon with Jeanne Boucoiran.[29] Offie[30] keeps sending me American-made products, with the best wishes of Bullitt. Got a whole shipload via diplomatic pouch. I am touched by their undying consideration.

---

26. Claude Reibel, Deputy, then Senator and a member of the Senate's Defense Committee. In Vichy, in 1940, he voted in favor of the Marshal.

27. Paul Bénazet, Deputy, Senator, friend of Briand, and member of the Socialist Party. In July 1940, he voted in favor of granting Marshal Pétain plenary powers.

28. Georges Mandel's female companion.

29. She and Daladier married after the war.

30. Carmel Offie, one of Bullitt's associates in Paris.

From her vantage point in the park, Jeanne has formulated her opinion of the people working for the National Revolution: a bunch of greedy, incompetent, piggish informers.

I find the *Gazette de Lausanne* nauseating. In the name of anti-Bolshevism, they have stooped to fawning over Hitler and carrying "Vichy's realistic approach" even further. Poor old Switzerland. Just as in France, only the common folk are noble and brave. All those bourgeois politicians and businessmen make me sick.

At 4 A.M. I was awakened by the chirping of a nightingale, a kind of robin. I tried to lure it over with lemon peels and peach pits. When I was a child in Provence, I used to listen to the rhythmic singing of quail in the quiet of the fields. Over the plains of Limagne, the roosters are surely calling to each other right now. Here, there have been a few horse-drawn carts on the road to Riom, the voices of the guards behind the trees, and an invasion of fleas.

Recent communiqués from the Krauts reveal the ferocity with which the Russian Army is fighting. Western German cities have been bombed, and there have been considerable civilian casualties. Italian Generals have surrendered in Abyssinia.

Benoist-Méchin,[31] one of Vichy's Ministers, was in Ankara, soliciting Turkish assistance in Syria. He heard the Turks tell him, "You don't really expect us to grant a weak French nation what we have already refused a powerful Germany."

July 10, 1941

General Dentz in Syria has been ordered to request a truce.

Daridan came at 12:30 this afternoon. He told me that our losses in Syria were high, mostly among the officers. Ismet Inonu refused to grant passage to our reinforcements. What has all this gotten us? Could not this painful conflict have been avoided? Had the airfields in Syria been made

---

31. Jacques Benoist-Méchin, historian, Minister under Marshal Pétain, advocate of close ties, including military ties, with Hitler.

available to the Germans? Was this the opportunity that certain people had been waiting for?

The Russians continue to put up considerable resistance. I am surprised by the quantity of matériel that the Russian Army has as well as by the bravery of their fighting men. They have demonstrated heroism and genuine patriotism, just as they did in 1812.

They are still at one another's throats in Vichy, where a new ministerial crisis is looming, involving Huntziger, Achard, Bouthillier,[32] and so on.

Had an interesting talk with Daridan about possible peace terms: the reestablishing of legitimate democracies in Europe (for France, meaning the Republic), which is to say, governments that have the consent of the governed. As for territorial matters, there would be a much modified version of the Europe framed by the Treaty of Versailles. I fear that there is a little too much Congress of Vienna in Daridan's thinking. In any event, even if Hitler is eventually defeated, there will still be issues to be resolved between France and Germany. But then, can we really expect anyone to take our views into account given the way we withdrew to Bordeaux after the battle of the Somme?

Baudouin had met with Pétain and Weygand on May 29. The three agreed to push Reynaud out at the very first setback. They planned to move the government out of Paris, naturally, to avoid another Commune. Bouthillier and Chautemps were in on it.

Chautemps is in the United States in an unofficial capacity. They say he is getting paid $1,200 a month (40,000 francs). Pétain is rewarding him for his help.

July 12, 1941

4 P.M. Chauvel stopped by. His brother, a delightful fellow I very much liked, is gravely ill. His mother has come to Vichy and is supposed to dine with Marshal Pétain this evening. Chauvel is optimistic about the outcome

---

32. Yves Bouthillier, Finance Inspector and an associate of Paul Reynaud. He worked to bring Pétain to power and was named Vichy's Minister of Finance and National Economy in 1940.

of the war. Mme Chauvel witnessed a scene between Pétain and Darlan, and thinks that it won't be long before Darlan is gone.

The Germans have made a real killing: They got all of Polish industry cheap. They are preparing a military parade in Paris to celebrate the fall of Moscow, which is imminent. Reports have it that there remain no more than 200,000 German troops in France.

July 14, 1941

A radio broadcast from last night was reprinted this morning: "Once again July 14 will be celebrated this year." The first we had heard of it was in a communiqué from the Labor Ministry three or four days ago.

Of course, to listen to Pétain, France has been perpetuating a mistake for the last 150 years, which is what Maurras has been saying for the last 30. Maurras has at last discovered his finest disciple and scored his greatest triumph.

I couldn't find a French blue, white, and red flag to hang out of my window. Blum had better luck and came up with some tricolor ribbons. Brings back memories of July 14, 1939.

July 15, 1941

I saw Chauvel at 5 P.M. Sunday evening. He had dined with Pétain in his villa two miles from Vichy, in the company of his mother, Mme Chauvel; Ménétrel[33] and his son, Benoist-Méchin; and a naval officer from Pétain's staff and his wife. It turned out to be a wearisome dinner, because of Benoist's lecturing and the clowning around of Ménétrel, whom Pétain nearly had leave the table. Pétain is partially deaf, which meant that there could be no general conversation involving everyone. He had some very harsh words for Ménétrel, although none of this prevented him from displaying a hearty appetite and downing half a bottle of white wine. After dinner, he went for a walk in the park with Mme Chauvel, who is an intimate of his, and spoke to her of his loneliness. He said he hoped he

---

33. Bernard Ménétrel, Pétain's adviser and physician.

wouldn't die before signing the peace treaty, lest France be thrown into frightful chaos.

Weygand, whom Pétain can't stand, would like to succeed him. Darlan, whom Pétain doesn't like, is working at it harder and harder, and scheming more and more. Laval hasn't completely given up either. And in addition to these people, he said, there were a number of highly suspect and dangerous groups in Paris.

Pétain also talked to her about Catroux and de Gaulle. They might have been motivated by patriotism in the beginning, but now it is all a matter of pride on their part. Their actions in Syria were ignominious. Pétain refused to discuss their claims.

"From a purely military point of view, the British were pathetic in Syria. If 200,000 Germans were ever to land in England, it would be all over for them.

"The Russians are very good soldiers and what is more, they are considerably better armed than had been thought. Nonetheless, the Germans will take Leningrad, Moscow, Kiev, and the Caucasus. By occupying the 'exploitable' part of Russia, they will be able to make use of her mineral and oil resources, her grain, her oils and dairy products, and her industrial machinery. Russia will probably break up as the result of civil wars. Moreover, Japan will very likely enter the war by the end of the month. All of this should come to pass by the end of August, after which Hitler will launch his invasion of England, primarily by air. All of Europe's industrial capacity is now geared to replenishing and upgrading the German war machine.

"There is no doubt that British and American aviation has made great progress, both qualitatively and quantitatively. Nonetheless:

"1. In the end, the outcome of the war will be decided on land, and the British foot soldier, just like his commanding officers, isn't worth much.

"2. Roosevelt has encountered stiff resistance and in any event, the American soldier is even more inept than his British counterpart.

"3. Even if Hitler does not attempt to invade England, he could unify Europe and then wait it out, however long it takes. Closing the European market to England and America would be even more effective than the naval blockade."

Tuesday morning, in spite of Ménétrel, Pétain conferred individually with Mme Chauvel's son, my lawyer.

Chauvel told him that I had decided to seek a trial or, failing that, my temporary release. Pétain agreed that the situation was deplorable. He added that the trial was making him ill and said that it was the work of Marquet, which, he claimed, was one of the principal reasons why he forced him out of his government. He added, however, that he could not "under the present circumstances, authorize my release, because the government has learned of plots to kidnap the prisoners in Bourassol. To release them would be to jeopardize their safety, especially Blum's." He went on to say that "another solution to the problem will have to be found, such as an island, like Corsica." But he said he needed a few days to think about it and discuss it with Barthélemy. He asked Chauvel to take back both my letter and Ribet's, and to wait two weeks or so.

He said he himself would get back in touch with Chauvel. He asked him about M.L.[34] and was happy to learn that she had remained faithful and devoted to me.

July 19, 1941

Renée Blum informed me that a decision has been made to transfer us to the island of Porquerolles, where we are to be housed in reconditioned barracks. This was revealed two or three days ago, during a press conference. Blum thinks that the situation will be worse there. I am not so sure, but I'd like to ask Chauvel about it. It was from Porquerolles that I left on August 15, 1938, before the Munich crisis.

July 21, 1941

There has apparently been a counterorder; we will not be going to Porquerolles.

---

34. Edouard Daladier's female companion.

July 22, 1941

According to Jeanne, Radio Paris, which is to say the Krauts, has announced plans for our transfer to Porquerolles, with this added comment, "Undoubtedly so that they can be more easily kidnapped by a British vessel." American radio carried the same item. Judge Lagarde, however, told Jeanne that they had never seriously considered that option, which is the real truth. The rest is just so much hot air.

July 24, 1941

Talking with Blum through the window, I mentioned the tenacious resistance put up by the Russians. For the last few days, the names of the same cities keep reappearing in the communiqués, which is an indication of the ferocity of the fighting. It is now a matter of whether the Russian Army will be able to regroup its forces and continue fighting east of Moscow. If it can do that, victory is a real possibility.

At 4:30 P.M. Susset and his lovely wife came to see me, loaded down with presents. Spent two joyful hours in the company of friends. Susset was told by a German officer that the invasion of England was planned for August 20 and that all coastal ports would have to be cleared by that date.

Communiqué from the Havas Agency: We have agreed to meet Japan's ultimatum. The government acts as if it were proud to have been able to capitulate once again. They asked for an armistice supposedly to save the Empire. Is there anything left of our Empire?

Pétain went to Aix, where he went all out about Darlan and had something bad to say about every one of his Ministers. The demagoguery of a slick politician.

Passemard just informed me that Dormoy was assassinated in Montélimar.

July 31, 1941

Pierre's birthday.

At 11 A.M. Mme Reichenbach[35] came back from Montélimar where she had attended funeral services for Dormoy. They were held on Monday at 7 A.M. and carried out as if it had been the burial of a guillotined criminal whose unclaimed body gets carted to the cemetery from the basket into which it's dropped.

At first, the Secretary-General from the Prefecture and the Police Commissioner were deferential toward Jeanne Dormoy,[36] but after a phone call to Vichy, the only thing they were interested in, as they themselves said, was "getting it over with."

Dormoy's killer is a woman. She had a room in the same hotel and placed a bomb in his bed, between the mattress and the box spring. The bomb went off at two in the morning. He was torn to shreds. Blum feels that Vichy's attitude is as much a product of their fear as of their hatred. Such is the way the Nazis operate.

August 2, 1941

The Russians are still holding out. If we had continued fighting in North Africa, the war between Russia and Germany would have offered France a second opportunity to regain her freedom, the first being the Italian defeat in Cyrenaica.

Jean returned from Vichy, where he saw Brinon in the park, a fat man bearing his fat with pride.

What new German demands has Brinon joyfully brought back to the men of Vichy? The occupation of Casablanca? Dakar? Bizerte? All, naturally, for the salvation of our Empire.

---

35. Léon Blum's female companion. They married in 1943.
36. Marx Dormoy's sister.

August 5, 1941

I learned from Jeanne that Dommange has been arrested. His closest associate had informed on him; he had two grenades in his house.

It reminds me of Gaston Boissier's writings on informers in the days of Tiberius. Mutatis mutandis—we have improved on it since.

5:30 in the afternoon. Mazé came, talked about the heroism of the Bretons. They have put up a veritable "united front" in the cities and villages. The anticlerical Mazé is even on the same side as his parish priest. There are always fresh flowers on the graves of the fallen British pilots. Groups are being organized in the Occupied Zone. Then, at the other end of the spectrum, there are Landry and his Cagoulards.

With the packages I had received from my American friends, I was able to invite Mazé to stay for dinner.

August 7, 1941

Saw both Jean and Mazé. The latter showed me a copy of Sumner Welles's[37] speech denouncing Vichy's policies, which go well beyond the conditions agreed to in the Armistice, and threatening a break in the traditionally amicable Franco-American relations.

The Parisian press is aflame. Read some absolutely vile articles by Déat, Brinon, and Marion,[38] Chief of Information.

August 8, 1941

From my window, I tried to offer Jacomet some measure of comfort. A report filed by that wretch Cunin had left him beside himself. He had broken down in a fit of crying that drove his daughter to despair and was even a cause of concern for the guards. I spoke to him through the bars, while he was on the pathway in the courtyard, in front of the primitive toilets

---

37. Welles was Roosevelt's Under Secretary of State.

38. Paul Marion, first a Communist, then a Socialist, then a member of Doriot's Fascist Party, the PPF, with which he broke after Munich. He sided with the Vichy government and was appointed head of Propaganda and Junior Minister in the Information Ministry. He was imprisoned at the end of the war.

there. What could make for a more appropriate setting for a discussion about the trial? I joked with him and made fun of Cunin. I threw in a few new touches about Lagarde, the judge who has just had one of the witnesses done away with. I showed him who was really on trial here and appealed to his energy. When he left, he moved with determination and at a brisk pace.

August 9, 1941

Jean saw Chauvel in Vichy. Dampierre, a Minister, cabled from Budapest to say that the Germans had hit a snag in Russia. It's the beginning of the end. They will end up being defeated.

The cable was shown to Pétain, Weygand, and then Darlan, with the latter snorting, "It's just a bunch of crap."

Chauvel did not get to see Pétain. The issue of the moment is whether France will allow the Krauts to occupy Dakar, Bizerte, and Marseilles. The last Cabinet meeting was suspended until Monday, at which time a decision will be made. I am convinced that the matter had already been decided at the time of Brinon's trip. They are simply trying to figure out how to package it. Rumor has it that Weygand has opposed the move, but I don't believe a word of that.

Pétain and Weygand made a public appearance at the Grand Prix de Vichy. They were hailed by the crowd at the weigh-in.

August 11, 1941

An old friend of mine from Carpentras, Albert Josselme, came all the way up here but couldn't get permission to visit with me. Jean told him to stand behind the gates where he could see me when I went out for my walk. We waved to each other from afar. He gave Jean two packs of Boyards for me. Jean had to console him; he was crying and calling to me.

August 13, 1941

Renée Blum filled me in on the broad outlines of Pétain's radio address: total adherence to the doctrine and the practices of the Nazis. I read a printed version of it shortly thereafter in *La Montagne*.

1. Pétain's admission of his miserable failure.
2. Responsibility for the failure placed on the republicans and the Freemasons. The *Journal officiel* published a list of the supposed opposition leaders: Juvanon, Fabien de Champoille, and Paul Perrin, all of them poor souls who never had any influence whatsoever.
3. Adherence to Nazi principles and a condemnation of trusts à la Bergery.[39]
4. Submission to Germany in the name of collaboration.
5. Pétain's decision to pass sentence himself on those responsible for our defeat, which is his way of avoiding a trial with its public debates and comparisons. He claims he is "saving the honor of the Army," by which he means those incompetent leaders whose failings were revealed in the pretrial investigation.

2 P.M. Blum characterizes the speech as an explosion of furor and impotence. He interprets it as a sign that Germany is having serious problems. I think just the opposite. If there were a risk that Germany was about to lose the war, Pétain would never have burned his bridges. He still believes in a German victory, as he told his friend Mme Chauvel, only he doesn't say so outright, as opposed to Laval, who expresses his feelings publicly. Besides, Pétain has displayed considerable tact in his handling of the United States.

August 20, 1941

Desgranges[40] came to see me. He is a canon and an old war buddy, a magnificent human being. He refused to dine with Pétain and told Romier[41] and Moysset what he thought of their articles. He has been vigorously critical of the government's policies, especially their religious policies. He

---

39. Gaston Bergery, Centrist Deputy. He launched a weekly, *La Flèche*, and founded the Fascist "Frontist" Party in collaboration, most notably, with several former Communists. He was successively Vichy's Ambassador to Moscow and Ankara.

40. Canon Desgranges (1874–1958), militant priest in the Sillon movement as well as Deputy and republican. He fought brilliantly in World War I.

41. Lucien Romier, prewar journalist and right-wing author, Minister in the Vichy government.

has been praying for the victory of the democratic forces of the world and believes they will win. I find his courage and his boldness admirable. While we were together in this prison of mine, we enjoyed the memories of our camaraderie at Verdun.

6 P.M. Mazé has returned from the South. He met with Herriot, who hasn't changed. He is still upset at not having been arrested, although in his heart he hopes he won't be.

August 22, 1941

Génébrier has seen the high holy office manager of the high holy Minister of Justice, and Lagarde as well. They claim that there will indeed be a trial, but after the war!

August 30, 1941

Anniversary celebration of the Veterans' Legion, otherwise known as an exercise in how to create rifts among the veterans of the Great War.

Blum cleverly slipped me the following note: "In a recent speech, Cordell Hull claimed that France had misled the United States. America's aviation and naval production is now equal to that of Germany's; it will triple in a year's time.

"For a year, the French government took advantage of their Consul in Salonika by using him to spy on the British and the Greeks for the Germans. He found out about it when the Germans arrived in Salonika, whereupon he left to join the Gaullist movement in London. He has just made a statement to that effect on the radio."

September 1, 1941

I am suffering so from a painful abscess that I asked the Cour Suprême for permission to be seen by Dr. Bernard, who comes to take care of Blum. I was told that I would have to submit my request in writing, and that it could not be sent out before tomorrow. Not only will I get to keep my abscess for another twenty-four hours, but I'll also have the pleasure of hearing Dr. Bernard call upon Blum and leave without looking in on me. Oh, National Revolution!

September 9, 1941

Mazé has had a talk of vital importance with a friend of M. Nouvelle's; a meeting has been set for 6 P.M. If this isn't mere romantic fancy, it's terrific.[42]

September 21, 1941

Saw my son Pierre; he is more and more like Madeleine.

September 22, 1941

Spent the day with Pierre.

September 23, 1941

Saw Pierre and Marie and then Jean, who provided a picturesque description of his life in Marseilles. He is living with longshoremen.

Having been named Mayor of Annecy, General Cartier made the following obscene statement: "This is the first time since 1860 that the Savoie region has been united with the fatherland."

September 26, 1941

Jean left Thursday, Pierre and Marie Friday.

September 29, 1941

Judge Bruzin didn't even wait to have a look at Jacomet's excellent notes on the rearmament before submitting the completed indictment!

September 30, 1941

Claudius was even more responsible than Caligula for the debasement of power. In the most hideous way possible, he demonstrated to the Romans what favoring one race over all others can bring. Whither zealous obedience and the fervid desire to act the slave?

---

42. The reference is to Daladier's escape plans. A British plane would land in a nearby field and Daladier would escape with the head guard, Passemard, a member of the Resistance who was eventually caught, tortured, and killed by the Germans.

October 1, 1941

The government employee who has just read aloud to me the definitive version of my pretrial examination and the list of charges against me admitted himself that it was all a farce.

October 14, 1941

Perretti della Rocca, a former Ambassador, president of a life insurance company, a shady one at that, and head of the Political Justice Committee, presented his committee's report to the Marshal. I wonder whether they were able to look at each other without cracking a smile.

October 16, 1941

At 11 A.M. the head guard came and asked me to countersign a letter from Judge Lagarde. The indictment was to be presented to us at 5 P.M. today, after which we would have five days in which to respond. Then at noon, Pétain, in a statement broadcast on the radio, indicated that his decision regarding the actions to be taken against us would be announced at 7 P.M. At 6 P.M. we still had not received a copy of the indictment, which we were in fact never to receive. I will have been convicted without ever having had a chance to defend myself, as I have known I would be for a long time, ever since it became clear that France had not actually been defeated; she had been handed over to the enemy by a bunch of incompetent fools and traitors.

My thoughts are for my sons. They'll not lose courage, I know.

Having heard Pétain's address, Chauvel came to relay it to me. In a decision rendered publicly, Pétain has sentenced us to be imprisoned in the fortress of Le Portalet. He requested, moreover, that an even stiffer sentence be handed down by the Riom tribunal at the time of our trial.[43]

---

43. This is a long way both from the regrets Pétain expressed to Chauvel and the plan to send the defendants to the island of Porquerolles. It is highly unusual for a head of state to issue instructions to a tribunal publicly.

Our attorneys, Chauvel and Spanien, can't understand these contradictions. They have no idea of Pétain's hatred for republican regimes and for Poincaré and Clemenceau, who were so unerring in their opinion of him. He will never forgive them for not having named him Commander in Chief instead of Foch.

I heard that on October 13, Funck, one of Hitler's Ministers, gave a speech in Berlin: "Pétain will punish those who were responsible for the war as proof of his sincere desire to collaborate with victorious Germany."

Perretti della Rocca submitted the Political Justice Committee's report to Pétain on Tuesday, October 14. Every single member of that committee is a notorious reactionary. Some of them are particularly vicious, like Jassa, the epitome of the venomous cretin, and Vallin, a Deputy and member of the Croix de feu. Since Cassagneau had still not signed the indictment, one can only imagine the kind of fabricated and rigged dossier they based their judgment on. They have made a mockery of justice. The indictment was eventually signed on October 15, which just happened to be the day Pétain pronounced sentence.

October 17, 1941

Pétain's speech has been reprinted in the newspapers, and all of them ran the same headline. Will anyone ever have the courage to say that we were convicted before we even had a chance to read and respond to the indictment? Pétain actually invoked the principle of the separation of powers on the very day he violated it. Stranger still, he dropped the charge he has been making against me on the radio since August 13, 1940, namely that I had thrown France into war in violation of the Constitution. I was supposed to have gulled the entire Parliament. He was joined in this accusation by all the French Nazis, like Benoist-Méchin, Bergery, Déat, Montigny, and so on. The Parisian press, under German orders, has been accusing me of this unmercifully, as had Pétain, through the Legion and the newspapers it controls. In fact, Judge Lagarde never questioned me about anything else. All of a sudden, Pétain has abandoned this approach. Hitler is not going to like it.

Whether I am detained in a fortress in the Pyrenees or deported to a work camp somewhere, I shall not suffer as a result of that. I know that my sons and my sister, however much it grieves them, will be able to endure the ordeal. As for me, only the outcome of the war is of real concern. If Germany should be victorious, what would dying in the depths of some fortress matter? I would just as soon not survive, just as soon not have to witness the moral decline and the decay that would result. What meaning could life have, what would be the point of living then, even if I were free and no longer a prisoner? All that really matters is the ultimate victory or defeat of Nazi Germany.

Ribet came at 6 P.M. We drafted a protest to the "man sent by Providence," as His Eminence Cardinal Gerlier calls him.

October 18, 1941

My courageous friend Génébrier set out to see me as soon as he heard Pétain's announcement. We were speaking together about prewar politics, men, and ideas, when we were suddenly informed that Watteau, who is a General in the Reserves and a member of the Cour Suprême, had resigned. Other judges would appear to be on the verge of resigning. The government has let them know that if they do, they'll be sent to prison.

As for Charles Maurras, he is exultant. He continues to strike out against England and claims that this is Pétain's worthiest political act.

October 26, 1941

Laval: Moved from the cafe in Châteldon to a job as a school monitor and then a position as lawyer for revolutionary trade unions. Elected Deputy in 1914, he spent the entire war in the Chamber, even though he was only thirty-one. He spoke out against the expulsion of Trotsky in 1916. He was a defeatist, in favor of peace even back then (speech of July 1, 1917). According to Torrès, he was Mandel's contact with extremist groups. He became rich in the very midst of the war; defended a pathetic Malvy before the Board of Inquiry. During the Stavisky affair, he intervened with Mouton, the Director of Criminal Affairs at the Ministry of Justice, in favor of Hudelot's Foncière and Stavisky. Mouton lied to the Board of Inquiry, Mandel kept silent, and Loucheur died opportunely. In September 1939, again according to Torrès, it was Laval who staged the whole affair with

Portmann, Malvy, Monzie, et al., and sent Mistler[44] to Spain to meet with
Pétain.

November 7, 1941

Pétain has issued a statement: I have been sentenced to life imprisonment.

November 11, 1941

It's the anniversary of our victory in 1918. M. Belin has informed us that
there will be no official holiday this year, but we shall have the good for-
tune to see Marshal Pétain go to mass and have flowers placed at the memorial to the dead in Vichy. The Germans were probably afraid there
would be demonstrations. Once again, Unoccupied France will offer us an
abject example of servility, and once again their example won't be followed
in the Occupied Zone, where our victory will be celebrated as a day of
hope. The Republic has never known how to commemorate this great victory her fighting men won. Even the battle of the Marne, the greatest victory of them all, is only celebrated in some hole in the wall somewhere.
The commemoration of the Armistice was never more than a funereal rite,
with no mention whatsoever of the fact that it was signed at Germany's request. The Arc de Triomphe, which was dedicated to the magnificent victories of the nation, has become little more than a glorified sepulcher ever
since the Tomb of the Unknown Soldier was placed at its base. That som-
ber official parade on November 11, those huge wreaths they place on
tombs, and those lugubrious trumpet calls to the dead are just so many
burial rituals performed before a crowd huddled in meditation, as if at
graveside.

As I was sitting here thinking of the last war, of a time when the
French Army had real leaders, I was notified that there were to be no further visits after 6 P.M. At 7:30, the head guard came into my cell accompa-

---

44. Jean Mistler, writer, Radical-Socialist Member of Parliament and Minister in
Daladier's Cabinet in 1934. In Vichy, in 1940, he voted to give plenary powers to Pétain. He
was a member of the Conseil National.

nied by a handsome government commissioner in a spanking new suit. Looking as smug as Mistler himself, he solemnly informed me that at 6 A.M. the following morning we would be leaving for the fortress of Le Portalet and that we would be served a cold meal at noon. Whereupon, in his little priest's voice, he read aloud to me, punctuated by appropriate reverences, a statement from Pétain countersigned by Barthélemy. Then he bowed one final time and disappeared. How does the National Revolution manage to produce so many of these simpletons?

November 12, 1941

At 10 A.M., as a ribbon of light over the Clermont road fought to break through the torrential rain, a long procession filed into the prison: a police official, policemen, etc. There was a feeling in the air of an execution. After a good deal of time wasted in floundering, prattling, and formalities, we finally headed out. A lead car was followed by guards with machine guns and policemen, and then by our cars, in which we were each "protected" by a guard and a police official. Blum was ahead of me, Gamelin behind, and behind us were more police cars, more machine guns, and even an ambulance. All of these precautions had been taken for fear that some of the government's supporters had taken too seriously the Marshal's speeches and the campaign against us.

"My" police official was one of a well-known kind: a society man, who knew all the best people in those wealthy bourgeois circles where Hitler is revered. Their admiration for Hitler, which had long been kept under wraps, burst into the open the day he attacked Russia. Some of those people are actually indignant that the Pope has not given his blessing to this crusade and are absolutely convinced he will be unseated by council decree in Berlin after Germany's victory. Fortunately for us, we have the Marshal, who addressed the two thousand volunteer mercenaries of the anti-Bolshevik Legion. As they marched off in their German uniforms to fight the Russians, he praised them for saving France's honor.

My "traveling companion" had something to say about everything and everyone: the Count of Paris and his continuing claims to the throne, Weygand, et al. He finally came around to talking about the trial in Riom. He was clearly playing the game the way it is supposed to be played, frankly offering information in exchange for some he wanted to get from me. I obliged him. I told him that the Riom trial was no longer a matter of concern, since Pétain had already issued instructions to the judges. I told him I planned to spend my time in prison waiting for Hitler's defeat to be played out in a blast of Wagnerian horns and trumpets. As for Göring, Mussolini, Himmler, and Farinacci,[45] they would all end up escaping to Franco's Spain where they would join Pétain, Darlan, Laval, and Barthé-lemy in a reunion that would be nothing like the dethroned kings' dinner at the Carnival in Venice, which is recounted in *Candide*. Thus would the war end precisely where it had begun, in Spain. And the renascent Repub-lic, taking a page from the Bourbons, would launch its own Spanish expe-dition and bring them all back to France. That is what I offered my friendly companion: more than enough for him to file his report with the Director of the *Sûreté!*

A lovely road crossing autumn-colored forests took us from Clermont to Cahors, Gambetta's birthplace, where Monzie was later to settle. We then went through Souillac, the home of that wretched fellow Malvy, who after having been saved by the Republic, went on to betray it. A gambling addiction tripped him into venality, and he became an agent on the payroll of the Spanish Ambassador, Lequerica, as soon as diplomatic relations were restored with Spain. We passed through Auch, Mirande, Tarbes, Pau, and Oloron and were stared at everywhere we went by large numbers of curious onlookers and members of the Veterans' Legion, the French Nazi Party. I was surprised to hear so few jeers, although as we went through Barthou's territory, I heard one resounding "Bastards, Crooks" shouted by a well-dressed woman. That night, we drove down a winding road that ran along the Aspe stream, at the bottom of a hollow walled in by boulders rising straight up, and then moved on to the Fontaines d'Escot and the valley where Queen Margot, in the company of various lords and damsels, gamboled and prattled about love and the pleasures of life. We came to a gorge with a hellish bridge and saw a few stars twinkling over the

---

45. Roberto Farinacci began committing acts of violence for the Italian Fascist Party as early as 1922. He subsequently became the party's Secretary-General (1925–1926). He served as permanent liaison between Hitler and Mussolini during the war.

ridge across the way: the fortress of Le Portalet. The procession came to a halt.

Leaving our escorts behind, Blum, Gamelin, and I entered the fortress. In the glow from the headlights, I was pleasantly surprised to discover the presence of Bartalet, the same considerate and fearless fellow who had overseen my living arrangements in Chazeron, which was the worst period of my captivity. He had since then been appointed Commissioner of Police in Nancy, but the Germans had had him quickly removed from the position. This superb pilot from the Great War, who has remained undaunted and unyielding, was then named to a position in Pau, which is why he was there to take care of me at Le Portalet, making the hardship of my captivity easier to bear. I thanked him and we shook hands, as all those distinguished gentlemen from the police looked on.

Before leaving me, a Lieutenant in the guards told me that he too was from the Vaucluse. As it happens, I knew his father, who was a highly respected physician. They are friends of Lally-Nevière, who was the most generous of men, a man adored by all the peasants in the Aygues Valley, which was once a refuge for Calvinists. When I would go to visit him in Saint-Martin-de-la-Brasque, his servant, Némorin Pourpre, used to rush to get his drum, which he had bought in Avignon to while away his loneliness, and greet me with furious drum rolls, after which he would wipe his brow and shout out in Provençal: " I really got a kick out of that!"

I walked across the drawbridge and was greeted by the warden of the fortress, Commander Vidala, a disabled veteran from the Great War. He is a fine officer whom I had awarded an instructorship at the Saint-Cyr Military Academy in 1936. I tried to keep our encounter as short as I could, for I could feel all the warmth he still felt for me, which seemed even greater, given the ordeal I was going through and my shameful conviction. Vichy had unknowingly appointed an officer who was both a patriot and a republican.

As I was leaving, I ran into the dwarf who used to be the warden at the prison in Riom. He is Clémentel's protégé, a man who became a reactionary overnight just to keep his job. He let some sixty prisoners die of hunger this winter. He should roast in hell.

I went down the stairs to the fourth level of the basement, where we stopped in front of a massive door held by five bolts and a huge lock. There is a gendarme stationed in front of it night and day. I walked into a small, narrow room with a barred window that looked out onto a mountain stream with a monotonous gurgle and, beyond it, a sheer mountain face blocking the horizon. As General Laure once wrote, Marshal Pétain knows how to do things right. In this desert deprived of light and far removed from everything and everyone, I will receive no visitors, not even my sons, except over vacations, and I won't be able to offer them any comfort or take care of them when they do come. Pétain knows well that nothing could be more painful to me than that. He is hoping that by isolating me in this pit he will eventually drive me into some kind of depression.

In his October 16 diktat, he told the judges what their duties were in this trial. He thinks that by having us incarcerated far from our families and our lawyers he will be able to hamper us in the preparation of our defense and break down our resistance. I can do nothing about his judges, but I can do everything about myself.

As I do every year, I recalled, as the evening came to a close, a night in 1932, when in our little house in Garches my wife accepted death with a simplicity that was probably more heartrending for me than the anguish or horror of dying would have been. I relive that night every year on this date and hear her once again uttering her last wishes with a smile and a farewell.

November 13, 1941

I have been reading and working. I rest by putting my personal effects in order. Around 11 A.M. I went out for a little air on a windswept terrace of sorts. Seeing no point in turning around in circles in that narrow cage, hemmed in on all sides, I went back down to my cell. Vidala, the warden, was genuinely concerned about me. I tried to reassure him, but he later had a real promenade installed on the roof of the fortress.

During the afternoon, in an extraordinary display of baseness and childishness, the dwarf came to inform me of the regulations governing prison life. He claimed that this grotesque hodgepodge of rules was the work of Barthélemy, over in the Justice Department. I asked him for a copy of them, but he refused. Too bad—I would have loved to have sent them to the United States. Fate will apparently never reward Barthélemy with the glory he deserves.

November 16, 1941

Sunday. Chauvel was able to get in to see me at 2 P.M. Russia is still holding out. The United States has effectively repealed the laws imposing neutrality. He told me that Gamelin was ill and had been taken to a hospital in Pau. We looked out at the Aspe. A small group of children accompanied by their schoolteacher walked by. They stopped across from my window and shouted and waved a joyful hello to me.

November 18, 1941

Jeanne sent me a bouquet of violets and two packs of cigarettes. Got a letter of encouragement from my friend Gence d'Aubagne.

November 19, 1941

A gendarme and a cook who are both from Villeneuve met in my room to rail against the policy of collaboration and Nazism within France. They still think that Pétain is playing both ends against the middle, and that once the Germans show signs of faltering, he'll kick them out. I explained to them just who Pétain is—a vicious old man—and told them of the rancor he bears against Foch, Poincaré, and Joffre. I told them that in his preface to Chauvineau's book, Pétain spoke out against modernizing the Army, against armored divisions, against changes in the Army and in its officer corps. He even claimed that there was no way to get through the Ardennes, which was precisely where the Germans broke through, adding that if they ever tried, they would suffer terrible defeat. We all know what happened. On one point they agreed with me: that all our hopes lie with the United States.

November 22, 1941

The young gendarme from Villeneuve informed me that Weygand has been pushed into retirement (although they have made it look like an honor). The November 21 newspapers report that after a glorious career and fifty-six years of public service, General Weygand has decided to step down. He has been awarded a special commendation for meritorious service! He has not left Pétain's side since he got to Vichy, which coincided with an earlier visit from Abetz and Brinon. The news item from the Havas agency is a sparkling example of malaise, hypocrisy, and loutishness.

It reminds me of what the society-type police official who brought me here said about there being three problems:

1. Weygand, who does not want us to give up our bases
2. The Legion, which is modeled after the Nazi Party
3. The Count of Paris

Looks as if the Weygand problem has been resolved. One curious note was sounded here: In his retirement, Weygand will continue writing his memoirs. Which Weygand? The strict reactionary? The soldier? He is clear-sighted and has a gift for expressing himself, but his military knowledge is terribly outdated. He played a major role in ousting Reynaud and pushing through the decision to surrender in Bordeaux, in collaboration with Pétain, Baudouin, and Bouthillier. Consider the depositions he supplied for Riom—and his own ambitions. Pétain hates him, but he did not relieve him of his command gratuitously. Weygand was probably sacrificed to counterbalance the departure of Marquet and other pro-German types. He is at bottom just an African proconsul who succeeded in making a good name for himself with the Americans and the British, and in creating illusions about himself in the minds of French patriots; in sum, he's a Prefect masquerading as a General. Someday I'll have to put down in writing the nature of my relations with him in 1933, and his with Paul-Boncour and Pétain, and include reports from the Supreme War Councils of 1934 and 1935 and his letter to Reibel. He has also written a book about Turenne, which is mediocre. And then there is the speech he gave in Lille: "I was privy to Marshal Foch's secrets …" A marvelous example of political, military, and moral chicanery.

November 24, 1941

Blum managed to get word to me that the Germans have taken Rostov and that the British have gained ground in Libya. He added that Radio Paris has announced that Pétain is about to resign and be replaced by a General. I don't believe a word of it.

November 27, 1941

I am suddenly overcome with fatigue. I have been shivering and feeling nauseous.

December 7, 1941

The gendarme on duty came and told me: "Bad news. Japan is at war with the United States." I know nothing more.

December 16, 1941

Some of the fine gendarmes here came to say good-bye. They have been relieved of their duty at Le Portalet and will be moving on to Pau. They have been replaced by young, rather vulgar types.

The British are evacuating Malaysia. I always felt that if Japan were to enter the war, it would weigh heavily on the British. How will the United States be able to continue supplying them? Or China? or Russia?

December 22, 1941

Jean has come here from Grenoble, via Lyons, Avignon, Toulouse, and Pau. He is a wonderful lad, bursting with indignation and cheer. Grenoble is a veritable hotbed of patriotism and rebelliousness.

December 23, 1941

Hitler has appointed himself Supreme Commander in Chief, or rather, since he was already that, Supreme Commander with a direct and personal hand on things. This says a lot more about the failure of the German offensive in Russia than did his October 9 statement, in which he claimed success. Just as it was in ancient Germania, Hitler is trying to cultivate confidence in and devotion to his person.

December 24, 1941

At 7 P.M. Ernest, the young cook here, walked into my cell with a huge soup tureen. Since I never eat soup, I looked at him quizzically. He put a finger to his lips and left with his gendarme escort. When I lifted the cover, I found a magnificent Yule log![46]

Although Jean had lunched with me earlier, he managed to come back in the evening. I had saved a large slice of Ernest's Yule log for him.

December 25, 1941

Mazé[47] came, faithful as always.

---

46. A cake in the shape of a log, traditional Christmas fare.
47. The escape plan was dropped following Daladier's transfer to Le Portalet.

1942

[The prisoners are once again in Bourassol prison. They were brought back to stand trial in the courthouse in Riom, just a few miles away.]

January 2, 1942

The press has reprinted Marshal Pétain's New Year's Day address—an avowal of impotence. We have come a long way since the bravado that followed the signing of the Armistice. How sweet the National Revolution was ... while there was still a Republic.

January 5, 1942

At 11 o'clock this morning, I spotted Blum standing at his window. He looked relaxed and rested. He had hated being in Le Portalet, because of the hordes of guards who would come into our cells ten times a day and shadow us whenever we went out on the terraces. This, of course, is what prison life is all about. He smiled and reminded me of Bazaine's captivity on Sainte-Marguérite Island, where he enjoyed the company of his wife, his children, and his orderlies. I told him that the difference between that fellow's treatment and ours is proof that we are not traitors; if we were, the French-speaking Nazis who are running our country—after having handed it over to the Germans—would have afforded us the same pleasant lifestyle that comrades in treason always reserve for each other.

We also spoke about the trial. In spite of our having been brought back to Bourassol to be made available for Vichy justice, Blum doesn't believe we'll ever see the inside of a courtroom. He asked, "Can you really expect the government to be so stupid as to hand us the stick to beat them with?"

I replied: "The government is probably a lot stupider than you think; in fact, if Napoleon is to be believed, it's the stupidest form of government of all, since it is a military government. Remember what he told Roederer about military regimes? The French will not stand for them. Moreover, after the resounding speech Pétain gave on October 16, when he sentenced us before our trial, he couldn't go back on his word even if he wanted to. How could anyone think otherwise?"

Still, Blum felt that in view of the crisscross appointments that sent that sorry creature Lagarde to the High Court of Appeals as head prosecutor and brought Caous from there to preside over the Cour Suprême, there was reason to think that the case would be deferred. Caous is a man who likes to wield authority, and Blum feels he'll wield enough of it to have the case postponed indefinitely, "pending a more complete investigation," which is what the government really wants. I told Blum that I didn't believe any of that. Caous was brought in because during the last war he was the man who demanded the death penalty for those poor firing squad victims that history refers to as the Vingré Martyrs, which was a horrible tragedy. It is true, however, that after having demanded the death penalty, Caous voluntarily joined a fighting unit.

We then turned to the most recent depositions and the evidence that had been compiled to date. At the outbreak of the war, Blum had been critical of my record at the War Ministry. He told me now that he had not fully appreciated what I had done during that three-year period. If he had not himself seen the Examining Magistrate's file, he could never have even guessed that arms manufacturing had received so sizable a stimulus. He thought that we should have instituted currency controls after Munich. I had to remind him that the Senate had brought down the government in his second term as Prime Minister precisely over that issue. Moreover, currency controls would have created problems not only within France but above all in our relations with the United States and England, with which we had signed a monetary agreement in 1936. At any rate, could we possibly have used more than the 65 billion francs that had been earmarked for arms manufacturing?

It was a bright, sunny January morning, so conducive to outdoor conversation that we went right on chatting, with me in the courtyard and Blum standing behind the bars of his cell.

I asked him what he knew about the conditions under which Reynaud had resigned in Bordeaux. Blum asserted that Reynaud had not lost his majority in the Cabinet. The discussion there had already gone on for a long time, as I recalled it, when they recessed for three hours, with the debate over Chautemps's proposal resuming at 10 P.M. That is when it was agreed that Lebrun; Herriot, the President of the Chamber of Deputies; Jeanneney, the President of the Senate; and all the Ministers would board ship at Port-Vendres and leave for Algeria. Pomaret, the Minister of the Interior, even offered to give me a ride in his car, an offer I declined, preferring to leave with the Members of Parliament traveling on the *Massilia*. Blum confirmed these facts, but with one correction. Jeanneney had departed earlier and was already in Toulouse when he was called back to Bordeaux. Of course, while Parliament and the Cabinet were being led down this garden path, while people were assuring us with their hands over their hearts of their heroic resolve to continue the war from North Africa, telling us that our powerful Navy was still intact and how we had more than a thousand modern aircraft, the Armistice was secretly being negotiated with Germany through Franco's Ambassador, Lequerica.

I went back to my "apartment." The newspapers were carrying a Reuters dispatch, dateline Washington, January 3: "Twenty-six nations have issued a joint statement, pledging not to negotiate a separate armistice or peace with the enemies and to commit their full resources to the defeat of the members of the Tripartite Pact." These governments in exile are far more loyal and reliable representatives of their temporarily enslaved countrymen than the traitors the Nazis have installed in their place. That France alone did not join in signing that statement makes Pétain's grim New Year's address all the more appalling.

January 9, 1942

"The ocean liner *Lamoricière*, victim of a violent storm, has sunk off the coast of the Balearic Islands, as it was making its crossing from Algiers to Marseilles." That is the boat on which I was brought back to France from Morocco. I had left Casablanca by train and been warmly greeted by railroad workers and soldiers, in spite of Prouvost's[1] and Baudouin's slanderous remarks about me and their attempts to incite political assassination.

---

1. Jean Prouvost, founder of *Paris-Soir* and supporter of Marshal Pétain.

I was accompanied on the trip by Forneret, the Moroccan Chief of Police. Forneret was one of the first to come to Blum's aid after the Royalist attack on his life during the funeral services for Bainville. In 1936, he became associated with Salengro.[2] He is a devoted follower of Noguès and in all likelihood a Freemason. When Pétain took over, Forneret hoped to hold on to the excellent job he'd been awarded under the Popular Front. I had occasion to visit his magnificent police station in Rabat, which is more lavishly outfitted than any police headquarters in France. I would be very surprised if he were kept in the position. He always acted kindly toward me in Morocco and has always been restrained in his efforts to stay in the good graces of those now in power, efforts that have probably been unsuccessful. We parted company in Rabat, where I was met by policemen from the Algiers division of the *Sûreté*, there to assure my "protection." As it happened, they were both republicans and patriots. The heat was oppressive. Soot from the engine showered onto every compartment of the train, where the crowds of passengers massed together were dripping with sweat.

In Bel-Abbes, I was greeted by the Subprefect, come to share with me briefly his contempt for our having surrendered in Bordeaux and for the men who had handed over France in order to destroy the Republic. The train stopped in Maison-Carrée, where the gentlemen from the *Sûreté* decided that we would get off, on the grounds that in Algiers there might be demonstrations or incidents. Guillermet, former Subprefect in Carpentras and the man who started me in my career in politics, received me in the middle of the night. He was dressed in white. They put me up in a hotel on the top of a hill. The following morning, I was awakened by military bands, the regimental marching of soldiers, and the roar of crowds setting off to welcome Admiral Abrial, as the newly appointed Governor of Algeria made his grand entrance into the city. I knew what it was like to be welcomed by the French and Islamic populations in Algiers, having been received there in 1939, but today, I was a prisoner in a second-class hotel, not allowed to leave, day or night, as per the orders of Chevalier, the local

---

2. Roger Salengro, Socialist politician and Minister of the Interior. His suicide came in the aftermath of a campaign to defame him orchestrated by right-wing and far-right-wing newspapers, among them *L'Action française* and the weekly *Gringoire*.

Prefect, with whom I used to have considerable dealings. I objected so strenuously to those outrageous conditions that Chevalier eventually grew ashamed of himself, at which point I simply went off to dine at the seaside home of a kindly employee from the Prefecture.

At noon the following day, I boarded the *Lamoricière* with my son Jean. We traveled under destroyer escort, with the ship avoiding its normal course and hugging the West African and then the Spanish coastlines on its way to Marseilles. These precautions had been taken because the British had plans to intercept the ship and take me to London.

On our arrival, my son Jean set down the following account: "When our ship reached port in Marseilles, there was a welcoming committee on hand—workers, longshoremen, and agitators screaming and shouting threats, 'Cowards, deserters, traitors.' My father pointed to a fat character screaming his lungs out and laughed as he rolled himself a cigarette. Just as we were pulling alongside the dock, I heaved a sigh of relief when I saw Mazé coming on board to get us. We managed to get out safely through an office and fled in Giaccobi's truck before the mob could catch us. Giaccobi is a good and well-meaning fellow; he had taken care to load iron bars in the back so that we could defend ourselves, but hadn't bothered about the damaged rear wheel that forced us to stop every mile or so. It was a hairy experience, but our friends at the dock hadn't thought to follow us. We made it to Orange, where Diard had the courage to put us up, and where we learned rather quickly who our real friends were. Those first few days, there was no need to set additional places at the dinner table."

January 10, 1942

At 4 P.M. Dr. Mazé arrived, visibly upset, from Châtelguyon, where Jeanneney had asked to meet with him at 11 in the morning. In a discussion they had had four or five days earlier, Mazé found Jeanneney well disposed both toward him and toward me. Today, on arriving, Mazé was informed that he would not be received before 2 in the afternoon. Jeanneney probably needed all that time to prepare the "audience" he was about to grant him, in which, after criticizing Pétain, the Vichy government, and the Riom trial, he complained bitterly that I had never actually ordered an offensive in September 1939, that I had not issued Italy an ultimatum, that

I had come to Gamelin's defense, and so on. In sum, the President of the Senate leveled a scathing indictment against me, which he concluded by expressing his regret that Reynaud had not taken over from me as head of the government a lot earlier. Mazé was so infuriated that he snapped back violently. He probably should have just let it pass, but who ever heard of an infuriated Breton who could control his temper? Mazé was absolutely fuming, and to be fair to everyone, he laid it on Reynaud too, criticizing him for having brought Pétain into the government and having appointed Weygand Supreme Commander, in other words, for having chosen the hangmen who put the cord around his own neck after all those sleazy dealings in Bordeaux that brought about his downfall. He also criticized Reynaud for having surrounded himself with notorious defeatists, like the pro-Fascist Baudouin and the Cagoulard Bouthillier, whom he appointed Minister. Those two started betraying him from their very first day on the job. Gamelin at least would have remained a good soldier and executed the order calling for the organization of resistance forces in North Africa.

Mazé, who was still out of control when he related all of this to me, said that Jeanneney was so flustered that he couldn't find anything to say. I did my best to calm him down, but it wasn't easy. He added that, on the other hand, he had been very warmly received by the staff employees of the Chamber of Deputies and the Senate, whose offices had been moved from Vichy to Châtelguyon. They told him to offer me their respects and to ask me if there were anything that they could get for me to make my detention less unpleasant. Once again, the "little people" were giving a lesson in magnanimity to those who were supposedly their superiors.

Jeanneney is a mediocre sort whose surface severity impressed the high livers that more often than not Senators are. I was on good terms with him until the winter of 1939, when he actually did want us to launch an attack against the Italians, a point on which we were in total disagreement. I explained my position on numerous occasions before parliamentary committees and the War Committee. On the basis of all the intelligence coming out of Italy that September, it was clear that under the influence of the Crown, the Catholic church and various working-class organizations, the Italian people were opposed to going to war on the side of Germany. In fact, it was precisely because Hitler couldn't draw Italy into the war against Poland that he ended up turning to Stalin. Count Ciano was clear in his talks with François-Poncet,[3] our Ambassador to Rome, that it was his desire to work with us in maintaining Italy's neutrality. We had also signed an attractive trade agreement with them in October and ordered large amounts of equipment through their Air Force Ministry, which we had begun receiving at the end of 1939.

To be sure, we knew that if France were ever to suffer defeat or be dealt a truly debilitating blow, Mussolini would very likely make the political choice, as any jackal would. But no one in the military doubted the strength of the French Army or the solidity of France's fortified and well-organized defenses. Wasn't it enough to have to fight the powerful German Army? Did we have to go looking deliberately for a second enemy, one whose Air Force and above all whose Navy could inflict serious damage and sever our communications with North Africa?

However, if we assumed a purely defensive posture, four or five divisions plus the troops manning our fortresses would have been enough to defend the border in the Alps, and another five or six divisions would have sufficed to hold the coast and the lines that I had had fortified in southern Tunisia. The troops thus spared from duty in the Alps and North Africa could have been concentrated in northeastern France, which would have been our wisest course of action.

For all these reasons, launching an offensive against Italy appeared to me inappropriate, however weakened their forces were after the conquest of Abyssinia and their participation in the civil war in Spain. It also struck me as an unjust and gratuitous act, considering that the Italians had kept out of the war despite their alliance with Germany. I felt that the war would go on for a long time and that what had begun as a limited conflict would expand into a war between large coalitions of forces, eventually boiling down to a war of attrition. My idea was to hold the line in the North and the Northeast and to go on the offensive if the Poles managed to hold out against the German attack that winter and the following spring, as our military leaders believed they would. That would have been

---

3. André François-Poncet, French Ambassador to Berlin until 1938, then Ambassador to Rome.

the time to go on the offensive, in close cooperation with the British Army and above all, the British Air Force; that was my idea of how the war should be conducted. I should add as well that I was privy to the telegrams the British government was receiving from Sir Percy Lorraine, their Ambassador to Rome, and that they echoed those being sent to us by François-Poncet. Lorraine, too, was firmly opposed to any action being taken against Italy. Moreover, no one at any time, either on the War Committee or during Cabinet meetings, had ever proposed or even alluded to such an attack, with the exception of Jeanneney—during Parisian dinner parties. Whenever positions involving real responsibility were offered to this "man of iron," he always turned them down.

All of this was so futile, anyway. Couldn't Jeanneney have directed his outrage at matters closer to hand, like the dissolution of certain institutions guaranteeing freedom, which has now been officially ratified by the National Assembly in Vichy?

According to a British broadcast picked up in Châtelguyon, the Russians are just thirty miles outside of Smolensk. It seemed to me that that was far more important than Jeanneney's warmed-over rancor, and Mazé agreed.

February 4, 1942

5 P.M. Ribet met with Minister of Justice Barthélemy in Paris to discuss the possibility of bringing his file and various other documents with him to Riom for the trial. He was told that the Germans had been insisting that lawyers' files be submitted to their Embassy for a quick and "obviously superficial" review, in the presence of the lawyers themselves. Ribet strongly protested. He suggested to Barthélemy that he simply pass a law eliminating lawyers' rights to privileged communication altogether. When he refused, as we had agreed, to hand the file over to the German Embassy, Barthélemy sputtered and whined. He claimed he was doing everything in his power and that he was opposed to there being a trial at this time, but said that Romier had forced it on them. Whatever the truth, if the Germans insist on reviewing our file, we'll drop our defense rather than comply.

February 5, 1942

Ribet ran into Monzie at a lawyers' meeting about some case. The author of *Ci-devant* has switched sides once again. He no longer believes the Germans will win the war. Marshal Pétain's failure to find a place for him equal to his talents has made him an embittered man. If I have understood correctly, he would like to write another *Ci-devant*, this time with the Marshal as the prime target. Ribet filled me in on some of the juicier parts of Monzie's youth. More recently, he testified against Chaumié, who had given him a medal when he was Education Minister. As he was waiting for his turn to testify, Jouvenel[4] went over to Monzie and pointed to the *Légion d'honneur* ribbon he had pinned to his lapel. Monzie immediately removed it and then went in to testify against the very man who had given it to him. He also testified against me last year. Of course, I merely appointed him Minister.

February 6, 1942

Mazé, Ribet, and his wife came around 11:30. Mme Ribet repeated a conversation she had had with Bénazet the night before at the Hotel Pailleret, near Riom. To get away from his wife, Bénazet had told her he was going there to testify. He had been merciless when he testified against me at the Riom tribunal in the summer of 1941, the main thrust of his testimony being an attempt to prove that if he had been appointed War Minister or Air Force Minister, or better yet both, France would have repelled the German attack and been victorious. Since that time, after having expected to be named, at the very least, special counsel to Marshal Pétain, he has been removed from both his mayoralty and from his seat on a regional council. Furthermore, he has been denounced as a Freemason, which is why he is now a Gaullist. He showed Mme Ribet his latest deposition, in which he states that our military leaders alone, by virtue of their incompetence, were responsible for France's defeat; that we had 2,500 modern aircraft and 4,000 tanks, which they proved incapable of putting into operation; that there were all those traitors who wanted France to be defeated so that

---

4. Bertrand de Jouvenel, economist, philosopher, and essayist.

the Republic could be destroyed. He said he knew at least one of them personally, a classmate from the Saint-Cyr Military Academy. Pétain's police keep him informed. If Pétain doesn't personally apologize, Bénazet will pronounce so stinging an indictment of him that the very walls of the Riom courthouse will shake from it.

Today is the anniversary of the Fascist demonstrations of 1934, the first significant attack on the Republic. The mob included the curious and the stupid. Good people, driven to anger by the press's blown-up accounts of the Stavisky affair, had taken to the streets to demonstrate alongside French-style Fascists, all of them straining to force their way into the Senate and the Chamber of Deputies. Among the working classes, it is now thought that the men of February 6 took their revenge by surrendering in Bordeaux, and that they handed France over to the Germans so as to finish off the Republic. Laval was the man behind the Stavisky affair, as Torrès has ably demonstrated.

February 8, 1942

Had lunch with Jean, who talked about his life in Grenoble. We spoke of Hitler and the coming spring offensives, probably into the Caucasus and Egypt. Like Napoleon long before him, Hitler will be forced to recruit auxiliary troops: Romanians, Hungarians, Slovaks, and Poles, a veritable international army under the orders of the German High Command. This is why Göring and Ribbentrop went to Budapest. If Germany should fail to defeat Russia, the breakup of that international army will herald Europe's revolt.

February 9, 1942

At around ten this morning I opened my window to take in a little cold air and Guy La Chambre interrupted his walk in the courtyard to come over and chat with me. He is pleased about the upcoming trial in Riom, which will offer him not only a chance to defend himself in front of the nation, but also a pleasant diversion from his present life. Unfortunately the cells that have been set aside for us and that Marshal Pétain's government has been so kind as to furnish with a wooden table and a cane armchair are infested with lice and fleas.

La Chambre claimed that the heads of the Air Force lied. At the time of the battle of the Meuse, 2,000 fighters were available to them, but Corap's forces had only 2. Our military commanders didn't recognize the seriousness of the battle until it was virtually lost. We still had 2,500 modern aircraft left when the Armistice was signed.

February 10, 1942

American and British airplanes have dropped some 3 million extremely well-written propaganda tracts over Occupied France. They were probably well received. They do justice to the efforts made by the French.

A news item from Alsace relates in moving terms the Alsatians' resistance to nazification there, in spite of German brutality. There were demonstrations in Mulhouse and Colmar on November 11, even though laying wreaths on the graves of soldiers was officially prohibited. Boys eighteen and older are being sent to German camps and subjected to intensive military training, in preparation for being shipped out to the Russian front. Girls are being sent to Germany and Norway. All able-bodied men are being given roles in civil defense. They have set up concentration camps bursting with Alsatians; they have persecuted nuns in Ribeauvillé and they are demanding sworn allegiance to Hitler. Nonetheless, a great many young Alsatians continue to make their way into Unoccupied France at night.

February 17, 1942

The trial was supposed to open in Riom today, but when Ribet pointed out that this was Mardi Gras, the judges decided not to put on their costumes until the day after tomorrow.

February 19, 1942

We left Bourassol for the prison in Riom. It made for an imposing procession, with motorcycles at the lead, five cars, one for each of us plus the inspectors from the *Sûreté* at our sides, and a vanload of helmeted and armed guards from the new state police force, Pétain's SS.

The streets were dotted with curious souls, looking on the whole sympathetic toward us. When we reached the prison, we were met by the warden, a gentlemanly sort, who deep down disapproves of the trial. We were escorted to our cells by Dumas, the head guard, whose southern accent resonated against the vaulting of the long, dark, and humid corridor. We passed the exercise yard, the sleeping quarters, the workshop, and a thick oak door with massive locks. At the end of the corridor, we took a long staircase down to our cells. Mine is spacious, dark, and, in spite of the iron stove that Dumas had had lit for me, ice cold. The walls have been recently whitewashed. I suppose the straw mattress wrapped in gray cloth and set onto a wooden frame could pass for a couch, but there are vermin running all through it. The rest of the furnishings include a wooden table, three zinc tubs, an old armchair and two straight-back chairs, one of which wobbles. Fortunately, there is a little electric lamp I can read and work by.

February 25, 1942

I awakened in a state of such extreme fatigue that I was incapable of going to the courthouse. I so informed the Head Magistrate, who had the medical examiner from Riom sent to my cell at 12:30. No sooner had the jailer closed the door behind him than the doctor began shaking both my hands and clasped his arms about my neck to hug me. I had to pinch myself when I realized it was Renard, an old classmate of mine. We used to have our meals together at old lady Bisoud's place down on Marseilles Street in Lyons. I had nicknamed him Montesquieu because they have the same profile. After listening to my lungs and heart with his stethoscope and taking my blood pressure, Montesquieu told me I needed a full week's bed rest. I blew up at him, just as I used to in the days of our youth. He finally gave in. We reminisced for a while about that distant past. He wanted to get me cigarettes, coffee, God knows what else, and absolutely insisted that I be given a week's rest. He headed back to the Cour Suprême, where the judges were awaiting the results of his examination before rendering their decision. What a pleasure it was to see him. If this were ancient Rome, I'd take his coming for an omen.

February 26, 1942

I've got a fever, a pounding headache, and a hacking cough that's going to rip my lungs apart.

February 27, 1942

Spent the day dozing in bed, feverish and fatigued.

February 28, 1942

The Riom trial opened, and I was cross-examined for the first time. I was still running a fever and was nervous, but as soon as they started asking me questions, I lashed back at them. Over and over, I battered away at all those contemptible traitors who had handed France over to the Germans just so they could bring down the Republic.

When court reconvened for the second session, I struck even harder, stopping only when I was too exhausted to go on. I could sense panic in the balcony, where the New Order's inspectors were observing the scene, and could hear the frightened rustling of judicial robes. The presiding judge took this all in with a calm demeanor, which resulted in his being attacked by the Nazi-controlled press. As far as he was concerned, an accused man who had already been sentenced by Pétain was obviously a guilty man, but in spite of that, he seemed to have maintained some honorable ideas about his profession. Every now and then, the judge sitting next to him would lean over and whisper something. I would have liked to have known what they were saying, but I went on pummeling away with increasing vehemence.

Then it was all over and the lawyers began congratulating me. The gendarmes saluted me as I walked out past them, as if I were reviewing troops. There is no mistaking the meaning of a gesture like that. Back at the prison, the guards shook hands with me and seemed delighted. They are good Frenchmen, good republicans. They had fired the iron stove in my cell, where Génébrier and Mazé were waiting for me, both of them bursting with enthusiasm. I was so terribly sleepy.

February 29, 1942

Off again to the courthouse for another session. In the prison's outer office, I ran into a war veteran under police escort, wearing his medals and stars from 1914. He had been working in Vichy when he suffered some sort of humiliation that led him to speak disparagingly of the government and Pétain. A policeman informed on him and he was given a three-month prison sentence and prohibited from residing in Vichy, where he had built a house. His children cried their hearts out. Oyez! Oyez! Make way for the Marshal's justice!

Back in the courtroom, I continued my attack, as Vichy's grim-faced bureaucrats, overseeing the judges, went about their voluminous note taking. Afterwards, I was returned first to the Riom prison, where the good folk there congratulated me, then to Bourassol, where I hoped to get some sleep. When I got there, Marie was waiting for me, smiling and bright-eyed and very happy about the way things had gone. I chatted with her and the Alsatian guard Ancel, who is a good man. Ancel told me that he had filled out the prison register, which he claimed was the only place where you could still find the words, "in the name of the people of France."

March 1, 1942

The sun was up and the sky once again a soft, subdued blue, but high up in a pine tree, my friend the Bourassol owl went right on with his nocturnal song, even well after the break of day. I went down to the courtyard and set off on my walk. From his window, Blum kindly asked me how I was feeling, and his daughter-in-law Renée read the text of British radio broadcasts to me. Then I spotted Mme La Chambre heading toward me. She shook my hand and asked to have a word with me. She had been ignoring me for the past two years. She is superstitious, the way theater people are, and probably thinks luck has turned my way. I went back up to my cell. She had brought me a nice chicken leg. I gave her a can of apricot jam in return. My two faithful companions, Roger and the doctor, who have been so courageous and patient, were in excellent spirits, as they have been everyday.

March 2, 1942

Another beautiful sunny day. After all the dreadful snow we had been having, it is as if the earth has come back to life. Bourassol's pigeons are once again sailing across the sky. In the cafes in Riom, people are drinking to the Fourth Republic, one freed of the fetters, the rust, and the parliamentary demagoguery that eventually made the Third Republic unrecognizable.

My lawyer, Ribet, dropped by to see me at 5 P.M. Listening to me talk for two whole days has apparently worn him out.

March 3, 1942

For an entire afternoon, I laid out for those finely robed fellows on the bench all the problems associated with harnessing our industrial resources and the various solutions I had painstakingly sought to implement. At the start, I had absolutely nothing to work with because in 1934, Pétain, as War Minister, had cut back the military budget that I had managed to get passed by Parliament when I was Prime Minister in 1933. Neither the judges nor the prosecutors knew anything about these matters, and they prudently refrained from intervening. If I failed in the industrial sector, how is it that the output of war matériel tripled over the winter months? It is a real stickler of a subject, but because I was completely absorbed by my desire to make everything perfectly clear for the stenographers, the journalists, the policemen, and the gendarmes, who were the true representatives of the French people in that courtroom, it appeared to the judges to be no more than a pleasant and interesting issue; I made no mention of the contemptible traitors in Vichy.

Gamelin was supposed to be cross-examined after me. He stated at the outset that he would answer no questions whatsoever. The presiding judge struggled for an hour to get him to talk, but to no avail. It was distressing and painful to watch, enough to make you sick.

March 4, 1942

Guy La Chambre was on the stand for the whole afternoon. For two hours, starting at 1:30, he went over his handling of the Air Force Ministry. The people on our side must not have been too pleased. Why didn't he go on the attack? The second half was better. At the time of the signing of the Armistice, there were 2,500 modern warplanes that had never seen action; they had been left sitting in hangars while our soldiers, pounded by bombs and strafed by Stukas, were begging for air support.

The accusations contained in the depositions given by Massenet, d'Harcourt, and other Air Force Generals like Le Chatelet were terribly damaging for La Chambre. He answered them point by point, graciously excusing the Air Force Chiefs of Staff for having spent their time reflecting on the future while the battle for the life or death of France raged on outside. His final statements were better still, as much in what he said as in the way he said it, and his concluding comments were excellent. I congratulated him and his lawyer, Cresteil, as well.

When I got back to the prison, the head guard came to chat with me. He is a generous and brave fellow, and the epitome of a Marseillais. Quite unexpectedly, he handed me a flask of pastis, out of friendship for me and probably also as a result of the defamation campaign they have been running in *Gringoire* for years, in which they portray me as an alcoholic. Afterwards, this very good fellow began raving about his two daughters, one of whom is a gifted stenographer and the other a law school student. I waved hello to them just a while ago when I saw them at the window of their quarters.

Thursday, March 5, 1942

I just learned today that on March 3, British planes bombed the Renault, Rosengard, and Salmson factories in Billancourt, where they have been manufacturing tanks and airplane engines for the Germans ever since the signing of the Armistice. The death of hundreds of innocent victims is deplorable, but why didn't the sirens sound the alert so that the people could take cover in the excellent shelters that had been provided for them? The German military command in Paris wanted them to be massacred, that's why.

La Chambre took the stand for the last time. He did all right from a purely oratorical point of view, but he praised Vuillemin and the Air Force Chiefs of Staff, and that was a little bit much. He also made a few treacherous comments about me and above all, Blum. As Mme Ribet observed, he was trying to find some loophole to sneak through to save his skin.

March 6, 1942

Young Commander Jacquot came in uniform to see me at the prison and, right in front of all the policemen, boldly handed me a present. Nothing touches me as much as thoughtful gestures of this kind that come from a real soldier.

The court had ruled that the minutes of the meeting of August 23, 1939, would be taken up in closed session. As soon as the presiding judge began his examination, I told him that I was prepared to discuss behind closed doors the diplomatic matters raised at that meeting, but not the military matters. When he insisted that we proceed, I calmly began discussing the diplomatic issues and had absolutely no trouble demonstrating that France had taken all steps necessary to maintain peace.

As early as May 16, 1939, we notified Poland that we would not go to war over Danzig, which the Germans knew well. They wanted war, wanted to destroy Poland and take one more step toward the total domination of Europe. Whoever wrote the article about Danzig under the name Bruère is a traitor. On August 23, 1939, I added, British air power compensated in part for the weakness of our own Air Force. I made reference to a speech Hitler gave on October 12, 1941, which shows that he chose not to invade England in the summer of 1940 because it would have meant committing and very likely sacrificing the entire German Air Force, which is proof of the size and effectiveness of the British Air Force. The meeting that was held on August 23, 1939, was above all given to bringing everyone up to date on events; in no way did it prevent us from subsequently devoting all our energies to saving the peace. To have cowardly resigned ourselves to let the attack on Poland stand would have brought dishonor on the nation. It was, moreover, an attack on France as well, for the only way to remain secure in the face of Germany's might was to defend the bridges over the Rhine or maintain the presence of a counterbalancing force in the East. I concluded by publicly stating that I was convinced that Germany would ultimately suffer defeat.[5]

---

5. Daladier turned his back to the judges and, speaking directly to the people in the courthouse, declared: "Germany suffered its first defeat with England and its second with Russia. There is no doubt that Germany will be defeated; it is inevitable. We must not let our confidence waver."

April 12, 1942

Rules governing the coverage of the trial in Riom as issued by the French National News Bureau:[6] "Wire services are not to carry any discussion of a political nature, any opinion bearing on the ongoing events of the war, any criticism of the government, any reference to actions taken by Pétain or even to statements he has made about the Army. Tendentious statements that can be construed as Gaullist propaganda will be subject to the severest penalties. Any person failing to comply with these rules will be immediately dismissed and turned over to the appropriate legal authorities."

April 14, 1942

Preparations were being made for our being moved to the prison in Riom, but my intuition told me that it wouldn't happen. At around 9:30 this morning, Commissioner Morel arrived with the latest issue of the *Journal officiel.* It included a legal decree adjourning the trial, pending completion of certain aspects of the investigation. All of Bourassol—prisoners, guards, and policemen alike—rang with laughter. At the time, the judges still hadn't heard about it; they were busy going about their preparations for the coming court sessions with all requisite seriousness.

At the main police station in Riom, Ribet's request for a gasoline coupon was genially turned down. He was told, "There is no need for it, counselor, now that the trial has been put off," and shown a copy of the *Journal officiel,* after which he raced over to the courthouse to inform the judges, who were totally in the dark. No one could find a copy of the *Journal.* Bruzin phoned the Police Commissioner but learned that he had given his copy to Morel, who had already left for Bourassol. So Bruzin, the Solicitor-General arguing the case, ended up calling the Bourassol jailhouse so that they would send him the *Journal officiel,* which was being shared with all the prisoners. Ever since, lawyers have been in and out of this place,

---

6. At the close of each courtroom session, the French National News Bureau issued similar orders accompanied by similar threats. See Appendix B: The Riom Trial, and Frédéric Pottecher, *Le Procès de la défaite* (Paris: Fayard, 1990).

some asking me to autograph their courthouse passes for them. Thus has come to an end Vichy's attempt, as orchestrated by Pétain and his Ministers, to place responsibility for France's defeat on the Republic. I have gone from accused to accuser. Since they had no way to respond to my accusations, they simply canceled the trial, but without setting us free, naturally.

Received a note from Jacomet: "Pétain has once again called for an armistice."

May 1, 1942

Tixier, a fine man and the owner of the Hotel des Voyageurs, sent me a small bottle of champagne to celebrate May 1. Jean sent me some lines from Walt Whitman's "O Star of France" (1870–1871):

> Like some proud ship that led the fleet so long,
> Be-seems to-day a wreck driven by the gale, a mastless hulk
> And 'mid its teeming madden'd half-drown'd crowds,
> Nor helm nor helmsman.
> Star crucified—by traitors sold,
> Star panting o'er a land of death, heroic land,
> Strange, passionate, mocking, frivolous land.
> O star! O ship of France,
> Sure as the ship of all, the Earth itself.

May 3, 1942

The Japanese have taken Mandalay. Supply routes have been cut off and the invasion of India is imminent. Nehru has been preaching passive resistance and nonviolence. Cripps's mission was a total failure. After the war, the British Empire will survive only at the cost of far-reaching changes, and even then its survival is open to question. This is the final chapter of a splendid story.

May 4, 1942

For two hours starting at 9:00 this morning, a lawyer named Baraveau and a court reporter named Paulin were at Bourassol questioning me about the progress made in our military buildup between 1936 and the end of 1938, and the fact that by the spring of 1939 we were six months ahead of schedule. That matériel, however, never made it out of the warehouse. I answered their questions, then read a statement I had prepared refusing to continue to be a part of this farce of theirs. Has the trial been suspended, or hasn't it?

There have been reactions to the Riom trial. The Italians are indignant over the testimony given about the battle in the Alps. They would like to lay claim to Nice, Corsica, and Tunisia. As for the Russians, they have been enjoying themselves at both Blum's expense and mine: the bull of the Vaucluse at Munich, they call me. And just what were *they* prepared to do for Czechoslovakia? They did nothing but equivocate, as is evidenced by the diplomatic cables of the period. The Americans, via radio, have been emphasizing the courage of the men who stood accused in the Riom courthouse and who effectively put Hitler and Pétain on trial. All of France knows what went on there. Our actions haven't gone unnoticed by the international community either.

Hostages are being executed in Norway, Belgium, Yugoslavia, and France. Just before he died, a Communist named Semard wrote a remarkable letter. He had informed the British of the plans of commando groups and collaborators.

But what had really been missing until now was the kind of contribution Chautemps has just made in the *Nacion de Buenos Aires:* a testimonial to Pétain, whom he helped bring to power, followed, naturally, by a violent diatribe against Laval. He's got two irons in the fire.

I believe that the Allies have a very good chance of winning this war.

May 5, 1942

Roosevelt gave a remarkable speech on April 28. I read both the English version and the French translation. He spoke of the struggle to maintain a humanitarian form of democracy. After Canada voted heavily in favor of joining the conflict, Vichy issued a despicable commentary on Quebec's supposed dissidence. Their interpretation of the facts is pure falsification. The majority of the people in Canada and an overwhelming majority of Canada's men in the military are in favor of sending combat troops overseas. The Anglo-Saxons are the only people to have understood what democracy is and to have practiced it. They have clearly been influenced by religious principles, most notably by those of the Protestants. Can there be true democracy, and the idealism and the necessary sacrifice it demands, if people do not hold to some sort of religious conviction? Prior to the war, I worked with Cardinal Verdier, Monsignor Beaussart, and Canon Desgranges to bring about a reconciliation between republicanism and Christianity, without which we could never become a great nation. There were, to be sure, numerous obstacles to overcome, but Nazism and Bolshevism did their part to help us. Basically, we tried to move in the same direction as the early Renaissance had, by seeking a purified religion, more focused on human concerns. The Humanists effectively helped destroy that movement by forcing the Catholic church to harden its position into what became the Counter-Reformation, which eventually led to the creation of the order of the Jesuits. The way the Cardinals acted after the Armistice and made Pétain into "the man sent by Providence" is sure to revive anticlerical sentiment, which will be extremely difficult to quell.

May 6, 1942

At around 12:30 at night, a lovely, clear night, British aircraft flew over Bourassol. I could hear the sound of their engines flying low in the sky. Was it a reconnaissance flight over the Michelin factories? A raid on Genoa and on into an Italy protected by the well-defended Rhone Valley? Or better still, could it be … ? In all events, the ack-ack started pounding away, probably from Clermont and Aulnat. Everyone in Bourassol was looking out the window, as were the people in all the surrounding villages. Whatever was the mission of those mysterious aircraft, the people of France were at their side as they streaked across the sky.

May 7, 1942

Had several long conversations with Léon Blum, who has been suffering from sciatica for a month now. We spoke about the future. He outlined what he felt the political and social consequences of the war would be. He believes that the work we began in 1936 will be continued, work that, sadly, fell victim to demagoguery. After the agreements signed at Matignon, we were frustrated by the rhetoric of the unions, just as we had been constantly undermined by the rhetoric of Members of Parliament, which started as far back as 1910 and reached its peak in the years just before the war. Sooner or later, it was bound to undo the Republic. Consequently, in creating the new institutions of the Fourth Republic, we must focus specifically on erecting insurmountable barriers to demagoguery, by basing those institutions on the American Constitution and British practices. The majority of people in France think that once the British and the Americans win this war, we will be back to the good life they knew in 1936. We cannot afford to tolerate facile solutions.

May 8, 1942

In Clermont-Ferrand, at a meeting conducted by General Lenclud, Colonel Perré,[7] former Commander of the Second Armored Division, which he made into an excellent fighting unit during the war, lectured officers from the area on the role played by his armored division. Then he moved on to address the Riom trial, which, fortunately, he said, focused primarily on the lack of matériel. That left the Army looking just great! But, he added, it is important for you to know, just between us, that matériel was not lacking. We were defeated because we were not mentally prepared for war. In sum, his analysis was no different from Colonel Allerme's. His talk, which was given with General Lenclud's approval, caused quite a stir among the young officers there. Doctor B. was present to see it. He told Blum that he would take the stand should ever the trial in Riom be reconvened.

May 9, 1942

On Monday, Japanese admirals were in Vichy negotiating their plans to occupy Madagascar, just as they had done before occupying Indochina. For once, the British were on time. On the very same day, their fleet positioned itself just off Diego-Suarez.

---

7. During the trial in Riom, however, Colonel Perré stated that his tanks had given him complete satisfaction.

At a luncheon given for the regional press, Laval made a speech that the French National News Bureau characterized as moving. He believes in Germany's ultimate victory. "If we believed differently, we might as well have handed over power to the men being tried in Riom." If there is a negotiated peace settlement, it will cost us just Alsace and Lorraine. If the Germans dictate peace terms, it will be a lot worse.

May 11, 1942

The most horrible catastrophes can occur, war can spread to every continent on the planet, millions of people can be dying of hunger, and Réal Del Sarte will go on, unchecked, dotting the land with the garbage he calls sculpture. The war has made him richer and richer. Most recently, Chambéry and Limoges have each been graced with a Joan of Arc, fully as unattractive as the ones that came before them. The only thing missing in all this was for Pétain to glorify the artist. Now even that has been done. When will we ever be able to rid our town squares of these grotesque statues—Joan of Arc, Joffre, Alexander—and replace them with real works of art? I read an excellent article by Thierry Maulnier in *Le Figaro* on the ravages wrought by academicism over the last half century. Pétain is the Réal Del Sarte of politics.

May 12, 1942

Laval has been in power for a month now, brought back by the German Embassy in Paris and the French newspapermen on their payroll. Actually, from the time the rough going in the Russian campaign began, there have been two clans vying for Hitler's favors: Ribbentrop and the moderates on one side, and the hard-liners—the Gestapo and the High Command—on the other. The heavy German losses in Russia have led Hitler and the hard-liners to adopt a more aggressive approach and force France to join them in an anti-Bolshevik alliance and, by so doing, assume a more overtly hostile position toward the British and the Americans. With the war becoming more and more difficult for the Germans, the French fleet has taken on increasing value. Ribbentrop and Abetz would like to see a French government that still has some influence over public opinion, a government headed by Laval. The Gestapo and the Army would prefer an authentic French version of Norway's Quisling. A month ago, Pétain was forced to surrender as a result of the campaign orchestrated by the German Embassy in Paris, Brinon's efforts, and the threats that appeared in the Parisian press. Of course, he had had practice at it. See that these matters are attended to, gentlemen, the hard-liners said, and let's hope your M. Laval's actions are not limited to words.

Laval and Abetz have taken a common stand, proposing that in exchange for further material advantages, Germany release French prisoners of war and ease the formalities restricting movement between the Occupied and the Unoccupied Zones. They would present France's pro-German approach as the profound desire of the people, by reestablishing regional councils and bringing into the government noted pro-German Members of Parliament, such as Monzie, Bergery, Marquet, and Lamoureux. It took Laval forty-eight hours, almost as long as it used to take before the war, to put together, or rather to fail to put together, his government. Pétain remains basically hostile to Laval, and the people in his entourage have done what they can to destroy Laval's career. Pétain insisted that he keep Barthélemy and Romier. As for the Germans, they have demanded posts for Bonnard[8] and Marion. In Parliament, people were so convinced that this great new government would not last long that they all made themselves scarce. But there was no way for Laval to retreat from his position, and now that a month has gone by, his situation would seem to be highly compromised. There are several groups against him: the Marshal and his clique, the Royalists, the clergy, and, of course, the Army. People in France have generally become either defiant or irritated with him. His pal Mussolini, troubled by the manifest loss of the support of the Italian people, is laying claim to Tunisia and Corsica. The Gestapo and the German High Command are asking Hitler exactly what he thinks he can gain from backing a man as wasted and out of step as Laval. Abetz is starting to worry. Doriot and Déat are watching him closely, getting ready to take his place as soon as the first occasion presents itself.

---

8. Abel Bonnard, writer and supporter of Marshal Pétain, who named him Minister of Education.

May 14, 1942

As a side story to last month's ministerial crisis, Senator Reibel made his play, the same Reibel about whom Mme Poincaré would squeeze her nose and say, "Pooh, Reibel" every time his name was mentioned. He is a kind of Charles Humbert, but less colorful, less intelligent, and decidedly more corrupt. He had the backing of Brandt, the man whose name is stamped on mortars he didn't really invent. Having brought discredit on himself in the Senate, Reibel got the bright idea of going to Vichy a few weeks ago and huddling with Du Moulin de Labarthète, one of the birdbrains close to Pétain. His brilliant scheme was to eliminate both Laval and Darlan and replace them with the team of Barthélemy and Reibel. Outside of these two conspirators, there was only one person capable of taking this business seriously: the aviator Fonck,[9] Göring's friend. Fonck headed off for Paris, absolutely delighted to be playing a role in this affair, and went about congratulating himself in front of everyone he met. He was arrested and had his papers confiscated, whereupon the master plan was uncovered. Abetz became frightened and sent Brinon to Vichy to deliver an ultimatum to Pétain: either Laval or a Quisling-like Doriot. Pétain, panic-stricken, agreed to meet with Laval in Randan Forest. We all know what happened after that.

May 18, 1942

Mussolini returned to Rome after having spent six days in Sardinia. Before leaving, he went to kneel at Garibaldi's tomb!

June 6, 1942

Chauvel was consulted by one of his Jewish clients, a war orphan who lost her father in 1914 and her husband in 1940. She has two children and wears a yellow star of David, which is considered a sign of infamy by the people who made wearing it mandatory.

There was an announcement in today's newspapers from the Legion of French Volunteers Against Bolshevism: "The maximum age for enlist-

---

9. René Fonck, pilot and hero in World War I.

ment has been moved up to forty and the minimum age is now eighteen," *Dépêche de Toulouse* (June 6).

June 7, 1942

Midway. At 9 A.M. Mme Reichenbach brought word of a British radio broadcast announcing a major American naval victory. Three Japanese aircraft carriers were sunk, along with three submarines and fourteen other warships and transports. The Midway Islands are the outposts of the Hawaiian Islands, more or less equidistant from Japan and California, 2,200 to 2,400 miles away. We'll have to wait for more complete reports; we can't forget what happened at the Coral Sea battle. But if these facts are true, they will give an enormous boost to America's war production, which is already substantial. It will boost morale in England and Russia as well. Still, the consequences of an American victory would be felt most deeply in Germany, where Japan's triumphs, which have been stunning indeed, have been repeatedly exploited by Germany's propaganda agencies to off-set the grimness of the war in Russia and the appalling losses the Germans have suffered there.

America's decision to intervene in the war was hard on the German people, for whom the ghosts of 1918 are still quite alive. Goebbels ridiculed it, telling his fellow Germans that this time, thanks to the Führer's genius, America's intervention would go for naught. "The Japanese will take care of those Yankees from New England and hog merchants from Chicago. Those people have all sold their souls for dollar bills, refrigerators, and mass-produced automobiles. Every Babbitt they send off to war will end up as food for the fish at the bottom of the Pacific." It made for a great story in the Kraut press and on their radio. Too bad. Now they'll have to find something else.

British radio also hailed the Libyan exploits of a Frenchman, Colonel Kœnig.[10] French people can take great comfort in what he has done,

---

10. General Pierre Kœnig, commander of the heroic Free French Resistance Forces fighting Rommel.

which will be of considerable importance in the peace negotiations. Kœnig and a few others like him will counterbalance the Georgeses, Requins, Bessons, and Weygands. He has brought glory back to our flag. I saw Jacomet from my window. He told me how overjoyed he was with the news—a sign of the times. "It's all over for Germany," he said and then added, "Midway, Libya, and the statements I have been submitting to the judges ... they're finished!"

June 9, 1942

Mme Reichenbach told us that British broadcasts, last night and again this morning, have been alerting the French people in the Occupied Zone to an impending Allied landing. They've been told to withdraw from combat areas and not to participate in any way, and that subsequent broadcasts will announce the time for them to take action. The news spread throughout Bourassol and drew considerable attention from every quarter. Blum takes this to mean that aerial bombings are imminent. I think it will be another few days yet. Could this signal at long last the liberation of France? Are there leaders anywhere in the ranks of our young Army capable of throwing themselves into the fray and bringing freedom back to their country and honor back to their flag? J.B. confirmed this evening that German soldiers have been notifying people living in restricted areas, which is to say along the coast, to be prepared to leave their homes.

June 12, 1942

The newspapers have reported that Molotov[11] has returned from a trip to London and Washington, where agreement was reached over plans for the continuation of the war and postwar peace terms. According to Russian, American, and British radio, ten points were agreed to, among them: not to sign separate peace treaties; to supply each other with material support; to establish a second front; not to seek territorial gains; to form a twenty-

---

11. Vyacheslav Molotov, the Soviet Union's Commissar of Foreign Affairs.

year alliance (barring the creation of an effective international peace organization); not to intervene in the internal affairs of other nations.

As Blum went down the list of these various points, he stopped to express his pleasure over the last one. That matter had been of particular concern to him, and he was now relieved. He exclaimed, "Now we'll be able to rebuild the world." In his joy, he must have forgotten that there was a similar clause in the agreement signed by Stalin and Laval.

Sumner Welles gave a Memorial Day speech in Arlington Cemetery. It was an impassioned and moving expression of the guilt Americans feel for the position they took in 1919 when peace terms were being negotiated, for their isolationism, and the frightful consequences it had for Europeans.

June 17, 1942

"Marshal Bazaine on trial, the Monarchy or the Republic on trial—in their differing forms, these all reduce to one and the same phenomenon: France questioning herself, peering into the confusion to define her role in what happened in the past and her perspectives for the future," *La Revue des deux mondes* (1873).

The Riom trial was in no way a 1940 remake of Bazaine's trial. Pétain was careful to exclude any inquiry into the functioning of the military. In the minds of the people who engineered this—Pétain, Laval, and their valets—the Republic and the Republic alone was to be put on trial, but from the very first day on, I made a point of putting Pétain on trial. Unfortunately, I didn't get the chance to go as far as I would have liked. Pétain panicked again and called for another armistice.

Thursday, June 18, 1942

Pétain gave a speech yesterday that was broadcast over the radio several times throughout the day. It was supposed to commemorate his coming to "power," a word that has been so weakened that it is no longer really applicable. Anyone wishing to find out exactly what the conditions were surrounding his rise to power has only to consult the proceedings of the Riom trial, Elie Bois's[12] account of the crisis in Bordeaux and how Reynaud took flight, and, let us not forget, Montigny's book *Toute La Vérité!*

It is now manifestly clear that there was a criminal plot to hand France over to the enemy and that it succeeded because there were enough cowards to go along with the plotters. The idea was to deal a death blow to the Republic and replace it with some form of fascism or Salazarism. An agreement with the Germans had been reached probably as early as May 25 and in all events no later than June 15, but Pétain and his accomplices went about preparing the government's transfer to North Africa, under the pretense of organizing French resistance there. Lebrun, Jeanneney, and Herriot were to go by land, the loyal Members of Parliament by sea. The latter group were all later to be accused of having fled; that's the now well known story of the *Massilia*. As for Darlan's role in this business, at first he was taken in as well, as is clear in the cables he sent General Noguès: "Set up a command post for me in Rabat, next to yours."

June 19, 1942

Pétain's speech seemed curious at first. The flourish we had come to expect was replaced by the muffled trill of a Magic-less Flute. The man who gave France "the gift of his person" has begun to fear that the gift hasn't worn well, which is why he blamed the bureaucrats for the poor results of his two years of absolute power. Our national Tartuffe declared that the Jews and the Freemasons were responsible for things having gone so poorly. The speech must have been either prompted by Laval or reworked by him, and it didn't want for shrewdness. Laval, after having been arrested on Pétain's orders on December 13, 1940, and released only after Hitler's direct intervention in the matter, managed to get the Marshal to acknowledge a long list of failures brought on by his predecessor, Admiral Darlan, and the Ministers who became the underlings of that brainless head of state. It's a nice piece of work; add to that the fact that the French are good people, born naïve. Oh, the Marshal is such a fine man! He tells us the truth. He is

---

12. Elie Bois, Editor in Chief of the *Petit Parisien* prior to the war.

so honest, so good. He has been as much a victim as we are of that gang of administrators, Prefects, distributors, and swindlers, etc. Another case of Orgon feeling sorry for Tartuffe after the latter has confessed to having tried to seduce the former's wife.

June 20, 1942

My friend the owl was flying about at daybreak from the pine tree to his nest and back. I heard the familiar call I used to hear at nightfall when I would come back from the Riom courthouse.

June 22, 1942

Tobruk has fallen. Just this past winter, Blum assured me that the Germans would run out of gasoline by May! In spite of all the communiqués from the front and the reports in the British press, he's still reserving comment, on the grounds that we couldn't pick up British radio yesterday.

June 23, 1942

Laval's latest speech is couched in terms of the inevitable. Had he already foreseen a few days ago Mussolini's ultimatum and Hitler's threats? The man is so extraordinarily soulless. I can't think of any words to describe what moves him other than the Italian *vilta*. Jacomet, who is absolutely indignant, thinks the speech is proof that Laval was already a traitor both before and during the war. He spoke mainly of Bolshevism, in an attempt to incite fear and appeal to the bourgeoisie. Yet it was Laval who negotiated the 1935 pact with Stalin that allowed for the creation of the Popular Front. It's quite a way from Kienthal (or Stockholm) to Vichy; just look at the speeches he gave in 1916 and 1917. Everyone in Vichy is up in arms. According to the orderly of General Bridoux, the War Minister, the part where Laval decried General Giraud's escape was received especially badly in the Ministry and throughout the Army.

Chauvel ran into Flandin, who thinks the Germans will be defeated and that they and the British will be the war's principal losers. He anticipates several months of Communist agitation following the war, but feels that it will be quashed rather easily when the country as a whole rises up against it. Communism will fall into disrepute, along with neofascism and the neo-Nazism of the collaborators, after which we'll witness a return to a Republic freed of extremists. In other words, Flandin will live to see the dream of a Democratic Alliance—his party—come true!

Flandin believes that in his district, the Riom trial seriously cut into the government's popularity. What could have been more absurd than having politicians tried in the courts? The judges were obviously going to be overwhelmed by the people they were judging. Since the high court had been dissolved, they should simply have carried out the Marshal's sentence and left these men to rot in Le Portalet. Flandin concluded by saying that if an election were to be held today in his circumscription, Daladier would carry it easily.

In *Les Nouveaux Temps*, that traitor Luchaire and someone named Guy Crouzet are demanding a people's court for us, so we can be sentenced without judicial proceedings. It's all perfectly logical, given that he believes that Germany's victory will bring good to both the world as a whole and France individually. Luchaire, Crouzet, and Mallet basically run the paper, along with Lassguiwer. Du Moulin de Labarthète gave a speech about the Frenchmen working in Germany, praising them for the quality of the work they have been doing for the Germans.

Sunday, June 28, 1942

I have a very low opinion of Stafford Cripps and the Australian Minister whose fears led to the breakup of the forces in Libya. The Japanese have given further proof of their cleverness by feigning an attack on Australia and India while marching into Chiang Kai-shek's China, gaining a foothold on the Aleutian Islands, and preparing to intervene in Siberia.

Blumel[13] came to spend the day with Blum. The Portuguese police had turned him over to the Spanish, whose uniformed brutes beat him when he refused to answer their questions. He was imprisoned in Spain before being handed over to Vichy, then sent to an internment camp in southeastern France, and finally released.

---

13. André Blumel, Daladier's Chief of Staff.

The picture he drew of Spanish prisons, where three years after Franco's victory there are still almost a million political prisoners, was in marked contrast to what has generally been presented to the world as the retribution taken against a handful of terrorists and Bolsheviks by a victorious, broad-based, national movement. He said that executions were being carried out daily and that the prison halls rang with the *Marseillaise* and the Communist *Internationale*.

In the Pyrénées-Orientales and the Hérault, the people (among them, Badie) have been putting up admirable resistance, above all among the lower-level civil servants. Laval's speech was met with indignation. Large numbers of farmers are reportedly refusing to deliver their produce to the official redistribution centers; they are convinced that most of it ends up in Germany. In Nîmes, they are selling *Combat*[14] in the streets. Several people have been arrested.

June 30, 1942

German and Italian forces have taken Mersa Matruh and another 6,000 prisoners. Air raids are being carried out over Alexandria. Will the Egyptians go to war against England? And what about the Turks? Papen is undoubtedly trying to lure them with visions of Armenia, Syria, and Palestine. What is the explanation for Britain's collapse?

Australia's Labor Party Prime Minister, who took over from Menzies, has been bluffed by Japan into pulling his troops out. In any event, England is on the verge of being run out of the Mediterranean. The Italian fleet will be able to operate in the Atlantic, and their bombers, which have already gone into action there, will be given the means to do even more damage.

The Russians have put up heroic resistance in Sebastopol. Timoshenko has been counterattacking.

In France "All Parisian high society was at Longchamp. ... Attendance records were broken. ... The prize at the weigh-in was raised ... women had on absolutely ravishing outfits." All this while workers, forced

---

14. A Resistance newspaper.

onto the unemployment rolls as a result of the closing of 1,500 factories and the shipping of raw materials to Germany, have to sign up to work for the victory of the Third Reich.

July 1, 1942

Met with Reverend Father Dillard,[15] from the Society of Jesus, who has taken over for Candan in giving Gamelin confession. He expressed the desire to see me also, if I was so inclined. I was happy to receive him and was quickly won over by his directness, his candor, and the loftiness of his heart and mind. He has traveled a great deal; knows the United States, Italy, and Germany well; and is an admirer of the youthfulness and the idealism basic to Americans and so often misunderstood by Europeans. He holds Roosevelt in great esteem, on perfectly legitimate grounds. Talked about what he had done during the war as commander of an artillery unit on the Meuse (a support group for Etcheberrigaray's 102nd Division). He is unforgiving in his judgment of the High Command and the leaders who lost their heads—and never found them again—as soon as Germany attacked. Thinks that the Germans will ultimately go down to defeat, that they will take one tumble after another before the final catastrophe. Also thinks that the British Empire is doomed and does not share Candan's enthusiasm for Japan.

He said the Vatican is hostile to Hitler and to Mussolini (which I knew) and that the overfed and overpraised farmers in France had fallen victim to material values. He finds the workers to be the most attractive part of the population. He spoke of the heroic death of Communists at the hands of German torturers: "They died like true Christians." He feels that this war marks the failure of the bourgeois values incarnated in tax inspectors, capitalists, engineers from L'Ecole Polytechnique and politicians from Sciences-Politiques, etc. He fears that there will be bloody incidents once it's over, and that, as a result of the current government's stupidity and the church's naïveté, there will be a resurgence of anticlerical sentiment.

---

15. The Reverend Father Dillard, a Jesuit who volunteered to work in Germany. Informed on, he was deported to a concentration camp, where he died.

July 13, 1942

Le Roy Ladurie[16] issued a vehement statement, reprinted in *Le Temps*, about the manner in which vegetables have been brought to market: "At the beginning of July, at the very height of the vegetable season and after the splendid work done by our farmers, the public markets are bare, store shelves are empty, and goods are being sold at outrageous prices; the only people profiting from this situation are those with special privileges and the idle rich. Given the hardships people are facing, this is scandalous."

Every man is his own best judge. Le Roy Ladurie, one of the principal prewar demagogues in matters of agrarianism, is in perfect position to draw up an indictment of his bankrupt policies. He can go right on rattling his cardboard saber and rereading his *Philippics*.[17] One after the other, he castigated the farmers, the distributors, the storekeepers, and the consumers. He spared no one except himself. He should come here and look out my window onto the farm worked by Poles. He'd witness the continuous procession of barterers who, under the eyes of the garrison that surrounds Bourassol, come to exchange tobacco, shoes, or, if they have to, money for ham, eggs, poultry, milk, butter, and so on. It is the perfect illustration of what has resulted from the economy as structured by these "National Revolutionaries," a bunch as corrupt as any group of smugglers.

Last night, I reread Herriot's excellent books on the Lyons revolution. "For their revolution to succeed, the lower classes must be led by a core of incorruptible men." You're not going to find any of those at the Bank of Worms or among those well-heeled demagogues of the Agrarian Party. Farmers are starting to take seriously all the theories that the Mathés, the Le Roy Laduries,[18] the Achards, and the Dorgèreses went on ranting about before the war, in what was a pure attempt to use the farmers

---

16. Jacques Le Roy Ladurie, farmer and Marshal Pétain's Agriculture Minister.

17. Demosthenes' exhortations to the people of Athens, in which he accused them of apathy and of failing to live up to their glorious past.

18. Gabriel Le Roy Ladurie, financier and member of the Worms conglomerate. He had close ties with Paul Reynaud (1940), then with Admiral Darlan. Edouard Daladier considered him to be the kingpin in the plot against the Republic. He was affiliated with the Synarchie, a secret organization working to seize power.

as a political stepping stone. To date, there hasn't been a word out of Caziot, even though he is second in command at the Ministry of Agriculture and sticks closer to Le Roy Ladurie than his shadow.

Le Temps ran a four-column spread on the ceremonial oath-taking of the Rhône chapter of the SOL,[19] France's version of the SS, so to speak. The speeches that were given there, the oath they took on bended knee (not even Hitler came up with that), the remarks made about the kindness and generosity the German people would show the French, using Poland as an example of it—it was all enough to make you sick. We must really have sunk awfully low for so abject a performance to be possible, even in the wake of our defeat, on Terreaux Square in Lyons.

July 14, 1942

The Riom trial will not be reconvened, neither to assign blame for our having gone to war (the court effectively dropped that charge for lack of evidence), nor to assign blame for our defeat; on that score, the most recent documents demonstrate the overwhelming responsibility of our Generals. Laval's idea is to put La Chambre and possibly Jacomet under house arrest and either have Reynaud and Mandel brought to Bourassol or find a house for all five of us. Pétain, in contrast, wants to ship us off to Le Portalet. For two years now, they have been dragging me through the mud without giving me a chance to defend myself. The traitors have been taking shots at me to their hearts' content, Pétain most of all, followed by the Doriots, Déats, Carbuccias, and Fontinis, not to mention the Marquets, Aliberts, Baudouins, and company. In the early court sessions, I demolished the testimony of their phony experts and their phony witnesses, but that didn't faze them. They simply gagged us, starting last April. Since then, the admissions made by those who were truly responsible for our defeat and piles of staggering documentary evidence have continued to pour in. Even the judges appointed by Pétain and Alibert to conduct the pretrial investigation had to conclude that France was not defeated; France was

---

19. The Service d'Ordre de la Légion, an organization of shock troops created by Pétain and his Ministers.

handed over to the enemy. That truth will have to be buried in the moats around Le Portalet.

Bousquet[20] asked Génébrier, "How do you know Laval doesn't think that Germany will ultimately be defeated?" Thoughts like that are sure to provide him with terrific evenings galore.

They say that the Count of Paris[21] is a man with nothing to recommend him. He has a few stirred-up Generals in his entourage, all as mediocre as he. He came to see Pétain to express his astonishment at not having been made King of France. "I have been waiting for eight years," he told him. Nothing could be more unpleasant for that conceited old man, Pétain. As is his wont, he didn't let it show and sent the Count to see Laval.

July 15, 1942

American radio was absolutely magnificent yesterday. Roosevelt delivered a short, powerful address and the Senate adopted a resolution glorifying France and France's fight for freedom and pledging to restore France to its former greatness and wipe tyranny from the face of the earth. It had all the resonance of the best pieces written in the days of the *Convention*. I received a telegram Bullitt sent me from abroad. "The day will come when we'll be singing the *Marseillaise* in a France once again free and strong." They also read on the air a long excerpt from a *New York Times* article.

There have been large patriotic demonstrations in the major cities in Unoccupied France. Thousands of people sang the *Marseillaise* in the streets of Lyons, Grenoble, Marseilles, Toulouse, Montpellier, Nîmes, and Avignon. Shooting out of windows in Marseilles, SOL members killed four people and wounded several others.

---

20. René Bousquet, a former Prefect named Superintendent of Police in Vichy. At the end of the war, he took a position with the Bank of Indochina. Tried by the High Court, he got off with a token sentence and was immediately granted amnesty. Many years later, he was charged with crimes against humanity. He was awaiting trial when he was gunned down in his apartment in Paris in June 1993.

21. The Pretender to the French crown, in exile until then.

July 18, 1942

Jean showed up unexpectedly at 5 P.M. He told me about the July 14 demonstration in Grenoble, where five to six thousand people turned out, among them Abbot Desgranges. They shouted, "Down with the Krauts, long live France, long live de Gaulle, long live the Republic," and held off the SOL.

They call this version of the country legal? With a bunch of people in charge who were traitors before and during the war and again in Bordeaux? With the fraud they perpetrated in the National Assembly? With Generals who turned and ran or turned traitor and came back dishonored from Germany? With the capitalist concentration of wealth in the hands of trusts and the Bank of Worms, all of it now legalized and sanctified by a government order shutting down 1,200 businesses? The result has been that great numbers of workers have been forced to go to Germany to find work. And all this rottenness sits there under the banner of a collaboration effort undertaken for Europe's salvation.

July 19, 1942

They say that Pétain is just about senile in the afternoon. He remains lucid for two to three hours a day. He is surrounded by a bunch of nonentities, with General Campet at the top of the list. His whole entourage—and Pétain at times, too—is hostile to Laval. Behind this clique at the Sévigné Pavilion there is another one gravitating around Weygand and especially around Giraud, who is motivated by his dual hatred for Germany and democracy. Half of these people envision a military dictatorship à la Franco, the others a *Consulat*, lacking only a Napoleon to head it. Laval would have liked to pursue his servile policies toward Germany by putting up as many working-class front men as he could come up with: a union leader brought back to power; Lagardelle, brought in to replace Belin; parliamentarians in the style of Bonnet, Monzie, Mistler, Chichery, but the boys refused to go for it; they preferred to promote their own interests. He had to fall back on Bergery, Belmont, Reibel, and that bunch. Paul Faure[22] has written a book proving that everything that has been done since the National Assembly convened in Vichy was illegal. He had Susset give me his best regards.

Laval has been trying to broaden the role of the regional administrative councils. He has gotten nowhere with the Germans, who have in fact split into two clans: Ribbentrop, Abetz, and those who would pick France clean little by little, and the Army officers, who would simply slit her throat. The latter have Hitler's ear. Anyway, Hitler hates France. The Army officers have made a mockery of everything Laval has tried. So how does one get into their good graces? By mobilizing against the British and the Americans if they attempt a landing in France? By sending troops to Syria to support the Germans if they decide to invade? The question was put to General Frère, who responded that the French Army would never agree to dishonor itself in that way. They almost dismissed him for making those comments, but eventually backed down. He has been firmly opposed to the creation of the Tricolor Legion[23] and spoken against it openly on his rounds of military inspections. It is obvious that the German Army officers favor Doriot over Laval, although it is probably just a game. Outside of the groups in Marseilles and Nice, the PPF doesn't have that many members—two to three thousand adventurers all told, according to the Prefect of Police, who also said that it would not take much to wipe them all out.

Vichy was clearly upset and worried about the July 14 demonstrations, especially those held in Lyons, Marseilles, Grenoble, Clermont, Montpellier, and Nîmes, where waves of human beings flooded the streets. Popular demonstrations of this sort could only have been made possible at the present time by deep-seated feelings of rebellion and the growing sense of a veritable and profound national unity that extends from Communist workers to Catholics. It is our duty to see to it that the true great-

---

22. Paul Faure became Secretary-General of the Socialist Party after the break with the Communists in 1920. He held ministerial positions under Blum and Chautemps. Prior to the war, he was a pacifist. He did not participate in the vote of July 10, 1940, in Vichy but later became a member of Marshal Pétain's Conseil National.

23. A French Legion created to fight alongside the Germans, against the Allies.

ness of this national sentiment is preserved. I stand prepared to risk my life to oppose the manipulations and rhetoric of partisan politicians and stave off any attempt to thwart what is in effect the greatest national movement in all of French history. Perhaps our defeat was a necessary step for us, but not at all in the way that it is presented by Pétain and his cliques of hypocrites and traitors.

Laval would like to have the Riom trial suppressed. He has had Vals closed and disbanded. Every little fluctuation of contemporary history has had its repercussions on this trial, which has proven to be an event of major importance.

July 21, 1942

Last night in Riom, Génébrier ran into Commander Jacquot, who is a member of General Frère's staff and who has kept the General apprised of his meetings with my associates from the very outset. Frère is politically right-wing, but he is a fine and patriotic soldier. Jacquot still believes that Germany will ultimately be defeated, but not because of a shortage of raw materials, equipment, or workers. He thinks they will lose because they are going to run short of men and sacrifice their youth. By drawing recruits from among the able-bodied male population aged seventeen to fifty, they can raise 15 to 16 million men. If the Russian Army isn't surrounded and destroyed—and it seems clear that Timoshenko has understood the need to retreat—Germany will be facing yet another winter campaign that will inflict more frightening losses, at the very time that America is completing its preparations.

Jacquot is opposed, quite correctly, to the creation of a second front before next fall. He would prefer to wait until the following spring. I totally agree with him. He thinks that the French Army will join up with the Americans and bring with them twenty or so divisions outfitted with infantry gear but without airplanes and tanks, which the Americans will have to supply. I fear that the French Army's role in the liberation of France is little more than a lovely dream in the minds of our young officers.

July 24, 1942

Génébrier spent the day in Vichy, where they are still at one another's throats, but they keep on fighting without ever delivering any death blows. If they did, the species would have become extinct long ago. Pétain's entourage is now led by his doctor, Ménétrel, a high-society Royalist who is being stroked nowadays by Bonnet and the Count of Paris.

His court includes a few Jesuits and, every now and then, Du Moulin de Labarthète, a wait-and-see reactionary. Then there is General Laure,[24] alias Calamity Jane; Laval; and the Doriotists grouped under Darnand's[25] aegis, where the rifts have become serious ever since Valentin's departure. Génébrier also saw Jael, who believes that Vuillemin and Georges will be indicted once the new investigation is completed. He is a young fellow, still naïve.

On his way back to see me, Génébrier stopped off at the courthouse to get passes. Bruzin has become quite kindly and cordial. When Génébrier thanked Caous for having been so gracious during the trial, Caous was moved to tears. He said he would never have agreed to preside over it if he had known it was going to be suspended.

Jacques Kayser[26] came to see me. He has moved to the area around Villeneuve-sur-Lot. He told of the reawakening of public conscience that has followed the Riom trial and Laval's rise to power.

Young Raphaël-Leygues has put my photo on the desk in his law office … next to Darlan's!

August 2, 1942

The trial is the only thing Jacomet can think of, and it will never be reconvened. There is no point in trying to discuss England or the events in Russia with him. Within a few seconds, he is back talking about the trial and the scandalous way the trusts, the capitalists, the High Command,

---

24. General Emile Laure, Commander of the Ninth Army Corps in September 1939, then, temporarily, in May 1940, of the French Eighth Army. He was Pétain's Chief Administrative Officer. In 1943, he was imprisoned in Germany.

25. Joseph Darnand, Chief of Vichy's Militia. He was executed after the war.

26. Jacques Kayser, attaché in Daladier's Cabinet from 1938 to 1940.

Weygand, and a few other ogres treated him. The truth is that I have known very few men in my lifetime who were genuinely concerned with anything other than themselves. Nowadays, Jacomet spends every minute of his time at Blum's window, whereas he used to consider him a visionary and a danger to the people around him. But our resident prophet has complimented and flattered him and above all praised his wife. His bereft wife is doing her best too, by piling on the chocolates, the potatoes, and the apricots ... the most recent props for the most recent dance form of the most recent Salome.

August 3, 1942

Ribet, who has come down here to spend his vacation at the Hotel Pailleret, came to see me at 4:30 P.M., bringing news from Paris. The Germans arrested 8,000 Jews, who were to be deported to Cracow. The women were hauled to the Vélodrome d'Hiver after having been brutally separated from their children, who looked absolutely dazed and frightened to death as they were piled onto trucks and herded to detention centers. It was unbearable to watch. Some mothers went mad. An employee at the Prefecture of Police told Ribet that when two police inspectors arrived to arrest a Jewish woman and her two children, she threw them out of the window and jumped out to her death after them. Marshal Pétain offered the services of his police force and the National Guard to help carry out this ignominious act, and it's just one more in a whole series of outrages. He personally handed over Communist hostages to be executed by the Germans. Barthélemy, the Minister of Justice, placed their heads right onto the chopping block. The National Revolution has planted its roots in blood and infamy.

The renowned lawyer Pierre Masse, a Senator and, if I am not mistaken, a former Junior Minister under Clemenceau, was interned in the camp in Drancy for several months. He held up admirably. He was supposed to be deported to Cracow, but because he'd been keeping the records of the personal effects removed from Jews at the time of their arrest—watches, pens, money, etc.—and recording as well the formal requests made so that objects of value could revert to family or friends, a high-ranking Nazi policeman accused him of fraud. This turned out to be a godsend. He was sent to La Santé prison to be tried by French authorities. Ribet has been untiring in his attempts to help him. With the aid of a state prosecutor named Gabolde, who is incidentally a collaborator and a supporter of Pétain, he managed to extend Masse's imprisonment in La Santé beyond the date on which he was to be deported to Cracow. Ribet went to see him before leaving for Lyons and found him as courageous and steadfast as ever.

Before the trial, I insisted that Perretti della Rocca, the former Ambassador who headed the notorious Council of Political Justice that met in Vichy in October 1941, be made to testify. After having read the table of contents of the prosecutor's lengthy indictment, in which a good two-thirds of the figures cited are false, Perretti proposed, in agreement with Pétain, that we be sentenced to life imprisonment within the thick-walled medieval fortress at Le Portalet. When Perretti retired, he got himself appointed Chairman of the Board of Française Capitalisation, which is a finance company on the order of Séquanaise and which has had a considerable number of run-ins with the legal authorities over the last few years. He was named to head the Council of Political Justice through the good graces of Pétain and appointed thereafter Vice President of the State Tribunal in Paris by Barthélemy. Now he is under the threat of an indictment for fraud. Ribet had a look at the investigators' report, which is brutal. He said he would send me a copy of it. Moreover, he will be assisting Lemaire, counsel for the liquidators. This should get him a seat right up front to admire Barthélemy's efforts to rescue Perretti. The testimony to be given at the Riom trial by the head of the Council of Political Justice and the Chairman of Française Capitalisation is looking juicier and juicier.

Georges Bonnet has been working with the Nazis. He recently had dinner with a few high holy German lordships, each of them incidentally in the charming company of a woman from French high society. For the moment, the Germans are preoccupied with getting their hands on Portuguese coal mines whose stock is jointly held by the French, the English, the Portuguese, and so on. The British would like to get control of these mines too. Bonnet is doing whatever he can to help the Germans, which is just more of the same. I made a similar judgment about him when I read his latest deposition, which is in effect a confession.

Chichery is going around telling everyone that Laval won't do anything without consulting him first.

Ribet heard from one of his friends who had recently dined with Maillefaud, Deputy Chief Judge of the Cour Suprême, that I had torn the prosecutor's indictment to shreds and totally dominated the proceedings.

August 6, 1942

Admiral Abrial has been taking his traveling circus from city to city, giving crude, vehement anti-British propaganda talks. The heads of the Legion take these occasions to spew forth their hatred for the Republic, the Jews, the Freemasons, and Churchill. I can't say whether Abrial made a hero of himself at Dunkerque, but he has certainly made a jackass of himself with the violence of his verbal attacks. It is sad to see so highly decorated a naval officer stooping to the role of German propagandist.

August 7, 1942

Ribet and his wife were out for a walk with Bénazet in the gardens of the Hotel Pailleret when all of a sudden a limousine drove up and Laval stepped out. Policemen piled out of a second car and surrounded him. Ribet knows Laval well; they're on a first-name basis. He went up to him, followed by Bénazet.

Laval: So this is where you are. Come to see your client.

Ribet: Right, and to get some rest, too. Did you know that the Count of Paris was here yesterday?

Laval: Yes I know. He came by plane from Morocco to see Pétain, who sent him on to see me. I am going to have dinner with him, then I'll put him back on a plane to Morocco.

Then Laval spoke of the Riom trial, which he claimed hadn't dealt with the right issues.

Laval: They should have tried the people responsible for the war. France was the instigator, as I have been saying everywhere I go. And I could have prevented it from ever happening, if only they had let me take the floor in the Senate on September 2. The responsible parties should be put on trial along with the defendants in Riom.

Ribet: So bring the case to court. I don't think there is a judge in France who would agree to dishonor himself in that way.

Laval: We'll see about that soon enough. In any event, we're in the midst of a worldwide revolution. There is a choice to be made between fascism and Bolshevism. And when I say Bolshevism, I mean democracy as well.

At that point another car pulled up, with the Count of Paris, Ménétrel, and an Air Force Colonel from Pétain's Cabinet, followed by a swarm of policemen. Laval and his guests went into the dining room, where a table had been set for them. It was 8 P.M. and beautiful outside, but for fear of an attempt on their lives, the policemen closed the shutters and the windows and they dined by lamplight.

August 12, 1942

"A sacred relief effort has begun." "An intense, emotional moment was lived yesterday morning at the train station in Compiègne." An unknown number of repatriated prisoners and volunteers who had offered to work for Hitler embraced each other. The *Marseillaise* and a speech by Laval were right on cue in celebrating this act of treason under the mocking or disdainful eye of Von Ritter, the leader of the German workers' front. In a speech dripping with hate, Laval offered a defense of his treason. He termed those pitiful deals a triumph of his genius. A total of 50,000 farmers will be released from Prussian prisoner-of-war camps in exchange for 150,000 French workers who will go to Germany to promote their war effort.

When Laval came to power, he was what Voltaire used to call "everyone's daddy." He opened his arms to friends and enemies alike and hugged them warmly. Then, as soon as the first problem arose, the real Laval would rise to the surface: vicious and, wherever possible, insolent. It's mind-boggling to hear that in speaking with Ribet in the gardens of the Hotel Pailleret this past Friday, August 7, at 8 P.M., while waiting for the Count of Paris, Laval once again spoke of me in the same terms reported by Dignac and again by Bousquet in his talks with Génébrier: He claimed that he holds me in high esteem and is concerned about my safety.[27]

August 19, 1942

The Germans have now reached the Don and positioned themselves all along its banks. The ferocious fighting around Stalingrad rages on, but everywhere else the Germans have assumed a defensive posture. They have set up a base of operations with superior numbers of men and supplies between the Caucasus, the Don, and the Volga. The Soviets have launched diversionary counterattacks in Rzhev, Vyazma, and Voronezh, which have resulted in bloody battles but no appreciable strategic gains. We have clearly reached the critical point of the war. If there is still a Russian Army at the end of the summer and if the industrial centers in the Urals and Siberia are really what Butler said they were, 1943 could be the year of our victory. The future of the world is being decided at this very moment. If Germany should triumph, I will arrange for my two sons to leave for the United States, and rather than live in an enslaved France, whether I am free or imprisoned, I will have no choice but to put an end to my life.

The heat has been unbearable. To let in a little breathable air, Blum has propped his door open. I have done the same with mine and with the windows that face north, to give him a little bit of a breeze. Then I went over to chat with him. Once again the discussion centered on Germany and what would happen after the war. He went back over his feelings from 1919. We made two major errors then, he said. The first was in being so ungenerous toward the German people; the second, in allowing Germany's military, administrative, industrial, and capitalist structures either to remain functional or to be recreated, and thereafter in recognizing and dealing with them out of our fear of Karl Liebknecht, Rosa Luxemburg, and the inroads the Communists might make.

---

27. At the end of 1942, Laval told Jean Daridan that he would never let Daladier be deported to Germany. "If Blum and Daladier are forced to leave Bourassol, there's only one place for them to go, my place, Châteldon." In truth, Laval shipped them off to Germany in 1943.

Our first Ambassador to Berlin was Laurent, of the foundry owners' group, and the most highly respected German then was Hugo Stinner, a steel magnate from the Ruhr Valley. We can't afford to repeat those mistakes after this war. It would be good for Germany to be dominated by the working classes for a few years, under a regime analogous to the one created under the Russian Revolution. And we should demonstrate generosity toward that new Germany and not seek to destroy its unity.

I don't agree with Blum. There can be no lasting peace in Europe so long as Germany is dominated by the Prussians; if that state of affairs continues, a new war will break out twenty years from now.

Has Germany really changed that much in all this time? Isn't the essence of the Nazi doctrine already present in Fichte? I am afraid that Blum's ideas, which are attractive, to be sure, are just so many pipe dreams. He is right: We have to destroy the structures, but we also have to see to it that they are not rebuilt. Ancel, the prison guard from Alsace, knows the Germans a lot better than either Blum or I. I put the question to him. He didn't hesitate a second in answering: If we don't put an end to the Prussian domination of Germany, which we should have done in 1918, there is no possibility of a lasting peace.

Reverend Father Dillard came to Bourassol this morning. Gamelin, La Chambre, and Jacomet attended mass, while I lay outside, nude, on a blanket, taking in the hot sun.[28] Father Dillard came to see me after the church services and we chatted about the present state of the French Army's officer corps, which appears to him to be terribly mediocre. I heard that Blum took a snapshot of this dialogue in the sun.

August 20, 1942

Daridan, France's delegate at the Armistice Commission in Turin, dropped in out of the blue. He said that the Italians in Piedmont and Lombardy are absolutely exasperated with Germany's dictatorial attitudes. Their greatest wish is for the war to come to an end. Antifascist groups

---

28. During his hour's outing, Daladier would sometimes take sunbaths "top to bottom." The guards would remain off at a distance, which allowed him to speak without being overheard.

have been gaining ground, especially in Piedmont. Rationing has been imposed, just as in France. When word of the capture of Tobruk came, Mussolini took off to North Africa with fifty cameramen in tow to film his entrance into Alexandria. He grew indignant over Rommel's sluggishness and went and complained to Hitler. In any case, Daridan believes the Germans will be defeated by late 1943.

While in Vichy, Daridan met with Jardin, who admitted that his boss, Laval, had failed in every way. He would like to see Laval backed by a centrist party, which people have been dreaming about since the time of Louis XVIII and which I almost managed to create in early 1939, after the collapse of the general strikes. Anyway, the Germans take no notice whatsoever of the government in Vichy. Daridan said that the corruption that has taken hold in that town is absolutely appalling, and that goes for Pétain's staff as well, where every request for an interview is met with the question: "What's he offering?" The same holds true for the Ministries. Daridan brought me the kind respects of Revers, an anti-German French General, whose dream it is to be part of an "Armistice Army" expelling the Germans.

August 21, 1942

The press has reported a British sneak attack at Dieppe. *La Dépêche de Neuchâtel* carried dispatches from both London and Berlin. It was a large-scale raid, no comparison with the one carried out earlier at Saint-Nazaire, but it wasn't an attempted landing, as the Germans are claiming, which is perhaps regrettable. If the landing of a large force, protected by air power, had been attempted at several points on the coast, it is very likely that they could have gained a foothold. The conclusion to be drawn from comparing communiqués from the two different sources is that the Germans were taken by surprise and that Dieppe remained in British hands until almost four in the afternoon, when a division of German reinforcements arrived. A French officer from the Air Force base in Aulnat who witnessed the battle said that almost 200 German warplanes were shot down and that they had to bring in planes from as far away as Belgium and Holland. The people of Dieppe sided with the British, but they refrained from participating in the fighting, having been alerted by British radio that this was a reconnaissance mission and that they should take shelter and not intervene. Vichy and Berlin have been congratulating the local population so insistently that it's become a joke. General Stulpnagel has had 10 million francs run off for them on his presses. We'll see where they stand when the Americans and British attempt a real landing.

Americans victorious in the Solomon Islands. Riots in China. Heroic Russian soldiers and, two months from now, winter.

August 23, 1942

America's industrial war output. Fact: In June 1939, the United States manufactured only 224 aircraft, commercial planes included; in June 1940, 600; in May 1941, 4,000. Fact: In May 1942, more than 1,500 tanks rolled off the assembly lines. These figures demonstrate once again that it took between a year and a half and two years to bring the world's greatest industrial power to function at capacity. In France, the indolence of the different War Ministers in 1934 put our rearmament program a year behind the Germans'. If I had not demanded that the Finance Minister[29] order 4,500 airplanes from the United States before the war and at its outbreak, America would never have been able to turn out 4,000 planes in May 1941. This is all further proof that we could have and should have continued the fight from North Africa.

August 26, 1942

A recent law "eliminates the regulating agencies of the Chamber of Deputies and the Senate." Henceforth, civil servants and a commissioner appointed by the government will oversee the financial and administrative affairs of the two chambers. Legally, the powers of the legislative presidents and administrative officers expired on January 10, 1941. I never understood why Jeanneney didn't convene a session of the National Assem-

---

29. At the time, Paul Reynaud was Finance Minister. He considered the orders that Daladier had placed with the United States excessive. Daladier answered his criticism as follows: "If I can't get those planes, you'll have to find another Prime Minister, one who will make peace with Germany."

bly on that date to state for the record that Pétain had violated decisions made by the Assembly in Vichy.

I also ran across a particularly grotesque edict approving the rules governing the equally grotesque Francisque.[30] Members of this new order will now have to recite the following pledge: "I offer my life to Marshal Pétain, as he has offered his to France," etc.

August 29, 1942

At around 4 P.M. a truckload of SOL, the Legion's security forces, in other words, the Marshal's SS, passed by on the Clermont road. When they were in front of Bourassol, they started shouting, "Death to all cops." The cops in Bourassol did nothing. Probably just a whiskey-driven rivalry among thugs.

August 30, 1942

A parade of automobiles has been driving by here since eight this morning, official cars racing to get to the show they are putting on in Gergovie. Pétain wants to be both Joan of Arc and Vercingetorix.[31]

September 9, 1942

Génébrier spent yesterday, Tuesday, in Vichy with a number of his friends, some of whom are well informed. Deshuses's[32] loyalty to me has been magnificent. He told Génébrier of his plans in the event of a putsch by the German-backed Doriotists.

The real head of the Militia is Darnand, a brave and energetic hatchet man. Men have been dropping out of the Legion in large numbers. Those who have stayed are either Doriotists or Lavalists, like their leaders. And like those in the SOL, they were recruited from the ranks of Doriot's PPF.

---

30. A fraternal order instituted by Marshal Pétain.

31. The leader of the Gauls who in 52 B.C. held out against Caesar's troops during the siege of Gergovie, a site just a few miles from Clermont-Ferrand.

32. Deshuses, a young Subprefect and one of Bousquet's advisers. He was one of Daladier's faithful and courageous friends and assisted him in his attempts to escape in 1942. He helped members of the Resistance make their way into Switzerland.

Bombs have been thrown into Legion headquarters in Nice and Saint-Etienne. That explains why antiriot police are here at Bourassol: They think the Doriotists might try to exact revenge.

Saw Spanien, as well informed and friendly as ever. It seems that Laval is being simultaneously attacked by two opposing groups, not counting the republicans. On one side, there are Doriot and his party, backed by the Gestapo and the Nazi Party. In his recent talks with Laval, Doriot hadn't backed off from any of his demands: a military alliance with Germany, participation in the war under the leadership of the Germans, and the total and immediate institution by force of a Nazi regime in France. Doriot doesn't have many people behind him, just a bunch of adventurers, murderers, and hoods, but if the Germans should ever choose to, they could very easily set him up as *Gauleiter* in Paris.

Laval is also opposed by the Count of Paris and some Army Generals, who are doubtless spurred on by Pétain and his entourage, with Ménétrel right behind them. Far from taking the plane straight back to Morocco, the Count spent several days at the Bourbon-Busset château, where he met with Ménétrel, Alibert, General Laure, General Giraud, General Frère, General Bridoux, the War Minister, and others. Their plans are as vague and paradoxical as they are grandiose, and the inherent contradictions have not slowed them down any. The Army officers have shown no more genius around a table than they did on the battlefield. Their idea is to rise up against the Germans while remaining hostile toward the British, and they take pride in being in agreement on this with the Prince of Piedmont.

France would become a monarchy, ruled by military men, mostly mediocre sorts who have been discredited. Conceived under the hot Moroccan sun, the plan has received the stamp of each of these drawing-room heroes in succession, which raises anew a question that has until now defied answering: How is it that French military thinking has been mired in such mindlessness over the last twenty years?

Laval is forced to maneuver his way through all of this intrigue while fighting off a patriotic, republican movement that continues to grow as the war goes on. He also needs to win Hitler's support, lest the latter unleash Doriot. He knows perfectly well, and he admitted it at a luncheon for schoolteachers, that Hitler hates France, adding that for proof one has only to read *Mein Kampf.* At the most recent Cabinet meeting, in addressing the problem of the limited number of volunteers leaving to work in Germany, he proposed invoking the July 11, 1888, law relative to the organization of the nation in time of war, which allows for the requisitioning of the population. Workers would be drafted by the government and sent to Germany. Three Ministers rose to protest: Bichelonne, Le Roy Ladurie, and Lagardelle. There was even a rumor going around Vichy that they had resigned, but for the moment, anyway, Laval has not forced the issue.

An edict dated August 25 decrees the annexation of Alsace-Lorraine by the Third Reich, which is a direct violation of the Armistice Commission's agreement to address this matter at the time of the peace settlement. The French government addressed a letter of protest to the Germans and showed copies of it to Deputies from the region. Laval is reported to have thought of having it published, but he didn't go through with it.

French Cardinals, Archbishops, and Bishops have condemned the barbaric anti-Semitic acts that are being committed. Their pastorals were read aloud either inside churches, in spite of the law forbidding them to do so, or on the steps in front of them. The Nuncio also issued a protest in the name of the Pope. This is all to the Catholic church's honor, but it hasn't stopped the government from going even further. A missionary priest from Lyons, whose name I unfortunately don't know, refused to turn over to Angély, the Prefect in Lyons, Jewish children he had taken in. He was imprisoned but escaped. History shows that for a French government, no act is fraught with greater peril than arresting priests, but here again history has obviously taught us nothing.

September 10, 1942

5 P.M. Roger Génébrier has come back from Vichy, where he saw Bousquet. The Krauts have dropped Doriot. They had it in for him, first of all, because of the wild nightlife he's been enjoying, notably at the Lido, where he spends his evenings drinking in the company of jewel-bedecked whores; secondly, because after giving innumerable speeches about the so-called Bolshevik Legion and putting on the German uniform, he never dared venture near the front lines when he finally went out there.

September 13, 1942

Chauvel dropped by for a quick visit around 5 P.M. We were supposed to meet on September 8, but when he got to the train station, he saw machine guns on the platform and a General on the roof, and when he walked over to the post office to phone, he spotted more machine guns and soldiers on the sidewalks. The people in Vichy, who have seen it all, offered as an explanation the threat of an attack by Doriot and his buddies. But it would also appear that bombs have been thrown into the Lyons and Saint-Etienne headquarters of Doriot's party and of the Legion—which more often than not are one and the same—and that there is the fear that there will be other, similar acts.

This evening, Bourassol had the honor of being visited by a Brigadier General named Delmotte who inspected the guardroom with all the skill and method of a Battalion Sergeant. He pointed out that the walls weren't high enough and the locks not strong enough. He asked whether visitors were searched and whether their identification papers were scrupulously checked. The guard Passemard, who is a former Army Sergeant, told him that he followed the orders given to him by his superior, the warden of the Riom Penitentiary, and that he wasn't interested in hearing about any others. The General quickly beat a retreat, which was apparently nothing new to him. Gendarmes have arrived to reinforce the policemen here, but now we'll never know whether it's Doriot they are afraid of, or our escaping.

September 14, 1942

Three men showed up late this afternoon and introduced themselves as associates of that ninny Barthélemy. Members of his personal staff or prison officials of his? From the looks of them, as seen through the bars on my window, I would have sworn that they were real-life copies of Javert, the notorious police inspector from *Les Misérables*. But these are precisely the cruel martinets that Barthélemy has been recruiting as leaders and advisers ever since he started guillotining people who had been sentenced to a few months in prison for some minor political offense. Fear must be rippling through every ounce of that fattened prig's flab. The three Javerts started asking questions and making comments. They, too, talked about the walls and the locks, and they were coarse, if not quite vulgar. Then they said that reinforcements would be sent, which turned out to be so; two new guards came to bolster the forces in Bourassol. They said hello to me, and we chatted for a while. They are both loyal patriots. Let's face it, you just can't find a nicer bunch of people than prison guards.

September 15, 1942

I found Blum visibly preoccupied. His son Robert, who was captured while commanding an artillery battery and cited by the Army for his bravery, has been moved to a camp near Lübeck where conditions are reputed to be particularly harsh. He lives by himself at one end of the barracks, with Stalin's son alone at the other end and a guardroom between them. The Germans have grouped together the Socialists, the Gaullists, and the Communists. For two hours a day, Robert Blum can be visited by his friends in the camp, providing that they sign up the day before. He has the use of a piano and is allowed to go for walks, as long as there are guards right behind him. What does this brutal isolation augur for the future? I can sense that Blum fears that at some point the Germans will persecute the son to get at the father. Or could it be that the Germans are anxious about a possible uprising, now that there are so many prisoners and that they are in contact with the Socialist and Communist workers who went to Germany as part of the infamous "relief effort"? That would explain Robert Blum and Stalin's son being held in isolation. That's what I told Blum, without much conviction, unfortunately.

September 16, 1942

Bousquet came to see me. He had first stopped by to tell La Chambre that he would soon be released on his own recognizance, which, for form's sake, would be announced as being put under house arrest at a site of his choosing. I was happy to hear that they had made this decision, which, among other things, makes it obvious that our Air Force wasn't responsible for our defeat. I regretted, however, as I told Bousquet in no uncertain terms, that similar measures were not taken for Jacomet, but I could see that the possibility hadn't even been considered.

Bousquet spent almost two hours with me. I have known him for a long time. He is intelligent and kind and highly devoted to Maurice Sarraut. He was the Prefect in the Marne before the Armistice and acquitted himself very well. To his mind, our Generals were not up to their duties. They abandoned their troops and never understood the first thing about German tactics. General Thierry, for example, and others like Giraud and his staff officers went around trumpeting their contempt for democracy and insulting republicans, Mayors, and regional councilmen, all of which had a deplorable effect on the local populations. The RAF stationed in Reims took off as soon as the first bombs hit; the French command groups took off a day after the very first battles, leaving their troops with neither orders nor lines of communication. The French Air Force took no action whatsoever against German bombers. Waves of ragamuffin, unarmed French soldiers could be seen retreating everywhere, looting villages along the way. Then came the German Army: orderly, disciplined, powerful, and proper, which explains why they were welcomed by the locals. According to Bousquet, at that point, France was primed for a policy of collaboration with Germany.

The line France had taken at Montoire, the line promoted by Laval, became inoperative when he was arrested on December 13, which was the work of Peyrouton, Alibert, and, Bousquet said, the British as well. Laval had gotten the Germans to accept the presence of a French Army in North Africa that would fight off the English and win back the territory that had been lost. Laval was arrested by Peyrouton's surrogate police force, which planned to kill him, claiming he had tried to escape. He was saved by the police and the Germans.

Bousquet had more to say. He felt that any attempt to go back to the line taken at Montoire would meet with the worst kinds of difficulties. The country is divided. People don't understand. Some are pursuing hard-line, reactionary policies without even looking at the reality of the situation, whereas others think that although we are weaponless, we should tell the Germans to go to hell. As for the masses, they are not interested in anything other than putting food on their plates. The government is caught between the Germans, who are demanding and contemptuous at the same time, and public opinion, which is feeding on fantasy and chasing mirages.

At least he, Bousquet, was able to halt the execution of hostages, or so he claimed.

He thinks the Germans are in a position of great strength. They have organized the conquered Russian territories and harvested huge wheat crops there. With the Germans having reached the Volga and the Caucasus, their front lines are now even better structured for the Russian winter. After that they will invade Iraq, Syria, and Palestine, while Rommel attacks Egypt from the West. England will once and for all be driven out of the Mediterranean. Germany will then unify Europe according to the plans drawn up by Hitler's brain trust and say to the United States: "Do you want peace? You don't? All right then, come and fight."

Right, right. I had gotten Bousquet to talk. I answered by saying simply that in spite of their power, the Germans would be defeated in the end, probably after a long, drawn-out war. Bousquet then spoke of the trial. I reminded him that among its consequences, it had brought down Darlan's government and in so doing greatly benefited Laval, even though it was Laval who had determined in August 1940 that there would actually be a trial.

Saturday, September 19, 1942

Along the wall at 3 P.M. the hot sun was beating down on the nettles and the droppings of the livestock they keep at Bourassol. I went to sunbathe, nude, in the exercise yard. Croquez, a lawyer in Ribet's office who pleads at the High Court of Appeals, showed up unexpectedly, in his spiffy gray jacket, starched collar, and white shirt with cufflinks. Too bad for counselor Croquez. I didn't get up. I had him pull over a chair into the burning sunlight. It wasn't long before his head started to turn red. He tried to shade himself as best he could with an elegant little handkerchief but wasn't too successful. Tapping two Gauloises out of a pack, he offered me one. I put it away for later. One of these days, though, he is going to bring me Belgian tobacco. He said he had just arrived from Belgium and Holland and was taking a few days' rest at the Hotel Pailleret. He had met with Devèze, Carton de Viard, and others. All of them are convinced that they'll be free of the Germans as of next spring. The King still considers himself a prisoner in his castle and all Belgium is behind him. Pierlot, their

Prime Minister, in an address from London, let it be known that he did not recognize the legitimacy of any of the acts performed by the occupying powers. With the exception of Degrelle and the 50,000 Walloons and 50,000 Flemish traitors he has with him, the Belgians are unanimous in their resistance. Croquez also had a chance to visit Ostende, which he found very poorly defended. The Dutch are even more savagely hostile, and the Krauts are repeatedly confronted by gestures of contempt, even in the most ordinary aspects of daily life. The Dutch aren't about to forget that the Germans destroyed Rotterdam without declaring war.

Croquez dined with Bouffet, a Prefect from Normandy, who told him about the attack on Dieppe. Violent hand-to-hand fighting went on in the city streets while British planes, dominating the skies, knocked out the antiaircraft guns and the artillery along the coast. British tanks rolled several miles inland. The Germans had to call in air support from planes stationed in Belgium, Holland, and France and send in a division of reinforcements. The British pulled out around 5 P.M. What was the point of this half-hearted attack that was more than a commando raid but still far short of a full-fledged landing? To set up a bridgehead? With Russia fighting so heroically, if there isn't a serious landing attempt after the coming equinox, then something fundamental has broken down in the British High Command.

Croquez saw his friend Barthélemy, who is so full of himself he is going to burst. He brought back a perfect definition for the National Revolution: blue-blooded terror, black market, and rose-colored glasses. I asked Croquez if Barthélemy realized that he would probably be guillotined after the war, just like all those poor souls he has been sending up to the State Tribunal with orders to have them sentenced to death that same day, while the executioner and his helpers go about sharpening the blades. Croquez looked at me utterly flabbergasted. I repeated the question: Is he aware of the consequences that this royal reign of terror will have for those administering it? He said that Barthélemy told him that the Germans had summoned him to Paris and told him, with all due courtesy, that he would be held personally responsible for bringing in ten death sentences a day, to be handed down by the State Tribunal and carried out immediately, failing which they themselves would handle matters and execute a hundred people a day, among them Barthélemy's friends. "He should have resisted; he should have protested and done everything possible," I said. Croquez answered that Barthélemy's wife would rather he *didn't* do everything possible. She had been dreaming her whole life of being a Minister's wife, and now that she was, she planned to keep it that way.

Croquez is no longer a collaborator. Now he is a member of the Resistance. In the winter of 1940, he was singing the praises of Laval and a few unscrupulous Radicals like Lamoureux and Chichery, who is beneath contempt. He explained how theirs was the only viable political approach. Everything is different now. Now he sides with the Resistance; he's a Gaullist and an Anglophile. When he goes to have dinner at Olivier Jallu's, one of his Germanophile colleagues, and Mme Jallu raises her glass to honor the Marshal, Croquez puts in loudly, "Timoshenko." Our friend Croquez has changed clients; he has gone over to the other side. Congratulations, counselor.

But I was set on making him pay for his past mistakes. While he went on talking, I moved to the side of my blanket, bringing him directly under the sun's rays. He stretched his handkerchief and tried to use it as a parasol. His head was quickly turning fire-engine red. I asked him if he would care for a tub of delightfully iced Bourassol water, but he preferred to return immediately to his hotel.

September 24, 1942

René Besse, my former Pensions Minister, came at 2 P.M. and spent three hours with me. His right arm had been amputated at the shoulder as the result of wounds he received in the war. He was dripping with sweat, having come on a bicycle one of his colleagues in Riom lent him. After we hugged each other, he took his sleeve in his teeth to remove his jacket.

I have never met a more loyal or more proudly patriotic man in my entire life. What a pleasure it was to look into his face, open and candid, and hear once again his distinct, clear voice. The day will come, he said, when France will be proud to have gone to war and to have been the first to have risen up against those who tried to rule the world. Unfortunately, our armies were led by commanding officers from the preceding war, not by real leaders. They were bureaucrats, more concerned with their typewriters than with the enemy.

In the Lot, in the midst of the rout, he observed a number of Generals, including General Lenclud, who was calling himself "Commander of the Dordogne front"! It was, Besse said, a pathetic performance. The man was without will or energy and was incapable of inspiring his men.[33] I told Besse that this same General was pitifully ill at ease in testifying against me at the Riom trial, obviously wanting nothing better than to get out of there as quickly as possible. They have probably retired him since then. If they had wanted to get real leaders, they would have had to promote Battalion Commanders and Lieutenant Colonels to the rank of General. Before the war, that was unthinkable, and they refused to do it during the eight-month standoff from September 1939 on. Besse also spoke to me about the National Assembly and about Vichy, where no one had the courage to object to anything.

Besse is struck by the amount of ground the Communists have gained, especially in the Occupied Zone. He fears that there will be very serious incidents once the Germans evacuate Paris. Monzie is now living in the Lot. He is still just as flighty and capricious as ever and seems to have been discredited as a result of the visit he paid Ambassador Abetz. Monzie had his wife appointed City Councilwoman in Souillac, while he divides his time between Cannes and Paris in the company of Edmonde Guy.

September 26, 1942

Received a large crop of cable messages from J.B. They will all have to be burned, unfortunately. Russian radio has published excerpts from letters that German soldiers killed in Russia never got to mail. They refer to the living hell they were going through at the Battle of Stalingrad, which has been going on for a month. Many of the letters from Germany relate the destruction wrought by the Allied bombing of German cities.

---

33. Besse did not know that General Lenclud's son had been killed at the front just a few days earlier. Moreover, it has since then been established that General Lenclud played an important role in the Resistance.

Radio Free France broadcast the speech of a Socialist, Brossolette,[34] who left for London with Vallin,[35] a Deputy from the Croix de Feu Party. Vallin was one of the most rabid members of Vichy's Council of Political Justice. Without having looked at the file or hearing the accused men defend themselves, he suggested to Pétain that we be imprisoned for life in some dungeon. Either de Gaulle is not very well informed or he is not too choosy about the company he keeps.

September 28, 1942

Benoist-Méchin has been dismissed by Laval. He left, but not without threatening Laval before going. He was pro-German before the war, then became a supporter of Nazism during it, as Commander Ragaine, a witness at the Riom trial, pointed out in the wonderful letter he submitted.

Trouble is brewing at Bourassol. There are only three guards in all and they can't get along. Try and get a league of nations to work!

It appears that Vallin broadcast a talk over British radio. He felt the need to address a message to Herriot, under house arrest at his home in the Isère, and greetings to all prisoners. He won't get any greetings back from me. I find it obscene for de Gaulle to have given him this role. It has the foul smell of political maneuvering.

October 9, 1942

7 P.M. Le Trocquer came and spoke with me on the bench at the foot of Bourassol's linden tree. He confirmed what sweet little Simone had told me this morning: The court had denied the request that La Chambre be released on his own recognizance. Le Trocquer met this morning with the most important, or rather the two most important, judges. They told him that French judges had a sense of dignity and found the government's attempt to pressure them into releasing La Chambre totally unacceptable. Caous, the presiding judge, asked Le Trocquer: "Who is this fellow

---

34. Pierre Brossolette, journalist who joined the Resistance in 1940. Upon his arrest in February 1944, he committed suicide rather than risk informing on his comrades.

35. Prior to his decision to leave for London, Charles Vallin had been faithful to Marshal Pétain and a fervent supporter of the National Revolution and the Armistice.

Bousquet? He can't possibly be a lawyer." Bursting with pride, his face blown up like a balloon, Le Trocquer started pouring it on. This was a historic occasion; it signaled the awakening of France's magistrates. I have rarely had so good a laugh.

8 P.M. After taking his constitutional, Blum knocked at my door and came in, which was highly unusual. Right off, he informed me that de Gaulle hadn't been in London when Vallin arrived and had nothing to do with the obscene radio greetings that Vallin had had the nerve to send prisoners in France. He added that as soon as he got back to London, de Gaulle sent Vallin on a mission to Equatorial Africa with the rank of Captain. This confirmed my suspicions that Blum is in close contact with de Gaulle, probably through the news sources in Clermont (*La M.*, V., Fabre),[36] where his lawyer Spanien has an in.

Guy La Chambre, whom I have nicknamed the Bourgeois Gentilhomme, has been walking up and down the paths in Bourassol. Three days ago, he ordered Passemard to bring down a heavy trunk and his foot locker, where he had stowed his Commanding Officer's uniform—that makes two wars he has spent safely away from the action.

October 11, 1942

At 9 A.M. the Reverend Father Dillard drove up in a fancy Delahaye powered by a wood-burning engine. Highly symbolic: The slick body represents Catholicism, the wood-burning engine, the internal workings of the Church. Dillard came to console La Chambre, whose request to be released had been turned down.

October 13, 1942

Jean came around 10:30 in the morning and recounted the foolishness of the Youth Camps.[37] People are trying to get him to enroll. He had interesting stories to tell about his travels.

---

36. Probably *La Montagne*, central France's principal newspaper, and the two men who ran it: Alexandre Varenne and Francisque Fabre.

37. The Youth Camps, with Pétainism as the moving spirit, replaced military service.

Blum gave me the typewritten text of the speech Churchill gave in Edinburgh. I found it elegant in its form, sober, and moving. We have survived the first year. A new chapter is opening before us. The grandeur of these islands and of our Empire is to have held out alone and to have given ourselves the time to arm and organize and patiently assemble the invincible forces of the civilized world.

There are massacres throughout Russia and Yugoslavia. In Kiev 54,000 people were executed the day after Hitler marched in.

We have reached a turning point in the war; there can be no doubt about that now. The Vatican has just issued a statement reminding Catholics that although the Church, eternal and universal, does not concern itself with political regimes, it does not condone regimes that limit freedom of thought and engage in persecution.

There have been strikes in cities all over France: Villeurbanne, Grenoble, and Clermont.

The Germans battled Mihailović's forces for several days in southern Bosnia and had to bring in armored divisions. Germany was furious over Vichy's wait-and-see attitude when the British and Americans were threatening Dakar. They're fighting in Croatia; there are fires and incidents of sabotage in Belgium and executions in Norway and Poland.

A new assault will be made on Stalingrad to preserve Hitler's prestige.

A grotesque communiqué has been issued about the resistance shown in Madagascar.

8:30 P.M. Spoke with Blum about the speech Laval made to a Senate committee meeting in closed session on March 15, 1938. In an attempt to seize power, he presented himself as an enemy of the Germans and the only person capable of getting Russia and Italy to stand up to them. That was the same argument he made to Deputy Laroche during their train ride from Châtelguyon to Paris.

We raised the issue of our relations with Italy. Baudouin told Blum of his meeting with us, Mussolini's request, and his own trip to Rome, when he met with Ciano. He told Blum that although I was highly circumspect, I had not completely severed our ties. It was agreed that I would give a speech and that Mussolini would respond to it favorably. I did make that speech and Mussolini did prepare his, but then the Prince of Hesse, the

King of Italy's son-in-law, suddenly showed up in Rome, probably carrying demands from Hitler. Mussolini never gave his speech.

October 20, 1942

Pétain was in Avignon, speaking to the farmers' union. He told them: "My friends, don't let yourselves be fooled into thinking that I can do what I want. I feel like this ... " whereupon he crossed his forearms on his chest, like a man in chains. Then he went on to tell his astonished audience: "Above all, don't repeat to anyone what I just said. If they ever heard about it in Vichy, I would be whipped when I got back there." He got a cold reception, except from the mercenaries from neighboring regions who had been ordered to attend.

Legueu, a former associate of mine, came to see me. His parents were close friends of Pétain's, who used to lunch at their house once a month. Legueu was a member of Pétain's staffs in Bordeaux, Clermont, and Vichy. He quit at the same time as General Bineau, disgusted with the people in Pétain's entourage. He made a point of mentioning General Laure's stupidity.

Legueu fought brilliantly in the war at Jacquot's side, after having spent time with him at Command Headquarters, which Major General Bineau once referred to as "a paradise for madmen." Legueu also pointed out the extraordinary difference between the bravery our soldiers displayed every time they had real leaders and the failings of the High Command. On the Seine, near Senlis, they would be given orders to fight and told not even to consider the possibility of a retreat. Then in the evening, they would be told to pull back.

Legueu has doubts about an Anglo-American victory. He thinks the British are not intelligent enough and that the Americans are not willing to make the effort necessary to win.

Finally, he spoke about how extremely serious the financial situation had become and the inflationary spiral we were in. Vichy hasn't the slightest clue; Cathala, the Minister of the Economy, is optimistic. It is basically a continuation of the moral collapse we witnessed in the bourgeoisie between 1914 and 1939.

3 P.M. Claude Perchot stopped by. He is in the Resistance and confident. He confirmed the information I had received. He thinks the war will soon be over. I am not so sure.

November 1, 1942

Spent the morning disappointed and conjecturing as to why Pierre hadn't come.

Gamelin told Jacomet that prior to the trial, Darlan had sent General Revers to see him, to ask him to incriminate me by putting responsibility for our defeat on the civilian government and the republican regime. That is supposedly when Gamelin decided not to answer any questions.

I am tempted to check whether General Revers actually visited him, and when. In any event, Gamelin's attitude shortly before the trial was quite different. His defense rested on the claim that he had not been supplied with what he had requested. So much for me. As for his subordinates, and in particular General Georges, they simply had not carried out his orders. Later, though, he must have reflected on the testimony given by the production managers and engineers, which stood as proof of the quantity and quality of our weapons. Three days of court hearings and my violent attacks during those opening sessions did the rest. In contrast, in the time since the trial was suspended, he has submitted excellent responses to written depositions and direct testimony given against him by various Generals. He also told Jacomet that, back when all this started, a Senator from the Ariège who was present with him at Gaboriau's told him that Pétain did not intend to target him, so as to avoid a Gamelin versus Georges slugfest and spare the Army.

Jean came at around 11:15 A.M. with a radio built by Abel Farnoux, who lives in Carpentras. He sneaked it past the guards in a large sack filled with foul-smelling vegetables, which was enough to evade a search. I put on the headset, wrapped myself in a huge greatcoat to muffle even further the noises around me and tried to bring in every station I could. Thus did I reestablish contact with the outside world, from which I had been separated for two years. No gift could have been finer.

November 2, 1942

All Souls' Day.

November 5, 1942

This morning, Ancel[38] brought me impressive news. At midnight, Sottens broadcast a communiqué from Cairo. The British appear to have defeated Rommel's Army, which is now in retreat, and taken some 9,000 prisoners. German ships bringing reinforcements and supplies were sunk off Tobruk. Will there be a second half to this brilliant offensive, launched from Chad into the oases of southern Tunisia? Large numbers of men and warplanes have been brought in through Liberia and over the new African highway. Large numbers of American troops have landed as well. A second front would appear to have been opened in Africa.

Stalingrad is still holding out. Timoshenko has made successful thrusts both south and north. The feeling I have been getting for a month has thus been confirmed: The Germans have begun their descent down the road to defeat and ruin, bringing with them the traitors here in France. Vichy is in a funk. The press has been barred from publishing the Cairo communiqué and was almost prohibited from publishing one from the DNB[39] announcing the capture of a German General commanding an armored division. If Laval's idea of negotiating a compromise peace settlement at Russia's expense was ever a real possibility—and I don't think it was and never did—it is much less a possibility now.

Pierre came by at 2:30. His eyes have been hurting him terribly. In spite of that, he performed brilliantly on the oral part of the *baccalauréat*. All of a sudden, in the middle of the questioning, Jardillier, who was examining him, asked, "How is Edouard doing?"

November 11, 1942

It has been bleak and gray. I was given to think back on the Armistice and what happened when my division's regiment, stationed around Origny-

---

38. A guard at the prison, hostile to Vichy.
39. Deutsches Nachrichtenbüro, German News Bureau.

Sainte-Benoite, heard the news. Beneath the surface joy at no longer having to risk one's life and at being able to go back home, free of apprehension, you could sense a certain disappointment. Some of the men were actually open about it. A young schoolteacher stated proudly that under the First Republic, France had said that it would never enter into negotiations so long as the enemy remained on our territory. He was accused of being a die-hard extremist. That was also Pétain's feeling at the time. At the Elysée Palace, at the end of the traditional meal that would follow the July 14 celebrations, Pétain would often tell us how much he regretted that the Armistice had prevented General de Castelnau from launching an all-out offensive that would have driven the German armies back across the Rhine. He used to criticize Foch for having too quickly aligned himself with Wilson's position. I wonder what he thinks about that now. During this past night, he got a letter from Hitler informing him that the German Army would cross into Unoccupied France today and occupy coastal zones along the Mediterranean. Hitler is convinced that the Allies are preparing a landing. Of course, he will continue to respect the sovereignty and independence of the French nation. Pétain and his government will be free to set up in Versailles, as they have long desired to do. Shades of Grippeminaud.[40]

This morning, Marshal Von Rundstedt, escorted by armed soldiers, went to see Pétain to reaffirm Hitler's decision. The Marshal vehemently protested against this violation of the Armistice and at around 11 A.M. Vichy radio broadcast his emphatic response. The two years in which we had been violently criticizing his collaboration with the enemy were seemingly swept away. What would he do? Take a plane to Algiers?[41] Call all Frenchmen to unite and resist? Call on the world at large to bear witness to the Nazi dictator's new breach of faith? Was that too much to ask of his

---

40. In one of La Fontaine's fables, a weasel and a rabbit call on the cat, Grippeminaud, to settle a dispute between them. The cat puts an end to the dispute by eating them both.

41. After the Allied landing in North Africa, people in the Marshal's entourage suggested that he fly to Algiers. Pétain told them that his doctor had advised him against flying. They then suggested that he step down, but he refused. See General de Serigny's memoirs.

advanced years? And that being the case, why not declare himself a prisoner of the Germans and relinquish a power that was just for show, anyway? Hours went by. Vichy radio remained silent. The solemn statement of protest was not repeated. The telephone rang here. It was the Riom Penitentiary on the line, dictating orders: All visits by relatives and lawyers were to be suspended; no newspapers were to be allowed in the prison; surveillance was to be doubled. Its meaning was clear. Our moment of elation was crushed by the brutally painful news of yet another capitulation. After digesting his lunch, Pétain changed his mind and decided to shame himself anew.

Remaining Chief of State is the only thing that really matters to this selfish and conceited old man. There was an admirable stand to be taken. He could have declared himself a prisoner of the Germans or left for Algiers by plane and broadcast an appeal to all Frenchmen to take heart and unite; he could have called for the world to take note that Hitler was once again violating his word. Instead, he thought about it, and in the end, this prisoner of his own self-image preferred to remain the "merry old King" under German protection. And that's not the last such act he'll favor us with. Clemenceau and Joffre were absolutely right in their judgment of France's "victor at Verdun."

Bourassol is all astir. Mme La Chambre came at the usual time, highly agitated. I asked the Lieutenant in command of the garrison what orders he would issue if the Germans were to march through the prison gates. He replied that his operating procedures did not cover that contingency and that he would phone for instructions. The prisoners began discussing the idea of leaving, of conspicuously walking out through the gates. One thought that the guards would just let us go. I didn't believe that at all. That was pure fantasy. The guards despise Vichy, but they are old-fashioned soldiers for whom an order is an order. So the choice was between making our way through the barbed wire and racing to Riom on foot, which at 11 o'clock in the morning would have been a futile exercise, or calmly and bravely awaiting the arrival of the Germans, which was what I resolved to do. Having reached that decision, we went back to our rooms. I burned some papers and asked to have my cigarettes, tea, coffee, and the other precious possessions that my good friend Hippolyte[42] had sent me from America, as well as the excellent liqueurs that my brave friends from Toulouse had brought me, stored away in an obscure attic that young Simone told me about. I had the other hired help, Marcelle, take this diary to a neighboring farm, along with other documents that I didn't want to destroy.

Then someone started shouting, "The Krauts are here!" I went down to see, but it turned out to be just the power of suggestion having its way with Mme La Chambre. She and Mme Reichenbach were in fact asked to leave the premises. The guards at the gate were turning away my son Pierre. I raced over to talk to him. He was calm, as I would have wanted him to be. I urged him to return to Riom and make note of the bearing, the physical state, and the equipment of the German soldiers who would soon be making their way through the city.

Time passed. It was 2 P.M. before the first German column appeared, heading down the Clermont road, with armored vehicles at the lead, automobiles with officers, and then Citroën trucks packed with armed soldiers standing in the rear. They were followed by a large detachment of men on bikes, Czechs and Poles, word had it, who had been drafted to fight under the Nazi flag. They moved slowly, fifteen miles an hour at most, sometimes at an even slower pace. A few trucks had broken down while climbing the hill. It was an impressive showing, but this was not the German Army of 1940. The troops heading south to the Spanish border would take three days and three nights to get there.

November 12, 1942

The procession of German troops has gone on. I watched them from the center walkway in the prison as they headed down the road. A lot of them looked very young; others were apparently recruits from German territories overseas. Could it be that Germania was already feeling the shortage of men? The local population in Riom reacted with absolute dignity. They

---

42. Daladier's pseudonym for William Bullitt.

too had sensed the difference between this Army and the one that had marched through their city in June 1940.

Then I noticed a car with a chauffeur and two impeccably dressed civilians standing in front of the entrance to the Bourassol jailhouse, looking sinister with their hats jammed tight on their heads: the Subprefect and the Superintendent of Police. I had to walk right past them to get back into the "castle," as they were gesturing broadly toward the barbed wire, the farmyard, and the screened gate, which they subsequently had padlocked. They also claimed that we were not watched closely enough during our daily walks. New guards and soldiers were brought in to tighten security.

La Chambre and I wrote to Bousquet to complain about these restrictive measures, which were totally gratuitous. Blum complained strenuously in a letter to Barthélemy. Le Trocquer and Spanien, who were the only lawyers present, went off to object to our being harassed in this way, but Barthélemy, groveling and gutless as usual, just raised his arms in the air and asked them to understand that there was nothing he could do about it. Meanwhile, Contencin, who managed the penitentiary system and was somewhat concerned about managing his future too, declared that the measures prohibiting visits did not apply to the prisoners' families and legal counsel.

November 13, 1942

Had lunch with Pierre and J.B., who told us about what had gone on in Vichy on November 11. Marshal Von Rundstedt showed up at Pétain's door with an armed escort and dismissed the French guards on duty; they didn't return until the Germans had left. In the course of the first exchange between the two Marshals, Pétain protested against the violation of the terms of the Armistice. Had he finally been aroused? No. That afternoon, he backed down. Did he do so because of pressure from Laval, who had just returned from Munich? I think these two cronies are still in cahoots, only Pétain would have liked to have made some gesture for the loyal patriots in France. After that, he made another great sacrifice and once again gave the gift of his person to France.

At 4 P.M. Le Trocquer met with Laval, who rejected the possibility of our being released from Bourassol, claiming that it would result in new hardships for France. Nevertheless, he accepted full responsibility for our safety.

Meanwhile, in Algeria, Darlan ordered soldiers, sailors, and airplane pilots to join up with the Anglo-American forces, in accordance with the Marshal's true desire, which he alone was capable of interpreting. There is some of the Artful Dodger in everything this Gascon does.

November 14, 1942

I picked up a radio broadcast from Moscow and heard London radio in Italian. As for Vichy's broadcasts, they are hailing the Anglo-American landing in Algeria as the beginning of a true military collaboration, a real alliance between France and Germany. Together they will defend Africa and the French coast against the British and the Americans.

Received good news about the way the French troops in Africa were being trained and how they performed in combat, a fact that will have great bearing on the future. Victories will mean more to France than all the speeches in the world.

November 17, 1942

According to the terms of the June 1940 Armistice, the Vichy government was to be allowed to maintain an Army of 100,000 men to preserve law and order. When the Germans marched into the Unoccupied Zone, General Huntziger commanded all men to remain within their garrisons. The Germans burst into barracks, gruffly ordered the soldiers to disperse, and seized their weapons, their equipment, and the war matériel that had been concealed. French officers, above all General Frère, who had anticipated leading these men into action when the time came, watched their hopes evaporate before their eyes.

Weygand has been arrested, after having refused the American High Command's offer to join forces with them. Pétain has accused Giraud of disloyalty and duplicity. In Algiers, Darlan has stated that at the request of General Noguès and in compliance with the Marshal's true wishes, he was taking command. There is no way I can make my way through this labyrinth of contradictions. We lost lives; men were wounded; we lost our best ship, the *Jean Bart*, which I had had such a difficult time getting funds to build. This was our ungallant last stand.

November 19, 1942

Pétain has renewed his order to the French troops in Africa to repel the Anglo-American invasion!!

Friday, November 27, 1942

Jean came by around 9:30 this morning, spirited as always. He was able to catch the train in Lyons because a girlfriend drove him to the station. Unfortunately, it was already too late when he got word by telegram; he was supposed to have been phoned Wednesday evening. It cost us a whole day and effectively compromised the plan that had been worked out Wednesday. Maybe that is just as well, since P. had been discussing Le Trocquer and Spanien's plan at the National Café in Clermont with just about everyone who came along. Guy La Chambre's wife told me herself that it was the subject of conversation in cafes all over Riom. Still, if Jean had been able to get here Thursday, we might have been able to manage, although somewhat differently.

I was looking out my window around eleven when I spotted a group of German soldiers standing at the foot of an electric-power pylon a few yards from the Bourassol outer wall, and others stationed all around the castle. Suddenly, the door flew open and a tall German Captain with a revolver on his belt appeared on the threshold, followed by a soldier with a rifle and a submachine gun. "This German officer," the prison guard explained, "has come to verify that you are here." The Captain bowed, looked closely at me and withdrew.

Had lunch with Jean, who left me to catch the train for Vichy, where he was to meet with P. After he had gone, I got another visit from the inescapable Subprefect, his Superintendent of Police, and an officer from the gendarmerie. They huddled in the north yard, gesticulating broadly. In the end they decided to bar all visits and limit our daily walks. Imagination is obviously not their strong point.

I learned that Bousquet ordered that everything possible be done to prevent the Germans from setting up inside of Bourassol, everything short of using force. Will the young Police Superintendent's arguments carry the day? At 5 P.M. I went jogging in the farmyard. I spent the evening reading a book by Gignoux and listening to the radio. Impossible to pick up New York and London. Heard a broadcast of Hitler's letter to Pétain.

Saturday, November 28, 1942

The news coming out of Russia is good; they are still driving forward. In Tunisia, Anderson's First Army, which includes sizable numbers of French troops, is just ten miles outside of Tunis, according to Sottens. Yesterday, at three in the morning, after having opened fire on the German and Italian troops invading Toulon, the French scuttled their own fleet. I imagine we are supposed to take this as an act of heroism commanding our respect, but didn't our Navy deserve a better fate? Darlan's responsibility in all of this is appalling.

November 29, 1942

At 7 P.M. I was visited by three other officers from the gendarmerie, including a Commander. I couldn't figure out what they wanted, probably because they didn't know what they wanted either. Jean called. He had met with Bousquet.[43]

December 4, 1942

Darlan has set up a government in Africa and declared himself Head of State, on behalf of the Marshal, of course. He has got a kind of Colonial Executive Council with him: Noguès, Boisson,[44] and Giraud, along with a pseudo-ministry of three or four members. I had no idea that this little sailor had so much guile in him. De Gaulle and the National Committee in London have protested to the British government and several Members of the House of Commons have raised a hue and cry. Eden has responded by saying that Darlan's power is only temporary. Eisenhower, however,

---

43. Bousquet told Jean Daladier that the police would protect the prisoners in Bourassol from the German troops.

44. Pierre Boisson, Governor-General of French West Africa.

made an announcement to say how pleased he was to have Darlan's support.

Roosevelt referred to his previous statement in which he said, basically, that the Americans would use all the means at their disposal and accept help from anyone ready to provide it. It would be up to the people of France alone to choose the form of government under which they would live. Strange that Moroccan radio hasn't been jammed.

Confirmation has come in from everywhere that the Germans had no trouble at all getting their hands on considerable amounts of equipment, clothing, shoes, etc., stored in our barracks and supply depots. Nothing had been secreted away. Eyewitnesses claim that there was enough to clothe and equip 100,000 men.

December 6, 1942

Spent a lovely day with Jean, who is a lot more mature than I thought. He is a fine young man, somewhat of a swashbuckler. The desire to go off and fight is still burning inside him. He'll have plenty of time for that.

December 7, 1942

Spent the day with Jean, who got a tube for my radio, which I have been hiding with greater and greater care. I wouldn't have known how to get one.

Sottens confirmed that the Americans had suffered defeat in Tunisia, apparently as a result of the superior training of the German troops and their superior air power. Sicily has become a veritable aircraft carrier, with squadrons of fighters and Stukas brought in from the Russian front, where the winter has left them free to be used as reinforcements in North Africa. There are only 125 miles separating Sicily and Bizerte.

It has become painful to listen to the verbal fencing between the Moroccan radio and the Gaullist broadcasts. Can you imagine what it would have been like if Homer's heroes had had access to the airwaves? De Gaulle wrote a long article for *La Marseillaise* that was broadcast on every station. The controversy is sure to have a nefarious effect on the French living in Africa and the Moslems. All those Christians seem to have forgotten the parable about the return of the prodigal son, and the scripture about the sinner who repents and the eleventh-hour laborer in the vineyard. I have no respect whatsoever for Darlan; I find him thoroughly despicable. Nonetheless, I am given to wonder what de Gaulle would have done if he had been commanding a division in France at the time of the June 1940 invasion, instead of on a mission to London.

December 8, 1942

At 3:30 P.M. a German captain came in, with an officer from the gendarmerie behind him and another lower-ranking gendarme in front. He was in Bourassol again to verify that we were actually there. Short in stature, his hair cropped close, he ceremoniously entered each of our cells, read our name off a paper he was holding, turned, and left.

A young Lieutenant of Alsatian descent told me that he had been summoned to the German Commandant's office this morning, following incidents between French and German guards. The Captain notified him that he himself, on orders from his Commanding General, would come to inspect Bourassol between 3 and 4 P.M. The Lieutenant replied that unless otherwise ordered by Vichy, he would meet force with force, after which he left to inform the Subprefect and the Captain at the Gendarmerie, sowing panic everywhere he went. In the end, they decided to let the Germans have their way and accompany them on their rounds. The procession reached Bourassol at 3:30 P.M., at which time the prison fell under German control. So now we know exactly what Laval's word was worth when he told Le Trocquer that he would guarantee our protection.

December 12, 1942

Churchill gave a wonderful speech, with a passage devoted to the immortal grandeur of the Commonwealth, reaffirmed in its having withstood adversity while France lay prostrate. He evaded the matter of British air support in France during the battles on the German and Belgian borders. Look at Vuillemin's testimony and the orders he was issuing at a time when the replies coming out of the British Air Ministry were totally at odds with what Chamberlain had pledged; or look at the exchanges with Paul

Reynaud in his office at the Quai d'Orsay, while we were busy burning documents. The answer the British gave Reynaud at his home in the middle of the night was practically insulting.

Churchill said he was delighted that the Germans are now occupying all of France. He claims it will serve to unite the French, after which he praised de Gaulle. The truth is that the British were saved by the United States, and of course also by their own Air Force, during the most spectacular period of the war. Why Hitler didn't attack England in the summer of 1940 is something I still haven't figured out.

We have been informed that Léon Blum, Paul Reynaud, and I are to be taken to Germany. In truth, I have been expecting this since November 11.

December 14, 1942

Pétain has written a letter to Hitler to express his gratitude for the new disgraces inflicted on France. He said he is now prepared to forge a military and political alliance with the victors and has put Laval in charge of working out the details. At no time throughout the trip from Paris to Bordeaux in June 1940, at no point on the way to Brittany and across the Touraine, Charente, and Gironde regions, when he often mingled with the crowds and was greeted as we drove down country roads and through cities, did I ever hear Pétain call for peace. The only time he did that was when he was conspiring with the other traitors. There is an analogy here with what happened in 1815 following Waterloo, a similar split between the people and their leaders.

December 15, 1942

It has been one dreary day after another. This morning, I had the pleasure of receiving Daridan. His subtle and witty irony has given way to an uncustomary vehemence. He found the presence of German police around the château sickening, and the attitude of the Cour Suprême despicable. He felt that once the Germans had violated the separation between the Occupied and Unoccupied Zones, the court should have met, released us provisionally, and dissolved itself as a body, instead of waiting for Laval to dissolve it. The French have offered no resistance whatsoever, and the

Germans have responded to their servility with increased scorn. Daridan has decided to take a leave of absence.

"Come on, Daridan. Tell me about your Italian friends."

His eyes lit up behind his glasses as he began unleashing his irony on the Fascist militia, the King—who can't go into the bombed-out cities of Turin and Genoa without hearing crowds shouting, "Pace, pace!"—and Mussolini, who has been stiffed until now and is still waiting for his tip. He painted a whole series of such portraits; he has become a master at it. What light and joy filled this room of mine, where the sun rarely shines.

Then he read Lord Gort's report on the British Expeditionary Force during the campaign in France. I copied down several excerpts; I'll want to comment on them later.

I was really sorry to see him go. He left me a clipping from *Le Moniteur*, Laval's newspaper, with the transcription of the press conference Laval gave yesterday, stating: "I *want* Germany to be victorious. ... The people who are counting on an American victory refuse to see that Roosevelt is bringing with him the triumph of the Jews and the Communists. People are free to wish for whatever they want, but I intend to crush them, whatever it takes." He referred to the way our two nations had been faithful to the spirit of collaboration, when in fact Germany has been violating the terms of the Armistice from the very beginning. Yet Laval has read what Goebbels wrote just as I have: "If the French knew what our peace terms included, they would have nothing left but their eyes to cry over it." France would shrink back to its 1450 borders. We'll never be able to collaborate with the Germans without first having rooted out Nazism. Laval is in so far now that he'll go through right to the end.

Received greetings from Louis Marin,[45] a proud patriot from Lorraine.

---

45. Louis Marin, President of the Republican Federation from 1925 to 1940 and several times a Minister. He refused to be a part of the Vichy government. He made it to London in 1944 and was a member of the Provisional Consultative Assembly in Algiers.

December 18, 1942

Catroux was interviewed in London by the Anglo-American press. A certain conceit came out of it, that of a man wounded in his pride and threatened in his ambitions. He pounded away at Darlan's presence in Africa, which he said jeopardized communications within the Anglo-American Expeditionary Force. In other words, if there were anything in it for him, Darlan would betray the Allies. Wrangling of this kind is not likely to encourage the French people of North Africa to join in the fight alongside the Anglo-Saxons.

De Gaulle's merits are beyond question, but this bickering shouldn't be tolerated. As for Darlan, he proved to be far more skilled when he was interviewed by the Anglo-Americans in Algiers. He claimed that the political approach he had adopted in France had been forced on him by events. He said that once the war is over, he will return to civilian life and let the people of France decide what form of government they want and who they want running it.

There is good news about the training our French troops received in Africa and the way they acquitted themselves in combat, a fact likely to have considerable importance later on.

December 19, 1942

Roger Génébrier had lunch with me on his way back from Vichy, bringing me good wishes from Louis Marin. He had met at length with Bousquet, who informed him that Laval had left for Paris and was thereafter to head for Munich to see Hitler, apparently to discuss the creation of a military draft to bolster the German forces, either by protecting maritime zones against a possible Anglo-Saxon landing or by relieving German troops occupying territories that now stretch from the Balkans to Norway. The French government would move its offices to Paris and the line separating the two zones would disappear. This would make Laval's plan a reality and would effectively result in an earnest collaboration, with Germany playing the beneficent suzerain and France the vassal at long last brought under control. Déat would be given a Ministry, but certainly not Interior, with control over the police force; trust is not the strong point of this group. All political parties, which is to say the only party that exists, Doriot's party, would be dissolved. Differences still remain between Pétain's entourage and Laval's. "We should move cautiously on this," Bonnefoy said. "After all, the old man could issue a new constitutional decree and chuck it all out the window."

December 20, 1942

At 7:15 A.M. Sottens announced that according to a late-night communiqué from Moscow, the Russians have won a major victory at Voronezh and broken through the German lines at two points. They have advanced an average of about forty miles along a front fifty-five miles long. There are some 10,000 German dead and as many prisoners, and the Russians have also destroyed a great deal of matériel. The strategic importance of this victory is obvious: Now they will fix their sights on Kharkov. But to date, after initial successes, every Russian attack has been beaten back by German counterattacks. We are still in the picador stage; we have got a long way to go before the matador makes his entry into the arena.

Radio message from Pope Pius XII.

Gaullist radio has announced that the Germans have been routed, but they have been announcing this every time the Russians attack. Their propaganda is clearly ill conceived. They must think the French are all simpletons. Fortunately, the American War Secretary Stimson has made a more objective assessment and clarified the situation without attempting, and rightly so, to obscure the difficulties. *That* is sound propaganda. The British do it similarly. Italian radio, in contrast, is as grandiloquent as ever. According to their announcer, just about everything in the United States is Italian. Nothing would ever have been built in New York without the Italians—bridges, railroads—they did everything. The very conquest of America might have been the work of Italians.

Finally, we were graced with a message from Marshal Pétain, in which he summarized in his quavering voice the results of his bankrupt policies.

December 25, 1942

I just learned that on December 24, at 3 P.M., Admiral Darlan was assassinated in Algiers by a twenty-year-old Frenchman. Six bullets from a handgun, fired point-blank.

I spent a lot of time with Darlan in 1933, when he was an adviser to Georges Leygues, my Minister of the Navy. He was a man consumed by vaulting ambition. Darlan came to see me when Leygues died following a long and painful illness. I had gone to see Leygues several times in his villa in Saint-Cloud and found him steadfast and courageous in facing death and abounding in the affectionate civility with which he had always favored me. When Leygues died, Darlan called me from my office and informed me of his passing with a flippancy that he was forced to curb when he sensed my sorrow.

In 1936, with Gasnier-Duparc's consent, Darlan pushed out Admiral Durand-Viel, getting him to retire early in exchange for who knows what. Darlan was lavish in assuring Blum of his devotion to him, but after we had reviewed troops somewhere, on May 11, if I am not mistaken, he told me how Pétain had snickeringly said to him, "So Darlan, I see you got yourself appointed Admiral of the Popular Front." In those days, Darlan was merciless in his sarcastic remarks about "the senile old man."

He didn't get along with Campinchi, the Minister above him, and worked on both General Bourret, who was very close to me, and above all Clapier, my Chief of Staff, dropping in on them, lunching, and dining with them. Darlan wanted to become head of the Joint Chiefs of Staff for National Defense, which was absolutely absurd.

I ran into him during maneuvers in Normandy. He was a doer, quite intelligent, and closely supervised our naval construction there. His hatred for Campinchi was ever increasing, and he tried to go over his head through the friendly contacts he had made with Clapier. However, the loss of his aide, Tavera, who had a lot more horse sense than he did, left him severely handicapped. In 1939, during the famous August 23 meeting at which we discussed the possibility of France's entering the war, he stated that the Navy was ready and that their Italian plans—for Genoa, Rome, and Naples—had been finalized. He hadn't understood any more about the role air power was to play than the Army Generals. Our two aircraft carriers, the *Béarn* and the *Teste*, were outdated; still there is no doubt in my mind that we outclassed the Italians. In 1939, he set himself up as a minor potentate in Maintenon, with a private train.

As soon as Reynaud took over, Darlan began playing the sycophant again, criticizing Gamelin. On May 19, having been disappointed at not having been named to replace Gamelin, he turned on Reynaud, but cautiously. He was simultaneously working both ends: resistance and capitulation. On the resistance end, he agreed with and ended up organizing plans for the Members of Parliament to leave for Morocco on the *Massilia;* he even cabled Noguès, the Governor-General in Morocco, to set up a command post next to his from which he would lead the resistance in North Africa. At that very same time, Vuillemin was issuing an order to have 2,000 planes flown to North Africa. Then Darlan turned traitor, refused to bring the fleet to Noguès, and became a collaborator.

After the palace revolution of December 13, 1940, he went to see Hitler. Once Laval was back in power, Darlan was relegated to the simple role of Commander in Chief of the Armed Forces. Since he was anti-British, he decided to try out the Americans. I still remember what he said about the British Admiralty and Admiral Pound. During the Supreme Council meetings in London and even more so in Paris, he couldn't keep his sarcasm in check.

Did he actually urge Marshal Pétain to resist on November 8, as he kept on claiming? In all events, that the French fleet chose to oppose the American landing during the first few days is totally incomprehensible. If Darlan and Noguès were in agreement, how could they have sent hundreds of officers, soldiers, and sailors to a useless death? If they weren't in agreement, how does one explain the sudden turnaround? The key to the puzzle lies in Pétain's November 11 address, in which he protested the movement of German troops into Unoccupied France. Marion intervened to stop that address from being broadcast, and Laval, who returned from Munich in the early afternoon, approved his decision. He declared in that statement that France was no longer bound by the conditions of the Armistice, which explains the turnaround in Africa. Laval managed to have Darlan, Giraud, Boisson, and Bireau stripped of their French nationality and handed them over to Vichy's "newspapermen," without either a trial or a sentencing. What is more, neither Noguès, Chatel, nor Bergeret[46] lost his citizenship.

De Gaulle was furious. They were absolutely out of control on the radio every night. The British press got into it. There was a great stir in the House of Commons. The realistic Americans, in contrast, remained unruffled. It was clear that Darlan served the French and Allied cause in North Africa. If the Anglo-Saxons had continued to encounter resistance, they would have lost at least a month, and the entire undertaking could have been compromised, for the Germans would have had the time to regroup.

A war council in Algiers has decided to execute the assassin. They have refused to disclose his name "for reasons of military security." His father is French and his mother Italian. Is he a Fascist? A Doriotist? One of the boys from the Youth Camps? A Gaullist? There have been all sorts of conjectures, especially in light of what Darlan is supposed to have said to the officers who rushed to his side: "It is useless. The British have attained their objective." Of course, that information came through the Stéfani Press Agency. Reuters offered bizarre comments, basically expressing pleasure at the assassination, which would pave the way for a centrist agreement between de Gaulle and Giraud, with the latter taking charge of the French fighting forces and de Gaulle assuming control over political and diplomatic matters. On the other side, Roosevelt condemned the assassination.

December 26, 1942

On her way out, Mme Reichenbach stopped off to tell me that she had decided to sew marks into the shoulder pads in Blum's overcoat and offered to do the same for me.

---

46. General Jean Bergeret, Air Force Brigadier General, member of the French delegation at the signing of the Armistice and Air Force Junior Minister in the Vichy government from 1940 to 1942. He left for Algiers at the end of 1942 and was appointed Commander in Chief of the French West African Air Force. He was dismissed by de Gaulle, arrested at the end of 1943, and eventually spent several years in prison.

December 30, 1942

Léon Blum told me that his lawyer, Le Trocquer, had gone to Vichy to see Bousquet, which was a mistake. First of all, because both Laval and Bousquet despise him and suspect him of belonging to a Gaullist organization in Clermont; second and most important, because there is no point in just going through the motions; the government in Vichy decides what to do on the basis of what it thinks will please the Germans most. Le Trocquer asked for permission to meet with Blum in his capacity as lawyer. Bousquet denied his request, saying that when Laval returns from Paris he will inform the Cour Suprême that it has been dissolved. The court would have done better to dissolve itself when the Germans moved in to occupy Riom.

What will become of us? Jacomet and La Chambre will doubtless be placed under house arrest. But what of the three of us, the men sentenced by Pétain: Blum, Gamelin, and myself? There is no way to send us back to Le Portalet, so we'll be shipped out to Germany. I have no doubt about that now, in spite of everything that's been promised by Laval and his cronies. Blum, however, thinks that we'll remain in Bourassol, which will be made into a fortified compound. I remain skeptical.

It doesn't really matter much anyway. The end of this year has been wonderful. The Allies have taken the initiative. The Russians are relentlessly hammering away at the front, taking a page from Marshal Foch. In the time since the beginning of the offensive, German losses have reached 300,000 men. The threat of an attack on Rostov has increased, and Rommel has been forced to draw back even further west. Moreover, just as I had predicted, the rate at which ships and planes are being built in the United States has continued to accelerate.

The word on Herriot is not at all good. He is thoroughly depressed. They have imposed restrictions that are simply loathsome. He has the right to have one three-hour visit per week, with a policeman present, and two letters a week.

December 31, 1942

Today is the last day of a year that witnessed the opening, then the suspension sine die, of the Riom trial, as ordered by a government in panic and frightened by its own stupidity. All they have left are Maurras and Déat. All France is now under the enemy's heel, all our colonies occupied. This is precisely the catastrophe that Pétain claimed that he had been sparing us ever since the betrayal in Bordeaux. We are no longer dealing with the "disinherited King" or the "merry old King of nowhere." Pétain definitively dishonored himself on November 11, 1942.

The Germans have gone into a slow downhill slide. After having achieved almost total domination of the world in 1941, they are now irreversibly heading into the abyss. It will of course not take place without terrible convulsions, but defeat and the invasion of Germany are inevitable. The initiative lies with the Allies on every front, which is why yesterday's traitors and cowards can be seen popping up here and there. North Africa appears to them to be a particularly propitious setting in which to shift allegiances. In Africa, they are even expecting the arrival of Peyrouton and Chautemps.

LEFT: *Daladier at age twenty-eight, when he was a history teacher(1912)*

BELOW: *Daladier as a soldier in the French Infantry (1914)*

Daladier (above the X) in the Foreign Legion during World War I

Prime Minister Daladier (right) and General Bourret, during an inspection of the front lines (1939)

Minister of War Daladier visits the front (1939)

Mayor Daladier greets a constituent in Avignon

ABOVE: *Birthplace and early childhood home of Daladier in Carpentras*

LEFT: *Daladier, in the garden at his home, overlooking the Rhone River*

Parliamentary Deputy Daladier at his desk (1955)

Daladier in later years

1943

January 15, 1943

Vichy radio has announced that the "relief corps" is making great headway. The number of volunteers leaving to work in Germany is increasing daily!

This morning, Mme L.C. related a story told by her "carriageman," M. Gilbert. He had taken the train to Clermont to buy a horse for butchering. Antiriot police and German soldiers herded him and all the other passengers into the waiting room. Forty yards away, on the public squares and the streets leading to the station, women and children were screaming and crying. Every so often, when the crowd would regroup and march on the station, the police would disperse them with the butts of their rifles, as the amused German soldiers looked on. The police were under orders to stop the protesters from overrunning the station and lying down on the tracks to prevent the trains from leaving, as they had done in Montluçon. On the platform, workers were lined up in rows of twos, with guards and German soldiers on either side. As each train pulled out, people would start singing the Communist *Internationale* and shouting, "Down with Pétain" and "Death to Laval."

January 22, 1943

At around 3 P.M. Bourassol was rattled with bursts from automatic weapons and exploding hand grenades. I got the feeling, though, that they were firing blanks. I saw Lieutenant Niepven prancing about on his handsome horse, his gold bars shining in the sunlight. I later learned that these were maneuvers to ward off possible aggressors from the North ... but the Germans had already invaded Bourassol last November!

Last night, a broadcast from Algiers announced the appointment of Peyrouton, Vichy's fascist ex-Minister of the Interior, to a position in the government in Algeria. The Gaullists have protested, and their outrage is perfectly legitimate. It was Peyrouton who organized Pétain's personal police force and masterminded the plot that ended with Laval's arrest. In Algiers, he will be up to his neck again in personal intrigue, unless Giraud manages to bring him into the Count of Paris's camp. It is unfortunate that Roosevelt wasn't informed of just how deplorable a choice he is.

January 28, 1943

Two thousand local assemblies have been dissolved; 800 Mayors and Deputy Mayors have been removed from office: These figures are an indication not only of what the men in Vichy have done, but of their very reason for seizing power in the first place. The words "National Revolution" are hardly devoid of meaning; nor are the piles of decrees, laws, and various measures that have been enacted.

January 29, 1943

At the Riom trial, our Generals testified that the French Army had not been provided with shooting ranges. Right here, in Riom, the Germans have been taking rifle and antiaircraft target practice, using live ammunition.

January 30, 1943

Pierre came. He is brave and involved. He told me that the Italians had pulled out of Carpentras.

It's the tenth anniversary of Hitler's rise to power, the day he was named Chancellor by Marshal Hindenburg. At 11 A.M. it was announced that Göring would address the nation; at 11:15, that he would address the nation in a few minutes. It was about noon when he actually spoke, the British having decided to mark this anniversary by bombing Berlin in broad daylight. This is what they call British humor: making Göring wait until the end of the air raid. The people of Berlin must have had no trouble measuring the difference between January 1943 and January 1942 or 1941. Now they can reflect on Göring's famous challenge to the British Air Force.

The lines taken by Briand and Stresemann, England's blindness, and America's isolationism all made it easier for the clauses of the Treaty of Versailles to be broken. Inflation and the destruction of Germany's middle class created a favorable climate.

There is something permanently and specifically German in Nazism. One has only to read Fichte's *Addresses to the German Nation.*

Hitler's paramount error was to have attacked Russia instead of invading England.

February 2, 1943

On January 30, Hitler, Göring, and Goebbels were already eulogizing the dead at Stalingrad, hours before their actual capture or death. The Russians continue to push forward along a vast front. Stalingrad is this war's Verdun, but more decisive and even crueler. The German Army is retreating along the entire front, and they are retreating slowly, perhaps more slowly than they'd like. Maybe mechanized armies have a harder time withdrawing than their earlier counterparts. How do you stealthily pull out all that huge machinery?

It is "victory or death," the Nazi leaders are now saying, borrowing a phrase from the French Revolution; earlier they had compared themselves to Napoleon for military genius. In any event, they have hidden nothing from the German people, although they may have exaggerated somewhat the gravity of the situation to trigger a burst of popular energy. Now that a compromise peace settlement is no longer a possibility, the Nazi leaders will be asking their people to make an enormous effort. The only thing that can save Hitler would be for the Russians to pull out of the war, once they have liberated their own territory and strengthened their influence over Poland, the Baltic States, Bulgaria, and Romania. In the eighteenth century, Berlin and Frederick II were spared when Czar Paul pulled out, but I tend to think that Stalin's vision stretches further than old man Kutuzov's.

While the world tragedy is hastening toward a climax, the phantoms of Vichy have kept right on with their ridiculous pantomime: Pétain has stripped Bergeret and everyone else who went to Africa of their *francisque gallique* decorations, a medal he made up himself. He has given his blessing to France's SS. Joffre, Foch, and Clemenceau were right in their judgment of the man twenty years ago.

Ever since the Americans set up Giraud in Algiers, the same Giraud that Reynaud wanted to name Supreme Commander, the English and Eden have found themselves in a very uncomfortable position.

It is obvious that the Americans' realistic approach has led them to endorse Giraud and Peyrouton in order to gain the support of officers like Noguès and Boisson, who are conservative but nonetheless favor democracy. And the Americans are the ones running operations in Africa.

February 9, 1943

Mazé showed up unexpectedly. He spoke of his odyssey, the American High Command, and new plans.[1] I'm worried about my sons.

Around noon, the presiding judge, Caous, called Bourassol to announce that Jacomet and La Chambre were to be released on their own recognizance. Then a car drove up with the warden of the Riom Penitentiary. Mme La Chambre was deeply moved, absolutely overjoyed, but the rest of the afternoon was spent on the phone with Bousquet, the Superintendent of Police. Apparently Laval had not yet submitted the court's decision to the Germans. Bousquet feared there might be incidents. So, instead of spending the night in a hotel, Jacomet and La Chambre had to spend it here.

Around 8:30 P.M. they came into my room. They were joyous, exultant. Neither one of them had a word or a thought for me, even though I was going to remain a prisoner. They said that their release was proof that the charge of their having ill-prepared us with arms and equipment had been dropped. On that score, they were right.

---

1. After having opposed plans to escape as long as the Riom trial was in progress, Daladier was now prepared to go to London, as Churchill, Eden, and de Gaulle had been urging him to do. Pierre de Vomécourt, who was later arrested and deported, served as liaison. Because a plane could land no closer than the area around Châteauroux, the principal difficulty lay in covering the distance between Riom and Châteauroux at night, without being caught.

February 10, 1943

The day went by without our "releasees" making it out of here, and yet they had donned their finest clothes for the occasion. Both of them were getting increasingly edgy, especially when their wives couldn't keep from showing how concerned they were and started asking preposterous questions. A guard named Fouilland chose to express ironically his doubts about their ever leaving, which didn't help matters. I found out this evening that the court recorder, Théry, had come with an order for their release, but that Brun, the Prefect, notified them that Laval would be going to Paris tomorrow to inform the Germans and request their authorization. Back to prison they went. Another guard, Young, who goes by the book, even bolted their doors shut, despite their vehement protests.

Neither one of them has had a considerate word for us these last two days, yet they should feel at least partially indebted to me for their release. Didn't I praise them at the trial? Wasn't I the one who tore apart the charges that we were not properly prepared to go to war?

Is man fundamentally evil, as the Church teaches us, and as is the contention of my old friend Dr. Renard, who came and spent the rest of the day with me?

After dinner, sweet little Simone, who was waiting on us, told me that Jacomet was becoming demanding and La Chambre even more condescending than before, and that it was making her sick.

February 11, 1943

I think Giraud and Peyrouton see things as Pétain does and that at the end of the war they'll head for Vichy and sing, "Maréchal, nous voilà."[2]

Why wasn't de Gaulle with the British and American troops when they landed in Algiers? I can't figure it out.

---

2. Literally, "Marshall, here we are," with "ready to serve you" implied. This was the song that all French schoolchildren sang in honor of Pétain and that became a kind of national anthem. The allegiance to and reverence for an individual leader was one of the typically Fascist aspects of the Vichy regime.

February 13, 1943

Had a final important talk with Mazé at 2 P.M. He left at 5. I pray that he'll succeed.

February 15, 1943

The Archbishop of New York is being received by the Primate of Spain, a meeting not without importance.

The *Richelieu*, a powerful 35,000-ton cruiser, whose construction was finished at my insistence, has just reached New York after first being damaged at Dakar and then crossing the Atlantic through a horrifying storm. The cruiser *Montcalm* and other ships made a similar journey, thus, along with the ships that had already gone back into combat, saving the honor of the French Navy.

The Russians have advanced to within five miles of Kharkov. Berlin claims that its forces have simply withdrawn from positions that had become useless and that were not actually threatened, and that they have inflicted terrible losses on the Reds. Try and figure it out.

The Bourassol owl is back.

February 17, 1943

3:30 P.M. Suddenly, Bourassol was all astir as a car with two magnificent chauffeurs pulled in. Out of it, in all his majesty, stepped the honorable Superintendent of Police. I assumed that he had finally come for the two men who had been freed, but I could hear people yelling and women's voices squealing above the men's vociferous protests. Doors opened and slammed shut; then the halls rang anew with the noise of shouting. Fouilland, an old veteran from North African campaigns, filled me in on what was going on. After Jacomet and La Chambre had gotten all of their personal effects together this morning, in anticipation of their definitive release, the Superintendent of Police came and read them a new order from the Minister of the Interior. Instead of being released on their own recognizance, they were placed under house arrest and, worse, here in Bourassol. They both refused to sign the order, fumed at the Superintendent of Police, and began railing against poor old Young, accusing him of being responsible for everything. They must have forgotten that this poor old head guard had been threatened with losing his job for having failed to bolt our doors shut these last few days.

Fouilland came up to see me later to express his indignation and his fear that Bourassol would be transformed into a site for prisoners placed under house arrest, in which case Blum, Gamelin, and I would be handed over to the Germans. In other words, as Horace wrote, "Quieta non movere."

February 20, 1943

Goebbels gave a speech that was highly structured and forceful, which is in fact characteristic of all his speeches. He emphasized the extreme danger that the unexpected strength of the USSR represented for the Reich. He said that stopping them would require the total mobilization of Germany and the neighboring countries. "Let the people rise up," he said. "Let the storm loose its fury." Of course Goebbels, no more than any other orator, was not about to lift the veil covering the cordial relations between Russia and Japan.

I'll have to reread Spengler.

Jean came at 2 P.M. We discussed Mazé's plan.

February 22, 1943

There's been a new episode in the soap opera about our "releasees." This time, Jacomet and La Chambre were actually expecting to leave sometime today. People were running all over the place, with no one minding especially about us. The Germans have had their attention focused too sharply on Bourassol. They could end up moving in here or taking their guests to Germany, without so much as a nod to the decisions of Vichy's Cour Suprême.

Jean left at 1:30 P.M.

February 23, 1943

Daridan related his meeting with Monsignor Suhard[3] and Monsignor Chapoulié,[4] in which they distanced themselves from Pétain with all due ecclesiastical unction. They are worried about what will happen after the war. Will the Church be able to hold on to the gains it has made? Wouldn't it be in the Church's best interests to relinquish certain overly spectacular favors it has received? According to Daridan, the Church is leaning toward the idea of relying on the Socialists as protection from the Communists. At the Vatican, they no longer believe that Germany can win, but they are concerned about a Soviet victory.

February 25, 1943

This General Giraud of ours is either a Royalist or a Fascist, depending on circumstances, but in every instance he is antirepublican. That is his meeting ground with Pétain, Maurras's boy, the "Monck" whom the Action Française group couldn't find on February 6, 1934.

Following the assassination of Darlan, who had promoted himself as anti-Fascist and anti-Nazi in Africa, Giraud sided for a time with the Count of Paris, the Pretender to the French throne. The latter made a visit to Algiers, but in the face of the vehement protests from the Gaullists in Algeria, the British, the Americans, and the democratic factions in Algiers and other cities, he was forced to turn back to Spanish Morocco. Thereafter, Peyrouton and Flandin freed the Gaullists, Communists, and Spanish Republicans imprisoned in Algiers. Stay tuned for more.

Stalin has stated that the Red Army has no mission beyond that of liberating its national territory. This reassured the moderate elements, who had been clearly shaken by Vichy's constant talk of the Red peril—Europe submerged under a flood of Bolsheviks. They have been relentless in milking Laval's pet themes: the German as civilization's soldier; Hitler as the knight of Teutonic order, etc., etc. Stalin's speech obviously comes in response to this propaganda. He was also highly ironic with regard to the

---

3. Cardinal Suhard, Archbishop of Paris.

4. Chapoulié was a Bishop and the Episcopate's liaison with the government.

Anglo-Saxons, above all the British, calling for them once again to launch an offensive in the West. The sword of honor that King George had cast for Stalingrad is not enough to satisfy him. The insolence with which it was accepted by Kalinin, the "little father" of Soviet peoples, was magnificent.

March 2, 1943

Senator Maroselli[5] has arrived in London. He made a statement, which I couldn't hear very clearly, about the military reasons for our defeat, which he ascribed to the inferiority of our Air Force, in spite of the tenacious efforts that he, Maroselli, had made. One more example of someone who thinks he's the center of the universe.

March 3, 1943

Gamelin came to see me at 9 A.M. He had had a visit from his lawyer Arnal, a former classmate of the prosecutor, Cassagneau. At a gathering with Cassagneau, Barthélemy, and Caous, the presiding judge, Arnal learned how furious the Germans were when they found out about the court decision releasing the two prisoners. It took a full two weeks of negotiations between Hitler and Laval just to get the two of them placed under house arrest.

Caous and Cassagneau are relieved that we too didn't ask to be released on our own recognizance, for if we had, the court would have found itself in the position of having to order us freed and, in so doing, of handing us over to the German authorities. They're nonetheless reserving the right to release us when the Anglo-Saxons land in France.

As for me, I never even dreamed of asking to be released on my own recognizance, which serves no purpose in practical terms and represents a feeble, contrived compromise in terms of justice.

Sooner or later, the world of French jurisprudence will have to recognize that from 1919 to 1939 no Minister of War did what I did for our national defense. In September 1939, no French statesman could have left

---

5. André Maroselli, Radical-Socialist Senator.

France open to an accusation of breach of promise without inflicting on the nation a dishonor greater even than defeat. In 1939, there was nothing for us to do other than become involved in a war that Hitler wanted.

March 4, 1943

Jacomet and La Chambre came by to see me at 6 P.M. They had been notified by the Regional Prefect that the German military authorities have refused to authorize their release.

That was inevitable. The only thing that will come out of this business will be the sterner conditions the Germans will impose in Bourassol. How could anyone have believed for as much as a second that at a time when the war in Russia has taken an irreversible turn, the Germans would allow the French government to free two men who are standing trial? It just goes to show how much sway even the most childish illusions can have over intelligent men.

The actual consequences weren't long in coming. At nightfall, the Gestapo arrived to relieve the German soldiers stationed here. There are now twice as many guards, all of them Gestapo.

It is their intention to keep Mme Fouilland, the cleaning lady, from leaving Bourassol every evening to go home. The German captain demanded that the head guard bring him the visitors' register, which he examined in detail and put his mark on.

Ever since the court's decision releasing the two of them, I have been expecting us to be sent to Germany. "Quieta non movere."

March 5, 1943

There have been more incidents at the barriers set up at the entrance. The Gestapo tried to keep one of the guards, Ancel, from returning to his job. Mme Reichenbach and people who have been coming here regularly received a thorough going-over. All of this is highly significant.

March 10, 1943

Vichy has been mobilizing French youth to serve the German cause. They're handing out travel papers for Silesia, Poland, and Sebastopol. Soon they'll be handing out German uniforms. It's reported that thousands of young men have sought refuge in the Alps. Pétain is paving the way for the Communists.

March 31, 1943

Around 10 A.M. Bousquet, the Superintendent of Police, and a thoroughly dejected-looking Génébrier came into my room. I knew right away that Vichy had backed down. Bousquet confirmed as much, saying that Laval had held out for as long as he could, but that the Gestapo was convinced that the British and Americans were plotting to kidnap us. Bousquet explained that we would be lodged in perfectly suitable quarters and that we could correspond with the outside world through him and even take someone along with us to Germany. I thanked him, but that wasn't the issue. I had nothing to say about the decision the Germans had made. However, I had plenty to say about the attitude of the government in Vichy, which was the sole responsible party in all this. A German Colonel with the Gestapo walked in and quite courteously repeated what Bousquet had said. Génébrier, my friend in need, agreed to carry out my last wishes if that became necessary. Jacomet stopped by briefly.

Our departure was set for 12:30 P.M. I went down to the outer office where a number of French officers saluted me. I answered back with the refrain, "Maréchal, nous voilà." The three prison guards reacted with dignity. This time, I found myself sharing a car with Blum.

On the road to Aulnat, I spotted Génébrier. He waved a final goodbye in my direction. When we arrived, they put us in a room where we spent the whole day. There were gendarmes, sentries, and searchlights all around. We met up with Léon Jouhaux,[6] whom they had brought in from Evaux-les-Bains; he would be traveling with us. Got news of Herriot, who had been taken with his wife to the Seine-et-Marne. There was some improvement though—we had our meals together.

---

6. Léon Jouhaux, union organizer and leader of the CGT union.

April 2, 1943

Left Aulnat. Five cars. Jouhaux didn't come with us. Went through Montferrand, Bourassol, Riom, Moulins, Nevers, La Charité. Saw well-equipped German soldiers. Went on to Montargis.

There seemed to be no men anywhere in the region. Shops were closed. Drove on to Fontainebleau and Paris. I was overcome with a feeling of anguish; the city seemed to have been chloroformed. Drove up the Avenue d'Italie—empty—to the Gobelins, onto the Boulevard Saint Michel, where there was some activity. Rode by Vilmorin's plant shop on the quay.

Reached the Place de la Concorde. Went down the Champs Elysées, passing in front of number 32, where I had lived with my father-in-law for several years after the Great War.

Sent a salute that carried all our hopes to the Unknown Soldier.

In Maisons-Lafitte, I was recognized by a few civilians, which didn't sit well with our German guard.

Came to a house surrounded by guards and sentries, who had orders to shoot if we got close to the garden gates. Dinner at 8 P.M.

April 3, 1943

Left Maisons-Lafitte at 8 A.M. Went by car, with two armed soldiers.

Reached Le Bourget at 9 A.M., where several civilians recognized me. A little human warmth.

Arrived in Mannheim at 11:20 A.M., but we were kept locked on the plane until 7 P.M. Took off, with orders to land in Frankfurt. Had dinner at the Air Force base, where we were courteously received by the officers. Had sausages and tasteless coffee.

Left for the Weimar region by highway at 10:30 P.M. Got there before dawn.

Around 6 A.M. we were welcomed by a Gestapo Commandant, tall, well built, and cordial. He reminded me of a British officer. "Horresco referens." He assigned us rooms; I settled into mine.

Day was breaking on the plateau, over the forest of pines. From my window I could see a sentry with a police dog and beyond them fences, barbed wire, and more sentries and dogs. There were bars on my windows but done in better taste than those at Bourassol. We were cut off from the world and life in France, but no more so than a million other French prisoners and the French youths that had been taken to Germany.

France will rise again. That is the only thing that matters.

April 7, 1943

Snowed all day. At 11 A.M. I went for a walk outside the house, stepping over the roots of the pine trees. The sentry was right behind me with his police dog.

Had lunch at 1 P.M. We could only bring in two stations on the radio. What are the Germans getting out of keeping us sequestered here?

Jouhaux talked to me about workers' lives and the strikes in the old days over sardine nets and the rotating nets in Concarneau. He also sketched a few portraits of some working-class activists: Rivelle, Vignaud, and Gautier.

Won't this war herald Asia's entry onto the international stage?

Will Europe be able to go on living by and for itself without lowering its standard of living?

Got two 20-gram packs of Croatian tobacco.

April 9, 1943

There was a storm last night. Soldiers were shouting and dogs were barking. The pine trees are covered with snow.

April 10, 1943

The camp Commandant came to see us at 4:30 P.M. He was as helpful as he could be within the limits of his prerogatives. It's a huge camp, with 20,000 SS, all of them volunteers. Before the war, it held three divisions; today it holds twenty. The men undergo training for seventy-five days and then leave for the front. There's a lesson in that for the French High Command.

A lot of the men are sick, even though the authorities go to great lengths to see to the well-being of their soldiers.

The food, which is the same for officers and enlisted men alike, is healthy and plentiful, and the diet well balanced. The pay and the child benefits are high. Many of the soldiers come back from Russia having saved up a considerable amount of money. They try to do more or less the same for the workers, with certain advantages clearly favoring the soldiers. There's a lesson in that for the French working class.

The Commandant told us that there were now a million French workers, men and women, at work in Germany, and that they had proven to be productive and conscientious once they got used to the factories.

He mentioned productivity records that French workers had broken.

April 15, 1943

Jouhaux is relatively realistic. He fears that through overcapitalization, the United States will eventually dominate Europe economically and thereby politically. He is opposed to granting independence to the colonies, although he believes that we should maintain an open-door policy.

Jouhaux is a proponent of international treaties and a multinational defense; he foresees American capitalism leading the world under a new banner. Blum actually waxes lyrical. He's very much taken by Wallace's[7] views. He thinks some compromise will be reached between communism and a modified version of private ownership. Like Jouhaux and myself, he believes that there will have to be a genuine federation of European nations. I am of the belief that it will take time to rebuild France and that the political system of the future will have to be different from the last one. We'll have to choose between a British-style parliamentary system and a presidential system.

April 18, 1943

Palm Sunday. This was a major day of celebration in Provence, with olive trees and boxwoods. Part of the greatness of Christianity. In the current war, however, the Catholic and Protestant churches have once again fallen short of their mission. The political parties of the Left erred significantly

---

7. Henry Wallace, successively Secretary of Agriculture and Commerce under Roosevelt.

in ignoring the religious problem and the place it holds in France. There was a tendency to confuse secularity with secularism, which is a caricature, or rather a denial, of secularity.

April 21, 1943

De Gaulle made a formal statement on the radio, a typical Minister's declaration from the old school, in which you do your utmost to reconcile all interests and satisfy all concerned parties. It contained a mix of Communist and conservative catch phrases: the exploitation of our common wealth, a renewed and reformed Republic, protection for large families, etc.

Blum was enthusiastic about it: "He has never spoken so clearly." He probably put in some of those phrases himself, with the help of his friends in Algiers. In all events, he has given up the idea of calling back Members of Parliament and reconvening the National Assembly for a few days.

De Gaulle has appointed himself Head of the Provisional Government in all free territories of France. He has named Ministers and Junior Ministers to assure himself of support from all parts of the population. This will be followed by a Constituent Assembly, to be ratified through elections, and finally by a definitive government. I am in agreement on all points except the re-creation of a Popular Front, to which I am violently opposed because of the duplicity of the Communists. I am also opposed to a return to political parties, which, given the present international situation, would favor the Communists.

Blum doesn't believe that a British-style parliamentary system is suited to France. He sees no drawbacks in reestablishing political parties so long as we opt for a presidential system. He says it would be impossible to govern in association with a party tied to a foreign power, but he believes that Stalin has given up the idea of leading a world revolution and is now interested in becoming a great national leader. I remained highly skeptical as I listened to his prophesies. I believe precisely the opposite.

According to Jouhaux, the Communists have assured de Gaulle, "We are with you heart and soul." That is exactly what they told Blum in 1936.

April 22, 1943

The regional newspapers are filled with obituaries every day: "Fallen for the German Fatherland." "Died for the Fatherland, the German people, and the Führer." "Gave his young life for the Fatherland." There are lists of the dead from March and April and statements of appreciation from families who have received condolences. The stoicism of the German people during this third year of the war is undeniable. The fall of Stalingrad was met with an officially decreed period of mourning. Foreign countries have grossly underestimated the extraordinary degree to which Nazism has been instilled in the German people and their youth.

April 24, 1943

Had a sumptuous dinner: meatballs, potatoes, lettuce, and two eggs. I have been trying to get the new radio to work.

A massive attack on Tunisia would appear to be imminent. In Russia, there has been heavy fighting on the Donets. On the other hand, there has been no further word on Timoshenko's offensive. The tragedy has now spread to the entire world. As for Gamelin, he continues telling tales of his days in the Middle East and his memories of Brazil. He is writing his memoirs. According to him, we lost the war for lack of resolve. Facing the dynamism of the Germans, public opinion in France was divided, the middle classes had forgotten their mission, and political intrigues were raging among Pétain, Weygand, and Georges. He noted the failings of our fighting men and above all their leaders. Patriotism had become a matter of circumstance. The only thing he neglected to mention was the crisis in military thinking.

April 25, 1943

Easter Sunday. It's bitter cold out and foggy. Read some newspapers: *Je suis partout*, *La Gerbe*, *L'Echo de Nancy*, *Le Nouveau Journal de Bruxelles*. In the latter, there was a piece on the funeral ceremonies for Paul Collin, the Belgian Déat, and the speech given by Degrelle. This was already a Nazi movement well before the war began.

198

The Belgian newspaper went back over the abominable Katyn Forest massacre, where 10,000 imprisoned Polish officers died.[8] Their bodies, with their hands tied behind their backs, were piled up in long, deep trenches. The officers had knelt at the edge of the ditch and been shot in the neck.

April 29, 1943

Had a medical examination, with a curt, distant doctor, a General by rank, who seemed to have swallowed a sword, and another younger one, who was only slightly less arrogant, plus an interpreter who didn't know any French. There were measuring instruments laid out all over the table; you would have thought it was a scene from *Doctor Knock*. They listened to my lungs, took measurements, and urine samples—the whole business. It was far more comical than anything else.

Dr. Hauffmann, however, has been courteous and kind. He brought me a package and letters from Jean, Pierre, and M.L. I was quite moved by the letter from Jean, delighted to see what a brave lad he is. The Commandant told us that Mandel would be brought here, close to Blum. Blum quipped that "they were going to turn the place into a ghetto," but he took comfort in the news and on the whole everyone was pleased. As for us, we are going to be taken into the Tirol, not far from Innsbruck.

April 30, 1943

We said our good-byes this morning at the forest lodge of the camp. We chatted with the two men who waited on us, one of whom was from the area, the other a Croatian who told us about his seven children and showed us their photos. He is a Croatian volunteer SS.

At around 6 P.M. we got a call from the Assistant Commandant; our departure had been postponed again. Instantly, everyone started speculating, as if to see who could come up with the most imaginative explanation. I had fun claiming that under threats from Pétain and Laval to resign, the

---

8. The Polish officers were killed by the Soviets, who have only recently admitted responsibility.

Germans had agreed to send us back to France; either that or they had discovered an Anglo-American plot in Innsbruck. My first suggestion spawned others, and Gamelin began gleefully pulling ideas out of his brain like a magician pulling omelets, bottles, and rabbits out of a hat.

May 2, 1943

Awakened at 4 A.M. for a departure at 6; waited uselessly until 8. There had apparently been some misunderstanding in the transmission of orders. Dr. Hauffmann came by; he had just returned from the Tirol. Finally, we were on the highway. In the suburbs of Munich, we spotted a detachment of French prisoners looking proud and determined. We drove on very quickly along the quays.

All the SS NCOs were on hand for our arrival at the "castle" in Itter.[9] Went through a first gate with bars and locks, then a second one identical to the first, but with armed sentries. Beyond a small, triangular courtyard lay a raised inner yard 150 feet long and 100 feet wide, dotted with shacks and sheds. I was deeply moved when I saw two rows of prisoners go by, forty men or so with their heads shaved, wearing gray shirts with large brown stripes, similar to what prison laborers used to wear. Each had a number stamped on the left side of his chest. There were men of all ages, some of them just kids, others quite old. Some of them were political prisoners; their faces brightened a bit when they saw me. Received a few friendly smiles from some who obviously recognized me. They were quickly dispersed by SS NCOs who came running up from the chapel that had been transformed into dormitories and refectories. The sight of these men is powerful. It's part of the same chain of suffering, torture, and infamy that links the centuries. I went up to my room on the fourth floor, number 19. It reminded me of the Portalet fortress where Pétain had had us imprisoned, but with fresh air and a view of the mountains.

---

9. Near the Tirol and the Dachau concentration camp.

May 11, 1943

It has been reported that Franco offered to serve as a mediator to end the war and that the British and the Americans rejected his offer. Some of the guards who have been keeping us informed told us that "two gentlemen would be arriving tomorrow." I told my companions that it would likely be Reynaud and possibly Herriot and that Hitler would then tell them—or us: "I am holding you hostage. You, Reynaud, you're to work on Churchill and get a compromise peace settlement with him; you, Herriot, you work on Stalin and Roosevelt; you, Daladier, on the Radical Party; and you, Jouhaux, on the unions. I'll give you a week, after which you'll be shot."

Jouhaux was sulking. Gamelin was beside himself: How could I have omitted him in so important a matter!

May 12, 1943

At around 3 P.M. Reynaud and Borotra[10] arrived from Berlin, after having spent two days in Weimar, where they had left Mandel with Blum.[11] That Borotra has remained loyal to Pétain prompted violent attacks from Reynaud, which allowed him to overlook the fact that it was he, Reynaud, who had brought Pétain to power.

May 13, 1943

Our discussions at meal times carry over into the evening. Borotra is full of life, impassioned, and open-handed. We have been relentless in teasing him about his collaboration with Pétain, to whom he remains devoted. In his eyes, France was fortunate to have come upon Pétain in 1940. "What would have happened without him?" We answered that what would have happened was exactly what happened in Norway, Holland, and Belgium and even in Greece and Serbia. Borotra goes running and does strenuous

---

10. Jean Borotra, industrialist and tennis champion prior to the war, served as Vichy's Youth and Sports Minister. He was arrested by the Germans and liberated in 1945.

11. Blum and Mandel were both deported to Buchenwald. Blum spent two years there, receiving special treatment. In 1944 Mandel was transferred to Paris and eventually handed over to the French Militia and executed.

physical exercises every morning at seven. The German SS watch him admiringly.

Hitler sent a message to Von Arnim's Army. The undeniable bravery of the Afrikakorps was not enough to prevent bitter defeat.

May 14, 1943

Churchill made an important speech before the American Congress. He has sent General Giraud an eloquent and noble telegram. As I said in June 1940 in Bordeaux, and then again in Morocco, it is in Africa that France will reclaim its greatness. The shame of Sedan will be drowned in the Mediterranean.

This morning Reynaud was set on explaining to me how Pétain had begun conspiring as early as May 29, 1940, by trying to lure away Mandel over a few lunches at the Café de Paris. Reynaud told me that he had resigned in the hopes that Lebrun would call him back, but that he hadn't received the backing of either Jeanneney or Herriot. He added that Weygand had told them, "In three month's time, Germany will have wrung England's neck like a chicken's." He talked about the *commune blanche* in Bordeaux, adding that Marquet and Monzie had done everything they could to prevent the government from going to North Africa. He also mentioned Belin's role. He emphasized that it was a vast operation, a real conspiracy. Reynaud also accused Bouthillier, but for some reason left out Baudouin, and yet he had brought both of them into the government.

May 17, 1943

Once again, Reynaud spoke to me about Pétain's maneuvering. Pétain had told Monzie in April, "They'll soon have need of me." Once he got a government post, he began trying to draw certain Ministers into his corner, among them Mandel. Reynaud repeated to me one more time that Pétain had taken Mandel to lunch at the Café de Paris, even before the Germans launched their offensive. After the German attack, he asked Reynaud to get rid of me, invoking the Army's feelings about me. Paul Reynaud, along with everyone else in his entourage, was absolutely delighted with what this so-called maneuvering augured for me. He hadn't noticed the shadow on the wall, that of the noose they were preparing to use on him once I had been pushed out.

In the May 13 edition of *L'Echo de Nancy*, I came across the citation General Bridoux, Minister of War, read to the Legion of French Volunteers in Tunisia for having fought against the Allies: "For having engaged the enemy in combat on the 14, 16, 17, 23, and 25 of April 1943 alongside German troops; for having offered staunch resistance to a powerful assault led by tank-supported infantry; and for having counterattacked in hand-to-hand combat with grenades and bayonets. Although two-thirds of their men were lost, they carried out their orders, gaining the respect of yesterday's foes and today's comrades in arms," in other words, the Krauts.

I also read the short speech Admiral Esteva gave on Vichy radio on April 20, in which he reminded everyone that he had set up his command post in Bizerte in May 1940 and that he had remained in Tunisia for three years, loyal to the Marshal.

Pétain replied to him, which I also saw in the papers: "You have placed the principle of loyalty above all others. As fearless and above reproach as the knight Bayard himself, you have been faithful and true. There lies within your inner nature that spiritual strength without which no man can display heroism and selflessness."

Ribbentrop wrote Esteva, too: "Your work has allowed for the cooperation between the various parts of the Tunisian population and the German and Italian garrisons to proceed smoothly. In so doing, you have aided the powers of the Third Reich in the performance of military operations. I offer you the thanks and the gratitude of the representatives of the German nation."

At least Admiral Esteva felt somewhat uncomfortable when it came to returning their thanks. He pointed out that he had merely followed his government's orders: "In the present instance, I did nothing more than serve my country, as I have done throughout my life."

May 18, 1943

At 3 P.M. I took a bath in a kind of fountain where the water was around 50 or 55 degrees. A young German officer took one right after me. We agreed that the water was just too cold.

May 20, 1943

Took another bath in the fountain at 4 P.M. The Germans would have liked to follow my example, but the cold water was too much for them.

May 21, 1943

At 10 o'clock last night, the guards tried out their new searchlights. My whole room was illuminated by beams coming in from the South and the West. They will probably soon be trying out their new barbed wire, followed by their new police dogs.

May 22, 1943

I just heard an important piece of news: The voluntary dissolution of the Communist International has been decided by a meeting of representatives held in Moscow. It's a shrewd move, designed to reassure public opinion in the countries bordering on Russia as well as in Algeria, England, and throughout the world. In some countries, like France, it may lead to the fusion of the Socialist and Communist parties, which is Blum's old dream. It seems to me we would do better to question their ulterior motives. Jouhaux is delighted with the decision. He sees only good things coming out of this, both in the long term and the short.

May 23, 1943

In the time since Giraud has been in Africa, de Gaulle has been engaged in a veritable campaign to round up support in France from every political party. The last to join him is Queuille,[12] who while in Bordeaux, according to Reynaud, was in favor of signing an armistice …

Jacquinot,[13] Maroselli, and Gouin[14] are among those who had hopped on the bandwagon earlier. De Gaulle is trying to impress Giraud by handing all these men microphones and sending them up to the front lines

---

12. Henri Queuille, Radical who initially supported the Vichy regime.

13. Louis Jacquinot, conservative Deputy from the Meuse from 1932 to 1940. He was Under Secretary on the French Committee of National Liberation in Algiers. From 1944 to 1946, he was Minister of the Navy, then Junior Minister.

of his London radio broadcasts. But Giraud now has with him an Army of some 100,000 men, many officers, and the prestige of the victory in Tunisia, which, although it clearly doesn't efface our shame, offers nonetheless bright hopes for a fresh start. Why should he yield to de Gaulle? The Allies will align themselves with one or the other of these two men, on the basis of their own plans.

June 1, 1943

Chatted again with Reynaud last night. I reminded him of the proposition Churchill communicated to Bordeaux through de Gaulle on June 16, 1940. Reynaud was surprised; he didn't know I was aware of it. Their phone call had been picked up in Bordeaux and a transcription was included as evidence at the Riom trial. Churchill wanted to bind the two countries together and make them inseparable. Reynaud said that he noted down everything Churchill dictated to him and read it aloud before the Cabinet. Pétain, Weygand, Chautemps, Frossard, and the rest accused him of wanting to reduce France to a part of the Commonwealth. That is when, instead of having the other Ministers resign, as was both the rule and the custom, Reynaud himself resigned. How could he have turned power over to these people without so much as putting up a fight? Now he says he expected Lebrun to call him back, but that when the time came, Jeanneney and Herriot didn't support him. Whereupon Lebrun, unsettled, called in Pétain, and the rest, as they say, is history!

The following day, June 17, de Gaulle left for London and embarked upon his career as a politician. Reynaud added that de Gaulle is an intelligent and highly ambitious man, whereas Giraud is a soldier.

At this point, Gamelin launched into new scathing attacks on General Georges. In March 1936, at a time when the French government seemed inclined to oppose Germany's reoccupation of the Rhineland, Georges, or so said Gamelin, was sending emissaries to various newspapers to have them write that it would be absurd to get involved in a war. This is sup-

---

14. Félix Gouin, Socialist Deputy from 1924 to 1940. He served as President of the Constituent Assemblies in Algiers and Paris in 1944–1945.

posed to be the explanation for Henri de Kérillis's article that appeared in *L'Echo de Paris* in which he opposed any form of armed intervention. Georges was both Pétain's and Weygand's protégé. The sole reason behind all that business about creating a National Defense Ministry separate from the War Ministry, and consequently creating two distinct military commands, was to promote Georges to a command position in the Army's Ground Forces and keep him in active rank beyond the retirement age of sixty-five and even until sixty-eight. Their machinations got nowhere in the Chamber of Deputies. However, their schemes were played out by Weygand's and Georges's boys in the Senate, most prominently by the renowned M. Fabry, former War Minister, and "honest" Claude Reibel. They eventually won over the Senate's Armed Forces Committee and the joint session of the Senate's three military committees.

But all of that is past now, as is Gamelin's criticism of Georges's serious mistakes and failings during the war. It is enough to read the evidence accumulated at the Riom trial to be convinced of Georges's shortcomings and of just how disastrous a choice Pétain and Weygand had made.

It is equally undeniable, though, that in leaving for Algiers, Georges, this eleventh-hour resistance fighter, has taken a step of major consequence:

1. It has dealt a serious blow to the Vichy government and to Laval's policies, which bear Pétain's stamp of approval. (Nonetheless, I personally don't exclude the possibility that Georges and Pétain see eye to eye on this.) It has had considerable effect on parts of the reactionary bourgeoisie and on a great many officers who until now have loyally supported Pétain's official policies.

2. It is sure to infuriate Hitler, who will think that he has been duped and won't accept Vichy's failure to have had Georges placed under tight police surveillance in Chambéry.

3. The Americans and the British were undoubtedly aware of Georges's decision to leave. Jean Monnet must have played an important part in this affair. For France's bourgeoisie, even if not, obviously, for the democratic elements in France, the fact that Georges has joined the Algiers Committee will have considerable impact. He has also strengthened Giraud's position in relation to de Gaulle's.

All of this makes me think back on my relations with Monnet. I appointed him to head the Joint Purchasing Committee during the war. He was at first very much an admirer of Paul Reynaud but grew hostile toward him when Reynaud became Prime Minister. He had close ties with Roosevelt and Bullitt. Then there is the story of his commercial enterprise in Shanghai. Much to his credit, he gave up an important post at the League of Nations to revive the business his father had founded, which was going through very difficult times.

June 5, 1943

De Gaulle's speech at 9:30 P.M. was pompous. Giraud's, although five minutes too long, was excellent: simple, moving, and very much to the point. Must have been written by Jean Monnet. He mentioned Metz and Strasbourg and the prisoners of war. He alluded to the heavy losses in Russia, probably inspired by his meeting with Litvinov. The Committee's 11:30 A.M. meeting ran more than two and a half hours. It was similar to those morning Cabinet meetings that used to run on beyond 1 in the afternoon, after which a statement would be issued hailing our unanimity.

Now that de Gaulle has arrived in Algiers, a huge battle for power is being waged, even though an agreement in principle was reached under pressure from Churchill and Roosevelt. De Gaulle wants to be head of the executive branch of a provisional government to be instituted in France by him, after the Allied landing. He seems to have drawn recruits from the National Committee in London. The plan had the backing of Blum, Jouhaux, and Grenier, a Communist who declared, "We are with you body and soul." Awakening to the fact that there were also Radicals in France, they rounded up Queuille and Maroselli, then people like Jacquinot, Vallin, Viénot,[15] and so on. Noguès has resigned and been replaced by Puaux.

---

15. Pierre Viénot, Socialist Deputy. He was Under Secretary for Foreign Affairs in Léon Blum's government in 1936. He voted in favor of the Munich Agreement in 1938 and joined the Free French forces in 1942.

June 11, 1943

The city of Pantelleria surrendered at noon. All day long we have been deluged with speeches on the radio, pouring in like the Tirolean rains: "the first piece of Italian soil," "the Italian Navy was nowhere to be seen." The Gaullist radio announcers are clearly right out of the Homeric hero school, with this minor difference: They do their fighting with microphones, on the air.

At 8 P.M. Henri Bénazet, a former announcer from Paris, was back on the air in Algiers. He is another one of those who first supported Pétain and even testified against his employer to placate Vichy. Everyone of us found him grotesque. In his excitement, he gave himself away and attacked the former Republican system in the typical style of Pétain or Laval: "a Republic of comrades and profiteers." Knowing what kind of a man he is didn't diminish our stupefaction at hearing his insults coming over Free French radio.

June 16, 1943

An SS General showed up; his visit had been announced yesterday. At around 11:30 A.M. he went to the room that Reynaud and Borotra have dubbed their office. He was received by Reynaud, Borotra, Jouhaux, and Gamelin, the latter acting as if it were a military school inspection from his days as a cadet at Saint-Cyr. Paul Reynaud had put on a sparkling, long-tipped white collar. I had hoped to avoid this ridiculous ceremony, but they sent Jouhaux to get me in my room, where I was reading Forster.

I went in, received greetings, listened to the conversation already in progress. "Living conditions are just fine here," Paul Reynaud was saying, but then he asked for three packages that had been mailed from Bordeaux but hadn't been given to him and for the jewelry box that had been stolen. They didn't spare us the standard gestures of shocked surprise. Borotra filled me in on what had been discussed earlier. The Germans have agreed to allow Jouhaux to bring his secretary here, and we had word of Blum and Mandel, who are doing well. Borotra went on to say that since the Germans want the conditions in Itter to duplicate those in Bourassol, we should be allowed to have visitors here, as we did in France. I told him that as far as I was concerned, I would absolutely refuse to add anyone at all to the number of prisoners already housed in this "castle."

The General and his escort went off to lunch; I went off for a walk. I watched them as they went into the dining room. All the NCOs in the garrison were invited to lunch with them. There isn't another Army in the world whose practices are so democratic. Gamelin felt the need to say that the situation was the same in the French Army: "Whenever a noncommissioned officer in my brigade carried out a mission or performed some act of heroism, I would invite him to dine at my table."

June 18, 1943

8:35 P.M. To our absolute astonishment, the announcer on Algiers radio unleashed a diatribe against the French Committee of National Liberation, lambasting the divisiveness that is paralyzing the committee and the jealousies and the ambitions of the Generals on it, and expressing regret over the disrepute into which France has fallen in the eyes of the nations of the world. The announcer's vocabulary seemed to be that of the Communist Party. We had the impression that he was transmitting the violent criticism of the Communist deputies currently in Algiers, who have to be upset at having none of their members represented on the committee.

Thereafter, the announcer launched into an epithet-filled tirade, reminiscent of political rallies of the past, to explain the reasons we had been defeated, apparently for an audience of the ignorant. Without naming him specifically, he attacked General Giraud and, above him in rank, General Georges, as the representative of a High Command hostile to engines, tanks, and airplanes, a High Command that had carried the doctrines of defensive strength and fixed fortifications to the point of superstition. Without intending to and without knowing he was doing it, he also attacked de Gaulle, who is a strong supporter of a professional army, by criticizing our Generals for not having had enough faith in the people to create a people's army.

It would not take much to tear all this grandiloquence to shreds and impeach the Communists and denounce their traitorous acts. But what is important here is the simple existence of the criticism and the conditions under which the announcer voiced it. If Laval were clever enough, if he had a competent and reliable Information Minister, there is no telling how much he could capitalize on all this sorry infighting!

June 19, 1943

In France, they have been making much of the announcement of Léon Blum's coming marriage. People are convinced the Allies are using us to draw the French closer to the Germans and bring them to sue for a compromise peace settlement, which is what Vichy thinks as well. Vichy, meanwhile, is falling apart. Word has it that Platon has been arrested. Ménétrel has left. Many of the Chiefs and Deputy Chiefs of Staff have been getting themselves appointed Subprefect or even better, when they can manage it. Gangrene has set in. Vichy is dying a death like Louis XVIII's: Every day, one of Louis's bones would break or one of his fingers drop off onto his deathbed. Throughout it all, Pétain has gone right on receiving delegations and looking over his gifts.

June 23, 1943

Our two Generals here have sent Stalin a telegram congratulating him on the anniversary of Russia's entry into the war. It seems to me that they, and along with them Churchill, Roosevelt, Benes,[16] Sikorski, and so on, should also have sent one to Hitler, who is really the man responsible for Russia's entering the war. There is just no justice in this world.

June 27, 1943

Fog shrouded the mountain tops until noon. In one of his speeches from Tunis, de Gaulle said something that was quite accurate: "In 1940, France succumbed in isolation." The greater part of that speech was excellent.

---

16. Edward Benes, President of Czechoslovakia until June 1938. He subsequently took refuge in London.

July 2, 1943

Christiane Mabire, Paul Reynaud's secretary, arrived at noon along with Marcel Granger, the brother of Giraud's son-in-law. Mlle Mabire had been imprisoned in Berlin since December 1942, living in a cell, in isolation, with no light but daylight and no news from her family. All she heard were the cries of a woman being tortured. She was gaunt.

Granger had been living in Tunisia. He was arrested in April by the PPF, Doriot's party, while he was planting chickpeas. The Germans took him in a Junker plane to Naples and from there to Dachau, near Munich. At first they had him in a prison laborer's uniform and in a cell; then they transferred him to another building. They sent him to work in the fields where there were 800 Poles, 200 Germans, and quite a few priests, several of whom had once been Alsatian separatists. The Germans have named a Canon and sent him to replace the Bishop in Metz.

There were also two British officers in the camp, one of whom was chained in his cell. After having first subjected him to brutal conditions, they suddenly eased up. There are large numbers of Communists in Dachau; they know we are here. The mix of people of all nationalities and from all walks of life is incredible. The new Europe, in prisoner-of-war camps.

Granger left us dumbfounded when he told us of the existence of crematoriums and the experiments with various gasses they perform on prisoners. When prisoners arrive at the camp, their entire bodies are shaven. They are read a list of possible punishments and forced to go twenty-four hours without food. The SS threaten to hang them by their wrists for an hour and to flog their kidneys between five and twenty-five times. No one can withstand twenty-five blows; they die before. He said there were SS who would grab a prisoner's cap, toss it in the air, and then shoot at it, and the prisoner as well, as he ran to retrieve it. They live piled together in barracks, with beds one on top of the other, wooden bowls, wretched soup and food that is hardly edible, and barely enough of it to survive. He told horrifying stories about the Polish block and the Russian prisoners they had brought back from the front, locked in boxcars for five days, without food or fresh air or sanitary facilities.

Granger had spent much of his life in Tunisia. He spoke highly of Peyrouton, who had been Governor-General there, and regretted his decision to resign, which he claimed de Gaulle and Giraud had unsuccessfully tried to refuse. After the defeat in 1940, Granger accepted a position as head of the Legion. He had been present during my trip to Tunisia in 1939 and told me that no other Prime Minister had ever received so warm a welcome. Before the war, he had been a member of the PSF, Colonel de La Roque's party.

I saw Granger again this afternoon. He spoke to me of his life in Tunisia. He frequented a club where a hundred or so naval officers used to gather, most of them Anglophobes. They broke out the champagne when the *Bismarck* sank the *Hood*. The majority of them felt that Giraud was a turncoat, devoid of honor, who had betrayed the Marshal. They were all devoted to Darlan and Pétain, in that order. When the Germans arrived, they welcomed them with open arms. According to Granger, they were all pure products of the Naval Academy, every last one of them anti-republican. In contrast, the engineer officers were almost all republicans, and there was sharp antagonism between the two groups.

July 11, 1943

At 8:30 this morning, I heard the news about the American-British-Canadian landing in Sicily yesterday. The terrain is difficult, rugged, with inland plateaus rising high up to the mountaintops in tiers. The coastline is rocky and the coastal plains don't extend very far inland. The Italians have been heavily reinforcing their fortifications for the last several months. There are said to be about 150,000 Germans and 350,000 Italians on the island. The antiaircraft weapons, attack planes, and one armored division are apparently German as well. I would have thought the Allies would sooner attempt a landing in Greece or even in Flanders.

On the Russian front, the battle rages on with increasing intensity. So many people are dying these days in Russia, in the Mediterranean, and in the Pacific, just to mention these few areas. At day's end, I reread the Polish blue book's account of diplomatic events as they accelerated after March 15, 1939, with the destruction of the Czechoslovakian state. That is really the date that marks the start of the world war.

Today, I received a great many books and presents of all kinds. My friends have been generous.

Some of the prisoners left this morning and Russians have arrived. The Russians look emaciated. One of them is very ill, many of them are very young. Their faces are closed and hardened.

July 12, 1943

According to a communiqué, the landing on Sicily is proceeding successfully with the taking of Syracuse and ten other localities. The Anglo-Saxons have advanced twenty miles inland, but the real counterattack is yet to come.

In Gamelin's view, the Allies have gone the difficult route and taken the bull by the horns. They might have been counting on the fact that they would be facing principally Italian soldiers, but it is possible that the Germans will blunt the Russian offensive and send enormous air support to Sicily. We shouldn't let our imaginations run wild.

July 14, 1943

To remind us that today is Bastille Day, the German authorities have ordered the Commandant of the castle to close off the western terrace, to which we previously had access, with doors with iron bars and padlocks. There we were, corralled in between the walls and the fountain, when Dr. Hauffmann arrived, all smiles. Needless to say, he had nothing to do with it … he knew nothing about it … I think it's just as well that way.

July 18, 1943

A speech by Sforza, the new Secretary-General of the Italian Fascist Party, was broadcast on every Italian radio station this evening. I have a good command of Italian and I have rarely heard so poor a speech. It was a deplorably long mix of whining and blustering.

His leitmotif: We must resist, resist. He must have used the word once a minute. It's worth noting that he said that the Fascist Party proudly claimed responsibility for the war. Also worth noting was his desperate appeal to all those who had profited from the Fascist regime. The speech makes me more and more convinced that Italian morale is very low. The only question is whether the Germans can still put the pieces back together. The explanation for the success of the Allied landing and the advances they have made in Sicily lies in their overwhelming air superiority.

The Russians are apparently ten miles outside of Orel and moving on the railroad lines at Briansk. I doubt that they can continue to push forward without stopping sometime in the next few days to catch their breath.

July 23, 1943

At 9 P.M. I was visited by the officer-dentist who had already made a good impression on me a month ago. He immediately examined the area causing me pain and proposed to take care of it right away. He takes the train to Dachau and said he wanted to leave at 6 A.M. the following morning because he had a lot of work. We went downstairs three flights to find the sergeant in charge of the sanitary corps. He led us across a courtyard into a remarkably well equipped medical unit. The dentist submitted me to a second examination and was especially careful not to jar me, to spare me any pain. He then explained clearly and precisely what he planned to do. I put myself in his hands, with total confidence. A few seconds later he had already pulled out two teeth and the bridge they supported. He is an outstanding technician and a man of charm and politeness. Thanks to him, I'll be able to get some sleep tonight.

July 25, 1943

At 8:30 P.M. Paul Reynaud and Borotra came into my room while I was reading Falloux's *Memoirs*. They told me that they had just heard on the radio that Mussolini had resigned. He is supposed to have tendered his resignation to the Emperor-King on July 23 and been immediately replaced by Badoglio[17] (a well-known anti-Fascist who is very close to Gamelin). Guariglia, the Italian Ambassador to Paris, has been appointed Minister of

17. Marshal Pietro Badoglio, anti-Fascist leader of the Italian High Command and Governor-General of Abyssinia. He was the head of state throughout the final days of Fascist Italy.

Foreign Affairs. Italy is in a state of siege. The people, which means the Fascists as well, have been prohibited from bearing arms. Secretary-General Sforza is reported to have organized an insurgent movement, which was quickly put down. For the Italian people, these events offer the promise of impending peace. There are apparently huge crowds gathered on Saint Peter's Square and around the Vatican.

Mussolini's downfall awakens memories of Munich: theatrical speeches and the Corsican knife business. He resented my trip to Corsica, claiming that I had brandished a knife at Italy in a threatening way. What utter nonsense! I also remember what Laval and Baudouin undertook to do, none of which succeeded. Traditionally, there are two approaches to Italy's relations with France: that of Mazzini, Crespi, and Mussolini, on the one hand, and that of the Piedmontese and the Garibaldians, on the other.

The current turn of events finds Italy renewing its friendship with the British and perhaps developing cordial relations with France, the latter possibility being contingent on their renouncing all claims to Tunisia.

I am also reminded of my meeting with the British in Abbeville in 1939: the Salonika affair, Chamberlain's and Percy Lorraine's illusions about Italy, and their attempts to get me to yield. Naturally, it was up to France to make sacrifices, in the hopes that Mussolini, once sated, would be able to calm Hitler down. They tried for months to get me to give ground, but on that occasion, I was able to hold them off.

July 27, 1943

Before he resigned, Mussolini is said to have convened a meeting of the Fascist executive council last Saturday with Grandi, de Bono, Sforza, and all the other leaders who were there when it all began. After twenty years of effort and domination, it had all come to this. Is there an analogy here with the abdication of Napoleon, abandoned by all his Marshals? I never thought the end would be so pathetic. I thought Mussolini would either offer ferocious resistance or choose to die. Maybe events didn't exactly happen as they have been reported.

July 30, 1943

I am wondering whether Italy won't be drawn into a Communist movement. Heard another version of events in Italy related on London and Brazzaville radios.

There was a meeting of the Fascist executive council last Sunday. Mussolini presented the military plans for defending northern Italy that had been worked out in the Führer's headquarters. That triggered sharp opposition and scenes of great violence. Mussolini left for the countryside, to reflect on the situation and develop a new plan. The King had him brought back. Their talk lasted an hour, after which the King had him arrested.

The King then brought in Badoglio, who dissolved the Fascist Party and all its various offshoots and had the members of the Fascist executive council incarcerated. Suddenly that evening, waves of people began pouring into Rome, which had been virtually deserted until then, to demonstrate against Mussolini. These are, needless to say, the very same people who acclaimed him twenty years ago.

Badoglio isn't suing for an armistice. On the contrary, he asked the Germans to send in forty divisions to defend all of Italy, but it isn't possible to drain that many troops from the Russian front and the Balkans.

Italian political parties have called on Badoglio to convene a duly elected legislative body. The red flag is flying over Milan. The Germans occupy Trieste, Fiume, and the Istrian peninsula, as well as the principal communication routes.

August 7, 1943

So many events have transpired this past week! What serious playwright, from Aeschylus to Shakespeare, could have imagined such a drama, or rather such a tragedy? The masses are no longer playing the role of Greek choruses: They have been directly drawn into the action, with their misery, their despair, and their suffering.

Mussolini has abdicated; thousands of Italian soldiers have thrown down their arms and deserted. The Russians have recaptured cities the Germans abandoned after long and bloody battles. Airplanes are raining death onto huge metropolises like Hamburg, as local populations flee in terror. Berlin is being partially evacuated while Guariglia and Ribbentrop are meeting in Verona. It has been reported that Hitler met in Berchtesgaden with the top leaders of the party and the Army. It brings back memories of the sermon the Bishop of New York gave at Easter in 1939.

And throughout these dramatic days, the serenity of the Alps endures. Peace dwells on the mountaintops. The sun is shining down on the vast tiered plateaus; peasants are bringing in the hay.

August 8, 1943

Six Germans showed up wearing red armbands. They asked to take the place of political prisoners, all of this under the watchful eye of an SS woman dressed halfway like a man, with a gigantic butt and a hard and unsightly face.

Talked with Gamelin tonight. He repeated to me that Georges had made one error in not bringing his reserve troops into action as early as May 10, and another in assigning command for the entire front, including even the Second Army, to an incompetent General. He swore once again that if the French government had refused to allow us to come to the aid of Belgium, he would have resigned. It was a matter of honor, he said, and of the commitment he had made to the Belgian King. He also said that from a military point of view, the area between Wavre and Namur offered the best terrain for stopping tanks, far better than our northern border. Moreover, with the addition of Belgian, Dutch, and British troops, we would have been an even match for Germany. And we could have held on to our industrial basin, too. Marshal Ironside had told him, in one of their conversations, that with England itself directly threatened, the British would no longer send troops or airplanes into France.

August 12, 1943

There was a magnificent storm last night. The mountaintops would suddenly be illuminated by lightning, the thunder would echo back and forth between the narrow mountain valleys, then blasts of rain would pelt the walls and windows of the castle. The searchlights on the watchtowers made a pitiful contrast, making me think of a line from Vergil, "And suddenly there appeared a sign from the heavens."

August 17, 1943

According to Brazzaville radio, the Germans have launched a powerful counterattack on Kharkov, where they have brought in considerable reinforcements, and the Russian advance has been halted. Are we now witnessing, with this latest Russian offensive, what we have seen with all those that preceded it? After marking great initial successes, will it peter out just as they reach the heart of the German position?

After the first months of the war, it became obvious that armored divisions were ineffective as they had been used in Poland and France. Tanks, in coordination with infantry troops and attack planes, have to be supported by artillery fire, both before and during an assault. Artillery has to be moved forward in coordination with every advance. Isn't Germany's air inferiority, which we observed in the Allied offensive in Tunisia, a result of the Germans' having moved their factories into forests and quarries; and the result of their vast effort to decentralize, which has still not been completed? Or is it a result of the priority they gave last year to the construction of locomotives and submarines?

Once they no longer have women and children to worry about, won't the civilian populations in Germany find a way to cope with the bombings, just as people coped with artillery fire in 1914–1918 in Reims, Arras, Revigny, etc.?

What is the situation in Russia really like after two years of war? And what would Stalin do if, in the absence of a real second front, Hitler were to propose to withdraw from all of Russia, from the Baltic States and parts of Poland, and to accept the propositions made earlier by Molotov, turning the Balkans into a Russian sphere of influence? ...

The Allies have made a serious mistake in pushing the King and Badoglio back into Germany's embrace, with their demands for an unconditional surrender and their condescending words, "Let Italy fry in its own fat for a while."

It took 3,000 ships to transport 300,000 men from Africa to Sicily. How many will it take, and how long will it take, to transport 600,000 to the Italian mainland? They must be counting on the material effects of their bombing of the major Italian cities and its effect on the morale of the population.

Brazzaville radio has announced a forthcoming meeting between the leaders of the Axis powers and stated that Badoglio has offered his apologies to the German government for the violent incidents against German citizens in Italy. He promised to compensate all those who suffered material loss. The Germans are fortifying the plains of the Po Valley and concentrating troops there—the wonderful result of the Allies' spectacular intransigence. Meanwhile, Pucheu[18] has been arrested and imprisoned in Meknes. Communist Party meetings are no longer outlawed in Algiers. Thirty-five Communist deputies are strutting about there, the same thirty-five who, in 1939, on Moscow's orders, played right into Germany's hands. And that fine fellow Queuille is presiding over the commission examining the records of twenty-five Tunisian civil servants accused of collaboration.

At around 1:30 P.M. twenty-five flying fortresses flew over the Inn Valley at an altitude of 10,000 feet. Impressively, with the greatest of ease, they headed southwest, toward Italy. There was no cannon fire. The sentries gave the alert and the garrison set up their machine guns, but it was a bit of a joke, since they only have a range of 2,500 feet. Some of the soldiers were indignant at seeing their nation's airspace violated so casually. Far off in the distance we could hear the sounds of bombs bursting. At around 2 P.M. everything was back to its usual calm.

7 P.M. I learned on Ankara radio that the Allies had entered Messina, which, according to a German communiqué, had been evacuated by their troops with all their equipment. "A retreat comparable to the most splendid of victories." A few more victories like those …

There is heavy fighting in the suburbs of Kharkov. The Russians continue to move on Briansk.

---

18. Prior to the war, Pierre Pucheu had had close ties with La Roque, then with Doriot. In Vichy, he was successively Pétain's Minister of Production and of the Interior. In 1942, he went to Algiers to join forces with General Giraud. He was arrested, sentenced, and executed by firing squad.

August 20, 1943

Jouhaux came back for dinner from the hospital in Innsbruck, where specialists are looking after his heart. He had seen artillery, tanks, and troops moving on to Italy, and young vigorous soldiers, spirited and well equipped. There were flowers in the barrels of their rifles and artillery pieces. The soldiers were singing joyfully. Both the soldiers and the officers were twenty to thirty-five years old, all of them veterans exuding strength and confidence. While captain Hauffmann was off making a few purchases, Jouhaux saw a truck pull up in front of a restaurant where two employees began loading barrels. Jouhaux overheard one of them say in perfect French argot, "I got a date with a chick at two o'clock at the center," as our little Frenchman, either a volunteer worker or a war prisoner released from a stalag, went on complaining that it was already after two and he was going to miss his date with his chick. Spoke briefly with Jouhaux, who had nothing at all to say about the war, or France, or the future. Visibly soused, Jouhaux claimed that the captain of "the castle" was Bavarian. Now that's important news.

August 23, 1943

The Labor Party has won a landslide victory in the Australian elections. In South Africa, a few days ago, the elections were marked by the overwhelming success of General Smuts's party. People will continue to speak of the decline of the British Empire and the defection of the various colonies, etc. In truth, what stands out most is the incomparable greatness of this community of British peoples. Of course, the soldiers there voted, just as American soldiers will soon be voting in Sicily, North Africa, and England. Can anyone really be that sure that the German Army and the German people would vote for their present government and a continuation of the war? In France in 1918, would we have voted for Clemenceau, and for him to carry on the war to the very end?

Can anyone really believe in all seriousness, even for a second, that those millions and millions of Anglo-Saxons, from Greenland to the South Pole, who have constantly supported the war effort in elections, have been manipulated by the Jews in New York and London? Those Jews would have to be prodigious geniuses to pull that off, in which case they really would deserve to run the world!

In truth, England and America are real democracies, but without class struggles, or rather without the demagoguery that has been corrupting France since 1900. Along with Renan, I believe that the methods and the spirit of Protestantism are among the essential reasons for this profound difference. … Beyond that, what does it matter if there are "differences between Protestant denominations," which has been the major argument advanced by Catholics since the time of Bossuet?

August 24, 1943

In Germany, it has become impossible to work because of the air raids to which the people are subjected nightly, sometimes at midnight, sometimes at 2 A.M. As soon as the sirens sound the alert, they have to take two suitcases and move into designated shelters. The consequences of these raids are obvious in terms of morale and productivity, which is why the decision was made to evacuate a million Germans, half of them to Poland, the other half to Austria. The government considered withdrawing to Vienna, but in the end only the various Ministries scattered and set up in areas surrounding Berlin.

August 25, 1943

I am beginning to find meals at our guest table unbearable. It's as if we were on a motionless ocean liner. I am going to have to go to Innsbruck for medical care.

September 1, 1943

Nitti[19] and Giorgini have arrived.

---

19. Francesco Nitti, Italian statesman, several times Prime Minister. An anti-Fascist, he left Italy in 1924. He was incarcerated by the Germans during the war. In 1948, he was reelected Senator.

September 3, 1943

Anniversary of the declaration of war.

At around 5 A.M. Lebrun and François-Poncet arrived. The latter was smiling, looking calm and peaceful as if he were in one of the drawing rooms of his embassy. Lebrun bore the signs of the fatiguing journey; his face was pale, his features sunken. He is seventy-one years old and had traveled all night and part of the following day, beginning on Thursday at 7 P.M., and hadn't had anything to eat.

At 11:30 A.M. last Wednesday, the Italian officer in charge of the surveillance of Lebrun's villa and the troops quartered at the Caisse d'Epargne bank, suddenly came and told him that he was free to go. In La Tronche, at just about the same time, an Italian Colonel was making a similar statement to François-Poncet. He added that once the Italians began their withdrawal from the Grenoble area, he would be pleased to take him to Florence, so as to avoid his falling into German hands, an offer that François-Poncet gladly accepted.

A few minutes later in Vizille, a German officer and several soldiers with submachine guns, arriving directly from Lyons, with an Italian soldier seated next to the driver as their guide, burst into Lebrun's villa. While the German officer went about informing him that he was under arrest and ordering him to come with him without delay, the soldiers kept their submachine guns pointed at him and his family, who had come running up to see what was happening. He was whisked away in a car after barely having had the time to pack two suitcases. The car drove through La Tronche, where they arrested François-Poncet under similar circumstances.

September 7, 1943

Anniversary of my arrest at La Vernue, as well as those of Reynaud and Gamelin. We celebrated with a bottle of cognac that Reynaud had received and a magnificent box of mint and fruit candies that my sister had sent me, along with other wonderful gifts. The candies were a big hit.

September 8, 1943

At 10 this morning Brazzaville radio announced that Italy had surrendered unconditionally. Badoglio issued a statement saying that the superiority of the enemy forces had compelled his government to request an armistice.

At 9:15 P.M. London radio added a few details. The negotiations had begun in a neutral country and been continued in Sicily between Allied and Italian military leaders. Terms had been finalized on September 3, but it had been agreed not to make the signing public until the Allies judged the moment propitious. The military clauses of the settlement have been kept secret. The Italians have committed themselves to respecting political, economic, and financial terms that are to be worked out subsequently. Italy has declared that it is prepared to defend its territory against all acts of aggression, whatever quarters they may come from.

There was joy in Itter castle. Nitti and Giorgini were very moved. Had they remained free just a week longer, they could have tried to make it back to Rome. "I have been in exile, waiting for the collapse of fascism, for the last twenty-one years." Actually, Italy's fate was already sealed when they lost Tunis.

Germany is not about to throw in its hand. They'll organize defensive positions in the Apennines, the Alps, and the Po Valley. But then what will Italy do? Admiral Cunningham has called on Italian ships to move on to Allied ports or to be scuttled.

On the radio and through tracts dropped by plane all over Italy, the Italians are being asked to join the Allies in liberating their country. The appeal to them is cast in sober and moving terms.

At 8 P.M. German radio announced the news of the surrender of the Italian government. At 9, the DNB began heaping abuse on Badoglio and his Ministers.

This is the end of fascism. It is the end of the Triple Alliance. It is the end of an era: the end of arbitrary rule, barbarianism couched in scientific terms, and the deification of brutal strength. This is the twilight of the false gods.

German radio stations are broadcasting a statement addressed to the Italian people by a "national Fascist government" whose seat and makeup remain unspecified. Nitti thinks the leader is probably Farinacci, who voted against Mussolini because he found him too soft. Farinacci had been arrested earlier but escaped to the German Embassy in Rome. While the *carabinieri* were surrounding the building, he made his way out in an embassy car, disguised as a German officer, and went on by plane to Germany. The statement on the radio was made in Mussolini's name and in the name of everything the Fascists had achieved. Badoglio, who was already being held responsible for the defeat, was accused in the strongest terms of being a traitor. They called on the Italians in the Army and the Air Force to continue the fight alongside their brothers in arms to save the honor of the Italian nation. We must fight back in order to save our honor and "drag our country into the war." These words appear to me to speak volumes about the Italian people's desire for peace at all costs. The station played the Fascist hymn, which is none other than the song of the Italian *Arditi*, the Italian assault troops from 1914 who used to sing it as they marched at our side.

The Allies have landed in the area around Naples and in Sardinia, but from my point of view, the Balkans remain the grounds on which to launch a real offensive, if there is a way it can be done.

For our benefit, all the SS radios in the castle broadcast the Fascist hymn all morning long.

Nitti doesn't believe the new Fascist government will be able to do anything. To my mind, this is the final step in giving this world war the look of an international civil war.

London radio recalled the war in Italy in 1940, citing the victorious resistance put up by five French divisions. They mentioned my personal struggle to eliminate the war zone in the Rhone Valley and transfer the divisions in the Alps to the Northeast, and Gamelin's, Georges's, and Prételat's obstinate refusal. Given the movement of the French forces in Belgium, it was incumbent on us to reinforce the pivotal areas. Not doing that was the major mistake, the principal cause of our defeat. How much damage were the tanks and Stukas really going to inflict on fortifications that had been built years before and had been constantly improved? Add to that the incredible overestimation of the Italian forces by our Military

Intelligence in the War Ministry and the Air Force and the overestimation of Belgian forces by the "famous" Colonel Laurent.

September 10, 1943

The day began with a broadcast of the Fascist hymn throughout the building. I can almost sing it now. At 7 P.M. once again on Brazzaville radio, we heard about another great Allied success: their taking control of the port of Taranto, where there were probably only a couple of squadrons left. Actually, the Allies have been taking their time in Calabria, even though the armistice went into effect on September 3, although it wasn't officially announced then. They have barely gotten anything out of it other than a few landings in the area around Naples. Italian naval vessels have remained in their ports, and with the exception of seven ships that made it to Gibraltar, they are being attacked by German airplanes.

No landings have been attempted in Sardinia, occupied Corsica, or the area around Rome. According to a German communiqué reported on Lausanne radio, the Germans continue to occupy Rome, Genoa, Trieste, Dalmatia, and Albania. They are supposed to have disarmed the Italian occupying forces and moved them to detention centers in France, east of Toulon and Nice. The Italians in the Savoie crossed over into Switzerland. On the other hand, the Italians are reported to be holding Turin, Milan, and Venice. Mussolini is said to be imprisoned on Maddalena Island, north of Sardinia, and the Germans are making every effort to free him.

At 8:30 P.M. Hitler gave a speech. I didn't recognize his voice. François-Poncet said he did recognize it but that Hitler was so emotional it didn't sound like him. He praised Mussolini, the great Italian, the creator of the new Italy, and his faithful friend. He mentioned the undying support that he and Germany had given Italy, even though Italy had not honored the Pact of Steel and had not entered the war in September 1939. He had backed the Italian Army in Greece, Africa, Sicily, and Calabria, but he had been betrayed by Badoglio and the Judeo-Masonic forces as early as September 1939. Those forces, he said, were now triumphant, but their triumph was precarious. Nothing had been lost in Russia. Germany was still the master of Europe and was forging new weapons to fight off the terror raining down from the skies. All of Germany was as one with the Führer and the Nazi Party.

Giorgini told us how Mussolini had made a deal with three Greek Generals to buy the war against Greece for 250,000 million. The Italian Army was supposed to march right in without firing a shot—a military cakewalk. Their disappointment, their anger, and the losses they incurred were all the more bitter.

He also told us that while under arrest, Mussolini supposedly wrote to Badoglio to thank him for the consideration he had been shown and offer him his services. So much time has been wasted by the Allies since that July 25 when he was imprisoned.

An article in a German newspaper that we received today refers to "Badoglio's and the House of Savoy's ignoble treason." It says that their betrayal surfaced with the Anglo-American landing in Sicily, which could never have succeeded without the complicity of certain Italian divisions commanded by Generals who were part of Marshal Badoglio's band of traitors. The article went on to say that the second act of infamy lay in waiting for the moment that most favored Europe's enemies before announcing the armistice that had actually been signed on September 3. Badoglio had effectively handed an ally over to the enemy.

September 13, 1943

A German bulletin announced that German paratroopers had rescued Mussolini from the hotel in the Abruzzi where he had been held prisoner. The news sent shock waves through our little community. Mussolini is going to make a triumphant entrance into Rome and take back his place at the Palazzo Venezia. Can anyone explain to me why the Allies left him in Abruzzi? Does this mean that the Italians refused to hand him over, which would in that case honor Badoglio and the King of Italy? More and more I am beginning to think that if England does win this war, it will have to be the work of Divine Providence.

The Americans have run into stiff German resistance forty miles south of Naples. Montgomery's Army went off somewhere south of Calabria to conquer Taranto, Brindisi, and Bari while the Germans were taking Rome and Naples and disbanding Badoglio's Army.

Badoglio and the King of Italy fled Rome on Wednesday September 15 and went to an Italian division's headquarters near Lake Albano. From there, they fled to Sicily on a twin-engine plane. The Germans burst into the headquarters only moments after their departure.

September 20, 1943

A Lieutenant-Colonel doctor came to see me—an astounding visit. We spoke about the way the war had evolved. He stated that the British were fighting for the benefit of the United States and the Soviet Union. Even if victorious, England would come out of the war so drained and would remain that way for so long that it would cease being one of the world's great powers. The British would be abandoned by their colonies, who would turn toward the United States. They would lose India, without which they would be no more than a second-rate power. They would lose their markets abroad and the dominance of the pound.

I answered that the British were confident of their victory and that they probably didn't have the slightest doubt about the loyalty of the nations of the Commonwealth. In any event, I told him, one thing was certain: Either any offer of a peace settlement accompanied by threats and intimidation would be rejected out of hand by the British or I knew nothing about the character of the British people. Similarly, there might well be clashes and problems between the United States and England, but they were of little consequence in terms of the deep-rooted, indestructible solidarity binding the two nations.

The Colonel came back to his idea about a compromise peace settlement with the West. In connection with this, he told me that Laval's government had no backing in France, that although Laval was extremely resourceful, the people had no confidence in him whatsoever, which was an extreme handicap for someone expected to implement a policy of collaboration.

I asked him if he thought that a defeated Germany, occupied by and paying ransom to the victorious nation, forced to turn over to that nation great numbers of her citizens as hostages, many of whom would die facing firing squads or in concentration camps, and stripped moreover of two wonderful provinces and precisely those she held most dearly, if he

227

thought that Germany would agree to collaborate with that victorious nation? He replied that as long as the war continued, painful experiences were inevitable. All of that would disappear, he said, if peace were reestablished with the West, adding that Hitler had been far more lenient than the German High Command had wanted. Moreover, he added, within France, collaboration is associated with politically and socially reactionary ideas that violently conflict with the innermost feelings of the French people, as the Germans realize full well.

The doctor repeated that Laval had no backing whatsoever but that I, in contrast, he said as he bowed, continued to maintain a large following in France. I thanked him, telling him that all the credit should go to Pétain who had sentenced me, before the trial ended, to be deported for life and who, seized with panic, had halted the Riom trial because, in spite of all the precautions he had taken, he found he was becoming its principal focus. I was forced to add that if I did continue to enjoy a certain popularity in France, the German government had also contributed to it by bringing me to Germany as a prisoner, in defiance of international law and of Germany's own commitments.

Today's German press, I went on, is condemning Badoglio and accusing him of having tried to hand Mussolini over to the British. Didn't Pétain hand me over to Germany? Hasn't the Gestapo locked me up in Itter castle? The doctor answered that those were matters he could not discuss and asked me if I had any particular wishes. I answered that I never had any particular wishes and that Epictetus was now my favorite author.

He bowed and saluted, but I reminded him that the examination for which he had come was supposed to be of a medical nature, and that ever since I had arrived in Germany I had been suffering from visual and auditory problems, as I had explained to him. He politely contended that it was far too late to do anything then, for he had to return to Munich immediately, but said that he would come back the following Saturday with his instruments. What was the purpose of his visit? Who ordered it?

Badoglio has given a statement asking the Italian people and the Italian Army to combat the German invader and free the homeland from oppression by fighting alongside the Allies.

I am uneasy about this. This is the same man who, after having signed the unconditional surrender on September 3, was telling his former allies as late as September 8 that the news about his surrendering was a fabrication of British propaganda.

September 25, 1943

François-Poncet was visited today by one of Himmler's lieutenants. His wife had written Mme Göring, who had gotten Himmler to agree to transfer her husband to a villa where he could be joined by his wife and children, but where he has to promise to remain until the end of the war.

October 1, 1943

The September 26 *Parizer Zeitung* carried an article entitled "Benes's Crowns[20] Rolled in the Streets of Paris." The bulk of the article consisted of excerpts taken from the archives of the Czech Foreign Affairs Ministry, which the Germans had seized when they marched into Prague. According to these files, Benes and, on his instructions, his Press Chief, Jean Hajek, were royally subsidizing substantial portions of the French news media. For some twenty years, French newspapers and certain key figures received large subsidies from the Ministry's press and propaganda fund.

Some of the subsidies went to well-known news organizations and journals: L'Agence Economique et Financière, L'Agence Fournier, L'Agence Radio, *L'Ere nouvelle, Excelsior, L'Exportateur français, L'Information financière, Le Journal des débats, La Presse associée, Le Peuple, Le Monde slave, Les Annales, L'Europe nouvelle, Liberté, L'Information, Marianne, Messages, L'Ordre, Paris-Soir, Pax, Le Petit Parisien, Regard, Revue bleue, Revue mondiale, Le Temps, Volonté.*

The amount of the subsidies varied for each newspaper and also varied according to the times.

---

20. Unit of Czech currency.

The article then lists subsidies logged in Benes's hand, under the heading, "For Dr. Osusky in Paris for 1922." M. de Lapradelle, Professor of Public Law, received considerably more money when it was learned that he was the founder and publisher of *Droit international* and *Vie des peuples*.

These payments continued through 1938. In that year of crisis, Benes sent two million crowns to Ministers in Paris and London. Following Munich, it seemed necessary to cut down on expenses. Two days after Benes resigned on October 8, 1938, Hajek wrote Osusky that he was to distribute these moneys only to groups of particular political importance, such as *Le Temps, Les Débats, L'Information*, ... E. Tapounier, X. Vallat, L. Weiss.

Actually, that news pales in comparison with the sensational revelations about the Italian and German subsidies. According to Nitti and Giorgini, Italian subsidies to Frenchmen and French organizations totaled more than 28 million francs in just one year, with the two men receiving the largest amounts being Bailby[21] and Bourrageas.

October 28, 1943

This evening, the news was confirmed in a pompous and pretentious speech by Pierre Bourdan, French radio's strategist in London, "a rout, a debacle, a catastrophe." Jean Oberlé also spoke, denouncing the Munich Agreement on this, the twenty-fifth anniversary of the Czechoslovak Republic, and attacking me personally, "who stood up in his car, like a dictator." This fellow was unaware that I was standing in that car to keep women and children from being struck, as had already happened several times starting from the moment we drove out of Le Bourget Airport. Most important, though, is that a centralized Czechoslovakia was simply not a viable alternative. The system Benes adopted and sustained was a disaster.

October 29, 1943

At 9:15 P.M. Roosevelt announced that the Moscow Conference had come to an end and was a glowing success.

---

21. Léon Bailby, journalist with *Le Matin*.

November 1, 1943

A Socialist Party meeting was held in Algiers, with Le Trocquer presiding. A motion of sympathy and loyalty to Léon Blum passed by acclamation. They talked of working in cooperation with the Communist Party and creating a multinational organization to prevent all future wars.

François-Poncet commented, "It's funny. These are the same expressions they used in 1918." Nitti added, "I already heard all that at Versailles, and I am just as skeptical now as I was then."

9 P.M. A bulletin from Moscow. After a meeting that lasted twelve days, agreement has been reached on a common approach to shortening the war. I noted in particular the plans to oversee the institution of democratic regimes throughout the world. Those guilty of massacres and atrocities will be handed over to the various Allied nations and judged according to their respective laws. Russia has agreed to act in cooperation with the Allies. Nothing was said about France. There was no word on Poland, and nothing about Japan. We'll have to wait and see.

November 7, 1943

All the mountains are covered with snow. It has been snowing in Itter as well, but I still managed to play ring tennis with Mme Brenklein and Jouhaux. Suddenly we heard a military band and artillery fire. Flags were flying over city hall. They were celebrating their dead from 1914–1918. It brought back memories of November 7, 1918, when I was in the area around Origny-Sainte-Benoite. I remembered the German envoys arriving at a little villa at the outskirts of La Capelle.[22]

When the conditions of the armistice were announced on November 11, the troops were not delirious with joy, as I had expected. They had the feeling that their victory was incomplete; they saw themselves escorting the German Army back to their homes. The peace treaties of 1919 carried

---

22. As a Lieutenant in 1918, Daladier received the German envoys who had come to ask for an armistice and led them to his superiors. He had begun the war in 1914 as a Sergeant in the Foreign Legion. He was awarded the *Croix de guerre*, three citations, and the *Légion d'honneur.*

the seeds of the following war. The conditions were at once too harsh and too lenient. The gravest error was to strengthen German unity and destroy Austria-Hungary. What will the peace treaties of 1944 herald? A Slavic victory?

The Germans were celebrating their heroes. The people of the village of Itter went to church. Six Privates and two NCOs delegated from the castle garrison went too. What could they all have been thinking, in their little church, as they called forth memories of the national disaster of 1918 at the very moment the Russians had just stormed Kiev and after two consecutive years of German retreat? At 1 P.M. I listened to a highly measured Roosevelt-like speech given by Stalin. No word on the Baltic States or Poland.

Mme V. is in tears. Her brother was killed in Russia.

November 10, 1943

There has been another change in the French Committee of National Liberation. Giraud and Georges are no longer members, but Giraud remains Commander in Chief. De Gaulle is president. He appointed the following *commissaires:* Queuille, Catroux, Philip, Le Trocquer, Marin, Jacquinot, d'Astier,[23] Massigli, René Mayer, Mendès-France,[24] Bonnet, Jean Monnet, et al.

It looks like a third Blum premiership, and once again without the Communists, who will probably go on playing the game they always play. It includes Socialists and Generals who are notorious Laval supporters. That gives us in France, in Vichy, a German party, and in Algiers, on the

---

23. Emmanuel d'Astier de La Vigerie, founder of the Resistance movement Libération Sud. He went to London in 1942. In 1943, he was appointed Commissioner in the Security Department of the French Committee of National Liberation and in 1944, Interior Minister in the Provisional Government.

24. Pierre Mendès-France, Radical-Socialist Deputy in 1932, Under Secretary of Finance in Blum's second Cabinet. He supported the Munich Agreement in 1938 and was an Air Force pilot in the war. In 1940, he left for North Africa on the *Massilia*, as per the decision of the government in Bordeaux. He was sentenced to six years in prison but escaped and went to London, where he flew missions with the RAF. He was Finance Minister in 1944 and headed other Ministries thereafter. He was Prime Minister in 1954–1955.

whole, a Socialist Party. The irresponsible influence being exerted by the Communists behind the scenes is significant.

I had a talk with Nitti. He is an elderly man of vast experience and great subtlety, in the Italian tradition. He explained that he passed for a Germanophile in France because of his staunch opposition to the Treaty of Versailles as well as to anti-Russian policies. He felt we had to find a modus vivendi with Germany, which remained a strong and populous nation in the very heart of Europe. "We are not going to make them disappear," he said. "We have to find a way to live with them." He felt reciprocal concessions would have to be made by England, Russia, Germany, France, and Italy. He had always had a low opinion of the Socialists, both in France and in Italy, and had been kept fully informed of the Soviets' plans by Carlos Ferrari, a Captain in the *carabinieri* who had gained the Soviets' trust by passing himself off as an anarchist. Nothing had happened since to make the Socialists rise in his esteem. Nitti was highly critical as he listened to the propaganda on the radio. He believed that after the war, England would be terribly weakened, Italy and France would be in ruins, Germany too. He felt there was probably a secret agreement between Japan and Russia and thought there would be an explosion of anti-Semitism throughout the world and above all in the United States, which was good reason for us to remain calm and reflective and not fall into crude traps.

Badoglio was right to refuse the King's offer to abdicate.

November 11, 1943

This should really be our national holiday.

Anniversary of 1918. Deep in thought, thinking about Origny-Sainte-Benoite, about La Capelle, about the future, too. The Gaullist propaganda is becoming more and more incredible. Their methods are unpleasant and have needlessly offended Churchill and Roosevelt.

There was a review of Allied troops in Algiers. Who reviewed them? De Gaulle or Eisenhower? The radio said nothing on that point. Meanwhile, for the first time ever, France has been excluded from the negotiations going on in London, where Russia, England, and America are determining the world's fate. We were defeated in 1814 and 1815 and even invaded and occupied, but France nonetheless played an important part at the Congress of Vienna. De Gaulle hasn't even been summoned to London. Stalin could have insisted that he be present, since he has recognized the Algiers Committee. Our only hope is that Churchill and Roosevelt will still be alive and still be in power when peace arrives.

November 13, 1943

Establishing an international monetary system is a distant goal. The first step is to assign as stable a parity as possible to the various currencies. Our first task therefore will be that of determining the domestic purchasing power of each currency, which will be difficult to do, given that price indexes have lost all real meaning. We also have to see to it that this same domestic purchasing power is not subject to wide fluctuations. A stable exchange rate means stable prices. The prewar period offers numerous examples of price variations. Excessive protectionism, such as that practiced by the Americans, can only weaken the stability of the international monetary edifice.

Moreover, no international monetary system will be possible until we establish definitive parity between the dollar and the pound. Without a definitive solution to that problem there would be no point in holding an international monetary conference.

We could create a single international currency even if gold didn't exist. The only people opposed to doing so are the English, who are major producers of gold, and the Americans, who hold large stores of it. If the Americans continued to buy gold at a fixed price, the metal would have the same fixed exchange rate with the international currency the dollar has. There is no reason then to link the gold issue to the debate over whether to have an international currency.

November 17, 1943

The experience of the American and British landing has shown that it would be equally difficult for them to make headway in Burma or in the Pacific archipelagos that have been lost. Japan is vulnerable only from the air. Stalin, though, far from turning over airfields to his allies in the fight against Germany, has regularly been locking up stranded American pilots.

234

What decisions were made in Moscow with respect to Japan? Has Stalin secretly committed the Soviet Union to join the fight against Japan if and when Germany is defeated? Or will he remain neutral and leave the door open to a vast propaganda campaign in Nationalist China, where there are still Communist Generals and armies? Will he offer his support to the Japanese if they promise him India and part of China in exchange? China alone represents one-quarter of the world's population. Whatever the case, no valid conjectures can be made as yet about what a peace settlement will entail, at least not until the Anglo-Saxons demonstrate that they have learned something from the lessons in tactics and strategy that were given to them by Rommel and other Marshals of the Reich, and that they are just as good students as the Russians. Nitti agrees with me.

November 18, 1943

As they used to say at the time of the French Revolution, some of the smaller countries, like Bulgaria, Romania, and Yugoslavia, are sisters of the Republic! It is significant, as Goebbels pointed out, that the statement issued after the Moscow Conference mentions Austria's independence but says not a word about Russia. "*Pravda*," Goebbels added, "was right in stating, just prior to the conference, that the western borders of the Soviet Union were of as little a matter of concern for the Anglo-Americans as the borders of Canada and California were for the Soviets." But what would become of Germany then? Driven by despair or by a hatred for democracy even greater than their hatred for the Soviets, overrun by Soviet agitators who would find recruits and supporters among former Communists and among those freed from the concentration camps, Germany too would declare itself a Soviet Republic and become a member of the great federation of the Union of Soviet Socialist Republics, just like the little neighboring states.

In fact, one could well conceive that in the wake of major upheavals within France, Italy, and Spain, all of Europe would gradually join such a Soviet-style European federation, with variations for individual nations; but then one would also have to accept the notion that England and America would stand by idly. But won't they be giving all their attention to the war with Japan?

The importance of Japan's victories in this war has been grossly underestimated. The key Pacific and East Asian positions of the British Empire and America collapsed in just a few days' time. To date, only Chiang Kai-shek's China has held out.

November 19, 1943

Nitti told Giorgini, "If we are shot by firing squad, you'll see how I smile and remain calm."

Had another long talk with Nitti about the war. He dismissed Germany's chances for victory long ago. British and American involvement has been essentially limited to bombings, but the Russians have poured huge numbers of men and huge amounts of matériel into the war. Nitti's thinking is almost exclusively directed at the postwar period. He came back to his major thesis: We can't afford another Treaty of Versailles; this time we have to allow for the existence and the legitimate aspirations of a great German nation living at the heart of Europe. He recalled the errors committed in 1918: the creation of a Czechoslovak nation, the independence granted to an Austrian state that wasn't viable and wished to be part of the Reich, and the "fabrication" of a huge Polish state that included Danzig and Upper Silesia. (In this connection, he revealed to me that Sforza, the son of a low-level civil servant, under the influence of a Polish countess who was his mistress, became a count as the result of a bureaucrat's error at the Ministry.) Nitti sided with Millerand, who disagreed with the way Lloyd George ignored the results of the plebiscite in fixing the line separating Upper Silesia.

I agreed with him; I voted against the Ruhr. In May 1939, I let the Poles know that France would not go to war over Danzig, and it was not over Danzig that France did go to war. And if Germany should be defeated, this victory and the victory of 1918 will have nothing in common, for the victor will be Soviet Russia. Nitti agreed. He said that the real question is, what does Stalin want? The West or the East? I personally think he wants both. To the west, he will put back together the empire of the czars: Finland, the Baltic States, and Warsaw, where he'll resort to well-known means to set up Soviet Republics.

November 21, 1943

Talked with Nitti. He has the appearance of an old man with a serene philosophy of life, not unlike the sages of ancient Greece, philosophizing in the gardens of the Academy with the friends of Socrates or Marcus Aurelius. Only this is Itter. I am very interested in what he has to say about the period following the last war and the French statesmen he met. He spoke about his conversations with Briand, whom he advised to give back the Saar without calling for a vote. Briand refused, citing the opposition of M. de Wendel and company. Nitti admired Briand's intelligence and subtlety and his sensitivity to public opinion. But, he said, "like all Socialists, he only governed to get applause." To my mind, after the curtain calls, this great actor would forget his role as soon as he had his topcoat on. Nitti went on to say that Briand was a liar and that he had corrupted French politics. I would sooner say that through his speeches and his acolytes he was one of the great corrupters of the public mind. His famous rallying cries haven't been forgotten: "Roll back the cannons. So long as I am here, there will be no war." Peycelon[25] handled the corruption end of it and didn't leave himself out.

Nitti cited a conversation he had with Colonel House, a confidant and friend of President Wilson. Wilson told House that if he had been aware of the secret treaty signed by Briand and the Czar in 1916, America would never have entered the war. Nitti mentioned Briand's major speech from 1916: "We don't want German territory, we don't want as much as an inch of it. We are at war with the German government, not with the German people, etc., etc." Briand also spoke about liberating Poland and oppressed nations. At that very moment, Paléologue,[26] who naïvely recalled this in his book on the Romanov's final journey, was meeting with the Czar, on Briand's orders, persuading him to agree to a secret treaty. France would accept all of Russia's claims—the annexation of all of Poland, Constanti-

---

25. Gilbert Peycelon, one of Briand's close associates.

26. Maurice Paléologue, diplomat and Director of Political Affairs in 1912. He was Ambassador to Russia from 1914 to 1917.

nople, and the Straits—and in return, Russia would agree to allow France to annex the left bank of the Rhine, including close to 14 million Germans. "The Bolsheviks published this treaty and a number of others, provoking President Wilson's ire." Nitti said that greatness in statesmanship required respect for moral principles.

A few days ago, I received a visit from Captain Höner[27] of the Reich's Security Police, who specifically oversees Itter castle and the prisoners here. He was very friendly when he came into my room and inquired about my health. Then, very abruptly, he stated that he had been ordered by the German authorities to insist that I take advantage of the offer that had been extended to me the very day I arrived, to have the company of some friend, or rather some female friend, as two other prisoners at Itter had done. I thanked him for this gracious officer and begged him to convey in turn my thanks to the German authorities for their marked and kind insistence. But I reiterated to them what I had already stated several times: that I consider myself to be what I actually am, a French prisoner, one of the innumerable captives in the stalags and oflags. Do my compatriots have the right to have the company of their wives or their girlfriends? When they do, I'll get back to you.

November 29, 1943

Nitti's departure. Yesterday, Nitti was informed by the Captain that he was to leave for a pleasant hotel where he would enjoy far greater material comfort. Nitti protested and asked to remain at Itter, where he had found spiritual comfort, which was, in his eyes, far more important than material concerns. Today, he was forced to leave in spite of his protests. He was very sad; tears welled up in his eyes. I tried to get his departure postponed by explaining to the Lieutenant of the SS patrol that had come for him that it was cruel to ignore the wishes and the state of health of a seventy-five-year-old man. We were gathered together in Nitti's little room; he had packed. On his bed, which, small as it was, took up almost the entire room,

---

27. Captain Höner's visit should be seen in conjunction with the doctor's visit on September 20. On orders from Berlin, both adroitly sought to learn whether Daladier would subscribe to some form of collaboration with Germany.

lay a cheap-looking suitcase and a few cartons that constituted everything he owned, he, a man who had several times been Minister and even Prime Minister of Italy.

His departure pains me deeply. I had come to appreciate more and more the gentle wisdom of this courageous old man. Following a cruel period of exile and the loss of a daughter, Nitti had made a reputation for himself throughout Europe with his knowledge of Oriental languages. He had been abruptly abducted from Paris, where he was forced to leave behind his sick and elderly wife and his son, the Director of the Pasteur Institute. He possessed to the ultimate degree that moral resolve that allows man to overcome adversity. Since our nightly chats began and I was favored with all his kindness and courtesy, how many times did I regret never having had occasion in Paris, before our captivity, to encounter this great Italian.

December 4, 1943

The Japanese greeted the statement issued at the close of the Cairo Conference with considerable sarcasm. They pointed out that in spite of the contentions of the Anglo-Saxons, Japan, far from being prepared to surrender unconditionally, has held on to all its phenomenal conquests. Not one of them has been breached or even seriously threatened.

December 8, 1943

Left for Innsbruck at 7:30 A.M. Thick fog and ice on the roads. We stopped at Wözel to get gas. It reminded me of a trip I made long ago with Dulot and our visit with a former burgomaster. We passed truckloads of soldiers and antiaircraft batteries. The stores were open, but the only merchandise in them was in the windows. I reflected on the stupidity of the predictions Gouin and Moch had made in the spring of 1942. We arrived in Innsbruck at 9 A.M., pulling up in front of the Gestapo building. At the hospital that was adjacent to it, I got an impression of cleanliness, order, and discipline. I found myself face to face with the otorhinolaryngologist: a young, dark-haired, kindly fellow, unaffected and polite. Mlle B. served as interpreter. He thoroughly examined my ear and treated it right away. Would it be necessary to operate? First, he wanted to get an X-ray. He handed me a slip for the radiologist in Building 2, directly behind the administration building.

The Gestapo has been worried that I'll be recognized. It finally had taken an order from Captain Höner to get me treated in Innsbruck, after three months of waiting. They're still afraid the British might pull something off. That is why they had given me the name Dietrich. The admission papers I was carrying were made out that way, but there was no first name. Mlle B. christened me Heinrich. So it was Heinrich Dietrich who went off to see the radiologist. A few yards away, I heard someone say in German, "It's really funny how much Dietrich looks like Daladier." I pretended not to hear. They are perfectly capable of turning me into the Man in the Iron Mask the next time. They took several X-rays but said I wouldn't get the results until the following day. Undaunted, I went back to the specialist. He kindly offered me a cigarette and recounted a few things about his area of specialization. He was familiar with the work of an old friend of mine, Maurice Vernet. He said he deplored bureaucratic mix-ups and that he would let me know if an operation were necessary, one way or the other.

December 9, 1943

They have just delivered machine guns and cases of grenades and ammunition to the castle. On the brighter side of things, my ear doesn't hurt anymore.

December 16, 1943

The British government has declared that it is in no way bound to the King of Greece. Hence, the British are leaving Greece to be sovietized. Finland, the Baltic countries, Bulgaria, Romania, Hungary, Yugoslavia, and now Greece. The Russo-Czech agreement is not without interest: It provides the avant-garde, the bridgehead, the platform from which Russia's Air Force can carry out its surveillance and perhaps even its battle missions.

From the Near East and Central Europe to the Adriatic; from the Aegean Sea in the South to the Baltic in the North: a Europe under Russian influence. The Anglo-Saxons have given up the view they had traditionally held.

December 17, 1943

Went back to Innsbruck. As we came into town, sirens sounded. People were hurrying about in the streets. They were coming out of the shelters. The siren had sounded the end of the alert.

This was another false alert, but there have been numerous bombings, the last one from about sixty American planes dropping their bombs from 10,000 feet. The train station and a military hospital were destroyed. There were sixty dead, mostly women and children. In the heart of the city, Marie-Thérèse Street, which had been so gay and welcoming in peacetime, was particularly hard hit, notably the Hotel Marie-Thérèse, where I once stayed with Dulot. Trenches were being dug in the outskirts of the city. Women and children were being evacuated from surrounding areas. I saw no sign of fright or nervousness on their faces, only expressions of calm and resolve. The National Socialist Party leaders have maintained their authority and are leading by example.

Nothing seemed to have changed at the medical center. I got the same impression of orderly bustle in a beehive of activity. I saw the same doctor, and he received me with the same kindness as before. I ran into a young French artilleryman, a prisoner in a khaki uniform, who was just walking about from one room to the next.

On our way back, we stopped at an inn, as we had the first time. Prices were high and there wasn't much choice—potatoes and rye bread—but our ingenious captain had got a pork chop from a farm.

December 20, 1943

There have been a great many radio broadcasts about the execution by hanging, in front of 50,000 people in Kharkov, of the two German officers and the Russians who were sentenced to death for having killed large numbers of people by asphyxiation. They had transformed a truck into a gas chamber. Russian propaganda is using the same techniques the Germans used when they uncovered the mass graves in Katyn Forest.

Maurice Schumann gave a bombastic speech, bombast having become the characteristic sign of the Gaullist radio station that allows you to distinguish it from the others. He extolled the Moroccan, Algerian, and

French troops fighting alongside the Americans in Italy, although to date no battles have actually been fought.

A few outposts are captured and it becomes an exploit worthy of Homer. Their attempts to glorify France make it look ridiculous. They are back promoting the myth of an Army on the Meuse, in May 1940, fighting without equipment. No mention of the panic and the cowardice that had seized them at the time of the opening battles, and at the time of some of the closing battles, too. It is their way of pounding out a mea culpa on someone else's breast.

December 21, 1943

Hungarian radio has announced that the new weapon being built by the Germans is a cannon that fires 12(?)-ton shells that can destroy everything in a radius of thirty miles. These cannons are to be set up on the western coast, supposedly to destroy London. In Russia, Stalin is reported to have decided to change the lyrics of the *Internationale*, which no longer reflect Russia's situation. But the *Internationale*, with these changes, will remain the national anthem!

This evening, the SS garrison celebrated Christmas a few days early so that they could all be together for a dinner among friends before some of them went home on leave. The supply manager had bought them a deer, which the Czech cook spent the day preparing, sending odors of venison wafting throughout the castle, and filling every room in the place right up to the rafters. The dinner was held in a large room on the second floor from which the ping-pong table had been removed. Each man found a little box on his napkin, with jam, fruit, cigarettes, and fifty marks. The soldiers sang until midnight. Most of them sang on key; many had lovely voices. The SS sent us some stewed venison as well. It was excellent.

December 23, 1943

Another trip to Innsbruck. We were on the road by 8:30. We passed a lot of trucks heading in the opposite direction, loaded with beds, furniture, women, and children. It looked like France at the end of May 1940. There were clearly a number of similarities, but this was all done with order and discipline. The German authorities had decided to evacuate the women and the children. We drove through the city to pick up a hundred liters of wine at a store next to the train station. Saw considerable damage everywhere. Here and there, shops and hotels had been reduced to piles of smoldering rubble. I noticed purple placards on all the abandoned houses: "Looters will be shot." Large apartment houses were split in two as if by an axe. Workers and soldiers were already out clearing away the debris. The people looked serious and sad, their faces impenetrable and taut.

The Gestapo said that more than a thousand people had been killed, once again a result of bombs dropped from an altitude of 10,000 feet and intended to work total destruction. If the Germans really do come up with a new and terrifying weapon, which they have been talking about for months now, there will be indescribable joy and enthusiasm throughout Germany. There are signs of collapsed buildings everywhere in the city.

At the clinic, there was a great deal of activity. The specialist asked me, "Why war?" I gave him Dietrich's answer. I was received there with the same open smiles and cordiality as before. At the police station, in contrast, faces were closed.

We went quickly back to Itter, without stopping at the inn, where trucks were parked out front. That evening, we went about exchanging Christmas gifts, as best we could. Mlle B. called out the names. There were flowers from all of us for Mme M. as a gesture of thanks. I had made a few gifts of my own: a bottle of Châteauneuf-du-Pape for the women prisoners who wait on us (they were delighted), a tin of sardines for the waiter, and a bottle of champagne for the Czech cook and the Serbian handyman. I feel a lot closer to them than to some of the others. I gave a few cigarettes to the accountant who had earlier given me some tobacco. I was able to hand out jam and chocolates as well. I could see J.'s face and hear his objections already, once I had my back turned.

It has taken time in a German prison for me to come to the realization that my father-in-law, Dr. Laffont, was right when he would say that only two things motivate men: pleasure and self-interest. My Rousseauian or idealist philosophy is only valid for humble people, not for the false elite assembled here, with two notable exceptions. I should act accordingly, counter to what I have done throughout my life. It is a little late, though, for me to have realized it. I was struck again by what Dr. Heckel told Debeck when he was giving me boxing lessons, "Make him mean."

December 24, 1943

I have continued to have great games of ring tennis with Borotra. I spotted him at 3 P.M. breaking the ice in the courtyard. I went down to help. As they used to say, he is a true gentleman. He'll garner affection and respect for France wherever he goes. Following the enlightened instructions of this wise *polytechnicien*, I began pouring wheelbarrowfuls of sand over the courtyard, which he spread about with consummate skill. We had a wonderful time until nightfall. We played until we couldn't see the ring anymore. It is a game that doesn't cost much and is easy to set up. It should be made more popular. This ring tennis idyll will have been our best distraction from captivity. This evening, I went to the dining room that the women had decorated under the supervision of the German Captain and his wife. They showed great consideration in inviting the French prisoners to their Christmas Eve party. Between the two windows to the east hung a portrait of Hitler. Gamelin was shocked.

Having paid them a visit, I returned to my cell, where I dined alone, as was my custom. Memories surfaced of Christmases of my childhood: mangers with little figures in them. I thought of the molds for Christmas figures that Raphaël Mouletin used to make. I remembered as well Christmas in the little house in Garches, where the fireplace was surrounded by toys for Jean and Pierre; and then, too, Christmas in 1914 in Verzenay, and in 1915 in Arras; and I thought of Canon Desgranges, my friend and war buddy. Christmas 1943 brings the duel between the Slavs and the Huns from which there will emerge, for Europe and for the entire world, a revolution whose form has not yet taken shape, but still a revolution far less important than that of Christ's.

At around 8:30, Granger came over and told me stories of his days in Tunisia and his captivity in Dachau. He's a fine man, highly patriotic and brave, a wonderful example of the average Frenchman. He was highly appreciated in Dachau, even by the SS in his cell block, and all the more so, of course, in his bunker. The stories he tells are fascinating, but he has no desire to write them down. After he had gone, I read Sombart's *German Socialism.*

December 25, 1943

I was awakened at 7 A.M. by a little black-headed titmouse. He comes to the window facing west to pluck seeds out of the little butter box that Susset sent me. The noise of the butter box clinking against my window is my alarm clock. At 1 P.M. we once again exchanged good wishes and thanks. Had soup and starches yet again. This is probably the reason I thought all those women were pregnant—why they're generally so huge. One of them was arrested and beaten for having been seen with Poles. I learned this morning that they had discovered that another of them was here by mistake, but that they refused to release her for fear she would reveal that we were being held here. The Iron Mask again. I have been interested and amused by the SS pamphlets that are clandestinely being circulated throughout the garrison. They are typewritten notes. One of them reads like this: "If Germany is defeated, those SS who bring three new recruits to the Nazi Party will receive permission to resign. Those who bring in six will be given permission to resign and will additionally receive a document certifying that they never belonged to the party. Those who bring in nine will receive a document certifying that they spent time in a concentration camp."

A second pamphlet is entitled, "The Führer's Speech of 1955."

"Given on the occasion of the establishment of a common border with Japan and of the steps taken by Major Churchill and Commodore Roosevelt to have their countries officially admitted as colonies of the Third Reich. Pledges of devotion have come in from Lieutenant Colonel Pétain and Lieutenant Stalin. Rosenberg has been elected Pope under the name of Pius XIII, and Goebbels, who is now living in Jerusalem, has been appointed Grand Rabbi."

1944

January 1, 1944

The snow has been falling for three months, compounding the mournful feeling of loneliness that comes with spending the holidays in captivity. Will this new year bring peace? I think not. Germany is still strong. This year will be decisive, though. In Vichy, there has been another palace revolution. Pétain is now flanked by Darnand and Philippe Henriot.[1]

January 8, 1944

This morning, Captain Vinner told me that he had been ordered to go to the Wörgl train station tomorrow to pick up Clemenceau, the son of the Tiger, and Colonel de La Roque! I was so astonished that I made him repeat it, which he did. Then I burst out laughing. He did too. The noise brought Granger from his room, to find out what was going on.

Granger then explained to the Captain that there was going to be trouble in Itter-city, while pretending to sight an imaginary rifle and yelling, "Bang, bang." Vinner went, "Bang, bang," too, laughed heartily, and left us. I reassured Granger that since La Roque would side with Weygand and Clemenceau with Reynaud, the balance of power would be maintained.

I have never met Clemenceau. I heard a little about him a long time ago, from Ignace and several others. Apparently, the only thing he inherited from his father was his name. I saw La Roque only once, very early one October morning in 1936, in the passageway of the train that was car-

---

1. Philippe Henriot, the principal radio voice for Vichy propaganda. He was a right-wing Deputy who in 1935 spoke out against the Franco-Soviet Pact. He collaborated with Marshal Pétain in 1940 and was later Laval's secretary. He was executed by the Resistance on June 28, 1944.

rying me back from Biarritz. A short, pale, rather flabby fellow, he was standing outside the door of his sleeping compartment, between two bodyguards, watching the sun come up. After that, he came to the dining car to have his café au lait and smoke a pipe. I concluded that he was not a threat to the Republic.

On the whole, he has had quite an eventful life. He enlisted in the infantry and fought bravely in 1914. He was wounded twice, twice cited for bravery. In this war, one of his sons was killed in air combat over the Meuse, the other was seriously wounded. He founded a political movement whose purpose seemed to be the creation of an authoritarian, antiparliamentarian, hierarchical republic, with the reinstitution of corporations as the basic approach to social issues. Anyway, that is what I could make out of it, that along with something of a neo-Boulangism. Although the movement attracted a number of old reactionaries who had been saddened or grown indignant over the fighting among political parties, it mainly drew on the young middle-class men and women who were victims of the economic crisis. They were fed up with the constant changes in Ministers and the way people carried on in Parliament, and also by the scandals of the time, which, even if they were blown entirely out of proportion and exploited for political gain, were all too real.

La Roque was primarily concerned with keeping control of his movement. Chiappe,[2] Tardieu,[3] and Laval wanted him as their Lieutenant, or Recruiting Officer. He couldn't very well refuse to be a part of the February 6 events, but he participated without enthusiasm, as if he had resigned himself to it. It took no more than some Head Sergeant and a few antiriot policemen posted on Palais Bourbon Square for La Roque and his followers to keep right on moving and abandon the idea of storming Parliament.

---

2. Although Prefect of Police in 1934, Jean Chiappe was aligned with the rioting right-wing parties. He had been overly indulgent in dealing with Stavisky and those handling the swindler's defense. As Prime Minister, Daladier dismissed him, but Chiappe lent his support to the February 6 rioters.

3. André Tardieu, conservative politician, hostile to parliamentary forms of government, Prime Minister in 1929, 1930, and 1932.

This is why Maurras and Daudet[4] —and they weren't the only ones—accused him of being soft, if not quite a traitor.

After February 6, he became one of Doumergue's close acquaintances. That was his period of greatness. The man was the undisputed master at organizing motorized rallies. He could marshal thousands of automobiles on vast prairies without a single accident or breakdown. The grandeur and the flawless formations of his parades humbled his rivals: Pujo, Doriot, and the Bonapartist Taittinger,[5] who since that time has taken on both a position as city councilman and numerous layers of fat.

Little by little, La Roque's parades attracted the various groups of the splintered political Left. Then the Radical Party broke with Doumergue at their convention in Nantes, in spite of Marchandeau's[6] zeal and the predictions about all the wonderful things the future augured. A few days later, the savior, wearing a beret and escorted by police, sneaked out of his house on the Avenue du Bois by a side door and headed back to Tournefeuille. By July 14, 1935, the Popular Front's marches far surpassed those of the Croix de Feu. La Roque can thus be seen as somewhat of a founding father of the Popular Front, whose members were frequently—in fact, most of the time—not in it voluntarily.

After June 1940, La Roque became a National Adviser and, considerably later, one of the special counsels to Pétain, who borrowed a great number of his stock phrases. La Roque was apparently high on the list of those playing the wait-and-see game. Once the Russian campaign bogged down in 1941, he became convinced that Germany would ultimately be defeated, which provoked Laval's ire and made him suspect in the eyes of the Germans, eventually leading to his arrest.

---

4. Léon Daudet, Alphonse Daudet's son, writer and journalist/editorialist for *L'Action française*. At the time of the February 6 incidents, he published articles supporting the riots and advocating racism and political assassination.

5. Pierre Taittinger, industrialist and conservative Deputy. In 1924, he founded the Fascist Jeunesses Patriotes. He supported Marshal Pétain in 1940 and was imprisoned at the end of the war.

6. Paul Marchandeau was a Radical-Socialist Deputy. He was several times a Minister under Daladier. In 1940, he voted to grant plenary powers to Marshal Pétain.

La Roque's arrival has generated still more talk. Reynaud considers him a traitor, primarily because he waged a vigorous campaign against him in the elections of May 1936, which Reynaud won by a hair, but also because he collaborated with the Marshal. Gamelin follows in Reynaud's step like Saint Roch's dog. Jouhaux hasn't forgotten the insults and the threats that were heaped on him by the Croix de Feu. I was subject to them too. Didn't they call me a murderer and an executioner? Borotra and Granger, who were at one time members of the Croix de Feu, have remained loyal to their former leader.

I was better off listening to the radio. The Russians have continued their powerful push forward. They've moved beyond Poland's 1939 borders. Waldeck-Rochet, a Communist Deputy, gave the kind of speech I had heard many times before, from Grenier, Fajon, Gresa, and others. He talked about uniting all Frenchmen and reaching out to the Catholics. France first! Unite, unite! He must have gotten confused and pulled out one of those all-purpose jobs from May 1936. Or maybe Marty[7] just hadn't sent him his copy of Moscow's latest speech. There wasn't a word in it about purging anyone. Or perhaps in spite of himself, Waldeck-Rochet just couldn't help remembering that wonderful statement that appeared in a July 1940 underground issue of *L'Humanité*, "The Communists are in favor of Franco-German collaboration"; unless it was the one from March 1941, "General de Gaulle and that whole crowd working for Britain's financial community would like the French to go to war for the City." As opposed to what the *roi galant* used to tell us in song, it is not just women who are fickle.

Sunday, January 9, 1944

At around 1:30 P.M. Colonel de la Roque and M. Clemenceau arrived in Itter. Borotra went to greet them, followed by Reynaud. They welcomed them and shook hands.

---

7. André Marty, leader of the 1919 mutiny on board a French vessel sent to the Black Sea to fight the Bolsheviks. Granted amnesty in 1923, he was subsequently elected to Parliament as a Communist and went on to play a major role in the leadership of the Communist Party. He participated actively in the war in Spain. He left France for the Soviet Union in

A little after 2 P.M. a frenzied Gamelin came running into my room, his face flushed with emotion. Clemenceau had told them that in the camp in Eisenberg, from which they had just come, La Roque had offered the Germans his personal cooperation as well as that of his party, the PSF, in fighting the Communists. He had written to Himmler, the head of the police and the SS, to propose his services. The Germans had circulated copies of the letter at the camp, provoking strong reactions from the French prisoners. On hearing Clemenceau recount this, Reynaud had exclaimed, "If I had known that, I would never have extended my hand to La Roque when he arrived," and Gamelin, whose hands were still unsullied, thank goodness, said that from then on he would refuse to shake with him.

I asked Gamelin if he had seen a copy of the letters to Himmler. I asked him if he, Gamelin, had proposed to Clemenceau that he confront La Roque with these accusations, with us present. He admitted he hadn't. "Go and ask Clemenceau if he stands behind his accusations," I said. "Then we'll so advise La Roque, so that he can have a fair chance to defend himself. Once that has been done, we'll have the right to form our own opinion." Gamelin ran out of my room even faster than he had come in, looking for Clemenceau.

I went downstairs to play some ring tennis. I ran into Mlle Mabire and heard her version of La Roque's act of treason. I asked her if she had seen the letter to Himmler. "No," she said, "but Clemenceau has read it." "Fine, then he can share it with us, but with La Roque present. Short of that, I prefer to withhold judgment, not being one of those who rejoices at the thought that France has yet another traitor in its midst."

Then it was Borotra's turn. He came up to me in his sandals, in the snow: bare legs, shorts, and a polo shirt. I asked him if he was aware of what was being said about La Roque. He said he had been apprised of the situation by Mlle Brenklein. News travels fast in Itter. He had protested to her that it wasn't so and protested again to me, indignantly.

1939 and in 1943 headed the Communist Party's delegation to the French Committee of National Liberation in Algiers. He was excluded from the Party in 1953, in what remains one of the major "affairs" of this kind.

I was about to toss the ring over the net when Gamelin came running up, even more flushed than before. He had spoken with Clemenceau, "that tall old man walking over there, stiffly, holding his head erect as if it were the Holy Sacrament." Clemenceau reaffirmed what he had said but was not prepared to state so publicly, not yet. In effect, he was hedging, but without withdrawing his accusation. I found that reprehensible and said so. Gamelin took off again, going from one person to another to tell them that maybe the new inmate wasn't a downright bastard after all. Borotra was delighted. Had a wonderful game of ring tennis.

Went back to my room and read Lucas-Dubreton's book on Marshal Ney. I was struck by the similarities between the Prussian High Command at the time of Iéna and the French High Command in May–June 1940: the same closed inner circle of old men; the same inability to regain control of themselves on the battlefield; the same panic at the first impact and no desire other than that of laying down their arms. Just look at Weygand's admissions as recorded in the transcript of the Riom trial. Of course, eight years after Iéna, the Prussian Army came marching down the Champs-Elysées.

Somebody was knocking at the door—Borotra—to ask me if I would agree to meet with Colonel de La Roque. Given what had transpired, there was no way I could refuse. How different he looked from 1936. The German prison camp had left its mark; hunger had shriveled him. He had been kept in isolation for months, in cells infested with vermin in Moulins and Fresnes and at Cherche-Midi, without news of his wife or children. Then in the German camp at Eisenberg, he was put on a starvation diet, as were all the other French prisoners. At least he got word there about his wife and three surviving children.

La Roque was indignant in denying what Clemenceau had been saying about him. He stated that on their leaving Eisenberg to come to Itter, General Altmayer,[8] the highest-ranking French officer in the camp, acting under German authority, had assembled all the French prisoners and pub-

---

8. In 1939, General René Altmayer was Commander of the Tenth Sector. He was relieved of his command in September of that year and returned to active duty on May 21, 1940, as Commander of the Tenth Army. He was a prisoner of war.

licly congratulated the two of them for having offered so fine an example of dignity and steadfastness. La Roque also told me that he had never ceased lodging protests with the Germans for his arrest and that of thirty-five of his Parisian associates who were also in captivity. He is convinced that Laval induced the Germans to arrest him, to keep him away from Marshal Pétain, whom he had seen frequently over the previous months. In this connection, La Roque told me that in his opinion, Pétain had long since ceased believing in a German victory. Pétain was playing it smart. He was making ready to call for the Resistance forces and all Frenchmen to unite, just as soon as the hour of liberation began to toll.

I told him I bought absolutely none of that. For Pétain, the defeat of France was an opportunity to realize political ambitions he had been nurturing since 1934, when, during the premiership of Doumergue, he began mustering the support necessary to take Doumergue's place. That is how he came to sound out Jouhaux for a Ministry. He's a crafty, guileful, and devious man who has been using his military prestige, partially drained now, and, even more so, his image as a true and loyal old soldier to carry out his endless intrigues. He wasn't even above disavowing overly compromised associates, like Commander Loustanau-Lacau,[9] whom I had been forced to relieve of his duty in 1937. After the defeat, Pétain didn't utter a word of protest about the annexation of Alsace and Lorraine, in direct violation of the Armistice. Worse still, right after the Germans violated the very Armistice he had presented to the nation as having been negotiated "with dignity and honor," he went to Montoire to drink his cup of shame right down to the dregs. Similarly, there wasn't a peep out of him when the Germans crossed into the so-called Free Zone on November 11, 1942. It makes for a sorry end to a long life.

---

9. Georges Loustanau-Lacau conspired within the Army to bring the antidemocratic Right to power through insurrection. He was disciplined by Daladier. He joined the Resistance in London and in France and was eventually deported to Germany. He was elected Deputy in 1951.

Monday, January 10, 1944

La Roque and Borotra came to see me this afternoon to show me copies of the letters the Colonel had sent the German authorities. First I read the one he had sent Himmler, which had served as the basis for Clemenceau's accusations. There was not the slightest trace of the supposed deal: If I am released, I and the thousands of French men and women I lead will collaborate with you in fighting communism. La Roque read the others. They were not very well written; I would have preferred another style too, but they were the letters of a man who held passionately to his newspaper, his achievements, and the leadership of his party and who, above all, wanted to see his image of Pétain redeemed through patriotic resurrection—Pétain, our man of Bordeaux, Montoire, and November 11, 1942!

He persists in thinking that Pétain is shrewdly stringing the Germans along, just as Stresemann once did with the French. That upset me, and I told him so. Nonetheless, I reread those letters and really didn't see anything in them that could be taken for any sort of an offer to collaborate with the Germans. Borotra and Granger agreed.

Then he read aloud two letters from French prisoners in Eisenberg, one of them an admirer of Louis Marin, the other a Communist sympathizer. Both thanked him for having comforted them and spoke of their friendship and the trust they had in him.

As far as I was concerned, the Clemenceau business was finished. It was up to La Roque to share these letters with the "lords" of Itter, if he thought it was worth it. But was it really necessary, given that Clemenceau had chosen not to make a public accusation?

To my mind, the matter was closed, but it took yet another turn after dinner. As the radio broadcast we were listening to was about to end, Paul Reynaud told us that he had seen Clemenceau earlier in the evening and that he had once again repeated his accusations; he stood by what he had told Gamelin. Reynaud added that instead of expressing indignation and protesting strenuously, La Roque was holed up in his room. But why on earth should he protest, if Clemenceau himself had told Gamelin that he wasn't prepared to make a public statement? Whatever the case, this had to stop. I said that the two men should have it out with each other tomorrow so that we could get this over with, one way or the other. The atmosphere was already strained enough. I told Reynaud that the only way to put an end to this business once and for all was for the two men to talk it out face to face, and the sooner the better.

Tuesday, January 11, 1944

Here's the epilogue of our little drawing room comedy. At the end of the evening meal, La Roque stood up to say that he wished to respond, without mincing words, to everything Clemenceau had been saying about him for the last three days. A very emotional Borotra read aloud all the letters that La Roque had written to the Germans. There was disappointment on several faces around the table, ironic smiles on others. Clemenceau rose in turn and said that he had never seen those letters and saw nothing wrong with them. However, he went on, La Roque's attitude at the camp in Eisenberg was highly suspect. That, he claimed, was the opinion of the interpreter and many of the prisoners there.

La Roque responded. He said that he had shown Clemenceau several of those letters before giving them to Altmayer, the French General in the camp. Jehin, the interpreter, had entrusted him with confidential messages. And General de Gaulle's brother, who was also a prisoner in the camp, had hugged him as he was leaving and assigned him several missions. I said to myself that if a de Gaulle, be he short or tall, skinny or fat, svelte or hunchback, had put the stamp of patriot on La Roque, even those who were most difficult to satisfy would salute.

Reynaud, however, after a friendly exordium in the purest Ciceronian tradition, said that the matter deserved closer examination. One reading was not enough; there would have to be more. He suggested that La Roque submit the letters to him, Reynaud, and me for further study. La Roque responded that he stood prepared then and there to reread every last letter involved, and there weren't many of them, and that he would reread them as many times as we wished and answer all questions pertaining to them, but he said he wanted to have it done with, then and there. Nobody could blame him for feeling that way.

I spoke up, saying that my initial reading of those letters sufficed and that I had found nothing in them to support the claims M. Clemenceau had made, first privately, then publicly. He had failed to provide proof of the specific accusations he had made, namely an offer to Himmler of the PSF's cooperation in fighting communism. As for La Roque's collaboration with Pétain and support for his policies, this was clearly not the setting for a debate, with the Germans looking on sardonically. It would be up to the people of France, and to them alone, to judge. Since no one had anything further to say, as La Roque duly noted, everyone went back to his room.

As I was heading back to mine, La Roque, whose room is close by, told me that he and his father had once had a run-in with another Clemenceau: Georges, "the Tiger." Around 1898, Colonel de La Roque's father was what they used to call a Naval Artillery General. It was in that capacity that he had opposed the purchase of torpedoes manufactured by a British company, Armstrong, finding the prices excessively high. Clemenceau violently attacked him in Parliament and the Minister of the time insisted that the order be placed. La Roque's father chose to take a leave of absence.

Much later, in 1918, Clemenceau was on a visit to the French troops in Flanders who had just blunted the German offensive. When he arrived at the division command post to which La Roque was assigned, he inquired about officers deserving medals or promotions. The name of Captain de La Roque, who had already been wounded and cited for bravery several times, was mentioned repeatedly. Hearing the name, Clemenceau winced and refused. La Roque added that he knows Clemenceau's daughter quite well. Mme Lemaire-Clemenceau is actively involved in the social work done by his party, the PSF.

January 14, 1944

L'Humanité makes for highly interesting reading. Since the beginning of the year, Communist leaders have been voicing their displeasure with de Gaulle and Gaullism while continuing to proclaim themselves faithful supporters. This is exactly what they did to the first Popular Front government. They began by praising Léon Blum to the hilt, then criticized his halfheartedness and eventually accused him of inertia, if not quite treason. At the Clichy riots, they shouted, "Do something, Blum." They continued organizing strikes and sit-ins in factories, in spite of the Matignon pact and collective bargaining. "Planes for Spain," they chanted, but in the factories, they worked only thirty-seven-hour weeks and turned out a mere 30 planes a month, while the Germans were producing 600.

They are using the same tactics in North Africa. "Long live de Gaulle!" Deputy Grenier said. "The Communist Party is with you heart and soul!" That's even better than in Blum's days. For the last few weeks, their criticisms, which remain measured and are still more insinuation than indictment, have begun showing through their praise. The Algiers Committee isn't purging fast enough. The traitors are still alive. Nothing changed when cautious Henri Queuille, whose very prudence made him suspect, relinquished his seat as President of the Purge Commission in favor of Communist Charles Laurent, known for his combativeness and for having organized a general strike of civil servants. People have been removed from office, but there hasn't been a single execution. The traitors have to be brought before firing squads. The Communists are demanding a court-martial, probably similar to the one Laval and Darlan organized in France, so that they can pronounce death sentences and without further legal ado execute the guilty parties—those named by the Communist leaders.

January 21, 1944

At Vichy's instigation, a law has been enacted in France creating courts-martial with three-judge panels presiding. Their role will be limited to determining whether "terrorist crimes" have in effect been committed and whether the guilt of those arrested is manifest. If so, the guilty parties are to be executed immediately. In the event of contrary findings, the accused will be judged by the appropriate courts.

A recent decree has given Darnand authority over all police organizations.

January 28, 1944

There follows a list of the principal stages in de Gaulle's relations with the Communists:

September 24, 1941: Stalin declares that should the situation present itself, de Gaulle alone would be France's spokesman.

September 28, 1941: De Gaulle sends a congratulatory telegram to Stalin on the occasion of the anniversary of the October Revolution.

January 13, 1943: Grenier, a Communist Deputy from Saint-Denis, goes to London to offer de Gaulle the support of the Communist Party.

January 15, 1943: Speaking on London radio, Grenier repudiates all non-Gaullist leaders of the North African Resistance.

In February: The Gaullist Committee in London requests and obtains the release of twenty-seven Communist Deputies.

March 30, 1943: Molotov meets with Garreau in Moscow. Their talks deal with the Communists' support for de Gaulle.

May 1, 1943: A Communist Party manifesto issued in London calls on all expatriates to support de Gaulle.

June 24, 1943: An envoy from the Soviet Union arrives in Algiers. The decree dating from September 26, 1939, dissolving the Communist Party, is repealed.

August 27, 1943: Moscow recognizes the Algiers Committee as the official government of France

October 1943: Marty arrives, followed by Vyshinsky.[10]

January 31, 1944

Interesting account of Britain's bombing campaign. Sixty cities have been designated for destruction because of their war industry. Debatable. They added that these bombings have kept the greater part of the Reich's fighter planes in the West and in the skies over Germany, in other words, out of Russia. By doing so, the British have contributed greatly to the success of the Russian advance. The Royal Air Force will thus have played an enor-

---

10. As Public Prosecutor in the Soviet Union in 1936, Andrey Vyshinsky was the state's principal voice during the prewar purges. He served as Minister of Foreign Affairs from 1949 to 1953.

mous role, first by preventing the invasion of England and, in 1943, by favoring the Russian offensive.

It didn't work that way for France in June 1940, despite Britain's promises.

February 1, 1944

In Italy, General Clark has sent a very fine letter of congratulations to General Juin.[11] Schumann gave a good speech about pan-Germanism and the rifts separating the Allies in 1918.

The weather has been really lovely. I had run out of wood and at 8 A.M. went down to the courtyard to get some. When I got back, I found that unsightly hag in my room. I gave her hell and sent her running.

February 6, 1944

February 6, 1934, remains a significant date in the Fascist press throughout the world and notably in France. I am reminded of what the postman in Orange used to say, "In August 1940, they pulled off the coup they had botched on February 6."

La Roque came to see me at 5:15 P.M. He told me that the attempted coup of February 6, 1934, had been organized by Maurras, Lebecq (President of the National Union of Veterans), Taittinger, Pinelli, and Bunau-Varilla,[12] but not Chiappe. The conspirators, who would brazenly speak to each other on the phone, had decided to exploit the Stavisky affair. When I removed Chiappe as Prefect of Police, they realized that they would have to make their move immediately or run the risk of being indicted.

---

11. General Alphonse Juin (subsequently promoted to the rank of Marshal), Commander of a mechanized division in 1939, the French Forces in North Africa in 1941, and the French expeditionary force in Italy in 1943. He was named Chief of Staff for National Defense in 1945.

12. Maurice Bunau-Varilla, Editor in Chief of the all-powerful *Le Matin*. The Germans authorized the newspaper to begin publishing again as of June 17, 1940. When Bunau-Varilla died in 1944, he was replaced by his son. After France was liberated, *Le Matin* was outlawed and its presses confiscated.

La Roque met with them several times in a cafe near the Hôtel de Ville, but he wasn't interested in marching on the Chamber of Deputies. He didn't think his organization was strong enough. He had only a few thousand men behind him and the movement hadn't yet taken root nationwide. In Toulouse, for example, he had enlisted only seven or eight members. Most of his recruits were from Paris.

He decided to demonstrate separately from the other groups, on the Left Bank, and maintain his group's identity and freedom of action. He was flabbergasted when he learned that Lebecq's men had joined with the Communists in a plan to storm Parliament. The other conspirators were planning to force their way into the Chamber of Deputies and proclaim a provisional government. They thought they could get in through the cata-combs and the sewers,[13] which come up between the Chamber and the War Ministry. La Roque's refusal came as a disappointment to Maurras, who would subsequently accuse him of treason!

Late 1937: The same men, abetted by new accomplices, had put to-gether offensive and defensive plans to ward off the Communists. They had organized a coup d'état and intended to set up a new government under the presidency of Marshal Franchet d'Esperey. Pétain had preferred to wait and "see what the future would hold"; Weygand had turned them down.

Alibert (the same fellow who would be seconding Pétain in Vichy), Lémery,[14] Tardieu, Vallat, and the rest of the bunch had hoped that La Roque would provide the troops. Commander Loustanau-Lacau (Marshal Pétain's Chief of Staff) served as liaison between the protagonists.

La Roque refused, which incensed Tardieu; then he bought *Le Petit Journal*, which drew Bailby's wrath. That is why Tardieu set about cutting him down, first by attacking his military record, then by claiming that he had received money from slush funds. Ybarnegaray got various Interior Ministers to state that La Roque had never received secret funds. Pétain himself said that "La Roque's citations for bravery were for him sufficient

---

13. This was the plan that had been worked out by the CSAR (the Cagoule).

14. Henry Lémery, Deputy and Minister of Justice in the Doumergue government in 1934. In Vichy in 1940, he voted in favor of granting Pétain plenary powers and was ap-pointed Minister of the Colonies.

and conclusive response enough." Weygand refused to speak out against La Roque, who had been a member of Foch's command staff from 1920 to 1922. At a huge rally held in the Vélodrome d'Hiver, Ybarnegaray triggered an outpouring of enthusiasm by quoting Pétain's expression of esteem for La Roque. That's when Tardieu and his fellow schemers took their indignant protests directly to the Marshal. At two in the morning, a journalist working for the Havas News Agency warned La Roque that Pétain had sent them a letter stating that he had never personally had La Roque in his command and was thus incapable of evaluating his true merit. La Roque retaliated with a scathing letter addressed to Pétain and an article in *Le Petit Journal* published along with a letter from Pétain expressing his friendship for La Roque and the confidence he had in him as well as an autographed photograph of the Marshal with words of praise and affection for La Roque. Tardieu then raised the issue of secret funds and La Roque took him to court.

Basically, I think La Roque wanted to create a national movement and assume power legally, with the idea of instituting an authoritarian, corporate state.

In 1938, he approved the Munich Agreement, once General Debeney explained to him that we were not militarily prepared to defend Czechoslovakia on our own and that England was at best reluctant and incapable of undertaking any action elsewhere than at sea.

In 1939, he tried to get in to see me on several occasions. He met a number of times with Arago, who had gone to him on my behalf. He wrote me and later expressed his indignation at not having received an answer. He was summoned by Laval, who told him that according to his count, he would have 120 deputies in 1940. I can't believe that, unless Laval was including the seats of some of Marin's friends.

In Bordeaux in June 1940, Ybarnegaray offered him a position as executive officer of his two Ministries, Health and Family. La Roque said he would only accept if the job were not remunerated and if Pétain and Weygand concurred. But once again, Pétain demonstrated that he was not one to forget the past; he refused to give his assent.

La Roque went back to Pau and decided to take direct control of his newspaper in Clermont. He refused to have his troops incorporated into the Legion. Pétain came little by little to make his peace with him and borrowed a great many of his slogans, in particular the well-known "Work, Family, Country." They discussed plans for arms caches, but Pétain never followed through on them.

Laval can't stand La Roque's relationship with Pétain and is undoubtedly responsible for La Roque's misfortunes.

February 7, 1944

La Roque came back to talk to me about the lawsuits he filed against Tardieu for having accused him of receiving secret funds.

La Roque read aloud to me what he had written about this period of his life, which had been painful for both him and his family. I was interested in finding confirmation for the accounts of certain events that I had long judged suspect. The Republic never really had political police. I have often wondered what they actually do in the Interior Ministry.

"The accusations of corruption lodged against me represent an attempt to dishonor me, resulting from my refusal to participate in an illegal rebellion and lend the services of the members of the Croix de Feu, later known as the PSF, to the overthrow of the republican regime."

A violent press campaign was unleashed by Maurras and Daudet in *L'Action française* and by Bailby, Tardieu, Vallat, Henriot, and others. La Roque noted, "I refused to collaborate with L'Action Française. We were demonstrators, not rioters."

In 1929, La Roque created an Air Defense Committee, later to become the Air Defense League, with the aim of alerting the population to the dangers of aerial bombardment. He was financed by a modest 30,000 franc annual subsidy provided by Michelin. At the time, Marshal Pétain was Inspector General of Air Defenses. La Roque was on good terms with him, but in 1933, he "respectfully" criticized certain memos circulated by Pétain and recommending the purchase of gas masks that had not been thoroughly tested. General Laure, Pétain's Chief of Staff, then offered La Roque sizable subsidies from the Foundries Committee, the coal mining industry, and the Air Force and War Ministries, but with the proviso that La Roque devote himself exclusively to the League, accept Colonel Picot as one of its leaders, and above all withdraw from the Croix de Feu. Anyone could have seen through that. La Roque rejected their offer and even quit the League, despite Pétain's efforts to prevent it.

After February 6, 1934, in an attempt to exploit the aftereffects of the riot, a coalition of Fascist and Royalist organizations known as the National Front was formed. When La Roque declined to participate, Pétain, then War Minister in Doumergue's Cabinet, canceled his nomination for promotion to the rank of Colonel in the Reserves and removed his name from the list of those to be considered for promotion.

In 1935, however, Pétain renewed his overtures to La Roque. They began meeting frequently, every two months. The Marshal shared with him his political aspirations and his ideas for reorganizing the government, ideas he intended to put into effect as soon as he became Prime Minister.

Pétain's political ambitions came to life in the immediate aftermath of February 6, 1934, and expanded rapidly. He realized that given the Radical Party's opposition and the worsening economic crisis, the fall of Doumergue's government was inevitable. He set about taking steps to find the support he would need to accede to power. He got word to Jouhaux that he would like to meet with him and his associates. With me, he became so extraordinarily amiable that I found it excessive. In the Chamber of Deputies, he supported a bill limiting military service to one year, which Weygand staunchly opposed. Since his political objectives would bring him the support of the Right in any event, he was trying to appeal to the Left. But when Doumergue's government did fall, Pétain failed in his attempts to replace him. He chose to lie in wait for a more favorable occasion and discreetly offer his services, with his customary prudence, as head of a national, broad-based government.

He made it a point to be introduced into every possible circle and to place some of his people in all of them. He concerned himself with overcoming the obstacles that lay in his path and neutralizing whatever opposing forces he could not win over to his side. He didn't actually exclude the possibility of eliminating outright those opposed to him, if ever the situation were to present itself without incurring great risk, but violating laws and the use of force was never seriously considered. He was rather counting on the antagonism among political parties and their overall ineffectiveness. It was his wish to appear on the scene at some point as a conciliator draped in glory, with the discreet support of business groups and the bois-terous enthusiasm of certain veterans' associations.

In his talks with La Roque in 1936, Pétain told him that the Popular Front's victory would be short-lived, that the Left would inevitably go too far, and that the reaction of the farmers and the middle class would prove fatal. The hour would then be at hand for the victor of Verdun to come to the fore as a moderating force.

Those were the Marshal's words, but the acts of some of his associates belied them. Commander Loustanau-Lacau, for example, was involved in mobilizing an insurrection.

In April 1937, La Roque learned that under the pretext of fighting the Communists, officers in the garrison in Nice had secretly formed their own defense unit. He informed the Marshal in writing. No later than April 15, Loustanau-Lacau, accompanied by Captain Bonhomme, Pétain's or-derly, came to tell La Roque that his letter had not been passed along to the Marshal. Loustanau-Lacau then informed him that he had organized a supramilitary intelligence group to handle surveillance of the Communists and asked La Roque to participate. As he explained it, the Communists were preparing a takeover; he had proof of it. The Popular Front govern-ment was either powerless to stop them or an accomplice to it. The situa-tion called for a union of the large national political organizations—Doriot's PPF, Maurras's Action Française, the Republican Federation, and La Roque's PSF—to be supported by major business groups. To avoid pos-sible rivalries, they would create a National Committee on which each group would be represented by its leader, but under the presidency of a great military leader, that is, Marshal Franchet d'Esperey, since Marshal Pétain wasn't available. Either General Brécard[15] or General Altmayer would serve as Secretary-General. The organization would reach into ev-ery province. After serious and thorough preparation, on D day at H hour, the National Committee of this united Freedom Front would assume power to save France from the Communist peril. Commander Loustanau-

---

15. General Charles Brécard, former Cavalry Inspector who became the war chroni-cler for right-wing and far-right-wing newspapers: *Candide, Le Jour, L'Echo de Paris*, all of which were published with German authorization and oversight.

Lacau was insistent in trying to get La Roque to sign on, but the latter refused to take part in an operation tantamount to civil war.

A short time later, the Freedom Front was created. When La Roque failed again to respond positively to overtures made by Loustanau-Lacau and Bonhomme (both of whom were on Pétain's staff), they unleashed violent attacks against him, with Tardieu, Bailby, Abel Bonnard, Gillouin, Alibert, and Maurras proving especially caustic.

When, on July 14, 1937, La Roque announced that *Le Petit Journal* had become the property of his party, the PSF, the Freedom Front's attacks intensified. Bailby distinguished himself as the most vicious of all. La Roque mentioned once again the relentlessness with which Tardieu maligned him. He clearly represented the principal obstacle to the plot's success. There could be no united front without his followers. Tardieu, and the National Committee along with him, accused La Roque of accepting bribes and corrupting officials, with Tardieu claiming that as Prime Minister, he had personally handed La Roque money from secret funds. La Roque sued Tardieu for slander. That was the beginning of a series of lawsuits and an unusually violent press campaign.

Time went by. I became Prime Minister. My Minister of the Interior never once mentioned this secret organization called the Freedom Front. However, my military advisers informed me that General Gérodias,[16] Deputy Chief of Staff, had sent a message to Army corps and military sector commanders that included the translation of an old Spanish Communist Party paper. The paper described the ways in which to neutralize an army by overpowering its officers, as preparation for an insurgency. Gérodias's message said that these tactics would undoubtedly be employed in France. I expressed surprise and indignation that such a note could have been circulated without its having been communicated to me, General Gamelin, and General Colson. It had been intended to unsettle officers and their families and possibly draw them into political movements. I immediately ordered an investigation.

---

16. Paul-Henri Gérodias was Deputy Chief of Staff in 1936.

General Gérodias said that the message had been brought to him by Commander Loustanau-Lacau, acting on Marshal Pétain's behalf. He said he hadn't understood its political nature and had simply passed it along for its informational content. When Marshal Pétain claimed that he had never seen it, I decided to place General Gérodias on inactive duty, in spite of his personal merits; in effect, during this past war, he commanded his division brilliantly. I also decided to remove Commander Loustanau-Lacau from office. On learning of my decision, Pétain simply said, "I had been noticing for some time that he had been seeing too many people."

Near the end of 1939, La Roque was visited by Lémery, whom Pétain had dispatched to find out what La Roque would do if Pétain were to seize power, which he was seriously considering, with the approval of Laval and other political figures. It was their intention to negotiate a separate peace agreement with both Germany and Italy, with Spain serving as intermediary. The plan wasn't made public until June 1940, in Bordeaux, when it was put into effect. This had been Pétain's idea as early as May 25, 1940: Use the defeat to seize power. After Reynaud's downfall, Pétain emerged unopposed as the master of France. He immediately called on the men from the Freedom Front and the Synarchie: Laval, Baudouin, Lémery, Bouthillier, Brécard, and so on. He made peace with La Roque when he found he needed him, and made him his confidant. Of course that didn't prevent him from letting La Roque be deported.

Is that the final chapter of this story? I rather doubt it, given that, in spite of everything, La Roque remains devoted to Pétain. He just can't believe that behind the ignoble attacks on him lay a carefully concealed Marshal Pétain. Does he at least believe that Pétain knowingly let it all happen? Not even that. In his view, Pétain was duped.

February 15, 1944

Von Rundstedt has given Gamelin and other French Generals a lesson in warfare. He stated that the Maginot Line, because there was no depth to it and because its rigidity made it difficult to defend, was poorly conceived. Neither the fortifications nor the arms had been designed in response to the firepower of Germany's weapons. Above all, the line could be outflanked since it stopped in the middle of eastern France.

I remember the protests voiced by Pétain, Weygand, and the Supreme War Council when I expressed concern over this gap and suggested that we continue building further north. Pétain considered the Ardennes impassable. He even wrote that it was.

Von Rundstedt will have huge resources at his command. To repel an Anglo-Saxon landing, Hitler will strip the Russian front, if he has to.

March 4, 1944

Pucheu's trial opened today in Algiers. Prior to the war, he was a member of the Synarchie, along with Baudouin, Bouthillier, Barnaud, and others. Their idea was to establish relations with Germany and Italy, with a view toward the economic and financial domination of Europe. Their plan, or plot, probably began as early as 1936–1937. They were also very likely allied with the group that has stupidly been called the Cagoule. Pucheu and other members of the Synarchie had close ties with certain members of the Joint Chiefs: Prételat and Franchet d'Esperey.

They obviously played a significant role at the time of the Armistice, but once the golden age of the Bank of Worms came to an end in Vichy, probably as a result of setbacks in their relations with Germany or on Pétain's advice, these boys decided to try out the Americans. Even that vile creature Baudouin wanted to go to Africa, to join up with Darlan, and later Giraud, but either he couldn't manage it or he was overly wary.

Pucheu took the same route taken by Peyrouton and others who had been in Vichy, but he didn't have the support of the Anglo-Saxons. That support wasn't enough to keep the others from losing their positions, but at least it kept them out of a military courtroom, which is where Pucheu finds himself now.

What standing does this court have? General Weiss is serving as Public Prosecutor. I wonder what Blum's lawyer, Le Trocquer, thinks about it, given that he challenged the legality of Riom's Cour Suprême.

In my opinion, this trial should be held after the war, in an official court of law, with a lot of other men facing charges, too. The verdict, whatever it is, will have no value. It's probably just one of the many bones being thrown to the Communists. However despicable I may find the men of the Synarchie, I place the law and respect for the law above that.

Pucheu is charged with conspiracy against the nation and high treason. He is also charged with having carried out illegal arrests, abuse of power, and abuse of authority. As he stood accused, calm and in perfect control of himself, he began by challenging the court that was trying him. Having been asked questions relative to the request for an armistice and its acceptance, he tried to explain his position at the time, but he was not allowed to, his feelings being deemed irrelevant. Then he accused Laval of having committed the offenses that were being imputed to him. He stated that he had always been anti-German and that he had had some success in defending France's industry against German businesses. He claimed that he had ordered the arrest of members of the Gestapo. He had no response, however, to the charge that he had allowed the Gestapo and the SS to set up their offices in Vichy.

March 6, 1944

Huge Russian offensive north of the Ukraine. The rail link between Lvov and Odessa has been cut. Large amounts of matériel have been seized.

Pucheu's trial is still going on. We were given a long communiqué about the defendant and his statement. General Weiss claimed that Pucheu's position in Pétain's Cabinet was proof of "his complicity in the policies of collaboration." Pucheu replied that in 1941 the majority of Frenchmen supported Pétain and that Admiral Leahy and a representative of the Soviet Union were still at their posts in Vichy. Weiss shot back that that was no excuse for serving in Pétain's government.

At the second court session, they read a memo circulated by Pucheu, ceding control of France's textile industry to the Germans, and so on. None of this has anything to do with the execution of the hostages in Châteaubriant. Pucheu always made a distinction between the Gaullists and the Communists.

Pucheu stated that he had crossed the Pyrenees and gone to North Africa in answer to a call from General Giraud and that he had left behind his wife and children, who had since then been arrested by the Germans. It seems to me that the timing of this trial is particularly poor.

At the third court session, Giraud and Béthouart[17] appeared as witnesses for the defense. I have seen only an extremely brief and rather slanted summary of their testimony. On the other hand, the prosecution witnesses, most of them Communists—Grenier, Laurent—are quoted directly. They often got involved in violent disputes with the other witnesses, with the two groups lobbing accusations of lying back and forth. The Communists accused Pucheu of having handed Party members over to the German authorities and of having set up special courts. They also held him responsible for the Châteaubriant killings. The Communists admitted that they had no proof, but, they said, "We can smell it!"

March 8, 1944

There has been a terrifying daylight bombing of Berlin. There is talk of 3,000 Allied aircraft involved. These air raids bring back memories of the German bombings of London in 1940. Anglo-Saxon convoys are now making their way to Russia and the Mediterranean unobstructed.

Fourth courtroom session for Pucheu. Highly favorable testimony was given by Captain Begbeder, a former member of his staff, and by Giraud, who took the stand yesterday to state that it was at his official request that Pucheu had been called back to North Africa. Giraud and Pucheu had at times been very close.

In a terribly violent closing statement, General Weiss called Pucheu "the nazifier of France," "the pivotal man in the enslavement of the country." "He is the enemy of Stalin's men ... and yes, we owe our thanks to Stalin's followers, those men who are supposedly devils. I love those supposed devils, because they are saving our country." Weiss called for the death penalty.

Pucheu was found not guilty of plotting against the nation and its form of government. Conversely, he was found guilty, with no mitigating

---

17. General Maurice-Emile Béthouart commanded the expeditionary force to Narvik and thereafter the military zone in Rabat. He went to Algiers in 1942 and was Commander of the First Army Corps in 1944.

circumstances, of conspiring with the enemy, to which he had handed over our economy and our police. The charge of having chosen and/or turned over hostages was dropped. He was sentenced to death, and all his assets are to be seized. He has appealed the verdict. The summary of the closing statements presented on the radio was insufficient and skewed. All the arguments raised at the trial were mediocre. It was just so much nit-picking, with no greatness to it at all. The closing statements were feeble.

March 17, 1944

British artillery and aviation have reduced the ancient remains of Cassino to rubble. Once again, I find confirmation of Armengaud's theory that well dug-in troops can withstand aerial bombings.

Speech by Lord Halifax: "France shares with my country the honor of having taken up arms to meet its international commitments and defend freedom." "Our thoughts and our prayers are with the people of France. We are convinced that a strong, free and proud France will rise once again." "Whatever the future government of France may be—and that is for the French people themselves, when the time comes, to decide—we are glad to have in Algiers a body of Frenchmen who, working together, form a remarkable symposium of French opinion, insofar as that opinion can, in present circumstances, be vocal."

March 27, 1944

In Algiers, the National Resistance Council had the unusual idea of issuing a reminder that "France's principal goal is the struggle against the invading forces" along with a series of warnings aimed at "people circulating lists of collaborators, people writing letters informing on others and sentences handed down by kangaroo courts." It was followed by a plea for people not to do anything that might jeopardize the union of all Frenchmen. ... This comes clearly in reaction to Pucheu's trial.

The Consultative Assembly in Algiers—the government had chosen not to participate so as not to impede discussion!!—has decided on the structure of the future legislative body even though it was not itself mandated by universal suffrage.

270

March 31, 1944

The Russians are moving on Odessa.

Of particular note is the economic agreement between Japan and the Soviet Union over fossil fuels and the fishing grounds at Sakhalin. Japan has agreed to an increase in the fees they pay to fish there.

April 1, 1944

There have been new aerial bombings of Germany; the Russian Army continues to drive forward. The bombings are clearly helping them advance, by drawing away the greater part of Germany's fighter planes. The second front is in the sky. The Germans have understood the gravity of the situation along the southeastern front and are aware of its consequences.

Italy: Russia has recognized the government headed by Badoglio and King Victor Emmanuel, much to the dismay of the Anglo-Saxons, who weren't notified beforehand, and probably of the fiery Sforza, the Communists' ally. That explains why the Communist leader Ercoli, extending a hand to the Catholics and the military brass, gave a speech reminiscent of those Thorez used to make before he deserted: "The new government must include members of all the non-Fascist parties. In no instance, can we yield to the desire to wage vendettas. We cannot make the mistake of allowing for the massive elimination of officers. We need them to forge a union of all Italian people."

April 9, 1944

A beautiful sunny day. I watched people stroll by in the ravine, girls with soldiers, women, and children. Itter must have been a vacation spot before the war. There are traces here of religious customs that predate Christianity and that have survived over the ages.

The tribe (Reynaud, Weygand, et al.) held a banquet. Jouhaux didn't get back until 5 P.M., all lit up and giddy. I prefer to have my meals alone.

April 10, 1944

At 2 P.M. I learned that the Russians had reached Ruthenia, a former Czechoslovak province that was ceded to Hungary after Munich. They raised the Czech flag. There was a commemorative ceremony in London and speeches by Benes.

Ever since the retreat from Russia, the German garrison at the castle has been growing increasingly discouraged. An old veteran of the War of 1914–1918 said to me, "Don't they realize that the war is lost and that they have to make peace?" One officer said that he would take to the mountains with provisions; another that it was time to get out his civilian clothes. The younger ones, though, remain fervent and confident.

April 12, 1944

In a recent speech, Lord Vansittart stated that originally, the Entente Cordiale of 1904 was merely a mutual declaration of goodwill generated by the multitude of incidents that had been occurring daily. At the time, England had no wish to conclude an alliance, but had that alliance, to which they did ultimately agree, been forged then, there might never have been a War of 1914–1918. He added that the fruits of the victory of 1918 were lost because the Americans refused to grant France the guarantees that it sought concerning the Rhine.[18] Then the Americans stupidly withdrew, claiming it was not their province to intervene, and the British followed suit. During the French occupation of the Ruhr Valley, the British protests were fully as vehement as those of the Germans. Lord Vansittart added that in 1940, England was spared France's misfortune because it was separated from the continent by twenty miles of sea. France was condemned to suffer its horrible fate as a result of errors of which England was not entirely innocent.

He concluded by saying that it would be folly, and fatal on the part of the Allies, to undertake to reestablish order in the countries soon to be lib-

---

18. At the Paris Peace Conference, Lloyd George and Wilson did not support France's demand to occupy the left bank of the Rhine (see diary entries for November 11, 1942, and September 29, 1944). They agreed instead to the demilitarization of German territories west of the Rhine (the left bank) and a strip thirty miles wide east of it (the right bank). When Germany violated this provision of the Versailles Treaty by remilitarizing the Rhineland in 1936, England and the United States did nothing.

erated, for the people living in those countries have suffered far more than we have. He said that each of us must refrain from offending our friends by paying too much attention to the words of our enemies.

April 23, 1944

Spring has made a modest appearance in the Tirol; the light is playing upon the snow-covered mountaintops. What a wonderful morning! Suddenly, at 10 A.M. there was an explosion in the village. From behind my barred window, I watched as a villager in a deserted street prepared to fire another round from the cannon they use to signal the joyous or painful events that mark village life. More blasts shook the air. I learned that the cannon shots had been occasioned by the news that two of their sons had died on the battlefield. Then the church bell began to toll. I understand that the priest gave a moving talk and that all the women gathered in prayer were in tears. Itter has a population of only 400; 12 of them are now dead. Proportionately, that works out to 2 million deaths for Germany.

Last night, in one of the village inns, the castle garrison celebrated Hitler's birthday. One of the soldiers told me about their party: beer, wine, and to top it off, a Roman-style orgy with eight women playing the role of bacchantes ... of course the SS do it standing up.

April 25, 1944

The bombing of Europe continues on an increased scale. Airfields in Dieppe, Metz, Nancy, and Dijon were hit. In Itter, yesterday, sirens sounded the alert all day long. Fires have been raging through Ludwigshafen, Mannheim, and Munich. The "Sanitär" got a postcard from his family. "All we can say is that the only thing we have left is our lives." He is a good man and was terribly shaken by the news.

Aerial reconnaissance missions are being flown from the Baltic to the Danube. I also heard stories about the exploits of the French Resistance, much of that news false or grossly exaggerated. Were we not told that in the Ain, the Germans lost 500 men and had 700 wounded, whereas there were only 74 French deaths?

April 26, 1944

The massive bombings have continued without letup. There is fierce fighting between Lvov and the Carpathians. Meanwhile, in London, a ceremony was organized at the Alliance Française. Benes was received by Dejean,[19] the Algiers Committee's delegate in London, and by Viénot, and General Kœnig was present. Dejean condemned "the servility with which the governments who signed the Munich Agreement had backed down; backing down was to become the program of the Vichy government." Benes deplored the fatal error of all those who considered the negotiations at Munich to be of limited import. Then he praised de Gaulle for having raised anew a French flag that had been betrayed.

The Czechoslovak government was pleased to recognize the Liberation Committee as the true representative of France, which, he said, in a liberated Europe would regain its place of strength and honor among the leading nations of the world. Then Viénot concluded by lauding Benes. He attributed the error of Munich to "a feeble-minded government devoid of courage and foresight." Viénot himself voted in favor of the Munich Agreement! Apparently neither the United States nor Great Britain was represented at the ceremony.

April 27, 1944

In London, Pierre Dac, who, prior to the war, was a well-known humorist, was heard threatening collaborators with the death penalty. There is no shortage of surprises, that's for sure.

As for Pétain's tour of France, it has been learned that he spent the night in Melun. Then he went to Notre Dame for the funeral rites of the victims of the Anglo-Saxon bombings of Paris's 18th Arrondissement. The trip was announced twenty-four hours beforehand, allowing the Prefects time to alert the staffs of the collaborationist parties and get out the Pari-

---

19. Maurice Dejean, career diplomat, one of Paul Reynaud's associates in 1939. He was Director of Political Affairs for Free France and National Commissioner of Foreign Affairs from 1940 to 1942. In 1944, he served as French delegate to the Allied governments based in London.

sian population. By 9 A.M. the French flag was flying over the Hôtel de Ville and a large security force was in place. Pétain left city hall a little before ten, in a huge procession heading for Notre Dame, where he was met, naturally, by a huge crowd. After the ceremony, he returned to the Hôtel de Ville for lunch, then began receiving various delegations, notably the beef porters from the Halles market. Following that, he went out onto the balcony and addressed the assembled crowd. He spoke about Paris in mourning, the confidence the government and the people must have in each other, and the day when peace would return. It was a perfect example of how not to commit yourself. There wasn't a single word in it that could have failed to draw applause from patriots.

May 10, 1944

Massive bombings are continuing with no letup over France, Belgium, Luxembourg, and the Gulf of Genoa. This is today's heavy artillery preparing the ground for battlefields to come. So many flourishing cities will be reduced to formless ruins. How can anyone not be heartsick at the thought of the women and the children there? These are wars of mass destruction; real hell is being wrought on a scale equal to that of our technological advances.

Addressing the House of Commons, Churchill stated that 6,670 American airplanes, 5,050 British tanks, and large amounts of matériel have been delivered to the Russians. England has lent them 80 million pounds, following a tradition set by Pitt, the banker of coalitions. Add to that the American aid, in the form of lend-lease.

"Jeremiah" Schumann has spoken out violently again against Pétain and his trip to Paris. That was followed by a series of official communiqués that formed a tangled web of contradictions.

May 11, 1944

Emmanuel d'Astier de la Vigerie spoke in Algiers about the Resistance and how they see their role in the coming landing. The forces inside France are to be called the FFI. He noted that in the time since the Armistice was signed, 20,000 Frenchmen have been executed by the Germans. He threatened Monzie, Bonnet, and Frossard, who remain staunch supporters of the Marshal and are preparing to install a new republic in Paris. Once again, d'Astier is striking out at shadows.

May 14, 1944

Joan of Arc Day. The new successes won by the French fighting in Italy, in spite of the desperate counterattacks launched against them, are the best commemoration possible.

May 15, 1944

Both the British and American press are filled with heartfelt praise for the French troops commanded by General Juin. His performance has been excellent.

May 16, 1944

Spoke with La Roque about the Synarchie. He talked to me about a plan that Le Roy Ladurie of the Bank of Worms, Pucheu, Baudouin, Bouthillier, Barnaud, and others had devised in 1937. The idea of these anti-Communist promoters of Anglo-Saxon capitalism was to rally political moderates to collaborate with the Synarchie under the leadership of a well-known military leader. Offers were extended to Pétain, who turned them down, and Weygand, who likewise refused. Franchet d'Esperey accepted. It is quite possible that Pétain remained a substitute choice, since Loustanau-Lacau, who was on his staff, monitored these events closely. La Roque refused to be a part of it. He told me that Pucheu had at first been inclined to side with Doriot, but that he dropped him as soon as he had proof that Doriot was being subsidized by the Italians.

May 28, 1944

Lisbeth and Andrea said good-bye to me. They had come to work at the "castle" after having first been deported to a camp; now they were being sent back. Lisbeth is German. She was imprisoned for having married a Jew prior to 1933. After Hitler came to power, she sought refuge in France, in Paris and Lyons. She is about forty-five years old and very bright. She is frail in appearance, with a look that is intentionally closed and lifeless. She finds the Bolsheviks as criminal as the Nazis. Andrea is a young blond-haired woman from a good family, married to a Russian Jew. She is meeker and less intelligent than Lisbeth. Lisbeth said to me: "La Roque is a Fascist! Why did they arrest him?" Then she said: "I hope you'll get to return to France. I know how much they love you there." Going back to the camp is hard on both of them.

Louis Marin spoke on the radio. Finally a speech from a patriot whose only thoughts are for his country.

June 4, 1944

After violent street fighting in the suburbs of Rome, the Eighth Army entered the city, where they encountered no resistance whatsoever. How grand an event this is, and how many memories it evokes! I spent several years in Rome, working on my thesis on the cities of Renaissance Italy. German columns have been sighted north of Rome, in disorderly retreat. The Allies have seized the Alban Hills and the road from Rome to Pescera, on the Adriatic. They took full control of the capital last night. General Clark made the following statement, "It is thanks to the fighting men of France, Britain, and America that this day has come." And thanks to General Juin's men, the shame brought on us by Huntziger, Georges, and Gamelin, if not entirely erased, will at least have been largely offset. In Europe's eyes, thanks to these men, France looks like a warrior again. Clark added that Germany's Tenth and Fourteenth Armies had been defeated. In Rome, delirious crowds cheered the Allied soldiers, above all the French soldiers. They are France's finest ambassadors. The friendship the people of Italy hold for France is alive again, now that the Fascist gangrene has been eradicated. The two countries will have to work together during the peace negotiations. The Pope made an appearance on a balcony at the Vatican. This has also been a victory for the spirit of Christianity, if not for the Christian religion. There is greatness in this historic moment. The only thing missing was the splendid presence of Nitti.

Pétain traveled to Lyons. France's Fascists have left him in the dust, as they have Laval. Now their sole allegiance is to Darnand, Henriot, and

Déat. They no longer take the Vichy government seriously. In the absence of an Allied landing, the continued bombings have had an obvious effect on morale.

According to Monte Carlo radio, Mendès-France, who has been in Washington since May, has resigned, having failed in his negotiations.

Won't the principal Allied landing take place in Italy, where they hold sixty miles of coastline and control the entire country?

June 6, 1944

The Allied landing began in Normandy at midnight, with thousands of airplanes filling the skies. They met neither antiaircraft fire nor German planes. Four thousand boats are advancing behind smoke barriers, in spite of the presence of high-speed gunboats. There is talk of bombings carried out by waves of 10,000 planes dropping 10,000 tons of bombs. The landing took place at 7 A.M. on the left bank of an estuary of the Seine, between Villers-sur-Mer and Carentan. They have moved several miles inland. There is fighting around Caen. That they were able to take the Germans by surprise has been attributed to the effectiveness of previous bombing runs that destroyed communications throughout the coastal zone.

June 8, 1944

Intense battles continue to be waged south of Bayeux and on the outskirts of Caen. American reinforcements have been sent to the area around Carentan. The fighting seems to have been limited to the German troops already in the area and the Allies who landed the first day. Neither German reserves nor the greater part of the landing forces have yet to be engaged. The Germans are expecting a larger-scale landing elsewhere. After four days of combat, the Anglo-Saxons have not been thrown back into the sea. In fact, they have managed to make significant progress inland.

June 11, 1944

The Americans have made great advances in the Cotentin peninsula. British columns are moving beyond Bayeux onto Caen. Other British units have joined up in the vicinity of Carentan with the paratroopers who landed on the peninsula.

The Allies have made a major push north in Italy, halfway to Florence. And they have sealed the Moroccan border facing Spain. In anticipation of a massive landing in the Gulf of Genoa?

There has been considerable British and American news coverage describing the joy and the emotion in the areas that have been liberated. There was a huge demonstration in Bayeux, in spite of the fact that the Germans were still close by. People put on tricolored armbands with the Cross of Lorraine and shouted de Gaulle's name.

In an interviewed with F.I.,[20] de Gaulle strenuously objected to Eisenhower's statement denying his representatives the right to govern the liberated parts of France. It is a violation of French sovereignty, de Gaulle said; the people have already spoken.

It has been raining outside, but oh, the joy in our souls!

June 13, 1944

10:30 A.M. The alert sounded. Bombers and fighters flew over the mountains, some on to Munich, others toward Innsbruck. ... More women and children about to be killed. Another alert sounded at 10:30 at night. We watched them as they flew over the "castle" and then again on their way back around 3 A.M.

June 23, 1944

According to Sottens, the Russians have launched their offensive.

Spoke with La Roque, who told me that at the time of his lawsuit with Tardieu, his former commanders, Pétain and Weygand—who is currently imprisoned with us here—pretended not even to know him, the same Weygand who used to have lunch at the home of Pozzo di Borgo.[21] When the Armistice was signed, La Roque was at odds with the Marshal. He said

---

20. L'Agence Française Indépendante

21. Pozzo di Borgo, rich Corsican landowner. He and General Duseigneur founded the Union des Comités d'Action d'Extrême Droite. His resignation from the executive committee of the Croix de Feu caused considerable fuss. He was closely aligned with François Coty.

he suffered more under the Vichy government than he did with the Popular Front.

June 25, 1944

The sun has finally come out again.

Bernanos has addressed a message to the "people of France," just a simple little message to the entire nation. Is there anyone these days who isn't addressing messages to "the people of France"? This one is solemn and as vague as they come: spiritual values ... economic injustice ... noble Normandy. A slew of stock images squeezed into a few lines. The unbelievable conceit of all these expatriates in America and elsewhere.

Fortunately, the events actually unfolding are far more palatable. Saw a review of the British press and articles from the *Times* and the *Manchester Guardian*. Bands of patriots in Occupied France, and in particular in Normandy, are risking their lives attacking the Germans. Resistance groups have been paralyzing the movement of their armored divisions. Many of their members had been imprisoned during the Occupation; and there were others who were executed. Read an excellent article in the *Sunday Times* about the simple and prideful dignity with which French patriots welcomed their liberators. Their war correspondent wrote that "there were no hysterical scenes. Standing before the ruins of their homes, the people were calm and proud. They talked with the Canadians and the British and expressed their admiration for England, for having held out in 1940. The British, they said, had been saved by the Channel, for they were not armed or ready to fight. Then Hitler got the insane idea of invading Russia." This article has led to a series of others in which people admit to having underestimated the French. Have the Anglo-Saxons finally begun to see things clearly? They still have to explain where their Air Force was during the Battle of France.

June 28, 1944

Philippe Henriot was assassinated by men pretending to be militiamen come to protect him. He was killed in his bedroom, with his wife looking on. Laval made a speech about it and Pétain sent his widow a letter, all of four lines long. Pétain hasn't said a single word implying that he and Henriot were in any way aligned, although Henriot was his Minister of Information. The man's ego is monstrous, politically as well as personally. It wouldn't surprise me if he were busy cutting a deal with the Americans.

July 9, 1944

A milestone would appear to have been reached with today's events. The Russians are advancing on eastern Prussia and Poland. The push stretches over a front three hundred miles long.

In Italy, several miles outside of Ancona and Livorno, the Allied advance has intensified.

In Normandy, they have taken Caen.

It would appear that the Germans waited too long to cut loose and evacuate some of the territory they occupied. They are suffering today from an inferiority of the worst kind, one that will cost them the war: inferior numbers of men.

In Normandy, it was inevitable that the Allied advance would stall, given the hedgerows, the marshy terrain, and the sunken lanes. This is a war for infantrymen, and the Germans have had much more practice at it.

I had thought the Allied landing in the Cotentin was only a first phase designed as a cover for the real landing: in Flanders or the Gulf of Genoa, or both.

July 14, 1944

Another July 14 in captivity, the most painful of them all, when I consider all the tragedies that have befallen my country. There's something terribly oppressive in the silence of these mountains, in this peacefulness, in the solitude. It has been a day spent in despondency.

This evening, I learned that Mandel had been assassinated. The German government had handed him over to the French, probably to be held as a hostage following the assassination of Henriot. According to Vichy, he was killed during an escape attempt contrived by "resistance fighters" as he was being transferred to some prison. Memories of Mandel have been racing through my mind. He was present throughout my political career.

While in Morocco, both of us tried to win General Noguès over to the side of the Resistance; and both of us tried, in vain, to reach London. We were imprisoned together and brought to Germany together.

July 15, 1944

Jean Oberlé gave a thoroughly mediocre funeral oration for Mandel on British radio; Monte Carlo radio has been spewing forth vile remarks about him. His assassination hasn't given rise to a single statement of protest, neither by the United Nations[22] nor in any of the capitals of the nations allied in the fight against Nazism, although Nazism is what killed Mandel. During the last war, he was Clemenceau's secretary, and he adored the man. He even took a bust of Clemenceau with him when he went to prison. I can hear a dispute going on between the son of the "Tiger" himself and Jouhaux. Michel Clemenceau is a horse's ass; there's just no way around that. I am more and more struck by how narrow-minded he is and by his inability to see that there's anything in this world other than himself.

René Payot has moved his chatter over to Swiss radio. He is now as pronounced a Gaullist as he was a Pétainist. He spoke of the "disaster in the East"—those were the words he actually used.

Von Rundstedt has given up his command for reasons of health. Actually, there was a difference of opinion: Rommel wanted to attack the Anglo-Saxons as soon as they landed and push them back into the sea; Rundstedt wanted to wait until they had moved further inland. His error has proven fatal. Almost the entire German High Command has been replaced.

July 17, 1944

According to an SS who was there, yesterday's air raid in Munich was carried out by several hundred planes. It was the fourth one over the last five days. The city is in flames. The losses were even more horrible than they

---

22. The twenty-six signatory states, which in their Declaration of January 1, 1942, resolved not to make peace separately and to form an international organization to replace the League of Nations.

might have been, and more cruel, because the evacuation of children had just begun when the bombers appeared in the sky. It was a dreadful spectacle.

In eastern Germany, the population has begun fleeing before the oncoming Russians, who are only fifteen miles away. Great numbers of Germans are making their way out of the Baltic States.

July 18, 1944

The Captain went to Munich to attend funeral services for his brother. The city had been devastated; there were no buses and no cars. He had walked through the debris for two hours to get to the improvised morgue where his brother's remains lay when more bombs fell and razed it to the ground, with all the dead bodies pulverized in the explosions. No services were held. He returned to Itter totally demoralized.

Mandel was handed over to Vichy when the Resistance kidnapped Chevalier, a former Minister and Dean of the Humanities division of the University of Grenoble. The man was half senile, but Pétain was very attached to him, which is why they offered Mandel as a hostage.

Jouhaux pointed out to me that Renan and Nietzsche, starting from totally opposite points of view, both concluded that the creation of a unified Europe was a necessity. We would be wise to get at it soon, or there will be nothing left of it: no cities, no industry, no universities, no museums. Even as we spoke, the sky above us filled with hundreds of American bombers and fighters.

After the Allies took Ancona and Livorno, General Kesselring, the Commander of the German forces, was awarded "oak leaves." Apparently, every army has its strange customs. The Germans are now in serious trouble in the Baltic, and eastern Prussia is threatened with imminent invasion. They have made the same mistake Napoleon made when he failed to pull out of Spain before heading down the road to Moscow. How could Germany have expected to prevail on so many different fronts?

July 21, 1944

It has been a beautiful, sunny day. After a while, the contrast becomes oppressive, but what can be done about it?

Last night, there was a dynamite attack on Hitler's headquarters. A bomb went off about six feet away from him. He escaped with just a few bruises, although several members of the High Command were wounded. He went right back to work and met with Mussolini. A little later, Göring arrived. The news has had a major effect on the prisoners in Itter, both the men and the women, but it's impossible to discern any sign of it on their faces. Living in the camps has taught them to say nothing and remain impassive. Some of them have been tortured.

A. described various forms of torture: a pail clamped over a prisoner's head and pounded with a hammer, the strappado, as many as three days straight without bread or water, slow death by starvation and exhaustion, crematoriums, gas chambers. I would never have believed that there could be such abominations in Europe. Centuries of effort and progress have been wiped out. We've gone back to the Inquisition and the Wars of Religion.

Hitler made a statement following yesterday's failed attack on his life. It involved, he said, "a small clique of unhappy Generals." The architect would appear to have been General Von Beck, who has apparently been executed. Göring made a statement, too. As for Goebbels, he feels it was the work of the Intelligence Service. A report from the DNB lists the names of the Generals who were seriously wounded and those who were wounded only slightly. It was followed by a long article on the men really responsible for the attack: the various Secret Services, Roosevelt, and his two accomplices, Churchill and Stalin. "That they are forced to resort to murder is proof that they are powerless militarily." No mention in this long article of the Generals Hitler and Göring denounced, neither Von Beck nor the others.

The importance of this plot is obvious, and the timing highly significant. These were, moreover, Generals who had been decorated by Hitler himself, some of whom had distinguished themselves during the war. Himmler, the head of the domestic forces, has ordered Germans to shoot any suspect resisting arrest or attempting to flee.

July 30, 1944

The Russian Supreme High Command is actually concentrating the greatest part of its resources, not in those areas that protrude into eastern Prussia, but in Poland, along a front stretching 120 miles from Brest Litovsk to Bomberg. In Grodno and Hannas, they are holding their positions without attempting a breakthrough. The Russians intend to cross the Vistula and attack Warsaw. Their aim is to:

1. Cut off the German retreat in the Baltic states;
2. Enter eastern Prussia;
3. Outflank Warsaw;
4. Cross the Carpathians and move into Slovakia.

The *maquis* have clearly been effective in disrupting German operations behind the lines in France. De Gaulle's efforts and those of the Resistance have been far from futile. Dissension remains, however, this time between the Communist *maquis* and the others, and for the British these divisions are a matter of concern.

August 3, 1944

At 8 P.M. a glowing Jouhaux came and announced the capture of Rennes and Dinan. Is there another Westphalia Treaty in the making, with Stalin taking the place of Louis XIV? Or will there be a democratic settlement that will really bring us peace?

The breakup of the German states is a very real possibility. Once the Prussian cement is gone, they might well revert to independent nations. Anything can happen as a result of or during the invasion of Germany. The opposite possibility can't be overlooked either: that of a German nation holding to its unity and "going Bolshevik" to preserve it.

Jouhaux continues to emphasize the overriding importance of economic issues in the postwar period. I tend to attach greater significance to psychological elements, like the sense and spirit of nationalism and, above all, the Soviet Union's desire to exert a preponderant influence over Central Europe.

The Americans have taken Rennes, where the German garrison surrendered. In spite of their lack of experience, the Americans have made their landing a success, but they won't be able to organize a second one in Flanders, as I had hoped. It hardly came as a surprise that Turkey has broken off diplomatic and economic relations with Germany.

In the "castle," anger and dismay are rife among the SS, while the deportees are experiencing a secret joy.

August 6, 1944

There was just one sunny spell throughout the entire gloomy day, a break in the cloud-filled sky. But Granger told me that the Americans are fighting just outside of Brest and that they have reached the Loire.

La Roque told Reynaud that he has learned from a very reliable source that the Germans have decided that whatever happens, neither Reynaud, Weygand, nor I is to be harmed. I find it all quite amusing. How people reveal their true selves in times like these! To my mind, given the cataclysm that is now imminent, I can't imagine how our lives could be spared. But what does that matter, if Nazism is destroyed.

August 15, 1944

The Anglo-Saxons landed between Toulon and Cannes this morning.

August 19, 1944

The German Army has met disaster in Normandy, as a result of the overwhelming superiority of Allied air power. This is precisely the reverse of the situation in the spring of 1940. Similar causes have produced similar effects.

The German Seventh Army is almost entirely encircled in a pocket around Falaise. They are trying to break out.

The coastal fortifications in Provence were no more successful at stopping the Allies than the Atlantic Wall.

De Lattre de Tassigny is making his way up the Rhone Valley. Little by little, Marseilles, Toulon, and Hyères have been turned and outflanked.

August 20, 1944

It has been a wonderful sun-filled day, but in Paris patriots are battling with the Germans. Images flash through my mind of the Paris I saw on March 31, the skeptical Paris just before the war, and the working-class Paris, once so antimilitaristic. So many strangely different looks in the space of a few years, each of which has proven equivalent to centuries.

August 21, 1944

In the Vaucluse, Perthuis has been liberated.

The Resistance has taken control of Vichy; I heard it on the radio. Their playing the "Marche Lorraine" is a little much. There was a speech on the peacetime organization of France. It sounded like Cassin's[23] voice. Laval's Cabinet is apparently in Belfort. There hasn't been a word about Pétain. What a way to end a life.

August 22, 1944

The noose around Paris is tightening. The Allies have taken 50,000 prisoners in Normandy and 15,000 in Provence. What would happen if the Allies were to mount a drive on France's eastern border?

Toulon, Hyères, Bandol, and La Ciotat—towns that bring back memories of various periods of my life—have all been liberated.

Bouisson[24] was taken prisoner by the Resistance forces in his villa in Saint-Raphaël. The radio broadcast claimed that he had confessed to receiving 30,000 francs a month from the Germans. How strangely naïve of him, and how implausible it seems for a man as cynical as he. His role in gross cases of corruption did terrible damage, as did the petty insolence he displayed as President of the Chamber of Deputies and his obsequiousness

---

23. René Cassin (1887–1976) joined de Gaulle at the time of the Armistice. He was a member of the Consultative Assembly in Algiers in 1944.

24. Fernand Bouisson, industrialist, Socialist Deputy, and President of the Chamber of Deputies from 1927 to 1935. He was Prime Minister for seven days in 1935. He sided with Marshal Pétain in June 1940 and voted in favor of granting him plenary powers.

toward those who held power. Few men have done as much as he and Tardieu (both of whom were seconded by Laval) to bring about the decline and discredit of parliamentary government. He was very close to Laval and played a thoroughly despicable role at the National Assembly in Vichy. "I want the names of everyone who has abstained to be published in the *Journal officiel*," he is reported to have said. What surprises me most is that he decided to wait out the storm in Saint-Raphaël. What delusions could he have had about the hatred the Communists have for him, not to mention the contempt he has inspired in every loyal patriot for so long now?

August 23, 1944

Paris has been liberated after three days of street fighting led by the French Forces of the Interior. Ordinary policemen have taken over the Prefecture. Jouhaux claims the Commune is having its revenge, and there's some truth in that. This will go down as one of the great dates in French history.

August 25, 1944

Leclerc's division has marched into Paris.

August 26, 1944

Cavaillon, Avignon, Carpentras, and Orange have been liberated; I have put on my Sunday clothes. De Gaulle gave an excellent speech.

August 29, 1944

Following the arrests of Taittinger and Paris's city councilmen, Sacha Guitry, Stéphane Lauzanne, and Carcopino are now behind bars as well.

September 1, 1944

Five years from the day the Germans marched on Poland. In spite of the appeals being made by the insurgent Polish forces in Warsaw and the Poles now in England, the Russians have done nothing to supply them with weapons, ammunition, or food, although they are just a few miles away.

For me, today marks the anniversary of Verdun. My thoughts go back to the fighting in 1916. In Verdun, even though we were pounded by the bombings, we were able to crawl out of our holes and repel their attacks. What a monstrous bloodbath it was.

September 3, 1944

Five years to the day I declared war on Germany. Cause for meditation.

September 4, 1944

At 8 A.M. Gamelin came into my room to bring me news of the American advance, news I had already heard the night before. Then he switched to the arrests and shouted, "What they're doing there is stupid because we are the ones who are going to pay for it." Now there is a cry straight from the heart!

The Germans won't be able to hold out more than a few weeks longer. They have turned to challenge the Allies too late, like a boar who has already lost too much blood. Which means that the second half of the great human tragedy is about to get under way. Who will win out? The authoritarian approach to organizing a society, Moloch's cruel and unfeeling new State, or men who are free but disciplined? We're into one more round of Athens versus Sparta, Rome versus Carthage, the great confrontation that has taken on a look of the eternal. Will we see an authoritarian state ruling over enslaved men or a land of the free? The latter is worth dying for.

September 5, 1944

Rumor has it that the Nazi leaders have taken refuge in Madrid.

September 6, 1944

Now it's de Gaulle who is being compared to Joan of Arc on every radio station. Not a word about Pétain. There are more and more arrests. Maurras is behind bars.

September 15, 1944

The Russians have finally decided to help the Warsaw insurgents.

Brazzaville radio has been abject in commenting on Maurras's arrest. They had the nerve to say that the Third Republic should have outlawed L'Action Française!

A warrant has been issued for Pétain's arrest.

September 17, 1944

London is celebrating the fourth anniversary of the RAF's victory over the Luftwaffe. In 1939, I thought that the British Air Force and, above all, their fighters were very powerful. But what does one make of Vuillemin's extraordinary inability to do anything during the Battle of France?

September 18, 1944

Baudouin (enthroned by Reynaud) played a decisive role in the surrender in Bordeaux; they were all at his house when the decision was first made. He betrayed his own Prime Minister in the very midst of the fighting; he glorified Pétain on the radio, and Pétain kept him on as Minister, relieving him simply of his position as Chief Executive Officer of the Indochina Bank. It's interesting to compare his fate with that of Carcopino, who has been arrested.

September 19, 1944

Some people in Itter would like to see a new Treaty of Westphalia, but a pact like that could work only if we went back to the demographics of the time, when France had the largest population of any country in Europe, twice that of Germany. It's absurd to imagine France annexing the Saar Valley and the left bank of the Rhine. Today, there is a strong sense of national unity in Germany. Moreover, a Germany broken up into small pieces would run the risk of being sovietized. We would see Russia's domination spread throughout Europe. Stalin would succeed where Hitler has failed. A federated German nation is not inconceivable.

September 24, 1944

Le Roy Ladurie and Worms[25] have been arrested. Now we have reached the inner circle of plotters. I think that prior to the war, out of their hatred or fear of communism—which, as of late 1938, no longer posed any sort of threat at all—these two men were laying the political groundwork within France for an alliance with Germany. They wanted to install a regime grounded in Nazism. And of course they were prepared to leave Germany free to reign over Central and Eastern Europe. I am convinced that their group—Le Roy Ladurie, Worms, Lémery, Alibert, Brécard, Loustanau-Lacau, which is to say Pétain, and some adviser from a line of Protestant emigrants with a French-sounding name that I can't remember—was working in close contact with the German Embassy. The war offered them a magnificent opportunity, "a divine surprise." Pétain wanted an armistice immediately, as early as May 19, and Weygand by May 25. The Worms group had links with the Synarchie—Bouthillier, Devaux,[26] Leca,[27] and Baudouin—as well as with people in Reynaud's entourage, who trusted them. These weren't traitors in the ordinary, traditional sense, but rather men eager to accept defeat. Emigrés in their own land.

Needless to say, Dormoy and after him Sarraut knew nothing and did nothing about any of this. In the time since the end of the other war, with the sole exception of Schrameck,[28] France has never had a real Minister of the Interior.

---

25. Hippolyte Worms, Director of the Worms conglomerate: banking, munitions, and brokerage. He was a Pétainist in Vichy, a collaborator in Paris, and a Gaullist in London.

26. Gilbert Devaux, Finance Inspector and Assistant Director of Public Accounting. He was Paul Reynaud's Deputy Chief of Staff.

27. Dominique Leca, Finance Inspector. He was twice Reynaud's Chief of Staff, first in the Finance Ministry (1938), then when Reynaud became Prime Minister.

28. Abraham Schrameck, Senator and Minister, first of Justice and later of the Interior (1925). When Ernest Berger was killed, Schrameck began legal proceedings against Charles Maurras, who had made death threats against Berger. In Vichy, in 1940, Schrameck voted in favor of granting Pétain plenary powers.

September 25, 1944

For the last few days, snow has begun covering the top half of the mountains. The cows have moved back down from the elevated pastures to the plains. I now hear cow bells jangling in the night. It makes me think I am back in Provence.

In Holland, the Germans have launched a counterattack against a British airborne division in Arnhem. The British have put up stubborn resistance west of the Rhine, between Aix and Cologne, and along the Moselle, in the gap at Belfort.

Fierce fighting continues in Warsaw.

September 29, 1944

Churchill made an important speech in the House of Commons: "I have not forgotten that the promise of aid that Britain and America made to France in 1919, which led France to give up its demand for a border on the Rhine, was not ratified by the American Senate, and that peace failed as a result. I know that France, with her small and declining population, stood across from a powerful neighbor.

"In the course of the twenty years that followed the first war, my opinion regarding the vital necessity of maintaining the alliance that unites France and England never wavered."

October 2, 1944

Resistance in Warsaw has ceased. The city is being evacuated. Having been abandoned by the Russians and having had terrible difficulty establishing links with the British, the decimated insurgent groups have given up the fight. The repercussions felt in the United States and Britain will be painful. General Bor has been taken prisoner.

October 7, 1944

I watched the SS go rushing about the "castle." Red flares went off. It was all either preparation to ward off a commando raid or a positioning exercise in anticipation of an attack from the village or from down in the valley.

The maneuvers lasted two hours, and enlisted men and officers alike went through them in dead seriousness.

Peyrouton, Flandin, and Bergeret have been indicted for treason.

October 9, 1944

The Dumbarton Oaks conference has ended with the creation of an organization for international security: the United Nations. It will feature a Security Council with five permanent members, one of which will be France. Resolutions will require a two-thirds majority. The organization will have at its command a military air force as well as a sort of council made up of the head military leaders of various nations. ... In short, after thirty years of mistakes and debates and after another world war, the ideas Léon Bourgeois promoted as France's representative in 1918 have finally won out. If the Anglo-Saxons had adopted them in 1919, the fate of the world would not have been the same.

The present war marks the end of a period of history that began in 1792—the era of independent nations. Nations will now have to be integrated into federations and, above all, vast economic systems. The well-being of the masses will have to be assured. The partitioning of Germany, which certain Britons and Americans have been talking about, is an absurd proposition. Once the war is over, the Anglo-Saxons will be anxious to demobilize. England has already called back its miners and many of the workers in its major industries. We can't be drawn into playing the role of world gendarmes.

October 11, 1944

In a recent speech, Goebbels was remarkably effective in turning to his advantage various articles and statements calling for the Allies to flatten Germany, apportion its territory, occupy it up to the Elbe in the East and the Rhine in the West, and deport millions of its workers.

I have seen a great many trains go by the last few days, but they are often pulled by steam-powered locomotives.

October 14, 1944

In a radio broadcast, de Gaulle hammered away at the same themes we heard in Nancy, Lille, and Rouen. He appealed to everyone to keep working; the war isn't over yet. He appealed to people's sense of discipline. He was trying to reach the more committed members of the Resistance and above all obtain the support of people in the middle. The truth is that a choice will have to be made between furthering the cause of a social revolution or putting an end to it. Probably the only thing de Gaulle can do right now is evade the issue.

For example, with regard to the way the various parties will be represented in a broadened Consultative Assembly, there is talk of using a sort of proportional system: seven Communists, fifteen Socialists, twenty-three Radicals and Christian Democrats. Why the strange coupling of Radicals and Christian Democrats? And why weren't seats allotted to every Member of Parliament who voted against Pétain or abstained? This all smells of backroom deals, and history shows that machinations of this kind have a short life span. Just look at the *Directoire*.

As for the reality of our situation here, it was brought home to us by the Captain. He told us that any prisoner attempting to escape during an air raid would be shot.

October 17, 1944

Twenty-four new SS and three NCOs showed up, carrying machine guns and ammunition. They dug trenches around the "castle" and positioned their weapons. Then they established visual communications with the garrison in Wörgl, about two or three miles from here as the crow flies, where an SS battalion is stationed. Everything was done with speed and discipline. Do they fear an Anglo-Saxon commando raid or an insurrection from the Tirol?

In this autumn season, there remains the contrast with the beauty of nature: the gold of the maple trees and the birches amid the darker colors of the pines, all of it enveloped in a light mist. There is a magnificent maple tree just beneath my window. The snow has begun to cover the lower parts of the mountains. Soon, it will blanket the "castle" and its courtyards. Another winter to be spent here.

October 19, 1944

The trade union convention and the speeches made by Morgenthau and Cripps have strengthened the Nazis' grip on their people and firmed the nation's resolve. They have got the Germans convinced that their cities will all be destroyed and that they're going to be deported. Yet Stalin handled Romania and Bulgaria so skillfully.

October 20, 1944

The Captain got drunk tonight. He threatened the Czech cook, telling him that he'd be the first to get it and that we'd be next in line. Instead of a cooked meal, he made him serve us tiny bits of meat and leeks, a portion of rubbery paté, and a few dried-out potatoes.

October 21, 1944

It has been reported that on his trip to Moscow, Churchill agreed that henceforth the Soviet Union would control certain areas once under French influence: Romania, Greece, Poland, Yugoslavia, etc. This agreement has to be seen in the light of the one Churchill worked out with Belgium and Holland.

October 22, 1944

A delegation including Vincent Auriol went to see Jeanneney to protest the highly unusual methods he had used to exclude from the Consultative Assembly certain Members of Parliament who had voted against Pétain in Vichy. I'd be interested to hear what Jeanneney had to say, he *not* being one of those who voted against Pétain.

October 25, 1944

De Gaulle has been complaining in the Paris press that the Allies have failed to give the French the amounts and kinds of weapons they need to wipe out the remaining pockets of German resistance. He is right. The situation is paradoxical. There are still 60,000 Germans in Lorient, La Pallice, and Le Verdon.

The Cabinet has decided to grant Algerians the same rights enjoyed by French citizens living in Algeria. That reminds me of Proudhon's well-known comments from 1848 about according universal suffrage to Frenchmen. There are 900,000 French citizens and 7 million native Algerians. Of course, the French there have always opposed reforms every step of the way. These are just stalling measures, not real progress.

October 27, 1944

All around me, I have been watching the SS hurriedly work to reinforce their defenses, setting up machine gun nests and felling trees to block the routes leading up to the "castle." There have been practice alerts. The Captain informed us that they would be using two different alarms: one to signal aerial bombings—in which case it would be up to us to decide whether to take shelter in the cellars, with the understanding that if we didn't, it would be at our own risk—and another to signal a ground attack—in which case we could either go down to the cellars of our own accord or be taken there by force.

October 28, 1944

Roosevelt has announced a major naval victory and a successful landing in the Philippines. A few days ago, Churchill decided to send part of the British fleet to operate in conjunction with the United States in the Pacific, against Japan. Shows the importance of Asia. De Gaulle has issued an order for the creation of a volunteer force for the liberation of Indochina.

November 2, 1944

All Souls' Day. Soon I too will be in Père Lachaise, resting in peace. The Captain has taken away our radio to stop us from listening to short wave broadcasts. Now we'll only be able to get German stations.

November 5, 1944

Reynaud was visited by the fat German girl who used to be his reader. They had lunch together with Mlle Mabire, who was not entirely thrilled about it. Later, we watched them stroll by: Reynaud, with a woman on each arm, and Gamelin solemnly bringing up the rear, as the Germans looked on and chuckled. They repeated their laughable performance later in the afternoon.

November 7, 1944

Gertrude is a prisoner working in the "castle." She has just received a letter from her lawyer informing her of her release, scheduled for mid-November. The poor girl is delighted, but she is sensitive enough to hide it so as not to depress those around her who haven't been so fortunate. Gertrude hopes to go back to Leipzig and move as close to Weimar as she can, to be near her French boyfriend, who is a prisoner there.

The Germans continue to stage military operations to defend the "castle." Now they are busy fighting off paratroopers camouflaged with tree branches, sneaking in through the ravines.

November 10, 1944

Churchill and Eden continue to repeat mechanically their pat phrase demanding Germany's unconditional surrender. Yet even now the Allies are giving refuge to Germans who used to run the country; these men could govern the country again. In his dealings with Finland, Romania, and Bulgaria, Stalin gave them an expert lesson in subtle diplomacy—and what a lesson it was! Are we witnessing the intellectual decline of Britain's ruling class and the Foreign Office?

November 21, 1944

A major French victory: The French have reached the Rhine. Eisenhower has sent congratulatory telegrams. The Americans have broken through twenty-five miles of the Siegfried Line in an area around Cologne. Gertrude, who is still here, said to me, "It is terrible to find yourself rejoicing over the misfortunes of your own country."

November 23, 1944

The French have entered Strasbourg.

November 28, 1944

De Gaulle has arrived in Moscow with Bidault and Palewski. He has begun talks on a Franco-Soviet pact and participated in others dealing with the breakup of Germany. He is distancing himself from the British.

November 29, 1944

I dreamed a great deal about my son Jean last night.

There has been street fighting in Brussels. The Communists have been demonstrating against Pierlot, who has demanded that they turn in their weapons.

December 4, 1944

According to Paris Radio, Germany, acting through Switzerland, informed the French government that the lives of French hostages held in Germany would be directly linked to the fate of the collaborators in France.

The Russians have reached Lake Balaton.

December 6, 1944

Last night, Churchill spoke to the House of Commons about the events unfolding in Greece. The Communists have taken a number of steps designed to bring them to power: organizing general strikes, attacking and taking over police stations, preventing trucks and boats from unloading food supplies, and so on. Churchill declared that Greece must move forward with a general election under fair conditions, and that until such time, Britain would unflinchingly assume the burden of maintaining stability. He added, "Left-wing elements and the Communists are responsible for the bloodlettings."

December 8, 1944

Following Churchill's speech on the events in Greece, his government was forced to call a vote of confidence. He won out, with 270 in favor and 30 opposed, but the majority of the Labor Party members abstained, which is a good indication of the extent to which the policy of improved relations and cooperation with Moscow has gained in popularity.

As for the Americans, they have ruled out any form of intervention in the internal affairs of Greece.

December 11, 1944

A moving ceremony, chaired by Joliot-Curie, was held at the Sorbonne to commemorate the role played by intellectuals who had given their lives. The American press, above all the *New York Times*, has been just as enthusiastic as yesterday's *Times* over the Franco-Soviet military alliance and the mutual aid agreements that have just been signed. They see them as a complement to the pact between Britain and the Soviet Union—a guarantee against future German acts of aggression that is in perfect harmony with the goals of a broader, international peace organization.

Whatever the case, there has been a change in the Anglo-Saxon attitude toward France, so it's just as well. Now they will probably indulge us a little more when we ask for ships, tools, and supplies. I read an excerpt from an article in which Lippmann, who had just returned from Europe, paid homage to the people of France. The fellow has improved a little. Others will begin changing their tune as well. No one is saying what General Smuts said a few years ago, that France was a second-rate nation with no influence. We have once again become, in Churchill words, "one of the world's leading powers."

Still, it's Greece that has really been drawing my attention. The Communists have taken over the greater part of Athens and said that they will not lay down their arms until Papandreou resigns. There is talk of 10,000 armed Communists in Athens.

At the Labor Party convention, Bevin staunchly defended Churchill's policies. "You don't govern with sentiment." They deem the situation in Greece intolerable. The Communists signed an agreement, then went back on it. The leadership of a country cannot be left in the hands of a bunch of armed men. Greece is effectively our first test.

December 14, 1944

On his return from Europe, Walter Lippmann wrote a long article in New York sharply criticizing Churchill's policies with regard to Greece and Belgium. As is his wont, he also offered a little instructive advice to Europeans and every government around. I find his tone highly objectionable. He added, "The governments in power in 1939 failed in their duty to defend the independence of nations." Another prime example of American impertinence. Why didn't the Americans intervene in September 1939 or June 1940 instead of waiting to be attacked by the Japanese? Of course, at the time, isolationism was a virtue. Actually, elections should have been held immediately in every liberated country. Lippmann is sarcastic in belittling the growing influence of communism throughout Europe. A few months from now, he will be able to measure the validity of the theories he expressed, with his usual conceit, in 1943. He still hasn't understood that at this very moment a powerful movement is at work, drawing Europe toward communism.

December 17, 1944

The terms of the Franco-Soviet pact have been made public. There is the standard phrasing one finds in all mutual aid pacts, but it also includes a twenty-year military alliance, similar to the one with Great Britain. They have agreed to counter any German attempt to extract revenge, or even any semblance of such an attempt, which is to say that they reserve the right to intervene in the makeup of future German governments. So as to avoid the appearance of a bilateral treaty, they have chosen their words carefully and made constant reference to the United Nations. Even so, there is also an unusual clause, the fifth or sixth one, that prohibits both countries from entering alliances formed against either of them. That can hardly benefit anyone other than the Russians. What kind of coalition could conceivably threaten them in the future, and for what reason? They must have in mind a coalition including Britain or the United States, or even both of them, that might be formed in the event of some serious conflict in Asia. Russia can hardly be considered vulnerable other than from within Europe, where an Anglo-German-French coalition could pose a serious threat. Is this clause the work of a highly cautious man or is it an indication of Russia's political designs over China? Doesn't the wording suggest that there are secret appendixes? It certainly seems strange that so brief a document required de Gaulle to spend all that time in Moscow, engaged in lengthy negotiations. There are probably secret agreements about the Rhineland, the Saar Valley, eastern Prussia, Poland, and perhaps the Dardanelles and the Balkans.

I have just this moment heard that the Germans have broken through the Allied lines south of Aix-la-Chapelle and driven fifteen miles forward, in a wedge twenty miles wide. They have moved into Belgium and Luxembourg. There were violent air battles, in which they are reported to have lost 130 planes.

December 19, 1944

The Germans continue to drive forward. They have moved beyond Stablot in Belgium, which represents an advance of twenty miles, and are supposed to be using new weapons. General de Lattre gave an eloquent speech about the French Army retaking Alsace—a sober, moving speech, elegant in its very simplicity.

Stettinius, the American Secretary of State, has issued a statement about Poland that is pathetically hypocritical. He claimed that the United States never guaranteed any European country's borders. According to him, we would do better to put these matters off until after the war, when they can be taken up in the United Nations. Yet he knows well that Russia has just recognized the Lublin Committee as Poland's sole representative.

In Teheran in 1942, did the British reach agreement with Stalin over Russia's new western borders? In all events, that is what Molotov now claims. The Polish Cabinet in London has refused to enter into any form of agreement with the Lublin Committee.

December 20, 1944

The Senate met in Paris and approved the Franco-Soviet pact by unanimous vote. There was a lot of talk and a lot of enthusiasm, but few direct references to the document itself. As I suspected, the important part is the one that did not appear in the Moscow texts: the agreement over the partitioning of Germany.

Russia's hold will stretch over Central Europe and the Balkans—it will be the greatest sphere of influence on the European continent. Populations will be shifted about as they were in the days of the Pharaohs.

The German offensive that began six days ago into Belgium and Holland has been stopped by the Americans, north and south. Eisenhower's objective: to transform the German offensive into a nightmarish defeat.

At the Radical-Socialist convention, Chautemps, Bonnet, Palmade, and Mistler were excluded from the party.

December 24, 1944

Christmas Eve. Just as they did last week, squadrons of bombers continue making their way to Innsbruck and Munich. There isn't a cloud in the sky.

Several speeches were given tonight, notably one by Roosevelt, but it was the Pope's address to the College of Cardinals that really caught my attention. The text of the speech was given on Swiss radio. The Pope:

1. Offered praise for true democracies but said there were countries whose system of government, although claiming to be democratic, was totally alien to democracy;
2. Condemned dictatorships;
3. Said that while armies were carrying out their work of destruction, men were joining together to lay the foundations for a future peace. He paid homage to the efforts of these men;
4. Recognized that the peace settlement to come would necessarily include war reparations, but said it must not lead to the permanent enslavement of the vanquished peoples, which would run contrary to our efforts to bring justice to the entire world;
5. Recognized the legitimacy of the punishment to be meted out to individuals guilty of criminal acts, but said that there must not be wholesale condemnations of groups.

In its broadcast out of London, the BBC omitted the fourth point and the second part of the first one, in other words, all that might be construed as casting doubt on the democratic nature of the Soviet regime. Who would have believed that the Pope would one day be censored by the BBC?

December 25, 1944

It now appears that the Americans have completely halted the German offensive in the West. I note, however, that after four years of war, and although opposed by an Army of overwhelming superiority, supplied with great amounts of equipment, tanks, and planes, the Germans were nonetheless able to unleash a surprise attack of unexpected violence, over particularly difficult terrain in the Eifel region, and drive the Allies back forty miles in just a few days. The analogy to be drawn with Sedan is obvious. This should put a clamp on the criticism that has been lodged against the French Army, criticism which was particularly bitter in American newspapers under Walter Lippmann's byline.

December 29, 1944

Churchill and Eden have returned. They are going to ask the King of Greece to accept Papandreou's resignation and the institution of an Archbishop-led Regency.

1945

January 2, 1945

We have had even heavier snowfalls; twenty inches of snow blanket the courtyard. A few groups of SS have gone about cutting a narrow path through it, while others have been clearing off the roofs that might otherwise collapse under the weight, all of it accompanied by playful laughter and shouting and horseplay as old as time itself. The sky is clear and the sun is shining on the mountaintops.

The lead-in to the speech was dramatic: All boys sixteen and seventeen years of age are now officially members of the Army; almost all of them enlisted voluntarily. The youth of Germany have long been prepared to make the supreme sacrifice, and now that time has come.

He began speaking. I could barely recognize his voice. It had once been so powerful, so modulated too, as it would alternate in throaty tones between moments of pathos and moments of irony, before culminating with a burst of triumphant fanfare; that forceful voice of his that from town to town, over a period of ten years, won over all of Germany. This evening, that voice revealed fatigue and deep concern. As I listened, I wondered whether it was really his.

He explained that he had not addressed the people of Germany since the attempt made on his life on July 20 because all his energies had been devoted to organizing the military campaign. "During this past summer, we altered the course of fate." He reminded his listeners of what he had said at the Reichstag on September 1, 1939: Germany will *not* be defeated. The Allies had predicted that the war would end this winter; they had even worked out details for the partitioning of Germany; that was because they don't know what Germans are made of. "We are prepared to make every effort necessary; we shall never surrender," he said, indulging in some predictions of his own. And as is the case with all oracles, this one invites comment, too. I actually do not believe that Hitler will ever surrender. He will either die leading his last remaining troops in battle or put an end to his own life. He won't bring dishonor on himself by taking flight, as William II did.

He went on to lash out at the Allies' tactics—the bombing of cities, the coldly conceived, premeditated massacre of women and children, intended to break down the morale of the country and its fighting men. He reviewed the casualty figures, and he could not hide the fact, he said, that they had made a powerful impact on him, too. But German industry is continually producing new weapons, he said. Their new fighter planes have firepower and fly at speeds heretofore unknown. Then he unleashed a resounding condemnation of the free enterprise system and glorified the new, egalitarian state that would demand sacrifices of the German people and necessitate further suffering. Finally he launched into his grand conclusion, but what a disappointment it was! Belief in miracles and faith in God Almighty, who would bring victory to "those who deserve it most" by virtue of the purity and dignity of their sentiments and their thoughts. The people of Germany will reshape the world. The speech lasted all of twenty-five minutes.

He concluded his program of operations for the military with a similar appeal to God Almighty: "We are fighting now for the very existence of the German people. The Jews and the plutocrats are seeking to wipe our country off the map, by reducing us to slaves and sending 15 to 20 million Germans to Siberia, and by making our western provinces part of France and our eastern provinces part of a sovietized Poland. Morgenthau, that Jew who is Roosevelt's Secretary of the Treasury, actually wants to destroy Germany's industry. ... Their monstrous plans stand as justification for everything I have done.

"The fighting will become more and more intense. The setbacks we have suffered are the result of a series of betrayals and the collapse of the Italian-Hungarian front on the Don in 1942. The July 20 attempt on my life marks a turning point. That conspiracy will be the last. There will never be another November 9. ... Our enemies would do well to understand that they will pay for every inch of German soil with torrents of blood. ... I have never been as confident as I am now." Then he threatened to annihilate anyone within Germany who attempted to weaken or undermine the magnificent resistance of the German people. He followed that once more by an appeal to divine Providence.

All of Germany was listening tonight—the soldiers on the front lines, the old men and the women in the ruins of their bombed-out cities, the peasants in their peaceful villages or in their isolated farmhouses. For six months they had been waiting—first in stunned impatience, then with a kind of anxiety—for word from the man who had so frequently brought them news of victories, those won in the fight against unemployment and the war on poverty, and those of the Reich's triumphant entrance into capital after capital of the nations of Europe.

Rumors had been spreading that Hitler was paralyzed or dead. He had to go on the air, but the voice that the people had been waiting to hear for so long had changed; it was almost a monotone. He brought them not one single reason to hope.

To be sure, the German Army will fight on heroically, as long as their leaders choose to lead them into battle. But on this the first night of the new year, are there not among them, and among the leaders of Germany's economy as well, some who are wondering whether the moment hasn't come for Germany to follow a different path, not the road to death and despair that Hitler has just laid out for them?

Before listening to Hitler's speech, I picked up some news items. A committee of Polish Communists, most of whom had been living in Moscow for quite a while and who had returned to Poland with the Soviet Army, has just set itself up in Lublin as the country's provisional government. A Polish newspaper printed in London, the organ of the Peasant Party, has protested both against Russia's annexation of Lvov, Poland's great industrial center, and the fact that armies of a foreign power have established a government without the Polish people having spoken. They called for a free and independent Poland. The Polish government-in-exile in London has also protested. The British, however, have remained silent, whereas France has gone as far as to assign this provisional government, if not an official Ambassador, an Observer, which amounts practically to the same thing. It has been the subject of scandal in many British newspapers, where de Gaulle and his government have come under sharp attack. The United States has not recognized the government in Lublin, but that has not kept the people in power there from routinely going about their work. After having expressed their gratitude to the Russians—which was only natural—and labeled the Polish émigrés in London Fascists—which was inevitable—they have begun dividing up large estates among poor peasant farmers—which is far more serious.

Saturday, January 6, 1945

Last night, I listened to the Swiss journalist René Payot's weekly program on political and military events. He spoke about France as if he held some veiled official capacity. Gamelin told me that in 1940 and later as well, *Le Journal de Genève* ran a number of Payot's articles on the military that, without ever naming Gamelin, were clearly indictments of him. Through mutual friends, Gamelin provided Payot with documents that proved that the figures he had been using were erroneous. Payot refused to give them credence, saying only that he had got *his* figures from General Weygand. Now he has a job as a Gaullist propagandist in French-speaking Switzerland.

Payot praised statements made by de Gaulle at a recent session of the Consultative Assembly. Another speaker there had attacked Jeanneney for having supported the naming of Marshal Pétain as Prime Minister in Bordeaux, at the most dramatic moment of our nation's history. The speaker attacked Jeanneney further for having later praised Pétain on the Senate floor in Vichy, and for having matter-of-factly chaired the National Assembly session and personally called for the vote, without voicing the slightest objection, that gave Pétain plenary powers and allowed him to destroy the Republic. In covering for the former President of the Senate, who has since been named one of his Junior Ministers, General de Gaulle maintained that in June 1940 there were several different views of what the best interests of the country entailed. Given the Army's refusal to continue the fight from North Africa, suing for an armistice was a legitimate option. In every one of his previous speeches, de Gaulle had been saying exactly the opposite.

Tuesday, January 9, 1945

Over the last few days, the situation in Alsace has become one of great concern. The Americans have been drawing off units from the Saar Valley, in all likelihood to support their slowly progressing counterattack in the Ardennes. The Germans have taken advantage of the situation and gone on the offensive; they are now threatening Strasbourg. They have crossed the Rhine to the south of the city and are only fifteen miles away. The news has left France terribly shaken.

Vladimir d'Ormesson,[1] writing in *Le Figaro*, and Paul Bastid,[2] in *L'Aurore*, among others, have been reminding people that the war is not over yet, and that all our efforts must be subordinated to the work of liberating the country. But what can France do if the Allies won't arm and equip French soldiers? How is it possible for them not to want to make forty French divisions battle ready? If Strasbourg were to be lost again, it would be a national disaster.

The Polish government in London has protested the methods it claims are being used by the Communist government in Lublin: the tyranny of a police state, the suppression of all democratic freedoms, and, behind the lies proffered for the press and the international community, the institution of a despotic reign of terror. The Lublin government has retorted by issuing a decree stripping "the Fascist leaders of the expatriate government" of their Polish nationality. The Poles are fighting among themselves amid the ruins of their homeland. It is a terribly sad story for all of us who admire the courage and patriotism of this martyred people, who truly appear to be victims of fate.

How is one to know what is best for them? Only truly free elections, jointly organized by the three major powers with all the necessary guarantees, could have allowed the Polish people to express their preferences.

---

1. Vladimir d'Ormesson, conservative journalist, named Ambassador to the Vatican in 1940 but dismissed by Vichy. He was named Ambassador to Buenos Aires in 1945 and to the Vatican in 1948.

2. Paul Bastid, lawyer, Deputy from the Cantal, and Commerce Minister in Léon Blum's government in 1936. He was a member of the National Resistance Council in 1943–1944. Editor in Chief of *L'Aurore*.

Most likely, a coalition government would have emerged. But for at least the last two years, Great Britain, clearly, and the United States, apparently, have abandoned Poland to the powerful sphere of Soviet influence and allowed it to be reduced to a veritable protectorate. With the dictatorship of the proletariat and the physical destruction of the middle class, we shall soon be told once again that "order reigns in Warsaw."

Thursday, January 18, 1945

Last Sunday, January 14, the Russians began mounting another formidable offensive along a front 250 miles long, stretching from eastern Prussia to Silesia. If you include the men still involved in the siege of Budapest, that would make 5 million men, organized into seven separate armies, marching from the Baltic to the Danube. I am now convinced that the war will come to an end this year, perhaps before winter.

More and more, Germany's leaders have resorted to terror as a means of governing the people. In Vienna, the Gestapo is supposed to have fired on factory workers demonstrating against the decision to remove machines from Austria and send them to Germany. During their retreat from Poland, the Germans summarily executed civil servants. And last Friday, in an act of unprecedented cruelty, five Frenchmen were shot, in retaliation for the execution of collaborators in Alsace and elsewhere in France. German radio stated that there would be similar acts of reprisal as long as the execution of collaborators continued. On Tuesday, Algiers radio replied that "the work of French justice would not be delayed." Isn't this absurd? Are French patriots currently held by the Germans going to die because French traitors are being sentenced to death? Is that what justice demands? Of course not. This is just one more reason, and there are a great many of them, for postponing the greater number of these trials until the end of the war, when they can be held in official, legally constituted courtrooms, after calm and order have been restored.

At a time when present circumstances have nothing in common with those that France faced in 1793, there is far more urgent work to be done than this parody of a revolutionary tribunal. They might as well make executions public again! I am surprised that certain former deserters haven't been demanding it.

Churchill gave an excellent speech to the House of Commons. He re-iterated the Allies' demand for an unconditional surrender, but, he added, "We are not monsters and we have no intention of destroying Germany or enslaving its people." I am absolutely convinced that if the German people had a clear idea of the conditions under which the Allies were prepared to make peace, unrest might very well break out within Germany. Obviously, they have to be anticipating terribly exacting conditions. Still the phrase "unconditional surrender" is too humiliating and too vague. It has allowed Nazi propaganda to raise the specter of the total destruction of the coun-try, to refer constantly to the Jews' desire to annihilate the Germans, and to maintain, unopposed, that there is no other way out for Germany than to defend itself desperately, to the bitter end. Death is to be preferred to the slow, agonizing tortures to which the Allies are preparing to subject them. Churchill was absolutely right to say what he did. The term "uncon-ditional surrender" doesn't really mean anything.

From the details Churchill provided about England's contribution to the war effort, there would seem to have been only sixty-seven divisions of British soldiers engaged in combat on all fronts combined. In 1918, there were sixty-two divisions just on the front lines in France. Now in 1945, there must be ten British divisions in India, twenty or so in Italy, and five or six in the Middle East, which would leave only thirty divisions fighting in France, not counting, obviously, Canadian troops.

To be sure, these figures reflect only their ground forces; the numbers of men engaged in action in their Air Force and Navy are surely quite high. Nonetheless, it is highly unlikely that the British and Americans can mount and sustain a major offensive in the West without increasing their numbers significantly. As of now, there are probably no more than 100 divisions in all. In 1940, France alone had 110 divisions in action. British losses would appear to be similar to those of the Americans: 300,000 wounded, 57,000 dead. It is clearly the Russians who have suffered the heaviest casualties, with numbers beyond comparison with those of the Allies.

Saturday, January 20, 1945

It was extremely difficult to bring in anything on the radio today. Fortu-nately, I had two copies of *Das Reich*, from December 24 and 31. I know of no European political weekly that is as lively, as diversified, or as well documented about international affairs. Obviously, its function as a tool for spreading Nazi propaganda has to be kept in mind, but even with that, I always find it extremely interesting. In these two issues, Goebbels examines the passivity with which Churchill and Roosevelt have gradually allowed Stalin to achieve the domination of Europe, not to mention Poland, Romania, Bulgaria, Yugoslavia, and Czechoslovakia, which are just so many more or less—and generally not very—disguised Russian protectorates. The pressure being exerted by the Bolsheviks is increasingly strong, even in countries liberated by the Allies.

The Anglo-Saxons had hoped to use Russia to bring down Germany, but Germany's downfall has effectively led to the triumph of the Soviets in Europe. The Franco-Soviet agreement totally nullifies the pact among Western nations that England had been seeking. Even if victorious, Great Britain will be reduced to a second-rate power. Of course Dr. Goebbels has yet to explain why Germany entered into an agreement with the Bolsheviks on August 23, 1939.

Wednesday, January 24, 1945

They are fighting in the suburbs of Posen. The Russians are now only 150 miles outside of Berlin.

Thus, in one of those dramatic reversals of which history offers so many examples, the Slavs are invading the vast eastern plains that had for centuries been subjected to callous and implacable German colonization. We have entered that period of history that Renan had predicted in letters written to his "master" Strauss, during the war of 1870. East of the Elbe, and even more so east of the Oder, one still finds Slavic place names, typically Slavic settlements, with their characteristic villages organized around a large circular plaza lined with houses opening directly onto the fields, and large estates, all of them spoils of Germanic conquests. There can be no doubt that the Russian and Polish Slavs will divide eastern Prussia among themselves or that the new Polish nation, Russia's western outpost, will occupy territories stretching westward up to the Oder, and the ethnic Germans living there will be forced to leave their homes and settle in a defeated, dismembered Germany. For geographers, the Oder has always marked the border separating the two Germanys: one to the west with deciduous trees, one to the east with evergreens; one with small farms, one with the huge estates of country squires; the Germany of the ethnically pure and the other Germany in which, in spite of repeated conquests and domination, Slavic islands attached to the *Lander* have survived intact. Nothing will remain of the achievements of the Knights of the Teutonic Order, or of the accomplishments of the great Margraves of Brandenburg, whose statues are still traditionally visited by the schoolchildren of Berlin, where they line one of the principal paths in the Tiergarten.

The day before yesterday, the Germans reported that after they took the bodies of Marshal Hindenburg and his wife to Berlin from the crypt of the monument in Tannenberg where the two lay, they destroyed this grandiose memorial to Hindenburg's victory over the Russians in 1914 and the liberation of eastern Prussia. The news of that destruction will echo painfully in the hearts of the German people. It marks the end of a great period of both German and European history. After centuries of the Germanic race's expansion toward the East, after centuries of accumulating wealth and glory, the hour of the Slavic expansion toward the west is at hand. It won't be long before Moscow's soldiers come marching into Berlin, but this time the period of military occupation will be a long one.

The Germans are withdrawing in the West, too, driven back by the American counteroffensive. They have been forced to give up the territory they had won back in the Ardennes. Obviously, this is nothing like the generalized, precipitous retreat in the East. West of the Rhine, which remains a formidable barrier, the Germans have retained the vast fortified zone incorrectly called the Siegfried Line.

To break through these powerful fortifications, or to neutralize and move beyond them, the Allies will have to commit greater numbers of men and matériel. They apparently thought last summer that the Germans were exhausted and prepared to lay down their arms. The Americans then mounted a powerful offensive in the Pacific, against Japan. They won't be able to launch a general offensive on all fronts until next spring, and it alone can bring Germany to surrender.

Heard quite a bit about France this evening; unfortunately all the news is sad. France is suffering from hunger and cold and cruel deprivation.

There are more than half a million unemployed in France and more than a million people reduced to part-time work, even though 2 million Frenchmen, the youngest and the hardiest, are either prisoners or workers in Germany. In this major crisis, which has spared no one, gravest of all is the almost total absence of virtually every means of transportation. The winter has been harsh, but coal remains piled in the mine shafts because there are neither locomotives nor coal cars to transport it. Similarly, agricultural regions are finding great difficulty shipping their produce to urban centers where people are starving. But what can the Ministers who are being criticized be expected to do? Or the prefects who are being blamed, or the civil servants who are being taken to task, given the almost total lack of locomotives and railroad cars? It seems to me that all our efforts should be aimed at obtaining some from the Americans and the British, whatever the cost. This is not the time, to say the least, for the political controversies we so often get embroiled in with them.

The efforts to supply food and fuel have generated considerable criticism, but judging from press releases and the debates in the Consultative Assembly, apparently not so much as what has been called "the foot-dragging in the purges." François de Menthon[3] has come under attack a number of times. He has been accused, if not quite of being overly indulgent, of being a "moderate," although judging from his speeches, he sees himself as a direct descendant of the uncompromising likes of Fouquier-Tinville. In the Consultative Assembly, they have made no effort to temper their expressions of displeasure. They find him timid and lazy in meting out justice and characterize him as a man who simply goes by the book. Yet it doesn't seem to me that the fellows on the firing squads have been especially affected by the general crisis in unemployment.

---

3. François de Menthon, who had left France to join forces with de Gaulle, was the French Committee of National Liberation's Commissioner of Justice and then Minister of Justice in 1944. During the purge trials, he proved to be scrupulously conscientious.

On the radio today, they gave out specific figures: Forty thousand people accused of crimes and collaboration with the enemy have been languishing in French prisons for the past several months. Two thousand people have been tried, and 1,800 of them were convicted, including 340 who were sentenced to death. The activities of 20,000 of the people now being held are under investigation. The 114 courts set up specifically to handle purge trials hand down 60 sentences a day. At this rate, it will take two years to bring to trial all the people held, that is, if some of them are not previously released and of course assuming there aren't additional arrests.

Given that timetable, it is understandable that people have grown impatient. But it is equally understandable to hear complaints and objections of violations of basic human rights from men who have been living piled together for months in prison cells or internment camp barracks, without knowing exactly what they have been charged with, without ever having met with the Investigating Magistrate, and at times without there even being an actual case file on them.

Treason is the most abominable of all crimes. Any Frenchman who turned over other Frenchmen to the Gestapo deserves the death penalty. Many of the contemptible traitors who participated in the enslavement and the oppression of their own country have managed to flee to Germany. Some of them have been pointed out to me right here in the towns around Innsbruck, militiamen and "French" (sic) Volunteers Against Bolshevism, who have put their uniforms back on and gone back to spying and informing on people, this time for the Tirolean Gestapo. They have seen to it that some of the poor souls in the camps have ended up facing firing squads. But if they don't return to France after the war, there will be no way to punish them.

Everyone who was able to get out of France before the Liberation did so. In view of that, couldn't we quickly sift through the cases of the 40,000 currently in French prisons and hold over for trial only those who have criminally conspired with the enemy?

Of all our wounds, this is the most painful and the most grievous of all, which is why it should be lanced, without delay, so that the healing process might begin, without delay. It seems to me that the only possible approach is to separate crimes from misdemeanors and quickly mete out punishment for the former even if it means that those guilty of the latter benefit from a relative indulgence. Whatever is decided, it is thoroughly unacceptable for France to allow people to be held in prison without trial.

January 28, 1945

I wouldn't be at all be surprised if the policies the Soviets will soon be implementing were conceived and elaborated long ago. Their plans call for the Red Army to enter Berlin and remain there as an occupying force. They are probably holding a friendly German leadership in reserve. They will set them up in power immediately following the military collapse of the Reich. It will naturally include leaders resigned to the annexations and harsh conditions that come with military defeat: the annexation to a sovietized Poland of states to the east and southeast of the Oder; the Rhine as the military frontier of France; devastating war reparations in the form of raw materials, machines, and laborers. As a Soviet satellite—and the Soviets will have need of Germany's conversion industries—the German government will be able to save whatever there is to be saved and preserve their future. It wouldn't surprise me to see the war end that way, with Russia the master of Europe. The Allies would protest, you say? Nothing would be easier than to present this new Russophile government as the will of the people, which is to say, the workers and the farmers. Even though the concept of universal suffrage is totally foreign to the Soviet regime, they're very good at working it and using it to their advantage.

What is more, I think that the idea of a treaty with Russia, even one involving tough conditions such as these, would very quickly find considerable backing in Germany. Germans admire the power that dominates them, even the power that crushes them. It would have been so easy for France, in 1918, to arrive at a practical settlement with Germany. Stalin is not about to let the chance slip away. It will allow him to achieve the domination of Europe without firing another shot. Even if Churchill and Roosevelt have foreseen these grandiose schemes, and that is far from certain, they don't have the means to prevent him from carrying them out. This would mark the end of Great Britain's place as one of the world's leading powers. England would be reduced to a leading position among the nations of the second tier, and British influence in Europe would wither.

Such could well be the result of the overblown rhetoric and the short-sighted vision that have framed the Allied approach. In the place of realistic and humane terms, the Allies have demanded unconditional surrender and threatened to reduce Germany to so many potato fields. Whatever happened to Britain's legendary tact and the political flexibility of yesteryear, when balance and moderation were foremost in British minds? It is as if their political leaders had adopted the style and the spirit of an Ezekiel or a Jeremiah, along with the belief that maledictions and threats are enough to bring order to this, the most prodigious of world revolutions since the fall of the Roman Empire.

Tuesday, January 30, 1945

This is the twilight of the gods; there is utter consternation in Itter castle, our prison. All the radios have been locked up in the Commandant's office for the last few days, probably to keep the garrison's morale from caving in, but in spite of all the precautions, disastrous news reports continue to filter through. The SS can see the clenched jaws and the faces of their two commanding officers; their strained and downcast looks tell them just as much as they could ever learn from listening to field communiqués.

An officer arrived sometime during the night, a relative of the castle warden. He has difficulty getting around on his two canes, the result of wounds sustained on the Russian front. He has been assigned to the quartermaster corps. He arrived in so frenzied a state that all the soldiers were soon buzzing around him. He had just returned from a mission to Prague, where he had found the situation extremely tense. The Gestapo were on edge and unable to keep up with events. The cafes and all other public establishments had shut down. In short, Prague was a city on the verge of revolting against its oppressor. The SS were deeply stirred by the grim images conjured up by this disabled veteran, now convinced that two years ago his blood had dappled the snows of Russia to absolutely no purpose at all.

This morning, as I was cautiously making my way over the ice-covered ground, I could see dejection on the faces of the sentinels and consternation in the eyes of the soldiers as they busily went about their chores, as they do every day. In the kitchen, where I occasionally go to chat with the young Czechoslovak cook, the four women prisoners who assist him were beaming, as if they could already feel the winds of freedom caressing their faces. The young Czech who waits on the SS and hears and sees everything told me that we had to be on our guard. Some of the SS were talking about suicide. Others planned to seize all the food supplies, drink all the beer and the few bottles of wine that are kept in the cellar, get drunk, and shoot us. The two faces of Germany.

I heard a summary of the French press on the radio. It is generally felt that the final offensive won't be launched until the spring. The military experts—a race I had thought extinct, but that has apparently been given a new lease on life—laid out plans for the Russian Army and offered advice, with all the authority that their war school diplomas and armchairs confer on them. First the Russians will make this move, then they'll follow it with this one. These experts should have learned from the almost five years of war that boldness is the principal asset of Russia's military leaders, just as it was of France's revolutionary Generals.

If they have a chance to march on Berlin, you can be sure that they are not going to wait to hear from Churchill and Roosevelt. It won't be long before both of these gentlemen realize the irreparable error they committed in failing to rearm France these last six months. There should be fifty French divisions along the Rhine right now. But that is another story.

Thursday, February 1, 1945

Caught in the vise. The news we heard last night was of considerable moment, and it was confirmed this morning. The vise is squeezing them ever more tightly.

Goebbels has been given command of the defense of Berlin. How is he going to stop them when everywhere else the most formidable fortifications have crumbled under the Soviet onslaught? Riots are on the verge of breaking out in the major metropolitan areas. Starving refugees from eastern Prussia have been pillaging food stores, and the SS have opened fire on them, spilling the first drops of blood. Will Berlin be able to hold out as Leningrad and Warsaw did? Or as Budapest is still doing even now? Whatever Goebbel's personal energy, whatever the fanaticism of the Nazis, what can they possibly do to hold back the storm?

With the same admirable political skill that they have demonstrated throughout the war, skill that stands in such stark contrast to the total disregard of psychology in the Anglo-Saxon camp, the Russians have been appealing to the German people to rise up against the Nazis, whom Soviet propaganda has already begun differentiating from the rest of the German population.

The Committee for a Free Germany, which the Soviet government set up in Moscow, with General Paulus and other high-ranking officers at its core, has been operational for a long time. You can be sure that they'll move into Berlin on the heels of the Red Army, just as the Polish Committee in Moscow followed the Red Army into Lublin. And you can be just as sure that they will do everything they can to sovietize Germany. This is the beginning of a new chapter in world history, but to judge from the summary of the news I heard, the incredible events unfolding on the battlefield don't seem to have captured the attention of the French press. For them, the main issue is whether France's provisional government and the provisional National Assembly, both of them self-appointed, have the right to implement structural reforms that would rework the nation's social fabric.

Le Monde claims that they don't have that right, that the people of France must be given a voice. They feel it legitimate to assume that many Frenchmen chose not to join Resistance groups precisely because they were opposed to the revolutionary changes being proposed. They see a clear distinction between patriotism—the fight against a foreign oppressor—and social revolution. *Combat* and another newspaper, *Le Populaire*, which is the organ of the Socialist Party, have vigorously attacked *Le Monde*'s position.

One could hardly have expected otherwise, given that France is now going through a period when "legality is on leave," the period Léon Blum thought would be so highly favorable to the establishment of a socialist system.

In *Combat*, they wrote that "a revolution in social conditions is a necessity." In *Le Populaire*, they said we have a unique opportunity to revolutionize France from the top down, in orderly fashion, whereas later we shall find ourselves obliged to make revolutionary changes from the bottom up, with nothing orderly about it at all.

Thus do they call for the nationalization of banks, electric companies, insurance companies, the transportation sector, and heavy industry. After all, aren't the people in the Resistance the real France? In any event, such are the issues of the heated and engaging debate now going on in France, which have the added virtue of making us forget that the war is still going on. Nationalizations don't frighten me. In fact, I nationalized the arms industry and paved the way for the nationalization of the railroads. But I find nationalizations outdated. There are more flexible and efficient ways in which to shape a new economy.

Even though I have no fondness for *Le Monde*, which is little more than a revamped version of *Le Temps*—the voice of the prewar cliques of the privileged and the powerful, with little new other than a change in its discredited name and its defeatist publishers—I agree that the people alone can make such decisions. There should have been elections within the three months following the Liberation. More than ever, I am a supporter of democracy, a believer in its spirit and its methods. The people writing in *Combat* and *Le Populaire* are "totalitarians" who don't dare acknowledge it. No one has spoken about the revolution in values, although it underlies the other one.

The National Front's convention is still going on. Two million Frenchmen of the most varied leanings are represented there, with speakers as different as Jacques Duclos[4] and Debu-Bridel,[5] François Mauriac, and Joliot-Curie.

I have seen excerpts from speeches calling for a wealth tax and the replacement of old banknotes with new ones, with the idea of holding down inflation, at least partially, by asking those with cash savings to make con-

---

4. Jacques Duclos, Communist Deputy whom the Party put in charge of various surveillance missions. He was sentenced to three years in prison in 1932. When the pact between the Soviets and the Germans was signed in 1939, he was called on to bring Party members to accept it. He was active in the Resistance and regained a seat in Parliament after France was liberated. He went on to play a major role in Communist Party affairs.

5. Jacques Debu-Bridel joined the Resistance as a moderate in the group Libération and was a member of the Consultative Assembly.

siderable sacrifice. There have been speeches in support of nationalizations and the farmers' movement as well. We'll have to wait and see what they resolve to do in the end.

Of all the French newspapers, at least from what I can gather, the Communist *L'Humanité* is the only one exclusively concerned with the war. They keep calling for the creation of a large French Army. And they are right. There is simply no way to overstate how deplorable it is that Free France is not now a presence on the Rhine, with fifty divisions or more. But that was up to the Allies.

Did the Allies actually believe last summer that the war would be over in a matter of weeks? Were they alarmed by the suddenness with which the French and the Soviets concluded a separate agreement? Whatever the reason, it is too late now.

As for fielding a large army of occupation forces on the Rhine, that is another problem altogether. It will require little more than a large police force. If all the able-bodied youth of France are sent to keep watch on the Rhine, who will be left to rebuild the nation?

February 2, 1945

The battle for Berlin rages on. The Russians have brought in reinforcements and the Germans are busy digging antitank trenches and shelters.

More than a million Germans from Silesia and Pomerania are making their way back to the capital in below-zero temperatures. They are blocking roads, paralyzing troop movements, and sowing panic along the way.

Yesterday, the Russians were sighted just forty miles outside of Berlin. The Nazis are determined to defend their cities in house-to-house fighting, if it comes to that.

Word has it that the foreign diplomatic missions have left the city and that German government services have been moved into either Bavaria or the Tirol.

Here too, it is possible that we will forced to evacuate Itter "castle." We might well be transferred somewhere near Berchtesgaden, so that as the tragedy winds down to its conclusion, we, too, can play our role. Hostage or victim?

The progress made by the Russian troops has quite naturally exalted the Communists and promoted their cause everywhere. Marcel Cachin commemorated the liberation of Stalingrad. Along with the Anglo-Saxon landing in North Africa, the liberation of Tunisia, and the landing in Italy, that victory marked the turning point of the world war.

I am convinced that de Gaulle entered into agreements with Blum and the Communists as early as April 1943. In fact, he made a speech at that time that I heard while I was in Weimar.

Le Monde and the economist Charles Rist[6] have been attacked in an article in *Le Populaire*, Blum's mouthpiece, for having dared to criticize the wealth tax. In 1932 and 1934, Rist erred totally in opposing devaluation at a time when it was unavoidable. He himself admirably admitted his error in his testimony at the Riom trial, an event so rare that it is worth noting. I think he is wrong again now. The issue is neither the desirability of a wealth tax nor the various problems it would generate. It is rather a matter of whether there exist any other effective means for cleaning up the nation's financial situation and whether there is any way to avoid such a tax. To my mind, this tax is both inevitable and insufficient.

Finally, in *L'Ordre*, Emile Buré[7] has taken his turn at playing the biblical Jeremiah: "Woe unto the bourgeoisie should they oppose these reforms; woe shall befall them, just as nobles and clergymen suffered at the time of the Revolution." The bourgeoisie has heard all this before.

In contrast, the Communists are going about skillfully reassuring public opinion, most notably the middle class, where people become so quickly alarmed whenever they feel their property or savings are being threatened. The Communists are looking to win majority support by pre-

---

6. Charles Rist, free enterprise economist, Deputy Governor of the Bank of France from 1925 to 1929.

7. Emile Buré, Socialist journalist with extremist views. He joined Clemenceau's camp before World War I. In the period between the wars, he ran *L'Eclair*, then *L'Avenir*, then founded his own newspaper, *L'Ordre*, which was centrist but staunchly anti-German. He was hostile to Daladier. During World War II, he took refuge in the United States, where he started a newsletter, *France-Amérique*, with Henri Torrès. (See the February 21, 1945, entry for one of the reasons for Buré's hostility toward Daladier.)

senting electoral slates in combination with the Socialists, the Christian Democrats, and others, after which, little by little, they'll take full control.

To get the votes of those who are not Communists—since the votes of Party members are not in doubt—all you have to do is avoid frightening them. After all, you don't catch fish by blasting your hunting horn on the riverbank. You catch fish by cleverly preparing your bait. Or as Captain Traint, one of the first French Communists, used to say: "When you want to pluck a chicken, you don't go chasing after him, there are too many risks involved; it's a lot smarter to offer him a little tasty chicken feed. Then there's no problem later on, when it's time to pull out the knife."

That's why Duclos, Billoux,[8] and others have been all sweetness and light since the Liberation. As Orgon said in *Tartuffe*, "What gentility!" Look at what Duclos and Billoux told a gathering of Communist physicians in Paris. There wasn't a single word about the Soviet regime and not the slightest mention of a social revolution. They said that there would have to be true democracy in France, that reforms would have to be carried out "in an orderly way, in compliance with the law, and by authority of the government." Then these wolves in sheep's clothing presented a moderate program of political action designed specifically for Mr. Average Frenchman, whose incurable naïveté and unflappable penchant for gullibility are well documented. Duclos and Billoux even spoke out against "carrying nationalizations too far" and in favor of the farmers, just as Stalin did—right before he shipped them off either to Siberia or those agricultural barracks they call *kolkhozy*. Better still, Duclos and Billoux criticized attempts to fiddle with our currency, which should be enough to reassure the people holding banknotes, at least long enough for the Communists to win a majority. On the other hand, when it comes to patriotism, there is no holding them back. They are intransigent, almost fanatical:

---

8. François Billoux. Communist Party member as of 1925, elected Deputy in 1936. In 1940, he was arrested for pacifist activity and condemned to five years in prison. He volunteered to testify against Daladier at the trial in Riom. He made his way to North Africa, where he was a *commissaire* on the French Committee of National Liberation and a member of the Consultative Assembly.

The Franco-Soviet pact takes precedence over everything. I can just hear the ecstatic little bourgeois nationalist joyfully murmuring, "Ah, that Duclos ... say what you will, he's really a good man."

Thus does Captain Traint's chicken lick his lips as they bring him his feed, without ever considering the terror reigning in Poland, Bulgaria, and the Baltic. ... As the British press has been saying, "These regions are now shrouded under an impenetrable veil of mystery and silence."

February 5, 1945

The Americans have captured Manila. The Anglo-Saxons have turned matters around in their fight against the Japanese; they would like to finish them off without having to turn to the Russians for help. They have made considerable progress in Burma, where the old Silk Road has been re-opened. Their victories will have tremendous impact throughout the world, at least on those who understand that the ultimate goal, of both the Anglo-Saxons and the Slavs, is the domination of Asia.

In a ceremony recently held in Moscow, amid great pomp and pageantry, the famous Alexis was anointed Patriarch of All the Peoples of Russia. Alexis had first sided with the Soviets years ago, bringing "religion's workers" into the Party ranks. Orthodoxy has thus become an effective tool in the Russians' drive for the domination of Eastern Europe.

The French press continues its commemoration of the victory in Stalingrad. Jean Richard Bloch sees that victory as proof of the superiority of Marshal Stalin and the Bolshevik system over the Nazis! By playing super-patriot, the Communists have stifled the few protests that have been voiced over the Party's role in 1940 and before. Time will bring matters into perspective.

For the moment, there has been no word on Paris, American, or British radio about the countries "liberated" by the Russians.

Is Soviet Russia using the war to pursue its goal of world revolution? Is it actually possible to reconcile Western humanism and Russian communism?

The only information I have comes from excerpts from the Allied press reprinted in quotation marks in German newspapers.

324

VB[9] published parts of a telegram to the *New York Times* that their Sofia correspondent was able to cable to New York only after he had gotten out of the country: "A government including representatives from all four major parties has in fact been formed, but it is actually the Communist Party, which has control over the police, the militia, and the Ministry of the Interior, that holds the reins of power."

Terror reigns in Sofia. In two special courts set up in the capital, they have been putting on trial not only the Regents and Ministers who had collaborated (along with most of Parliament, in fact) but also democrats like eighty-year-old Mouchanov and seventy-year-old Bourend, both of whom had been fighting the Germans these last several years.

No one is talking about referendums or free elections.

Terror reigns in Poland as well. The British have offered to grant citizenship to Polish soldiers who fought in the Allied ranks and now wish to return to their homeland. That "protection" says it all.

It is the same story in Romania. The fact is that Churchill intervened only in Greece, where he prevented the Communist ELAS[10] from seizing power. Churchill is reported to have put out an official report detailing the atrocities committed by the Communists there.

The reports coming in remain to be confirmed, but there can hardly be any doubt about the general tendency.

Whatever happened to the Atlantic Charter and all the solemn declarations made by the Allies? If the point of this war was to defend democratic freedoms from the threat of Nazi dictatorship, doesn't it follow that it remains the Allies' duty to reestablish these freedoms in the liberated nations?

---

9. *Völkischer Beobachter* (People's observer), daily newspaper that served as the semi-official organ of the Third Reich.

10. The Army of the EAM, the National Liberation Front.

February 12, 1945

The woman who serves as quartermaster for the "castle" went to Magdeburg, where her house had been destroyed. When she got back, the horror was still visible in her eyes. Her stories make you shudder.

At 11:30 P.M. I heard a communiqué detailing the Yalta Conference. I took notes. The fundamental principles were stated clearly and unanimously: "The Premier of the Soviet Union, the British Prime Minister, and the President of the United States have jointly examined the matter of the political and economic reconstruction of Europe, including nations that were allied with Germany. They have agreed to aid these nations, through democratic means, in resolving whatever economic and political problems they may have. These nations must be allowed to establish democratic institutions. ... All three nations are committed to bringing about free, secret-ballot elections and universal suffrage."

February 21, 1945

In particular, the Yalta Agreement calls for a strong, free, and democratic Poland. In Britain, twenty-two Conservative deputies offered an amendment: "The House of Commons would like to express its regret at not having been able to prevent the transfer of the territory of an Allied nation to one of the great powers, this transfer being contrary to several treaties as well as to Paragraph 2 of the Atlantic Charter. The House regrets as well that the government was not instituted through free elections." Twenty-five Members of Parliament voted in favor of the amendment, 396 against. In contrast, the Yalta Agreement was approved unanimously.

The *Daily Telegraph* would like to know why, after the signing of the Yalta Agreement, mass arrests were carried out in countries "occupied" by the Soviets.

There has been a Roosevelt–de Gaulle incident. Every French newspaper has backed de Gaulle's refusal to go to Algiers to meet with Roosevelt, at the latter's request, on his return from Yalta. De Gaulle considered it humiliating for France. I am not so sure.

Roosevelt sent back a stinging response; Churchill's was sharper still: "We met to discuss our own affairs. The three powers that have been bearing the brunt and burden of this war over the last four years are not about to grant anyone a say as to whether they can meet whenever and wherever they wish or take joint action to bring about an end to the war."

As for Poland's independence, I don't think Churchill seriously believes there is "freedom and independence in today's Poland." The Red Army set up a Polish government after a sham general referendum. Poland will become Russia's western outpost. It would be more honest and straightforward to say that without Russia's participation in the war, Poland would have remained off the map. But that is still a far cry from the democratic pronouncements contained in the Atlantic Charter.

The same people who continue to criticize the Munich Agreement of 1938 are accepting annexations that are far more serious and definitive, and at a time when they, as opposed to us, are *not* in a position of weakness. Quite the contrary.

The meeting being held in Alexandria is of major consequence. Churchill and Roosevelt have brought together the Emperor of Ethiopia, the King of Egypt, and representatives of Syria, Lebanon, Iraq, and Saudi Arabia. These regions are of vital importance to the British Empire. Should there ever be a Third World War between Russia and Great Britain, the Middle East will be one of its principal theaters.

The British have resurrected their grand designs for a pan-Arabic confederation, now that the French have been chased out of Syria and Lebanon. Syria and Lebanon were never of vital interest to France anyway.

The French press has been speaking with virtually one voice. Before the war, the French press was corrupt, but as a rule newspapers acted independently. There wasn't a single Prime Minister or Minister of the Interior or Foreign Affairs who would have been so crude as to withhold from newspaper publishers who attacked his policies the monthly subsidies he received from secret funds. Occasionally, very rarely actually, and even then only temporarily, when attacks got too violent or became too personal, they would hold back an envelope or two. Even I had that experience, with Emile Buré, who never forgave me for it. Still, the truth is that newspapers followed their own political line—that of their party, or their publisher, or the business group that owned them. No one was ever required, as has often been claimed, to back government policy, not even those who were being subsidized regularly from secret funds. In this respect, the ministerial musical chairs that they used to play back then worked to strengthen the custom of noninterference.

I have no idea how things actually work today. It seems as if there are more papers than there used to be, even though there are fewer readers, as a simple result of the deportation and imprisonment of some 2 million Frenchmen still in Germany. The higher cost of everything can't have failed to have repercussions on the cost of running and printing a newspaper. Consequently, it is highly likely, in fact inevitable given present circumstances, that many newspapers could not survive without financial assistance from the government. Censorship remains, and not only in military matters, at least to judge from the vehemence with which it has come under attack. Still, given that no newspaper could have made it onto, or back onto, the stands without the government's approval, and given that most of them could not continue to publish if the government were hostile to them, the reality of the situation is that the greater number of journalists have to be considered bureaucrats. Only when peace is restored will freedom of the press really return, if it ever does return, along with other human freedoms that tend to atrophy when systems of law are in recess. So it is that the entire French press has endorsed General de Gaulle's refusal to meet with President Roosevelt in Algiers. The Information Minister deserves to be congratulated on the discipline he has instilled and the impressive united front the press has shown.

Could the war have been won without the involvement of the United States, which the French press tends to overlook? They should have a look at what the German press has to say about it: Despite the resistance of American isolationists, Roosevelt managed to convince his nation to throw its people and its resources into the battle for freedom. The official reasons given for turning down the invitation to Algiers are so sordid that several papers have strained to find others: It would seem that the head of the provisional government has foiled a plot against the nation, that although France had not been asked to participate in the Yalta Conference, they tried to enlist de Gaulle's support by getting him to go to Algiers. That is clearly not the issue. Generosity and gentlemanliness are often more productive than prideful self-righteousness.

March 1, 1945

Roosevelt's speech to Congress is first and foremost a display of his consummate skill as a statesman. He would like to avoid the stumbling block that proved Wilson's undoing. Wilson presented his work as that of the Democratic Party. At Versailles, he surrounded himself exclusively with Democrats. Then the bill he sent up to Congress failed to pass by a mere six votes. Roosevelt has been careful to point out, over and over again in fact, that peace cannot possibly be the work of one political party, that it is the work of every American, and that it requires the sustained efforts and understanding of everyone who participates in America's democracy. He was careful to include Republicans in the delegation going to San Francisco.

Moreover, American public opinion has apparently shown no restraint in criticizing what the Soviets are doing in Finland, Poland, and the Baltic States. Soviet expansionism throughout the world has become a cause for concern in American industrial and financial circles.

Unlike Churchill, Roosevelt was not about to accentuate the problems; on the contrary, he tried to minimize them. But he was careful to emphasize, tactfully, the agreement reached by the three major powers for the establishment of democratic institutions in liberated countries, an agreement that also stipulated that there would be no zone of influence dominated by any one of them. But are these statements reflected in the reality of the situation? The speech was apparently very well received by the Congress and the press. Roosevelt stated in particular: "It was Hitler's hope that we would disagree, but never before have the major Allies been more closely united. All our military plans were worked out together in detail. ... From now on, we shall be engaging in the massive, systematic bombing of Germany in direct support of Soviet Armies. ... We appeal to the German people to understand that unconditional surrender does not mean the destruction of Germany. It rather means an end to Nazism and militarism, the punishment of war criminals, and war reparations in kind." Roosevelt said nothing about forced laborers. "We have reached thoughtful agreement on Germany, Poland, and peacetime arrangements. ... Poland is a good example of our joint action. The Polish government will be reorganized and then recognized, after which general elections by secret ballot will be held."

He concluded by pointing out the need for the United States to accept its responsibility in creating a peaceful world order. "Ours must be a new era in the history of mankind."

March 3, 1945

Paris is mired in tedious debate. There is controversy on all sorts of issues, with voices coming from all quarters.

Germany is marked by panic and despair, and by its relentless determination as well—a fight to the death. Courts-martial are being held with only one outcome: the death sentence. The choice that remains is that of the means: firing squad, beheading, or hanging. Goebbels said that he would prefer to die and see his children die rather than become a slave. They are stirring up fears of catastrophe, destruction, and mass deportation.

According to rumors circulating around here, the German Army is preparing to mount a last-ditch resistance and concentrate its forces in two areas: one in the North, in an area including Hamburg and the Jutland; one in the South, in Bavaria and the Tirol. So in ancient Germania did they circle the wagons, with their wives, their children, and their war trophies inside.

April 12, 1945

2:35 P.M. A squadron of twelve planes flew over the "castle" at low altitude. I didn't see a single woman out working in the fields. Calm was restored by 3 o'clock. Jouhaux came to see me. He had set out for the hospital in Innsbruck yesterday at 5 A.M. It is just a short distance away, but he didn't get there until 4:15 in the afternoon.

The chaos in the train stations is terrifying. Women and children refugees are piled on top of each other, without either food or facilities. Sometimes the stations are bombed, and they all dash madly for the shelters and the trenches. The tracks have been cut at several points along the line. The railroad cars are old and dilapidated, with broken windows. Jouhaux overheard an old *Feldwebel*, wearing an Iron Cross, say that it was all over, that there wasn't a single officer left on the front lines, and that it was criminal for the government not to sue for peace.

April 13, 1945

Roosevelt is dead. Death came at three in the morning, following a cerebral hemorrhage. The commentary by the British was excellent. Roosevelt was a true believer in democracy, a man who served humanity. The goals he set forth in 1942 have almost all been reached. His wonderful voice will long be heard throughout the world. Along with Lincoln, he is one of the great figures of modern times. I remember his phone calls, his attempts to strengthen our Air Force, his words of encouragement as he told me to hold on until he could convince his countrymen to go to war against the Nazis. His associate, my friend Bullitt, proved to be the most faithful and most helpful of friends.

April 14, 1945

M. and Mme Cailleau arrived in Itter last night. Her maiden name is de Gaulle; she is apparently the sister. This morning, Mlle Mabire paid her a visit at the earliest hour propriety allowed and promptly launched into a diatribe against the traitors in Vichy.

Just as Mme Brenklein was coming up to offer her services as well to our newly arrived guests, Mme Cailleau began sharply replying that in June 1940 Frenchmen could very easily have had a different view of what their duty to the nation was, whereupon Mlle Mabire quickly moved on to praise General de Gaulle and the Prime Minister (Reynaud), who was the first to argue in favor of mechanizing the Army, who supported de Gaulle, etc., etc.

This afternoon, I was out for a walk with Jouhaux when I spotted our new prison mates. Mlle Mabire and Reynaud were still clinging to their sides. Mme Cailleau is a distinguished and very personable woman. She spoke in measured terms of the fatigue and suffering she had gone through following her arrest. She had been separated from her husband throughout the ordeal, he having been sent to Buchenwald. But Mme Cailleau didn't have a chance to say anything further. Reynaud and his companion led her off for a walk around the ramparts, hanging on her every gesture, drinking in her every word. As Mazarin said long ago, the Frenchman is a born courtier. Now that battle lines have been drawn in the war to win her over and influence her, the twists and turns of it just might offer us a little amusement. M. Cailleau, the mere prince consort, stood peacefully by throughout; he wasn't snapped up the way she was. He was playful and spirited in describing his experience in Buchenwald, although it must have been excruciatingly painful. While in Saint-Etienne, he had done volunteer work with the prisoners there, in an attempt to ease the hardship of their captivity. "I never once suspected," he said, "that I would come to know similar conditions firsthand, and all the worse for me."

When they were transferred, in the heart of winter, the Germans left them nude in their cattle cars to make sure they wouldn't escape and gave them practically nothing to eat.

The camp was located a few miles outside of Weimar, Goethe's city. There was even a statue of the great German poet right outside. What he described to us in the most measured terms was absolutely horrifying. Twenty thousand deportees subjected to starvation, illness, beatings, and humiliations, and at times outright torture. Most unbelievable of all, the Gestapo set up a whorehouse right next to the camp. On Christmas Day 1944, after lunch, the block leaders were asked over the camp loudspeakers to supply a list of people who were interested in going there. Will anyone ever be able to fathom the German mind?

April 20, 1945

It's Hitler's birthday today, a national holiday if there ever was one. But this year, all we got was a speech by Goebbels stating that Hitler never wanted anything other than peace, that all he had ever been looking for was a place in the sun for Germany. Then he said: "The evil coalition of Bolsheviks and plutocrats is about to collapse. Fate has intervened to remove the head of this enemy coalition, just as it had earlier intervened to spare the Führer so that he might continue the work Providence had called upon him to carry out." The word Providence came back seven times. ... This was followed by the placid description of what life would be like after the war—after Germany's victory in the war. Such was the first part of the trilogy. Events were to furnish the other two.

Looking out my barred window these last few days, I have been watching the exodus down the road that leads from Wörgl to Hofgarten:

automobiles with mattresses on the roofs, people on foot loaded down with Tirolean knapsacks, and frazzled women dragging starving children by the hand. Sometimes the women stop at farmhouses and ask for a piece of bread, but the farmers just raise their hands to the sky. They have nothing left to give them. When traffic gets bottled up, people simply lie down in the ditches on the side of the road; when it clears, they get up and start out again. Millions of people are fleeing over the few German roads that remain open, down through the narrow corridor that, for a few days more, will carry them from the North to Bavaria. Other roads, both to the east and the west, are already under Allied control. Soon all of Germany will be occupied by Allied troops. Thus has the grand dream of dominating all of Europe come to its disastrous end.

Germany has been defeated. All countries come to know the whims of fate, or as Frederick the Great used to call it, His Majesty Chance.

Then there's the third part of the trilogy. For the last few days, London radio has been describing the horrors of the concentration camps with tragic sobriety. General Eisenhower has issued orders to have all the civilian authorities in neighboring towns led through them, so that no one can remain ignorant of the cruel and sadistic acts that were committed there, both during the war and well before it. Germans suspected of being anti-Nazi were probably tortured even more than those deported from other countries. The stories of those who escaped and the photographs taken of the camps have been met with prolonged shrieks of horror. In a cruel twist of fate, the proof of these ignominious atrocities has been released throughout the world on the very day Hitler is celebrating his birthday, in the company of the few handfuls of fanatic Gestapo and party members that remain. The documentation is so unimpeachable that even the Germans will be forced to recognize the truth.

Germany's defeat appears everywhere as the great liberation of mankind. Hundreds of thousands of prisoners, people deported from every nation, have set out to regain their homelands.

Here in Itter, confusion and fear are running rampant. Lieutenant Stephen can already see himself in Siberia. The woman in charge of the female German prisoners has been pouring out her distress to them. She's preparing herself for life in a Russian prison camp, where she'll have to put on the same kind of convicts' clothes her prisoners have been wearing for the last four years.

The SS and the soldiers of the Wehrmacht have been eyeing each other hostilely. It seems that Germany will be spared a civil war only because of the presence of foreign occupation forces.

Evidence keeps pouring in. They have seized concentration camp logs, interviewed eye witnesses, and taken photos.

The description of the camp at Dachau that appeared in the British press corresponds exactly to what I heard, when I came to Itter, from prisoners who had been held there. The Nazis had institutionalized concentration camps and torture long before the war; it was one of their tools of government. Thereafter, they introduced them throughout whatever parts of Europe they conquered. As the war progressed, as the setbacks they suffered worsened and the restrictions on food supplies tightened, they left their prisoners with just enough rations to starve by.

In Buchenwald, the Americans were able to evacuate some 5,000 people who were gravely ill, but there remain all those poor souls who can't be moved, who are dying at a rate of 40 a day from tuberculosis, typhus, and harrowing physiological deficiencies.

In the camp at Belsen, the Americans discovered corpses of women piled almost 6 feet high, in a row 250 feet long. A hundred other women and countless children stricken with typhus and tuberculosis were found lying on lice-infected wooden floors. Here, as in all the other camps, in what was clearly part of a calculated plan, the Nazis carried cruelty and sadism to new heights, by seizing every available opportunity to humiliate and degrade their captives.

In other camps, as the Allies closed in, prisoners who attempted to escape were shot by the hundreds or died in barracks set aflame by the SS. But the worst might yet be to come when Dachau, the camp near Munich, is liberated.

April 24, 1945

The names of the prisoners held in Itter "castle" were picked up on a German pirate radio. The hairdresser in Hofgarten told Mme Brenklein, adding, "We can only remember one of them, Daladier." When did the hairdresser hear this broadcast? What does one make of it?

April 25, 1945

This is the sixth day of tremendous street fighting in Berlin. They are even fighting in the subways, where the Germans have set up machine guns and even field artillery. The resistance they have put up borders on the fanatical; sixteen-year-old boys have been thrown into the battle. They are being bombed from the skies; artillery shells are raining down on them. To the east, the city is in flames.

Patton is now just forty miles outside of Munich. The French have reached Lake Constance.

April 29, 1945

At 5 P.M. I learned that Mussolini had been executed by firing squad, along with his mistress and seventeen Fascists. His body lies exposed in the street.

It is a sun-filled evening; the cherry trees are in blossom. Wisps of smoke mount skyward from mountain chalets. The Americans are now only forty miles outside of Innsbruck, not very far away at all. There is fighting in Munich between the Nazi authorities and the civilian population. The climax is at hand.

I went downstairs at 6:30 and ran into Borotra, who greeted me with, "Have a nice walk, Prime Minister." Ten seconds later, a blast went off. I ran to the parapet, as did Borotra, but then he scaled it and started running madly down the hill. The SS began firing at him from a few yards away. He took the barbed wire in stride as more and more shots rang out and the SS began their pursuit. 7:20 P.M. Borotra was brought back. He had probably twisted an ankle, given the way he was limping. He had once tried a nighttime escape, on a Sunday about a month ago.

The "castle" was in an uproar during the night. Violent fights broke out around three in the morning. I saw the captain go down and begin shouting orders. It was impossible to sleep.

April 30, 1945

The Russian flag is flying atop the Reichstag.

Last night, the Commandant of the camp at Dachau came to Itter with his direct subordinates, their wives, and their children. Before fleeing the camp, he had had 2,000 people shot. He is obese and apoplectic, with the face of a brute. His second in command is tall and fat, a real thug.

May 2, 1945

The Commandant from Dachau had barely settled in when he committed suicide. Ever since Hitler's suicide,[11] the garrison is like a body without a soul.

May 3, 1945

At 6:30 this morning, a little titmouse came into my room and started fluttering around me, as if to say good-bye.

At the time of his arrest, Pétain said, "I was never involved in politics." The comedies and tragedies of life.

I learned that the body of the Commandant from Dachau was put in a pine box, but the box was too big for the doorway to his room. Four soldiers removed his boots and dragged his corpse across the floor. On the ground floor they put the body in a sack and stuck it in the coffin. This morning, the priest from Itter refused them permission to bury him in the village cemetery.

May 4, 1945

They are actually fighting right near us, in Wörgl. The SS Commandant of the "castle" had me informed that as part of their retreat, the Germans would make a stand at Itter. He asked me if I wanted to leave with them. I refused. They put on civilian clothes and took off on bikes, after having handed me a corporal's pistol. Around 3 P.M. I took advantage of our jailers' departure and went for a walk in the village. Large numbers of soldiers passed by in orderly fashion. A lot of them were very young. None of them

---

11. Hitler committed suicide on April 30.

showed any signs of despondency, even less of disaster. I spotted the priest, not in religious dress, and a very beautiful young blond girl. In an inn, a young man in civilian clothes introduced himself as a German officer in charge of an antiaircraft battery. "This is the second time the Jews have won out," he said, "but we'll get them next time."

At around 5 P.M. I came upon Borotra and La Roque in the village. We met a young, very nice and very intelligent airman, twenty-three years old. ... He was worried about our safety. He was afraid that the SS who were falling back would try to take the "castle" and kill us. Horns started honking from within the "castle" walls. We ran to see what was happening and found an American captain there with five or six other men, in a tank. A German major with fifteen soldiers also appeared on the scene, having come voluntarily to protect us. Lee, the American Captain, was crude in both looks and manners. Gangel, the German Major, on the other hand, was polite, dignified, and distressed. If Lee is a reflection of America's policies, Europe is in for a hard time. There were toasts and a good deal of bustling about. We were joined by two Austrian resistance fighters wearing armbands and toting guns. Quite a strange gathering.

For the help we got, and maybe even for our lives, we owe our thanks to Andrea, the German deportee who worked at the "castle" under the Quartermaster. When the Germans took off and released their prisoners, instead of taking flight and hiding out, Andrea headed for Wörgl by bike. A battle was being waged there between the Americans and the SS. Everything was in utter confusion, but that didn't seem to faze Andrea, who went to see the German Major and explained our situation to him. The Major made contact with the American Captain and they both left for Itter to help us. In any other circumstances, a story like that would be unbelievable.

May 5, 1945

This morning, two bullets whistled by my ear and landed in the wall behind me.

At 10 A.M. I was walking in the courtyard with Jouhaux when they began lobbing shells into the "castle" from the South: Austrian 77s or 88s. They honored us with about fifteen of them. One of them went through Gamelin's room ... and was followed by machine gun fire. We hurried back inside the "castle." All the phone lines were cut. The American Captain set up machine guns along the wall, but his tank was destroyed by a shell, as it sat on the stone bridge. The German Major deployed his men and set up his machine guns and his armored vehicle. A lull in the action prompted the Major to move into the doorway to observe the situation. Suddenly, he slumped to the floor. A bullet had gone through his heart. It had struck him dead on the spot. His right hand trembled a bit, then fell motionless. The nobility of this man, this German for whom the war was over! He had risked his life to help French prisoners, his enemies.

The situation was getting worse. At around 12:30 P.M. Captain Lee gave Borotra information about American troop movements and sent him off to try to bring back reinforcements. Clemenceau and La Roque busied themselves firing randomly into the woods, although they hadn't actually seen any Nazis.

I went up to the second floor where two of the German soldiers who had come with the Major had taken up positions, with their rifles resting on the window sills. They pointed out German soldiers firing at the "castle" from a few hundred yards away, near the little electric plant, on the edge of the forest. The two soldiers returned the fire. I took advantage of a moment of calm to exchange a few words with our defenders. They told me in German that they were Polish. When I told them that I was French, one of them started shaking my hand while the other pulled a bottle out of his coat and offered it to me. It was a bottle of Fernet Branca; where the devil did he ever get that? I drank a bit; it was really bad. Then he laughed and told me that Hitler was kaput.

Suddenly he stopped laughing and shouted, "Panzer!" Five tanks were approaching. We watched them turn onto the road leading up to the "castle." The SS attackers vanished; these tanks were American. They had been alerted and guided by Borotra, who was now wearing an American uniform. The unit with him was a company, maybe a little bigger. The American Colonel appeared, a big, strong, nice fellow. We greeted each other cordially. As we were thanking him, war correspondents from American newspapers began taking photographs. Then we introduced the German soldiers who had fought to help us, and the corpsman with them. They were immediately released. Other French prisoners began arriving, they too having been liberated by the Americans. One of them recognized me and said that we had once been together at a branding in the Camargue, back in the days when they were still marking wild bulls.

Then we all moved down toward the tanks and the automobiles. The people from the village had gathered in the town square. Austrian flags were hanging from the windows. An old antiques dealer from Berlin, who had taken refuge in the area with his daughter, told us, "We have been liberated, too." I noticed that Resistance fighters from Wörgl were there as well.

At 7 P.M. we headed down to Innsbruck, free at last. We were shown to the Command Post of the General leading the 103rd Division, Anthony McAuliffe. That was the heroic division that had been surrounded in Bastogne. The General had in fact been on leave at the time, in the United States. He immediately had himself flown back and parachuted into the middle of his troops. His encircled division eventually broke out. He greeted us in princely, kindly fashion and honored us with a candlelight dinner in his Tirolean villa.

May 7, 1945

The General called the Army and asked for a plane to carry us back to Paris, but the First French Army insisted on handling our transportation. That is why we ended up leaving by car for Augsburg, where Patton's Seventh Army headquarters was located. We moved from the enthusiasm of the Tiroleans, joyous in spite of the bombings and the buildings reduced to rubble, to the hostility of the Bavarian population, mainly old men, women, and children. Their hostility was written on their faces. Many of them turned their backs as soon as they sighted American vehicles.

Augsburg is a city rich in palaces and churches, one that played a major role in the history of civilization and intellectual history, above all in the fifteenth and sixteenth centuries. The city had been subjected to massive bombings. A flood of trucks, cannons, and tanks were making their way through it, heading for the front.

We arrived at 7 P.M. and went to the Seventh Army headquarters, but no one was there. Our convoy set out again, this time for the suburbs. We stopped in a neighborhood of lower-class housing. German officers, now prisoners, could be seen standing at windows. We strolled around a playing field to pass the time. At 8:30, Captain Lazare showed up, sporting a fine red garrison cap. He didn't say much, laughed a lot, and told us he would try to find an apartment for us. We didn't see him again. We went back to Headquarters, where a French captain set us up at the Kaiserhof, which was practically deserted. Captain Lazare reappeared and informed us that we would be leaving the following morning at 10 A.M. sharp for the Headquarters of the First French Army at Lindau, on Lake Constance.

May 8, 1945

At 11:30 we were still waiting. After having paced up and down the sidewalk, I went to sit down in the officers' mess in the Kaiserhof. As I glanced toward the door, I saw my son Jean. I hadn't had word from him in almost two years. I thought I was hallucinating, but it really was Jean. This was the most wonderful moment of my life.

General Patton, one of the greatest commanders in the American Army, came in. He was unaffected and cordial. I expressed France's admiration and gratitude for all that the Americans had done. "No need to, not at all," he said. "You were the ones who showed us the way in 1917."

We left for Lindau. News of our liberation had been spreading. Ribet, my lawyer, was there to greet us, along with Soupiron, a reporter from Lyons who had followed the Riom trial, published accounts of it, and written *Bazaine contre Gambetta*. I remember having shouted at one point during the trial, "The way things are today, Gambetta would be in prison and Bazaine would be an official in the government."

Then I saw Bullitt, wearing a French Commander's uniform. We hugged each other. Oh the memories that awakened!

At 10 P.M. I had a friendly chat with General de Lattre. He left me to talk at length with Weygand. Two planes had been brought in: one for us, one for Weygand, La Roque, and Borotra, whom they intend to put on trial upon their return to France.

I went off peacefully on my own, in my son Jean's car. We went to his regimental Command Post.

Jean had joined a *maquis* in the Jura Mountains, where he had been shot in both legs. He was helped out by patriot farmers, then finally picked up and attended to by Dr. Charlin, a good man who helped him get across the border into Switzerland. Jean later returned to France to join the Alsace-Lorraine brigade, commanded by my good friend Jacquot.[12]

We had lunch at Jacquot's Command Post, in the company of his officers, all of whom were from *maquis* in the Corrèze and Dordogne. They told deeply moving stories.

We left the following day with my son and Jacquot and passed trucks carrying deportees and former prisoners, rolling along now in joyous song. A lot of them were very young. At Brisach, we took a pontoon bridge over the Rhine. There we stopped. There were young soldiers all around. As we set foot on French soil, a Lieutenant bid us welcome to France. Some of the men recognized me, men from Fos-sur-Mer and the Gard. We stood and chatted together on the banks of the Rhine. They were all volunteers. One of them, who had been a *maquisard*, had been tortured by the Germans.

Alsace is everywhere bedecked with French tricolor flags, just as it was in 1914. In Mulhouse, I saw Alsatian women in traditional dress, some of them very beautiful. Crossed the Vosges via Bussang Pass, drove through the streets of Remiremont, lined with the blue, white, and red colors of France. Stopped at a farmhouse to fill the car with water. Having recognized me, a man came up to us with his sons and daughters. "Welcome, welcome," he said. "We still love you ... more than ever."

We stopped around 10:30 P.M. in Vrécourt, in front of Jacquot's house. His mother was expecting us, a sturdy, energetic woman, seventy-five years old. She told us gripping tales in the simple words that befit the stark occupation years. Then she cracked a few eggs and served up two delicious omelets.

We got back on the road. It was dawn when we arrived in Paris, a silent Paris whose symbols of victory were still illuminated, a deserted Paris, perhaps more moving than it would have been had the streets been filled with joyous crowds.

---

12. This is the same Commander Jacquot who had come to visit Daladier, in the prison in Riom in 1942, dressed in military attire.

Appendix A
France's Principal Modern Weaponry

Weapons	June 1, 1936	Sept. 1, 1939	May 1940
60 and 81 mm Brandt mortars	450	7,500	9,980
25 mm antitank guns	1,280	3,800	6,000
Tracked armored vehicles	700	3,800	6,000
47 mm antitank guns	0	411	1,280
Blockhouse antitank cannons	0	518	[a]
12 ton Renault, Hotchkiss, FOM tanks	0	1,780	2,665
20 ton SOMUA speed tanks	0	261	416
16 ton D1 tanks			150
20 ton D2 tanks	17	50	260
30 ton B, B1, B1[b] power tanks	17	172	387
Machine guns: AMR (7 ton), AMC (7 ton), and AMD	0	407	866
Fortified defense weaponry	0	96	[a]
Small caliber (20, 25, 40 mm) anti-aircraft weapons	0	321	2,140
Modernized 75 mm antiaircraft weapons	25	400	[a]
Modernized 105 mm antiaircraft weapons	0	124	[a]
New 75 mm antiaircraft cannons	38	392	[a]
90, 94, 100 mm antiaircraft cannons			40
13.2 mm antiaircraft machine guns			1,360

[a]Production terminated.

[b]Second series.

Source: Document furnished by Edouard Daladier after the war to Parliament's fact-finding commission.

Appendix B
The Riom Trial

Jean Daladier

[*Directives for the Press*[1]

All newspapers are to publish excerpts from the Riom indictment preceded by an appropriate introductory paragraph, no later than April 26. These excerpts are to be taken from the brochure previously distributed to the media and outlining the principal charges. This press release is intended to spur sales of the full-length version of the prosecution's indictment, soon to be made available in bookstores.

Be sure to emphasize the prosecution's arguments.]

The Riom trial[2] was one of the most shameful and one of the saddest trials in our history. It was shameful in that Marshal Pétain sentenced Daladier and his codefendants to life in prison simply on the basis of a recommendation made by the Political Justice Committee chaired by Perretti della Rocca, whom he, Pétain, had appointed (see the diary entry for October 14, 1941).

The Vichy government then set up a tribunal to hear the case. Daladier was to answer to the principal charge of having declared war on Germany! The pretrial investigation was actually conducted along these lines for months. The charge was later changed to having failed to prepare France for war. With the exception of General Gamelin, who would, incidentally, refuse to say a word during the trial, only civilians were indicted.

---

1. Addressed to journalists by Vichy government bureaucrats. Throughout the trial, Vichy issued directives to the press as well as to many witnesses and magistrates. This is the directive dated April 24, 1942.

2. See Frédéric Pottecher, *Le Procès de la défaite* (Paris: Fayard, 1980).

All facts predating 1936 were barred from the courtroom, which is to say, all facts pertaining to the period when Pétain was War Minister and a member of the Supreme War Council.

Most pathetic of all, the trial ended when Hitler publicly demanded that it be suspended, at a time when Vichy could already sense how counterproductive it had been.

Quite a sorry business, this trial. I was there. After each session, newspapermen were given directives to be followed under threat of penalty. They were not to mention Pétain or his associates; not to mention Free France or certain Generals. The trial was especially sad in that men who had acted bravely in 1914 took the stand to deny any responsibility whatsoever, as per the script that had been written out by Vichy. Because they were not allowed to consult their notes, a number of these witnesses were shown to be mistaken or lying and ended up looking like fools.[3]

At the beginning, people were lining up to testify—career officers, politicians, even Communists. But after Daladier virtually took over the first few sessions, volunteers were hard to find.

Very few men—and they are all the more noteworthy for it—took the stand and simply told the truth as they saw it, as did for example M. de Moustier,[4] whose opinions in fact conflicted with Daladier's. As for the rest, what hatred and incompetence they displayed. What base flattery they showed toward Vichy, what scorn for the British, what blindness in their estimation of Germany's strength.

As soon as his cross-examination began, Daladier revealed unusual audacity in the face of the Germans present in the courtroom. "Germany intends to use the sentences pronounced against us for propaganda purposes, and demand admissions of guilt from its victims. ... France should be the one admitting its guilt. ... The way things are today, Gambetta would be in prison and Bazaine would be an official in the government." That set the tone for the rest of the trial. The man who stood accused was to become the principal accuser.

---

3. Roger Génébrier, *Le Procès de Riom.*

4. A Deputy and a member of the Resistance. He was deported and died in the camps.

Daladier had to bear the burden of practically the entire trial, since he alone had command of all the facts and knew all the people involved.

During a subsequent court session, he declared: "Germany met its first defeat when it proved incapable of invading England. It has met a second defeat in Russia. Germany will be defeated, that is now inevitable. We must not let our confidence waver."

When the Presiding Judge interrupted, Daladier pretended to yield to his point, but he held the floor and came back even stronger.

Tanks and Antitank Weapons

Presiding Judge: There were only 2,848 tracked infantry vehicles; we needed 3,765 of them.

Edouard Daladier: On May 1, 1940, we took delivery of 6,200 tracked vehicles. According to General Picquendar, 1,200 of them remained in storage depots and were never used, like the 500 tanks the Germans captured in Gien, along with considerable amounts of other matériel.

Bruzin, the prosecuting attorney, shifted the questioning to tanks. "Production figures refer to 3,446 tanks."

The Presiding Judge reiterated the myth, debunked by both France's Military Intelligence (Colonel Rivet) and German Generals, to the effect that the German Army had between 7,000 and 8,000 tanks. (They actually had around 3,000 tanks.)

Daladier stated that when he was appointed War Minister in 1936, France had only 34 tanks! In 1940, 3,500 had rolled off factory lines, including the 2,800 tanks that were in combat position, along with 500 other armored vehicles. The Germans attacked with only 3,000 tanks. (General Guderian confirmed these figures.)

Our tanks were split between the infantry and the cavalry. They were not used to capacity; they were even used to protect bridges; 2,400 tanks were assigned to the infantry, the remainder to the cavalry.

Daladier went on: "General Doumenc was the first to suggest a modern-day strategy for using tanks, as early as 1928. General Guderian adopted his ideas in 1934."

In fact, the Army adopted Marshal Pétain's theories. "Our approach is the correct one," Pétain said. "Tanks are best used in support of infantry. There is no point in throwing armored vehicles into the wilds."

General Georges, the Commander in Chief, and General Dufieux, the former Tank Inspector, agreed with him. For example, the High Command halted the construction of thirty-ton tanks. Certain appropriations were never spent.

Several Generals voiced their opposition to these outdated theories, but they were not heeded. Daladier mentioned that General Billotte had warned that the Germans would deploy five armored divisions, either in Lorraine or west of the Meuse, and use the same strategy they had put into effect in Poland. Billotte stated: "We have at our command one armored division, three heavy-armor units, and more than forty light-armor battalions. Technically and numerically, our superiority is clear." [*At the end of this court session, the press was instructed to omit these comments.*]

Although the Military Command had sole power in determining the weapons they used and the quantities they required, Daladier noted that he had gotten them to create one armored division. It had taken two years to decide on a field for military maneuvers near Nancy, and Daladier actually had to go there himself to get it done. "Our tanks were spread out everywhere, and thrown into battle in little bunches," he said in conclusion. "The problem wasn't our matériel; the problem was our approach to conducting a war."

After a series of exchanges, Daladier made a similar demonstration for our antitank weaponry. "There were 15,000 antitank guns," he said. "Many of them remained in storage dumps. After the Armistice was signed, we handed over 2,500 cannons and 1,200 armored vehicles to the enemy."

Then the Presiding Judge accused the defendant of responsibility for the insufficient number of mines.

Edouard Daladier: It was the High Command that put an end to the production of mines! Now they are trying to hold me responsible for it.

The prosecutor himself had to admit that it was so.

At a later session, General Keller, the Tank Inspector, was called as a witness for the prosecution. He repeated that the Germans had attacked with 6,000 tanks (as we have seen, historians have shown this figure to be erroneous) and said that given that imbalance, there was nothing our military commanders could have done.

Edouard Daladier: Is the witness aware that in 1935 the Chiefs of Staff scrapped an order for thirty tanks, and that in 1936 they simply neglected to order them from the Renault Company? The witness has no knowledge of these facts? Then maybe the witness is aware that the Chiefs of Staff put off placing orders for Hotchkiss tanks for over a year?

General Keller: Undoubtedly for lack of funds.

Edouard Daladier: They had all the funds they needed, in particular 300,000 francs that had to be carried over to the following year because no one had spent them. It was the same story with the 1937 cannon, the 1938 model. Its production was delayed two years because the people in the Tank Division were six months late in making a decision.

General Keller: Then you'll have to put your question to those people.

Edouard Daladier: I'll ask my questions whenever I like; I don't answer to you. To these figures we should add 600 British tanks.

General Keller flashed a smile.

Edouard Daladier: The mention of British tanks brings a smile to your face, does it? We have just seen what they can do in the area around Tripoli. Go ahead and laugh if you want, we'll see who'll be laughing ten or fifteen months from now! Did you, General Keller, communicate to your superiors the same black picture you've painted for us here?

General Keller: Of course.

Edouard Daladier: To whom did you communicate it?

General Keller: General Gamelin.

General Gamelin, indignantly: You never told me that. Do you hear me, never!

Court was adjourned. General Keller waited for General Gamelin and moved forward to greet him. Gamelin refused his hand, saying: "I shall never shake hands with you again. You're no man at all."

When Colonel Perré, whose tank division had fought brilliantly, took the stand, he testified that he was satisfied with the tanks, satisfied with their sturdiness, their armor, and their speed. However, he criticized the radio equipment, saying that there were too many different models.

Presiding Judge: M. Daladier, do you have any questions to ask of the witness?

Edouard Daladier: I have no questions to put to real military commanders.

The matter of a conspiracy within the Army surfaced during the cross-examination of General Gérodias, who had conducted himself ably. He mentioned, in particular, having been sanctioned by Daladier for having circulated throughout the Army a memorandum outlining a Communist putsch that directly threatened military officers and even their families.

When asked by the Presiding Judge where the memorandum had come from, the witness replied, "From Commander Loustanau-Lacau, of Marshal Pétain's staff." His response electrified the courtroom.

Fortifications

Daladier was accused of having been shortsighted in the area of fortifications. He answered by stating that he had committed 2.5 billion francs to building fortifications, adding, "I tried to have their construction continued further north on several occasions, but the Supreme War Council rejected the proposal each time, adopting the motion of its Vice President, Marshal Pétain.

"In spite of the opposition, I managed to have funds set aside for fortifications as early as 1933. When I was back in the War Ministry in 1936, I had an additional 300 million francs put in the budget for 1937, even though Belgium had backed out of its alliance with us. I made on-site inspections of everything that was being built and personally brought the matter to the attention of the High Command, but Marshal Pétain stated that the enemy would never be able to advance over this sector. [*Directive to the press: Delete the passage referring to Marshal Pétain's statement about this sector.]*

Similarly, in Parliament, each time deputies moved to have our fortifications extended further north, Marshal Pétain succeeded in blocking them. His hold over Parliament was undeniable.

Better still, in 1939 and 1940, General Billotte pointed out our vulnerability in this sector. The High Command took no notice of it.

An airman was called to testify. On May 8, 1940, he had flown over the Ardennes and spotted hundreds of German tanks moving on France, headlights ablaze.

Subsequently, Commander Caillet would affirm that in 1940, he had sealed off the two roads over which the Germans would later advance, by building walls and laying oak trees over them. On May 5, just a few days before the attack, he was ordered by the Second Army's Headquarters, commanded by General Huntziger (Pétain's War Minister at the time of the trial), to dismantle these barriers.

It was by these same two roads that the Germans reached the Meuse.

Conduct of Operations

The Chiefs of Staff believed neither that the Germans would attack with armored divisions nor that they would choose to attack through the Ardennes. One of the witnesses, General Etcheberrigaray, was in command of a B Series division (reserves) in this area. Two other B Series divisions were based at the point where the Germans attacked. The regular Army troops remained either in Alsace or in the East.

One further example: Our troops moved into Belgium in the daytime rather than at night, as military regulations stipulate. Daladier, who was there, said: "I didn't see a single German airplane, not one sign of an armed intervention. I thought that we had fallen into a trap."

General Prioux so notified his superiors, to no avail.

The errors committed by our military commanders surfaced again and again throughout the trial.

During the sixteenth court session, one of the prosecution's own witnesses, General Hering, acknowledged that Daladier's accomplishments were considerable, whereas the Ministers who had preceded him had done nothing.

In answer to a question from the defense attorney, Ribet, Hering stated that during a meeting of the Supreme War Council, Daladier had advocated the use of armored divisions and air power in combined operations. Unfortunately, the Council wasn't even able to reach agreement on what should constitute an armored division.

Aviation and Antiaircraft Weaponry

Guy La Chambre, who was Air Force Minister from 1938 to 1940, was called to testify. "In 1937," he said, "our industry was turning out only thirty-five planes a month. It was a craft industry; I even had to order machines from abroad. The High Command didn't really take aviation seriously. For example, we were forced to reduce our work force by 50 percent.

"In 1938, M. Daladier offered me the most useful kind of support there is, namely appropriations of 5 billion francs. The result was that by June 1940, we had 2,500 warplanes."[5]

General Massenet de Marencourt took the stand. "The Chiefs of Staff had locked up all our planes in hangars. I took it upon myself to put together fighter patrols. I even found the turret guns and machine guns we needed in Châtellerault." The witness gave other examples as well.

With regard to the planes ordered from the United States, Guy La Chambre said that "for reasons of security, the High Command asked us to have them delivered to Casablanca rather than to France, although there were neither assembly plants nor adequately trained personnel in Casablanca." Everything had to be improvised. Daladier was not even notified of the decision, although it was on his initiative that planes had been ordered from the United States.

---

5. It is generally agreed that there were 2,176 airplanes on the front lines, in addition to 550 British aircraft, not including the planes based in England. The Germans had approximately 4,500 aircraft. In 1940, France was producing 500 planes a month. That, taken together with the British output, meant either that the Allies were already outproducing the Germans or that they would outproduce them sometime in 1941.

Antiaircraft Weaponry

General Marescaux, a former Commander of antiaircraft defenses, testified about the major deficiencies in his units. He said that he had brought the seriousness of the situation to the attention of his three superiors: the Artillery Inspector General, the Director of Artillery, and the Inspector General for National Air Defense.

Marescaux said, however, that Daladier was not made aware of the situation until May 1938, at which point he immediately called Marescaux in. Within a few days' time, a 2.5 billion franc program for the construction of antiaircraft pieces had been launched. Then it was the experts' turn to show themselves incapable of reaching agreement. In the end, an exasperated Daladier had to impose the choice of a 90 mm cannon that had been designed in 1932 and that eventually proved to be an excellent weapon.

Nationalizations, Organization, and Legislation

Presiding Judge: You have been accused of failing to apply existing labor laws.

Edouard Daladier: France was stricken with an unemployment crisis. Many factory owners were offering their workers only thirty to forty hours of work a week. Moreover, in 1938, when I became Prime Minister, 130,000 workers were on strike. I negotiated with them; that was my duty. I appealed to public opinion; then I evacuated the factories without spilling a single drop of blood.

That ended the general strike.

Presiding Judge: But the strikers were hired back.

Edouard Daladier: It was a time to demonstrate generosity and unite all Frenchmen. We couldn't afford to lose men with expertise. As it turned out, by the end of 1938, half of the equipment had already been built. There were no production delays, quite the contrary.

Presiding Judge: You elected to nationalize certain industries for political reasons.

Edouard Daladier: I nationalized only ten factories. I also proposed government investment in private industry. M. Dautry, the Arms Minister, stated that "thanks to the retooling underwritten by the government, factories were able to provide the equipment needed at the time of the mobilization." In 1936, we appropriated 6 billion francs to stockpile industrial machinery and metals. We set up state plants. I tripled the number of new machines purchased from the United States. Working together with manufacturers, we created veritable industries in aluminum, cobalt, and magnesium. Similarly, after the general mobilization, output continued to increase, even though, without my knowledge and contrary to my instructions, skilled workers were called up who should have been left at their jobs in the factories. The production of equipment was three to four times what it was at the time of the mobilization.

The Presiding Judge cited a statement by M. Dautry characterizing France's industrial output as meager.

Edouard Daladier: If things were that bad, how does M. Dautry explain the rise in the productivity curve?

Colonel Rinderknech, writing to General Gamelin on June 2, 1940, stated that "there would be no reductions in munitions and matériel."

Of course, getting them to the front lines was something else!

Prosecutor: But you were the War Minister, weren't you?

Edouard Daladier: Once war was declared, the Supreme Commander was no longer under my authority. You'll have to put your questions to General Georges and the Army's commanders. What demands for matériel did they make? They should have created commissions to determine the state and quantities of our war supplies.

(On August 6, 1945, General Picquendar testified that in October 1940, he had seen equipment sitting in depots and even out in the fields. That matériel, with an estimated value of between 15 and 18 billion francs, could have outfitted twenty-four divisions—enough to arm three hundred thousand men. A full third of this equipment, the General said, fell into German hands when they invaded the Unoccupied Zone in November 1942.)

As of the twenty-fourth court session, Marshal Pétain issued a decree suspending the trial. Of the three hundred witnesses who were to appear, only thirty-six had been called. It had become clear, both in France and abroad, that those actually responsible for the defeat were Marshal Pétain; his War Minister, General Huntziger; and our military commanders, since they alone were in charge of defining strategy, directing operations, and choosing the kinds and quantities of weaponry to be used.

It had been shown that the French people and their civilian Ministers had provided the military with all the moneys that they had requested, and more.

The tribunal that had been created by Marshal Pétain and his government decided to release Guy La Chambre, the head of the Air Force; and Jacomet, who in his capacity as Secretary-General of Arms was in effect the head of France's ground forces. In view of the decision to drop the charges against these two men, how could one maintain that Daladier and Blum were responsible for the defeat?

How does one explain the fact that Daladier and Blum remained in prison, if not by a desire to appease Hitler and Vichy? In 1943, Marshal Pétain and his government would hand both men over to the Gestapo, who had them imprisoned in Germany.

And once again, how does one explain the fact that, even today, what were revealed to be lies and errors during the trial in Riom are still given credence by a great many Frenchmen?

Appendix C
Biographical Timeline

1884	Born in Carpentras, into a family of craftsmen, originally peasants, who had settled in the Vaucluse region of France in the seventeenth century.
	Attended middle school and high school in Lyons, on scholarship.
	Received the highest score ever achieved until then on the *agrégé* examination in history.
1909	Appointed to a position as a history teacher in Nîmes.
1911	Elected Mayor of Carpentras on the Radical-Socialist ticket at age twenty-eight.
1913	Founded a far-left, republican newspaper, *Germinal.*
1914	Having volunteered, served as a Sergeant in the Foreign Legion. Was awarded the *Croix de guerre*, three medals for bravery, and the *Légion d'honneur.* Promoted to Lieutenant in 1918.
1919	Elected to Parliament on the Radical-Socialist ticket.
1923	Voted against Poincaré's decision to send French troops to occupy the Ruhr Valley.
1924–1926	Appointed Minister several times, including Minister of War in 1925.
1932	Published the first paper calling for the nation to rearm (one in a collection of papers).
1933 (Jan.–Oct.)	Prime Minister. Won support for the nation's first rearmament program. Toppled by the Socialists, who opposed his rearmament program, and the Right, who criticized his social reforms.

1934 (Feb.)	Appointed Prime Minister a second time. Stood up to the rioters, who failed in their attempt to storm the Chamber of Deputies. Failed to win adequate support for his proposed stand against them. Stepped down in the absence of a majority in Parliament.
1936	Regained the leadership of the Radical-Socialists and, by supplying the party's support, brought about the victory of the Popular Front. Launched the first vast rearmament program as War Minister in Léon Blum's government.
1936–1938	Served as Minister of Defense on several occasions.
1938 (Apr.)	Appointed Prime Minister for a third time. Signed the Munich Agreement in September.
1939	Declared war on Germany on September 3.
1940 (Mar.)	Resigned.
(Mar.–May)	Minister of Defense, then Minister of Foreign Affairs, in Paul Reynaud's government.
(June)	Left for North Africa with Mendès-France, Campinchi, Mandel, and several Members of Parliament to carry on the fight from there.
(Sept.)	Forcibly brought back to France and imprisoned.
1942	Sentenced to life imprisonment, then tried in Riom.
1943	Imprisoned in Germany.
1945 (May)	Liberated.
1946	Reelected to Parliament from the Vaucluse.
1946–1958	Served concurrently as a Member of Parliament and Mayor of Avignon.
1958	Resigned from all political offices.
1970	Died in Paris.

About the Book

The French Prime Minister who signed the Munich Agreement in 1938 and who one year later led his country into war against Hitler's Germany, Edouard Daladier was arrested by the Vichy regime and imprisoned in France and Germany until the war's end. As a pastime and a catharsis, Daladier wrote.

He wrote about what had happened to him and to his country, about day-to-day conditions in captivity, and about what he could glean of the anti-Nazi war effort through newspaper accounts, from the visits of his friends and family, and from his well-hidden radio receiver. He wrote of the accusations made against him by his former protégés and comrades-in-arms; and of his trial, during which the charges oddly metamorphosed from having declared war on Germany to not having sufficiently prepared France for battle (the charges were of little importance, as the verdict had been previously decided).

Ever the statesman, Daladier wrote most of all about his hopes and fears for France and Europe—which hung so heavily, at first, upon the battlefield successes of the British, American, and Allied forces; and later, upon the Allies' refusal to recognize in Soviet power the danger of the very totalitarianism that they had been fighting to eliminate. At the war's end, witnessing the devastation of Germany, Daladier wrote with a poignant sympathy that is unexpectedly moving.

Daladier's notes remained forgotten and unpublished until twenty years after his death, when they were discovered and compiled by his son Jean. They are presented here in English for the first time. By turns sorrowful, enraged, humorous, and philosophical, this lively narrative gives fresh insights into the tangled politics of the era.

Edouard Daladier was born in Carpentras in 1884. He was elected to Parliament as a member of the Radical-Socialist Party in 1919 and named War Minister in 1925. Thrice named Prime Minister (1933, 1934, and 1938), it was he who signed the Munich Agreement for France in September 1938. From March to May 1940, Daladier was successively Minister of War and of Foreign Affairs in Paul Reynaud's government. When France was overrun in June 1940, Daladier left for North Africa with the hope of carrying on the fight from there. He was forcibly returned, arrested, and imprisoned by the Vichy government, which brought him to trial in Riom in 1942, then handed him over for deportation to Germany in 1943. Daladier remained in captivity there until he was liberated by the Allied forces. After the war, he was reelected to Parliament and served as Deputy and Mayor of Avignon from 1946 to 1958. He died in Paris in 1970.

Jean Daridan, who provided most of the annotations to the original French edition, was a good friend of Edouard Daladier and remained close to him during the war. A diplomat who began his career in 1932, he was also a member of the staffs of two Prime Ministers, Edouard Herriot and Joseph Paul-Boncour.

Arthur D. Greenspan is Professor of French at Colby College.

Index